PRACTICAL APPLICATIONS OF DATA COMMUNICATIONS

A User's Guide

Edited by Harry R. Karp, Founding Editor, *Data Communications*

PRACTICAL APPLICATIONS OF DATA COMMUNICATIONS

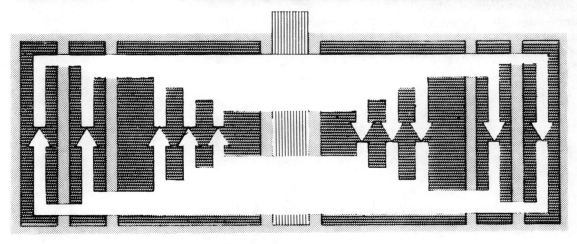

A User's Guide

Edited by Harry R. Karp, Founding Editor, *Data Communications*

Electronics MAGAZINE BOOKS

McGraw-Hill Publications Co.
1221 Avenue of the Americas
New York, New York 10020

ELECTRONICS BOOK SERIES

Also published by *Electronics*
with *Data Communications* **Magazine**

• **Basics of data communications**
• **McGraw-Hill's Compilation of Data Communications Standards**
• **Data Communications Procurement Manual**

Library of Congress Cataloging in Publication Data

Main entry under title:
Practical applications of data communications
   (Electronics magazine books)
   Includes index.
   1. Computer networks. I. Karp, Harry R., 1922-
            TK5105.5.P72.   621.38   79-27239
ISBN O-07-606653-3

CONTENTS

PREFACE

The technology of data communications—in particular the development of architectural and protocol concepts—has proceeded at great pace during the last several years, aided by advances in large-scale integrated electronic circuits and ubiquitous microprocessors.

The upshot has been the rapid, effective, and low-cost exploitation of data communications networks, large and small, by industry, commerce, and government—and soon in the home.

Most of the major activity in data communications has been reported in *Data Communications* magazine. This book is based on reprints of articles published during the last few years, organized into eight key categories of advancements and activities.

Like its predecessor, *Basics of Data Communications,* this book reflects both the efforts of the authors of the articles and the contributions of the editorial staff of *Data Communications.* Thanks also go to Brunny Ayala, Fred Sklenar, Colin Ungaro, and Janet Eyler for their help in getting this book through the many phases of production and quality control.

—Harry R. Karp,
Founding Editor,
Data Communications

Part 1
Architectures
and protocols

General-purpose protocol integrates different networks

Do-it-yourself network architecture frees the user of terminal protocol and constraints

Patrick J. Nichols
Telcom Inc.
Vienna, Va.

Protocols

To save a lot of money, sometimes it is necessary to spend a little first—as an organization with several small, separate networks would do well to remember. For, by integrating the various pieces into one large, cohesive network, a company can save as much as $1 million a year.

The money spent goes partly on installation of a high-speed "backbone" network to integrate existing networks, and partly on a general-purpose network-control architecture, which is an extended version of a bit-oriented advance data-link control. With these innovations, the operating procedures and the multitude of different terminals used on the various networks need not be replaced. Most of the user's investment is protected, yet cost for lines and operating can be reduced drastically.

The backbone network takes advantage of such state-of-the-art techniques as locating concentration devices and message switchers at suitable geographical sites (nodes) and using high-speed links between the nodes. The general-purpose network-control architecture will permit any of a variety of terminals—with different codes, speeds, and protocols—to communicate with concentrators, while a concentrator and a message switcher communicate with each other with the advantages obtained from a bit-oriented link protocol.

This architecture has been developed for a large Government agency, which maintains four large Teletype-oriented communications networks and several smaller, but similar, networks, as well as a computer-to-computer network. The new, integrated network will consolidate these individual networks and eventually will interconnect with other communications networks of both national and international scope.

The agency's present setup is typical of the common situation in which a communications system consists of several distinct networks, each organized by functional purpose or communications characteristics, and each of which contains a particular class of terminal. These classes can span the range from low-speed, five-level-code, teletypewriter terminals using the 83B3 protocol, to medium-speed intelligent terminals using either seven-level ASCII or eight-level EBCDIC codes with a block-oriented ANSI protocol, to high-speed computers using a bit-oriented SDLC-type protocol.

There would be considerable savings achieved

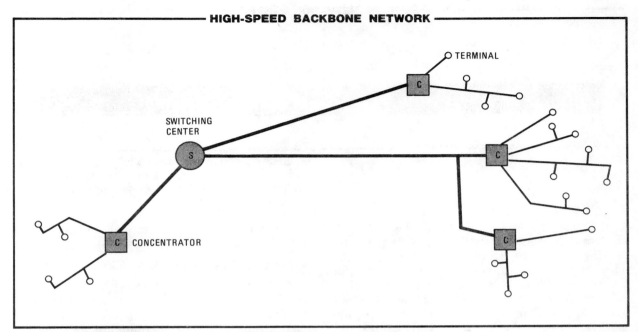

TERMINAL

SWITCHING
CENTER

S

CONCENTRATOR

C

1. General-purpose network-control architecture works over the backbone network (color) and makes the network independent of a terminal's own code, speed, and protocol characteristics.

by the integration of such independent networks into a single, coherent network of greater capability. Efficiency can be improved, interaction between networks can be realized, and message transfer times can be reduced. Furthermore, the network architecture, even though it can be implemented within the message switch and concentrators, is substantially independent of constraints of the host computer and terminal equipment.

Here, integration means the development of an additional communications network, which acts as the high-speed backbone network as well as the controller for the existing networks. With proper planning, redundant circuits may be eliminated and others can be multiplexed at the concentrators onto the higher-speed, more efficient network circuits. This backbone network, by its very nature, requires the use of a highly flexible, efficient, bit-transparent link protocol such as IBM's synchronous data-link control (SDLC). Furthermore, bit transparency through the backbone network becomes vital when it's necessary to transfer a mix of codes of different levels and code-independent messages. In short, the general-purpose network-control architecture combines efficient network control and data-link transparency.

Of the various configurations possible for a backbone network, a star-shaped layout with central control and switching and remote concentrators will efficiently handle store-and-forward message applications (Fig. 1). In such a network, the control architecture will take charge of its primary, or trunk links (the color lines in the illustration).

However, both the concentrator and the switch will service existing secondary links from terminals at each terminal's own speed, code, and protocol. That is, each multidrop line in the network can handle one class of terminal, but the concentrator can interface with and service different multidrop lines for different classes of terminals.

This geographical, rather than functional, organization of terminals from different networks requires compatible hardware and software in order to interface to the various mixes of terminals that exist in the integrated network. Properly configured and programed, a concentrator will supply this capability.

Network savings

The advantages of such a hybrid, general-purpose approach to network control can be great. Most apparent is lower costs. For example, the traffic from the numerous Teletype and other low-speed lines in older networks may now be merged into a smaller number of multiplexed, medium-speed communications circuits. These primary circuits will range in speed from 2,400 through 9,600 bits per second over synchronous, voice-grade, dedicated circuits. The result is a greatly reduced monthly circuit charge.

Another saving is that associated with maintaining existing equipment. Usually, upgrading a network using another approach requires that such equipment as terminals be modified or completely replaced to maintain compatibility with newer protocols, such as SDLC. Or equipment might need

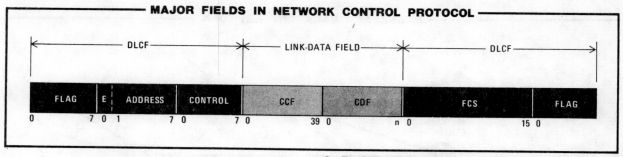

MAJOR FIELDS IN NETWORK CONTROL PROTOCOL

DLCF				LINK-DATA FIELD		DLCF	
FLAG	E	ADDRESS	CONTROL	CCF	CDF	FCS	FLAG
0 7	0 1	7	0 7	0 39	0 n	0 15	0

2. Each frame starts and ends with an 8-bit flag, and the details of the network-control information are contained in the subfields of the communications-control field, denoted as CCF.

to be upgraded to handle the increasing work load of a particular network nodal point. Here, however, existing equipment usually is adequate: it is the network itself that cannot handle the increase in the number of terminals or nodal points.

Should new equipment be added when integrating networks using GPNCA, the choice of equipment can be made on the basis of cost, options, and performance—and not on its ability to meet a particular bit-oriented protocol or to operate at a higher (usually unnecessarily high) data rate. In other words, the cost of new equipment can be kept to a minimum because of the concentrator's ability to handle a wide range of input data rates, codes, and protocols.

There are also less tangible advantages to integrating networks. As an example, an upgrade of a network is transparent to the user because it is not necessary to alter operational procedures in order to communicate over the new network. The only difference that should be apparent is one of improved performance.

And the new network has considerable flexibility. Thus, the addition or deletion of equipment causes little, if any, impact on system operation. New terminal protocols can be easily absorbed into the network. Expansion should prove to be a minor effort, once the network has been established.

Finally, reliability and backup may be easily en-gineered into the network to yield almost any degree of terminal availability to the users.

How the architecture works

In the general-purpose network-control architecture, a message is exchanged between a concentrator and a message switcher, or between two message switchers, using a frame of bits in the sequence shown in Figure 2. The bit at the left is transmitted first. This frame is an extension of the one used in IBM's synchronous data-link control, but the network does not require the use of SDLC-type terminals (see "Synchronous data-link control," DATA COMMUNICATIONS, May/June, 1974). In this frame, the link data field is equivalent to the I field (information field) in SDLC. The link-data field, though, is itself divided into two fields, CDF and CCF.

CDF, for communications-data field, is a frame segment of any number of bits that carries the actual message. While it is similar in usage to the I field, the message can be in any code and thus is not restricted to the eight-level EBCDIC code required by SDLC—and successive frames generated by dissimilar terminals may have different codes.

The CCF, or communications-control field, is the key control element in transferring a message from one terminal to another through the concentrators and message switcher. Its numerous functions will

3. The communications-control field (CCF) allows many terminals on the same multidrop link to be addressed simultaneously because each terminal address is defined by a single bit position.

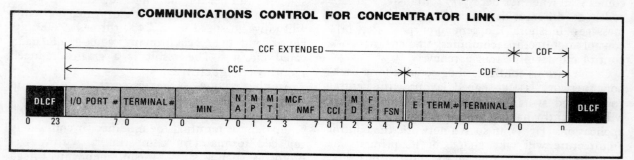

COMMUNICATIONS CONTROL FOR CONCENTRATOR LINK

DLCF	I/O PORT #	TERMINAL #	MIN	N A P	M P T	M T	MCF NMF	CCI	M D F	F F	FSN	E TERM. #	TERMINAL #		DLCF
0 23	7 0	7 0	7 0	1 2	3	7 0	1 2 3	7 0	1 2 3	4 7	0	7 0	7 0	n	

CCF EXTENDED — CDF
CCF — CDF

be discussed later in some detail.

First, though, it's important to review those aspects of the frame that serve as a point-to-point (say, concentrator-to-switcher) data-link control. These functions are denoted in Figure 2 by the two segments called DLCF, for data-link-control field.

The DLCF functions are substantially identical to those found in SDLC. This control field is not involved in message transfer or message-flow control through the network but rather provides frame control between adjacent backbone nodes. A flag, an 8-bit segment coded as 01111110, marks the frame's beginning. The flag is followed by an 8-bit address, with the setting of the first bit (E) used to indicate address extension. The remaining bits shown in Figure 2 as 1 to 7 thus allow up to 2^7, or 128, addresses for different I/O ports within the message switches, concentrators, and other devices in the backbone network. The setting of the E bit allows further 8-bit address groups to follow the first address field, providing any number of communications-processor addresses.

The control field is used for such things as acknowledgment of correct or erroneous frames and for frame numbering for link control, while the frame-check sequence (FCS) is a 16-bit cyclic-redundancy-check block that evaluates the accuracy of the received frame. The frame ends with another flag.

Carrying network control

As mentioned, the communications-control field is the frame segment employed to transfer a message from a sending terminal through all intervening concentrators and switches to the addressed terminal. It has two variations, one for a link between a concentrator and a message switch and another for a link between two switches.

When used in a concentrator-to-switch link (Figure 3), the CCF contains five 8-bit octets, comprising the first 40 bits of the link-data field. The first octet stipulates the addresses of up to 256 ports of the concentrator (or switch). The next octet selects the terminal number on the multidrop line connector to the selected port number. Here, the terminal number is based on the setting of a particular bit position within the octet, so that the octet is capable of addressing any one, several, or all eight terminals at the same time. Thus the same message—such as an all-points weather bulletin—can be broadcast simultaneously. Extension to more than eight terminals is discussed later.

The message identification number (MIN) occupies the next octet in the CCF and allows for numbering of up to 256 messages.

The next octet serves several functions. Bit 0 is reserved for an optional network acknowledgment (NA) used to indicate the end-to-end message acknowledgment. The next bit provides a two-level message-priority (MP) indication. Bit 2 indicates whether the message type (MT) is a network-management message or an information message.

The next four bits (3–7) provide more insight to the nature of MT. When it is interpreted as an information message, MCF (message-code field) identifies any one of up to 32 message codes and formats appearing in the communications-data field.

When MT is interpreted as a network-management message, the NMF (network-management field) is interpreted as any one of up to 32 different network-management messages. Among them are such control messages as: demand retransmission of a message from the switching center; request the switch to hold the concentrator's traffic in order to keep the concentrator's dynamic buffer from overflowing (network throttling), and inform a switch of line and terminal faults.

When eight or fewer terminals are served by one multidrop line, the CCI (communications-control indicator) is set to 00. But when more than eight are on the line, the CCI is set to 01 and the CCF is extended by adding one or two octets (the sixth and seventh). If two octets are added, then the first bit in the sixth octet (E) is set, which means that another octet of terminal addresses follows.

As shown in Figure 3, then, up to 23 terminals (our particular implementation restriction) can be addressed on the same line at the same time. It

4. In the switcher-to-switcher backbone link, the communications-control field selects the appropriate addressed switcher and the addressee switcher from among those in the network.

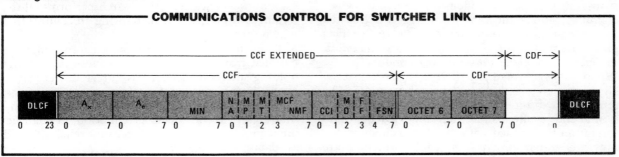

COMMUNICATIONS CONTROL FOR SWITCHER LINK

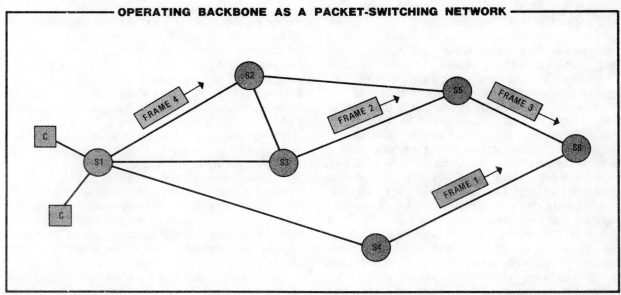

5. The general-purpose network-control architecture allows the network to operate in a packet-switching mode between different switchers when that mode can provide operational advantages.

proves more efficient to transfer the same message once per multiterminal line rather than transferring it once for every destination terminal. That is, using one-bit terminal addressing, concentrator buffering, and concentrator message control result in a lower network overhead.

The MD (multiple-dissemination) bit may be used on multidrop lines, or to indicate that a message is to be relayed to another node—as in a packet-switching network discussed later. The FF bit indicates the final frame of a given message, and FSN, 4 bits long, is used to number up to 16 consecutive frames in the message.

Switch-to-switch link

When the integrated network employs two or more message switches, the protocol structure between them is that shown in Figure 4. Once a message has been associated with a particular switching center, the address of the destination switch is placed in the first octet, called A_x for exit address. The entry switching center places its address in the second octet, A_e, for entry address.

On receipt of a message, the destination switch strips off the CCF intended for switch-to-switch communications and replaces it with a CCF suited to switch-to-concentrator communications. This procedure makes it possible for the entire network to operate in a packet-switching mode (Fig. 5). When a message made up of several frames is traveling between switching nodes, each frame may be sent over a different route, depending on the instantaneous traffic load at each node. Adequate information is provided with the CCF to effect such a message transfer. That is, each intermediate switching node examines the destination address and determines the best-path routing for the particular frame in transit.

The flexibility of the general-purpose network control architecture has other advantages. As mentioned, the message information contained in the CDF can be received in any one of up to 32 different code and protocol formats and can proceed unchanged in format through the concentrators and switches and to the receiving terminal. However, appropriate programing of the concentrator and message switch—say, through a look-up table—will permit the format to be changed to one suited to another class of terminal. In this way, the inherent flexibility of the network will permit two dissimilar terminals (code and protocol) to communicate with each other.

Usually, it is the message switch's responsibility to scan and interpret the incoming messages. The switch performs reformatting and code conversion if required and determines the destination address. The switch will likewise break up an incoming message into multiple messages, one for each input/output port associated with an addressee. For each of these messages, the switch performs all the logging, journaling, and accounting procedures that may be necessary.

Thus, billing and statistical programs may be handled from the single central message switcher holding such data on a mass-storage device. Since concentrators need not perform these functions, no mass-storage devices are needed for them—and this means a considerable reduction in management problems, as well as increased reliability and availability of the network. ∎

Large computer/communications networks demand a rational approach to their design under which host computers are considered simply as nodes on the network. The approach devised by IBM is called systems network architecture, or SNA, and was formulated and developed in recent years. DATA COMMUNICATIONS now offers a report on SNA written by people intimately concerned with its philosophy and technology.

Thomas F. Piatowski, Dale C. Hull and Robert J. Sundstrom
International Business Machines Corp.,
Research Triangle Park, N.C.

Data networks are growing larger, more complex and more essential. Already networks with hundreds of terminals span continents and oceans; soon networks carrying traffic between thousands of terminals will be common. And so a rational, organized and expandable methodology in network design and operation has become a necessity. Such a methodology is known as a network architecture.

A network architecture is like a computer architecture—with greater geographic dispersion. But it is far more important for the user to grasp the rationale for a network architecture than to understand the local, contained architecture of a computer. Networks, by their exposed nature, are vulnerable to failures and errors from many causes. What is more, traffic moving over networks with many links—among them possibly long terrestrial or satellite circuits—is subject to indeterminate delays in propagation. Errors and delays lead to the loss of coordination (or synchronization) between network components.

The network architecture must of itself be capable of detecting and correcting this type of problem. A network must also keep track, in real time, of the numerous states of each of its many resources and of the intricate movements of the hundreds of different messages simultaneously passing through it.

International Business Machines Corp. has developed an integrated set of solutions to the problems affecting networks, which it calls a systems network architecture or SNA. This development is providing a basis for present and future IBM communications products and programming support. And this basis, in turn, allows network designers and users to take advantage of SNA's straightforward and consistent data communications attributes, and to configure a large variety of computer/communications systems to meet present and future needs.

But SNA is more than merely a line of products. It is a fundamental concept laid out to accommodate all aspects of system definition, and network and transmission control. This article will not dwell on the various hardware and software products designed to be part of an SNA network. It will concentrate rather on the underlying architectural rationale, and on how SNA can overcome many of the problems that have up to now beset network operations.

Before the introduction of SNA, for instance, IBM had more than 200 communications products in the field, requiring 35 different teleprocessing access methods and 15 different data link controls. The resulting imcompatibilities reduced the effectiveness of network operations. If desired, SNA can be implemented by only one access method in the host computer and one link protocol in the net-

work. In the present product line, the access method may be the virtual telecommunications access method (VTAM) or the telecommunications access method direct (TCAM DIRECT), while the link protocol is synchronous data link control (SDLC). These and other software and hardware products are compatible because they conform to a common set of protocols embodied in SNA. This not only makes it easier for IBM to design its products but also simplifies the user's task in configuring, installing and operating an SNA network.

Provision is made in certain products to support both SNA devices and devices using binary synchronous communications (BSC) and asynchronous protocols. This can ease a user's move towards an SNA configuration.

Having only one access method in a host computer eliminates the disadvantages of duplicated function and storage requirements; and a terminal need no longer be dedicated to applications supported by a specific access method, a situation which limited the sharing of terminals and applications. Finally, having in the host computer a single access method and, more particularly, a single control point in the access method, simplifies dynamic network reconfiguration—for instance, when a network's mode of operation is switched from daytime to nighttime applications.

Consistent use of SDLC means that terminals supporting different applications can occupy the same communications link, so that transmission line costs may be reduced. Using only one data link control does away with duplication of function and storage requirements, such as for extra line control and error recovery code needed when more than one link protocol is supported by the same host computer or communications controller.

It is also possible for SDLC to provide higher throughput than previous IBM half-duplex line protocols because of its full-duplex transmission capability. Furthermore, SDLC provides more efficient control messages, such as polling, acknowledgment and end-of-transmission (EOT).

Under SNA, application programs need no longer be dependent on device and network characteristics. Changes in device types, locations, and addresses need not have any effect on user-written application software.

Remote job entry (RJE) stations supporting batch applications in the host computer, and formerly attached through point-to-point links, can under SNA be efficiently connected with several stations on the same link. Furthermore, traffic from different types of SDLC terminals can be interleaved on the same link. For instance, it is possible under SNA to interleave traffic from inquiry/response stations with that from RJE stations.

Error detection and recovery procedures have been developed to a high level within the various SNA protocols. Now, when an error is detected and signaled, powerful error detection routines can frequently identify its source.

Modular structure

A key structural and functional feature is that an SNA network is a protocol system that enables the reliable transfer of data between a number of end users. An SNA network also provides a wide range of protocols to control its internal communications and data manipulation resources, as well as those of the end users.

The basic components of an SNA network are defined independently of products or technologies, making it possible for a wide variety of products and applications to reside compatibly in the same network. And so SNA allows special or simplified products to operate along with general and more sophisticated products.

One result of SNA has been a great increase in what a network can do over anything IBM has hitherto had on the market. And this increase has been easier to achieve because of the modularity found in SNA hardware and software, as well as because of the high level instructions—called macroinstructions or "macros"—used for system definition. The modularity allows such functions as network control and device and link management to be implemented either in the software or the hardware, or in both, at various nodes in the network.

In the SNA hardware and software available at present, the control points are in the host CPUs. However, much of the physical management of transmission links, controllers and devices are in 370X-type communications controllers attached to these hosts. Figure 1 shows IBM's VTAM in the host CPU performing the control point function, and a network control program (NCP) in the communications controller performing the physical network management function.

The degree to which a user takes part in the set-

1. The communications controller performs some duties to relieve the host computer, but both share the work of network control and management.

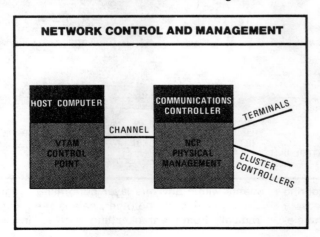

NETWORK CONTROL AND MANAGEMENT

ting up of his SNA network may vary considerably. As a rule, however, he will at least draw up a system definition. And in that case he will generate his own version of VTAM and NCP by describing, in macros supplied by IBM, the particular configuration of lines and devices in his network.

The NCP relieves the host by providing much of the management and control of the link interfaces. The NCP performs bit assembly and disassembly, code translation, error recovery, line and device tests, polling, and other physical management operations. An NCP is generated by coding a set of macros defining the terminals and lines attached to a 3704 or 3705 communications controller. For example, a user will code a macro for each transmission link attached to the communications controller. Parameters in the macro define such link characteristics as speed, link discipline (SDLC, BSC, start/stop), and the type of connection (point-to-point, multipoint or switched). Similarly, the terminals on the link are defined by macros whose parameters specify type of device, transmission code and other characteristics of the terminal.

After the macro statements are coded for NCP, they are submitted to the assembler at the host CPU. The macro statements are expanded by the assembler into tables which represent the network configuration described by the user. (During network operation, these tables are interrogated and updated by modules of executable code in the communications controller; these modules are provided by IBM for code translation, data link control and buffer management.) The output of the assembler is submitted to the linkage editor, so that linkage can be established during operation between the executable code and the tables defining the particular network.

The VTAM package is generated in a similar way. Macros define the applications that connect to VTAM, as well as the network operating rules and other characteristics of the control point. These macros are assembled and edited to produce an executable VTAM version.

The network is initialized by issuing a START VTAM command at the system console. First, VTAM is loaded into a region or partition at the host computer, where it initializes itself; next VTAM loads the communications controller by retrieving a copy of the NCP from a library at the host and writing it across the channel to the communications controller; then the NCP initializes itself—and the network is ready for action.

Control point

The control point of a network in SNA is called the system services control point (SSCP). In present implementations of SNA, the SSCP resides in VTAM or TCAM DIRECT in one or more host computers in the network. (This article describes SNA in a single-host configuration with one SSCP.)

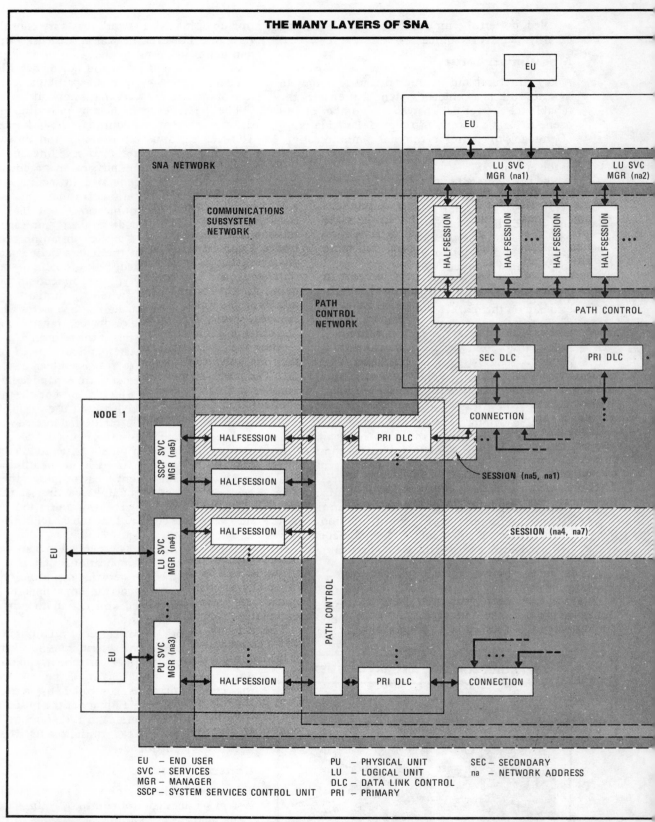

EU

EU

SNA NETWORK

COMMUNICATIONS
SUBSYSTEM
NETWORK

LU SVC
MGR (na1)

LU SVC
MGR (na2)

HALFSESSION

HALFSESSION

HALFSESSION

HALFSESSION

...

...

PATH
CONTROL
NETWORK

PATH CONTROL

SEC DLC

PRI DLC

NODE 1

SSCP SVC
MGR (na5)

HALFSESSION

PRI DLC

CONNECTION

...

SESSION (na5, na1)

HALFSESSION

HALFSESSION

SESSION (na4, na7)

LU SVC
MGR (na4)

EU

PATH CONTROL

PU SVC
MGR (na3)

EU

HALFSESSION

PRI DLC

CONNECTION

...

EU – END USER
SVC – SERVICES
MGR – MANAGER
SSCP – SYSTEM SERVICES CONTROL UNIT

PU – PHYSICAL UNIT
LU – LOGICAL UNIT
DLC – DATA LINK CONTROL
PRI – PRIMARY

SEC – SECONDARY
na – NETWORK ADDRESS

2. There are two equally valid ways of considering the structure of an SNA network. In one, the network is seen as a set of concentric layers, with all the elements within any one layer performing roughly the same function. In the other, data is seen as flowing radically from the transmitting end user in the outer

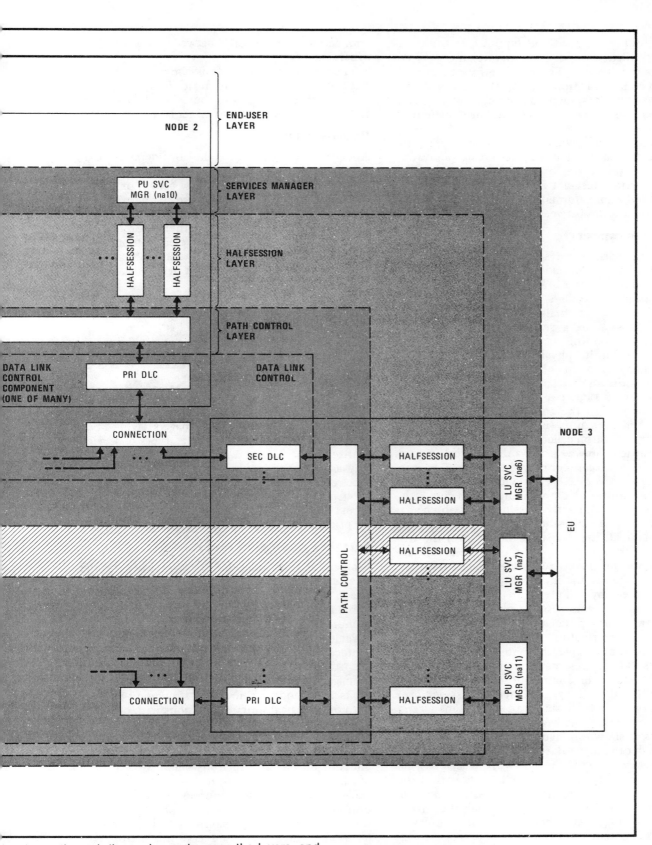

NODE 2

END-USER
LAYER

PU SVC
MGR (na10)

SERVICES MANAGER
LAYER

HALFSESSION

HALFSESSION

HALFSESSION
LAYER

PATH CONTROL
LAYER

DATA LINK
CONTROL
COMPONENT
(ONE OF MANY)

PRI DLC

DATA LINK
CONTROL

CONNECTION

NODE 3

SEC DLC

HALFSESSION

LU SVC
MGR (na6)

HALFSESSION

PATH CONTROL

HALFSESSION

LU SVC
MGR (na7)

EU

CONNECTION

PRI DLC

HALFSESSION

PU SVC
MGR (na11)

layer, through the nodes and across the layers, and
out to the receiving end user. Nested layers make up
subnetworks within the structure.

11

The SSCP performs three types of network services: configuration services, maintenance services and session services. These are performed in reaction to commands from a network operator (VTAM or TCAM DIRECT system console operator) to end-user requests, and to events occurring elsewhere in the network.

Configuration services include such operations as starting, shutting down, restarting, activating and deactivating the links and devices. Maintenance services test network facilities, and collect and record error information. Session services open and close sessions between end users.

A new perspective

There are various ways to view SNA. It can be thought of as a set of nodes—corresponding to hardware products such as S/370 hosts, 3704/3705 communications controllers, and a variety of cluster controllers and terminals—connected by links. Or it can be seen as a set of network-addressable units—corresponding to actual process modules—called logical units, physical units, and the system services control point. These are connected by the transmission subsystem network provided by VTAM or TCAM DIRECT in the host nodes, and supported by NCP in the communications controller nodes. And each unit (including the SSCP) is governed by a function called a services manager.

This article, however, views the network as pairs of services managers connected by protocol components called sessions. Each services manager lies in a network-addressable unit along with some of the logic used for each active session with which it is associated. Together, the network services managers make all the decisions that control the network resources—including not only the communications and processing resources used to transport messages but also the input/output and processing resources seen by end users.

Portions of each session provide appropriate communications protocols to coordinate the exchange of information between paired services managers. For example, the system services control point (SSCP) services manager monitors and controls the status of communications resources at each physical unit by exchanging messages over sessions with each physical unit services manager.

An overview of the basic components of an SNA network is shown in Figure 2. There are two ways to consider the network's structure. One is the concentric view, in which the network is seen as a set of concentric layers, with all elements within the same layer performing roughly the same function. The other is the radial view, in which the data is seen as flowing from an end user in the outer layer, through the nodes and across the layers of the network toward the inner data link control (DLC) elements, and back out to another end user. The hatched bands in Figure 2 depict two such radial

connections (or sessions) between different pairs of services managers.

The name of each layer is shown in its upper right corner. The designation in the upper left corner of each layer refers to the "subnetwork", consisting of that layer and any inner layers.

End-user layer

A logical starting point for the consideration of an SNA network is the end-user layer, outside the network proper. An end user is any person or process not part of SNA that wants to use the network. All end users are attached to the SNA network through nodes, to which they can be either external or internal. External end users are, typically, terminal or console operators, whereas internal end users may be application programs resident in a node and executed on a processor in the node.

The next layer, and first layer of the SNA net-

> ## " An end user is any person or process that wants to use the network. "

work itself, is the services managers layer. There are, as previously described, three types of services manager: the logical unit services manager, the physical unit services manager, and the system services control point (SSCP) services manager. These services managers communicate with each other across the inner layers of the network by using appropriate protocols to establish sessions.

Services managers layer

Each end user attaches to the SNA network through a logical unit services manager. An end user may attach to more than one logical unit services manager and a logical unit services manager may attach to more than one end user.

Each logical unit services manager supports protocols for two kinds of session. For sessions with the SSCP services manager, the logical unit services manager helps monitor and control the allocation of its local node resources in support of sessions with other logical units. For sessions with other logical units, the logical unit services manager helps monitor and control the allocation of local node resources, and may also provide other product- or application-dependent functions—such as the sharing of a printer among concurrent sessions.

Each node in Figure 2 contains a single physical unit services manager that supports protocols through which the SSCP monitors and controls the physical configuration and communications system resources associated with the node.

The network contains one or more SSCP services managers for monitoring, allocating and otherwise controlling the communications and data manipulation resources of the network as a whole, using information exchanged with each of the logical unit and physical unit services managers. In this way, the SSCP services managers can control the network's configuration and the status of all its sessions. (The network described in this article is assumed to have only one SSCP, so interactions between SSCP services managers in a multiple-host-computer configuration are not discussed.)

The boundary presented by each services manager to the inner communications network is completely specified. One key function performed by the logical unit services managers is to provide the functional bridge between the end users and the defined communications subsystem network.

Necessary concepts

Before describing the remaining layers, it is necessary to introduce the concepts of sessions, of addressing and of message units.

Sessions. The services managers are paired for the exchange of information by a logical connection called a session. For example, a session can exist between the services managers of the SSCP and each physical and logical unit, or between pairs of logical unit services managers.

Each session consists of two halfsessions—one at each end of the communications path—connected through a path control network. Each halfsession provides its own services manager with a number of sending and receiving protocols covering such features as session activation, traffic pacing, message-unit chaining, bracketing of transactions, and half-duplex or full-duplex send/receive nodes.

Within any session, one of the halfsessions is the primary and the other the secondary. In general, the primary halfsession has the capability to initiate more protocol features than the secondary, for example, it is the one that will resynchronize sequence numbers after a failure, such as a streaming modem, has been corrected.

The only direct communication between paired halfsessions is through the path control network, which is subject to transmission errors as well as to propagation delay. One principal function of a halfsession is to detect certain classes of transmission errors in the path control network and provide recovery aids. Another is to coordinate with its partner so as to compensate for any delays in the path control network.

Addressing. Each services manager has its own network address or "na". A session is identified by the network addresses of the two services managers involved. For example, session (na5, na1) in Figure 2 denotes the session between the services managers of the SSCP (na5) in node 1 and the logical unit (na1) in node 2; session (na4, na7) defines the session between the services managers of the logical unit (na4) in node 1 and the logical unit (na7) in node 3.

Message units. Messages flowing though an SNA network take various forms, depending on the point in the system at which they are handled. These forms are derived from the two basic message formats presented in Figure 3. The path infor-

3. Two basic formats are used for message flow in SNA sessions: one is the path information unit and the other the basic link unit.

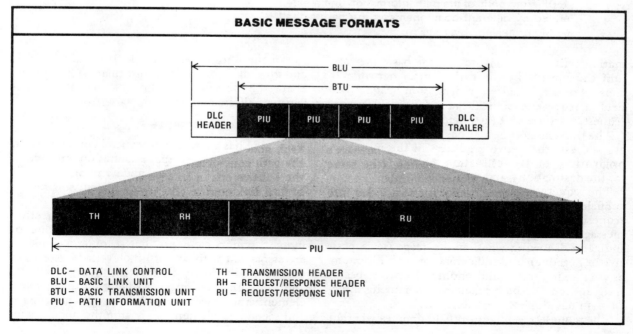

BASIC MESSAGE FORMATS

DLC – DATA LINK CONTROL
BLU – BASIC LINK UNIT
BTU – BASIC TRANSMISSION UNIT
PIU – PATH INFORMATION UNIT

TH – TRANSMISSION HEADER
RH – REQUEST/RESPONSE HEADER
RU – REQUEST/RESPONSE UNIT

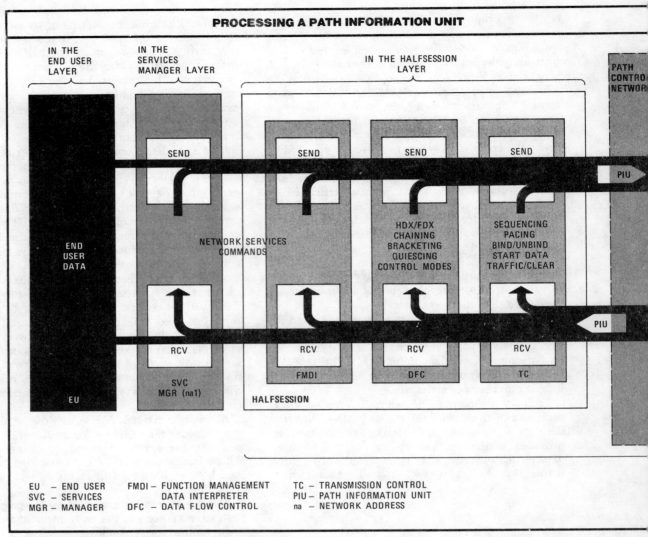

PROCESSING A PATH INFORMATION UNIT

| IN THE END USER LAYER | IN THE SERVICES MANAGER LAYER | IN THE HALFSESSION LAYER | PATH CONTROL NETWORK |

SEND   SEND   SEND   SEND

END USER DATA

NETWORK SERVICES COMMANDS

HDX/FDX CHAINING BRACKETING QUIESCING CONTROL MODES

SEQUENCING PACING BIND/UNBIND START DATA TRAFFIC/CLEAR

PIU

PIU

RCV   RCV   RCV   RCV

EU   SVC MGR (na1)   FMDI   DFC   TC

HALFSESSION

EU – END USER
SVC – SERVICES
MGR – MANAGER

FMDI – FUNCTION MANAGEMENT DATA INTERPRETER
DFC – DATA FLOW CONTROL

TC – TRANSMISSION CONTROL
PIU – PATH INFORMATION UNIT
na – NETWORK ADDRESS

4. Different parts of the path information unit are generated by different components in the partner halfsessions making up a session.

mation unit (PIU) in Figure 3 is the basic message unit transmitted by the path control network. It consists of three fields: a transmission header (TH) field, a request/response header (RH) field, and a request/response unit (RU) field.

The transmission header has three subfields: origin address (the network address of the message's originating point), destination address (the same for the destination), and sequence number.

The request/response header is also divided into subfields, including (as may be appropriate) a request/response indicator (showing whether the message is a request or a response), a response-type indicator (showing whether the response is positive or negative), and indicators for such functions as pacing, beginning and ending of chains, beginning and ending of brackets, and changing direction (in half-duplex operation).

The request/response unit field denotes whether the request/response unit (RU) contains either end-user data or control information to be exchanged by the corresponding services managers of partner halfsessions making up a session.

Path control network

Each node has a single path control component, in the path control layer, that attaches on one side to the halfsessions in its own node and on the other to data link control (DLC) elements supporting the basic connections between nodes (Fig. 2).

Each DLC component consists of a connection element, a single primary element, and one or more secondary elements. The secondary elements are associated with sets of link-level addresses that distinguish between distinct secondary elements and route link-level messages between the primary element and selected secondaries. Each primary and secondary element lies inside the node it sup-

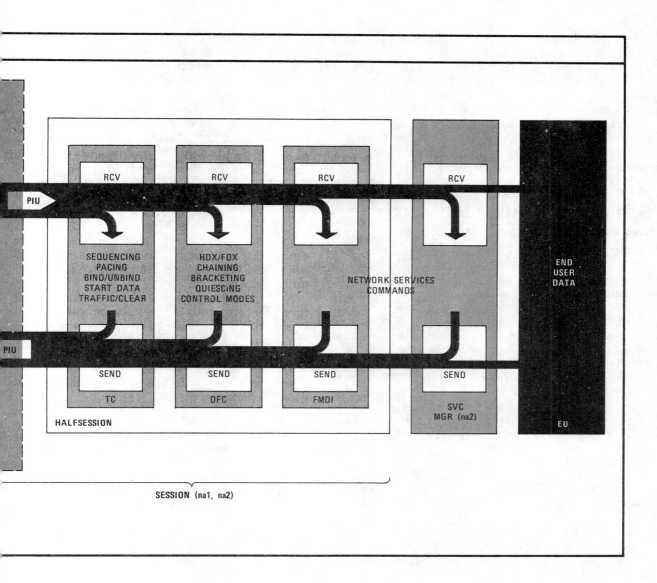

RCV   RCV   RCV   RCV

PIU

SEQUENCING
PACING
BIND/UNBIND
START DATA
TRAFFIC/CLEAR

HDX/FDX
CHAINING
BRACKETING
QUIESCING
CONTROL MODES

NETWORK SERVICES
COMMANDS

END
USER
DATA

PIU

SEND   SEND   SEND   SEND

TC   DFC   FMDI   SVC MGR (na2)   EU

HALFSESSION

SESSION (na1, na2)

ports, while the connection element, typically a transmission link, lies outside the nodes and transmits messages between nodes.

The DLC elements can be implemented by various physical and logical devices, producing such specific DLC protocols as System/370 channel, SDLC, point-to-point and multipoint.

Each DLC component coordinates the transfer of messages between the single primary DLC element and the set of secondary DLC elements, and provides link-level management and error recovery procedures. In support of these functions, the primary and secondaries can also provide buffering, as well as such connection functions as automatic dial and disconnect.

(For simplicity of illustration, Figure 2 highlights only one data link control component; in fact, there will be many DLC components active at any moment, and more than one DLC component may be used for a particular session.)

Messages exchanged between primary and secondary DLC elements typically have the basic link unit (BLU) format shown in Figure 3. The DLC information is contained in the DLC header and trailer. It provides link-level information to synchronize the primary and secondary DLC elements and supports link-level error detection and recovery mechanisms. User information lies in a message's basic transmission unit (BTU), which consists of one or more path information units.

The path control and DLC components together make up the path control (or common) network (Fig. 2). Each path control component routes path information units between its local halfsessions and its local DLC primaries and secondaries. The path control network does this in such a way that any path information unit (PIU) addressed to flow between paired halfsessions is properly routed and kept in first-in/first-out order in each session.

The path control components also support segmenting and blocking of path information over the DLC elements. The message units handled by the halfsessions, therefore, need not be the same length as those handled within the path control network.

The path control network, the innermost layer in SNA's set of nested subnetworks, transmits messages between paired halfsessions in such a way

66 Synchronization and management of halfsessions are internal functions. 99

that each halfsession appears to be directly connected to its partner. The synchronization and management of halfsessions are internal functions of SNA and need not directly concern the network user. It is useful, however, to understand broadly how halfsessions operate (Fig. 4).

Each halfsession performs various levels of resource management and data manipulation. A halfsession also provides coordination and error recovery mechanisms that allow both it and its partner halfsession to interact correctly, irrespective of their relative positions in the network. Thus, the protocols observed by paired halfsessions are the same whether the halfsessions are in the same or in different nodes, and the network user need not be concerned with the effect of error and delay in individual links.

Each halfsession layer is divided into "send" and "receive" components. As shown at the left of Figure 4, different parts of the path information unit (PIU) are generated by different components, such as the end-user layer, the services managers layer, and the halfsession layer.

Each PIU consists of multiple commands or responses corresponding to the complete set of fields and indicators contained in the transmission header, the request/response header, and the request/response unit fields. Each of these commands is strongly associated with one of the principal sublayers of the halfsession layer—for example, the pacing commands carried by the pacing indicator are associated with the transmission control layer. The commands associated with each PIU can be thought of as originating in the appropriate "send" components of the sending halfsession (Fig. 4). The resulting PIU enters and is transported through the path control network, and is delivered to the destination halfsession.

Halfsession components

Here each command part is routed to the corresponding receive component in the halfsession layer complementary to the sending layer. Each

component (described below) issues commands to initiate specific actions in the network. Representative commands will be described for each component of the halfsession layer.

Commands, actions and responses are generated as a result of internal or external events. For example, in response to a network operator signal, VTAM issues commands to the NCP during initialization of the network; these commands cause the NCP to prepare dial ports for incoming calls and to establish contact with remote stations. Other commands from VTAM cause a session to be activated with the remote end user, data movement to begin on the path, or a session to terminate. Commands are also issued by VTAM to remote stations to start data traffic, to resynchronize data flow after a failure in the link, and to perform other control actions in the network.

A key structural feature of SNA is that it gives functional responsibility for network management to individual layers or to components within a layer. Furthermore, error detection for any particular class of actions is performed in the layer responsible for those actions. In many instances, the recovery action is also implemented by the layer that detected the error.

This functional separation permits error effects to be limited, in many cases, to a specific layer or component. Without this structure, minor errors could be overcome only by terminating a transmission and restarting, with a consequent decrease in throughput and increase in communications costs on switched links. For example, DLC is functionally isolated and separated from the management of a session. The components that maintain a session's status are not immediately affected if a data link experiences transmission failures during the session. Once the data link has again become operational—for example, after a modem has resynchronized—the session may continue from the point of interruption.

The next three sections describe the key features of the components in the halfsession: transmission control, data flow control, and the function management data interpreter.

Transmission control. The transmission control component controls the activation of sessions, initializes data traffic, and paces and sequences data flow within sessions.

The principal command groups and protocols supported by the transmission control component are BIND and UNBIND, START DATA TRAFFIC, CLEAR, SEQUENCE NUMBERS, and PACING.

The BIND and UNBIND commands are sent by a primary halfsession to initiate the activation or deactivation of session. A set of parameters contained in the BIND command defines such key attributes of the session as request unit chaining characteristics, error recovery features, and whether the session is to be half- or full-duplex.

The secondary halfsession can respond positively or negatively, depending on whether or not it can support the session with the requested attributes. The UNBIND command performs the opposite of a BIND command, and deactivates a session.

The command START DATA TRAFFIC is sent by the primary halfsession to the secondary halfsession to signal that an exchange of user data is imminent on the already activated session.

A CLEAR command halts all user data flow and resets pacing and sequencing algorithms without deactivating the session. This command is useful in recovering from data flow errors without forcing session reactivation.

In a special field of the transmission header are the SEQUENCE NUMBERS, which tag the commands, including request/response unit (RU) data, that are carried in requests. The same numbers are inserted in the transmission headers of responses to correlate returned responses with their respective requests. The sequential nature of this field is exploited in certain operating modes where responses are to be returned only to certain items in a long string of requests. Sequencing is supported independently in each direction on the request data

5. Independent pacing and sequencing numbers lend stringent control—against excessive flow and errors—to messages moving between terminals.

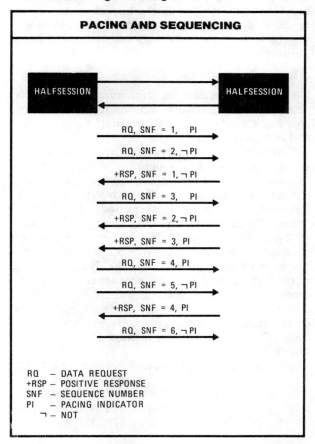

PACING AND SEQUENCING

HALFSESSION ⟷ HALFSESSION

RQ, SNF = 1, PI →
RQ, SNF = 2, ¬PI →
← +RSP, SNF = 1, ¬PI
RQ, SNF = 3, PI →
← +RSP, SNF = 2, ¬PI
← +RSP, SNF = 3, PI
RQ, SNF = 4, PI →
RQ, SNF = 5, ¬PI →
← +RSP, SNF = 4, PI
RQ, SNF = 6, ¬PI →

RQ — DATA REQUEST
+RSP — POSITIVE RESPONSE
SNF — SEQUENCE NUMBER
PI — PACING INDICATOR
¬ — NOT

flows between halfsessions. Halfsession sequence numbers are distinct from DLC sequence numbers, which synchronize one DLC station with another. Figure 5 shows an example of sequence numbering, as well as how pacing operates.

The technique called PACING allows a halfsession to control the rate at which it receives request data from its partner halfsession. Pacing is used when the receiving halfsession is unable to accept more than a certain number of data requests at a time, say because of a limited number of buffers. Pacing control information is then exchanged, using appropriately set bit indicators in the data request and response headers.

Pacing and sequencing operate according to the cycles illustrated in Figure 5. The sending halfsession initially may send up to N requests, where N is the pacing limit. The pacing request indicator is set on the first request in the series. If, after sending the Nth request, the sender has not received a pacing response indication it must cease sending data requests until this indication is received; at this point the sender can transmit another group of N data requests. If the pacing response indication has been received by the time the sender has completed a batch of N data request transmissions, the sender may go ahead immediately with the next batch of N data requests. A pacing response indication can be carried on a regular sequenced response to a given request, or on an unsequenced ISOLATED PACING RESPONSE when no regular response is scheduled.

In Figure 5, the pacing limit (N) is 3. (Note that in Figure 5 time progresses down the page.) The first request is assigned sequence number 1 (SNF-1), and carries the pacing indicator. Then the second request (SNF-2) is sent. Next, the receiver responds with SNF-1 to the first request, and the sender transmits the third request (SNF-3). Now transmission halts until, as shown, responses are received to the second and third requests. Receipt of a positive response (+RSP) to the third request with the pacing response indicator ON permits the sender to transmit more requests—numbers 4, 5, 6—and so on.

The pacing discipline does not apply to certain control requests; thus control of the session can be exercised even if the flow of data is halted by the pacing protocols.

Data flow control. In the halfsession layer, data flow control (DFC) components provide dynamic control within a session of the data transmission and manipulation resources allocated to the session at the time of its activation. The principal modes, functions and commands supported by the DFC components are SEND/RECEIVE, CHAINING, BRACKETING, QUIESCING and CONTROL.

The SEND/RECEIVE mode relates to the fact that, while the transmission control network is architecturally full duplex, at the DFC layer (and outward) data requests can be exchanged either in the full-duplex mode or in variations of the half-duplex mode. In half-duplex, when a sending DFC component completes its transmission of data requests, the component transfers control of sending to its partner DFC by setting the change-direction indicator in the header of the last data request sent.

The CHAINING function provides a mechanism through which a sequence of related data requests sent from one halfsession to another is logically treated as a single end-user message. In a business application, for example, requests relating to individual invoices may all be grouped as one chain for each invoice. The beginning and ending request in each chain is denoted by the begin-chain and end-chain indicator in the request headers.

The BRACKETING function provides a mechanism through which a set of data request chains and their responses, exchanged between two halfsessions, can be logically associated with a single transaction—for example in an airline reservation system, all the end-user messages in both directions for a flight reservation corresponding to customer data, flight inquiry, reservation confirmation and so forth, would be grouped as chains in a single bracket. The beginning and ending of each bracket is denoted by the begin-bracket and end-bracket indicators in the request headers.

The QUIESCE AT END OF CHAIN, QUIESCE COMPLETE and RELEASE QUIESCE commands are the control requests used to interrupt the flow of data requests between paired halfsessions for an indefinite time, without affecting the other control protocols of the session. These requests can be supported independently in either direction between the paired halfsessions. For example, quiescing may be invoked when a buffer pool is running out of usable space or when a printer has run out of paper.

A halfsession sends QUIESCE AT END OF CHAIN when requesting its partner to interrupt a data request transmission at the end of the current chain. The partner halfsession replies with QUIESCE COMPLETE to indicate that it has quiesced. As a result, data request flow from the partner ceases until resumption is requested by the original halfsession's sending of RELEASE QUIESCE.

The CONTROL mode has two options for request flows and two for response flows. The appropriate option depends on the application and is picked at the time the BIND command is given. In the IMMEDIATE REQUEST mode the sending halfsession can have at most only one data request chain outstanding to which no response has yet been received. In the DELAYED REQUEST mode the sending halfsession can have multiple outstanding data request chains. In the IMMEDIATE RESPONSE mode a receiving halfsession must respond to data requests in the order they are received, while in the DELAYED RESPONSE mode a receiving halfsession may respond to data requests in any order (the sequence numbers, in any mode, correlate the re-

sponses with the corresponding requests).

The request and response control mode alternatives present a tradeoff between data throughput and error recovery complexity. Sessions defined as immediate request and immediate response by the BIND command may have lower throughput than those defined as delayed request and delayed response because of the more stringent request/response interlocking; conversely the error-recovery procedures can be much simpler.

Function management. Data requests, as distinct from control requests, pass between function management data interpreters, which are connected in the same session by the data flow control (DFC) network.

For sessions between logical unit services managers the request unit content is provided by the end users and is processed by the function management data interpreters, which may provide such fa-

> ❝ SNA may provide such facilities as compression and display formatting. ❞

cilities as data compression and display formatting.

Sessions involving the system services control point (SSCP) use appropriate procedures in the SSCP function management data interpreters, as well as in those of the physical and logical units, to monitor and control the network's processing and communications resources.

Network services

Flowing between the function management data interpreters are network services requests and responses, classified as configuration, maintenance and session services.

Configuration services. Each physical unit services manager has a definite responsibility to monitor and control the data link control (DLC) components attaching to its node, and may also have to load and dump adjacent nodes.

Each physical unit services manager is assisted in its configuration service role by the SSCP services manager, which maintains over-all information on the network configuration and the dynamic status of the key communications components. The SSCP services manager keeps track of the network architectural components and indirectly controls these components by exchanging cues and data with each physical unit services manager, using configuration service requests.

The principal configuration service command groups are ACTIVATE LINK, DEACTIVATE LINK, ACTIVATE CONNECT IN, DEACTIVATE CONNECT IN, CONNECT OUT, ABANDON CONNECT OUT, REQUEST CONTACT, CONTACT, CONTACTED and DISCONTACT.

Command ACTIVATE LINK initiates a procedure at the receiving physical unit services manager to activate the primary DLC component specified by the link address parameter in the request. Conversely, DEACTIVATE LINK initiates a deactivation of the designated primary DLC component.

Certain commands are used with switched (dial-up) links. For example, ACTIVATE CONNECT IN requests the designated primary DLC component to accept any incoming connection or call, while DEACTIVATE CONNECT IN prevents the designated DLC component from accepting any further incoming connections, but will not end an ongoing call.

Command CONNECT OUT requests the designated primary DCL component to begin a connect out (dial) procedure, using such designated parameters as telephone number and number of retries if that number is busy or fails to answer. Conversely, ABANDON CONNECT OUT terminates the connect out procedure if it is still in progress. When a con-

6. A prescribed sequence of commands and responses establishes a switched (dial-up) link between one terminal and another in an SNA network.

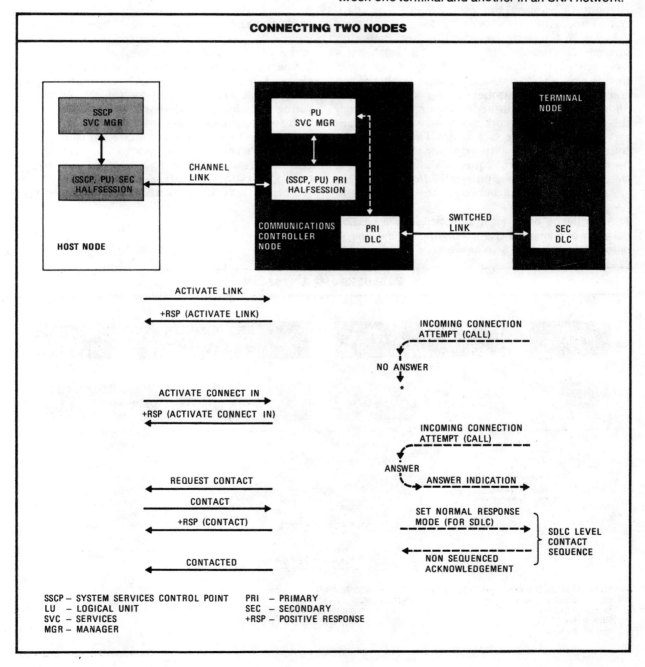

nection is made, whether through a "connect in" or "connect out" procedure, the SSCP services manager is notified by a REQUEST CONTACT command (identification parameters received at the DLC level can be passed with REQUEST CONTACT to identify a node calling in).

Finally, in the class of configuration services, CONTACT requests the designated primary DLC component to initiate DLC level contact and synchronization with the designated secondary component. When DLC synchronization is completed the physical unit services manager returns CONTACTED to the SSCP services manager. The command DISCONTACT causes link level contact to be abandoned between the primary and secondary DLC components.

Figure 6 demonstrates how these configuration services commands can be used to establish a switched (dial-up) connection between one node, in this case a terminal, and another, in this case a communications controller serving as a destination node. The destination node is connected through the path control network to the SSCP services manager in the host, the SSCP node. The physical resources to effect the information transfer have been set up before the sequence shown in Figure 6 starts. (In Figure 6, time progresses down the page.)

As shown, the link between the SSCP node and the destination node has been activated and a positive response to this action has been returned. The next event in the sequence is that the terminal attempts to establish a dial-up connection with the destination node. But the call is not answered because the ACTIVATE CONNECT IN and its positive response have not yet been completed.

When this command and its response have been executed, the next attempt to make the call is successful. Then, as shown, the necessary commands and their responses are exchanged so that the switched link is made ready for SDLC transmissions with sequenced acknowledgements. The desired session between the terminal and its destination node can now start.

Maintenance services. These command groups support tracing of trouble at the link level and the testing of network components.

Session services. These commands are exchanged by logical unit and SSCP services managers. They enable the SSCP to assist a logical unit in activating a session between itself and another logical unit so as to exchange end-user data.

The principal session services command groups are INITIATE and TERMINATE, CONTROL INITIATE and CONTROL TERMINATE, SESSION STARTED and SESSION ENDED, and BIND FAILURE and UNBIND FAILURE.

The INITIATE and TERMINATE commands flow

7. A sequence of commands establishes a session between a primary and a secondary logical unit in different nodes of the SNA network.

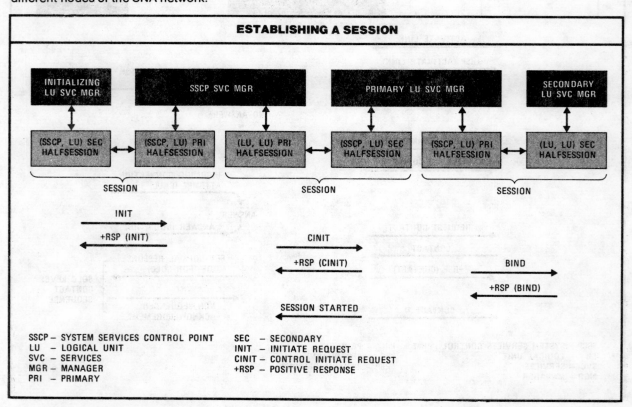

only from a logical unit to the SSCP. An INITIATE command requests the SSCP to authorize and assist in the activation of a session between the logical units designated in the command. Before acting on the request, the SSCP may determine the authority of the logical unit (or its end user) to send the specific INITIATE command. The SSCP also ascertains that the logical units designated in the INITIATE command, as well as the transmission path between them, are all in service and active.

Command TERMINATE requests that the SSCP authorize and assist in the deactivation of the logical unit session designated in the command.

The commands CONTROL INITIATE and CONTROL TERMINATE flow from the SSCP to selected logical units. The first requests the destination, or primary, logical unit to attempt to activate a session with a designated secondary logical unit by sending a BIND command. Values for the session parameters to be used in the new session are included in the CONTROL INITIATE command, which is typically sent by the SSCP as the result of having received an appropriate INITIATE command.

Command CONTROL TERMINATE requests the primary logical unit to attempt to deactivate, with an UNBIND request, its session with the designated secondary logical unit.

The last four commands flow from logical units back to the SSCP. The commands SESSION STARTED and BIND FAILURE are sent to the SSCP by the primary logical unit to indicate whether the BIND attempt has been successful or unsuccessful, while SESSION ENDED and UNBIND FAILURE are used in a similar manner with respect to UNBIND attempts.

Figure 7 shows a successful INITIATE/CONTROL, INITIATE/BIND sequence. Note that three sessions are involved. The two sessions to the left were activated prior to the sequence shown in Figure 7. The SESSION STARTED command is sent to let the SSCP know that the desired BIND has succeeded. In this way, the SSCP is kept up to date about ongoing activity on the network.

In general, the initiating logical unit (shown at the left) can also be either the primary or secondary logical unit shown in the example.

Protocol coupling

The principal components and command groups of SNA have been described as separate features, although they are in fact strongly interdependent. For example: No data can be validly transmitted on a session that has not been activated by a BIND command; no session can be activated between logical units that do not themselves have currently active sessions with the SSCP, as established by ACTI-VATE LOGICAL UNIT commands; no request or

response unit can be routed for transmission on a data link if the primary and secondary DLC elements involved have not achieved successful synchronization by way of the CONTACT and CONTACTED commands.

The effect of this SNA interdependency is two-fold. First, command senders are obliged to send only those command sequences valid with respect to all the protocol and state dependencies explicitly included in SNA. Second, command receivers are also obliged in many cases to check that received command sequences are valid with respect to the protocol and state dependencies.

What is more, SNA enjoys powerful error detection and recovery mechanisms in each layer of the architecture. Each principal component of an SNA network checks the input it receives from the network, or from end users by way of the services managers, for proper format and for consistency

> **" SNA enjoys detection and recovery mechanisms in each network layer. "**

with the current state of the newtork. And errors detected on received requests will result in a negative response, which includes a sense code describing the error. A set of request units (for example, LOGICAL UNIT STATUS) is also defined in SNA to describe various error conditions or to request error recovery assistance.

Once an error condition has been detected and reported, a variety of recovery procedures can be invoked through the SNA facilities, from total network restart, through individual link and node restarts, to specific recoveries within individual sessions at the bracket and chain level.

Finally, it is important to point out that since September 1974, when IBM formally announced SNA, numerous hardware and software products have been introduced which implement the architecture described here. Figure 8 shows the 3767 (background) and 3775 (foreground) communications terminals, both of which are part of the IBM 3770 data communications system. These and other SNA terminals provide a unified structure for handling complex teleprocessing tasks. Many networks using SNA have been installed, and the architecture itself has been expanded with IBM's recent announcement of support in SNA of multiple-host networking. These points illustrate the fact that SNA continues as the base for IBM's communications products and programming software. ∎

Making SNA work on existing on-line networks

Peter D. Rosenow, Crocker National Bank, San Francisco

Implementing SNA on existing nets requires careful evolutionary planning and the patience needed to keep one's eye on the rewards

Crocker National Bank, San Francisco, operates 358 branch offices spread over 201 communities throughout California. These offices comprise the third largest branch bank network in the country and, in early 1975, were linked by telephone and hardcopy computer output. It was then that management decided that if the bank's services were to be competitive and convenient, Crocker's customers should be able to bank at any branch, regardless of where their accounts were kept.

After this objective was defined, the bank decided, in July 1975, to go ahead with the creation of a 7,000-mile statewide retail inquiry system (RIS) that would link all Crocker offices through a network of computer-based inquiry terminals. The decision was part of a larger strategy aimed at providing management with a flexible technology base that would permit quick response to new initiatives, such as electronic funds transfer systems (EFTS) or retail point-of-sale (POS) facilities. A statewide terminal network, together with the projected Crocker Banking Card, was seen as a springboard for implementing future bank services.

IBM was chosen as the primary vendor for the network because its open-ended systems network architecture (SNA)—along with such mainline software as MVS (multiple virtual storage) and IMS (information management system)—allowed the bank to provide

the needed functions in timely fashion, while keeping future options open. The IBM 3600 finance communication system, operating under SNA, would provide the bank's branches with communications and terminal facilities for major transactions, as well as preparing the way for additional on-line customer-banking services. Moreover, under the announced launch program for the model 3600 terminal network, it was felt that IBM could provide effective support in achieving the bank's goals on schedule—a belief that was justified.

In July 1975, Crocker's San Francisco operations center operated three IBM System/370 model 158s, primarily for batch production. Teleprocessing facilities then consisted of three IBM 3270 data communications terminal networks, dedicated to such functions as IBM's timesharing option (TSO), Video/370 for data entry purposes, and an Intercomm application used by the investment department. These programs and services were supported by 66 IBM 3270 terminals—accessible through IBM's basic telecommunications access method (BTAM/TCAM), half of which were attached by local channels. Crocker had neither MVS nor IMS database management capabilities.

To implement the retail inquiry system and coordinate it with the existing facilities, four major steps were defined, some of which would have to be performed

1 Components of performance

Stress testing. *Before taking delivery of IBM's financial service terminals, Crocker tested the rest of the loop to see if it could take the load. With 20 branches on-line, the* *flow of teller transactions from a 3606 was simulated by a program in the 3601 controller. Tests were included for software host-system, combined, and application stress.*

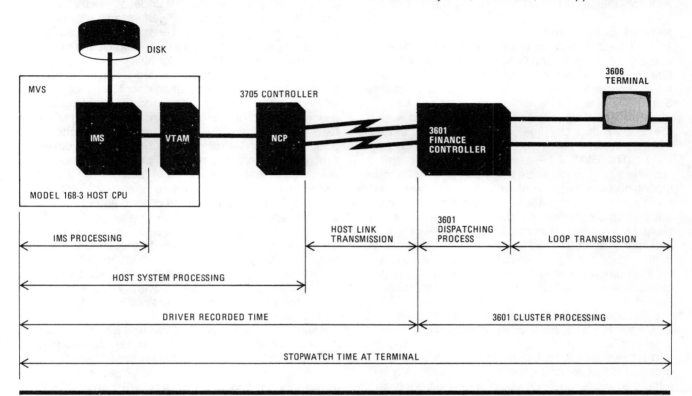

concurrently. First, the bank had to establish, at the San Francisco operations center, a centralized computer facility that would include larger mainframes with expanded main and disk storage, as well as network control capability. Next, Crocker had to plan, design, install, and test the physical RIS network. Third, there was the need to code, test, and install the RIS application programs to operate with IMS and VTAM (virtual telecommunications access method). Finally, the bank had to install IMS, MVS, VTAM, NCP (network control program) and ensure successful integration.

More projects in parallel

It is important to understand that, since July 1975, there have been many other significant projects undertaken in parallel with the on-line project. These projects ranged from the installation of the IBM check processing control system (CPCS) to the development of many applications for IMS under SNA. In total, RIS, plus more than 40 other new systems or major subsystems, were installed by Crocker's 107-member systems staff (with help from IBM) in two and a half years.

Within a span of 90 days—from July to October 1975—an applications team of 10 Crocker people, assisted by IBM engineers, installed the basic elements of a live RIS network in the San Francisco area. In that time, Crocker installed its first IBM 370/168 with four megabytes of main storage, the 3705 communications

controller with the network control program (NCP 3), the 3601 finance controller, type 3604 keyboard display teller terminals, and the application software for 97 RIS terminal functions. MVS 3.6, VTAM, and IMS/VS1.1.1 software was also installed. On the applications side, the customer database was converted to permit on-line demand deposit, savings, and Master Charge transactions from teller terminals.

The integration of MVS, IMS, and VTAM into an effective networking system was particularly difficult since the VTAM/IMS interface was not well understood. The bank learned how these complex software elements "shake hands" and advised IBM of required corrections. Crocker believes this should enable future users to install SNA networks with less difficulty.

In addition, Crocker coded a transaction simulator that ran in the 3601 controller and provided terminal users with a transparent full-function transaction capability for demonstration, test, and training purposes.

In a live demonstration for bank management, the data communications department displayed the full capabilities of a prototype RIS network consisting of a branch terminal, the 3601 and 3705 controllers, and the 370/168 host processor. It was shown that terminal inquiries against the live database could be initiated either by keying in the customer's account number or via the Crocker plastic debit card, which tied together the three major types of accounts.

Since the network was generated with a full set of SNA workstations, more terminals and controllers could have been deployed than were actually used. From a business point of view, a creditable terminal-based transaction capability that could be expanded with confidence was developed in only 90 days.

Network design criteria
The criteria for the design of the network had been worked out jointly by the Crocker technical staff and IBM, making use of a number of IBM simulation tools. When completed, a network of well over 600 terminals, distributed over 360 branches, was envisioned.

Among the major design factors considered were the host-link capacity, line costs, and the cost of the 3601 controllers which were to act as remote concentrators. The IBM 3601—essentially a small processor—was considered to be a key component because it controls both the transmission of data between terminals and the central processor, and—through user application programming—the functions of the attached terminals. To provide for future growth, the maximum size 3601 (56K) was selected. Other 3601 factors to be considered were loop speed and capacity, internal cycle speeds, and resource sharing capabilities between the 3601 program, loop slots, and logical units.

Based on these factors and allowing for growth, 4.8 kbit/s full-duplex trunk lines were chosen to communicate in SDLC between the 3705 controller at the host and the remote 3601s. Up to five 3601s could be dropped from each trunk line and five (potentially six) remote SNA branch loops could originate from each 3601 controller. Within each remote loop, four to five branches could be interconnected via two-wire 1.2 kbit/s voice-grade lines. This allowed between 20 and 25 branches to be connected to each controller.

Communications between the 3601s and the 3705 controller is in a "multipoint duplex" mode, rather than full duplex. In this mode, the 3601s cannot send and receive messages simultaneously, although there is two-way traffic on the trunk lines. In practice, this makes little difference, however, because the 3601 controller buffers and stores the message traffic from the various branch terminals in the loop, and upon being polled by the 3705, transmits all messages.

To determine terminal response-time characteristics, Crocker ran a network simulation, based on a maximum load of one transaction per terminal every 90 seconds, and a number of assumptions as to message length, transaction mix, etc. The simulation showed, for example, that with three 3606 teller terminals per branch, or a total of 300 terminals on a trunk line (for 100 branches), 90 percent of all transactions would have a response time of 6.3 seconds or less, and half the transactions would be done within five seconds.

Performance testing
Before the arrival of IBM's 3606 financial service terminals, the bank ran tests to document, tune, and stress-test the network for satisfactory performance under load. In early 1976, with about 20 branches on-line, a series of system tests—that included software function, host-system stress, 3601 controller/application program-stress, combined-stress, and regression tests—was performed. The major components involved in performance testing are shown in Figure 1.

The host system was tested under stress by the use of a 3601 driver program that generated a flow of teller transactions to the 3705 and host CPU at a predetermined rate and transaction mix. Response time was measured at the 3601 driver for nine levels of transaction complexity. Of particular interest was a series of tests to determine the operating characteristics of the 3601 controller and the associated user application program during high-volume transaction activity. These tests were performed with 20 operators and actual 3606 terminals. Two additional 3601 software drivers simulated high-volume transaction activity. Major tools consisted of IBM's measurement facility 1 (MF1), the IMS DC monitor, stopwatch timing, and IMS log tape analysis. Operators were instructed to enter transactions as rapidly as the response time allowed.

Results of tests with a single 3601 controller and a simulated traffic load equivalent to that from a 90-terminal 3601 cluster indicated a 3601 throughput of 1.9 transactions per second. Response time for 90 percent of inquiry transactions was 5.7 seconds or less, while for "update" transactions it was 9.1 seconds or less.

Tests with multiple 3601s indicated a throughput of 1.6 transactions/second (at 30 percent CPU utilization). Ninety percent of inquiry response times were 5.2 seconds or less, well within the target of five to seven seconds. Update transaction response time, however, was high, due to a direct access storage device (DASD) performance bottleneck at the host. This was traced to two high-activity databases allocated to the same disk media. As a result of the tests, the database was reallocated and additional tuning of the host was carried out.

Network expansion . . . and problems
Between January 1976 and the official Aug. 18 announcement date, 3606 terminals were installed in roughly 75 percent of the Crocker branches. This was said to be the first time that IBM 3606 terminals had been installed anywhere, and the first time that a 3606 application program had been written to run in the 3601 controller. A portion of the new 3606s were used as customer-operated lobby terminals, permitting customers to use their Crocker Bank Cards to inquire directly into their account balances from an automatic, unattended lobby terminal.

By the end of September, 450 3606s were installed in 358 branches, all running off 23 3601-1 finance controllers. In June of 1977, there was further expansion of the terminal network. Selected branches were equipped with the IBM 3614 automated teller machines (ATMs), permitting unattended self-service customer transactions for 19 hours daily. These transactions were also driven by the Crocker Bank Card.

During installation of the branch circuits, Crocker management experienced considerable difficulty edu-

2 First configuration

First attempt. In June 1976, the RIS network in Northern California had two IBM model 158s and one 168 responsible for all processing. However, each of the controller/processor systems ran alone. One system could not back up another in case of an outage and all three processors were forced to contend for the same storage.

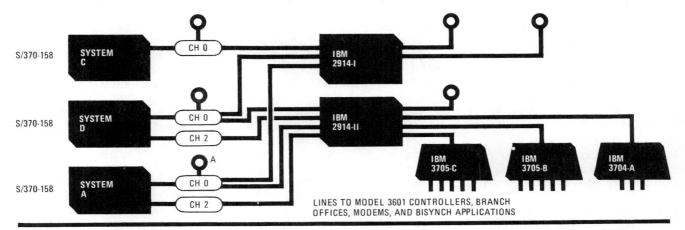

LINES TO MODEL 3601 CONTROLLERS, BRANCH
OFFICES, MODEMS, AND BISYNCH APPLICATIONS

cating local telephone companies in IBM's SNA loop technology. Each line within each loop had to be separately ordered and each one was separately billed at first. The telephone company asked that four-wire circuits be installed on the 3601 loops so that the phone company technicians could run loopback tests from their central office. This would facilitate rapid problem determination during outages. (Depending on the geography, in some cases it actually was more economical to use four-wire lines from the last branch back to the controller.) The installation of electrical outlets to power the IBM 3603 modems and 3606 terminals, which the phone companies didn't want to handle, had to be performed by contracted electricians.

Figure 2 illustrates the configuration of the RIS network and other services at the Northern California operations center (NCOC), as of about June 1976. The bank had two model 158s and one 168, two model 1 3705 communications controllers and one 3704, with channel switching provided by an IBM 2914. The entire RIS network ran under the NCP4 network control program in the 3705-C controller, which was connected to the model 168 with MVS 3.6 and VTAM1. Non-SNA (bisync) on-line applications, serviced by BTAM, such as Video/370 and Intercomm, ran under the EP 2.3 emulation program in the 3705-B controller, and were primarily used for timesharing (TSO) and test purposes. They were attached to one of the 370/158s.

An obvious problem with this configuration was that each of the controller/processor systems was unique and could not back up the others. In fact, major applications were dedicated to a single system and could not run in another. For example, if the 3705-C controller with the RIS network went down—which happened on occasion—the controller had to be repaired before the network could go back on line. Moreover, system error recovery and fallback procedures were inadequate. This was an unacceptable situation for a customer-oriented network. Total backup for the existing configuration, however, would have required six

very costly communications controllers. Crocker management and technical personnel also found that they had serious DASD contention, with each of the three processors trying to gain access to the shared disk facilities. As the transaction volume began to increase, all of these problems grew worse.

Conversion to dual backup

To overcome these fallback, error recovery, and contention difficulties, Crocker management used the months from June to December 1976 to convert the initial system to a balanced dual processor/controller configuration with full backup capabilities (Fig. 3). The conversion was a very complex task, since it required the phasing and integration of a variety of new hardware and software without interrupting ongoing operations. The two 370/158 processors were replaced by a second model 168-3, equipped with four megabytes of internal storage. To resolve the DASD contention, disk facilities were expanded and most of the model 3330 drives were converted to larger capacity model 3350s. Disk access was balanced by arranging symmetrical dual paths between the processors and disk storage. Two 3705 model 2 communications controllers (with 160K storage each) replaced the three existing controllers. Each of the new 3705-2s could handle the combined workload of the three former controllers.

On the software side, Crocker installed the MVS 3.7 operating system, VTAM II in the two host processors, and NCP5/EP3 in the two 3705 controllers. For a balanced configuration, the partitioned emulation program (PEP) was used, instead of running separate EP and NCP programs in the 3705s for BTAM and VTAM applications. PEP, however, is considered only an interim step before completing conversion of all existing BTAM applications to VTAM.

There were several problems involved in cutting over to the new hardware and software without taking down the whole system. While VTAM II could run with EP 2.3

and NCP4, the new 3705-2 controllers could not operate with the early versions of the software, and the old controllers could not run with the new software. After about six weeks, the conversion was completed, and the result was that the bank had achieved one of the country's first balanced dual systems with a full PEP (NCP/EP) capability in the 3705-2s. To allow switching of lines between the controllers without recabling the modems, a front-end, 32-position, digital switch from Cook Engineering was installed.

Since December 1976, further facilities' expansion has been achieved by installing an additional two megabytes of memory in each 168, for a total of six megabytes on each system. Another 32K has been added to each 3705-2 for a total of 192K each, and IMS 1.1.3 has been installed.

The resulting configuration (Fig. 3), with the model 2914 channel switches and the 32-position digital switch, provides a high level of flexibility. The load can be balanced between the two processors and 3705 controllers as desired. In effect, any line can go to either processor. The JCL procedures have be revised to reflect which 3705 is to be used for a particular on-line application. Referring to Figure 3, normally the RIS network and other on-line services run on the 3705-X controller and the "red" model 168-3 (the "red" system also supports CPCS and five 3890s), while TSO, test jobs, and batch work run on the 3705-Y and the "blue" model 168-3. At night, both processors may handle batch work.

In the event of host processor or controller failure, the network can be reconfigured to the "blue" system in less than five minutes. However, IMS restart procedures usually take another 10 to 15 minutes. Overall availability has been improved by error-recovery procedures that provide step-by-step instructions to recover from any major component failure.

Network management

Proper network management, including rapid problem determination and resolution, is crucially important in an on-line network. These functions are performed by console and master terminal operators (MTOs) in the San Francisco on-line control center. The center is equipped with a digital patch panel, trunk-line modems, two 3705 communications controllers, two system consoles, and a duplicate of every major component used in the network. In addition, the center contains complete network documentation, the RIS status control board, the IMS log tape drives, and a variety of test equipment, including a recording Spectron Datascope. The MTO can directly dial up each remote 3601 controller location and access a variety of diagnostic functions.

Because a break anywhere in a remote loop will cause the entire loop to stop operating, quick reporting and effective problem resolution of outages is a necessity. A typical outage incident is handled through six separate steps. *First,* the problem is either observed by the console operator as a result of self diagnosing software tests (run automatically every five minutes) or phoned in to the center by a terminal user. *Next,* the center's service desk personnel start the trouble report and run the initial problem resolution procedures (PRPs). These consists of calling each location on the faulty loop to determine the READY/SYNC-light status and instructing the teller at the terminal to run the 3606 modem wrap test and a remote sub-loop wrap test. The results are recorded on the trouble report and posted on the status control board. *Third,* if the initial PRPs have pinpointed the problem, the master terminal operator dispatches the responsible repair organization—either IBM, the telephone company, or the bank's own maintenance organization. *Fourth,* if the problem has not been isolated, further problem determination is performed. For example, the MTO may invoke the 3601 control-operator function and dial into the remote location to observe various system indicators, such as the system log, error counters, and device tests. *Fifth,* the MTO follows up on repair progress by requiring repairmen to call in at fixed intervals and, if necessary, invokes various escalation procedures. *Finally,* when the incident has been resolved, the failing component and cause of failure are identified on the trouble report, the length (in terminal hours) and severity (in total terminal hours lost) of the outage are recorded, and the status control board is cleared.

Weekly summaries

Summary reports of host and network outages, availability, and daily transaction volumes are prepared weekly. In a typical week during November 1977, for example, there were 18 network outages that amounted to 47.2 hours of downtime among the 578 installed terminals. Meantime to resolution, therefore, was 2.6 hours. Total network availability, based on scheduled terminal hours, for the week, was a highly acceptable 97.7 percent.

RIS network performance has steadily improved during the two years of its existence. Problems involved with installation of the model 168 and interfacing the early versions of the software put availability in the 80-95 percent range in 1976. Network availability during 1977, measured in available terminal hours, has averaged 96 percent.

Terminal response time currently averages four to five seconds. It has not changed much since June 1976, when the bank had a low-performance, relatively untuned system with about 370 terminals and only 49,000 transactions a week. It appears that the increased transaction volume—currently about 257,000 transactions/week—and increased performance have to some extent compensated for each other.

As mentioned earlier, a number of other Crocker Bank on-line services that use bisynchronous communications with BTAM now run under the partitioned emulation program in the 3705 controller. These are not accessible by SNA/VTAM applications and terminals. These processes are gradually being converted to VTAM and all new on-line applications are being written with a VTAM front-end. The Video/370 facility and the corporate CPU data links have already been converted to VTAM, with Intercomm to follow. Under IMS, a CPU to CPU data link to the Western States

3 Final configuration

Balanced system. The problems encountered in the first attempt were resolved by conversion to a complete, dual backup host site system. Two 158s were replaced by one 168, and contention was solved by increasing disk facilities. On-line SDLC functions use one processor, all others use the "blue" host. The 3705-2s route by availability.

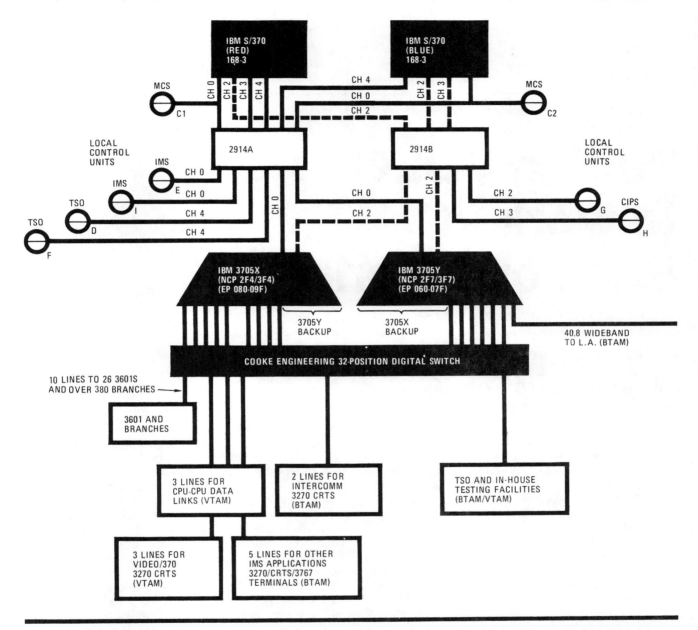

Bank Association (WSBA), as a VTAM application program, has also been implemented. This has been added to the RIS network, permitting tellers at remote branch terminals to make direct inquiries concerning Master Charge credit authorizations. An inquiry message coming in through the Crocker network is automatically switched to WSBA, with a response being returned in five to seven seconds.

Crocker Bank's intention is to integrate all on-line functions into the basic SNA framework, with the objective of allowing any Crocker terminal with the appropriate authorization to have access to any of the bank's on-line applications. In the past two-and-one-half years, a second-generation capability has been converted to a network of state-of-the-art systems and services. The bank's level of investment, and the human resources (about 40 man-years total) needed to establish the network, were relatively small. A good part of this success is due to the efforts of an outstanding development team, and to the work of a dedicated computer operations staff.

Crocker management support was—and will continue to be—based on the business value of the project and not on the technological innovation involved. ■

Putting SDLC to work at Bank of America

Herbert Chang, Bank of America, San Francisco

Ingenious network using three forms of synchronous data link control (SDLC) speeds bank's statewide service

To support its statewide on-line banking operations, Bank of America, headquartered in San Francisco, developed a distributed processing network with 48 General Automation 16/440 minicomputers running on both standard and variant forms of IBM's SDLC protocol. Three forms of SDLC were needed to make the network operate to Bank of America's requirements—and each variation fits neatly into its own niche in the network structure. The ingenuity of the bank combined with the flexibility of the protocol have made possible a data communications network that fits all the needs of a huge transaction-oriented organization.

The way the network is presently configured, the hubs of the bank's network are two distributive computing facility (DCF) centers, one in San Francisco and the other in Los Angeles. Within the DCF network is a hierarchy of minicomputers that form processing modules, modules that form centers, communications lines linking centers, and further communications lines linking the centers with the branch offices where the customer's contact with the network revolves around a teller and a transaction terminal.

To follow the path of network communications, the place to begin is at the processing module. A processing module is the basic operating unit in the distributive computing facility. It contains four minicomputers inter-connected by 1.2 Mbit/s communications links. A group of modules at the same physical location makes up a distributive computing facility center. All modules in a DCF center are also interconnected by 1.2 Mbit/s communications links. In addition, a dedicated module is available in each center to allow centralized operational management, monitoring of each module in the center, and connection to the external communications network. This dedicated module is known as the network operations center.

The four minicomputers that make up a module are functionally divided into two parallel pairs (Fig. 1). Two message-handling processors (MHPs) are responsible for the basic communications handling and message routing within the DCF. The pair of file management transaction processors (FMTPs) perform all of the data processing for messages received. The parallel pairs of processors provide undegraded system throughput even when as much as one half of the components within a module fail. For more details, see the panel "What's in a module."

Applications and their networks are distributed over different modules in the same DCF center based on the needs of the applications (Fig. 2). Also, an application may reside in a set of modules in two DCF centers and have its own external communications net-

1 Typical distributive computing facility module

Backup capability. *Each distributive computing facility center's basic functional unit is the module. The components of the module are parallel pairs of minicomputers for message handling and transaction processing cross-connected by 1.2 Mbit/s data links. The module will continue to function even if half of the unit's configuration fails.*

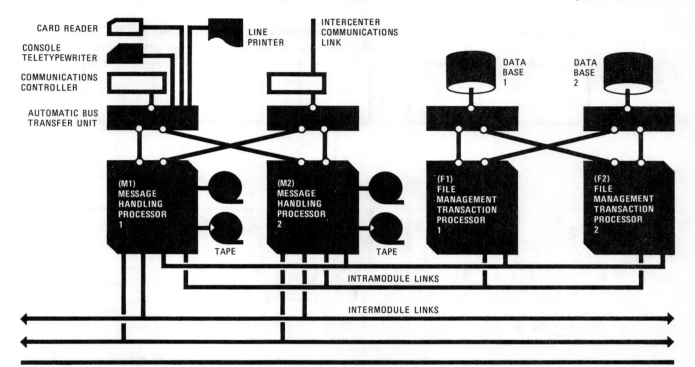

work distributed across several other modules.

A transaction may be introduced to the network through one of its modules and be processed by another. Or, several applications may reside in a single module with or without its own external communications network. Applications may share the external communications network of another application. In addition, an application may have its modules geographically distributed in more than one DCF center.

Because of this flexible arrangement of network sharing among applications, a message may be routed to several processors before it arrives at its final destination for processing. For example, a San Francisco customer may wish to cash a check at a Los Angeles branch (Fig. 3). The inquiry will arrive at one of the modules in the Los Angeles center (Module D, for example) and be routed to the module with the external communications link (Module E) to the San Francisco center. After arriving at the San Francisco center, the message is forwarded to the module where the data base of that account is maintained for processing. The response to this inquiry takes the path through Module C back to the terminal connected to Module D where the inquiry originated.

DCF standard message format

To allow for this type of distributed processing, a standard interface was adopted for all modules. The interface requirement is satisfied by the use of a standard message format (Fig. 4) throughout the internal net-

work of computers. Imbedded in the message is information that will allow the message to be routed to its final destination.

All the message-handling processors have sufficient logic to digest the information contained in a DCF standard message, allowing them to forward the message to its next destination..An incoming message will be converted to the standard message format before being routed to any module or processor in the distributive computing facility.

Three protocols for the DCF

The DCF now has two internal communications protocols and one external protocol. Synchronous data link control (SDLC) grammar was used to develop these protocols. SDLC was selected because of the following functional capabilities and characteristics:
- Transparency—the dependence of the communications link on code structure is eliminated, allowing for transmission of both data and control information essential for the efficient routing and flow of messages in the network.
- Bit-oriented transmission—the flexibility of this property facilitates the development of the message text since the user is not tied into any length of characters.
- Efficient operation in many types of communications environments—SDLC is designed to operate point-to-point or multipoint, full duplex or half duplex, and over communications lines with either short or long propagation delays. This allows maximum use of the commu-

SDLC variations. Along with a variant of IBM's synchronous data link control (SDLC) protocol for use within each module and for intermodule links that join processor sets to form a DCF center, intercenter links utilize a different variant of the protocol. External links that assure like modules run the same applications use a third variant.

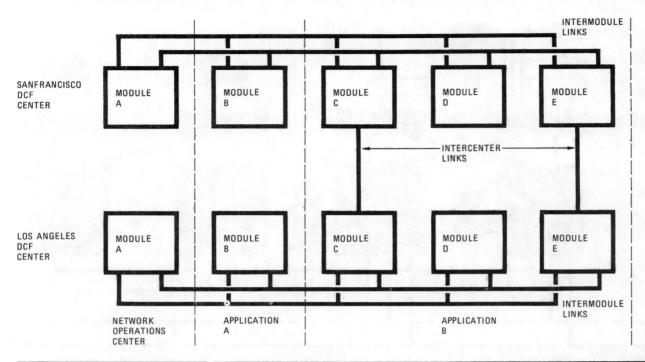

nications lines. The stations on the link may be either simple or complex in terms of intelligence.

■ Error checking and detection—SDLC allows for both redundant checking of transmitted data and automatic error detection. Error recovery may be handled for a station without having an impact on the ability of other stations to use the link during the error recovery procedures.

■ Open-ended structure of the SDLC addressing and control—this property allows enhancements and expansion of the network with greater flexibility and ease.

The SDLC grammar satisfies most of the goals inherent in the DCF design. Two internal SDLC protocols were developed to handle all internal communications needs. The structures of these two protocols are variations from standard SDLC. The third protocol, adopted for external network communications adheres very closely to the structure of SDLC.

For a detailed discussion of IBM's SDLC see *"Synchronous data link control,"* DATA COMMUNICATIONS, May/June 1974, pages 49-60.

The two internal SDLC protocols in Bank of America's DCF network support the intra/intermodule links which connect the processors within a module, and one module with another at the same locality. The external variant SDLC protocol has been adopted as the standard for communications with all terminals in the network handled by the distributive computing facility. These three protocols, as has been mentioned, have a common feature called a special message format.

The intramodule/intermodule protocol is used in communication between processors in the internal distributive computing facility network. It is implemented as a variant of standard SDLC. There are basically two internal paths. The intramodule link connects the four processors comprising a module, and the intermodule link connects all modules forming a DCF center. As such, all message-handling processors in a center are stations on the intermodule link while all processors within a module are stations on the intramodule link.

Station interaction

The stations on these links are minicomputers. Each link is capable of handling more than one line. Stations on each line are locally connected. The lines operate in a half-duplex mode and can run at speeds up to 2.44 Mbit/s. At present, the speed is 1.2 Mbit/s.

All stations on the link are secondary stations and all stations have equal status. If a station wishes to transmit a message, it must contend for the line (one of at least two for reliability). When one station obtains the line, it assumes the role of a primary station and begins its output to another station on the line. Since all other stations are then secondary stations they can only receive messages directed to them.

In the event of a sequence error during transmission, the set normal response mode (SNRM) command is used to reset the send and receive (N_S/N_R) counts of the station in question. The last and only unacknowledged message will then be retransmitted.

All information and control frames or messages are in the bank's variant SDLC format. Here, in addition to the presentation of the receiving station address, the sending station must include its own address in the message frame. The sending station address occupies the first eight bits after the address and control words in a standard SDLC format. Hence, a typical frame will take the form of a flag, a receiving station address, a control, a sending station address, an information frame (not present in control frames), a frame check sequence, and a flag.

Since processors within the DCF function autonomously, each processor must handle its own initialization. It must inform all stations on the link when it becomes operational. This is done by sending on-line commands to all other stations on the link. If a station fails to respond within a predetermined period, it is flagged as inoperative by the sending station. Periodically, the station will repeat the on-line command to the inoperative station. If a response is received, the station is flagged as operative and normal traffic can be exchanged between these two stations.

Two types of information frames are used. They are the sequenced (I) and nonsequenced (NSI) information frames. The I frames are used for all normal DCF message transmission. Each I frame received must be acknowledged immediately. The normal acknowledgement is in the form of a supervisory frame, receive ready (RR). However, if the receiving station is congested, it may refuse receipt of the message by responding

What's in a module

The typical distributive computing facility module consists of the following hardware:

Four General Automation GA 16/440 processors each with 128 Kbytes of memory. Two are for the message-handling processors and two for the file management transaction processors.

Four Wangco self-threading magnetic tape drives—two for each message-handling processor.

12 GA1579 synchronous data link control (SDLC) communications controllers for intermodule and intramodule communications. Four for each for the message-handling processors and two for each for the file management transaction processors.

400 million bytes of disk storage to be shared by the two file management transaction processors.

A group of peripherals for local operator communications (one line printer, one card reader, and one operations console teletypewriter).

Two GA 1575 SDLC communications controllers (multiplexed) for external communications needs.

Automatic bus transfer units (ABTUs) are installed to house critical non-redundant components such as the GA 1575 controllers and the disk drive units. Should one of the processors fail, the devices attached to the ABTU will be automatically switched to its companion processor. This design satisfies the reliability goals of the DCF architecture.

with a receive not ready (RNR) response.

Upon receipt of a RNR response, the congested sending station is flagged as inoperative and the initialization procedure is repeated. A congested station will refuse input but will continue to send messages in order to replenish its buffer supply.

Non-sequenced information frames (NSI) are used for only one reason, the loading of a message-handling processor (MHP). The MHP, by design, does not have any auxiliary random access storage. A special external read-only memory (ROM) is attached to each MHP. A program loader in the ROM loads the MHP from a library that resides on disk units in its corresponding file management transaction processor (FMTP). The program loader uses non-sequenced information frames to communicate with the FMTP for loading the MHP. A special form of acknowledgement is used for all program segments received. The acknowledgement is keyed into the loading process and is not handled by the link protocol. The link only acts as a vehicle to carry the program segments to the MHP. Therefore, NSI frames are never used in the intermodule link.

Inherent in the design of this link is a self-checking capability at each station. In order to insure proper operation of the link, a station periodically sends a status message to itself. This is possible because the processor can play the role of both the primary and secondary station during this exercise.

Intercenter SDLC link

The intercenter protocol is used to communicate between geographically separated DCF centers. It is a second variant of the standard SDLC procedure. The lines used are full duplex, point-to-point, running at 9,600 bit/s. A minimum of two lines are used on this link to provide fast and efficient transmission of messages, as well as for reliability. This link may be implemented on either the GA 1579 or the GA 1575 communications controllers.

Since both centers operate as primary stations on the intercenter link, the poll/final bit in the standard SDLC protocol loses its significance. Each station controls the input received from other stations.

Each station functions autonomously once it is initialized. Initialization is done by the exchange of set initialization mode (SIM) commands and non-sequenced acknowledgement (NSA) responses. A station is in the synchronization mode while it attempts to establish contact with another station. Once the NSA response is received as a result of a SIM command, the responding station is capable of accepting messages. At this point the responding station is in the receive ready (RR) mode.

Once a responding station is in the receive ready mode, informational—as opposed to supervisory—messages are sent on an unsolicited basis. Acknowledgement may be in the form of an I, RR, or RNR frame. A reject (REJ) acknowledgement is sent if an out-of-sequence condition is detected. Up to seven unacknowledged messages may be outstanding at any point in time. All messages must be acknowledged. Retransmission of unacknowledged messages will oc-

3 Path of an intercenter message

Banking transaction. A Bank of America customer with an account at a San Francisco branch can go to a Los Angeles branch with any type of transaction. Intermodule and intercenter data links are accessed by the branch through PCUs to connect a teller with the customer's files for fast information transfer and statewide service.

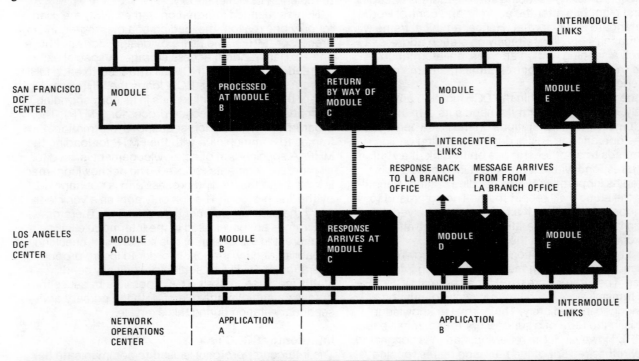

cur on receipt of an REJ or on a time-out basis.

Line activity is monitored on a periodic time-out basis and continued operation of the link depends on the regular exchange of I, RR, or RNR frames. If no activity is detected in a preset time interval, a control message in the form of an RR or RNR frame will be sent to the receiving station. The receiving station must respond with an I, RR, or RNR frame immediately. Failure to respond to the activity control message will cause the sending station to go into the synchronization mode. Once in the synchronization mode, all outstanding and/or undelivered messages will be re-routed to the alternate lines in the link. The lines in this link are spread over different modules in the center, thus affording additional reliability.

The receiving stations always control incoming messages. On receipt of a message, the congestion level of the message-handling processor is checked to make sure that the processor is capable of handling the message. If the processor is not able to handle the message, an RNR response will be sent immediately. Otherwise, the message will be accepted and no acknowledgement is given until the next outgoing message is transmitted. The next outbound message may be generated by the message-handling processor if the acknowledgement threshold of seven messages is reached, or if the link inactivity is reached.

The external SDLC link protocol is used to communicate with the bank's distributive computing facility's standard external network. To qualify as such, the message format must be a subset of the standard DCF message format. Since it is compatible with the general SDLC procedures, only highlights of the use of this protocol are covered.

The protocol is implemented on approximately 120 2,400 bit/s multidrop, full-duplex leased lines with an average of 12 stations per line. The stations are intelligent programmable control units (PCUs). Each branch office in California has at least one PCU. Each PCU, in turn, controls a set of teller terminals with numeric keyboards and small CRT screens, as well as administrative terminals with full alphanumeric keyboards and large CRT screens. This network has about 1,150 PCUs and 10,000 terminals. The link is effected on General Automation 1575 communication controllers. Each controller is capable of handling 16 lines.

The distributive computing facility acts as the primary station for the PCUs. A PCU on a line responds to either a unique address or a common broadcast address. The PCUs are always ready to receive messages from the primary station. However, they will not send any messages until they are polled. Once the DCF initiates a line, it continuously calls all the PCUs on that line's polling list. Polling is in the form of an RR or RNR frame. A PCU must respond to a poll message within a preset time.

After several repeated failures to respond to a poll message from the DCF, the programmable control unit will be flagged as inoperative and placed in a slow-poll mode. A PCU in the slow-poll mode will be called less

4 Standard distributive computing facility message format

Message unit. *The standard format of a Bank of America message allows communications at all network levels through the use of a common introductory frame. The whole message is for internal use, but special information embedded within it gives routing directions so that the proper applications programs receive the correct data.*

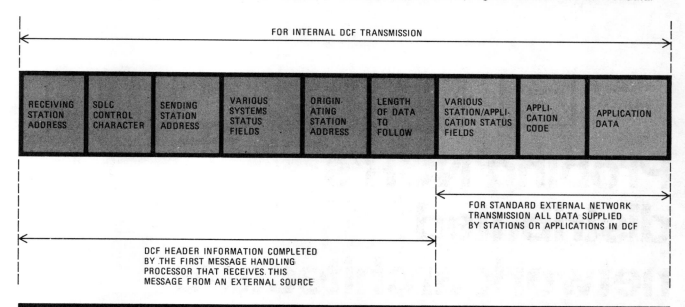

FOR INTERNAL DCF TRANSMISSION

| RECEIVING STATION ADDRESS | SDLC CONTROL CHARACTER | SENDING STATION ADDRESS | VARIOUS SYSTEMS STATUS FIELDS | ORIGIN-ATING STATION ADDRESS | LENGTH OF DATA TO FOLLOW | VARIOUS STATION/APPLI-CATION STATUS FIELDS | APPLI-CATION CODE | APPLICATION DATA |

FOR STANDARD EXTERNAL NETWORK TRANSMISSION ALL DATA SUPPLIED BY STATIONS OR APPLICATIONS IN DCF

DCF HEADER INFORMATION COMPLETED BY THE FIRST MESSAGE HANDLING PROCESSOR THAT RECEIVES THIS MESSAGE FROM AN EXTERNAL SOURCE

frequently than active PCUs on the same line. Once a PCU in the slow-poll mode responds to a call, it is automatically reset as operative, and normal traffic can occur between it and the DCF.

Since this is a full-duplex protocol, input and output must overlap and be asynchronous to maximize line utilization. Poll control messages take priority over normal output messages. Once a poll control message is sent the input line is reserved to accept whatever response may come in, while a normal output message is scheduled for delivery to any station on the lines that responds. The response to a poll can be either in the form of an I frame or any other allowable supervisory or nonsequential frame.

All messages must be acknowledged. All unacknowledged messages will be retransmitted. Output to a station will cease if a preset level of unacknowledged messages is reached. This level is a system-generated variable between one and seven, the maximum allowed by SDLC procedures. The DCF acknowledges all messages received from the PCUs. Acknowledgement is in the form of a supervisory frame (RR or RNR).

The load level of the processor is continuously monitored. If a certain level is reached, no input is solicited from the secondary stations. However, exchange of control information and output from the DCF is expected. In such instances, polling messages will be in the form of the RNR frames.

Down-line loading of PCUs
Perhaps the most interesting aspect of the use of Bank of America's external SDLC link is the situation in which the link-control functions of a secondary station are delegated to another program residing in a different

processor. This action is required because neither the message-handling processors nor the programmable control units have auxiliary random storage capacity. Because the PCUs are programmable and because Bank of America wanted to be able to centrally load new software or reload a failed PCU, the file management transaction processors have to be used for storage of the PCU software and for control of the loading process. If a PCU needs to be loaded, it will respond to any poll request with a request for initialization (RQI). The message-handling processor will transfer this request to an appropriate application in the file management transaction processor. This application will initiate the link control function of the PCU and it will be transferred to the message-handling processor by setting a flag in a message sent to the message-handling processor. At this time, the PCU will be taken out of the polling list. The message-handling processor will act as a vehicle for the application.

The application controls various aspects of the loading functions. The message-handling processor will poll the PCU on request from the application. However, it will not act on a response, but merely pass it back to the application. To provide control to the application, all messages sent to PCUs in this way will be guaranteed a response message, either from the PCU or generated by the message-handling processor as the transmission is completed. Any information generated by the message-handling processor will be in the form of stubs of the original messages from the application program. Once the specific function is completed, the application program will return control of the PCU to the message-handling processor. The activities of other PCUs on the same line are not affected. ■

Probing NCR's distributed network architecture

Frank B. Andrews and Chris G. Cooper, NCR Corp.

Among the newer entrants in the growing architecture arena is NCR/DNA, a communications concept centering on distributed network control

NCR's new communications system architecture—distributed network architecture (NCR/DNA)—embodies a set of concepts, methods, and disciplines which will guide the design of many future NCR products. NCR/DNA is being implemented in planned stages—beginning with the new 2140 electronic cash register—through the 1980s.

The architecture enables shared use of networks by potentially unrelated applications, with the apparent user benefits in terms of cost of operations. It is open-ended, permitting growth of networks and incorporation of additional teleprocessing functions without major disruptions to the network. NCR/DNA has been designed to incorporate modern data communications procedures, including X.25 support and a bit-oriented protocol compatability.

The architecture provides for decentralized control of distributed networks. The network supervisory functions provided by NCR/DNA are not essential to short-term operation. In this way, network operation is not vulnerable to any single element failure.

The concepts which form the basis for NCR/DNA are illustrated by logical growth from a simple telecommunications application to a large network. Figure 1 represents a number of terminals connected to a host processing system through two different communica-

tions lines. In this simple system, the communications hardware is integrated in the host. The host executes several different application programs which interact with corresponding functions in the terminals. The application and terminal functions address each other by logical addresses. This permits communications to take place without concern for line configuration or the particular communications protocols being used.

NCR/DNA provides a telecommunications procedure which is transparent to applications. The telecommunications access method software (NCR/TAM)—a facility of the host operating system—performs a number of vital functions, including support of high-level commands (SEND, RECEIVE). An end-to-end protocol is used to manage the network's information flow and to assure correct delivery.

Once the terminal network expands to a certain point, operating efficiency dictates off-loading much of the communications function from the host by incorporating a communications processor into the system, as depicted in Figure 2. With NCR/DNA, application programs are unaffected by this change, because communications hardware and operating system configurations are transparent to the application program.

More complex configurations may involve multiple host processing networks and multiple clusters of ter-

1 Basic system

Host-based. Communications hardware and software can reside in the host in a basic NCR/DNA configuration. The telecommunications software is transparent to users.

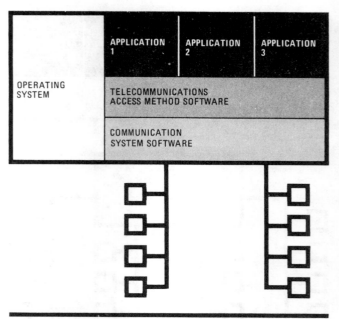

OPERATING SYSTEM

APPLICATION 1   APPLICATION 2   APPLICATION 3

TELECOMMUNICATIONS ACCESS METHOD SOFTWARE

COMMUNICATION SYSTEM SOFTWARE

minals as shown in Figure 3. In this system, any application program, whether it resides in a host, a cluster controller, or a terminal, is capable of accessing any other application. Communications processors, in this case, perform two functions. First, they serve as terminal tenders, and second, as node switches. The subnetwork containing node-switching processors and internodal communications lines constitutes an NCR data-transporting network (NCR/DTN). This network provides multiple paths for message routing and alternate paths in the event of node or link failure.

Each node processor in a DTN configuration shares in the task of regulating and directing message flow within the network. Further, the architecture is designed to distribute most control functions within the operational structure. As a result, NCR/DNA's network supervision must handle only exception conditions and requests from a human operator. In addition, supervisory functions are distributed between a local and a global supervisor. The local supervisor is replicated in each network node and is responsible for the links directly attached to that node. A global supervisor is responsible for handling network-wide exceptions. This distributed supervision creates a network which is less vulnerable to the failure of one element, as compared with a network oriented to centralized control.

Because NCR/DNA separates application processing from communications processing, the application programmer is insulated from the procedural aspects of communications. This separation is realized by using Cobol '74's message control system functions as a boundary between the application program and the communications environment. Moreover, all aspects

of communications protocol are handled in the operating system without involvement of the application program. All network configuration data is written into the operating system separately from the application programs, further insulating the applications programmer from the details of communications control.

This is an important feature of NCR/DNA, because it allows nodes to be added to an existing network without disturbing the status of users on the network. A basic criterion in the development of NCR/DNA is the accommodation of changing user needs and technological evolution. NCR/DNA provides an open-ended design which permits evolutionary changes to the architecture without major disruption. To accomplish this design, protocols are open-ended and the operational structure is highly modular—permitting extensions or replacement of network elements without impairing connectibility.

How NCR/DNA operates

NCR/DNA provides communications services for entities called "correspondents." A correspondent may be an application program or a man/machine combination (operator at a terminal). A correspondent need only request communications service and respond to his/its peer, if required. The communications system is insensitive to the content of exchanges between correspondents. It is only responsible for providing service upon request.

The operational structure of the architecture is depicted in Figure 4. This structure consists of functional elements or layers, peer layer protocols between correspondent machines, and interfaces between adjacent layers. The layer diagram shows two physically separated correspondents to illustrate the structure. This diagram does not include all functions which may be performed by the correspondent, and many other combinations are possible. Also, Figure 4 shows only communications functions. For each of the five layers shown, both an interface and a peer layer protocol exist. The interface specifications define the ground rules by which the services of one layer may be called upon by the layer immediately above.

A layer is a set of related functions which meets three conditions. First, a layer must have a specific hierarchical relationship with respect to other layers in a machine. Second, it must have well-defined interfaces between itself and its adjacent layers. And finally, it must be able to communicate with its peers in another machine.

Of these three conditions, the most basic characteristic is the functional-hierarchical relationship. Beginning at the correspondent (application), each successive layer consists of a composite set of functions that require the services of the lower layers. Access to adjacent layers is always through the standard access interface from a layer to its next lower layer.

Peer layers are layers in two different machines which provide like functions. Such layers may communicate with one another through peer layer protocols, such as NCR's data link control. The topmost layer in Figure 4—NCR's telecommunications access method

(NCR/TAM) — essentially acts as an adaptor between a user's programming language and the communications environment. Although user program access in NCR/DNA is designed primarily to support ANSI Cobol '74 for applications development, TAM can provide support for other languages as an option. The interface between TAM and Cobol '74 is the language's message control system (MCS) interface.

Implementation levels

There are three possible levels of implementation of this interface; the level chosen for a particular product is matched with the requirements of the application program as well as with the product's capabilities. The two higher levels provide full ANSI Levels 1 and 2 MCS features. Essentially, ANSI Level 1 MCS provides a somewhat restricted subset of the Level 2 MCS capabilities, and is limited to NCR's smaller processing systems. The lowest level, identified as Level 0, is a non-standard subset intended for use in the smallest of NCR's Cobol-programmable machines such as selected microprocessor-based terminals.

As a service to the applications programmer, NCR/TAM provides access to subroutines, for virtual-terminal support, which normalize the functions and formats of the various terminal devices into conceptualized classes of "virtual terminals." For instance, one virtual-terminal support subroutine can be used to translate Cobol to teletypewriter formats. This concept insulates the applications programmer from the specific function and format details of a particular model or type of terminal (e.g., code set, format control characters, number of line-fill characters required). These functions are not actually part of the communications functions of NCR/TAM; however, a gateway to this device-dependent code is provided.

The Cobol program itself interfaces to TAM through five Cobol verbs; ACCEPT (count), DISABLE, ENABLE, RECEIVE and SEND. Each verb references one or more data structures which are identified within the source statement containing the verb. Each such statement must refer to a communications descriptor (CD), which provides an area in which the program and NCR/TAM exchange information regarding the request represented by the verb. Typical information is the source or destination network correspondent (which is translated by TAM into network addresses), the length of the text being transferred between the program and TAM, and the status of that transfer. Additionally, the portion of the input queue structure being examined for input messages is named in the CD. TAM manages the queue structure, allotting messages to queues on a pre-defined algorithm. Basically, the algorithm relates an address to an queue.

TAM accepts and processes these user requests, which, in turn, cause TAM to make network service requests to its next lower layer — the communication system services (CSS in Fig. 4). Both the user program and TAM operate at the message and message-segment level, although TAM releases to CSS only completed messages, as defined by the end of message indicator with the SEND verb.

2 Adding a processor

Off-loading. *As the basic network grows, a communications processor can be added to off-load the host's communications chores for improved operating efficiency.*

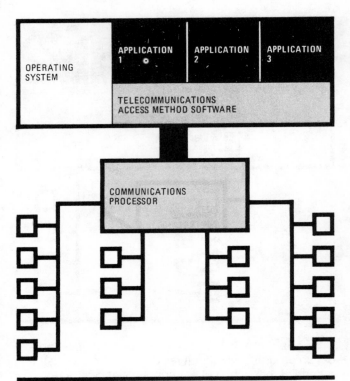

The CSS layer is responsible for managing communications between two correspondents (application processes or terminal functions). The sending TAM presents the message and the network logical addresses of the origin and destination to CSS, which then forms packets from the data and ships them to the receiving CSS through the communications medium. At the receiving CSS, the message is reconstructed from the packets and passed with a logical address to TAM for delivery to the correspondent.

At the CSS level, two types of communications are possible — unnumbered service or dialog service. Unnumbered service operates much like datagram service on public packet networks. For unnumbered service, a message's maximum size cannot exceed the network's maximum packet size. CSS forms a single packet and ships it to the receiving CSS. End-to-end assurance is the responsibility of the correspondents.

Dialog service — a major function of NCR/DNA — on the other hand, provides optional guaranteed in-sequence delivery of messages, data security beyond that normally associated with datagram type service, packetizing, reconstruction of messages longer than the network's maximum packet size, and end-to-end acknowledgment of transmission.

Traffic assurance functions are accomplished in the CSS as a portion of dialog control. By using a specific peer protocol, the two CSSs assure traffic integrity for each dialog in the transmission medium. The choice

Multi-hosts. *In its full-grown implementation, represented by a data transporting network supporting multi-hosts, NCR/DNA supplies network control for any on-line program. The application programs can reside in a host, a cluster controller, or in a terminal. Multiple path routing is available for communications in the event of node failure.*

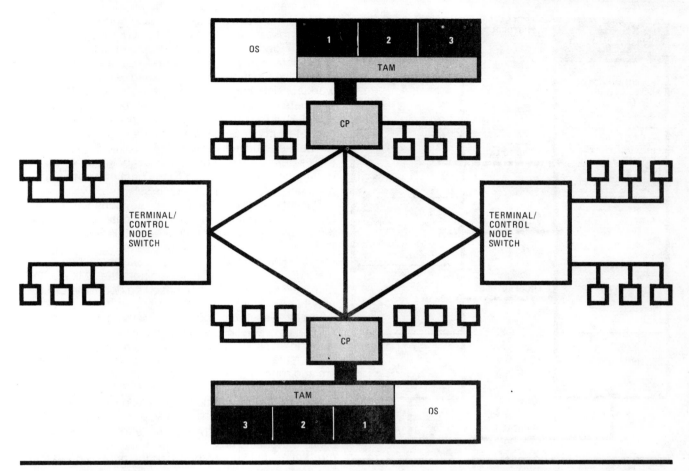

of the specific protocol set used for dialog service depends on the type of communications required. For each of these two correspondents, the specific protocol set will differ, although both sets are part of the same communications process. For instance, one CCS may require acknowledgment that a message was received, while the other may only need to be notified if the message was not received.

Dialog service flexibility

Dialog service messages entering or leaving the CSS may or may not be of optimum length for multiplexing. The architecture allows each implementation to use a packet size based on system performance requirements, rather than being limited to one format.

To provide acceptable response times for correspondents, the user may select a short packet size, requiring longer messages to be divided. The source CSS, in this case, will divide messages into packets, and the destination CSS will reassemble the packets into messages. In dialog service, the communication system services guarantee packet sequencing within a message and guarantee message order when required.

The rules of communications between the two CSS layers constitute the protocol. Communications are required to manage the four phases of dialogs (establishment, conversation, dissolution, and recovery). Elements of the protocol may be encoded within the packet header or, in other configurations, within the text of the control packets.

Recognizing that bit-oriented protocols—such as NCR/DLC—offer from one to three orders of magnitude lower error rates than byte-oriented protocols in a data communications network, the CSS peer layer emphasizes flow control rather than error detection and recovery. Flow control is achieved by using both special control packets, and by managing the number of packets which are outstanding in any dialog. Correspondents addressed in NCR/DNA are designated by a logical location, called a logical address, rather than by a physical address. This permits a correspondent to be moved physically in the data-transporting network without affecting any other correspondent which may communicate with it. Figure 5 details three packet formats. Figure 5A is the format for unnumbered service. The packet format is defined by a one-octet field

4 Layered structure

Isolated. Each peer layer is isolated from all other layers, but each can communicate with its corresponding peer layer in another machine via a peer layer protocol.

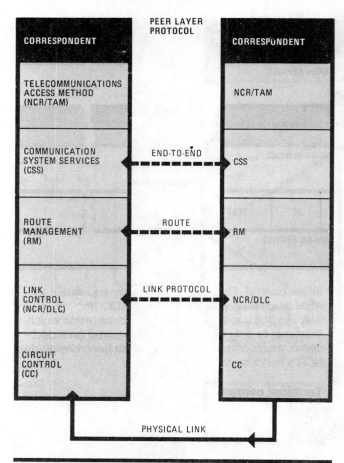

indicated as PF. The logical origin address (LOA) is the network identification of the sending correspondent. The logical destination address (LDA) is the network identification of the receiving correspondent. Both LOA and LDA may be two or three octets in length.

A basic packet format for dialog service is illustrated in Figure 5B. The packet number (PN) is a one-octet field containing a modulo-128 packet sequence number and an end-of-message flag as its high-order bit. A rotating window is maintained within the packet sequence number count. The size of the window is the maximum number of packets which may be outstanding at any one time for the dialog in question. Each time the oldest outstanding packet is acknowledged, the bottom of the window is advanced to the next unacknowledged sequence number, and the top of the window is advanced a similar number, permitting that many more packets to be sent.

Another packet format for dialog service is depicted in Figure 5C. An eight-bit field, known as the disposal and cause (DC) field, is used for control purposes in the event a packet is undeliverable. The DC field's high-order four bits define the means of disposal, while the low-order four bits identify the cause for the packet's being undeliverable.

Steering the packet

Route management provides the physical steering of the packet by converting the logical addresses to physical addresses. Three possible transporting mechanisms—dedicated line, public packet net, and NCR/data-transporting network—dictate a variety of alternative functions in route management. If the network consists only of locally connected links, the appropriate point-to-point, multipoint, or dial-up link is selected. If the transporting mechanism is a public packet-switching service, the header is appended to the packet, and it is delivered to the link. Finally, if NCR's data-transporting network is being used, the routing header is attached to the packet and the appropriate link for transmission is selected.

Packets enter and leave the route management (RM) layer at the top, and transport units enter and leave at the bottom. The primary function of this layer is to choose the proper output route from the node. In doing this, the RM layer will also reroute packets when a primary route is unavailable. In addition, the RM layer manages packet priorities, based on control information it receives from the CSS layer.

In simple systems, route management is limited to routing between links and communication system services. In an NCR/data-transporting network, route management includes adding and deleting route headers and routing between links at intermediate nodes in the network.

NCR's DTN is an optional service in which each piece of information (transport unit) shipped in the network is treated independently. DTN networks involve a multiplicity of nodes. Thus, a transport unit may pass through multiple nodes between the original node and the destination node.

The route management layer serving an entry point into an NCR/DTN network accepts a packet from communication system services and appends a routing header to form a transport unit, as shown in Figure 6. The physical destination address (PDA) is derived by interpretation of the logical destination address (LDA) in the packet. PDA is the address of the exit node for this transport unit, the node at which the other correspondent is physically located. POA (physical origin address) is the address of the entry node creating the transport unit.

The transport unit is then routed to the appropriate link for shipment to the exit node. At each node, route management examines PDA and selects the next appropriate link to move the transport unit toward the exit. At the exit node, the transport unit is recognized as belonging to that location, the routing header is stripped off, and the packet is presented to communication system services.

The routing header format (RF) field in the routing header is a one-octet field which defines the format and priority of the transport unit. The physical destination address (PDA) and the physical origin address

5 Packet formats

Structure. *Unnumbered service packets (A) include a field defining the packet (PF), a logical origin address identifying the sender (LOA), and a logical destination address (LDA). Basic dialog service (B) also includes the packet number (PN). In special dialog service (C) a dispose and cause identification field (DC) is added.*

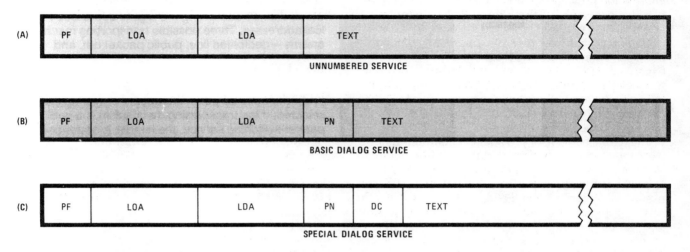

6 DTN transport unit

Priority. *The routing field (RF) in a DTN transport unit defines the packet's priority. PDA and POA define the receiving and sending correspondent address fields.*

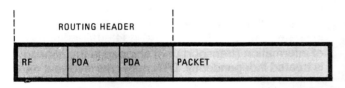

(POA) may be one or two octets in length. NCR/DLC is a bit-oriented data link control protocol and, as such, is a member of the family of protocols which include the international standard high-level data link control (HDLC), advanced data communications control procedure (ADCCP), and IBM's synchronous data link control (SDLC). All of these protocols are transparent; that is, the protocol is insensitive to code, word length, or content of the data transferred. Also, all of the protocols feature error checking on all information and control functions being transferred. Moreover, bit-level protocols can support two-way simultaneous operation, if a network configuration permits.

NCR/DLC can be operated in a normal response mode (NRM), an asynchronous balanced mode (ABM), and a mode called NCR in-house. NRM—the principal mode of operation of NCR/DNA terminals—implies that a primary station controls the link, with all other devices on the link being subservient.

ABM is principally used between switching nodes in the network or between two large processors on a point-to-point basis. The principal feature of a balanced mode is that both ends of the link share equally in link control. This mode is generally equivalent to ABM as defined within HDLC and ADCCP.

A specific subset of normal response mode which implements only those functions required on a dedicated, multipoint, short-haul link has been designated NCR's in-house mode.

Terminal communications
An NCR/DNA terminal is any man-machine interface device which uses NCR/DLC protocol and presents properly encoded packets to the network. In other words, an NCR/DNA terminal performs the subset of NCR/TAM and CSS functions applicable to a single terminal unit, and the functions of link control and circuit control. Packets from NCR/DNA terminals are accepted by the route management layer of the first node encountered, appropriately encoded as a transport unit (if required), and routed.

A mechanism known as entry/exit service is provided for interconnecting pre-DNA terminals to the NCR/DNA network. Such a service is developed for each type or class of terminal (e.g. teletypewriters) selected for interconnection. Entry/exit services are actually software modules which execute on the terminal controllers of communications processors. The interface from entry/exit services is the access interface to route management, at which point appropriately encoded packets are presented.

Network management
Most supervisory functions are performed by the local supervisor. The local supervisor initiates, monitors the progress of, and reports the results of network diagnostics. These network diagnostics provide the network administrator with the ability to rapidly isolate a problem to a specific network element (link or node) before requesting service from maintenance personnel.

The local supervisor can also read and control performance-monitoring counters and also supervise other software instrumentation.

Network description is initially provided to each layer and may be modified by the local supervisor. Typical information provided includes: poll tables, routing tables, logical-to-physical-address translation tables, and definition of pre-established dialogs.

The local supervisor receives reports of exception conditions and initiates appropriate action. Typical exception reports include repeated failure to respond to a poll (link control) and route failures, i.e., inability to use a primary route (route management). Most exceptions are resolved locally and, in addition, may be reported to the global supervisor.

The global supervisor provides for centralized network monitoring by a network administrator, central recording of exception conditions, and recovery from failures affecting large portions of a network. The global supervisor can request diagnostics and receive the results from a local supervisor. It can request the starting, stopping, resetting or reading of instrumentation. The global supervisor may redefine the network in order to, for example, add terminals, or to reroute around link or node failures. Network configurations may include duplicate global supervisors for backup.

Network generation

The NCR/DNA operational structure is supported by a set of user facilities that enable the user to define the network topology and the attributes of the entities comprising and using the network. These facilities are available through a language called NCR/network description language (NCR/NDL).

There are two distinct parts of NCR/NDL from the user's viewpoint. One part is concerned with the topology (physical configuration) of the elements of the network, the other with the correspondents using the network.

Description of the topology of an NCR/DNA network involves the definition of the physical nodes in the network, the connections (communications links) between them and the application processors, and locally connected links associated with each node. Physical terminal locations are also described in relation to the locally connected links to which they are attached.

Correspondents are described in terms of their (initial) physical location. The types of attributes which may be assigned to a correspondent include: the name by which it is known to other correspondents (including the supervisor), the rules governing inter-correspondent access (e.g. security considerations, maximum message size), the type of traffic used (dialog or unnumbered, relative priority), and the rights of the network control language with regard to correspondent attribute inquiry and modification.

The user, having configured the network, describes it, using NCR/NDL statements. These are inputs to an NCR/NDL processor, analogous to a compiler, which produces a set of data-structures in machine-readable form. A set of data-structures is produced for each node in the network, as well as a smaller set for each intelligent (programmable) terminal in the network. The data structures, containing the routing and correspondent information, are distributed to the appropriate nodes, terminals, and application processors at network initialization.

Distribution can be by physical media (cassette, flexible disk, magnetic tape, etc.) or by down-line load techniques. The method chosen depends upon the capabilities of the individual network components. Network initialization is performed under control of the network supervisor.

Network control language

As described earlier, the operational control of the network is normally effected by the local and global supervisors. However, for those exceptional conditions where a decision from an entity external to NCR/DNA is required, or where such an entity desires to influence the network in some way, dynamic control can be exerted through the use of the NCR/network control language.

NCR/NCL consists of a set of imperative and interrogative statements which can be submitted by either a designated (human) network operator or an authorized application process, while the network is in operation. In the former case, the entry is made through a designated terminal, and security checks are made to identify the requester; subsets of NCR/NCL capabilities may be identified for certain less-privileged operators. NCR/NCL statements issued by an application process are passed by communication system services to the local supervisor for subsequent processing by the local and global supervisors. Security checks are again performed on the identity and permitted capabilities of the process.

The network control language provides facilities for inquiring into the status of various elements of the network and for changing these elements. Included in the inquiry facilities are statements to determine the status of a logical address, a physical address, and path (links) between physical addresses. A logical-to-physical translation (and its inverse) can also be requested, so that, for example, an NCR/NCL user may determine the current physical location of a logical entity.

Modification of network

The imperative facilities of NCR/NCL provide for the modification of the network topology, including the addition and deletion of terminals in the network. (Terminals may be added in this manner only if a similar terminal already exists within the network.) Additionally, the capability of controlling the availability of logical addresses to the proscribed parts of the network is available. For example, a sensitive or secure application can be declared off-limits to certain terminals.

These facilities, essentially, modify some of the network attributes defined in NCR/NDL. Therefore, they are subject to rigid security checks by the network supervisor. These security checks are based on information provided at network generation time through NCR/NDL, and include information such as password and location checks. ∎

Packet-switched networks agree on standard interface

New international protocol rules on how to establish an access link, set up virtual circuits, and transfer data

Richard B. Hovey
Telenet Communications Corp.
Washington, D.C.

Networks

A standard protocol for interfacing host computers and data terminals to any packet-switching network is just a vote away from worldwide acceptance. When Study Group VII of the International Telegraph and Telephone Consultative Committee (CCITT) adopted Recommendation X.25 on March 2 in Geneva, it remained only for the full session of CCITT to vote final approval in October—and that approval is apparently a foregone conclusion.

Recommendation X.25, entitled *Interface between data terminals operating in the packet mode on public networks*, has already been adopted by four packet carriers. They are Telenet Communications Corp. in the U.S., Bell Canada, and the public packet-switching carriers in France and the United Kingdom. The four have already agreed among themselves to use the standard interface, both to connect users' computers to their domestic networks and eventually to interconnect their networks with each other so that the international data communications traffic may then flow freely without any complications for the network's subscribers.

What X.25 does, in essence, is to provide precise procedures for a host computer or a data terminal first to obtain access to a packet-switched network and then to establish one or more so-called virtual circuits through the network between it and another host computer or terminal.

Recommendation X.25 is based in large part on the design of Telenet's functionally equivalent host interface, which Telenet subscribers with IBM, DEC, and Honeywell computer systems have been using now for a year. Host-to-network interfaces meeting the specifications of X.25 are currently being tested. In these and earlier cases, either the carrier or an innovative user developed the necessary interface software. Recently, however, some manufacturers of host systems and some suppliers of communications software have decided to provide the interface as an optional enhancement of their standard products. Since this trend is expected to continue, employing such an interface will make a few technical demands on the user.

Nevertheless, the user should understand the main features of X.25 and how it enables existing computer systems to benefit from a public packet-switched data communications service. Data transmission services based on packet switching are quite different from those that use either dedicated communications links between points or circuit-switched data communications facilities. In the latter two cases, the user obtains a defined bandwidth (or bit rate, if it's a digital carrier) but he is free to choose his own mode of communication over the link—including speed, data format, protocol, and error control—provided that the two stations at opposite ends of the channel use precisely the same mode of communication.

With the packet-switched data networks, however, the sender of data does not establish a physical link with the receiver before starting transmission. Data, once received by the network, is sent to its specified destination by whatever combination of routes is fastest at any given instant. Data delivery is so rapid that the subscriber appears to have a dedicated, end-to-end, channel called a virtual circuit. To transfer data between the network and the user, the carrier provides a limited set of standard protocols, like X.25.

How a packet-switched data net works

To provide this service, the public packet-switched data networks typically operate central offices in major cities to which users can connect their computers and data terminals by means of telephone lines. These central offices contain computer-controlled interfacing and switching equipment and are connected to one another by multiple high-capacity communications channels.

A user's computer or terminal gains access to the data network through a communications line that connects it to a network stored-program computer. Those user devices that exchange data over this connection are described by the X.25 protocol as "data terminal equipment operating in the packet mode." Such equipment transmits data synchronously to the network in a standard format, called a packet. Then, at the interface, the data content of a packet may be reformatted by the network into smaller segments for internal handling. (Historically, the packet designation has been reserved for these internal segments. They are the packets that are switched, and they, in Telenet, are the basic billing unit. However, the somewhat different definition provided in Recommendation X.25 will be adhered to here.)

The segments of data are transmitted from node to node over the optimal long-haul paths. A technique of dynamically routing each segment individually along any one of several alternative paths minimizes end-to-end transmission delay and increases system reliability. At each switching facility along its route, a segment is checked for errors and, if necessary, is retransmitted. At the destination interface, the segments are reassembled into the original packet format and passed to the receiving station. The fact that the data is reformatted and complex routing and error-recovery techniques are employed within the network has no impact at all on the messages received by user.

Data travels through the switching centers, experiencing only a fraction of a second's delay from source to destination. Because of the buffering and flow control features of the X.25 interface, the physical characteristics (e.g., bit or byte orientation and speed) of the transmissions sent into the network can be different from those of the transmissions received at the destination. Perhaps more importantly, network-resident software for device support, called a terminal handler, can perform the packet-mode interfacing function on behalf of a device incapable of implementing an X.25-like protocol, whether the device is an asynchronous keyboard/printer, a hardwired binary synchronous terminal, or a host computer emulating such devices. Because of this capability, a packet-mode host can communicate with a large variety of packet-mode and non-packet-mode devices over its single synchronous connection to the public network [see "The user's role in interfacing to a value-added network," DATA COMMUNICATIONS, May/June 1974].

The sophisticated routing, monitoring, and error-correction techniques internal to the network are invisible to the host computer system. Similarly, to the extent that the interface to a packet-switched network is supported by his supplier of communications software, the user need not to worry about how he himself must modify equipment or software.

With the X.25 network access protocol, the network appears to the host system like a remote concentrator attached to the access link. Consequently the user is mainly interested in the relatively simple procedures and structures for transmitting and receiving data to and from that "concentrator." These procedures are defined in X.25 and are incorporated in the user's system in the form of software routines. Typically, the routines reside in a programable processor that serves as a front end to the host computer.

Although Recommendation X.25 is represented as a standard for general packet-mode terminals, its actual purpose is to enable teleprocessing computer systems in particular to communicate with many devices simultaneously and efficiently over public packet-switched networks. Public packet-switching carriers throughout the world have selected the virtual-circuit interface approach as being initially the most appropriate, since it exhibits the properties of a traditional switched or leased-circuit facility and burdens the user the least (see "Classes of packet network interfaces.") The interface therefore provides the means to address the many computers and terminals connected to the network, to rapidly establish virtual circuits among these remote devices, and to ensure the integrity of the data.

An intelligent terminal that communicates with only one other device at a time—such as a microprocessor-driven batch terminal or a buffered cathode-ray-tube display—could also use the X.25 interface to access a packet-switched network. But as a practical matter, a second standard interface specifically for the single-connection class of packet-mode terminals is under development.

For efficiency and economy, host computer systems are connected to the data network by single or dual high-speed lines. The physical and electrical signalling characteristics of this access circuit, as outlined in Recommendation X.25, do not ask anything new of the user since established standards like RS-232 are specified. However, because a single hardware connection is used, the software interface must be capable of exchanging data for numerous processes simultaneously over the physical connection (called the subscriber access link) between the host computer and the network. The interface must also allow both host and network to control the flow of data over that link, so that one does not overburden the other. These and other requirements must, of course, be satisfied with as little overhead of control information as possible.

How the network passes data

Figure 1 is a conceptualization of an end-to-end data transfer through a public data network—in this example, between a packet-mode (host) terminal and a non-packet-mode (teletypewriter) terminal. The hashed lines between modules apply to those functions occurring internally and, hence, invisible to the transmission process. The solid lines apply to those functions performed during transmission and thus controlled by the X.25 interface protocol.

As shown, the subscriber's software interface defined in X.25 consists of two distinct levels of control procedures:
■ The subscriber link-access procedure (function 10 in Fig. 1).
■ The packet-level interface (function 8A).
The purposes and requirements of these control procedures will be explained later. Meanwhile, note that Recommendation X.25 specifies a local, rather than end-to-end, protocol. That is, internally, the network may be taking data received according to Recommendation X.25 and wrapping it in a more complex protocol (function 12 in Fig. 1). At the destination, the data packet may be translated back to an X.25 protocol (function 8B in Fig. 1), or indeed some other protocol, such as the Telenet's present host interface protocol.

Each module in Figure 1 could represent a software program that performs a specific control task, sometimes in combination with hardwired logic. However, the real reason for imposing these modular boundaries is explanatory—to isolate for discussion purposes the function related to network communications, more than to suggest an actual implementation. There are, after all, a number of possible variants on the host system scheme shown, primarily determined by the sophistication of the communications hardware and, hence, distinguished by different distributions of modules between the host processor and front-end units.

What the user's software does

Figure 2 depicts the host system in more detail, stressing those modules directly relevant to network communications, in particular the packet-level interface embedded in the communications control software. Some of the functions performed by each software package are indicated. Between them, Figures 1 and 2 illustrate one possible packet-mode terminal—a host system configuration that allocates some of the data communications functions to a separate front-end processor. The additions to the communications software that are required for interfacing with the public data network are assumed to reside in the front-end processor. (Of course, if the communications interface were realized in a hardwired rather than software-controlled device, the extensions would be co-located with the access method in the central processor.)

The actual preparation, analysis, and processing of data for transfer over a public data network is performed by the subscriber's application programs. Such a software module is usually dedicated to a single teleprocessing task, which can be categorized as an interactive, inquiry, batch, or processor-to-processor application.

An application program may encompass one or more application processes. For example, when a time-sharing application is simultaneously servicing a number of on-line terminals, each terminal's operation requires a separate process within the host. A process can be thought of as a software routine that is invoked whenever there is an incoming or outgoing data flow. When data flow stops, the process is suspended.

The precise form a process takes depends upon the subscriber's application and is of little direct concern to the network providing the communications. The concept of a process is nevertheless useful because it helps define the level at which the Recommendation X.25 interface maintains independence of data transmissions. For instance, the establishment of virtual circuits, the flow control of data, and the multiplexing of data across the interface can all be thought of in relation to individual processes. Similarly, any communication through a public data network can be characterized as being between two processes. This may be obvious for processor-to-processor applications but, as Figure 1 suggests, computer-to-terminal communication is in fact communication between a host-resident application process and a network-resident terminal-handler process.

An interface between a host computer system and a packet-switched data network generally falls into one of three categories:

- Datagram interface.
- Virtual-circuit interface.
- Terminal-emulation interface.

The distinguishing characteristic of the datagram transmitted by the host is that it is completely self-contained. It includes the control information for the network and the complete address of the intended receiver. The network handles each datagram independently, so that each is delivered with minimum delay but without a guarantee as to duplication, loss, or relative sequencing. Hence, the receiving host is responsible for such tasks as identifying the source of each datagram, detecting and recovering lost datagrams, and putting them back into their original order of transmission, as well as processing ones returned because they could not be delivered. A datagram interface is attractive in research with network interfacing techniques because it does not freeze the entire communications protocol in advance.

Virtual circuit

With the virtual-circuit interface, however, the host sees a much more organized flow of data. As the name suggests, the network appears to provide a dedicated, point-to-point circuit between the host and such destination devices as another host or terminal. Rather than treating each block of data that is transmitted to the network as an independent entity, the virtual-circuit interface assumes that the communication between two points is characterized by a sustained sequence of such transmissions. Thus, a circuit is set up by the network's maintaining an association between a pair of source and destination addresses. Actually, in a packet-switching network, no real end-to-end physical transmission channels are assigned.

With datagrams, the network is strictly a transmission medium. With the virtual-circuit interface it also recovers data which has been lost, eliminates duplicated data, and orders the data that arrives out of sequence. The network and host also share the job of controlling the flow of data, stopping a sender from flooding the network or the receiver with data it cannot absorb.

A host computer system may set up more than one virtual circuit at any one time by associating a logical-channel number with each destination and using that number to identify the data exchanged with

---

In practice, the task-oriented messages in which these application processes deal are read from or written to symbolic stations (e.g., terminal devices or other host processors) by macroinstructions issued in the application program. These macroinstructions transfer control to the teleprocessing access routines that manage the actual receipt and delivery. To the extent that the user's application programs are isolated in this way from such telecommunication complexities as queuing or polling, they should not require reprograming to adapt them to a packet-service environment. It should be possible for a public data network to appear as just an extension or replacement of part of the existing communications environment.

Application programs are concerned primarily with data content. The complexities of telecommunications, however, result from the variable and random characteristics—not the content—of the data traffic to and from these programs. Concern for simplicity in applications programing often leads to a single teleprocessing access-method software package, which performs the necessary telecommunications functions on behalf of all the applications programs. This software may be supplied by the host processor vendor or written by the subscriber for a particular class of application, but in either case handles all communications-related functions like addressing, buffering, polling, error control, and code conversion. A common way of implementing a host interface to a packet-switched network is to have those interface software routines residing in the front-end processor emulate conventional terminal devices—something the teleprocessing access method "already knows about."

A similar approach is to add the X.25 interface on to a distributed network access method supplied by the vendor of his own manufacture. This has been particularly successful in the case of Digital Equipment's Decnet software, which makes the public, packet-switched service seem to the DEC host like part of the standard Decnet facility.

Gaining access to the network

As mentioned earlier, X.25 specifies two distinct levels of control procedures, the subscriber-link-access control and the packet-level interface. The main purpose of the subscriber-link-access control is to connect the host computer to the network. Information is transferred over the subscriber access link in a transmission block called a frame. As shown in Figure 3, some carriers (including Telenet) provide for two formats of frames—one for use with such new bit-oriented line-control hardware as synchronous data link control, and the other for use with such existing character- or byte-oriented hardware as binary synchronous communications.

A frame may contain a packet within its infor-

each. In contrast to datagrams, transmissions across a virtual-circuit interface need contain only the short logical-channel number.

Complete source and destination addresses are not necessary, since this information is retained by the network. In this manner, the virtual-circuit interface, like the datagram interface, can be implemented using a single physical access link between the host computer system and the network.

Since it is desirable to provide a communications interface that has the properties of a traditional switched or leased communication facility, public packet-switched networks initially will all offer virtual-circuit interfaces. These networks include Telenet, Bell Canada's Datapac network, the British post office's experimental packet-switching service, France's Transpac network, and Japan's Nippon Telephone and Telegraph public network.

Terminal emulation

The terminal-emulation interface is the final logical extension of the virtual circuit idea, in that the network takes over all the remaining responsibilities of the host, such as monitoring a logical channel and controlling flow. The host merely sends and receives serial character streams, as would a simple terminal with keyboard and printing capabilities. Indeed, the same interface is used for unintelligent keyboard terminals: hence the terminal-emulation designation. The host computer appears to the network—and conversely, the network appears to the host—as a simple terminal.

Maintaining several terminal-emulation interfaces simultaneously is analogous to maintaining multiple virtual circuits. However, one difference is that with the terminal-emulation interface, each virtual circuit is broken out by the network into a separate physical access channel. To minimize the cost, it is usual to equip the host site with an actual multiplexer, which presents the host with multiple physical connections but is itself connected to the network by a single access link. In the Telenet environment, this is achieved by a character-interleaved multiplexer called a Telenet access controller (TAC).

Because the network emulates terminals for which the host already has support software, the host can quickly and easily access the packet network. In comparison with a multiple-connection virtual-circuit interface, a terminal-emulation interface is less economical and less efficient. However, it has been found attractive in the context of a new commercial offering.

mation field. The main function of the frame-level subscriber-link-access control is to ensure that these packets arrive at and leave the network free of error. The frame-level procedure outlined in Recommendation X.25 is the high-level data link control procedure (HDLC) specified by the International Standards Organization. This protocol, when used with either bit-oriented or byte-oriented hardware interfaces, achieves a high level of error-free throughput between the host system and the network. Only those aspects of this procedure that relate to error control are discussed here, since the details of the data link control are adequately covered elsewhere [see "Synchronous data link control," DATA COMMUNICATIONS, May/June, 1974].

A 16-bit cyclic redundancy check evaluates the frame for any transmission errors that may have occurred on the subscriber access link connecting the host system with the network. A frame that is found to be in error is merely discarded; the HDLC frame sequence control technique ensures that it will be detected as lost and will provide for its retransmission.

The two frame sequences—one sent and one received by the host—are another level of information grouping used to ensure data integrity on the access link. According to the HDLC procedures, a host system counts and numbers each frame it transmits which contains a packet. This send-sequence count is known as $N(S)$ (Fig. 3). Since each frame is identifiable by this number, missing or duplicated frames are readily detected by the network and can be retransmitted. Similarly, the host counts each error-free frame it receives from the network; the receive-sequence count is called $N(R)$. The returned receive-sequence count acknowledges that frames up to that point have been received free of error. Otherwise, $N(R)$ requests that frames be retransmitted from that point. Since packets are contained within sequenced frames, the subscriber-link-access procedure guarantees the integrity of all packets transmitted to and from the network. This includes both packets that contain user data and packets that contain information for controlling virtual circuits.

Interfacing at the packet level

Once the host is connected to the network, orderly communication through a public network of the data contained within packets is achieved through a virtual circuit. The salient features of the protocol which controls these virtual circuits are discussed next.

The packet-level interface (function 8 in Fig 1.) is a different level of control from the subscriber-link-access procedure (function 10 in Fig. 1). The packet-level-interface control is embodied in the

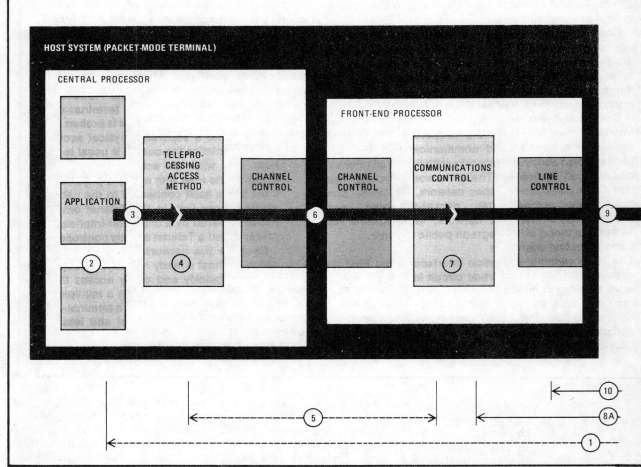

HOST SYSTEM (PACKET-MODE TERMINAL)

CENTRAL PROCESSOR

APPLICATION

TELEPRO-CESSING ACCESS METHOD

CHANNEL CONTROL

FRONT-END PROCESSOR

CHANNEL CONTROL

COMMUNICATIONS CONTROL

LINE CONTROL

1. Seventeen-step procedure details how different levels, or layers, of protocol make sure the applications-program process gets to the receiver, whether it's a terminal or a host computer.

1. Application-specific procedures control the exchange of data between the host system and the remote terminal. In this example, the host system is sending data to the terminal.

2. An application program prepares the task-oriented message (sometimes referred to as a logical message) and prefixes this data with the symbolic address of the destination terminal.

3. The data is transferred from the program's work area to an access-method queue, after an output macroinstruction is issued.

4. The teleprocessing access method handles the communications-related preparation, including code conversion, addressing, and queue organization.

5. The channel interrupts the controller program, which prepares the necessary buffers and

connects the access line to the network.

6. The data is transferred over the channel, typically a few characters at a time.

7. The communications control program handles network-related preparations. This includes affixing the logical-channel number which has previously been reserved for transfers to and from the terminal. The identification of the data by logical channel provides the means of concentrating transmissions to different destinations over the single access link to the public network.

8. The disciplines for assigning logical-channel numbers, as well as for managing the transfer of data over the virtual circuits that such an assignment defines, are part of a well-defined set of rules known as the packet-level interface.

9. The data is transferred synchronously over the

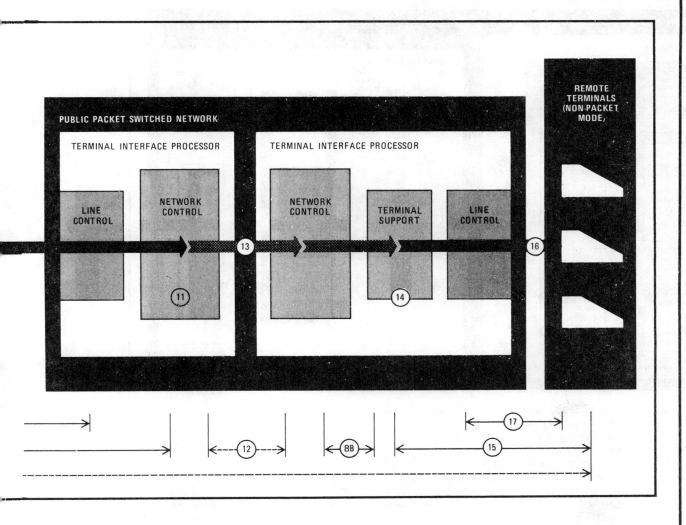

PUBLIC PACKET SWITCHED NETWORK

TERMINAL INTERFACE PROCESSOR

LINE CONTROL

NETWORK CONTROL

TERMINAL INTERFACE PROCESSOR

NETWORK CONTROL

TERMINAL SUPPORT

LINE CONTROL

REMOTE TERMINALS (NON-PACKET MODE)

communication line connecting the host to the network in blocks containing up to 1,024 characters of information.

10. The physical transfer of the data is handled by the subscriber link-access procedure which is primarily responsible for transmission error-detection-and-recovery procedures.

11. The network control program translates the logical-channel number to the actual network address of the terminal and selects the best route to that destination.

12. Protocols within the network control the store-and-forward transmission.

13. The data is transferred from one network node to another (perhaps in segments shorter than the original 1,024 characters) until the node connected to the terminal is reached. There the data from the host is reassembled into its original form.

14. The terminal handler process prepares and formats the data transmission for the terminal, accommodating the specific hardware and transmission-related characteristics of the particular terminal and line.

15. Procedures for managing the transfer of data between the network and the terminal can be specified from the terminal and/or remotely from the host.

16. Data is passed from the network buffers in the terminal interface processor to the terminal, where it is displayed.

17. The physical transfer of data to the terminal is conducted asynchronously or synchronously, depending on the physical requirements of the terminal.

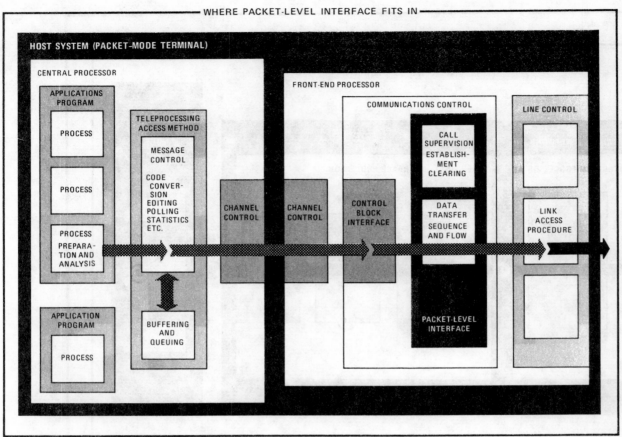

2. Usually a front-end processor handles traffic for the host computer, and the packet-level interface program fits into the front-end processor.

(continued from page 29)

packet, which may transfer information through the network, request a particular network operation, or indicate the result of an operation.

Methods and formats similar to the HDLC grammar are employed at the packet level for sequence and flow control. However, to support communication functions in a distributed network, this basic grammar is extended in the packet-level interface to include unique procedures and packet formats for, say, the establishment of virtual circuits. (The HDLC-like features of the packet-level interface are not to be confused with the point-to-point, full-duplex HDLC used as the discipline for transferring frames containing packets over the subscriber access link.)

Using the packet-level interface, the host system views the public network as providing a number of virtual circuits which it can link directly to processes in other host systems or to network-resident processes supporting terminal devices. As seen from the level of the applications process, a virtual circuit has general characteristics similar to those of a conventional switched or leased communications facility. As the name suggests, the network appears to provide the host system with a dedicated point-to-point "circuit" between the host and

a destination device (i.e., another host or terminal). Rather than treating each packet of data transmitted to the network as an independent entity, the concept of the virtual circuit assumes that any communication between two points is characterized by a sustained sequence of such trnasmissions. Thus, a "circuit" is set up by the network's maintaining an association between a pair of source and destination addresses. But, in actuality, no fixed end-to-end channels are assigned in a packet-switching network.

The virtual circuit is an end-to-end concept that describes the appearance of the network. At the interface, the host system can be thought of as accessing each virtual circuit through a logical channel. A host system may have more than one virtual circuit at any one time by associating a different logical-channel number with each destination and using that number to identify the data exchanged with each. Complete source and destination addresses are not necessary once the circuit has been set up, since this information is retained by the network until an appropriate command terminates the circuit. Thus the logical channel named in the packet can be conceived of as specifying an independent point-to-point data link associated with a

48

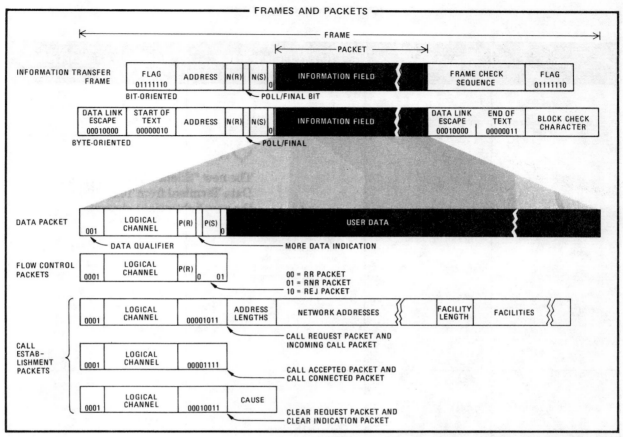

| | | | | FRAME | | | | |
| | | | | PACKET | | | | |

INFORMATION TRANSFER FRAME

| FLAG 01111110 | ADDRESS | N(R) | N(S) | INFORMATION FIELD | FRAME CHECK SEQUENCE | FLAG 01111110 |

BIT-ORIENTED — POLL/FINAL BIT

| DATA LINK ESCAPE 00010000 | START OF TEXT 00000010 | ADDRESS | N(R) | N(S) | INFORMATION FIELD | DATA LINK ESCAPE 00010000 | END OF TEXT 00000011 | BLOCK CHECK CHARACTER |

BYTE-ORIENTED — POLL/FINAL

DATA PACKET

| 001 | LOGICAL CHANNEL | P(R) | P(S) | USER DATA |

DATA QUALIFIER — MORE DATA INDICATION

FLOW CONTROL PACKETS

| 0001 | LOGICAL CHANNEL | P(R) | 0 | 01 |

00 = RR PACKET
01 = RNR PACKET
10 = REJ PACKET

CALL ESTAB-LISHMENT PACKETS

| 0001 | LOGICAL CHANNEL | 00001011 | ADDRESS LENGTHS | NETWORK ADDRESSES | FACILITY LENGTH | FACILITIES |

CALL REQUEST PACKET AND INCOMING CALL PACKET

| 0001 | LOGICAL CHANNEL | 00001111 |

CALL ACCEPTED PACKET AND CALL CONNECTED PACKET

| 0001 | LOGICAL CHANNEL | 00010011 | CAUSE |

CLEAR REQUEST PACKET AND CLEAR INDICATION PACKET

3. Frame, top, is used on subscriber access link, while packet types, bottom, establish calls, invoke logical channels, and handle data transfers.

single virtual circuit, and the packet-level interface is best thought of as a multiplexed point-to-point discipline. During normal operation, packets to and from remote stations may be sent and received at any time on any active, assigned logical channel.

Packet types

All transmission units regulated by the packet-level interface have a format called a packet and shown in Figure 3. Starting from the left, the first 4 consecutive bits provide the general identification. The next 12 bits specify one of up to 4,095 logical channels. Following this logical-channel field are the 8 bits of the packet-type identification field. As discussed below, the packet type may belong to any of four functional groups: data and interrupt, call establishment, flow control and reset, and restart.

If a user data field is present in a data packet, it is sent after the packet-type identification field and is not restricted in format or content. Moreover, in a packet, the maximum length of the user data field may vary among different networks, but in no case can it exceed 8,192 consecutive bits. (Note that these lengths are exclusive of bits which may be inserted during transmission and removed during reception to keep the subscriber access link trans-

parent and synchronize it periodically.) Although the call-establishment phase actually occurs first, it is more convenient to discuss the data-transfer phase first.

When a process internal to the host system wants to communicate through the public data network, the process is assigned a logical channel by the host system during call establishment, and a virtual circuit is set up through the network to the desired remote station. Similarly, if a remote station, such as a host computer, wishes to connect to the host, the network will select one of the host's inactive logical channels for the virtual circuit. Thereafter, packets to and from that station can be identified by the number in the logical-channel field of each transmitted and received packet.

The data-transfer phase

The packet-level interface is designed as a vehicle for transferring data contained in the user data field. Sequence and flow control of this data are achieved by using on each logical channel the same dual-sequence numbering techniques as used at the access-link level. In normal operation, data transfer involves the data and flow-control packet types. Only packets of the data type are given a P(S)

GROUP	PACKET TYPE	SENT BY THE HOST SYSTEM, INDICATING THAT...	RECEIVED BY THE HOST SYSTEM, INDICATING THAT...
CALL ESTABLISHMENT	CALL REQUEST	...the host is requesting the network to use this logical channel for a virtual circuit to the addressed remote station.	
	INCOMING CALL		...the network is requesting the host to use this logical channel to complete a virtual circuit from a remote station.
	CLEAR REQUEST	...the host is disconnecting itself from the remote station, terminating the virtual circuit and freeing the logical channel assigned.	
	CLEAR INDICATION		...the network is termintating the virtual circuit on this logical channel, usually at the request of the remote station.
DATA AND INTERRUPT	DATA	...the contents of the user data field are to be delivered to the remote station.	...the contents of the user data field were entered from the remote station.
	INTERRUPT	...the host is signalling an interrupt condition, bypassing the normal transmission sequence.	...the remote station has bypassed the normal transmission sequence to signal an interrupt condition to a higher control level.
FLOW CONTROL AND RESET	RECEIVE READY	...the host is confirming the receipt of data packets across this logical channel and is prepared to accept more.	...the network is confirming the delivery of data packets to the remote station and is prepared to accept more.
	RECEIVE NOT READY	...the host is confirming the receipt of data packets across this logical channel but is temporarily unable to accept any more.	...the network is confirming the delivery of data packets to the remote station but is unable to accept any more for that destination.
	REJECT	...the host is requesting the retransmission of data packets from the network.	
	RESET REQUEST	...the host is re-initializing the flow control parameters associated with this logical channel.	
	RESET INDICATION		...the network is re-initializing the flow control parameters associated with this logical channel.
RESTART	RESTART REQUEST	...the host is terminating all virtual circuits on all logical channels.	

or send-sequence number. The P(R) or receive-sequence number specifies the packet expected to be received next on the same virtual circuit and also implicitly confirms the receipt of the preceding packets. By this numbering means, the host and network continually report their P(R) and P(S) counts to one another for each virtual circuit.

The independent numbering of packets transmitted and packets received can accommodate a variety of bidirectional flow conditions that can arise during the exchange of information over a virtual circuit (for example, when a host transmits much more data to a terminal than it receives from the terminal). Independent numbering also allows complete end-to-end recovery, although retransmission of data packets is rarely required because of the frame-level protections.

The contents of sequenced data packets on a given virtual circuit may be assigned to one of two data levels by the 0 or 1 setting of the data-qualifier bit. In practice, this data qualifier distinguishes between packets containing raw user data—for display on a terminal, say—and those containing control data—perhaps to control the remote handler.

Flow control basically involves the stopping and starting of the transmission of packet sequences across a logical channel. For these purposes, there are three packet types: receive ready, receive not ready, and reject.

A receive-ready (RR) packet confirms sequenced data packets through a packet numbered P(R)-1 and indicates that the originating station (i.e., the station sending the RR packet) is ready to receive packet number P(R).

When the host gets a receive-not-ready (RNR) packet, it is being told there is a temporary busy condition and that no packets requiring buffer space can be accepted on this logical channel by the network. When the host sends an RNR packet, it indicates it can accept no more packets that require buffer space. In either case the RNR confirms data packets through P(R)-1. The originating station will send an RR or REJ packet when the buffer space necessary to continue is available.

A reject (REJ) data packet may be sent to request

transmission or retransmission of sequenced data packets beginning from a specified point. Because virtual circuits are protected from physical transmission errors by such different-level protocols as the frame-level subscriber-link-access procedures and internal network protocols, the request for retransmission of packets occurs so rarely that it may not be provided by all public networks.

The call-establishment phase

The call-establishment packets send call control information between the host system or terminal and the network—for example, the information needed to establish and terminate virtual circuits.

A call-establishment packet normally pertains only to the single virtual circuit specified in its logical-channel field. The packet-type identification contains one of several permissible codes indicating the operation to be performed on the basis of the packet. The basic commands are shown within functional groups in the table, along with brief explanations of their use.

Call-establishment packets typically occur in pairs. A packet from the host, for example, might request a specific action to be taken; the response from the network would acknowledge receipt of the packet and report on the status of the action. Cause fields contain codes for pre-defined conditions relevant to the control function. Similarly, supplementary information, specifying options associated with the action prescribed by the packet type, is contained in facility fields and user data fields. The position and interpretation of these fields are defined implicitly by the packet type and in general will be different for each.

As an example of a call-establishment exchange, consider a host system that wishes to be connected to a remote station. The host selects one of its inactive logical channels and sends a call-request packet to the network. This call request is addressed to the selected logical channel (i.e., a number from 1 to 4,095). A field within the call-request packet provides the network with the address of the host system or terminal device to be connected. Other facility fields may contain flow-control and billing information. When the virtual circuit has been established, the network returns a call-accepted packet. The network will thereafter associate the selected logical-channel number with the virtual circuit to the host system or terminal device, until an exchange of clear packets is performed to terminate that circuit.

In summary, the formal adoption of Recommendation X.25 as an international standard will give users the assurance that soon they will be able to employ packet-switching networks for both domestic and international traffic. The adoption will also give vendors of minicomputers and mainframe systems used as front-end processors and terminal controllers the incentive to implement X.25. ∎

Packet-switching networks seek bigger public role

Gregory Burch and Rubin Gruber,
Cambridge Telecommunications Inc., Bedford, Mass.

As X.25 protocol reaches 3270 users, resource-sharing, cost-saving benefits are spreading public packet network idea

With the internationally accepted X.25 protocol as the standard interface to packet-switching networks, a growing number of common carriers are providing public packet services. Recent developments make it clear that X.25 will become the standard protocol for all data communications: ITT recently announced that its ComPak public packet network will support X.25. ITT joins Telenet and Tymnet in the United States, while Bell in Canada, Transpac in France, Euronet in Europe, and Companie Telefonica Nacional de España (CTNE) in Spain have already announced their intention to support X.25 on their public networks. Further, mainframe and terminal manufacturers are beginning to announce new products with X.25 interfaces. The commonality of the X.25 protocol is providing the impetus for extending the benefits of packet switching to all data network communications users.

The X.25 standard defines the interface to a public packet-switching network for both host computers and data terminals. A detailed description of the X.25 standard, including how to gain access to the network, establish a virtual circuit, and transfer data through the network, can be found in "Packet-switched networks agree on standard interface," DATA COMMUNICATIONS, May/June 1976, pp. 25-39.

A significant observation is that the capabilities of X.25 closely parallel those of IBM's systems network architecture/synchronous data link control (SNA/SDLC). X.25 permits communications resources to be shared efficiently among a wide range of terminals and applications. Hosts can be easily interconnected to facilitate file transfers. Terminals can communicate with applications in one host, then switch to communicate with other central processing units (CPUs). Different terminals and hosts can co-exist within the same network. CPU loads can be balanced by relocating applications from one host to another. New services can be easily integrated into the network. In the event of a host failure, terminals can access alternate CPUs. Since existing conventional networks can migrate onto X.25 networks, the data communications user will have numerous opportunities to realize advanced communications functions (such as the file transfers and multi-host communications cited above) without having to replace hardware and upgrade host computer software.

Figure 1 illustrates the migration of conventional networks onto an X.25 public packet network. In the conventional network (Figure 1A), sharing of host resources and adding new terminals may require material

1 Comparing networks

Fewer terminals. *Operations of co-located terminals—though connected to different hosts—are combined into one terminal when the network makes the linkup.*

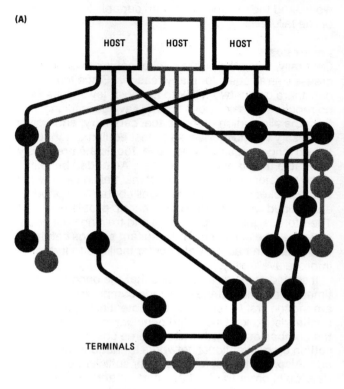

(A)

TERMINALS

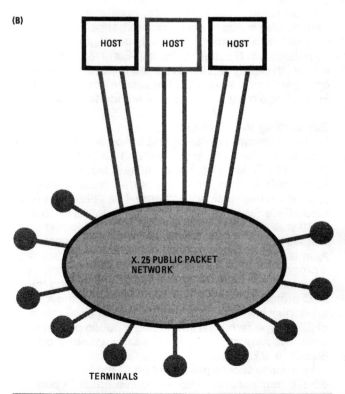

(B)

X.25 PUBLIC PACKET NETWORK

TERMINALS

program changes. And, if the number of terminals on a line is limited by software restrictions, adding a terminal may even necessitate adding a new line. Also, users at different terminals—but located near each other—cannot share long-line facilities which terminate at different hosts.

On the other hand, on the public packet network (Figure 1B), one terminal can access all application programs on any host. Also, because the hosts can communicate with each other, host load balancing becomes practical. Note that the one network is shared by many users, and that a new terminal is easily added. One more advantage of the public packet network is that the local links between the terminals or hosts and the network are more reliable (they are shorter and concern just one device) and are more easily serviced.

In Figure 2, the connection between the host and the network is shown in greater detail. Note that the communications controller—or front-end processor—connects to the network node by a single network link. However, this link handles many switched virtual circuits at the same time.

Balanced protocol
High-level data link control (HDLC), the communications control protocol component of X.25, is very similar to SDLC. Both are full-duplex protocols that provide significant improvements over IBM's binary synchro-

2 One link—many circuits

Linking the host. *The host's communications controller connects to its node with a single link, which handles all host-to-network switched virtual circuits at the same time.*

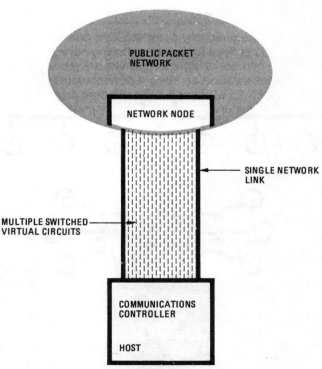

PUBLIC PACKET NETWORK

NETWORK NODE

SINGLE NETWORK LINK

MULTIPLE SWITCHED VIRTUAL CIRCUITS

COMMUNICATIONS CONTROLLER

HOST

nous communications (BSC) and the earlier start/stop protocols. They differ in that SDLC mandates a primary/secondary relationship for exchanging data, whereas HDLC assumes a balanced relationship. This difference, however, permits two HDLC components to be connected easily, which is necessary for network interconnect. One can expect to see, before long, connection taking place between networks of different countries, thus providing a user with multinational coverage. For instance, a host connected in the United States will be able to support terminals connected to another network in Europe as easily as a terminal connected across the street. Users will be able to interconnect several multinational host computers for such purposes as database sharing, update, and file transmission.

As IBM has stated, SNA defines a common method of supporting a broad spectrum of communications and network activities. Similarly, the X.25 counterpart, called packet level protocol, defines equivalent procedures for initiating, conducting, and terminating sessions. (A session is the time during which a user is connected to a computer.)

Admittedly, the packet level protocol is not as sophisticated as systems network architecture, but it is precisely for this reason that it can be adapted more easily to currently installed hardware and software. A drawback of SNA is that it is still based upon a conventional network and therefore lacks some of the inherent

3 Multidrop terminals

Multidrops. X.25 does not support conventional multidrop lines. But a logical multidrop of each terminal controller's line at the host computer's front end is equivalent.

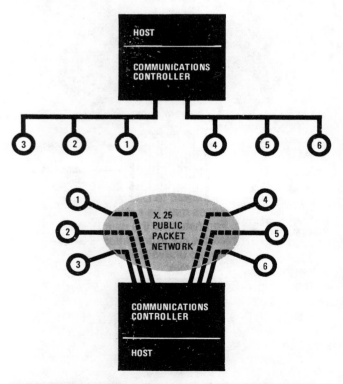

features of the newer public packet network.

In most situations, the degree of reliability and availability of public packet networks is higher than that of conventional networks. This is made possible by redundant hardware configurations in public packet networks and the multiple data path capabilities in case of line failure.

Lower costs
Generally, using the public packet network will decrease overall costs for many reasons. Since terminals can share one network link to the host, fewer links will be required. Less obvious are the savings resulting from the elimination of the space, cabinetry, and power necessary for the modems and test equipment that are no longer required. And gone, too, is the previously inevitable tangle of modem cables. An added benefit is the transfer of responsibility of maintaining a network to the packet carrier, who is usually better equipped and trained to investigate and clear up problems. Therefore, significant personnel and training cost economies can be achieved. The resultant savings can then be invested in backup data center facilities to further improve availability.

It should come as no surprise that the once regional timesharing and database service companies were among the first to recognize the potential of public packet networks. One of the principal restrictions to the companies' growth was the large costs involved in setting up conventional networks for nationwide coverage. Also, it often took too long for sufficient usage to develop in order to offset the start-up and maintenance costs. However, the availability of public packet networks, whose rates are usage-dependent (except for the host linkup), caused the cost of establishing such nationwide service to decrease dramatically. Yet, the new service was provided virtually overnight. And soon, as networks in North America and Europe are connected (which clearly would have been impossible without an agreed upon standard), the service company markets will again expand at little or no additional cost.

Supporting the terminals
Devices currently operating on public packet networks include the IBM 2741 and 3767, and ASCII Teletype-like terminals. More sophisticated and faster synchronous terminals also can be supported, without requiring changes in host-resident software. For instance, a Raytheon Data Systems X.25 terminal emulating an IBM 3270 was demonstrated by Cambridge Telecommunications Inc. at the recent Interface '77 Conference in Atlanta. This device exemplified what can be done with a programmable terminal. The 3270 emulator code in the intelligent terminal was modified by removing the BSC protocol interface and replacing it with the X.25 full-duplex interface. (For another recent application of 3270-type terminals interfacing a public packet network, see August 1977 DATA COMMUNICATIONS Short Blocks, p. 22.)

In order to successfully emulate all the functions of a 3270 terminal and to achieve comparable throughput, it was necessary to develop an extension to the

X.25 protocol. Packet protocol extension (PPX) was designed by Cambridge Telecommunications (CTX) to:

- eliminate polling through the network;
- eliminate redundant acknowledgements;
- convey terminal and controller status to the host;
- "piggyback" terminal status reports onto other terminal messages;
- permit each terminal to send a message to the host without waiting for a poll;
- synchronize terminal and host operations.

The X.25 3270 terminal is of special interest in that it illustrates some of the unique capabilities available with a public packet network. Although the terminal is permanently attached to the network, the session (making contact with the host through what is known as a switched virtual circuit) is not established until required by the terminal operator. To initiate a session, the user keys in the host number and identifies the application program—also known as the process—desired, much the same as when one dials a telephone number to converse with another party. Or a predefined number can be assigned to a single function key. The process could be a program such as IBM's timesharing option (TSO) or information management system (IMS). When the connection is completed, a virtual circuit has been established. Both the user at the terminal and the host application appear to be directly connected to one another, as if there were a private line between the two. When the session is completed, the virtual circuit can be disconnected and made available for other users. This virtual circuit capability provides the same functions as a switched IBM 3275 terminal. The capability is useful in low-usage applications where a dial-up or in-WATS circuit may not be economically justified.

Logical multidrops

In a conventional network, multiple 3270 controllers are frequently configured on a multidrop line for reasons of significant cost savings. However, X.25 does not support multidrop lines. Therefore, an equivalent 3270 controller configuration in an X.25 network requires a separate physical network link and virtual circuit for each controller. This situation might appear to create two problems which would tend to rule out many terminal configurations due to host software changes, or apparent higher costs. However, the first problem can be eliminated by logically multidropping the devices at the host communications front end (see Figure 3). And the second may be illusory. Usually, the speed of a multidrop line must be increased to compensate for the greater number of terminals in order to retain a desired response time. But when operation is on a public packet network, lower-speed lines and correspondingly less expensive modems can be employed, since only one terminal controller is attached to a line and the full-duplex nature of X.25 can almost double the line speed, depending upon the traffic flow.

The user may be better off without multidrop lines, for entirely different reasons. The trade-off of lowering line costs by configuring multidrop lines incurs many disadvantages. The inability to alter the configuration of a multidrop line without disrupting service to all terminals on a line sacrifices flexibility. The availability of multidrop lines suffers, since it is usually economically impractical to back up such a line. Frequently, a failure at one drop on the line impacts other drops on the line.

In effect, the multidrop line is analogous to the party line, which has all but disappeared. Moreover, as more public packet networks become operational, and more nodes are added, nodes will be closer to terminals. Thus, the economic advantage of multidrop lines, because of distance, will also disappear.

Network transition

The technique developed to link IBM hosts to the packet network was crucial to its success. The critical factor was that currently running host software and conventional network configurations should continue to operate without changes. Ideally, the transition method to be adopted would allow for easy expansion and migration from the conventional network to the public network. For IBM hosts, one of the ways of accomplishing this goal was to enhance the IBM 370X emulator program to support the concurrent connection of conventional network terminals and public network terminals. What evolved was a modified emulator program, called the data-network modified emulator program (DMEP), which required no changes in existing host software.

DMEP supports almost all IBM 360 and 370 operating systems, access methods, and telecommunications program products. The unsupported exception is IBM's virtual telecommunications access method (VTAM). Installation, system generation, program loading, and problem analysis are accomplished in the same manner as that employed with an unmodified emulation program. The terminals to be connected through the public network are identified by coding additional parameters during the emulation program system generation.

Once the program is loaded, communications between the 370X and the public packet network occur automatically over one or more high-speed data links. Session requests received from public network terminals are allocated to individual subchannel addresses—input/output (I/O) data paths between the host application programs and the communications controller—as if the terminals were connected through a hardwired 270X. In this regard, DMEP operates identically to the unmodified emulator program.

One advantage inherent to DMEP is that pools of subchannel addresses may be assigned to different host processes. For instance, the user may select either TSO or IMS. Messages are automatically sent to the terminal to indicate the unavailability of a process or that the host is inoperative

Once connection is made, data messages from the host are concentrated for delivery to the network over the network link. Similarly, data messages received from the network are de-concentrated and routed to the appropriate subchannel for processing by the 360/370 programs. The link is under the control of the HDLC protocol, and therefore passes messages in both directions simultaneously. By decoding control

4 Electronic mail application

Exchanging data. The necessary ingredients of an electronic mail system are CRT terminals for composing the messages, printers for receiving them, and storage for buffering. To achieve the greatest transmission switching flexibility and effectiveness, the terminal controllers are connected to an X.25 public packet-switching network.

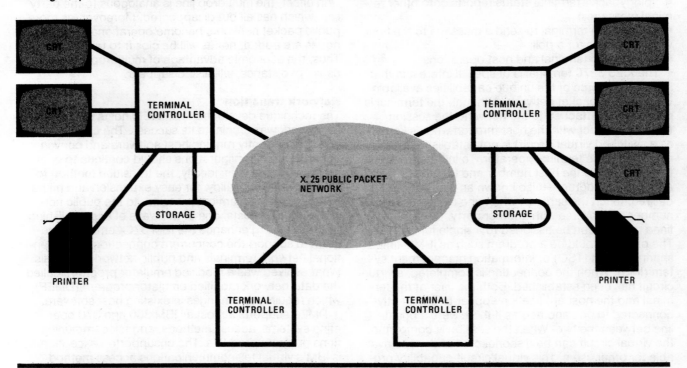

signals received from the network, DMEP presents the channel status, sense information, and control bytes necessary for the correct operation of the host software. Channel commands are executed and ended exactly as in 270X operation.

Optionally, when a new operating system is generated ("sysgen") by the user, the program can detect situations in which operation can be improved or assisted. Deleting extraneous program steps and expediting virtual memory log-on procedures are examples.

When the host, the terminal, or the network indicates completion of a session, the program terminates the connection and returns the subchannel to the pool, making it available for a new connection.

Controlling the network

Another capability of the X.25 network is an operator-oriented network control console. By keying in the appropriate command on a hardcopy or display terminal directly connected to the 370X, the user can query the state of any subchannel or line interface. Additional commands invoke traces (records of events, such as the interaction between DMEP and the network), list debugging information, display configurations, release locked subchannels, and log errors as detected.

Today's configurations of multiple networks supporting different terminals for different applications can be replaced easily by the X.25 networks. A single X.25 network terminal attached to the network, rather than to a specific host computer, can connect with a spe-

cific application and perform its operations. When complete, it can reconnect with another application, host, or even another terminal on the network.

Two hosts or more, connected anywhere in the network, can share jobs, share files, transfer files, offload tasks to each other, or act as backup to each other. It will not be uncommon to find users performing tasks on different processors, each best suited to a specific task. For example, a user can connect to host 1 to develop programs, compile those programs on host 2, execute those programs on host 3, and store and back up those programs on host 4.

Electronic mail and teleconferencing are readily accomplished on a public packet network. Even today, there are host computers on Telenet's network that provide capabilities of storing and retrieving mail. A terminal on an X.25 controller attached to a network can connect with a counterpart terminal or printer on the network to exchange information and data. Used together, the two terminals provide the necessary ingredients for an electronic mail system, as shown in Figure 4.

As the home computer market matures, computer service bureaus will seek an economic method to offer their wares to the public. Conventional private lines and even WATS lines are unworkable for this market. The user will demand access to all available services at a price that is comparable to monthly telephone charges. The only foreseeable vehicle for providing this link is a public data network. ∎

Matching teleprinters to X.25 packet-switching networks

Richard B. Hovey, Telenet Communications Corp., Washington, D.C.

The new user-level protocols X.3, X.28, and X.29 will facilitate the accessing of different asynch terminals to host computers

User-level protocols for the recently adopted X.25 packet-switching network interface standard are beginning to surface. The preface to these latest proposed standard protocols from the Consultative Committee for International Telegraphy and Telephony (CCITT) states: "The establishment in various countries of public data networks providing packet-switched data transmission services creates a need to produce standards to facilitate international interworking."

Recommendations X.3, X.28, and X.29 are the first of these new user protocols, and they are informally referred to as the international "interactive terminal interface" (ITI). They specifically relate to the support of low-speed, asynchronous (start-stop) teleprinter and display terminals by packet-switched networks. Popular teleprinters in this category include terminals in the Teletype, Texas Instruments Silent 700, and General Electric TermiNet series. Display terminals are represented by non-intelligent and quasi-intelligent product offerings of Lear Siegler, Hazeltine, Beehive, and Infoton. There are scores of others.

The new recommendations are significant logical complements to recommendation X.25, which first addressed the need for packet-switched data transmission standards. What X.25 does is to provide precise procedures for a host computer to obtain access to a packet-switched network, and then to establish one or more so-called virtual circuits through the network between that host and another host computer or terminal.

The role of the new recommendations can be understood by viewing the packet-switched network from the perspective of a host system connected to the network. For all practical purposes, the high-speed X.25 connection to a packet-switched network appears to the host computer as a connection to a remote, intelligent concentrator device, since the sophisticated routing, monitoring, and error-correcting techniques internal to the distributed network are invisible to the host computer.

The user is mainly interested in the relatively simple procedures and structures for transmitting and receiving data to and from this concentrator device. Since these procedures are defined in X.25, a brief review of X.25 may be beneficial.

The defined procedures are incorporated in the user's system in the form of software routines. Typically, the routines reside in a programmable processor that serves as a front end to the host computer.

The software interface consists of two distinct levels of control procedures: the subscriber link-access procedure and the packet-level interface. X.25 specifies

Controlling the packet assembly/disassembly functions

PARAMETER REFERENCE	BASIC FUNCTION	DESCRIPTION	SELECTABLE VALUES
1	PAD RECALL BY ESCAPING FROM DATA TRANSFER PHASE.	ALLOWS THE TERMINAL TO INITIATE AN ESCAPE FROM DATA TRANSFER PHASE IN ORDER TO SEND COMMANDS TO THE PAD.	0 (NOT POSSIBLE) 1 (POSSIBLE)
2	ECHO	PROVIDES FOR ALL CHARACTERS RECEIVED FROM THE TERMINAL TO BE TRANSMITTED BACK TO THE TERMINAL AS WELL AS BEING INTERPRETED AND FORWARDED BY THE PAD.	0 (NO ECHO) 1 (ECHO)
3	RECOGNITION OF DATA FORWARDING SIGNALS.	ALLOWS THE PAD TO RECOGNIZE DEFINED CHARACTER(S) OR THE "BREAK SIGNAL" RECEIVED FROM THE TERMINAL AS AN INDICATION TO COMPLETE ASSEMBLY AND FORWARD A PACKET.	0 (NO SIGNAL—TRANSMIT WHEN PACKET FULL) 2 (TRANSMIT ON CARRIAGE RETURN) 126 (TRANSMIT ON CONTROL CHARACTERS)
4	SELECTION OF IDLE TIMER DELAY	ALLOWS THE PAD TO TERMINATE THE ASSEMBLY AND FORWARD A PACKET IN THE EVENT THE INTERVAL BETWEEN SUCCESSIVE CHARACTERS RECEIVED FROM THE TERMINAL EXCEEDS SOME SELECTED VALUE.	0 (NO TIMEOUT) 1–255 (VALUE IN TWENTIETHS OF A SECOND)
5	ANCILLARY DEVICE CONTROL	ALLOWS FOR FLOW CONTROL BETWEEN THE PAD AND THE TERMINAL. THE PAD INDICATES WHETHER IT IS READY OR NOT TO ACCEPT CHARACTERS FROM THE TERMINAL.	0 (NO USE OF XON/XOFF—TRANSMIT ON/OFF) 1 (USE OF XON/XOFF)
6	SUPPRESSION OF PAD SERVICE SIGNALS	PROVIDES FOR THE SUPPRESSION OF ALL MESSAGES SENT BY THE PAD TO THE TERMINAL.	0 (SIGNALS TRANSMITTED) 1 (SIGNALS NOT TRANSMITTED)
7	SELECTION OF OPERATION OF PAD ON RECEIPT OF THE "BREAK SIGNAL"	ALLOWS THE SELECTION OF OPERATION AFTER RECEIPT OF A "BREAK SIGNAL" FROM THE TERMINAL.	0 (NOTHING) 1 (INTERRUPT) 2 (RESET) 4 (SEND "INDICATION TO BREAK") 8 (ESCAPE FROM DATA TRANSFER) 16 (DISCARD OUTPUT)
8	DISCARD OUTPUT	PROVIDES FOR A PAD TO DISCARD USER DATA RATHER THAN DISASSEMBLING AND TRANSMITTING TO THE TERMINAL.	0 (NORMAL DELIVERY) 1 (DISCARD)
9	PADDING AFTER CARRIAGE RETURN	PROVIDE FOR THE AUTOMATIC INSERTION BY THE PAD OF FILL CHARACTERS AFTER THE TRANSMISSION OF A "CARRIAGE RETURN" TO THE TERMINAL.	0–7 (NUMBER OF FILL CHARACTERS INSERTED)
10	LINE FOLDING	PROVIDES FOR THE AUTOMATIC INSERTION BY THE PAD OF APPROPRIATE FORMAT EFFECTORS TO PREVENT OVERPRINTING AT THE END OF A TERMINAL PRINT LINE.	0 (NO LINE FOLDING) 1–255 (NUMBER OF CHARACTERS PER LINE BEFORE FOLDING)
11	BINARY SPEED	ENABLES HOST TO ACCESS A CHARACTERISTIC OF THE TERMINAL WHICH IS KNOWN BY THE PAD. HOST CANNOT CHANGE THIS CHARACTERISTIC—"READ ONLY"	0 (110 BIT/S) 1 (134.5 BIT/S) 2 (300 BIT/S) 8 (200 BIT/S) 9 (100 BIT/S) 10 (50 BIT/S)
12	TRAFFIC FLOW CONTROL OF THE PAD BY THE TERMINAL	ALLOWS FOR FLOW CONTROL BETWEEN THE TERMINAL AND THE PAD. THE TERMINAL INDICATES WHETHER IT IS READY OR NOT TO ACCEPT CHARACTERS FROM THE PAD.	0 (NO USE OF XON/XOFF) 1 (USE OF XON/XOFF)

1 Data buffering by the network

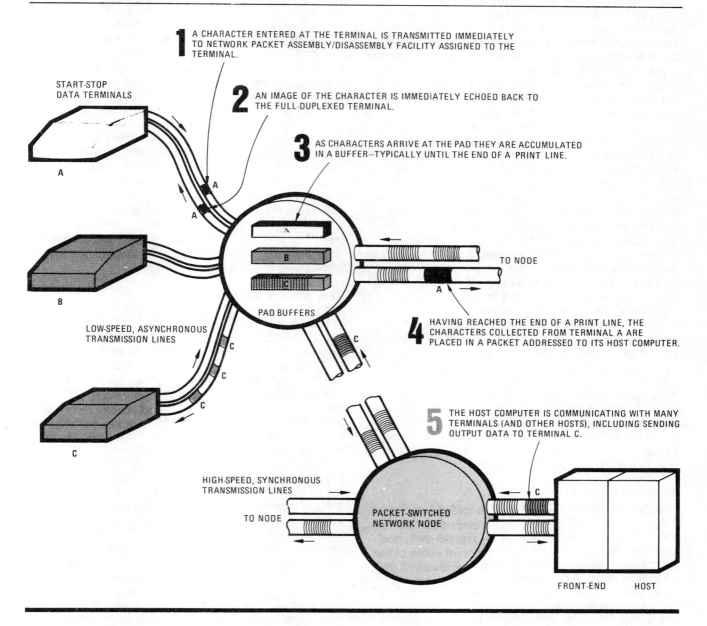

1 A CHARACTER ENTERED AT THE TERMINAL IS TRANSMITTED IMMEDIATELY TO NETWORK PACKET ASSEMBLY/DISASSEMBLY FACILITY ASSIGNED TO THE TERMINAL.

2 AN IMAGE OF THE CHARACTER IS IMMEDIATELY ECHOED BACK TO THE FULL-DUPLEXED TERMINAL.

3 AS CHARACTERS ARRIVE AT THE PAD THEY ARE ACCUMULATED IN A BUFFER—TYPICALLY UNTIL THE END OF A PRINT LINE.

4 HAVING REACHED THE END OF A PRINT LINE, THE CHARACTERS COLLECTED FROM TERMINAL A ARE PLACED IN A PACKET ADDRESSED TO ITS HOST COMPUTER.

5 THE HOST COMPUTER IS COMMUNICATING WITH MANY TERMINALS (AND OTHER HOSTS), INCLUDING SENDING OUTPUT DATA TO TERMINAL C.

START-STOP DATA TERMINALS

LOW-SPEED, ASYNCHRONOUS TRANSMISSION LINES

PAD BUFFERS

TO NODE

HIGH-SPEED, SYNCHRONOUS TRANSMISSION LINES

TO NODE

PACKET-SWITCHED NETWORK NODE

FRONT-END   HOST

---

a local rather than an end-to-end protocol. That is, internally, the network may be taking data received according to X.25 and wrapping it in a more complex protocol. At the destination, the data packet may be translated back to an X.25 protocol, or, indeed, some other host interface protocol.

The actual preparation, analysis, and processing of data for transfer over a public data network is performed by the subscriber's application programs. An application program may encompass one or more processes. For example, when a timesharing application is simultaneously servicing a number of on-line terminals, each terminal's operation requires a separate process within the host. A process can be thought of as a software routine that is invoked whenever there is an incoming or outgoing data flow. When the flow

of data comes to a stop, the process is suspended.

As mentioned earlier, X.25 specifies two distinct levels of control procedures. The main purpose of the subscriber-link-access control is to connect the host computer to the network. Information is transferred over the subscriber access link in a transmission block called a frame.

A frame may contain a packet within its information field. The main function of the frame-level subscriber-link-access control is to ensure that these packets arrive at and leave the network free of error. X.25's frame-level procedure is the high-level data link control (HDLC) protocol.

The other level of control procedure specified by X.25 is at the packet level. The control embodied in the packet is for transferring information through the network, requesting a particular network operation, or indicating the result of an operation.

Using the packet-level interface, the host system views the public network as providing a number of virtual circuits which it can link directly to processes in other host systems or to network-resident processes supporting terminal devices.

For more detail about X.25, see "Packet-switched networks agree on standard interface," DATA COMMUNICATIONS, May/June 1976, pp. 25-39.

The conceptual concentrator device (the network) accepts a connected terminal's individual characters of input data, accumulates several, then forwards this buffered data at high speed to the host computer. Figure 1 illustrates how this buffering mechanism operates. Terminal A's transmissions are being accumulated in A's assigned buffer at the packet assembly/disassembly (PAD) facility—described later—and assembled into packets addressed to A's host computer at the other end of the virtual circuit. Meanwhile, the host is shown sending data intended for Terminal C. The packets arrive at C's buffer at the PAD, where they are disassembled into the proper format for sending on to C. Terminal B is shown as idle.

As with any remote concentrator implementation, there are certain routine functions relating to the support of asynchronous terminals which the concentrator ought to provide in addition to buffering input data before forwarding it. Also possible, for example, are: echoing input characters (as shown in Figure 1, terminal A), editing buffered data, and padding output format effectors (providing "fill" characters so that a terminal has sufficient time for its mechanism to respond to non-printing format commands, such as carriage return, line feed, and tab).

Twelve functions

Recommendation X.3, in fact, sets forth 12 such basic PAD parameter functions to be provided for start-stop mode data terminal equipment by packet-switched networks. (See table.) An application of some of the functions is described later. Recommendation X.28 describes in detail the mechanism by which these functions can be controlled from the terminal, while X.29 specifies the mechanisms for control by the host computer. The 12 functions are by no means exhaustive, but rather define the basic set agreed upon internationally; the list can and doubtless will be expanded over a time, as agreement on additional needs evolves.

The result of this standardization is that a large number of host computers can all share the use of the conceptual remote concentrator—which is, in fact, a distributed nationwide network. The international significance is that a terminal in one country may connect to the local network, establish a connection through a host computer on a foreign network, and the foreign host will be compatible with the local network's terminal-support capability.

This terminal-support capability, which X.28 and X.29 together specify to be provided initially by the packet networks, is the packet assembly/disassembly or PAD facility shown functionally in Figure 1. In a

packet-switched network such as Telenet's, this PAD facility is itself isolated from the inner communications network by an X.25 interface, as shown in Figure 2. Also shown are the protocols used in establishing a virtual circuit between a terminal and a host. Circuits intended for other applications are pictured as part of the X.25 bundle. In addition, a table of parameters is shown within the PAD facility, with one table meant for each terminal connected to the PAD.

Because the PAD appears to the communications network functionally like another user's X.25 host, the inner communications network is able to establish X.25 virtual circuits among users' hosts and network (or users') PADs with complete symmetry. (The user may supply a PAD to support his own terminals.) Within the X.25 protocol, what a single X.25 virtual circuit ultimately provides, on an end-to-end basis, is an error-free, bi-directional data path. That is, when the overhead functions (or formats) associated with X.25 are stripped away, what is left is the equivalent of conventional point-to-point data circuits.

Two types of data

Data on a given virtual circuit may be classified as one of two types—and that is as far as X.25 goes. In practice, one of these two types is the raw user data passed between the host computer and terminal through the PAD, and the other type is the control data passed between the host computer and the PAD. Both types are transmitted over the same virtual circuit, to ensure the relative sequencing of user and control data in the store-and-forward environment of packet-switched networks. Recommendation X.29 is precisely the definition of the procedures and formats for the control data, when the terminal being supported is a start-stop (asynchronous) device.

The operation of the PAD depends on the values of a set of internal variables called PAD parameters, an independent set of which is maintained for each start-stop terminal, as mentioned earlier. The control mechanism consists of the ability to select the parameters by reference number and to read or set their values.

In typical Telenet packet network operation today, a host computer will routinely set the list of PAD parameters (see table) to those values suitable to the host application programs at the beginning of each terminal session. For most host computers, this is the extent of their interaction with the PAD facility. However, more sophisticated hosts may dynamically alter the PAD values during a session to adjust the network's management to meet the requirements of differing application program characteristics.

For example, during a session, a terminal operator might go from a manual line-at-a-time data entry mode to a batched cassette data entry mode. The host computer can facilitate his transition by making three changes: resetting PAD parameter 1 (see table) from a value of 1 (escape from data transfer stage possible) to 0 (escape not possible, therefore providing transparent data transfer); resetting parameter 2 from a value of 1 (echoes provided from PAD) to 0 (no echoing); and resetting parameter 3 from a value of 2

2 Virtual circuit protocols

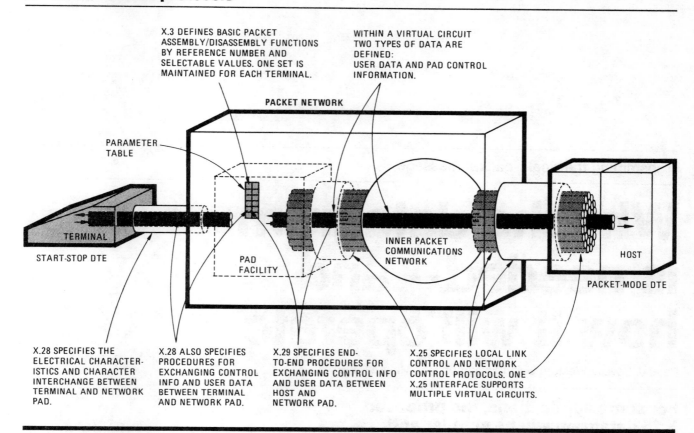

X.3 DEFINES BASIC PACKET ASSEMBLY/DISASSEMBLY FUNCTIONS BY REFERENCE NUMBER AND SELECTABLE VALUES. ONE SET IS MAINTAINED FOR EACH TERMINAL.

WITHIN A VIRTUAL CIRCUIT TWO TYPES OF DATA ARE DEFINED: USER DATA AND PAD CONTROL INFORMATION.

PACKET NETWORK

PARAMETER TABLE

TERMINAL

START-STOP DTE

PAD FACILITY

INNER PACKET COMMUNICATIONS NETWORK

HOST

PACKET-MODE DTE

X.28 SPECIFIES THE ELECTRICAL CHARACTER-ISTICS AND CHARACTER INTERCHANGE BETWEEN TERMINAL AND NETWORK PAD.

X.28 ALSO SPECIFIES PROCEDURES FOR EXCHANGING CONTROL INFO AND USER DATA BETWEEN TERMINAL AND NETWORK PAD.

X.29 SPECIFIES END-TO-END PROCEDURES FOR EXCHANGING CONTROL INFO AND USER DATA BETWEEN HOST AND NETWORK PAD.

X.25 SPECIFIES LOCAL LINK CONTROL AND NETWORK CONTROL PROTOCOLS. ONE X.25 INTERFACE SUPPORTS MULTIPLE VIRTUAL CIRCUITS.

(transmit on carriage return) to 0 (no special signal—transmit when packet is full).

Terminal-to-PAD interface

Recommendation X.28 specifies the interface between the terminal and the PAD facility provided by the packet network. The electrical characteristics and procedures for character interchange, for example, conform to present operation of asynchronous (start-stop) low-speed terminals and thus require nothing new. The significant standards are the operator-oriented procedures for the exchange of control information and user data between the terminal and the network.

Normally, at the beginning of a terminal session, the operator will be communicating with the network and will be required to provide the network address of the host computer with which his terminal is to be connected. Thereafter, the terminal-computer-terminal dialog can proceed just as if there were a direct physical circuit between the two. If the connection to the host cannot be completed, or is abnormally terminated, for example, X.28 proposes explanatory mnemonics to be displayed: **OCC** (occupied) transmitted to the terminal by the network, for example, is equivalent to the audible busy signal on the telephone system. Along with the standards for entering address information, X.28 provides standards for such options as network user identification and facility request information.

Command procedures are also available from the

terminal for altering the parameter values for individual network support functions. A typical command would be, SET 2:0 (set parameter 2 to 0). However, experience has shown that proper network initialization and host computer control of these functions eliminates the need for any such commands during routine operation. The result is that the user can adapt the network to his interactive terminal needs with ease and little training for additional tasks.

Finally, it should be observed that the PAD facility for start-stop terminals is only one of several conceivable such facilities. In addition to the expected expansion of the packet assembler/disassembler, it is anticipated that future recommended interfaces may standardize the functions required to support other generic classes of terminals—some of which are today operating over packet-switched networks. ■

Additional reading on interfaces and packet-switching networks:
■ Folts, Harold C. and Ira W. Cotton, *Interfaces: new standards catch up with technology,* DATA COMMUNICATIONS, June 1977, pp. 31-40.
■ Hovey, Richard B., *The user's role in connecting to a value added network,* DATA COMMUNICATIONS, May/June 1974, pp. 35-40.
■ Johnson, Timothy, *Projecting the future roles of packet-switching networks,* DATA COMMUNICATIONS, July/August 1976, pp. 18-23.

Why the datagram is needed—and how it will operate

Peter J. Sevcik, Western Union Telegraph Co., McLean, Va.

For some applications, the proposed X.25 datagram will be simpler and less cumbersome than the X.25 virtual circuit over a packet network

Demand for a simple, single-packet, network protocol has reached the point where new standards are being proposed to augment X.25. The new service is called datagram—or DG, for short.

Existing packet-switched networks and X.25 procedures for establishing virtual circuits—or virtual calls—have been described quite thoroughly (Ref. 1). What follows is a description of the somewhat similar datagram (DG) service, together with a comparison of DG with virtual-circuit (VC) service, developments in DG subscriber interfaces, and the proposed datagram standard. The details given here will probably change as a result of future standards work, but the concepts will most likely remain the same.

Packet switching was an experimental concept in the late sixties, became practical in the early seventies, and was being standardized by the mid-seventies. As early as October 1972, an informal meeting of packet-switch network builders (experimental and public) was convened at the International Computer Communications Conference (ICCC '72) in Washington, D.C., to discuss problems which occur when packet networks are interfaced.

The first international standards meeting (Ref. 2) specifically held to discuss the basic concepts of standardizing the new technology was the International Consultative Committee for Telegraphy and Telephony (CCITT) Rapporteur's group meeting on packet switching in Oslo, Norway, in August 1974. The purpose of that meeting was to identify the basic types of packet-switching services and their interfaces, and to determine what standards should be created. The two services identified were: virtual circuit and datagram. The United States delegation went on record that this discussion should not close the door to any other justifiable services which could be derived from this young technology

As a matter of fact, there was much discussion concerning the trade-offs between early standardization of a technology to get it widely used, or later standardization to permit more development and maturity. One decision reached was to limit the number of standardized packet services to two: VC and DG. Packet switching was, and still is considered by some to be, an experimental technology.

Work proceeded very quickly—relative to the usual pace of international standards organizations—on developing a virtual circuit interface for packet-mode hosts. The two primary motivations were that three networks were operational, and that the CCITT formalizes standards only every four years at its plenary meetings. The next plenary was to be in December

1976. So the alternatives were to get a standard in two or in six years.

Virtual circuits, as the name implies, are designed to functionally replace leased or circuit-switched data communications facilities. This was obviously the market with greatest potential. All of these circumstances led to the development of a virtual-circuit interface standard—which did not deal with the datagram mode of operation.

However, the datagram requirement did not go away. Actually, no sooner was the virtual-circuit interface standardized, than people started calling it too clumsy for some applications.

Fast select

One alternative which is currently under study is "fast select." The fast-select option permits quicker and easier connection establishment/disestablishment for short-duration calls. This will at best be a partial solution, since the virtual-circuit interface with all its connection overhead would still exist. Furthermore, the volume of virtual-circuit accounting information and the necessary circuit set-up traffic have been raised as potential difficulties in implementing fast-select service. Flow control (control of traffic volume to prevent overload) applies only to subscriber traffic. Fast select does not reduce the amount of control traffic. All of this control traffic would therefore become high non-flow-controlled overhead to the network if subscribers were to use fast select for very short (one- or two-packet) transactions. Also, it takes fast select longer to get a packet through the network than it does datagram.

The recent history (Ref. 3) of datagram standardization efforts starts with the work of a few members of the American National Standards Institute (ANSI) X3S3 committee's Task Group 7 on Public Data Networks, who formed an ad hoc datagram group. This group, which included W.E. Elden, Dr. V. Cerf, J. Wheeler, and the author, actively started to develop a proposal in the spring of 1977. A draft datagram standard was prepared by that November after a working document had been enthusiastically received and further refined at Task Group 7's October meeting.

The draft was discussed at the International Standards Organization (ISO) meeting in Cologne, West Germany, at the end of November 1977. This first international exposure helped shape a final proposal to the CCITT, which was ratified by ANSI's X3S3 committee, and most recently by the U.S. State Department. All this effort was in preparation for the CCITT data communications meeting in April 1978. The USA work, along with some other ISO contributions—namely from France—helped develop an ISO "white paper" to the CCITT defining what datagram service should look like. However, the paper does not ascertain if the transaction user would be better served by datagram or by fast select. The next crucial decisions on the future of an international DG standard will be made at the Geneva CCITT meeting in April 1978.

Datagram is gaining momentum and has the attention of the CCITT. There are several European PTTs (Postal Telegraph and Telephone agencies) which are

Table 1 Comparing vc and datagram

SERVICE DESCRIPTION	HOW PROVIDED	
	VIRTUAL CIRCUIT	DATAGRAM
BASIC UNIT	CONNECTION	MESSAGE
START AND END OF BASIC UNIT	CALL SET-UP TO TAKE-DOWN	SINGLE DATAGRAM PACKET
RELIABILITY	PROBABILITY THAT CONNECTION MAINTAINED	PROBABILITY THAT MESSAGE IS DELIVERED
SEQUENCE OF BASIC UNIT	VIRTUAL CIRCUITS NOT SET UP IN ORDER	DATAGRAMS NOT DELIVERED IN ORDER
SERVICE FAILURE AND NOTIFICATION	BREAK OF LOGICAL CHANNEL ADVISED BY NETWORK USING CALL ID	NON-DELIVERY NOTICE ADVISED BY NETWORK USING DATAGRAM ID

studying datagram as a possible future service offering. Although the Trans-Canada Telephone System once had datagram in its Datapac network, it was withdrawn because there was no standard interface and a not strongly enough defined need at the time. However, there are several private and experimental networks, such as Cyclades (Ref. 4) and Autodin II (Ref. 5), which currently provide a datagram user interface.

Meanwhile, there is a growing class of subscribers who want to purchase only basic packet transportation service from a common carrier. They either don't want to use any high-level protocols, or would rather build their own. The recent intensifying interest in large-scale distributed data processing systems operating on a national basis has generated a definite need for transaction-based networks. These new advanced applications of data communications are dropping old concepts like the "call"—in which time duration is a prime concern. There is no notion of a call in transaction services. Instead, there are many short, independent messages which must be moved in the new packet-network-related technology of distributed data processing (DDP).

Applying DDP

The most direct application of DDP uses short transaction message traffic such as point-of-sale, electronic funds transfer, credit checking, meter reading, reservation systems, directory searches, and inventory control. Process control systems also need an efficient means of transmitting aperiodic short messages, such as position, sensor data, alarms, and telemetry.

Table 2 Transportation analogy

PURPOSE	TRANSPORTATION	DATA COMMUNICATIONS
TO MOVE A LARGE NUMBER OF OBJECTS OVER A FIXED ROUTE, WITHOUT A RESERVATION	BUS ROUTE	DEDICATED LINE
TO MOVE A MODERATE NUMBER OF OBJECTS OVER A VARIABLE ROUTE, WITH A RESERVATION MADE FOR THE SERVICE	TAXI CAB	VIRTUAL PACKET-SWITCHED SERVICE
TO MOVE A SMALL NUMBER OF OBJECTS TO INDEPENDENT DESTINATIONS, USING VARIABLE ROUTES AND NEEDING NO RESERVATION	PERSONAL AUTOMOBILE	DATAGRAM PACKET-SWITCHED SERVICE

A datagram service matches these transaction processing requirements without the need for virtual circuit setup and clearing. Depending on the application, the use of permanent virtual circuits may be prohibitively expensive. (For example, more permanent virtual circuits may be required than can be economically supported by the network or the subscriber.) Or the interface procedures for virtual-call service (establishing and clearing a virtual circuit for each transaction) may be intolerably high in overhead (interface complexity, and time involved in completing the transaction).

The following illustrates how transaction-profiled subscribers will use a communications network:
■ Send short transaction messages (on the order of one or two packets each), with a short response—or none—expected.
■ Potentially, send the transaction messages to a large number of destinations over a period of several hours, without often retransmitting to the same destination. (For example, interarrival time of transactions to the same destination may be in the order of 10 minutes; interarrival time of transactions to any destination from the same subscriber may be about 0.1 second.)
■ Each transaction will consist of one packet, in order to incur the minimum overhead and delay in network handling and destination processing. That is, each time-sensitive transaction is independent and should be delivered by the network as soon as possible.

Datagram is both a packet-switched service and a subscriber interface to that service. The service can be defined in the abstract, or defined by comparing with virtual-circuit service. In abstract form, datagram

is a message service which begins and ends with the delivery of the message. Virtual-circuit service begins with the establishment of the virtual circuit and ends with the clearing of the virtual circuit. During the virtual-circuit lifetime, any number of messages may be sent and delivered in time sequence. During the datagram lifetime, exactly one message is sent and delivered.

Comparing the services
A direct comparison of datagram and virtual-circuit service is shown in Table 1. Note that both services perform similar operations, but on different basic units: connections and messages. The key purposes of the two services can then be reduced to:
■ Connection—a highly guaranteed pipeline for the sequential delivery of data.
■ Message—a highly probable delivery of one data unit.
The user has a clear choice between two services which have fundamentally different purposes.

A parallel can be drawn from the transportation industry to illustrate these different purposes, as shown in Table 2. The reservation referred to in the taxi service (analogous to VC) is the calling of the taxi company to get a car. In contrast, the average individual who owns a car need only get into it and go (analogous to DG).

Note that all the cited transportation systems operate side by side, using the same basic road network. The same can be done in a packet-switch network, which uses a system of trunks and access lines to provide both virtual circuit and datagram services "side by side."

Datagram service is therefore specifically geared to the transaction-profiled user. It is not that virtual circuits can't support transaction users; rather, they will be much better supported by datagram services.

A datagram definition
Datagram is not yet a standard, so no formal definition exists. But a working definition for the purposes of this article is:
■ A datagram is self-contained, carrying sufficient information to be routed from source data-terminal equipment (DTE) to destination DTE without reliance on earlier exchanges between source or destination DTE and the transporting network.
■ A datagram is delivered in such a way that the receiver can determine the boundaries—beginning and end—of the datagram as it was entered by the source DTE. The simplest way to achieve this determination is to deliver the datagram intact as one unit to its destination, but other methods are not ruled out.
■ A datagram is delivered to its destination with a high success probability, but it may possibly be lost.
■ The sequence in which datagrams are entered into a network by a source DTE is not necessarily preserved upon delivery at a destination DTE.
■ If a datagram cannot be delivered to the destination, or is detectably lost, the network will attempt to advise the source DTE through a "non-delivery indication." This notice indicates, to the best of the network's

1 Packet network interface options

Well-stacked. *Packet-switched networks can provide all of the required subscriber interface options by stacking the functions through protocol layering. Not all public data networks are being built in this manner, but the hierarchy of options which is shown here is probably the general form of future packet-subscriber interface architecture.*

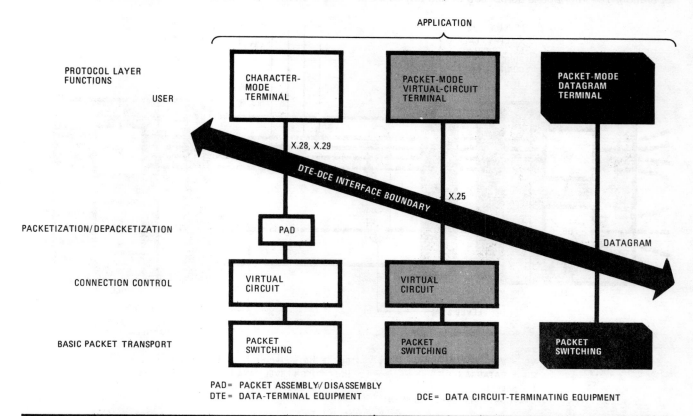

PAD = PACKET ASSEMBLY/DISASSEMBLY
DTE = DATA-TERMINAL EQUIPMENT
DCE = DATA CIRCUIT-TERMINATING EQUIPMENT

"knowledge," why the datagram could not be delivered. To distinguish among datagrams for the purpose of providing error indications, the network employs a DG identifier supplied in each datagram by the source DTE. Uniqueness of this identifier, if desired, is the source DTE's responsibility.

White paper development

At the recent ISO meeting in Cologne, Technical Committee 97, Subcommittee 6, Working Group 2 on Data Communications, developed a white paper (Ref. 6) for the CCITT defining, among other things, a "quality of datagram service." The quality of service description was intended to illustrate the types of parameters which are of concern to this organization of data communications users. The specific values of the parameters are the result of a very first attempt, and only indicate orders of magnitude envisioned by the group where no satellite links are involved.

The parameters and their initial values are:
■ The median transit delay between two subscribers is 0.2 second. This delay is measured between the time the last bit of a datagram is received by the source data circuit-terminating equipment (DCE) and the time the first bit of the same datagram is delivered by the destination DCE, in the absence of any other traffic or

inhibiting flow control to the destination DTE.
■ The maximum transit delay between two DTEs for 95 percent of datagrams does not exceed one second, with the same measurement conditions as the median transit delay.
■ The maximum transit delay between two DTEs for 99.99 percent of the datagrams does not exceed 10 seconds (same measurement conditions).
■ The probability of not delivering a datagram, but notifying the source with a non-delivery indication (NDI), and in the absence of any other traffic or inhibiting flow control to the source DTE, is 10^{-3}.
■ The probability of not delivering a datagram, and not notifying the source with an NDI, is 10^{-4}.
■ The probability of a network's duplicating a datagram is 10^{-4}.
■ The probability of datagram delivery to a destination other than the one specified is 10^{-6}.
■ The probability of undetected error for datagrams is 10^{-8}.

There are several subscriber interfaces being developed for public data networks. Collectively they are beginning to define a hierarchy of subscriber interface options. This hierarchy is depicted in Figure 1. The figure shows how packet-switched networks can provide all of the interface options by stacking the func-

2 The DTE-DCE X.25 interface

Working side by side. The proposed DTE-DCE interface provides for simultaneous virtual circuit and datagram operation. The interface is composed of one physical link, through which the three-level architecture of X.25 is applied. The datagram channel flow control is separate from that of the multiple virtual-circuit logical channels.

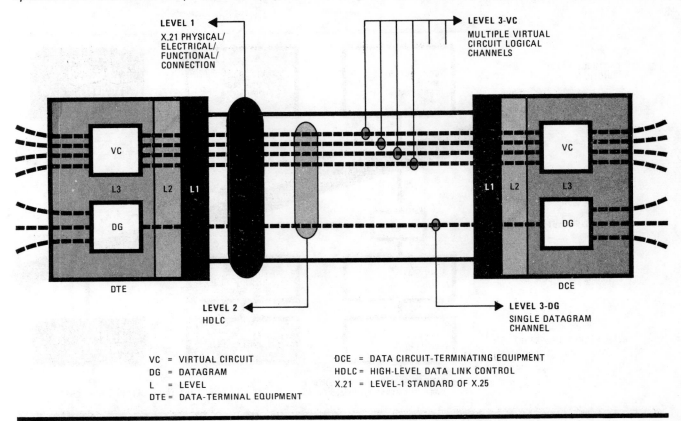

LEVEL 1
X.21 PHYSICAL/
ELECTRICAL/
FUNCTIONAL/
CONNECTION

LEVEL 3-VC
MULTIPLE VIRTUAL
CIRCUIT LOGICAL
CHANNELS

LEVEL 2
HDLC

LEVEL 3-DG
SINGLE DATAGRAM
CHANNEL

DTE

DCE

VC = VIRTUAL CIRCUIT
DG = DATAGRAM
L = LEVEL
DTE = DATA-TERMINAL EQUIPMENT

DCE = DATA CIRCUIT-TERMINATING EQUIPMENT
HDLC = HIGH-LEVEL DATA LINK CONTROL
X.21 = LEVEL-1 STANDARD OF X.25

tions through protocol layering. Not all public data networks are being built in this manner, but it is probably the general form of future architectures.

Character-mode terminals—the majority of today's terminals—must have their data streams packetized with proper headers and trailers on input, and the reverse process (depacketization) on output. As shown in Figure 1, the CCITT interface standard for this packet assembly/disassembly (PAD) function is X.28 and X.29. X.28 and X.29 also serve as network-to-human interface for the control and management of the virtual circuit protocol behind the PAD. This interface can support only one logical connection at a time.

Packet-mode terminals already produce packetized data. They interface directly to the virtual circuit function by means of X.25 (Fig. 1). X.25 supports many simultaneous logical connections, permitting the interleaving of packets to and from several destinations. X.25 also is the means by which the virtual circuits are established, managed through flow control, and cleared. (For more detail on how X.25, X.28, and X.29 apply to a packet network, see Ref. 7.)

The datagram packet-mode terminal will interface directly to the packet-switching facility (Fig. 1). The terminal also transfers interleaved packetized data to many destinations, and is managed by flow control.

But—as contrasted with the X.25 procedure—it does not make connections.

A formal proposal

Since the spring of 1977, a concerted effort by ANSI's Task Group X3S37 on Public Data Networks has generated a formal "Proposal for the Datagram Interface" (Ref. 8) to the CCITT. This document incorporates a proposed datagram interface specification into the current X.25 standard. The datagram mode of operation is fully complementary to virtual circuit mode of operation. The task group saw no need to invent new procedures where current ones would suffice. Furthermore, it is envisioned that if the interfaces were kept as compatible as possible, then terminals could easily be designed to operate in both modes. As a result, the task group's proposal includes: operation with the virtual-circuit mode only, datagram-mode only, and virtual circuits plus datagrams—all using a single interface.

The DTE-DCE interface proposal provides for simultaneous virtual-circuit (VC) and datagram (DG) operation, as depicted in Figure 2. The DTE is connected to the DCE by way of one physical link, through which the three-level architecture of X.25 is applied. Level 1 (Fig. 2) is the physical/electrical/functional link con-

3 Datagram states

Interstate commerce. *The datagram interface data transfer condition is divided into six designated states, as shown. The responsibility for the transition from one state to another, and the datagram successfully transmitted by the data-terminal equipment or data circuit-terminating equipment, are indicated alongside the transition arrow.*

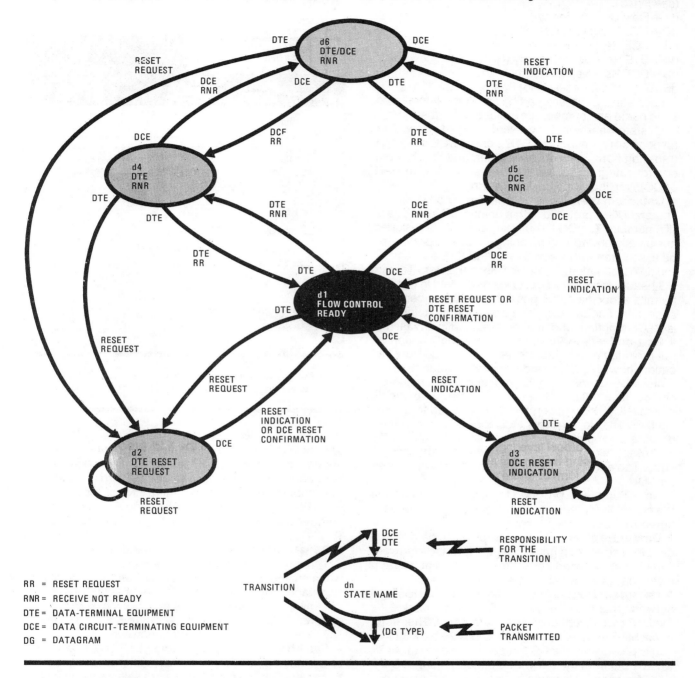

RR = RESET REQUEST
RNR = RECEIVE NOT READY
DTE = DATA-TERMINAL EQUIPMENT
DCE = DATA CIRCUIT-TERMINATING EQUIPMENT
DG = DATAGRAM

nection of X.21. Level 2 is the high-level data link control (HDLC), which controls the link flow of both VC and DG frames. Level 2 is insensitive to whether information frames contain VCs or DGs, and is independent of the Level-3 operations across the interface. All addressing, data transfer, and flow control of individual VC and DG packets are performed at Level 3.

The proposal suggests that there may be one or more logical channels, each separately flow-controlled through X.25 VC procedures. Additionally, there may be one datagram channel. The DG channel is flow-controlled separately from the multiple VC logical channels. Except for the special case of the restart procedure, the VC and DG operations are completely independent of each other. Virtual circuit and datagram control and data frames can be transferred (that is, multiplexed) across the interface in any sequence, pursuant to VC and DG procedures.

The salient points of the datagram interface proposal (Ref. 8) are:

■ **DTE-DCE interface states.** The DG interface data transfer condition is divided into six designated states (see Fig. 3).

d1—Flow Control Ready
d2—DTE Reset Request (RR)
d3—DCE Reset Indication
d4—DTE Receive Not Ready (RNR)
d5—DCE Receive Not Ready
d6—DTE/DCE Receive Not Ready

Each state is represented by an ellipse wherein the state name and number are indicated. Furthermore, each state transition is represented by an arrow. The responsibility—either the DTE's or the DCE's—for the transition from one state to another, and the necessary control datagram successfully transmitted by the DTE or DCE, are indicated beside the arrow.

■ **Datagram identification number.** Each Data Transfer DG is provided with a unique DG identification (ID) number. The DG ID number, being DTE-assigned, has unique end-to-end meaning when interpreted to be associated with a single "pair" of DTE addresses (origin/destination). A 12-bit field in the Data Transfer DG header format (DATAGRAM IDENTIFIER field in Fig. 4) permits encoding 4,096 possible DG ID numbers for each pair of addresses. The generation of the number is a DTE function, and may be assigned in any fashion.

■ **Non-delivery indication.** Delivery confirmation is not provided as a datagram service. Non-delivery indication, however, is a mandatory network function. When a DG cannot be delivered, and this condition can be detected by the network, a Non-Delivery Indication (NDI) DG is generated and delivered to the sending DTE. The Non-Delivery Indication DG returns the datagram ID number and the sending/receiving DTE addresses, along with a cause field and diagnostic code. Table 3 illustrates the current diagnostic codes for NDI.

An option is also provided to allow a user to disable the non-delivery indication on a per DG basis, or as agreed at subscription time.

■ **Datagram size.** DG sizes comply with the X.25 user data field sizes. At a gateway—the interface between two packet-switched networks—the maximum size of a user data field is 128 octets (8-bit bytes).

■ **Datagram fragmenting.** Fragmenting of DGs by the network prior to delivery to a DTE may be needed if the DTE can accept only short datagrams. Therefore, a mechanism for encoding from the MORE DATA indication is provided in the DG header (M field in Fig. 4) when a DG from the network is either the only DG or a DG fragment. An option is also provided for unique serial numbering of fragments, to support this function. However, as long as source and destination DTEs subscribe to the same maximum user data field size, no DG fragmentation should be necessary.

Combining of DTE DGs at the input of the network is not considered to be a datagram service characteristic, and is therefore not provided. Each DG at the network input is treated as an independent entity.

■ **Flow control.** The indicators defining the number of

4 Data transfer format

Formatting the data. *Consistent with virtual-circuit formats, data transfer and control datagram formats are uniquely identified with bits 8 through 5 of the first octet.*

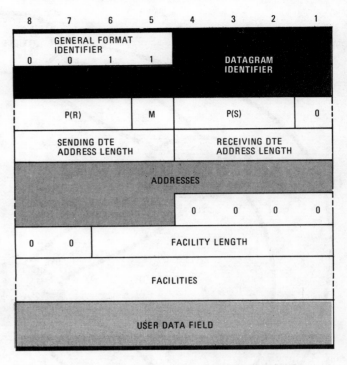

P(R) = PACKETS TO BE RECEIVED   P(S) = PACKETS TO BE SENT
M   = "MORE" BIT   DTE= DATA-TERMINAL EQUIPMENT

packets the network permits to be received—P(R)—and the number the user permits to be sent—P(S)—are called the windows of the flow control procedures. Flow control numbers have significance only to the applicable DTE-DCE combination. RNR stops DG flow while RR authorizes DG flow. P(R) and P(S) window number counters are independent of DG ID numbers (Fig. 4).

■ **Reset and restart.** Reset commands affect only the DG channel—not VC or other channels. However, when an interface supports both DG and VC operation simultaneously, a VC Restart triggers the DG Reset command automatically, thus effectively clearing all channels' flow control window counters back to zero. DG ID numbers are not affected, however.

■ **Facilities.** To enable optimizing DTE-DTE operation under varying conditions, certain optional facilities are necessary. While some options are selectable on a per DG basis, others may be designated at subscription time. Four optional facilities are presently defined: Throughput Class, Fragmentation, Closed-User Group, and Non-Delivery Indication Disable. Additional optional facilities that are being considered include Window Size Selection, Priority, Reverse Charging, and Reverse Charging Acceptance.

■ **Formats.** The formats for data transfer and control datagrams are consistent with virtual-call formats. Fig-

Table 3   Non-delivery diagnostics

DESTINATION CONGESTION
OUT OF ORDER
REMOTE PROCEDURE ERROR
INVALID DATAGRAM
ACCESS BARRED
LOCAL PROCEDURE ERROR
NETWORK CONGESTION
NOT OBTAINABLE

ure 4 provides the formats for a Data Transfer DG. The General Format Identifier code 0011 identifies the transmission as a datagram type. The DG identification number, or user's ID, occupies a total of 12 bits—4 through 1 in octet 1 and 8 through 1 in octet 2—and is analogous to VC logical channels. The coding of the DG RR, RNR, and Reset packet types are the same as the VC RR, RNR and Reset packet types.

If, as a result of this article, the advantages of datagram service are now more apparent to the user community, then it is suggested that users make their thoughts known to the standards bodies and common carriers. The more advocates that are known, the more likely it is that public datagram service will become a reality. ■

References
1. Hovey, Richard B., *Packet-switched networks agree on standard interface,* DATA COMMUNICATIONS, May/June 1976, pp. 25-39.
2. CCITT Rapporteur on Packet Switching, *Report of Meeting in Oslo,* CCITT COM VII, Document August 1974.
3. Elden, W.L., *Datagram Packet-Switching Interface Standardization for Public Data Networks,* Proceeding of Intelcom 77 International Telecommunications Exposition, Atlanta, October 1977, Horizon House.
4. Pouzin, L., *Virtual Circuits vs Datagrams—Technical and Political Problems,* pp. 483-494, 1976 National Computer Conference, June 1976, NY, AFIPS Press.
5. Sevcik, P.J., *Autodin II Subscriber Access Protocols and Interfaces,* National Telecommunications Conference (NTC 77) Proceedings, December 1977, Los Angeles, IEEE Press.
6. ISO/TC 97/SC 6/WG2, *Datagram Service and Interface* Contribution to CCITT Com VII Document, (Revised Cologne 26), Cologne, December 1977.
7. Hovey, Richard B., *Matching teleprinters to X.25 packet-switching networks,* DATA COMMUNICATIONS, October 1977, pp. 63-69.
8. U.S.A., *Proposal for the Datagram Interface,* Contribution to CCITT Com VII Document, December 1977.

Intelligent-network functions— who provides them?

Dixon R. Doll, The DMW Group, Ann Arbor, Mich.

Both the carriers and the vendors can provide network control functions, but users should be wary of paying twice, or losing control

Teleprocessing systems have historically involved well-defined functions performed by a common carrier on the one hand, and different, generally nonoverlapping functions performed by a computer vendor and independent suppliers of data communications equipment and terminals on the other. In recent years, the line of demarcation between functions provided by the carriers and by the computer vendors has begun to blur markedly. There is every reason to believe that such lines will disappear altogether in many instances.

As a result, problems can arise for the end user in future networks where either the carrier or the computer vendor is capable of providing many of the same functions. Not surprisingly, unless users carefully plan and implement such networks, much overhead can result, producing significant benefits for no one.

During 1977, the teleprocessing industry witnessed accelerated acceptance of the CCITT recommendation X.25 for interfacing to packet-switching communications networks. To briefly review the recommendation's essence, the first three layers of X.25 consist of a
- physical interface between data circuit-terminating equipment (DCE) and data terminal equipment (DTE);
- host access line protocol (physical link level);
- packet-level protocol for control and creation of virtual ports and circuits. This X.25 recommendation

surprised many people by attracting relatively broad support from many diverse organizations, in spite of many known shortcomings and details which have yet to be resolved. For example, X.25 is not designed to be a simple terminal interface. In spite of the recommendation's complexity, operation is restricted to just one physical access line—not yet permitting operation over multiple physical access lines. Another shortcoming is the relatively high overhead required for short messages.

But the present state of X.25 really consists of a set of recommended guidelines. There are many specific parameters of the protocol which have yet to be defined by the International Study Group of the CCITT, as well as variable parameter values which are left up to the particular countries and vendors to implement in their specific versions of the X.25 protocol. The danger in calling X.25 a standard at this time is that many individuals automatically infer ease of compatibility between two networks or devices which use the so-called same standard. There is every reason to be optimistic about the long-term future of compatibility between different packet-switching networks implemented using X.25. However, it would be foolhardy to suggest that any packet-switching network which implements X.25 will be readily interfaced to any other

1 Future network—carriers' view

Carrier provisions. *In order to provide a virtual circuit connection between terminals and computers, the packet carrier must perform elaborate network control functions.*

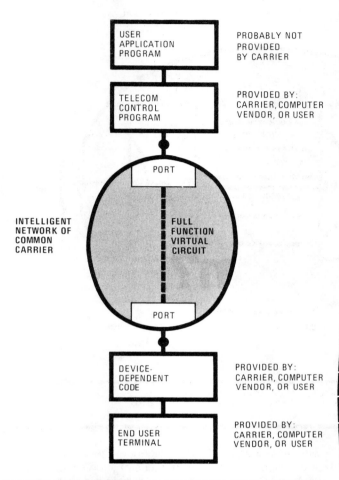

2 Virtual circuit functions

Rigid layers. *Private network architectures, rigidly layered, are generally based upon the premise that carriers provide only non-intelligent transmission facilities.*

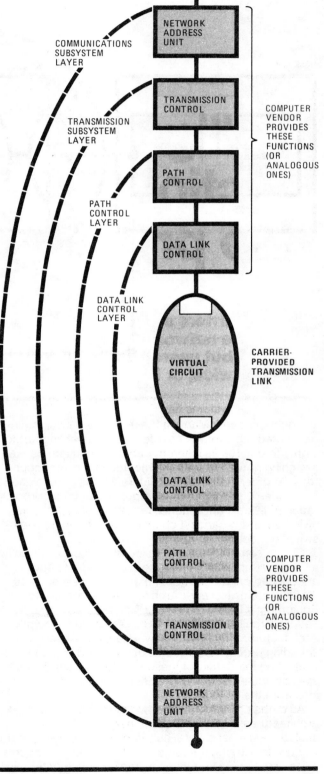

packet-switching network implementing X.25 without resolution of some very significant potential problems.

Some packet networks have already been interfaced from one country to another with X.25 being used at both ends. Experimentally, the interfacing was implemented, at a recent computer communications conference in Canada, between France's Transpac network and Canada's Datapac. Also, Datapac is currently interfaced with the United States' Telenet and Tymnet. These examples have proven the technical viability of network-to-network X.25 interfacing, but do not necessarily reflect the results to be met by others. Very careful advance coordination of detailed X.25 implementation approaches at each end was required—and will continue to be so in future interfaces of different X.25 networks. Nonetheless, end users and industry observers generally acclaim the emergence of some relatively widely accepted way for connections to be made to packet-switching networks. No user benefits from the absence of standards, and many consider the X.25 recommendations to be a very badly needed step in

3 Future network – computer vendors' view

A different philosophy. *To support his virtual circuit connections between terminals and computers, the computer vendor will provide very elaborate and complex schemes for logical channel establishment, distributing the control and data flow functions, and standardizing interfacing in the private network's addressable devices.*

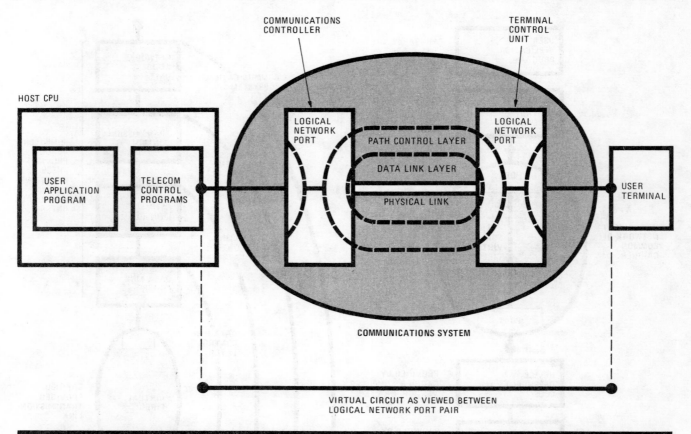

COMMUNICATIONS CONTROLLER

TERMINAL CONTROL UNIT

HOST CPU

USER APPLICATION PROGRAM

TELECOM CONTROL PROGRAMS

LOGICAL NETWORK PORT

PATH CONTROL LAYER

DATA LINK LAYER

PHYSICAL LINK

LOGICAL NETWORK PORT

USER TERMINAL

COMMUNICATIONS SYSTEM

VIRTUAL CIRCUIT AS VIEWED BETWEEN LOGICAL NETWORK PORT PAIR

the right direction. Many of the unresolved issues will be worked out over the next few years, enabling further clarity to emerge as different public and private packet-switching networks are implemented in different countries. Another important consideration in the resolution of standards problems is the requirement for incorporation of flexible approaches in the use of fast circuit-switched and broadcast channels, as well as packet-switching techniques.

On the computer vendor's side of the house, virtually all major suppliers of teleprocessing products have announced private networking architectures, such as IBM's Systems Network Architecture (SNA), Digital Equipment's Decnet, Univac's Distributed Communications Architecture, and NCR's Distributed Network Architecture, to mention a few. Users have been spending prodigious amounts of time studying and evaluating the details of these architectures and their specific implementations on announced product offerings from the vendors.

As of the end of 1977, the two most mature network architectures, SNA and Decnet, had each been installed on at least several hundred customer computers worldwide. Among the remaining thousands of uncommitted customers interested in implementing networks

with advanced levels of intelligence, there was considerable debate about the benefits of such schemes as SNA and Decnet. Much of this debate is natural and deeply rooted in the complexity and sophistication of these architectures, making it very difficult for people to quantify their benefits.

SNA and Decnet
To facilitate understanding of the elements of SNA and Decnet, the following major differences are noted. SNA is hierarchical—meaning a network of a small number of high-powered devices down to a large number of low-powered devices. Additionally, SNA is suited primarily to support terminal-to-network connections, although it can also be used—in a limited way—for computer-to-computer interconnections.

On the other hand, Decnet is a peer-coupled architecture. ("All nodes are created equal.") In a sense, any one network node can connect to any other node without requiring permission from a "third-party" node. Also, Decnet provides for a generalized real-time file transfer capability between different computers. So far, SNA has no general provision for this capability.

The future should witness slow, but broadly based acceptance of the private network architecture concept in countries where free and open competition exists in the public carrier sector. Users will find private networking approaches very attractive in applications where they wish to retain tight control over network operations. This situation holds where the users do not wish their network destinies to be placed in the hands of a shared public carrier network, and where they are very concerned about managing all resources impacting their own environment. Similarly, there will be substantial complementary needs for inter-organizational computing which can only be met through the use of public intelligent data communications networks. The evolving interface standards such as X.25 will greatly facilitate such inter-organizational networking needs.

The evolving conflict in the industry between public data communications networks and private data communications networks based on the architectures of the computer vendors, in essence, is a fracas over who shall provide the functions of the intelligent network. Packet-switching carriers wish to provide virtual circuit connections between terminals and computers, and also between computers connected to the network (Fig. 1). In order to accomplish these goals, the packet carrier must perform extremely elaborate distributed control functions in his network. These functions include all activities required for establishment, maintenance, and termination of the virtual circuits. In addition, there must be well-defined network-wide standards for the establishment of sessions, network addressing, and regulating the flow of data between the end-user devices and application programs. Packet carriers naturally think they should be responsible for providing and controlling all these functions.

Contrast this attitude with the general philosophy of the private networking architectures of the computer vendors. They desire to provide virtual connections to terminals and computers attached to the private network. To support these connections, the computer vendor will provide very elaborate and complex sche-

mes for logical channel establishment, distributing the control and data flow functions, and standardizing interface procedures which are used throughout the addressable devices or programs of the private network (Figs. 2 and 3). A logical channel is that portion of the virtual circuit which connects the user port to its adjacent packet-switching node. Note that the "full function virtual circuit" of the carriers' network version (Fig. 1) eliminates the need for certain parameters of the computer vendors' network version (Fig. 3). These parameters include most of the functions of the "data link control layer," "path control layer," transmission subsystems layer (network address function), and communications subsystem layer (transmission control function).

The computer vendors' view of intelligent networks can be summarized by the following: "We provide all devices and functions, except the physical transmission line." In comparison the common carriers' increasingly pervasive view of intelligent networks is: "We can provide all devices and functions (including telecommunications control programs), except the host CPU and user application program."

Conventional facilities
Private network architectures are generally based upon the premise that communications common carriers provide only non-intelligent transmission facilities such as conventional leased-line and switched offerings of the traditional marketplace (Fig. 2). The remaining necessary functions, such as data link control, path control, transmission control, and network addressable units (the last is from SNA and means units which can be reached by their unique addresses), would be provided by the computer vendor. These are the functions (Fig. 2) involved in the use of the network virtual circuit of Figure 3. Note that the specific function layers of Figure 2 correspond to those of SNA, but conceptual allocations of the functions shown are similar in other

4 IBM's interim solution

Compatible conversion. An example of function reallocation—necessitated by the use of a packet network—is the movement of polling from the communi- cations front end to the distant end of the network. IBM's implementation of this scheme makes the 3705 NCP X.25-compatible, and also adds a network interface unit.

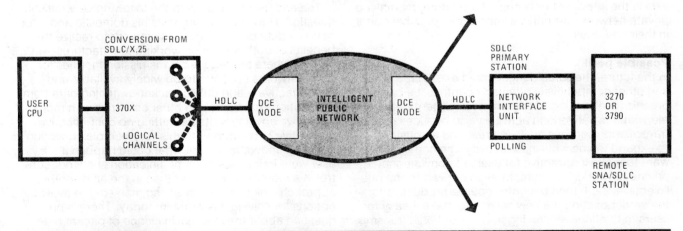

architectures. Clearly, the computer vendor assumes that the common carrier has been relegated to a traditional role. Also, all incremental intelligence functions should be provided in an elaborate distribution of network control functions across terminal controllers, distributed processing workstations, communications concentrators, front-end processors, and computer-based access methods. Viability of these architectures is thus based upon the assumption of cost-effective and widely available transmission services from the common carriers.

If the end user seeks to deal with intelligent networks, the question quite logically arises then about which functions should be provided by the common carrier, the computer vendor, and the independent data communications vendor (such as the terminal, modem, technical control, and multiplexer companies). In the present embryonic stages of this conflict, all major parties appear to be jockeying for position.

In a freely competitive market environment, the user should be free to choose whether he builds a private network, uses the public data network, or employs some combination of both in meeting his needs. Over the long term, the author believes that most users will find significant roles and justifications for the use of both private networking architectures and the public data networks. There is a substantial danger, however, that in their zealousness to expand their control and level of business activity, the public data communications network suppliers may cause the competitive private networking alternatives to become less attractive. Subtle or overt attempts may be used to make conventional leased and switched services more expensive or altogether unavailable for regular data transmission activities.

While there are yet no indications of such activities in the United States, there certainly are specific instances in a number of foreign countries, such as France, where PTTs have publicly stated their intention to phase out the availability of leased lines for data communications applications. Some of their reasons for such strategies are based on understandable concern over limited physical facilities availability. However, other reasons for such moves are clearly related to the increased control and function which they can provide in the intelligent networks of the future, by making private network alternatives impossible for subscribers in their countries.

Possible peril

In the future, the same danger could exist in the U.S.A. and other competitively oriented countries if a carrier organization seeking to expand its intelligent data communications networking activities also provides regular transmission services. In its interest and enthusiasm to expand the new business activity, the carrier will want to make it attractive for users of conventional private networking architectures to convert to the public equivalent. It then becomes counterproductive for the carrier offering the new service to make it easy for users to continue employing the conventional transmission services in a cost-effective way. Conventional

5 Logically layered network

Complex overhead. *The physical approach of Figures 2 and 4 results in this unnecessarily complex series of logical layers, due to the redundant functions provided.*

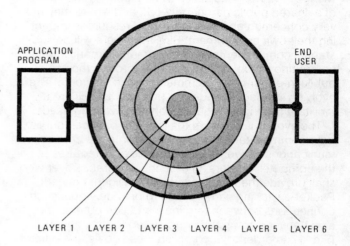

APPLICATION PROGRAM

END USER

LAYER 1   LAYER 2   LAYER 3   LAYER 4   LAYER 5   LAYER 6

LAYER	TYPICAL FUNCTIONS PERFORMED
1	PHYSICAL DTE-DCE INTERFACE
2	ACCESS LINK PROTOCOL FUNCTIONS
3	PACKET LEVEL FUNCTIONS (e.g. OF X.25)
4	"PHYSICAL" NETWORK CONTROL FUNCTIONS PERFORMED IN COMM CONTROLLER SOFTWARE
5	LOGICAL CHANNEL CONTROL BY COMPUTER VENDOR
6	LINKAGE OF LOGICAL CHANNEL PORTS WITH APPLICATION PROGRAMS AND DATA FILES

leased or switched lines critical to private networking architectures can thereby be made less attractive, either through pricing techniques or ultimately by service elimination.

The end user is faced with the following very difficult question: How does he organize his domestic and international data communications network to realize the benefits of both private networking architectures—in regions where the required transmission facilities for such networks continue to be widely available and cost-effective—and public packet-switching data communications networks—in other countries with more restrictive environments permitting no cost-effective alternative? The answer to this very complex question lies in an understanding of what could happen if the user were free to select communications network control in a modular way, rather than in the all-or-nothing approach which characterizes so many of the available options for solving this problem today. There is no question about the material influence of packet networks on the way users organize their teleprocessing

6 Packet network interface

Low overhead. To reduce overhead, the computer vendor would perform only the additional needed network operation functions not already instrinsically addressed by the public packet-switching network. In this way, the substantial duplication shown in Figures 2 and 5 could be at least kept to a minimum, if not gotten rid of altogether.

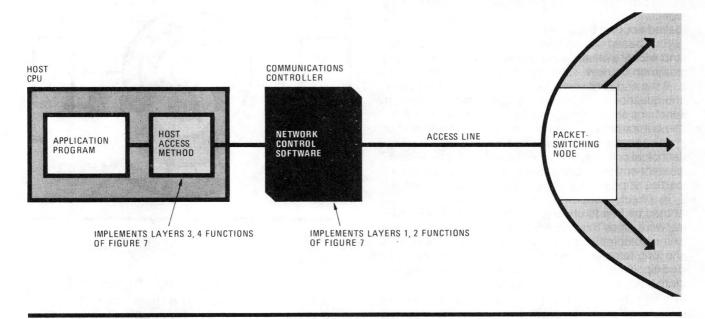

HOST
CPU

COMMUNICATIONS
CONTROLLER

APPLICATION
PROGRAM

HOST
ACCESS
METHOD

NETWORK
CONTROL
SOFTWARE

ACCESS LINE

PACKET-
SWITCHING
NODE

IMPLEMENTS LAYERS 3, 4 FUNCTIONS
OF FIGURE 7

IMPLEMENTS LAYERS 1, 2 FUNCTIONS
OF FIGURE 7

needs. Substantial re-allocation of function must take place when the user employs packet-switching services. For example, polling of remote terminals—traditionally from the host or attached communications front end—must now be moved to the distant end of the packet-switching network, since it is unrealistic to poll terminals through a packet-switching network. Consider Figure 4, which illustrates a method which has been recommended by IBM as an interim solution for enabling its French and Canadian SNA customers to connect through the packet-switching networks in those respective countries. At the central site communications controller, a software module extension to the 370X network control program (NCP) has been developed which converts the information from the basic 3705 NCP into a form compatible with the X.25 guidelines. Polling of the remote station controller has been moved out to the other end of the packet network, in an interface adapter. This adapter also converts the inbound data from the terminals into the form required by the packet network.

In the approach used by Raytheon Data Systems to attach its CRT terminals to the Canadian Datapac network, the Raytheon controller performs the functions of terminal control and the implementation of the X.25 interfaces, both in the same device. This is in contrast to the IBM approach of using two separate devices. Regardless of which way the packet network interface is provided, polling messages which would be generated in the 370X at the central site must not be permitted to enter the packet network. The user would have to pay for each poll message as though it were a data message. Also, each poll message would experience

unpredictable delays in traversing the network, resulting in excessive cost and poor performance.

What we have with the interim approach of Figure 4 is the addition of yet another level of conversion between the user's communications controller and the packet network. The packet network provides virtual circuits to its subscribers who interface in accordance with the X.25 protocol. As shown in Figure 2, external to the public data communications network, the computer vendor's equipment is similarly concerned with providing logical connections for session establishments generated by its end users. Note that the intelligent packet-switching network delivers a virtual circuit (Fig. 2) at the innermost layer. Transmission over this circuit involves multiple store-and-forward delays and transit times which are variable since they depend on packet network traffic patterns. Also note, in Figure 4, that there is a function redundancy, since the carrier and the computer vendor duplicate certain network control functions for virtual circuits (Fig. 2).

From a purely functional point of view, in an environment where the public data network provides the connections between the remote terminal and the central computer, many of the control functions in the rigidly layered architectures of the computer vendor are not needed. In fact, the physical approach of Figures 2 and 4 results in the unnecessarily complex situation shown in the corresponding logically layered network diagram of Figure 5. If such functions as network control, message routing, and session establishment are defined by X.25 and performed by the intelligent network of the public common carrier, then the end user certainly does not benefit from having them provided again by the computer vendor. In these situations, the end user would best benefit from an approach which involves the computer vendor and non-carrier suppliers performing only additional network functions needed for the network operation which are not already intrinsically addressed by the public packet network.

Implementing less

Such a low-overhead approach to interfacing packet networks could be based on the interfacing concepts shown in Figure 6. The network control software of the communications controller would be a natural place for implementing functional layers 1 and 2 of the corresponding logical network diagrammed in Figure 7. Layer 3 could be implemented either in the controller or host, depending on cost and overhead considerations. Layer 4 would most naturally be implemented in the host. In any event, the substantial duplication shown in Figures 2 and 5 could be at least minimized, if not eliminated.

The same potential overhead problem arises when the public packet carrier attempts to offer initial service to an existing private networking user, for example, of conventional binary synchronous communications CRT display terminals. The carrier needs to offer a transparent connection which will require no modification — or at least minimal modification — to any existing software running in the user's host or communications controller. Users simply cannot afford the major expense and disruption of rewriting and reconfiguring their existing network control software to use the packet network. And they certainly cannot afford to pay for the substantial overhead resulting from a duplicated function environment. And duplication would certainly occur if the packet network services were introduced without major reorganization of the user application programs, host access method, and communications controller software. This dilemma is, in fact, one of the major reasons the U.S. packet carriers have thus far provided support only for low- to medium-speed asynchronous terminals — which are character-oriented and easier to implement.

Packet carriers endeavoring to make it easy for a user to begin employing their networks must have a strategy that requires few or no changes in existing user code, by using approaches such as that shown in Figure 8. This arrangement requires few or no changes in existing user code, either in the communications controller or the host CPU. Network interface units must inhibit poll and select messages generated in the communications controller from passing through the packet network. If not, as was pointed out earlier, these messages would look like "data" to the packet network, and transmission charges for such non-data packets would be exorbitant.

At the opposite end of the virtual circuit, the interface unit must sense when the terminal has a message. Then the terminal's interface would relay the message through the packet network to the host site interface (which must contain substantial buffers). When the communications controller is instructed to poll that particular terminal, the stored message can be deliv-

7 "Cleaner" layered network

More straightforward. *Layers 1 and 2 would be implemented in the communications controller (Fig. 6), layer 3 in either the controller or the host, and layer 4 in the host.*

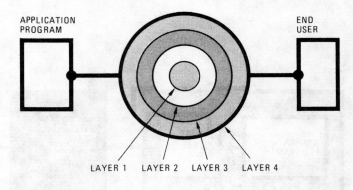

APPLICATION PROGRAM   END USER

LAYER 1   LAYER 2   LAYER 3   LAYER 4

LAYER	TYPICAL FUNCTIONS
1	PHYSICAL DTE-DCE INTERFACE
2	ACCESS LINK PROTOCOL FUNCTIONS
3	PACKET-LEVEL FUNCTIONS, CONTROL OF LOGICAL CHANNELS
4	LINKAGE OF LOGICAL CHANNEL PORTS WITH APPLICATION PROGRAMS, DATA FILES, AND END USERS

ered from the buffer in the host site interface. (An example of a product providing this capability is the Datapac-er manufactured by Daedalus Micro-Electronics in Scarborough, Ont. This product is to be used in making transparent connections through the Canadian Datapac network.)

Alternatively, users must develop their applications from scratch to take advantage of the intelligent public data networks. In higher-speed applications, there would appear to be only one viable solution to eliminating the duplicated-functions problem. That is for the user to design his entire portfolio of network applications from the beginning of the planning process on through to implementation, in a way which will result in all necessary functions being performed only once — as shown in Figures 6 and 7.

Regardless of which vendor provides the intelligent network control functions, there will continue to be substantial functional layers external to the network. These external layers should naturally remain the jurisdiction of the non-carrier vendors which supply the end-users with nodal processing, terminal, and database equipment. An example would be function layer 4 in Figure 7, which links the application programs and data files in the user's computers to the logical ports.

To the author, it seems foolish to think that common carriers can provide and maintain these highly complex

8 "Transparent" network interface

Easier for users. *To facilitate network use, packet carriers must require few or no changes in existing user code, either in the communications controller or the host CPU. Network interface units must inhibit poll and select messages from passing through the packet network. If not, these messages would push operating costs too high.*

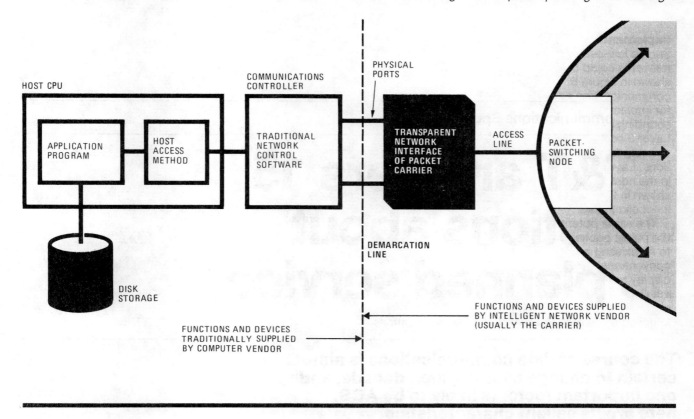

extra function layers which will be strongly dependent on the computer hardware, operating system, and storage devices at the user site. Even so, there are efforts under way in some research organizations of the common carriers to develop software-based access methods which would operate on user computers, thus being provided and maintained by the common carrier. Imagine the rather mind-boggling thought of calling the Bell System or PTT supplier to troubleshoot a problem in your mainframe access method software!

Efficiency unavailable

In summary, the major user problem arising from the present marketplace situation is that users do not see a clear indication of efficient modular network architectures becoming available. The user's best interest will be served by a free and open competitive marketplace in which he is able to choose from a broad range of cost-effective private network and public network solutions. Users should aggressively withstand any attempts by either the computer vendors or the public carriers to restrict their ability to interface to both kinds of networks, because such moves are not in the users' best long-term interest. It would appear that in some foreign countries certain attempts by the PTTs to force users onto their intelligent data communications networks fall into this category of being counterproduc-

tive. By the same token, the previously discussed interim interfacing solutions which have initially surfaced are also counterproductive, because the user is forced to pay for many of the critical network control functions twice.

The author believes strongly that solutions can be worked out in which computer vendors will offer modular network control and interface layers. In the environment of the future, it will be possible for the private networking architectures to peacefully coexist with intelligent public networks, which also play an important role in supporting the needs of interorganizational computing. There have been some initial attempts by certain vendors to enable the user to employ particular modules of control software in interfacing his private equipment to the public network, so that he pays only for the additional functions which are not already being provided by the common carrier. One recent development along these lines is the X.25 software interface which IBM has provided to its Series/1 users for accessing Canada's Datapac and France's Transpac networks. Substantial work still needs to be done by users in studying and defining their intra-company and inter-company needs for networking in the future. After these needs are more clearly recognized, some of the potential conflicts in the fight over function can then be understood, and usable solutions developed. ∎

AT&T answers 15 questions about its planned service

Compiled by George R. Davis, Data Communications

The course of data communications is almost certain to change over the next decade, and one important factor is likely to be ACS; here are its salient characteristics

At the end of 1978, AT&T submitted to the FCC an exhaustive document called "Responses to Information Requests of the Federal Communications Commission relating to Advanced Communications Service" (ACS). The 247-page report, along with its four appendixes, contains specific answers to questions posed by AT&T competitors, data communications and data processing users, equipment manufacturers, and the FCC itself.

Although much of the document is devoted to issues regarding regulation and AT&T finances, selected portions of it present the clearest picture to date of ACS's capabilities, scope, and limitations. The questions presented here represent queries about 15 major aspects of ACS. The answers are extracted from the "Responses to Information Requests" document exactly as submitted by AT&T, although for the sake of clarity, their order has been rearranged, irrelevant discussions deleted, and some editing performed to prevent any confusion in terminology.

1 How does ACS differ from a timeshared network; will timeshare suppliers employ ACS?

Commercial timesharing systems are designed to facilitate on-line program development, high speed calculations, database management, etc. Therefore, they incorporate on-line compilers, support a diversity of programming languages, and provide extensive database management features.

The design of ACS exhibits constructs [elements, functions] which would be unreasonable to include in systems providing general-purpose timesharing services. Customer data is accommodated by or moved through ACS in one of three forms. The call mode of information transfer results in the immediate movement of customer data through the network providing customers with service features which operate in the space domain. This data resides within the network for a relatively short period of time. The message mode of information transfer provides service functions which extend opportunities into the time domain. Accordingly, customer data resides within the network for longer intervals. Such data when resident in the network exists only in the form of messages. Each message within the network has associated with it a header which contains information necessary to accomplish the transfer process. This header contains space and time information permitting records to be kept of the movement of the customer data, the management of the data while it is resident in the network, and the ultimate transfer. A timesharing service would no more burden every element of its customer data with header information and handle all of its units of customer data by operating on parameters contained within such headers than would an office consider filing letters for later use by first inserting each into a separate envelope.

It is envisioned that both commercial timesharing services and their customers will benefit from ACS data communications service. As an innovative, efficient, nationwide, shared service which provides terminal compatibility, ACS should allow timesharing services to economically serve a greater number of customers.

2 What components will be in an ACS node and what function will each perform?

The following is a description of the ACS node-resident hardware:

- Data switch or tandem switch — Duplex minicomputer for routing and switching.
- Message manager — Duplex minicomputer with dual-disk storage units, each accessible from either minicomputer. One tape unit per minicomputer.
- Network access controller (NAC) — Microprocessor equipment that will terminate access lines and provide entry to the ACS network at a node. A remote NAC (RNAC) is a similar device, but at a location remote from the node.
- Central office access equipment — EIA interface & monitor panel: allows cabling the NAC to data sets.
- Miscellaneous data set frame: Used to mount miscellaneous data sets required for access. Data auxiliary set (DAS) frame: Used for mounting data auxiliary sets and pads for level adjustment. Cross-connect frame: Used to interconnect ACS access equipment.

The ACS nodes will consist of three principal elements: the data switch, the message manager, and access controllers.

The data switch is responsible for the routing and switching of data packets. It establishes logical paths through the network from origination to destination, directs the movement of information, and monitors traffic flow. As a monitor of traffic flow, the data switch functions to resolve local traffic congestion problems. Within each node, the data switch also serves as the coordinator of node maintenance activities. It maintains the status of node components and communicates with centralized network maintenance facilities. The data switch will be a minicomputer. It will be configured as a duplicated system.

The principal functions of the message manager are to store and manage messages for customers. In addition, the message manager stores customer communications routines and system programs. Noninteractive customized routines [see Question 8] are executed on behalf of customers in the message manager. The message manager performs ACS service functions related to authorization control and supports a wide range of administrative and maintenance functions for the node. The message manager will be a minicomput-

er. It will be configured as a duplicated system. The message manager system will be equipped with duplicated disk storage.

Access controllers in the ACS architecture include network access controllers and remote network access controllers. NACs terminate customer access lines at locations remote from nodes.

NACs provide terminal and host support and furnish line-handling capability by interfacing protocols supported by ACS and converting customer message data and commands into a network-standard form. NACs also perform the call supervisory functions such as setup and takedown, interpret network commands, and execute interactive customer-developed customized routines. The NAC transmits usage data to other network components for billing and preparation of traffic reports. The NAC also performs line tests for maintenance purposes.

An RNAC is used for remote areas where there are a sufficient number of customer terminals. An RNAC performs the same functions as the NAC and concentrates the resultant traffic to the node via a high-speed trunk.

NACs will also interface and support the two broad classes of host computer protocols, character oriented and bit oriented, and will provide for a range of options to allow customization of the communication capabilities of the subscriber's host.

NACs and RNACs will be comprised of microprocessor and minicomputer equipment.

3 What will be the physical configuration of ACS nodes, trunks, and access equipment?

The digital connection of an ACS node location to a digital data system hub office is highlighted by:

- Physical connection to the ACS network via a network access controller (NAC) and may be either digital or analog. Customer access to ACS is via Dataphone Digital Service under FCC tariff 267.
- Fifty-six-kbit/s trunks interconnected to the data switch. This type of trunk is used to connect RNAC to node, node to node, node to tandem switch, and tandem switch to tandem switch.

For an RNAC connected to a digital data system hub office, customer access to ACS is the same as at a node location.

Analog interconnections at a remote NAC location use analog facilities to connect the remote NAC to the node as well as to provide customer access via analog facilities.

The same arrangement applies at node locations, as well as connecting node to node, node to tandem switch, and tandem switch to tandem switch locations via analog facilities.

Existing facilities of the digital data system will be used to meet the combined needs of Dataphone Digital Service, Dataphone Switched Digital Service, and ACS. These services may share facility routes in the digital data system, but ACS will have dedicated channel assignments. Construction of new facilities for the digital data system may be required in the years beyond 1979 as the combined needs of the three services increase. Future digital facility needs are determined in the course of AT&T's normal network planning process. If, and when, it becomes apparent that specific new digital data system facilities are needed, AT&T and the Bell System Associated Companies will request appropriate authorizations.

ACS "access ports" and ACS "network ports" are synonymous for connections to the ACS network. The term access port is used to denote the physical point of access to (or egress from) ACS. All connections to the ACS network will be made via an access port, whether the connection is a Bell-provided service or a service provided by other carriers.

Constraints imposed on the connection of both AT&T equipment and non-AT&T equipment or networks (including those of other carriers) to ACS "access ports" will consist of limiting connections to equipment, communications systems, or networks with design and protocol standards which are compatible with ACS interface protocols, speeds, and codes. In addition, AT&T will not be responsible for installation, operation or maintenance of any equipment, communications systems, or networks provided by a customer or other common carrier connected to ACS.

Although present plans do not include use of satellite circuits for ACS, such use will be considered in the future depending on technological, economic, and customer usage considerations, subject to the appropriate regulatory approval.

ACS tandem switches, ACS nodes and remote network access controllers will in general be located proximate to digital data system hub offices so as to facilitate the provision of 56-kbit/s trunks which are used to interconnect the ACS network.

ACS tandem switches, ACS nodes, and RNACs may, in the future, be located proximate to digital data system end offices, although current deployment plans do not call for such location.

The chaining of intermediate office would be treated in much the same way as a digital data system end office.

The meaning, as it applies to ACS, of redundancy is the duplication of equipment and facilities provided to assure a high degree of service availability. The following features provide ACS with the necessary level of redundancy:
- Every data switch will be duplicated.
- Every tandem switch will be duplicated.
- Every message manager will be duplicated.
- Communication paths between node elements will be duplicated.
- Data written to "message storage" administered by the message manager will be written into two separate disk devices.
- Disjoint paths are provided in ACS trunking design.

Two "disjoint paths" can be thought of as logically equivalent, yet physically different, paths. These paths are designed to have as few modes of failure in common as economically practicable.

An illustration of this concept is the interconnection of ACS nodes. Any one node will physically be connected to all other nodes by at least "two disjoint paths." That is to say, if any one physical 56-kbit/s internodal trunk were eliminated, the network's internodal logical connectivity would remain complete.

4 How will ACS be accessed by users, and which terminal protocols will be supported?

Access arrangements from the customer's premises to the ACS service points will be provided by means of services provided under various tariffs of Bell System companies, independent telephone companies, and other carriers.

Under the present view of the ACS tariff regulations, services provided to a customer by an international record carrier (IRC) may be connected by the customer to ACS via either a private line service or the public switched network to an ACS service point. Further, the IRCs can be customers of ACS and connect their services to ACS via either a private-line service or the public switched network from their gateway operating center to the ACS service point.

The range of access speeds that will be allowed into the ACS network is as follows:
- For private line service, access to the ACS network will be provided at speeds up to 1.8 kbit/s asynchronous and 2.4, 4.8, 7.2, 9.6, and 56 kbit/s synchronous.
- For Dataphone Digital Service, access to the ACS network will be provided at speeds of 2.4, 4.8, 9.6, and 56 kbit/s synchronous.
- For public switched network services, access to the ACS network via a dial access port will be provided at speeds up to 1.2 kbit/s asynchronous and 2.4 and 4.8 kbit/s synchronous.

ACS does not provide protocol support for all terminals and computers. Initial protocol support for terminals and computers is based upon determinations as to customer demand and on market research. In the future, additional protocol support will be based on evolving user demand.

The following five classes of terminal protocols will be supported by ACS:
- Asynchronous contention - character mode
- Asynchronous contention - block mode
- Asynchronous polled
- Synchronous polled
- Synchronous contention

Each class includes a variety of well-known and widely used terminals. Support for each class will be based on parameters so that minor differences among similar terminals can be accommodated. Some parameters related to the physical device will be modified only by service order. Others may be dynamically altered on an individual basis.

For each of the five protocol classes detailed above, specific physical-line-control, logical-link-control, and operational-format-control aspects are supported. Support of the physical line includes electrical characteristics and data set signaling.

Support of the logical link includes handling the specific link protocol with its various options for polling, selection, and error handling.

Format control support provides an optional set of communication functions that can be performed on the data. These functions can be either data translations to reduce incompatibilities between end points (e.g., code conversion) or terminal enhancements which give the user capability beyond the hardware limits of the device (e.g., edits).

Three modes of format-control support will be provided in ACS:
- Class-specific mode
- Common mode
- Transparent mode

For a terminal operating in class-specific mode, ACS supports the full capability of the protocol for the terminal's class. ACS will automatically perform code conversion and, optionally under customer control, act on network commands in the character stream. Other functions like echoing and control character padding are activated or deactivated by the appropriate selection of parameters within a class.

For a terminal operating in the common mode, format control support is such that a remote terminal, host application, or network function may transmit (and receive) lines of characters to (and from) a terminal without concern for the specific format control support of the terminal. The common mode of support provides a level of communication across all classes of terminals that is similar to that of an unformatted teleprinter.

When operating in the common mode, data received from a terminal or host application is translated into the teleprinter-like format by ACS. For the asynchronous contention (character and block modes) and asynchronous polled classes, this translation is achieved by fixing certain parameters of the class-specific mode so that consistent mappings to the teleprinter-like format are achieved. For the synchronous polled and synchronous contention classes, ACS automatically translates data into the teleprinter-like format.

For a terminal operating in the transparent mode, ACS will not translate the data in any manner. However, at the customer's option, ACS will act on network commands in the character stream. ACS will provide physical line and logical link support, and the user is responsible for end-to-end compatibility of the format-control aspects.

Terminals in the asynchronous contention-character mode class are typically CRT displays or teleprinters. The protocol supported is the widely used start-stop contention protocol. Dial-in ports accessed via the public switched telephone network (either shared or dedicated to a customer), dial-out ports (dedicated to a customer), and private-line, point-to-point, asynchronous access arrangements will be supported for this class.

Full-duplex private-line access arrangements will be supported at 110, 134.5, 150, 300, 600, 1.2K and 1.8K

bit/s. Access line terminations at the customer premises will be with 108F or 202T data sets. Compatible customer-provided data sets may be used.

Full-duplex ports for dial access will be provided at 100, 134.5, 150, 300, and 1.2K bit/s. ACS will automatically detect the speed of the terminal. Access line terminations at the customer premises will be with 113A, 113C, 113D, 103J, or 212A data sets. Compatible customer-provided data sets may be used.

Half-duplex ports for dial access will be provided at 1.2 kbit/s. Reverse channel operation will be supported for break only. Access line terminations at the customer premises will be with 202S data sets. Compatible customer-provided data sets may be used.

ACS will support the ASCII, PTTC/BCD, and correspondence character sets.

The character structure for the ASCII character set will have the following format:
|start|seven information bits|parity|stop interval|
The parity bit may be specified as even, odd, or to be ignored. The stop interval may be specified as 1, 1.5, or 2 bits in length.
The character structure for PTTC/BCD and correspondence character sets will have the following format:
| start | six information bits | parity | stop interval |
The parity bit will be odd and the stop interval will be 1 bit in length.

Terminals in the asynchronous contention block mode class are buffered teleprinters and CRT displays that operate in the block mode. Otherwise, the operating characteristics are similar to those for the asynchronous contention character mode terminals. The physical line control support will be the same as that described for asynchronous contention, except 134.5 bit/s will not be supported.

The logical link control support will be the same as that described for asynchronous contention character mode for the ASCII character set.

The format control support will be the same as that described for ASCII terminals in the asynchronous contention character mode class, except echoing and local editing will not be provided, and terminal flow control will be.

Terminals in the asynchronous polled class are buffered teleprinters and CRT displays. ACS supports one or more asynchronous terminals on an access line. The number of terminals that can be connected to an access line is determined by ACS capacity limits. ACS manages the general operation of the line and is responsible for data transfers and error recovery. All transmissions are between ACS and the terminals; no direct intraline terminal-to-terminal transmission is allowed. All terminals on a multipoint line must use the same protocol and character set, and belong to the same customer. Full-duplex, point-to-point, and multipoint asynchronous private-line access arrangements will be supported at 110, 134.5, 150, 300, 600, 1.2K, and 1.8K bit/s. Access line terminations at the customer premises will be with 108F or 202T data sets. Compatible customer-provided data sets may be used.

ACS will support half-duplex, asynchronous, multipoint, centralized data-link-control operations based on "polling" terminals to pick up transmission and "selecting" terminals to deliver transmission.

The synchronous polled class applies to synchronous cluster-controlled and stand-alone data-entry collect terminals. These terminals can be either CRT displays with 12 or 24 lines per screen or printers. These systems use the two-way alternate, polled link protocol defined in ANSI X3.28-1976, subcategories 2.4 and B2, plus RVI [a positive response used to indicate that a high-priority message needs to be transmitted] and WACK [wait before transmit, positive acknowledgment—"temporarily not ready to receive"]. ACS supports one or more synchronous terminals on an access line. The number of terminals that can be connected to an access line is determined by ACS capacity limits. ACS manages the general operation of the line and is responsible for data transfers and error recovery. All transmissions are between ACS and the terminals. All terminals on a multipoint line must use the same character set and belong to the same customer.

Full-duplex, synchronous, analog and digital, point-to-point and multipoint, private-line access arrangements will be supported for this class.

Analog point-to-point access arrangements will be supported at 2.4, 4.8, 7.2 and 9.6 kbit/s. Analog multipoint access arrangements will be supported at 2.4 and 4.8 kbit/s. Access line terminations at the customer premises will be with 201C, 208A, and 209A data sets. Also, compatible customer-provided data sets may be used.

Digital point-to-point and multipoint access arrangements will be supported at 2.4, 4.8, and 9.6 kbit/s. Access line terminations at the customer premises will be with Bell System-provided data service units, or with Bell System-provided channel service units if compatible customer-provided data service units are used.

The logical link control protocol supported will be the binary synchronous communications (BSC) polled link protocol as defined in ANSI X3.28-1976, subcategories 2.4 and B2, plus RVI and WACK. Responses from the terminal may be segmented into blocks of not greater than 256 characters. Commands sent to the terminal may be any length up to 4,000 characters, but no segmenting into blocks will be performed by the network.

Synchronous contention class applies to batch and remote job-entry terminals. The protocol supported is the two-way alternate, contention link protocol defined in ANSI X3.28-1976, subcategories 2.3 and B2, plus RVI and WACK. ACS supports a single synchronous terminal on an access line.

Dial-in ports accessed via the public switched telephone network (either shared or dedicated to a customer), dial-out ports (dedicated to a customer), and private-line (analog and digital) point-to-point, synchronous access arrangements will be supported for this class.

Full-duplex private-line analog access arrangements will be supported at 2.4, 4.8, and 9.6 kbit/s. Access line terminations at the customer premises will be with 201C, 208A, or 209A data sets. Compatible customer-provided data sets may be used.

Full-duplex private-line digital access arrangements will be supported at 2.4, 4.8, and 9.6 kbit/s. Access line terminations at the customer premises will be with Bell System-provided data service units, or with Bell System-provided channel service units if compatible customer-provided data service units are used.

Half-duplex ports for dial access will be provided at 2.4 and 4.8 kbit/s. Access line terminations at the customer premises will be with 201C or 208B data sets. Compatible customer-provided data sets may be used.

The logical link control protocol supported will be the binary synchronous communications (BCS) contention link protocol as defined in ANSI X3.28-1976, subcategories 2.3 and B2, with RVI and WACK, plus additional features as commonly found in many BSC system applications today.

AT&T plans to offer a capability which would permit customers to support protocols not otherwise supported by ACS through use of customized communications routines. Such communications routines to be executed in ACS would need to be written in ACS's communications.

5 Which host-computer communications functions can be off-loaded to ACS?

ACS service features meet an important set of user needs by allowing a decoupling of the origination and termination stations engaged in message transmission, with a resulting independence of terminals and hosts in the time dimension. This decoupling reduces the terminal communications support burden experienced by hosts in many user network configurations today. As a result, the movement of certain communications functions from user host computers into the ACS network is supported. Just which functions are suitable for such relocation depends on the specific customer applications. The following list suggests some possibilities.

Polling—Since terminal output and host input need no longer be coupled in time, it serves no purpose for the host to furnish polling support. Moreover, even in inquiry-response applications where no time delay is specified, advance polling of terminals by the network and subsequent polling of the network by the host can generate efficiencies.

Device handling—Since terminals and hosts are decoupled, it is no longer necessary for the host to provide communications management functions for the terminal devices. Relocating the device handling into the network allows the host to accommodate a far greater range of terminal devices than would be likely if all terminal management functions are programmed into the host. The support of new devices is also more readily accomplished.

Broadcast—By maintaining current address lists within ACS, customer hosts need concern themselves only with the generation of suitable message text. Through the use of network mnemonics, the customer host becomes independent of customer network rearrangements which would otherwise require continual tracking of customer network topology. The complex physical problem is reduced to a manageable, logical one.

Authorization—ACS provides a sophisticated authorization arrangement which enables the customer to define private subnetworks within the shared service. This same logical capability extends opportunities for intercompany networking which is not realizable without this network function.

Format and validation routines—The decoupling of the terminal and the host which separates in time (often several hours and, on occasion, more than a day) terminal output from host input and which permits the network to consolidate messages entered by terminals into a single large message—which may be handled efficiently by serving hosts—obviates the need for host provision of format and validation support. Such support directly by the host is required in the first instance only because the host was used to support the class of terminals used by the customer for data-entry purposes. In addition, effective prompting through terminal displays reduces the skill level required of terminal operators, and immediate validation is essential because it is economical to correct operator entry errors near the source data. It is much less efficient to discover source errors several hours later (at a time and place distant from the source data needed for correction) after the message has been received by the host. The provision of network functions as outlined enables customers to make more extensive use of in-place (low-cost) terminals.

Error recovery—It is undesirable to burden a customer-host with the responsibility of providing communications management for the recovery of errors in a third-party network which is characterized by extensive distributed processing. Indeed, it is not clear how such error recovery could be handled by a customer host. When arrays of terminals were connected directly to a host, network error recovery was an important responsibility of the host.

Journaling—Customers may wish to keep abbreviated records of transmitted messages either at origination or termination locations. Such an activity has long been a feature of message switching systems.

6 Which and what types of terminal protocols will be available as emulation service in ACS?

The network emulates the following widely supported terminals:
■ Model 33/35 teletypewriter
■ IBM 3271-1, -2 cluster controllers
■ IBM 2780 terminal
Two terms used throughout this section are defined here:

Real terminal—When a terminal and a host computer converse via ACS, the terminal is referred to as the real terminal.

Emulated terminal—The terminal that the host computer "thinks" it sees at an ACS emulation interface is referred to as the emulated terminal. It is the network of emulated terminals for which the host computer must provide support.

The ASCII start/stop terminal emulation interface provides certain call features (but not message features) via a character-oriented interface in which the network appears to the host computer as if it were a series of asynchronous teleprinter access lines using start/stop contention protocol with ASCII code.

The interface emulates 110-, 300-, and 1.2K-bit/s asynchronous lines. The line interface looks to the host computer like dial-in lines, even though the actual lines used are dedicated. Operation may be half- or full-duplex, provided the host computer does not echo to the terminal.

The emulated terminal is a Model 33 teletypewriter, character-at-a-time, ASCII terminal. The real terminal can be any class 1, 2, or 3 terminal operating in its class-specific mode or any terminal operating in common mode. The real terminal also can be any class 1, 2, or 3 terminal operating in transparent mode, but the host computer software must be able to deal with the format control specifics of the real terminal.

The host computer can receive calls placed by the real terminal. Calls to the host computer are assigned to emulated terminals (ports) by a "hunt group" in ACS. Authorization checks are made at both ends of the call to verify that the originating terminal may call the host computer application. Either end may terminate the call, the host computer by dropping the "data terminal ready" lead on the data set interface.

Limitations to this emulation include:
■ Full-duplex applications in the host computer must disable echo.
■ While different speed lines may be used for the emulated and real terminals, care must be taken when doing so. The network will provide a buffer of 4,000 bytes; however, if the sender's output speed exceeds the receiver's input speed for a long enough period of continuous transmission, the buffer will overflow, and data will be lost.

The bisynchronous cluster controller emulation interface provides certain call features (but not message features) via a character-oriented interface by which ACS interacts with the host computer as if ACS were bisynchronous cluster controllers using the ANSI protocol X3.28-1976, subcategories 2.4 and B2, and compatible with the IBM 3270. Polling of the real terminals is performed by the network. The network responds to the host computer's polls without the polls traveling through the network; instead, the network responds to the polls with data already at the emulated terminal.

The host computer interface operates over synchronous private lines at 2.4, 4.8 and 9.6 kbit/s.

Both general and specific polling are supported. Both ASCII and EBCDIC codes are supported, though only one code may be used on a line.

The emulated controller is an IBM 3271-1 or -2, with display and printer devices attached. The emulated devices have buffers of 200 characters. The real terminal is a terminal in the synchronous polled class (Class 4) operating in class-specific mode.

The host computer can receive calls placed by the real terminal. Authorization checks are made at both ends of the call to verify that the calling terminal may call the host computer application. Calls to the host computer may be assigned to emulated terminals by a "hunt group" in ACS, or they may be addressed to a specific emulated terminal. The real terminal normally clears the call. However, ACS may clear the call from the host computer end (e.g., if there is a host computer failure).

Limitations to IBM 3271-1 or -2 are as follows:
▪ The host computer must never send a transmission block of more than 4,000 bytes. This is seldom exceeded with a 2,000 character screen.
▪ The customer must pre-specify the host computer's poll list. It is from the polling pattern that the network determines whether an emulated terminal, controller, or line is considered by the host computer to be down. When the host stops polling the emulated terminals, the associated call to the real terminal will be disconnected.
▪ If the host computer chains terminal commands, each command must begin with an SBA sequence.
▪ If the host computer issues terminal copy commands, the real terminals involved must be attached to the same physical controller.
▪ The emulated terminal is not designed to pass remote diagnostic tests which may be run by the host computer to test terminal hardware.

The network acknowledges commands before delivering them to the real terminal. If the data is undeliverable (e.g., illegal command or real terminal fails while data is in transit), the emulated terminal returns a status message (specifically, "device check, unit specify") to the host computer. Host computer programs can make use of this to deduce that the command was not delivered in a manner similar to the condition resulting from controller or device malfunctions.

For applications where the host computer expects the emulated terminals to be a single real terminal at all times, it is recommended that only one real terminal be permitted to call a given emulated terminal.

The Type 1 bisynchronous batch emulation interface provides certain call features (but not message features) via a character-oriented interface in which the network appears to the host computer, as if it were an IBM 2780 terminal.

The interface operates over synchronous private lines at 2.4, 4.8, and 9.6 bit/s. Both ASCII and EBCDIC codes are supported, as are EBCDIC transparent link-level procedures.

The real terminal is a synchronous contention (Class 5) terminal operating in class-specific or transparent mode. The real terminal need not use the same code as the emulated terminal, unless transparent mode or EBCDIC transparent link-level procedures are used.

The host computer can receive calls placed by the real terminal. Authorization checks are made at both ends of the call to verify that the calling terminal may call the host computer application. Calls to the host

computer may be assigned to emulated terminals by a "hunt group" in ACS, or they may be addressed to a specific emulated terminal. The real terminal normally clears the call. However, ACS may clear the call from the host computer end (e.g., if there is a host computer failure).

IBM 2780 type 1 emulation limitations are:
▪ The network acknowledges blocks from the host computer or the terminal before it delivers them at the destination. If the message is undeliverable, the emulated terminal returns an EOT before the acknowledgment of the last block in a string. Host computer programs can make use of this to deduce that the information was not delivered in a manner similar to the condition resulting from a device failure.
▪ The emulated terminal is not designed to pass remote diagnostic tests which may be run by the host computer to test terminal hardware.
▪ For applications where the host computer expects the emulated terminal to be a single real terminal at all times, it is recommended that only one real terminal be permitted to call a given emulated terminal.

The Type 2 bisynchronous batch emulation interface provides certain message features (but not call features) via a character-oriented interface in which the network appears to the host computer as if it were an IBM 2780 terminal.

The interface operates over synchronous private lines at 2.4, 4.8 and 9.6 kbit/s. Both ASCII and EBCDIC codes are supported as are EBCDIC transparent link-level procedures.

The real terminal sends ACS messages to the message arrival area (MAA) of the emulated terminal. These messages may be generated either by explicit use of the ACS message-sending capability or through a customized message-handling program. The messages are delivered to the host computer like a batch entry from a IBM 2780 terminal. The host computer may also send messages. To do so, it transmits prepared messages to the emulated terminal. The destination of each host computer originated message is specified in its header.

A type 2 limitation is as follows: The emulated terminal is not designed to pass remote diagnostic tests which may be run by the host computer to test terminal hardware

7 Which types of network languages will be available to ACS users?

Two levels of network languages are available: network-command level and problem-oriented level.

The network-command level allows the use of standard or custom capabilities and is designed for use by terminal operators. The command level can invoke an interactive or noninteractive customized communication routine (CCR). The network-command level consists of single-function commands which can perform such operations as originate call, send message, confirm delivery, survey MAA, and deliver message. In addition, this language can activate problem-oriented level CCRs which were written by the customer.

The problem-oriented level is designed to create programs for such message preparation functions as message management (consolidation and customized addressing), automatic routing, code conversion, field sequence rearrangement, form definition, data validation, and report formatting. The current composition of the problem-oriented level language includes the following four sub-languages.

Control—This sub-language enables customized control over the addressing, routing, and delivery of messages. It operates on messages as units of data and invokes other sub-languages where rearrangements within messages need to be accomplished. The control sub-language unites other problem-oriented level languages by maintaining control over data flow across customer-written CCRs. Using the control sub-language, special-purpose communications applications can be developed.

Form definition—This sub-language permits a customer to construct a form using an English-like language to act as an I/O interface between a terminal operator and an application. In particular, the forms designer can set the logical page and row lengths, input a field value, display text, move the cursor, set tabs, and define repeating groups. For input of field values, the forms designer will have control over display of text in the field before input, default field values, field justification, and fill.

Validation specification—This sub-language permits a customer to specify rules for input data using an English-like language. Field values may be tested for length, range, code set (e.g., alphabetic), set membership with explicitly specified sets, and structure. Tests and comparisons may be made contingent on the passing of other tests. Field values may be summed and the sum compared to a value. Changes to input fields are directed by the operator in response to error flags generated by this sub-language.

Report format—This sub-language enables the consolidation of messages, the rearrangement of data fields within a message, and code conversion necessary to make message control intelligible to target host or terminal application programs. The assembling of network management data into reports for delivery to customer terminals is another network function served by this sub-language.

In addition to writing their own network language routines for managing terminal and host use of ACS communications features, customers may utilize standard communications management packages available from ACS. These communications management packages may be customized through the designation of form definition statements and validation statements and parameters to control message flow. As an example of a terminal communications management package, a data-entry package will be provided to permit messages collected from different terminals to be validated, batched, and delivered as a single large message to prespecified destinations at intervals defined by the customer. As an example of a host communications

management package, a package will be p rovided which permits customers to collect usage and availability statistics associated with a host interface to ACS. As indicated by the preceding paragraphs, ACS network language is designed to facilitate customer customization of call handling and message entry, transmittal and delivery, and customer network management. As a practical matter, the limitations of the network language and the related price/performance characteristics of the service limit its usefulness to the communications purpose for which ACS is designed.

8 How much and what type of user customization will be offered with ACS?

The need for a high degree of flexibility in data communications solutions has been recognized for some time. Many large businesses have sufficient communications traffic to justify private networks specially designed for their business applications. This is really a form of customization. The inability to extend such capabilities to a broader community of interest (e.g., a firm communicating with its customers or suppliers) and the inability to share communications resources with others, especially at low-usage network end points, are shortcomings of existing customized networks.

By offering a new form of customizing, ACS reduces these constraints and also makes customization capabilities available to smaller firms. Most importantly, since the users are most familiar with their own communications needs, ACS allows the users to design and manage their own communications networks within ACS and to create new ways to use communications to enhance their operations.

Customers will implement the ACS customized features through the use of a series of communications problem-oriented sub-languages. (See question 7). These sub-languages are specifically designed for customization of message preparation, movement, and delivery. In contrast, data processing systems execute programs written in general-purpose languages such as Fortran, Cobol, PL/1, etc. Since the ACS sub-languages are specialized for communications, they impose practical limitations on noncommunications applications. It is unlikely that customers would attempt to program or reprogram their data processing programs into languages suitable for communications customization functions.

An arithmetic feature is included in the sub-language for input validation to allow the customer to verify the consistency of numeric fields in a message during the message establishment process. However, this sub-language does not enable automatic revision of fields found to be in error. Thus the validation specification sub-language would be useless as a computational tool for calculational applications such as accounting, scientific analyses, or engineering calculations. The form definition sub-language, as another example, has no usable arithmetic features, because such a capability is unnecessary for the communications purposes intended. Thus the ACS sub-languages themselves impose practical limitations.

If the ACS customer uses terminals which require that the network furnish prompting so that the customer can use less skilled operators to run the terminals, the customer must specify in an ACS customized communications routine what that prompting is to be. The customer stores in ACS a form definition statement which is used to prompt the customer operators as they prepare messages.

Likewise, the customer may establish in the network a data validation statement to provide confirmation that certain parameters of input messages prepared by the customer's operators are as intended.

For example, if one of the fields in a customer's form requires a name to be inserted and the name consists only of alphabetic characters, the customer may specify that the inclusion of a non-alphabetic character be detected and that the customer's operator be alerted. If the form contains an address in which a particular field should be numeric, the inclusion of a non-numeric character can be detected. If a particular numeric field is to be within a specified range, the customer may specify in a customized communications routine that it be checked. If field "three" is to be consistent with the contents of fields "one" and "two," that also can be checked. The data validation statement does not generate new information for insertion in customer messages; it can only check that the information introduced by the operator is as intended and alert the operator to errors.

Such validation is an important communications function since it frees the customer from the costly alternative of trying to correct operator errors at customer host computers after the message has been input to the network, batched for several hours, and distributed to several places. It is more efficient to detect and correct errors near the message source at the time the message is being entered.

For example, a control statement which governs the customized storage, addressing, routing, switching and delivery of messages must be furnished by the customer to provide storage, transmission, and delivery instructions for input messages. Should the messages be batched over the course of each hour in the day and then be shipped on an hourly basis to several host machines? Should the messages be batched over the course of the entire work day and be shipped in the evening to one, two, three, or even more host machines and terminals? Should subsets of these messages be sent to one set of computers and other subsets to other sets of computers? To accomplish the message communications described, a customer control statement must indicate how ACS should deal with the large number of data messages entered by the customer's terminals.

Additionally, a message handling statement provided by the customer assures that when the customer's messages arrive at the destination stations they exhibit the proper code and format. This capability recognizes that different host computers may require that the

fields within a message be sequenced differently. Different host computers may require that the communications code be different. One host computer may require ASCII code, another host computer may require EBCDIC code. Other codes may be involved. ACS needs to know how to handle the messages so that when they are delivered by the standard message delivery capability within ACS they are intelligible to the customers' application programs. Customers may thus avoid changing their applications programs or the way in which they operate their host computers today.

Implementation of a customized program will be subject to an administrative procedure which includes the following steps:

- Messages containing language statements are transmitted via ACS to the Network Language Center (NLC).
- The NLC evaluates the program and converts it into the ACS internal representation. An evaluation report is returned to the customer, including such information as syntax errors and program storage requirements.
- When the program is ready to be tested, the customer requests installation for the purpose of testing.
- The customer defines a subnetwork for testing purposes using the conventional ACS authorization control mechanisms.
- The NLC initiates the installation of the program within the customer's subnetwork on a temporary basis for test purposes only.
- The customer tests the program.
- Once the program has been tested successfully, and is ready for use, a standard ACS service order is prepared and processed to allocate the necessary resources and install the program in Customer Program Storage.

Several of these steps may be repeated during the test and installation process. Support personnel will be available to assist customers should they encounter any difficulties.

9 Will users of ACS be able to install subnetworks to handle local communications chores?

The logical structure which underlies the physical network of ACS permits the definition of customer subnetworks within the shared service and allows customers to exercise control over the connectivity arrangements and the use of network functions for terminals and computers within their subnetworks.

"Virtual subnetwork" is synonymous with "customer subnetwork" when used in connection with ACS. It refers to a customer-defined set of terminals, computers, and network resources such as storage areas belonging to or assigned to a particular customer account. Using the authorization mechanism provided by the logical structure within ACS, a customer may control the connectivity among such terminals and computers and the connectivity between specific members of such a set and other terminals and computers in the shared services. The authorization mechanism also permits the customer to govern the use of network functions and storage resources by terminals and computers within the customer's subnetwork. ACS network management reports will be furnished on the basis of "customer subnetworks."

Access arrangements can be obtained under various tariffs of Bell System companies, independent telephone companies, and other carriers.

The establishment of a subnetwork for a customer does not require that there be a physical connection between ACS serving points associated with the customer subnetwork. This "connection" is established only when information is to be transferred from service point to service point and then only during the actual instance of information transfer.

The customer, through network management capabilities controls the logical arrangement of his terminals and host computers. Therefore, one terminal and its respective access arrangements can be associated with several distinct and different subnetworks at the same time or can be associated with different subnetworks at different times of the day. The subnetwork construction is a dynamic capability under customer control.

The facility makeup connects the customer's premises to the ACS service point. These facilities can either be provided by the telephone company from those tariffs mentioned above or by other common carriers via their appropriate tariffs. Within ACS, for service-point-to-service-point transfer of information, the appropriate facilities can be either digital or analog channels in the existing Bell System network.

10 What type of logical addressing formats will an ACS user be able to implement?

ACS addresses communications applications in which customer messages need to be prepared at a large number of geographically dispersed terminals and then distributed to a number of host computers and other terminals involved in that application.

Every use of ACS is associated with a logical terminal identity. For example, when a teletypewriter attached to ACS is active, it has a unique logical terminal representation. Within a customer host, each active execution of a program constitutes a "task" which may require input obtained by data communications. When a "task" is actively communicating through ACS, it also has a unique logical terminal representation. The ACS message level host interface allows hosts to dynamically change the number of "tasks" which are actively communicating through ACS as the need arises. It also has a unique logical terminal representation. This flexibility provides the dynamic association between host "tasks" and specific logical terminals.

In the absence of ACS, users' hosts typically must statically define physical terminals with which they may communicate. Since "tasks" and physical terminals both correspond to logical terminals in ACS, greater communications flexibility is achieved for the host computer through dynamic association. Furthermore,

greater efficiency of the host interface to ACS is achieved since the transmission capacity of the access line may be shared by any host "tasks" which happen to be active.

11 Will ACS users be able to use network functions to manage remote and local databases?

ACS standard-and-customized-message-storage features are designed to enhance communications. While these features are appropriate for preparation and delivery of messages in data communications, they do not provide the means to develop relationships between items of data contained in different messages, or to retrieve directly from storage items of data from within messages as normally required for database management purposes. These functional limitations effectively limit the use of ACS for database management.

What ACS brings to the problem of auxiliary, or back-up databases, is a rapid, constantly available, effective means to communicate between primary and auxiliary customer databases, or with auxiliary customer databases when the primary one is unavailable.

No messages will be generated by ACS other than those required for network administration, management, and maintenance functions. The programming required to establish and handle such messages will be accomplished primarily by ACS personnel. However, where network management data, for example, is furnished for use by a customer, the customer may wish to format the reference data in a manner which suits the customer's needs. In such a case, the customer would develop a customization program for such formatting.

12 Will it be possible, or practical, for users to employ ACS as a data-storage facility?

The only way for a customer to store data within ACS is in the form of a message or a customized communications program. Programs may not be installed in ACS unless they are syntactically acceptable and conform to other specific requirements. While it is possible to include data within programs, it is impractical and uneconomical to consider such an approach for the purposes of storage and retrieval. Charges are incurred for the installation of programs and the time intervals associated with the installation process mitigate against such an application.

Multiple messages may be stored and edited for later transmission. In some cases, the user may delete the message without releasing it for transmission; however, it is anticipated that a message established in ACS will be transmitted because the design and resulting price/performance attributes of the service, as a practical matter, deters usage inconsistent with its communications objectives. A message established in storage can be returned to the originating station and, therefore, transmission could, in this case, take place solely between the ACS network and that originating station.

The user may subsequently desire to modify a message or review a copy before transmittal, in which case the user could retrieve the message for such purposes or the user might decide to delete the message. This capability is necessary for message preparation. However, it would be inefficient and uneconomical for a customer to attempt to use this capability simply as a means for data storage. The features and price/performance attributes of ACS are designed for the data communications functions of message preparation, transmission of calls and messages, and message delivery.

Multiple stations with authorization to access and to read and write messages in a single message area may access any message within that area. Messages, however, may be accessed only by message name assigned at the time of origination or by sequence number. The retrieval of messages from a message storage area (MSA) by other criteria is not supported in ACS.

It is expected that users, in many applications, will accumulate messages from a number of terminals in a particular MSA for a specific period (e.g., sales-order messages for a workday). The messages would then be sent to message arrival areas (MAAs) as associated with host computers or other terminals at a predetermined time to be available when the destination stations are ready to accept delivery of them. Further, as the ACS user community expands, order messages might be entered directly into a firm's regional MSA by its customers (under control of predetermined authorization arrangements). The content of a message might be read by a firm's regional sales office before releasing it for transmission to destinations. Messages found to be incomplete or not in the proper form for transmission could be removed from the MSA and not sent.

Customers may subscribe for storage on a network availability basis, specifying the amount to be reserved, and may use additional storage on a demand basis as needed and as available.

There is no "requirement" that messages stored in an MSA be sent within a specified time. However, a message established in ACS will be expected to be transmitted because it is uneconomical to hold a message for a long duration where there is no intent that it be sent.

13 Will ACS data maintain its integrity in the network?

In ACS, the telephone company will check customer customization programs for compliance with administrative requirements (e.g., naming) and syntax rules. More restrictive verification that customers are not misusing such programs to perform noncommunica-

tions functions is not practical.

None of the ACS capabilities involves the alteration of the information content of messages or data entered into the network by the user. There are instances where the form of the data is modified to facilitate the efficient preparation and transmission of messages through ACS. The customer's data may be modified in form while being established in the network to adhere to the network's data communications code, speed, and protocol. Further, in the course of establishing a message, a terminal operator may make an error (e.g., entering words or characters in certain fields which violate parameters prescribed by the customer) which should be remedied by the operator before the message is finalized and transmitted to the intended recipient. A validation and edit program alerts the operator to certain errors and permits the operator to correct them. During the message establishment process, information such as user identity, station identity, and/or date and time may be introduced into the message or its header automatically—under program control. The inclusion of such data is important for reasons of authorization control (i.e., privacy and security), as well as efficiency.

The customer can prescribe statements governing the customer's message flow in which message consolidation might take place. In such an instance, the chaining together of messages would result in the establishment of consolidated messages, fewer in number, providing efficiencies for the customer. The examples given above suggest the types of ACS features which might be considered to result in changes in form.

Inversely, the form of the data may be modified upon delivery to the recipient through speed, code, and protocol conversion, the use of forms to format data, and compression or similar conversion processes. Such modifictions are essential if data presented to network stations are to be intelligible—and if ACS is to provide broad compatibility

14 How much network management will ACS provide?

One of the major needs that ACS addresses is network management. In order for a user to adequately manage a network, the user is not only concerned with its operations and maintenance but also with monitoring the way it is used by its operators.

For network management of ACS there are no plans for any special interfaces to the AT&T facilities in the area of network maintenance. However, it is intended to equip the centers for network management with all necessary and appropriate interfaces in the area of network maintenance to allow the network management functions to be performed effectively. It is expected that all costs for such interfaces will be attributed in accordance with the extent to which these maintenance tools are used by ACS. It is not planned to make these interfaces available to other common carriers or those non-common carriers building private networks.

As presently planned, the ACS network control center (NCC) will receive network status information from each node via dedicated facilities. This information will be presented on status display devices.

The NCC will also have terminals connected to two separate nodes (for reliability) via dedicated facilities to perform network management functions.

There are three basic functions of the NCC. First, the NCC continuously monitors the network loading and status of various components (e.g., the trunks in the network using the status display devices).

Second, the NCC is responsible for implementing manual controls over the network (e.g., rerouting of traffic, using the terminals to eliminate network congestion and minimize the effect in the event of equipment failure).

Third, the NCC will use the terminals to coordinate the provisioning of all major additions (new nodes, trunks, etc.) and changes (new generic software) to the network.

15 On what basis will users be charged for service on the ACS network?

It is expected that four measures of use and cost assignment will be used by ACS for billing:
- A count of packets or bytes transported.
- Network resource units (NRUs).
- Kilobytes of storage, per some time unit (to be defined in the tariff).
- Elapsed time.

The packet or byte count will be used to measure the use of the transport facilities of ACS. NRUs will be used to measure the use of communications-management functions. Kbytes of storage multiplied by some time unit will be used to measure the amount and duration of demand storage. Elapsed time will be used in connection with public dial-in access, to allocate the cost of that access among the various users.

Packets will be counted for calls and bytes for messages because the cost of using the transport facilities is essentially proportional to the number of packets or bytes using them. NRUs are designed to measure the use of communications management functions. Storage is allocated—and universally measured—in bytes or kbytes. Thus kbytes of storage multiplied by some time unit will serve as the usage measurement for demand storage. Elapsed connect-time measurement reflects cost causation directly, based on proportional use of dial-in ports which are shared by many users.

The number of packet or byte counts will be determined during handling by the network. NRUs will be counted and accumulated upon use of ACS communications management functions. Storage usage will be measured when a request for demand storage, issued by the customer, is handled by ACS. Elapsed connect time will be measured from the time the customer seizes [establishes a path] a public dial-in port until the time the port is released. ■

Small is different

Concepts, strategies for local data network architectures

R.H. Sherman, M.G. Gable, and G. McClure, Ford Motor Co.
Research Laboratory, Dearborn, Mich.

For a data communications network covering a limited area, what's needed is a new architecture embracing contention, propagation delay, functionality

The number of microcomputers and minicomputers employed in process control applications has vastly increased over the past few years. Recently, a few organizations have expanded these applications toward fully distributed networks employing high-speed channels, with all users located in the same building complex.

Since the control for these networks is local, no central computer can bottleneck the data communications. Thus, higher data rates than those associated with larger networks are possible, since information is processed only by the communicating computers.

Local data network architectures—the backbones of these systems—are designed to implement functional control of several different process control environments. One local network architecture (LNA), used in Ford Motor Co.'s Research Laboratory in Dearborn, Mich., is typical of this new breed of architecture.

The requirements for an LNA-based process control network are more comprehensive than the requirements for conventional networks because of the wide use of heterogenous computers in Ford's manufacturing environment. Besides handling a wide mix of computers, the network is fully decentralized, with no single node more important than any other. Also, the net-

work's file system is decentralized and can contain automatic recovery features. A common protocol exists among all processors, which range from mainframes to microcomputers.

Historically, process control networks have been organized into star, multidrop, or ring configurations.

In a star configuration, one computer forms the center, acting as the network control (master), with separate lines to all other computers (slaves). These networks can be hierarchical, since a slave computer to one star can be a master computer for a different star.

One computer also forms the center of the network control in a multidrop scheme. In this configuration, a line is "dropped" to the other computers from a trunk. Communications are handled by polling (sequencing from one computer to another). Communication between computers is possible only by sending messages through the polling computer.

With a ring configuration, each computer is linked to two other computers in a loop arrangement. Messages from one computer to another are passed along by intermediate computers, which retransmit the messages. Usually, in a ring, a network master exists to delete messages that have not been acknowledged as received. Several difficulties arise when these configu-

90

1 Packet collisions

Wait. The retransmission delay (RD) in CSMA is the sum of packet n's collision time (y), packet n's normalized length (1), and the medium's delay/packet time ratio (a).

When both collision and carrier are sensed (CSMA/CD), the RD is simply equal to the average arrival time of the first data packet which collides with packet zero.

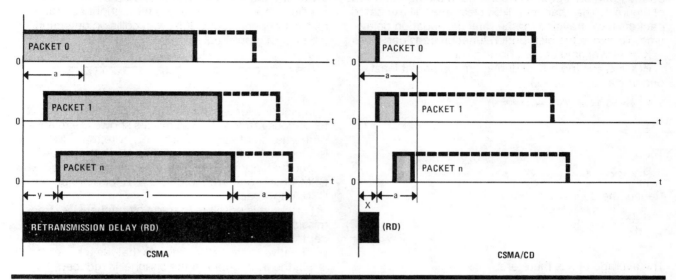

rations are considered for a manufacturing control system like the one used by Ford. None of these networks adapt well to full or partial communications failures. In the star, when a master fails, slave computers go off-line. To avoid the effect of a master failure, redundancy is required at all levels in the star's hierarchical control system. In the multidrop arrangement, if a polling computer fails, no other computers can communicate. In the ring network configuration, any computer failure inhibits communications.

Local data networks are better suited to a manufacturing control environment because they decentralize control communications with contention techniques. All computers share one medium, such as coaxial cable or a radio frequency, and the contention for the medium is locally handled by each computer.

One such network, the Aloha (Ref. 1) system, uses a broadcast channel with transmissions occurring at random. A refinement of the Aloha scheme, called Slotted Aloha (Ref. 2), provides a time slot for transmission which is shared by several computers. Transmission can only be initiated at the beginning of each time slot.

Network Systems Corp. (Ref. 3) uses a carrier-sense-multiple-access (CSMA) technique for contention. Retransmissions in CSMA are based on individually assigned time delays. To detect simultaneous transmissions, a message checksum is used. The average packet delay is decreased by increasing the transmission rate.

Yet another contention method is found in Ethernet (Ref. 4), used by Xerox. Ethernet handles contention by a carrier-sense-multiple-access scheme with collision detection CSMA/CD. Transmission in Ethernet is permitted only when an idle line (no carrier) is sensed. However, two or more computers may sense the idle line simultaneously, due to the propagation delay of the line. In this case, a message collision may result. If a collision is detected, the transmitters stop transmitting and wait a random amount of time, weighted by the network traffic, before retransmitting.

Contention comparisons

The choice of a contention scheme involves an analytical analysis, using models and simulation results which are available for several access methods. To begin the analysis, assume a Poisson traffic model in which the user can detect both carrier and collision. The channel can employ a nonpersistent protocol, which schedules packets in the following way. If the channel is idle, the packet is transmitted; if the channel is busy, the packet is rescheduled for transmission at some later time according to a delay distribution function which satisfies the Poisson traffic model.

In contrast to the nonpersistent user, a 1-persistent approach (Ref. 5) can be used. With this method, the packet is transmitted with probability-one (no delay before attempting retransmission) when an idle channel is sensed. The left side of Figure 1 depicts packets colliding in a CSMA scheme; while the right side shows packets truncated by the action of the collsion-detection logic. The throughput equation denoted by S for a nonpersistent CSMA without collision detection is:

$$S = \frac{Ge^{-aG}}{G(1+2a-ae^{-aG})+2e^{-aG}-e^{-2aG}} \quad (1)$$

where G is the arrival rate of new and rescheduled packets per normalized packet time, and a is the ratio of propagation delay to packet time. The duration for a successful packet transmission is $1+a$, and the average duration of idle is $1/G$. The minimum packet retransmission delay (RD) is illustrated by the solid color bar in Figure 1.

In the case where the user can sense both collision and carrier, the minimum retransmission delay is equal to X, the average time for arrival of the first packet that collides with packet 0, as illustrated in the right portion of Figure 1. The channel will be clear after all truncated packets have traveled for the total propagation delay time. To derive the distribution function consider:

X = arrival time of the colliding packet

P(X > x) = P (no arrival during time x, and at least one arrival during a − x)

$$P(X > x) = e^{-Gx}(1 - e^{-G(a-x)})$$

$$P(X > x) = e^{-Gx} - e^{-aG}$$

Then:

$$P(X \leq x) = 1 - P(X > x) = 1 - e^{-Gx} + e^{-aG}$$

Hence, the density function is:

$$\frac{d\, f(x)}{dx} = Ge^{-Gx} \tag{2}$$

The average of X is therefore:

$$\overline{X} = \frac{1}{G} - \frac{e^{-aG}}{G} - ae^{-aG} \tag{3}$$

The average duration of an unsuccessful packet is $\overline{X} + a$, and that for a transmission of a packet without conflict is $1 + a$. Therefore, the throughput equation for the nonpersistent CSMA with collision detection (CSMA/CD) protocol is:

$$S = \frac{Ge^{-aG}}{(1+a)(Ge^{-aG}) + (1+aG)(1-e^{-aG})^2 + 1} \tag{4}$$

In Figure 2 for a equal to 0.01, a plot of S versus G for various random access modes shows the relative performance of each. For large G, note that CSMA/CD is superior to other modes of operation. A channel capacity of approximately 0.952 can be obtained with CSMA/CD compared to only 0.815 for a nonpersistent CSMA approach.

Further, it is possible to trade off packet size, transmission rate, and propagation delay to obtain an acceptable level of performance. An analysis of throughput relative to the ratio a reveals that, as a becomes large, the throughput of the channel is reduced (Fig.

2 Comparing access methods

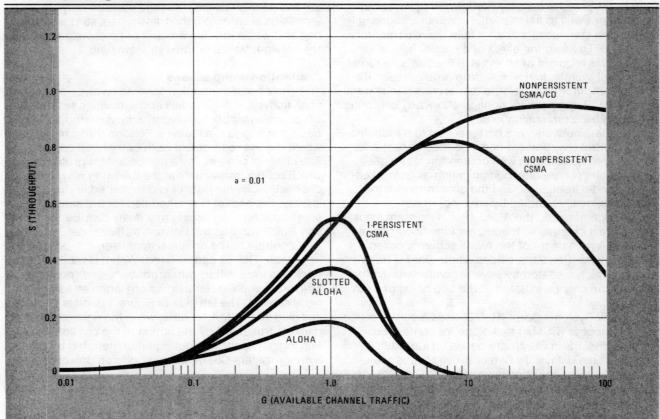

Fixed a. For a given propagation/packet-length ratio, CSMA/CD with a nonpersistent protocol yields the maximum throughput. As with most contention schemes, the throughput goes to zero when the system loading becomes too large, but note the slow rate of CSMA/CD's decline to zero. Parameters in this graph are normalized.

3). Hence, to effectively employ a carrier-sense-multiple-access scheme, it is necessary to maintain an a of about 0.01. Ford's LNA network uses a transmission rate of 1 Mbit/s with a maximum packet of 1K bits.

Collision detection is not performed directly on the encoded or modulated signal. If a design employs the amplitude or phase relationship of the transmitted signal for detection collision, it will probably be very sensitive to noise. In LNA, a band-spreading modulation technique is employed, which encoded the data using a ternary (base three) code of length six. The decoder classifies all 729 possible combinations of the code.

The correlation properties of this code permit collision detection to be performed by the *exclusive-or* function of the data transmitted and decoded by the receiver. The encoded signal also incorporates timing information which makes it possible to extract the data rate from the waveform to avoid problems with conventional clock synchronization techniques.

Coaxial cable medium

LNA uses the Ethernet CSMA/CD contention approach for a process control application, but with a slight modification. Communications connections in LNA are made between processes, instead of between hosts and terminals. Ford's communications channel— a branching bidirectional-passive tapped coaxial cable, shared in a multi-access scheme—is operated in a packet-switched mode. The number of users, limited by signal attenuation, and the number of port addresses is always less than 256. The transceiver amplification stages permit 25 dB (decibels) signal attenuation. This permits combinations of passive branching and non-directional taps. The propagation delay between any source-to-destination pair is a relatively small fraction of the overall network propagation delay.

The Ford net is designed for use in product testing, machine monitoring, power tool monitoring, product functional control, maintenance dispatching and energy management. With LNA, several of these applications can coexist on the network within one plant.

LNA is realized by using a communications interface between the user and coaxial cable. The choice of coaxial cable over more exotic media, such as fiber optic cable, is made for several reasons. Coaxial cable has a proven reliability, and while fiber optic cable users boast of excellent performance, in the manufacturing industry these applications are still limited. More importantly, coax is still less expensive than fiber optic cable, especially in large volume. The block diagram,

3 Changing propagation delay

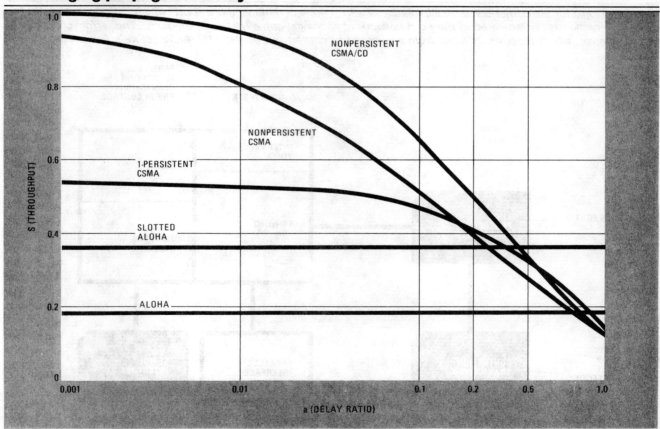

Varying a. *As a increases, network throughput falls, for any of the CSMA arrangements. For effective CSMA or CSMA/CD operation, a should be equal to, or less than 0.01. Keep in mind that a change in the ratio a can come about because of a change in the transmission medium's delay or a change in the time duration of the packet.*

Figure 4, illustrates the communications interface and its functions. The user accesses the interface through either a RS-232-C port or an eight-bit parallel port. The transceiver performs all the contention logic. The adapter contains a communications microcomputer which controls the logical message flows. The network includes a PDP-10 (DEC) computer, a microcomputer-controlled engine dynamometer test stand, a data-acquisition microcomputer on a machine tool, and a monitor computer.

Six-level structure

LNA provides: a scheme for resource allocations, a process naming function, and a means to initiate connections. Network addresses and resources are maintained by the user. When a process needs a resource, it can easily find it. Also, a new process can name itself in the network. For automatic handling of resource allocations, generic names must exist. These generic names for processes in the network are translated to network addresses by a LOG process. The LOG is a dynamic bookkeeping procedure which achieves resource management through a CATALOG—a file which contains both the generic name and the network addresses of processes and resources. Associated with

these names are resource costs, access privileges, and present attachments. For network reliability the LOG process and the CATALOG can be partially or completely replicated.

A CATALOG-update algorithm deletes network addresses when connections cannot be established. After recovering from a network fault, the LOG restores a state of agreement between replicated CATALOGs.

The architecture's organizational levels, shown in Figure 5, range from a user-level to a physical link level. In Ford's LNA-network the entire architecture is implemented, although the two highest levels—user and system processes—are still in the experimental stage.

The basic entity in the LNA-based network is a process. Processes communicate with other processes, and with machines, operators, and test stands in the manufacturing system. Process levels exist for both user and system jobs. System-level processes include mechanisms for task scheduling, communications, input/output device interfacing, and procedures to manage system resources such as files. User processes communicate with system processes to create an environment for operation of conventional applications.

File or message transfers between a set of processes are the responsibility of the communicating layers;

---

4 Interface block diagram

Logic. *The logic for the carrier-sense-multiple-access with collision detection is implemented in the Ford network at the transceiver, which receives its input from a synchro-* *nous-communications port which is connected to the coaxial-cable network medium. The error checking is carried out at the LNA architecture's link-protocol level.*

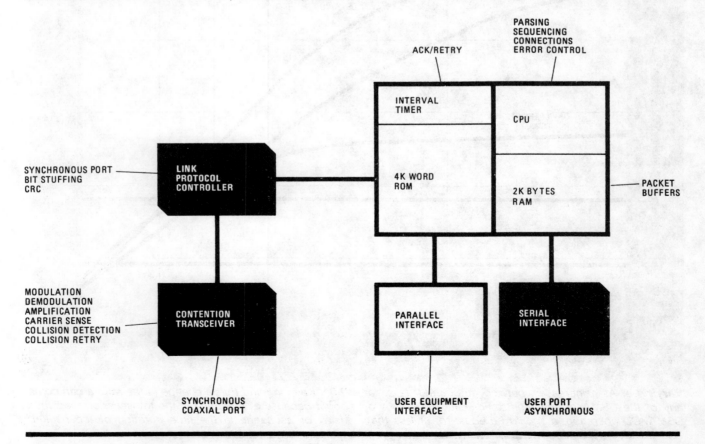

5 Functional layering

Organization. Six levels are defined in LNA, each with a unique role. The contention-control level, for instance, is responsible for the network's port-to-port message traffic.

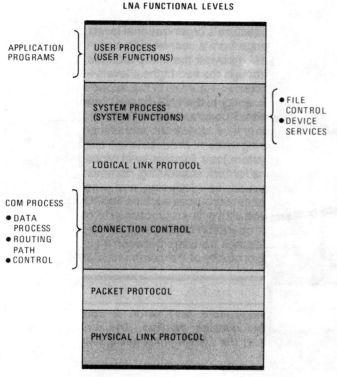

LNA FUNCTIONAL LEVELS

nevertheless, certain standard process-exchange procedures and formats are included in the network. These allow the user process to retrieve, store, and append data files, as well as to run certain utility software packages. The procedures also permit the user to make the necessary process-to-process connections and disconnections in a logical manner.

One example of a system process used to allocate and de-allocate processes and files is the LOG. The LOG process also controls access to the network addresses by users, thus controlling network security. The LOG command language is shown in Table 1.

Connection control

The basic connection of processes is established through a connection control function called COM. COM defines a port which is a unique network address and controls port-to-port message transfers. Associated with each port is at least one unique job. Ports are dynamically allocated and de-allocated. The COM function performs message-to-packet parsing, packet sequencing, buffering, and selection, positive acknowledgment, cyclic redundancy checking (CRC), and initial connection of processes.

To communicate with the connection control COM, a unique string is used to identify the logical link messages. The commands, which start with $COM ($ de-

notes a control character), are followed by a parameter list. These parameters are used to specify the initial connections, find the error conditions, test the operations, and impart special personality characteristics. The personality for buffer transmission is described by three statements which characterize how messages should be fragmented. These commands define the maximum packet length (LENG), maximum time before sending data (TIME), and a packet delimiter (DLMT).

Logging in

A user enters the network by logging in with his source network name (LOGI). Connections are established by assigning the destination network name (ASGN). The source and destination names are network addresses consisting of three bytes: the port identification (ID), the segment number (used to identify a specific local network when two or more local networks are connected through a gateway), and the user identification. For destinations on other segments, an entire route may be entered. The route is called the pathname and consists of gateway port identifiers, followed by the final destination name.

Three characters are reserved for network addresses:

* = the port name of the LOG process
? = don't care name of a port, process, or segment.
! = unassigned name of a port, process, or segment.

These characters are used to match the destination name of a packet with the name of a user. Either the unique name or a don't-care name must exist for the packet to be accepted. The assigned name is used in establishing a packet's destination. The assigned name can be changed by incoming packets to permit remote control of connections.

This logical-link protocol allows the user to define the data flow, routing, and path control to the COM process. The packet carries data from one port to another. Its length is variable from zero to 128 characters;

Table 1 The LOG process language

COMMAND	TASK
QU MARY LOCATION	FIND THE NETWORK ADDRESS OF THE GENERIC NAME PROCESS, IF IT EXISTS
QU MARY ENTER	ENTER INTO THE CATALOG THE GENERIC NAME PROCESS WITH ITS NETWORK ADDRESS
QU MARY EXIT	REMOVE FROM THE CATALOG THE NETWORK ADDRESS OF THE GENERIC NAME
QU MARY ATT FRED	ATTACH THE NAMED PROCESS TO THE REQUESTING GENERIC PROCESS
QU MARY DET FRED	DETACH THE GENERIC NAME PROCESS FROM THE REQUESTING PROCESS
QU MARY COST	PROVIDE THE NETWORK RESOURCE COST OF THE GENERIC NAME PROCESS

95

Distributed. One application of Ford's LNA-based network is engine dynamometer testing. A microprocessor on the stand collects engine performance data and communicates the information to the network's datalogger and file computer. If the file computer fails, the datalogger will continue to acquire and store data on the test.

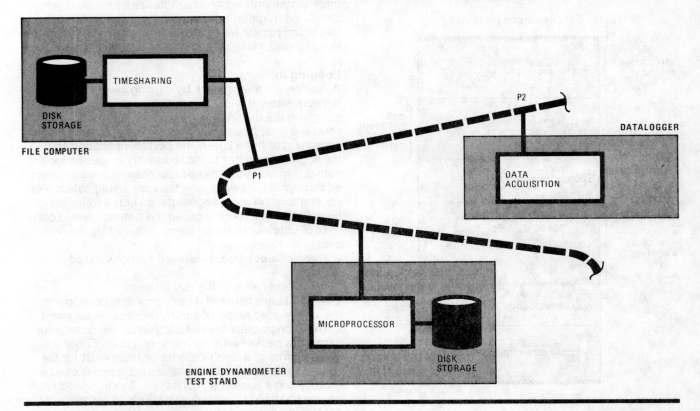

the packet format contains a link-protocol flag, a packet header, a data body, a CRC link-protocol check field, and a flag. The packet header is composed of the destination address, source address, and control field. The destination and source address fields are free-formatted, allowing gateway port names to be appended and deleted from the pathname.

Identification plan

The port name identifies individual adapters. The segment name is used for packet routing between local networks as it is in the link protocol. The user name identifies a specific process within a multiprocessing resource.

The physical link carries both the data and link control characters and must distinguish between them. Polynomial error encoding and decoding, synchronization, and information encoding for data transparency are all handled by the physical link protocol. These functions are performed by employing the CRC/CCITT error polynomial, the SDLC (IBM's synchronous data link control) flag for synchronization and bit-stuffing for data transparency.

Consider as an example LNA, the network shown in Figure 6. The engine dynamometer test stand uses a microcomputer to interact with an operator, to acquire data and to store data into a file. When a file-system

fault occurs, the datalogger can continue as usual without altering its acquisition procedures. The backup computer can store the data into its file and restore the primary file when the fault is cleared. A normal connection is made as shown in Table 2.

The datalogger enters the network with the network address, p2S1U1, where p2 is the eight-bit port name, U1 is the eight-bit user process name, and S1 is segment 1, (local network 1). The datalogger assigns the destination address for the data as p1S1U1. The file computer enters with its network address, p1S1?.

When data is sent, the packet is received by the file computer since U1 matches the don't care field, ?, which is then converted to the U1 field. The COM sends an acknowledgment, using only port names since the segment is known. On completion of the data transfer a # is sent as an acknowledgment to the datalogger. The file computer unassigns itself by entering p1S1? which allows other users to access the file system.

Automatic fault detection

An example of the logical link messages used in automatic fault detection and recovery is given in Table 3. The datalogger operates as in the earlier case; however, assume a communications fault is sensed by the backup computer. The backup computer immediately renames itself and takes on the role of the original file computer. End-to-end acknowledgements protect against lost packets during logical switching.

As an example of using the LOG process, consider the datalogger which doesn't know its network address, as shown in Table 4. The datalogger asks the LOG process for a network address by using its generic name Mary.

Mary's name is found to be p1S1U2 and the information returned to the datalogger. Next the location of John is requested and the reply received. An assignment to John's network address is made. This example shows the capabilities of acquiring network addresses from the LOG process.

Wide area LNA

When LNA networks are connected through gateways a wide area LNA results. The LNA's protocol is designed to accommodate interconnection of local networks. The gateway corresponds to two segments connected by a link such as a leased line. This approach can be particularly attractive when the link is a satellite which forms the backbone of the wide area LNA.

The major distinction between local networks, wide area local networks and global networks is the level or routing complexity. In local networks there is no routing, since all users have access to the packet destination name. In wide area local networks, simple routing is done by gateways. In a global network, front-end processors contain routing tables, protocol translation, and program buffer allocation and communicate with neighboring front-end processors for routing table updates.

Gateway functions between local networks include path building, address filtering, and fault control. Path building is the modification of the packet header during transmission of packets across a gateway. The gateway name in the destination field is deleted and the

Table 2   Normal process connection

DATALOGGER	COM PROCESSES	FILE SYSTEM
LOGI=p2S1U1		LOGI=p1S1?
ASGN=p1S1U1		
	p1S1U1;p2s1U1;0W;DATA →	
	← – p2;p1;0A;	
DATA	p1S1U1;p2S1U1;1W;DATA →	DATA
	← – p2;p1;1A;	
SENT	.	RECEIVED
	.	
RECEIVED	← – p1S1U1;p2S1U1;0W;#	# SENT
	p1;p2;0A; – →	
		LOGI=p1S1?

Table 3   Fault recovery

DATALOGGER	FILE SYSTEM	BACKUP
LOGI=p2S1U1	LOGI=p1S1U1	
ASGN=p1S1U1		
DATA	DATA	
SENT →	RECEIVED	
	"CRASH"	
	– – →	"CRASH SENSED"
		LOGI=p1S1?
DATA		DATA
SENT	– – →	RECEIVED
	"BACK ON-LINE"	
	LOGI=!S1!	
	ASGN=p1S1!	LOGI=p1S1?
	FILE SYSTEM UP – – →	DATA
		RECEIVED
		← – – BACKUP OFF-LINE
		LOGI=!S1!
	LOGI=p1S1?	
DATA	DATA	
SENT →	RECEIVED	

gateway name on the opposite segment is appended to the beginning of the source field. The gateway name is simply the port address, since this name is unique on each segment.

Address filtering is the process of recognizing a message that is to be transmitted across a gateway. This can be done for two types of packets.

The first has a pathname which is the complete route of the packet containing all gateway port addresses. The second type has only the three destination names: port, segment, and user process name. Notice that gateways have no knowledge of the network topology.

Fault control is provided both by error detection through time-outs on positive acknowledgments, and by error correction through gateway broadcasts for alternate routes. Unlike global networks, alternate routes are found by exploiting the broadcast nature of the contention medium, not by using routing tables.

Gateway routing

To illustrate the gateway strategy, consider a message sent from process U1 to process U2 in Figure 7. The destination name is a pathname which is received by the gateway, G1, as:

p2p1S2U2;p1S1U1;0W;data

which is acknowledged by the gateway as:

p1;p2;0A;

The gateway performs path building by removing

Table 4   The LOG process

DATALOGGER	COM PROCESSES	LOG PROCESS
LOGI=!S1U2		LOGI=*S1!
ASGN=*S1!		
QU MARY ATT --->	*S1!;!S1U2;0W;data	
	<-- !;*;0A;	
		LOGI=*S1U1
		ASGN=!S1U2
	<-- p1S1U2;*!U1;1W;data	MARY LOCATION p1S1U2
	*;p1;1A; -->	
LOGI=p1S1U2		
QU JOHN		
LOCATION --->	*S1U1;p1S1U2;2W;data	
	<-- p1;*;2A;	
	<-- p1S1U2;*!U1;3W;data	JOHN LOCATION p2S1U1
	*;p1;3A; -->	
ASGN=p2S1U1		

G1's name (p2 on segment S2) from the destination and appending the return pathname, p3, onto the source name field. Thus:

p1S2U2;p3p1S1U1;0W;data

This packet is acknowledged by the COM of user U2 as:

p3;p1;0A;

If the same transaction between U1 and U2 occurs without U1's knowing the pathname, then the message destination need only contain the network address. U1 sends the following message as seen by the gateway:

p1S2U2;p1S1U1;0W;data

which is acknowledged as:

p1;p2;0A

and retransmitted by the gateway, since S2 does not match the present segment, as:

p1S2U2;p3p1S1U1;0W; data

The message is received by U2 and acknowledged as:

p3;p1;0A

Now U2 has the entire route to U1 which is used to send from U1 to U2:

p3p1S1U1;p1S2U2;0W;data

Upon receiving the message at U1 the entire pathname is acquired:

p1S1U1;p2p1S2U2;0W;data

The address filtering, illustrated above, takes advantage of the medium when multiple gateways are on the same segment. Redundant paths from one user to another allow multiple packets to be received with a decision strategy to select the route.

One decision strategy is to select the route of the first packet received. Additional copies of the same packet are rejected, since the sequence number is the same. All packets with sequence numbers less than or equal to the current number are acknowledged. When a gateway does not receive an acknowledgment from another gateway along a route, the gateway can remove the pathname up to the final destination, and use the address filtering technique described above. A level count can be used to control the depth of search in the network. File control protects against lost packets. ■

References

1. N. Abramson, *The Aloha System- Another Alternative for Computer Communications,* R75-170, IEE Computer Society, Long Beach, Calif., 1975.
2. L. G. Roberts, *Extensions of Packet Communication Technology to a Hand-Held Personal Terminal,* AFIPS Conf. Proceedings, 1972 Spring Joint Computer Conference 40, 295-298.
3. Network Systems Corp., *Systems Description: Series A Network Adapters,* Pub. No. A01-000-00, Brooklyn Center, Minn., 1976.
4. R.M. Metcalfe and D.R. Boggs, *Ethernet: Distributed Packet Switching for Local Computer Networks,* Comm. of the ACM, July 1976, Vol. 19, No. 7, pp. 395-404.
5. L. Kleinrock, *Queuing Systems, Vol II: Computer Applications,* John Wiley and Sons, 1976.

7   Gateway

Interconnect. *Gateways allow two or more local networks to communicate. Here, Fred uses the gateway to establish a datapath for a message transaction with Mary.*

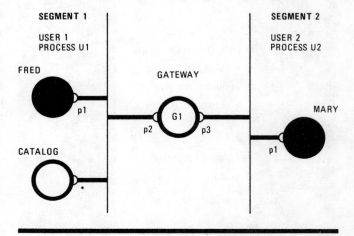

Part 2
Data link
performance

Equipment

Sharing the line: a cheaper way than multiplexing

Gilbert Held, U.S. Civil Service Commission, Macon, Ga.

But lower costs may mean a tradeoff in delays as terminals contend for access to the processor

Cost conscious company executives are always happy to hear of ways to save money on the job. One of the things a data communications manager can best do to make his presence felt is to produce a realistic plan for cutting down expenses. It may be evident that a single communication link is less costly than two or more. What is sometimes less obvious is the most economical and effective way to make use of even a single link.

Multiplexing is usually the first technique that comes to mind. But there are many situations where far less expensive, albeit somewhat slower, equipment is quite adequate. Here terminals are polled one by one through a "sharing device" that acts under the instructions of the host computer.

Typically, the applications where this method would be most useful and practical would be those where messages are short and where most traffic between host computer and terminal moves in one direction during any one period of time.

The technique, which can be called "line sharing" (as distinct from multiplexing), may work in some interactive situations, but only if the over-all response time can be kept within tolerable limits. The technique is not as a rule useful for remote batching or remote job entry, unless messages can be carefully scheduled so as not to get in each other's way because of the long run time for any one job.

Line sharing, then, is inexpensive—but has some limits to its usefulness in situations where a multiplexer, most likely a time-division multiplexer or TDM, can bring in more economic leverage. A TDM moves continously to sample in turn each channel feeding it, either bit by bit or character by character, and produces an aggregate transmission at a speed equal to the sum of the speeds of all its terminals. (Fig. 1a). A multiplexer operating character by character assembles its first frame by taking (for example) the letter A from the first terminal, the letter E from the second and the letter I from the third terminal. The next time round, the multiplexer takes the second character of each message (B, F and J respectively) to make up its second frame. And the sampling continues in this way until traffic on the line is reversed to allow transmission from the computer to the terminals. The demultiplexing side of the TDM (operating on the receiving side of the network) assembles incoming messages and distributes them to their proper terminals or computer ports.

A frequency division multiplexer (FDM) divides up the transmission link's total bandwidth into a number of distinct strips, each of which is able to carry a low-

1 Muxing vs. sharing

Multiplexer needs. *A time or frequency division multiplex system (A) requires one computer port for each terminal and a multiplexer at each end. A sharing system (B) needs only one computer port. Because it requires*

terminals to be polled, a sharing system can be cost-effective for interactive operation, but may not be so for long messages such as are likely to move in remote job entry or remote batch types of applications.

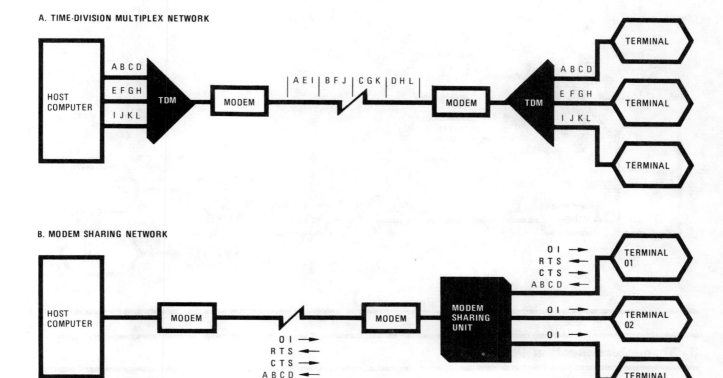

A. TIME-DIVISION MULTIPLEX NETWORK

B. MODEM SHARING NETWORK

speed channel. The FDM accepts and moves transmissions from all of its terminals and ports simultaneously and continuously.

A line-sharing network is connected to the host computer by a local link, through which the host polls the terminals one by one. The central site transmits the address of the terminal to be polled throughout the network by way of the sharing unit (Fig. 1b). The terminal assigned this address (01 in the diagram) responds by transmitting a request-to-send (RTS) signal to the computer, which returns a clear-to-send (CTS), to prompt the terminal to begin transmitting its message (ABCD in diagram). When the message is completed, the computer polls the next terminal.

Throughout this sequence, the sharing device merely routes the signals to and from the polled terminal and handles supporting tasks, such as making sure the carrying signal is on the line when the terminal is polled, and inhibiting transmission from all terminals not connected to the computer.

There are two subspecies of device used in this technique—modem sharing-units and line sharing-units. They function in much the same way to perform

much the same task—the only significant difference being that a line sharing-unit has an internal timing source, while a modem sharing-unit gets its timing signals from the modem it is servicing.

Remote operation

A line sharing-unit is mainly used at the central site to connect a cluster of terminals to a single computer port (Fig 2). It does, however, play a part in remote operation—when a data stream from a remote terminal cluster forms one of the inputs to a line sharing-unit at the central site, so as to make it possible to run with a cheaper single-port computer.

In a modem sharing-unit one set of inputs is connected to multiple terminals or processors, as shown in Figure 2. These lines are routed through the modem sharing-unit to a single modem. Besides needing only one remote modem, a modem sharing network needs only a single two-wire (for half-duplex) or four-wire (for full-duplex) communications link. A single link between terminals and host computer allows all of them to connect with a single port on the host, a situation that results in still greater savings.

2 Line sharing and modem sharing

Computer ties. Line sharing-units tie central site terminals to the computer, but modem sharing-units handle all the remote terminals. A line sharing-unit requires internal timing, whereas a modem sharing-unit gets its timing from the modem to which it is connected. In either case, access to the host is made through a single communications link—either two-wire or four-wire—and a single port at the central-site host computer.

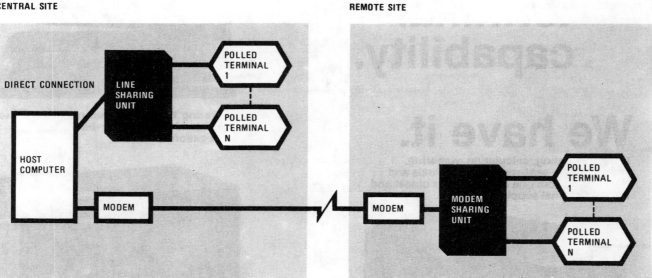

3 Through connection

Remote inputs. Line or modem sharing-units form a single link between host computer and terminals. This system contains a modem sharing-unit with inputs from the terminals at its own site as well as from remote terminals. A line sharing-unit at the central site can handle either remote site devices or local devices more than 50 feet away from the host computer, which is the maximum cable length advisable under RS-232-C standards.

Comparison of monthly rental costs

A. MULTIPLEXING	MONTHLY COST
TWO TIME-DIVISION MULTIPLEXERS AT $90 EACH	$180
TWO 4,800 B/S MODEMS AT $120 EACH	240
FOUR COMPUTER PORTS AT $35 EACH	140
LEASED LINE	1,000
FOUR TERMINALS AT $150 EACH	600
TOTAL MONTHLY COST	$ 2,160

B. USING A MODEM SHARING UNIT	MONTHLY COST
TWO 4,800 B/S MODEMS AT $120 EACH	240
COMPUTER PORT	35
MODEM SHARING UNIT	25
LEASED LINE	1,000
FOUR TERMINALS AT $150 EACH	600
TOTAL MONTHLY COST	$1,900

C. HOW PERCENTAGE SAVINGS INCREASES AS LEASED LINE COST DECREASES

COST	$1,000 A MONTH LEASED LINE	$500 A MONTH LEASED LINE
MULTIPLEXING	$ 2,160	$ 1,660
MODEM SHARING UNIT	1,900	1,400
PERCENTAGE SAVING	12%	16%

If multiplexing were used in this type of application, the outlay would likely be greater, because of the cost of the hardware and the need for a dedicated host computer port for each remote device. A single modem sharing-unit, at the remote site, is all that is needed for a sharing system; but multiplexers come in pairs, one for each end of the link.

The polling process makes sharing units less efficient than multiplexers. Throughput is cut back because of the time needed to poll each terminal and the line turnaround time on half-duplex links. Another problem is that terminals must wait their turn. If one terminal sends a long message others may have to wait an excessive amount, which may tie up operators if unbuffered terminals are used, although terminals with buffers to hold messages waiting for transmission will ease this situation.

Sharer constraints

Sharing units are generally transparent within a communications network. There are, however four factors that should be taken into account when making use of these devices: the distance separating the data terminals and the sharing unit (generally set at no more than 50 feet under RS-232-C interface specifications); the number of terminals that can be connected to the unit; the various types of modems with which the unit can be interfaced; and whether the

terminals can or cannot accept external timing from a modem through a sharing unit.

Then, too, the normal constraints of the polling process, such as delays arising from line turnaround and response, and the size of the transmitted blocks, must be considered in designing the network.

The 50-foot limit on the distance between terminal and sharing unit can make for a problem if terminals cannot be clustered closely. One way to get around this is to bring in a data communications interface option for the sharing unit the modem that allows a remote terminal to be connected with the sharing unit through a pair of modems (Fig. 3). This in turn allows the users the economic advantage of a through connection out to the farthest point.

It is advisable to check carefully into what types of modems can be supported by modem sharing-units, since some modems permit a great deal more flexibility of network design than others. For instance, if the sharing unit can work with a multiport modem, the extra modem ports can service remote-batch terminals or dedicated terminals that frequently handle long messages. (For a report on multiport modems see "Inverse multiplexing with multiport modems", DATA COMMUNICATIONS, January/February 1976, pp. 45-50.) Some terminals that cannot accept external timing can be fitted with special circuitry through which the timing originates at the terminal itself, instead of at the modem.

The prices of sharing units range from $500 to $3,000, depending mainly on the number of terminals that can be connected through the unit. At present this number varies, the most versatile units being able to handle up to 32 terminals.

As shown in the table, a typical multiplexing system containing a line leased at $1,000 a month (Section A) might cost the user $2,160 a month; a system with a modem sharing unit (Section B) would cost $1,900 a month, or 12% less. Because the leased line contributes the largest part of the system's cost, the percentage saved with a less expensive line can be even greater. For instance (Section C of the table), a line leased for $500 a month would increase the over-all saving to 16%.

Two more articles on sharing devices will appear in forthcoming issues. The first will deal with port sharing-units, which are used in polled networks for the programmed selection of the computer ports. The subsequent article will discuss port selection (or port contention), where the sharing unit provides random access to the ports under its control.

The most significant differences in the different types of sharing units lies in their placement and function, and in the options available to them. Unlike line, modem and port sharing-units, the port selection devices operate by time-sharing or contention.

Access to any one port is provided on a first-come, first-served basis whenever a port is available. With port selection, therefore, a large number of lines contend for a small number of ports. Users let go of a port by signing off in a way similar to that found in time-sharing and remote job entry applications. ∎

Making the most of digital data channels

H. D. Chadwick, Information and Communication Applications Inc., Rockville, Md.

Different thinking is called for on error bursts, bit-count integrity to take full advantage of improved performance

Digital data communications channels, such as AT&T's Dataphone digital service (DDS) and Datadial, formerly offered by Datran and now by Southern Pacific Communications, exhibit performance characteristics different from those found on traditional data communications channels consisting of a voice-grade line with modems. These differing performance characteristics call for different designs in the equipment selected by the data communications planner if he is to take advantage of the improved performance possible with digital communications channels.

The two most important factors that should be considered in the performance of digital channels are the extremely "bursty" nature of the errors on the channel and the possibility of the loss of bit-count integrity. Both of these may result from the fading phenomenon frequently occurring on microwave transmission. If multiplexer equipment is designed with these performance characteristics in mind, it is possible to achieve considerable improvement in the data throughput over digital channels when compared with the use of equipment optimized for transmission over analog links.

Conventional communications theory is based on the concept of independently distributed bit errors. The probability of an error occurring during any particular bit interval is independent of whether or not an error occurred at any time previously. The appropriateness of this assumption varies considerably with the nature of the medium used for transmission. For satellite channels, it is a good assumption; for data over analog channels using microwave or cable, it is not as good; and for terrestrial digital systems, it is poor.

The error performance of the terrestrial digital transmission links, which rely largely on line-of-sight microwave radios, tends to be characterized by two modes: in one mode, there are no errors at all; in the other mode, the error rate approaches 0.5 and there is no communication at all. Luckily, the error-free mode exists most of the time. During a small fraction of the time, however, the channel experiences an error burst that can last from a few bit periods to several seconds in duration. Figure 1 shows the relative frequency of bursts of different lengths measured on a 56 kbit/s circuit in the Datran system.

Throughput efficiency

Most higher-speed synchronous data communications applications use some form of automatic repeat request (ARQ) protocol. In an ARQ scheme—for example, stop-and-wait ARQ such as BSC, go-back-N ARQ such as SDLC (synchronous data link control), or selective-repeat as used in some new multiplexer de-

1 Most error bursts are 10—99 bits long

Bursty errors. Most of the time, the digital data channel is error-free, but when error-inducing noise occurs on the line, the length of bursts varies over a very broad range.

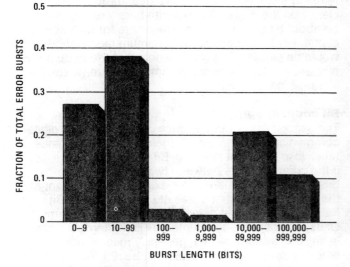

signs—one or more data blocks are retransmitted if one block is received with detected errors, thus reducing the channel throughput efficiency.

The throughput efficiency of a data communications system can be defined as the ratio of the average number of actual information bits received correctly in one second to the nominal bit rate of the channel. The actual information bits exclude overhead bits used for block headers and for such control functions as error

checking, as well as dead times when the transmitter is waiting for an acknowledgement from the receiver.

The throughput efficiency of a link depends upon the protocol used, the delay in the channel, the block length, and the probability that a block will be received correctly. Of these factors, the user has control only over the block length and, to some extent, the protocol. The delay and the block error probability are characteristics of the channel itself.

The objective, then, is to achieve the highest possible throughput efficiency on the channel by manipulating the factors that the user can control. The choice of protocol is a fundamental decision that is usually determined by the overall network design. In general, the full-duplex protocols (such as SDLC) provide higher throughput efficiency than the half-duplex protocols (such as BSC), particularly on circuits with significant propagation delays.

The choice of block length depends upon the characteristics of the individual channel. For the stop-and-wait ARQ protocol, the throughput efficiency can be expressed as:

$$TE = \frac{k - m}{k + R\tau} [1 - P(k)]$$

where TE is the throughput efficiency, k the total block length in bits, m the number of overhead bits in the block, R the data rate, τ the total channel delay (the time between the end of one block and the start of the next), and P(k) the probability that a block of k bits is received with one or more bit errors. This formula assumes that all errors are detected and that the acknowledgement channel operates without errors.

The equivalent expression for the go-back-N ARQ protocol (such as SDLC) is:

2 Digital channel features better error probability

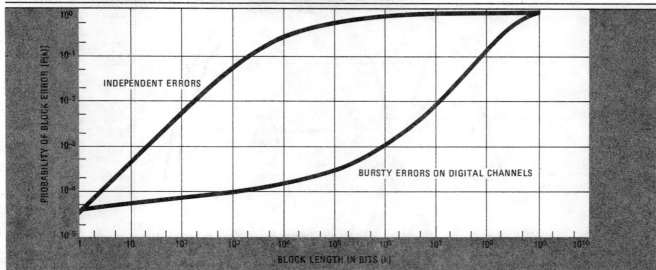

Much improved. The bursty-error characteristic of digital data channels has a much reduced probability of block errors in comparison with channels characterized independent bit errors—so that, by and large, throughput efficiency of digital data channels will usually be significantly superior to other practical terrestrial channel types.

$$TE = \frac{k - m}{k + P(k)R_\tau} [1 - P(k)]$$

and for the selective-repeat ARQ technique it is:

$$TE = \frac{k - m}{k [1 + P(k)]} [1 - P(k)]$$

In each equation it can be seen that an important parameter, over which the user has no control, is the block error probability, $P(k)$. $P(k)$ will always increase as k increases, but the way in which it increases depends upon the characteristics of the channel. For k equal to R, the data rate, $P(k)$ is one minus the error-free-second rate.

Figure 2 shows the block error probability as measured on the same 56 kbit/s circuit on the Datran network. Also shown for comparison is the block error probability that would result if the errors were independently distributed with the same average bit error rate. The digital circuit will exhibit superior performance at any practical block length.

Maximum throughput

If the block error probability is determined and the protocol and other factors are known, then the appropriate throughput equation can be plotted, as shown in Figure 3, for the 56 kbit/s Datran circuit. A delay of 100 millisec. and an overhead of 48 bits per block were used in calculating the throughput efficiencies. Also shown on the figure are the throughput efficiencies that would be predicted for a circuit with the same bit error rate, but with independent bit errors.

Now, each of the three types of ARQ protocol can be studied. Figure 3 shows that very high throughput

efficiencies can be obtained with the digital communications channels if the block length is chosen correctly. For example, if the circuit were assumed to have independent bit errors, a block length of approximately 7.5 kbit/s would be expected to produce a throughput efficiency of 34 percent with a stop-and-wait ARQ system. For this block length, the actual throughput efficiency on the digital channel with bursty errors would be about 51 percent. These values are for a 56 kbit/s circuit. For lower speeds, the optimum block length would be smaller. The curves show that the throughput efficiency will increase significantly with even a small increase in block length.

Bit count integrity

The second major performance characteristic of digital communications channels is their tendency to sometimes lose bit-count integrity. Bit-count integrity is lost if the number of bits between two distinguishable bits—the framing marker, for example—is different at the receiver from what it was at the transmitter. Bits have either been lost or inserted in the data stream. Of itself, loss of bit-count integrity is not terribly serious in an ARQ system, since it generally means that one block of data will be lost and must be retransmitted.

Loss of bit-count integrity is very significant, however, in a circuit where time-division multiplexers (TDM) are used. The high-speed-receive side of a typical TDM is maintained in frame synchronization with the transmit side of the corresponding TDM so that the multiplexer can distribute the incoming high-speed data bits to the correct low-speed channel. Frame synchronization is maintained in the TDM by observing that a known pattern, the framing sequence, occurs at predictable places within the incoming bit stream. When a loss of bit-count integrity occurs, the TDM loses this pattern

3　Bursty errors give better throughput

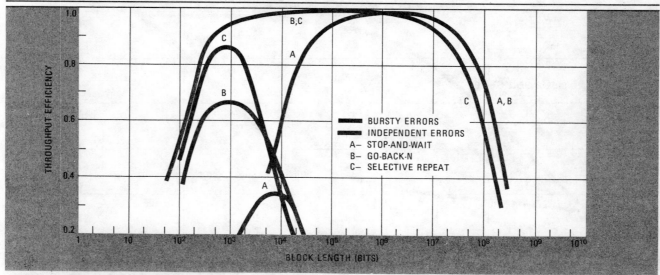

Channel performance. The actual throughput efficiency on data channels characterized by independent errors or bursty errors will depend upon block length as well as upon the type of protocol implemented on the channel. But over a wide range of block lengths, throughput efficiency will be better on bursty digital data channels.

in the expected positions and must, therefore, reacquire frame synchronization. Since the data on all low-speed channels is incorrect until synchronization is reacquired, the most advantageous scheme would be for the framing process to be very rapid. Figure 4 illustrates how the total number of errors on the output channels caused by a loss of bit-count integrity is reduced with a fast synchronization algorithm.

Error bursts in a TDM

Another consideration must be taken into account, however, in the design of a framing technique for a TDM: The time taken by a multiplexer to detect a loss of frame sync is inversely proportional to the probability that it will be fooled by an incoming sequence of errors. That is the reason why most existing TDMs do not have rapid reframing cycles. As stated before, errors on digital communication systems usually occur in bursts. A burst of errors which lasts longer than the synchronization loss detection time will cause the multiplexer to lose the framing pattern and to be fooled into the condition that frame synchronization has been lost, even when it may not have been.

When the error burst goes away, the multiplexer will reacquire synchronization, but, with most multiplexers, during the period between assumed sync loss and reacquisition, the output will be in error, as shown at the top of Figure 5. To combat false-frame synchronization loss due to error bursts, many multiplexer designs incorporate very long sync loss detection times. This

---

4 Losing bit count loses sync

Synchronization. *When a loss of bit-count integrity occurs, a time-division multiplexer may have its framing marker upset, so that data errors will occur during the* *time the TDM loses synchronization and reacquires sync. A time-division multiplexer featuring a fast-synchronization algorithm will yield a higher net throughput efficiency.*

SLOW SYNC ALGORITHM

FAST SYNC ALGORITHM

5 Fast syncing cuts data errors

Flywheeling. *A time-division multiplexer containing a flywheeling feature will reduce the period of data error because it will eliminate the sync-acquisition time. A TDM with a fast-syncronization algorithm yields a shorter error burst than a TDM with a slow-sync algorithm, so the time-division multiplexer again yields improved throughput.*

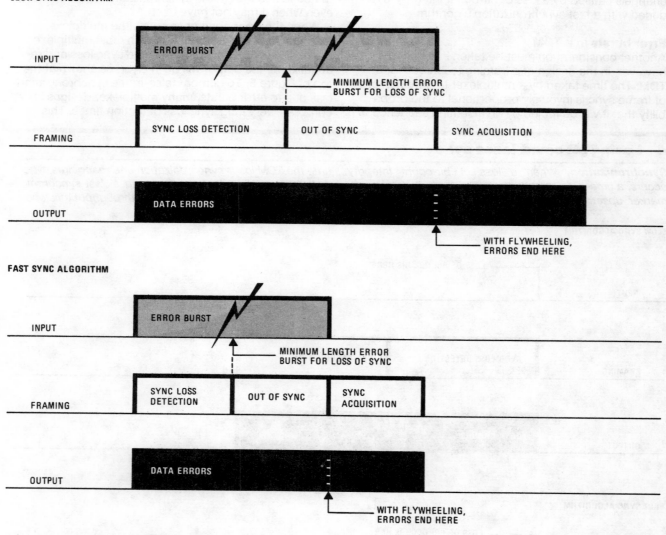

type of response, however, is exactly the opposite of the rapid response needed to combat bit-count-integrity losses most effectively. As shown at the bottom of Figure 5, a fast sync-loss-and-recovery algorithm will tend to lose frame synchronization more frequently because it will respond to shorter error bursts, but, since the output channel data will be in error anyway, this is of no serious consequence. The major problem is caused by the lengthening of the error burst between input and output caused by the reframing time.

The best multiplexer design, which would combat both error bursts and losses of bit-count integrity, would incorporate a "flywheel" effect between the input and the output, combined with a fast frame-synchronization-loss-and-recovery algorithm. The fast

frame-synchronization scheme would recover quickly after losses of bit-count integrity, but would lose synchronization frequently because of short error bursts. The error bursts, however, do not normally involve a loss of bit-count integrity, so that when the burst has gone away, the framing position is unchanged. The flywheel action would require the multiplexer to continue using the previous framing position even when frame synchronization has been lost. Only when synchronization is regained at a different phase position would the output framing position be changed. This flywheeling will make no difference for bit-count-integrity losses, since the sync loss-detection-and-recovery time will be the same. However, flywheeling will eliminate the stretching of error bursts. ∎

How to anticipate performance of multipoint lines

Ronald Zussman, Securities Industry Automation Corp., New York City

Equations representing the operation of multipoint lines are easy to solve on a programmable calculator

In any communications configurations, quality of performance must be balanced against cost, and an obvious way to cut back on network costs is to have a number of terminals share the line and the intermediate hardware. It is useful for the network designer to be able to compute the efficiency of his proposed configuration for the estimated traffic parameters, rather than wait until lines and equipment have been placed in service.

Among the shared-line techniques most often encountered is a multipoint (or multidrop) configuration, in which several terminals are connected along the one line, which leads to the host computer. Because it requires less hardware, multipoint line-sharing is likely to be less expensive than multiplexing, either with a time-division multiplexer (TDM) or a frequency-division multiplexer (FDM).

However, in multipoint operation the average response time is greater than that associated with either a TDM or an FDM. Excessive response time can well create serious user dissatisfaction in inquiry/response and message-switching applications.

Response time is sensitive to such network parameters as traffic throughput, line speed, delays at the controller or host computer, and length of input and output messages. The task of computing expected network performance can be rendered easier and more effective with the help of a programmable calculator. By using formulas representing a model of a generalized multipoint line, and entering the appropriate values of network parameters, designers can calculate the least expensive set of operating conditions that will satisfy the response time demanded in the particular application.

Through repeated use of this model, answers can be obtained to such important questions of design and performance as:

■ How does varying traffic throughput influence response time?

■ How does varying transmission speed influence response time?

■ Is a full-duplex line justifiable, in terms of performance and cost, as against a half-duplex line?

■ Should the host computer free the line after receiving an input message, or should the host retain control of the line until the corresponding computer output is ready for transmission?

■ What is the best priority assignment for different classes of transactions?

■ At what level does slow polling rate begin to degrade performance?

(Although the equations given later look rather

complex, they can be rapidly solved on a programmable calculator. In fact, a set of program and user instructions has been worked out for the Texas Instruments SR-52, TI-58, and TI-59 calculators—see the panel "How to get the multipoint simulation program"—and is available to users.)

Where a multipoint line is used for inquiry/response and message-switching applications, each transaction comprises two messages: the user's input to the terminal, and the host computer's output response.

In a mathematical model based on these circumstances, the overall rate for transactions arriving at the host from all terminals on the line is given as λ (in transactions per second), while the transmission speed is s (in characters per second). Tc is the sum of controller delay and computer processing time; Li the number of characters per input message; Lo the number of characters per output message; Ti the average line service time per input message, where $Ti = Li/s$; To the average line service time per output message, where $To = Lo/s$; and Ts the average line service time per transaction, where $Ts = Ti + To$. Line utilization (U) is found by multiplying Ts by λ.

A necessary interim calculation provides the ratio of output-to-input message lengths (N), where $N = Lo/Li$. The average time a transaction spends waiting for the line (Tw), is:

$$Tw = ((1 + N^2)/(1 + N)^2) \, U \, (Ts/(1 - U))$$

Ninety percent of the transactions have waiting times equal to or less than Tw(90%), where:

$$Tw(90\%) = Tw + 1.2816 \, \sigma$$

Similarly, 95% of the transactions will have waiting times equal to or less than Tw(95%), where:

$$Tw(95\%) = Tw + 1.645 \, \sigma$$

The average transaction response time, therefore, is:

$$Tr = Ts + Tc + Tw;$$

and 90% of the transactions will have response times equal to or less than Tr(90%), where:

$$Tr(90\%) = Tr + 1.2816 \, \sigma$$

Furthermore, 95% of the transactions will have response time equal to or less than Tr(95%), where:

$$Tr(95\%) = Tr + 1.645 \, \sigma$$

An important, though formidable looking, formula gives the standard deviation of transaction waiting and response time, σ:

$$\sigma = [((([4(1 + N^3)/(1 + N)^3]^{1/2} Ts)^2 U)/(6(1 - U))) + Tw^2/2]^{1/2}$$

Fortunately the programmable calculator can solve this in a moment once the input parameters have been entered on the calculator's keyboard.

The qualifications incorporated into the model are: that input and output message arrivals are random; that line polling time is much less than total response time; that either half-duplex or full-duplex line protocols can be accommodated; that half-duplex lines are restricted to interactive transactions with the same input and output message rates; that for full-duplex lines, input and output messages are modeled separately and that their rates, therefore, need not be the same; that lengths of input and output messages are constant, though not necessarily equal; that the sum of controller delay and computer processing time is fixed; and that total system waiting time and total system response time have normal distributions.

Twenty simulation examples of a multipoint network were worked out on a calculator, and are displayed in the table, "Six factors that affect multipoint operation." The examples are divided into six groups, indicating how the model can be used to answer the six questions posed earlier.

Varying traffic throughput

The first eight examples show the effects of additional traffic. As the number of transactions per second (λ) goes up, line speed (s) and controller-delay-plus-processing time (Tc) are held constant, as are input and output message lengths (Li and Lo); line utilization (U) increases; waiting time (Tw) and response time (Tr) become longer at a rapidly increasing rate once line utilization goes over 80%; finally, in Example 8, six transactions a second is more than the line can handle, because line utilization would then be 107.5%. An ideal set of conditions for multipoint lines occurs in Example 5: Line utilization is only 72% of capacity, which allows for some temporary peak load, and the response times are satisfactorily small.

Varying line speed

Line speed (s) is successively reduced through Examples 9, 3, 10, and 11. Utilization of the line climbs, and times increase as speed decreases. Although the effects of increasing λ or reducing s are similar, they are

How six factors affect multipoint operation

EXAMPLE NO.*	MODEL INPUT PARAMETERS					MULTIPOINT PERFORMANCE										
	λ	s	Tc	Li	Lo	Ti	To	Ts	U	σ	Tw	Tw (90%)	Tw (95%)	Tr	Tr (90%)	Tr (95%)
I. VARYING TRAFFIC THROUGHPUT																
1	0.5	1,200	1.2	65	150	.054	.125	.179	.090	.029	.010	.047	.057	1.389	1.426	1.437
2	1.0	1,200	1.2	65	150	.054	.125	.179	.179	.044	.023	.080	.096	1.402	1.459	1.475
3	2.0	1,200	1.2	65	150	.054	.125	.179	.358	.078	.058	.158	.186	1.437	1.537	1.565
4	3.0	1,200	1.2	65	150	.054	.125	.179	.537	.128	.120	.284	.331	1.500	1.664	1.710
5	4.0	1,200	1.2	65	150	.054	.125	.179	.717	.233	.262	.560	.645	1.641	1.940	2.024
6	5.0	1,200	1.2	65	150	.054	.125	.179	.896	.681	.891	1.764	2.012	2.270	3.143	3.391
7	5.5	1,200	1.2	65	150	.054	.125	.179	.985	5.003	6.999	13.411	15.229	8.379	14.790	16.008
8	6.0	1,200	1.2	65	150	.054	.125	.179	1.075	—	—	—	—	—	—	—
II. VARYING LINE SPEED																
9 (3)	2.0	2,400	1.2	65	150	.027	.063	.090	.179	.022	.011	.040	.048	1.301	1.329	1.337
10	2.0	600	1.2	65	150	.108	.250	.358	.717	.466	.524	1.121	1.290	2.082	2.679	2.848
11	2.0	300	1.2	65	150	.217	.500	.717	1.433	—	—	—	—	—	—	—
III. CHANGING TO FULL-DUPLEX OPERATION																
12	5.5	1,200	1.2	65	0	.054	.000	.054	.298	.033	.023	.065	.077	1.277	1.320	1.332
13	5.5	1,200	0.0	150	0	.125	.000	.125	.688	.246	.275	.591	.680	0.400	0.716	0.805
(7)											.298	.656	.757	1.677	2.036	2.137
IV. HOLDING THE LINE																
14 (1)	0.5	1,200	0.0	1,655	0	1.379	.000	1.379	.690	2.741	3.064	6.576	7.572	4.443	7.955	8.951
V. VARYING MESSAGE PRIORITY																
15 (3)	23.0	700	0.5	7	25	.009	.032	.042	.956	.433	.592	1.147	1.304	1.134	1.689	1.846
16	23.0	1,200	0.5	7	25	.006	.021	.027	.613	.027	.028	.063	.073	.555	.590	.600
17	2.0	464	1.2	65	150	.140	.323	.463	.927	2.531	3.388	6.631	7.551	5.051	8.295	9.214
18	25.0	1,200	0.6	12	35	.010	.029	.039	.979	.819	1.141	2.191	2.489	1.780	2.830	3.128
VI. VARYING POLLING RATE																
19	—	1,200	0.9	12	12	.010	.010	.020	—	—	—	—	—	0.920	—	—
20	—	1,200	0.01	4	2	.003	.002	.005	—	—	—	—	—	0.015	—	—

*NUMBERS IN PARENTHESES INDICATE EARLIER EXAMPLES TO BE REFERENCED FOR COMPARISON

more pronounced when s is reduced because service time (Ts)—as well as utilization—increases so rapidly.

Changing to full duplex

All lines considered so far have been on half-duplex operation. A full-duplex line is simulated in Examples 12 and 13. Here input and output transmissions go in separate directions to separate servers (the two-way line) and are therefore separately modeled. Controller-delay-plus-response time (Tc) is included only once—on the input side. The lengths of both input message (65 characters) and output message (150 characters) are entered as Li in these two examples. Cumulative system waiting time (0.298 seconds) and response time (1.677 seconds) are found by adding the input (Example 12) and output (Example 13) transmission results.

With the input parameters specified, full-duplex operation shows a marked improvement when compared with the half-duplex operation of Example 7; response time (Tr) is reduced from 8.379 to 1.677 seconds when Example 7's parameters are put onto a full-duplex line; in general, however, better performance must be weighed against the extra cost of converting from half-duplex to full-duplex operation.

Holding the line

Multidrop communications networks may be designed so that the computer holds the line after receiving an input message. This makes certain that the line is immediately available for the corresponding output, and so sometimes shortens response time. Otherwise, when the computer is ready to transmit this output message, it may find the line already tied up in servicing succeeding input or preceding output messages.

Holding the line can help or hurt performance. It takes less time to exercise the model than to experiment with the actual equipment. Example 14 uses the input parameters for Example 1, modifying them so that the line server is captured for both the total transmission and Tc:

$$Tc \text{ (modified)} = 0$$
$$Lo \text{ (modified)} = 0$$
$$\begin{aligned} Li \text{ (modified)} &= Li + Lo + (s \times Tc) \\ &= 65 + 150 + (1{,}200 \times 1.2) \\ &= 1{,}655 \text{ characters} \end{aligned}$$

The table shows that Example 14 has in fact a longer response time than Example 1. The lesson to be learned is that line holding by the host computer should be attempted only when unmodified Tc is less than unmodified Ts — which is not the case in Example 1, on which Example 14 is based.

Varying message priority

Classes of transactions with different priority levels can also be evaluated. On half-duplex lines, the model assumes that each transaction's input and output messages have the same priority. In full-duplex operation, however, different priorities may be assigned to a transaction's inputs and outputs.

Suppose that transactions in Example 3 have highest priority. They consume the first 35.8% ($U = 0.358$) of the 1,200 character-per-second line capacity, or 430 characters. If transactions in Example 15 are ranked next in priority, what remains to them is:

$$\begin{aligned} s \text{ (Example 15)} &= 1{,}200 \ (1.000 - 0.358) \\ &= 770 \text{ characters per second} \end{aligned}$$

Priority assignments are reversed in Examples 16 and 17. The full 1,200 characters per second is available to the high priority transactions in Example 16, leaving 464 characters per second for the lower priority transactions in Example 17:

$$\begin{aligned} s \text{ (Example 17)} &= 1{,}200 \ (1.000 - 0.613) \\ &= 464 \text{ characters per second} \end{aligned}$$

These results are not exact, however, because a preemptive priority is assumed that seldom happens in reality. Accuracy is best when high priority messages are kept shorter than those with lower priority (fortunately, this is usually the case) or when line utilization arising from high priority messages is low.

Example 18 assigns equal priority levels to the two classes of transaction used in Examples 3 and 15, and in Examples 16 and 17. The total arrival rate is:

$$\begin{aligned} \lambda \text{(Example 18)} &= \lambda \text{(Example 16)} + \lambda \text{(Example 17)} \\ &= 23.0 + 2.0 \\ &= 25.0 \text{ transactions per second} \end{aligned}$$

Li, Lo, and Tc are merged averages weighted according to the two arrival rates:

$$Li \text{ (Example 18)} = \frac{(7 \times 23.0) + (65 \times 2.0)}{23.0 + 2.0}$$
$$= 12 \text{ characters}$$

$$Lo \text{ (Example 18)} = \frac{(25 \times 23.0) + (150 \times 2.0)}{23.0 + 2.0}$$
$$= 35 \text{ characters}$$

$$Tc \text{ (Example 18)} = \frac{(0.5 \times 23.0) + (1.2 \times 2.0)}{23.0 + 2.0}$$
$$= 0.6 \text{ seconds}$$

Varying polling rate

Until now, only line contention and queuing have been considered, and so any polling time has been assumed to be smaller than transaction transmission time (Ts) and has been disregarded. If this is not the case, transaction response time (Tr) is dependent on the line turnaround time of polling messages.

The model itself can be used to determine when polling may be ignored, and when it increases response time. Using the number of polling characters as Lo and Li (or vice versa), the resulting Tr is the total time of an unsuccessful poll of one terminal. Then a conservative estimate of the average waiting time for a poll can be computed as follows:

$$\text{Average wait for a poll} = (M\text{-}1)/2 \times Tr$$

where M is the number of drops on the line.

Example 19 represents rollcall polling, with both the polling list and line protocol under software control. Assuming $M = 10$:

$$\begin{aligned} \text{Average wait for a poll} &= (10\text{-}1)/2 \times (0.92) \\ &= 4.14 \text{ seconds} \end{aligned}$$

Such a lengthy polling time obviously cannot be tolerated, and arises because Tc, and therefore Tr, are too long for communications purposes.

In Example 20, Tc and Tr have been reduced by means of an autopolling control unit or by hub polling. Here:

$$\begin{aligned} \text{Average wait for a poll} &= (10\text{-}1)/2 \times (0.015) \\ &= 0.07 \text{ seconds} \end{aligned}$$

which is consistent with the specifications required of inquiry/response and message-switching systems. ■

Bibliography

1. Thananitayaudom, T., *Communication system analysis and design using nomographs*, Report No. TR 21.566, IBM System Development Division, Kingston, N.Y. Oct. 17, 1974.
2. Martin, James, *Systems analysis for data transmission*, New York, Prentice-Hall, 1972 (ch. 36 and 37, pp. 553-640).
3. Held, Gilbert, *Sharing the line: a cheaper way than multiplexing*, DATA COMMUNICATIONS, March 1977, pp. 79-87.

Modems are capable machines, but where are they going?

Glenn Hartwig, Data Communications

Modem makers are split by two issues: some cite future uses of micros or LSI; others point to impact of DDS

By the time 1980 rolls around, some modem makers might be well on the way to making themselves invisible. The big push today, and for the near term future, is to make modems smaller, integrate them with data communications equipment, and at the same time give them vastly greater capabilities in the areas of self diagnostics, line diagnostics, and remote diagnostics through the use of microprocessor technology. Some modem makers are diversifying, with the idea of keeping modems only as a sideline product if AT&T's DDS network becomes widely accepted.

In both low-speed and high-speed modems, the trend toward minimizing the presence of the modem as a device separate from the terminal or the front-end processor is manifest among almost all large modem makers. Microprocessors and/or LSI chips on printed circuit boards are spurring this development. Looking farther down the road, several industry spokesmen acknowledged that their companies are already looking toward diversification as the only way to stay alive. Seldom, if ever, has there been such an apparent push on the part of an industry to see itself become an anachronism. William Myers, vice president of marketing for Prentice Corp., notes that the standard modem of today will continue to exist in some applications just as the punch card exists in data processing even

though tape and disk media are more efficient. The holdouts in data communications will be fewer, however, since the investment in new technology will be less expensive and will be more actively pushed by the terminal and front-end manufacturers.

To Charles Johnson, president of General Data-Comm Industries Inc., there is at least one gigantic flaw in this line of thinking. Says he, "The network dictates the technology, not the terminal." He feels that integrated modems are too limited in their ability to adjust to different speeds and protocols. "In the data communications industry, rapid change is disaster," he stated. "Once you build a terminal with an integrated modem, what's it going to talk to?"

Frank Lezotte, technical systems specialist for Intertel Inc., believes microprocessors expand the reliability of the modem by doing its housekeeping functions. Handling remote and local machine diagnostics and line diagnostic chores are where microprocessors really excel, he says. LSI chips have been used in place of microprocessors for diagnostics and to allow a single modem to do the work of two by giving the modem the ability to recognize more than one speed on inbound circuits. The use of an LSI chip instead of microprocessors is bound to be a short-lived experiment, said Lezotte. For one thing, "LSI gives you one shot to do your best job. If you've forgotten anything in your original design, you're dead." While a microprocessor can be reprogrammed to include new capabilities, the LSI chip is 100 percent hard wired. If anything is overlooked, or if new capabilities are desired at a later date, the LSI chip must be completely redesigned, rebuilt, and retested. This process is said to be too time-consuming and too costly to provide an adequate return on investment for both chip and modem makers.

On the other hand, GDC's Johnson and Dick Liberman, engineering vice president at Penril Corp., assert that microprocessors are only really effective in modems that operate at speeds above 4.8 kbit/s. To Johnson, LSI technology is good and the chips are taking hard knocks only from those companies that don't have them. Says Liberman, "LSI-based modems can be designed to adapt to special customer requirements if those functions that can be customized are designed to be outside the chip."

More than that, Ralph Lowry, director of marketing, Codex Corp., states, "My firm belief is that LSI chips can give you an edge because they're customized." While LSI has the performance edge, he says, microprocessors provide flexibility when it comes to making changes. He also noted that micros require more power for operation than LSI chips. He sees a tradeoff in power versus flexibility and says "the industry will

"You won't see too much of the plain old modem company anymore"

see hybrid use of micros and LSI" as a means of taking advantage of the best of each device.

Although the Bell 212A—an LSI based modem—that can operate at either 300 bit/s or 1.2 kbit/s and the Vadic VA3400, a microprocessor-based modem that operates at 300, 600, or 1.2K bit/s, are being touted as significant advances, Lezotte says that both are limited because they only operate as frequency shift key (FSK) devices, and with 1.2 kbit/s as their top speed they are both too slow for advanced applications. In Lezotte's mind, what's needed are low-cost, high-speed, bipolar microprocessors for use in higher-speed modems. Says he, "That's where the future is."

The near term future of the modem industry will center around feature competition rather than price competition, in the opinion of several manufacturers. Modem makers say they have taken the price of their product down just about as far as they can and the competitive base of the future will be the wooing of the user in the areas of speed, diagnostics, and compatibility.

With the growing use of microprocessors and LSI chips, chip makers such as Texas Instruments could occupy an increasingly important place in the world of data communications. Speculating on a possible invasion of his field by such large companies as TI, Lezotte acknowledged that it has the money and the technological expertise to take over. However, Lezotte

and William Myers believe that none of the chip makers have the service capabilities that traditional modem companies have, and the low profit margin and the wide variety of modem types needed to build a full-service base would make modems an unappetizing area for the chip-making giants.

John Rilling, vice president and general manager, Rixon Inc. disagrees with this scenario. According to Rilling, as the end of the decade approaches, microprocessors will be 10 times faster than they are now. In 1980, with a million elements on a chip, and the cost of the chips continually going down, the whole device will be so cheap that everything will be made in-house by the big chip makers. Says Rilling, "By the time modems are miniaturized to the point where they can be put on one 5-by-9-inch card, that will be the end of the modem business."

Packaging
Another aspect of the smallness of microprocessors and LSI chips is that it opens the way for the increased use of rack-mounting techniques at both central and remote sites. With the advent of racks comes the possibility of giving all modems in a rack a common power supply, common logic, and common diagnostic capabilities. As far as Lezotte is concerned, rack mounting will be common only at central sites because only there would the number of modems be high enough to justify the space savings that are the chief quality of the rack-mount approach.

As far as Ralph Lowry is concerned, there will be "more and more rack mounting done in installations that have modems only up to 2.4 kbit/s." Above that speed modems often have such built-in extras as multiplexers. For that reason they are harder to place on a single board for multiple installations in a single box. To rack mount high-speed modems, "Users will have to give up performance options for the sake of space," he says, and this would result in "no cost savings" for modem clustering.

Dataphone digital service
The impact of digital networks could produce a serious drain on modem makers or provide a bonanza, depending on whom you talk to. While the 300 to 1.2K bit/s data communicators would not be adversely affected by digital networks "DDS is the way to go at high speeds," Lezotte said. He added that, if DDS should expand and become popular, "specialists who make only high-speed modems would cease to exist."

Others seem to take a similar view. Thomas McShane, head of product marketing for Vadic Corp., believes that by 1980 as many as 50 percent of all computer communications ports will operate at 1.2 kbit/s, as compared with only 5 percent in 1978. The advent of good, low-cost printer terminals and the low cost of DDS at this speed will make the new digital networks popular for anyone interested in cost effective, interactive communications. The implication is that the attraction of DDS for low- and medium-speed users could aid in the slow but steady destruction of modem makers in the high end of the market.

John Samiletti, vice president and director of commercial products, Tele-Dynamics, believes that DDS will increase business for modem makers in the low-speed market. Although high-speed trunk lines will no longer require modems in a DDS environment, low-speed, local access lines to the nearest DDS outlet will still be needed and low-speed modems will flourish. GDC's Johnson matter-of-factly states that "DDS will double the market for datasets." Here he refers specifically to short-haul modems.

George Grumbles, vice president of marketing, Universal Data Systems, agrees with Samiletti's assessment. He sees DDS as, "enhancing the low-speed market" by allowing more people to become involved in data communications. The relatively high expense of using a modem and standard analog transmission lines would be needed only to connect a user to the nearest DDS "hub."

Even on short-haul routes for low- to medium-speed transmission to the nearest DDS center, however, there is a problem. According to Rixon's Rilling, the digital service unit (DSU) is the only way to access the DDS network and the only way to access DDS through a DSU is through another DSU on the user's property, or by way of a Bell (or Bell compatible) modem. Rilling foresees an AT&T lock on both the network and all access routes to the network. While the total demise of the modem industry expected by Rixon lies far beyond the end of this decade, the company says it is already looking for new areas in which to diversify.

George Kushin, director of marketing at Racal-Milgo, sees the same problem with DDS access and notes that his company will try to get Bell to allow independent interconnection to the DDS network through independent DSUs. If Bell complies, or is forced to comply, "Milgo would get into the area in less than a year." Other areas may also be attractive for modem makers with an eye to the future. Says Kushin, "You won't see too much of the plain old modem company anymore."

Penril's Liberman believes that modem compatibility is not really a very big problem. Most of the independents now have Bell compatible conventional modems. He also notes that the application of the DSU is similar to that of a short-haul modem. This is an area in which Penril is heavily involved, and one that he says is very active at the present time.

Prentice's Myers believes that his company will easily be able to develop new products to compete in the whole area of digital networking. On the other hand, he believes his company's future may depend on involvement in other areas of data communications. He mentioned his company's interest in multiplexing and diagnostics equipment as areas of future expansion.

Integral modems

While rack mounting will make modem installations smaller at central site locations, the modem at the remote site may altogether disappear from view. AT&T has announced that it will build modems into the terminals wherever possible — meaning that a single circuit board in the display or printer housing would eliminate the need for a separate space-consuming box.

Microprocessor and LSI technology would be directly responsible for shrinking modems down to PC-board size. AT&T, which has been successful with the LSI-based 212A multi-speed modem, has acknowledged the inflexibility of its unit and will go to a microprocessor-based small modem by 1980. In declaring that AT&T was premature in its commitment to LSI, Robert Hamer, product services marketing manager stated that "Bell will shortly drop its LSI orientation" and migrate to microprocessor technology.

On the question of modem integration, Racal-Milgo's Kushin sees the growth of user education as the key issue. "Users are becoming increasingly more sophisticated," he asserts. "They know more about prices and technical problems and are seeing the answer in integration." Not only will modems become incorporated in terminals, Kushin sees another aspect to growing user knowledgeability. "User sophistication is such that they can demand integrated networking systems (modems and diagnostic capabilities) from their vendors. Vendors who don't comply with these demands will experience a decline over the next few years," is his considered opinion.

Networking integration was also the subject of a comment by John Samiletti of Tele-Dynamics. It is his company's belief that a data communications network, "must be excellent and must have great diagnostics." In announcing a new area of expansion for his company, Samiletti declared, "Tele-Dynamics will provide a Codex- or Milgo-like network manager within the next two years. Within five years, Tele-Dynamics will carry the process a step farther and provide the network management system with its own minicomputer CPU power."

Universal Data Systems' George Grumbles sees the

"DDS will double the market for datasets"

"modem within the terminal" as a product that has been slow in coming and one that will not cut significantly into the "separate box" modem market. To him, the integral modem is strictly an OEM product designed to inflexible specifications. The integral modem in Grumbles' view is only going to be competitive in an end-user market where the users have a strict "hands off" policy toward their equipment. His final comment was, "The stand-alone modem will be used forever." Charles Johnson was more blunt. "Terminal and modem integration is a foolish idea. The whole concept doesn't make any sense when you realize that the modem will last at least twice as long as the terminal it's built into. The technology of the data communications industry is dictated by the network, not the terminal, and the modem is part of the network while the terminal is just the place where the network ends." When it comes to modems as separate boxes, "Our market will grow forever," is Johnson's determined and optimistic motto. ■

Interpreting SDLC throughput efficiency Part 1 —3 models

K.C. Traynham and R.F. Steen, IBM Corp., Research Triangle Park, N.C.

Three variations of SDLC are examined to see how they perform on several kinds of terrestrial and satellite links

Modern communications protocols, such as IBM's synchronous data link control (SDLC) and its variations, offer the prospect of improved network performance compared with older protocols. However, actual throughput efficiency depends on the best selection of a number of operating parameters, as well as on the error characteristics and propagation delay inherent in several alternative transmission links. The parameters and operating factors are so interrelated and complex that it is usually not wise to jump to conclusions about protocol performance.

What's needed, instead, is a clear understanding of SDLC operation and its performance under various operating conditions. To this end, three models are presented here, one for each of three possible variations and extensions of SDLC, which can be used to calculate throughput efficiency. Part 2 of this article, to be published next month, will analyze performance curves obtained by using these models.

The objects here are to present mathematical models which can be used to calculate batch throughput efficiency for various data link control (DLC) procedures and to use the models to study the efficiency of the IBM synchronous data link control and some hypothetical extensions to SDLC.

Throughput efficiency is the ratio of the time spent

transmitting original information bytes to the time spent transmitting all bytes, plus any time during which information cannot be transmitted. Original information bytes are bytes in the DLC information field, excluding those bytes retransmitted due to errors. "All bytes" refers to the total: information, control, and error recovery. Here, a byte is eight serial bits. Efficiency is measured in one direction only.

The models apply to steady-state batch transmission between two stations, so the link is assumed to be point-to-point. Both full- and half-duplex protocols are modeled, and five transmission links are considered. The terrestrial analog link consists of traditional analog ground facilities, while the terrestrial digital link assumes end-to-end digital transmission. The satellite link consists of only a satellite connection between the endpoint terminals, that is, the endpoint terminals are very close to the satellite earth station, such that little propagation delay and few line errors are introduced in the terminal-to-earth station link. The terrestrial/satellite link is composed of a satellite link with terrestrial (either digital or analog) facilities connecting the satellite earth stations with the DLC endpoints, such that the terrestrial medium makes a significant contribution to link error rate. (Although the terrestrial/satellite link is composed of two transmission media, it is consid-

Throughput efficiency models

Half-duplex normal response or asynchronous response modes—

(A) $TE = [(SBS)(FBE_{avg} - 1)/(SBS + 6)] \Big/ \Big[AD_{avg} + (FBE_{avg} + NPF_{avg})\Big(1 + \dfrac{ISD}{M}\Big) \Big]$

Full-duplex normal response mode—

(B) $TE = [(SBS)(FBE_{avg} - 1)/(SBS + 6)] \Big/ \Big[AD_{avg} + (FBE_{avg} + NPF_{avg})\Big(1 + \dfrac{ISD}{M+1}\Big) \Big]$

Full-duplex asynchronous response mode—

(C) $TE = [(SBS)(FBE_{avg} - 1)/(SBS + 6)] \Big/ \Big[AD + (FBE_{avg} + NPF)\Big(1 + \dfrac{ISD}{M}\Big) \Big]$

In Model A:

$$NPF_{avg} = \frac{M^2 + M - 2}{2M}$$

$$AD_{avg} = \frac{TOO}{M}$$

In Model B:
The values of NPF_{avg} and AD_{avg} depend on which of the three possible frame configurations (as illustrated in Figures 3, 4, and 5) applies.

Figure 3:

$$NPF_{avg} = 1.5 \times MPL - 2.5 + \frac{M \min r \,[TOF + MPL]}{MPL}$$

$$AD_{avg} = 0 \max r \left[\frac{TOF + MPL - M}{MPL} \right]$$

where r [ ] is defined to give the next integer greater than or equal to [ ], and max and min refer to the maximum and minimum functions (i.e., the larger "max" or smaller "min" of the two operands).

$$MPL = r \left[1 + \frac{(RTD \times BR/8) + 6}{SBS + 6} \right]$$

Figure 4:

$$NPF_{avg} = (M/2) - \frac{2 + MPL \times (MPL - M - 1)}{M + 1}$$

$$AD_{avg} = \frac{TOO + 0 \max (TOF + 1 - MPL)}{M + 1}$$

Figure 5:

$$NPF_{avg} = \frac{M^2 + 3M - 4}{2(M + 1)}$$

$$AD_{avg} = \frac{2 \times TOO}{M + 1}$$

In Model C:

$$NPF = (M - 1)\min r \left[1 + \frac{(RTD)(BR/8) + 6}{(SBS + 6)} \right]$$

where r [ ] is defined to give the next integer greater than or equal to [ ], while the min (minimum) function results in the lesser of its operands, so that NPF cannot be greater than $M - 1$ sender frames.

$AD = 0$	when $-1 \geq D$
$AD = 1 + D$	$0 \geq D > -1$
$AD = 1$	$D > 0$

where $D = \dfrac{(RTD)(BR/8) + 6 - (M - 1)(SBS + 6)}{(SBS + 6)}$

In all three models

$$FBE_{avg} = \frac{1}{[1 - (1 - BER) \exp 8 (SBS + 6)]}$$

where exp is the exponentiation function and BER is the long-term average of erroneous bits per transmitted bit. It is assumed that bit errors occur independently, a worst-case assumption.

---

ered to be a single link because such DLC functions as error checking and frame formatting are performed only at its endpoints.)

Each link is characterized by its bit error rate (BER) and round trip delay (RTD). Bit error rate is the long-term average of bit errors per bit transmitted, and round trip delay is defined to be the amount of time between the last bit of a given DLC frame (block) being transmitted and the first bit of its response being received at the sender. Along with signal propagation time, round trip delay includes the time necessary to generate and transmit a line-control response at the receiving end, as well as any delay in equipment between the endpoints. The basic models are written to allow the use of any error model, but the results described here assume simple error independence.

The models assume that a "Sender" desires to continuously transmit frames of SBS + 6 bytes to a "Receiver" which responds with six-byte control (no information field) frames, where SBS is the sender block size and the additional six bytes are SDLC frame overhead. Both Sender and Receiver transmit at BR (link

1 Half-duplex mode

Without errors. *An error-free sequence under the half-duplex mode in SDLC shows the Sender's transmitted frames (line SX) and the frames received by the Sender* *(line SR). After one round trip delay, the Sender's poll bit (labeled P) is acknowledged by the Receiver. The frame labeled 7F indicates frames 1—7 have been received.*

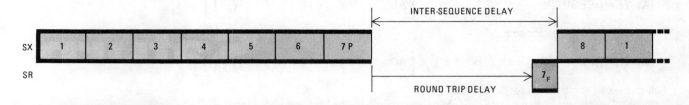

bit rate) bits per second. The DLC sequence number modulus architecturally limits the number of frames which a Sender can transmit before receiving a response, but the number of line buffers in the sending SDLC endpoint usually imposes a stricter limit. Each

Glossary

AD	Additional delay
ARM	Asynchronous response mode
ATF	Acknowledgement time in frames
BER	Bit error rate
BR	Link bit rate
DLC	Data link control
F	Final bit
FBE	Frames between errors
FDX	Full duplex
HDX	Half duplex
ISD	Inter-sequence delay
M	Maxout
MPL	Poll cycle length
NPF	Non-productive frames
NRM	Normal response mode
P	Poll bit
RTD	Round trip delay
SBS	Sender block size
SDLC	Synchronous data link control
TD	Total delay
TE	Throughput efficiency
TO	Timeout
TOF	Timeout in frames
TOO	Timeout overlap
TOS	Timeout in seconds

DLC endpoint has a characteristic maximum outstanding frames, or maxout, parameter, M, which is the number of frames that may be transmitted before receiving a response. M is usually determined by the number of frames of line buffering available, because each unacknowledged frame must be saved for possible error-correcting retransmission.

Throughput efficiency calculation

Throughput efficiency is the ratio of original information transmission time to total session time. Original information includes bytes in the DLC information field which are not retransmitted due to errors, while session time includes all time in which any information frames are being transmitted (either original or retransmissions), as well as time when nothing can be transmitted due to a maxout limitation in the Sender.

In any stream of frames, bit errors occur randomly. If a frame contains one or more bit errors, then that frame is erroneous and must be retransmitted. Here, the number of frames between (and including) an erroneous frame and the frame before the next successive erroneous one is denoted by the random variable FBE (frames between errors). The number of original information bytes in one such cycle (called an error cycle) is given by sender block size times one less than frames between errors:

$$SBS(FBE-1)$$

In SDLC error recovery, some frames are not "seen" at the receiver. These frames are called non-productive and their number is given by NPF. Thus, the number

2 Half-duplex error recovery

An error hits. *Frame 4 in the Sender's transmission contains and error. In HDX SDLC, the response the Sender will receive after one round trip delay is a request to* *retransmit frame 4 and the following frames. The Sender then will begin retransmission (frames 4′ and 5′ etc.). F in the response frame indicates "final"—no other response.*

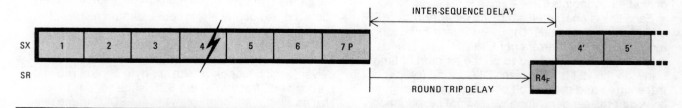

3 Full-duplex, no inter-sequence delay

Delay disappears. *In the full-duplex (NRM) mode with this short round trip delay, the Sender will receive an acknowledgement after he has transmitted only four frames. He must insert a poll bit in frame 5 in order to receive an acknowledgement of the transmitted frames 2 through 5. Note that two round trip delay periods occur.*

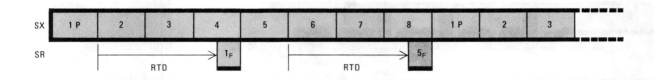

of byte-times consumed by an error cycle is given by sender block size plus six, times the frames between errors plus non-productive frames plus total delay:

$$(SBS + 6)(FBE + NPF + TD)$$

where NPF is a random variable giving the number of non-productive frames and TD is a random variable expressing the amount of delay (i.e., the time in which nothing can be transmitted) in the error cycle. Since FBE, NPF, and TD are random variables, the reported throughput efficiency figures are derived from the average number of original information bytes in an error cycle divided by the average number of total byte-times in an error cycle. Using the term avg to represent average values of random variables, the general model for throughput efficiency is:

$$TE = \frac{SBS\,(FBE_{avg} - 1)}{(SBS + 6)(FBE_{avg} + NPF_{avg} + TD_{avg})}$$

Synchronous data link control

The operation of IBM's synchronous data link control (SDLC) in its normal response mode (NRM) and some hypothetical extensions are reviewed next. It should be remembered that SDLC is only an architecture; for implementation details, including descriptions of the subsets of SDLC which have been implemented, the reader should consult product descriptions. The protocols described below are general enough that either Sender or Receiver, as defined here, can be the SDLC primary station. SDLC is able to operate in either half- or full-duplex mode.

In half-duplex operation (HDX), link endpoints (terminal, CPU, multiplexer, etc.) cannot transmit and receive simultaneously. (This condition may be imposed either by link or equipment restrictions.) Accordingly, after transmitting M (maxout) frames, the HDX Sender must pause to await the Receiver's reply, which normally arrives after one round trip delay interval. The Mth frame in each transmission has the poll bit (P) set to 1, indicating to the Receiver its opportunity to transmit. When the Receiver has no data to transmit (as is the assumption here), it simply acknowledges receipt of the data, using one frame, with the final bit (F) set to 1, indicating the last frame transmitted in response to the poll.

This process is illustrated in Figure 1, a time-line diagram of frames as seen by the Sender. The line labeled SX depicts frames transmitted by the Sender, while the line labeled SR indicates frames received. All time-line diagrams in this article assume a maxout of seven, and a sequence number modulus of eight. (Even though maxout is a property of the link endpoint, it cannot be greater than one less than the SDLC sequence number modulus.) For simplicity, these diagrams show responding frames to have the same number as the corresponding Sender frame. In SDLC, however, the response number is actually one greater than the corresponding Sender number. Likewise, SDLC frames are actually numbered from zero, but zero is not used in these diagrams.

Figure 1 shows half-duplex SDLC operation without line errors. When errors occur, the frame containing the error and any subsequently-transmitted frames

4 Full-duplex, with inter-sequence delay (ISD)

ISD returns. *In full-duplex SDLC with this intersequence delay, the Sender will receive a response after seven frames have been transmitted. He must insert a poll bit in the eighth frame to receive a response, but the round trip delay causes another intersequence delay before the response is received. The Sender can then retransmit.*

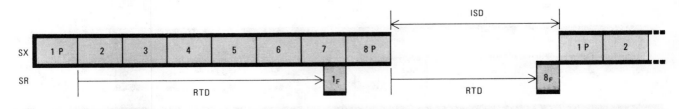

5 Full-duplex, with RTD longer than maxout

Longer delay. *When round trip delay is long relative to maxout, the Sender will receive the first acknowledgement some time after frame 7 has been transmitted. He must again insert a poll bit in frame 8 to receive a response, but the acknowledgment will not be received until after the longer round trip delay time has elapsed.*

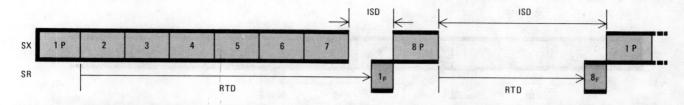

must be retransmitted, as illustrated in Figure 2. Frame 4 in Figure 2 contains one or more bit errors so that the Receiver will not "see" Frame 4 (erroneous frames are discarded in SDLC). When the Receiver gets an error-free frame with an out-of-sequence number (e.g., Frame 5 in Figure 2), it will require the Sender to retransmit the first missed frame, plus any subsequent frames, by sending a reject response (denoted by R in the diagrams). Upon receiving the reject frame, the Sender finishes any in-progress frame and begins the retransmission. For error-correction purposes, this article assumes that a correct frame always follows an incorrect one; SDLC, however, does not store out-of-sequence frames, so any frames arriving at the Receiver between an erroneous frame and its retransmitted correction are discarded.

All lost frames are not detected by out-of-sequence conditions. For example, if the last frame in a sequence of frames is hit, the Receiver will not see the frame (or the poll bit) and thus will not respond. Likewise, if the Receiver's reply is hit, the Sender will not see a response. These errors are corrected by Sender timeout. Each time the Sender transmits a poll frame, it initiates a timeout clock which runs for a predetermined interval. If the interval expires without a response being received, the Sender must take corrective action. Several courses are possible, but here it is assumed that the Sender retransmits all outstanding (i.e., unacknowledged) frames. In the half duplex mode, then, if a poll frame is erroneous, the entire M-frame sequence is retransmitted after a predetermined timeout. (This article assumes response frames are error-free.)

In half-duplex SDLC, then, the number of frames retransmitted due to one erroneous frame depends on the position of the erroneous frame in the M-frame sequence. For example, if the first frame in the sequence is in error, then all M frames are retransmitted; if the second frame is hit (and the first is not) then M-1 frames are re-sent. If the next to last or (M-1)st frame is hit, only two frames are retransmitted, but if the last frame (the one containing the poll) is hit, the entire sequence is retransmitted, according to the assumption described earlier.

Figures 1 and 2 show that there is always a period in half-duplex SDLC during which nothing can be transmitted. This time is called inter-sequence delay and consists of the time required for the last Sender frame to reach the Receiver, for a response to be generated at the Receiver, and for the response to reach the Sender. This interruption is normally the major reason for inefficiency in half-duplex protocols. In full-duplex operation there are methods to reduce and even eliminate this delay.

Using full-duplex SDLC, endpoints may transmit and receive simultaneously, thereby possibly avoiding the inter-sequence delay problem described earlier. Figure 3 shows a full-duplex SDLC exchange in which inter-sequence delay has been reduced to zero. Because full-duplex terminals may overlap transmission and reception, the assumed polling strategy is that polls are transmitted as soon as possible, so that there is a greater possibility of avoiding inter-sequence delay. However, SDLC requires that a poll not be issued to a given station until the previous poll to that station is

6 Full-duplex asynchronous response mode

No polls. *In full-duplex asynchronous response mode, the acknowledgements from the Receiver will begin after one round trip delay period. From then on, the Receiver will acknowledge each frame as it is received, so that the response will be received regularly, delayed by one round trip delay period. No poll bits are required in this instance.*

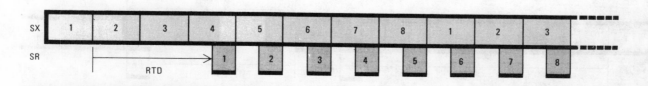

7 Full-duplex ARM error recovery

Errors not seen. *When an error hits frame 2 in asynchronous response mode, the Sender will receive an acknowledgement of frame 1 after one round trip delay. The error breaks the sequence and the next response the Sender receives is a request to retransmit frames 2 and following. The Sender does that and acknowledgments resume.*

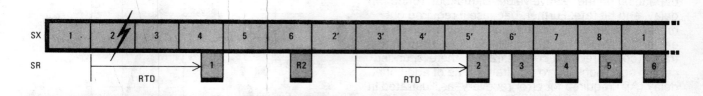

closed, either through receipt of an F bit or through expiration of a timeout. Thus, frames in full-duplex SDLC are acknowledged in groups (as shown in Figure 3) where the size of the group is determined by the magnitude of the round trip delay. Figure 3 illustrates full-duplex SDLC operating without inter-sequence gaps, but Figures 4 and 5 illustrate that full-duplex SDLC is susceptible to inter-sequence delay when RTD is increased, for example, by changing from a terrestrial to a satellite link. Figures 3, 4, and 5 also illustrate the three configurations in which frames and delay periods may appear on a full-duplex SDLC link. From them, one can also see that the inter-sequence delay period could have been eliminated by increasing the maxout parameter of the sending endpoint.

Because of its collective-response nature, full-duplex protocol error recovery is similar to half duplex, except that transmission sequences are defined by the magnitude of round trip delay rather than maxout. The number of retransmitted frames depends on the position of an error within a transmission sequence, and the possibility of a poll frame's being hit means that timeouts must be considered.

So far, the article has dealt with a specific data link control, IBM's SDLC operating in its normal response mode, which has been implemented and is described in References 1, 2, and 3. The following describes hypothetical extensions to the existing data link control which allow more efficient transmission on some contemporary data links. Each of these hypothetical extensions is included in later mathematical analysis.

One way of compensating for long propagation de-

lays such as those found on satellite links is to allow more frames to be transmitted before a response is received. This capability is included in the models by allowing the maxout parameter to vary up to 127, rather than the limit of seven imposed by the SDLC sequence number modulus.

Asynchronous response mode

Because many satellite connections will appear as point-to-point links, and because it is possible to design a more efficient protocol if one eliminates the requirement for multipoint support (and thus the poll-final bit protocol), a point-to-point protocol known as asynchronous response mode (ARM) has been hypothesized. The ARM protocol eliminates the requirement that a secondary station wait for a poll before transmitting so that, in ARM, a secondary may transmit whenever the need arises. Within the unidirectional data restriction imposed in this article, a full-duplex ARM exchange appears as shown in Figure 6. Note that each data frame is acknowledged individually, rather than collectively as in the two protocols described earlier. This allows, in general, a quicker response from the Receiver and, therefore, less susceptibility to inter-sequence delay.

Figure 7 illustrates full-duplex ARM error recovery. As before, the Receiver does not "see" the errored frame; rather, it realizes that a frame has been lost when it receives a correct, but apparently out-of-sequence, frame. Since it is assumed here that all erroneous frames are followed by correct frames, the time between transmission of an erroneous frame and re-

8 Additional delay (AD) in FDX ARM error recovery

With longer RTD. *When the round trip delay is longer, and frame 2 is hit by an error, an additional delay will be incurred. After the additional delay, the Sender will receive a request to retransmit frames 2 and following. The Sender begins this sequence in frames 2′ and 3′. The error recovery has been slowed by the length of the RTD.*

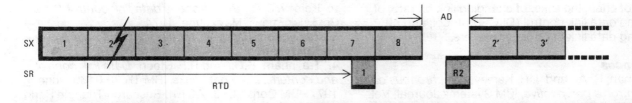

ceipt of the reject frame (asking for retransmission) is exactly calculable. For this reason, the number of frames retransmitted due to a single erroneous frame is also calculable (as compared with previously discussed protocols).

ARM is also susceptible to inter-sequence delay, depending on the relative values of maxout, round trip delay, and bit rate. Further, because it required one more frame-time (according to the assumption given earlier) for the Sender to be notified of an erroneous frame (compared to a correct frame), there is, under certain conditions, up to one frame-time of additional delay (AD) required for error recovery, as illustrated in Figure 8.

Both asynchronous response mode and the SDLC normal response (NRM) mode may operate either full or half duplex. However, from the point of view of this article, ARM and NRM perform equally in half duplex. This leaves three different protocols whose performance will be analyzed: full-duplex asynchronous response mode (FDX ARM), full-duplex normal response mode (FDX NRM), and half duplex (HDX).

Throughput efficiency equations are presented for each protocol in terms of the link parameters round trip delay (RTD), bit error rate (BER), and link bit rate (BR); and the endpoint parameters frame size (SBS), maxout (M), and timeout (TOF). The only relationship between the two classes of parameters is that timeout must be somewhat larger than the longest anticipated round trip delay. The throughput efficiency equations for the three protocols are contained in the panel "Throughput efficiency models." For a more complete treatment of the efficiency equations, the reader can obtain Reference 4 from the authors.

The second part of this article, to be published next month, will show the results of using these throughput efficiency models for the three protocols over a wide range of parameters, and will analyze these results in terms of realistic opportunities for data communications planners.

To get a look ahead, though, Figure 9 shows the general shape of the throughput-efficiency curve obtained by plotting the models as a function of Sender block size. The shape of the curve remains unchanged from plot to plot of the models as functions of various operating parameters, but the position of the curves relative to the axes varies markedly.

The rising segment in Figure 9, governed primarily by delay characteristics, shifts upward for links with small delay and downward for links with long delay. Similarly, the falling segment is affected most by the error rate so as to shift the curve upward for low error rates and downward for high error rates.

To be discussed and illustrated next month are the effects of changing links, of changing link bit rate, of changing data link control (DLC) protocol, and of changing data link control parameters. ∎

References

1. Donnan, R. A., and J. R. Kersey, *Synchronous data link control, a perspective,* IBM Systems Journal, Vol. 13, No. 2, 1974.

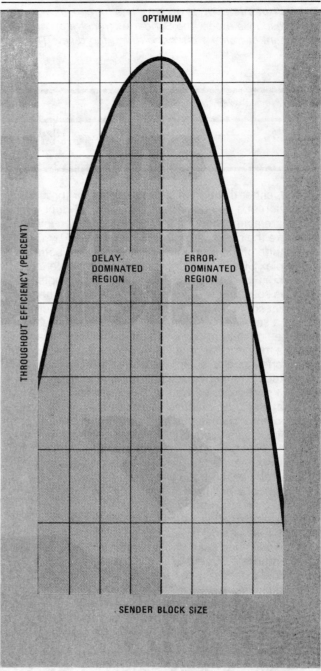

9   Typical throughput curve

OPTIMUM

THROUGHOUT EFFICIENCY (PERCENT)

DELAY-DOMINATED REGION

ERROR-DOMINATED REGION

SENDER BLOCK SIZE

The curves. *Although the general shape of the curves will remain unchanged, the curves' position relative to the axes will vary due to the variables affecting throughput.*

2. Kersey, J. R., *Synchronous data link control,* DATA COMMUNICATIONS, May/June, 1974.
3. IBM Corp., *IBM synchronous data link control General Information,* GA27-3093, March 1974.
4. Traynham, K.C., and R.F. Steen, *Data link control and contemporary data links,* IBM TR 29.0168, June 1977, IBM Corp. (E93/A010), Research Triangle Park, N.C. 27709.

Interpreting SDLC throughput efficiency Part 2—results

K.C. Traynham and R.F. Steen, IBM Corp., Research Triangle Park, N.C.

The three protocol models presented in Part 1 are used here to determine performance for varied links

Throughput efficiency of a data communications channel is determined by the kind of protocol employed, by a set of interrelated operating parameters, and by the characteristics of the transmission medium employed for the link. Part 1 of this article, published last month, presented throughput efficiency models for IBM's synchronous data link control (SDLC) operating full duplex in its normal response mode (NRM) for a hypothetical extension of SDLC called asynchronous response mode (ARM) also operating full duplex, and for half-duplex operation of both of these modes.

Now, the article continues with a description of five types of transmission links that may be used in practice, as well as a detailed analysis of the results obtained by exercising the models over a wide range of operating parameters. Each communications link is roughly characterized by its bit error rate (BER) and round trip delay (RTD).

The terrestrial analog link is the traditional voice-oriented communication facility. In this article, it is assumed to have a BER of 10^{-5} errors per transmitted bit and a near-worst-case RTD of 100 millisec. The delay value is taken from Bell System Technical Reference, PUB 41004, October 1973.

The terrestrial digital link is oriented toward the data communications user. Exemplified by AT&T's Data-phone digital service (DDS), the terrestrial digital link is assumed to have a BER of 10^{-7} and a near-worst-case RTD of 150 millisec. The delay value is given in Bell System Data Communications Technical Reference, PUB 41022, September 1974.

When SDLC terminals are located very close to the satellite earth station, the characteristics of the satellite link are determined almost entirely by the characteristics of the satellite path: BER = 10^{-7} and RTD = 700 millisec. The typical round trip electrical propagation delay in a synchronous satellite path is 520 millisec., but additional delay is incurred in the earth station for forward-error-correction encoding/decoding, data compression, concentration, etc.

Most satellite users will require some kind of terrestrial link to connect the terminal to the satellite earth station. If analog tails are used, then the bit error rate may be more like that of the analog link (i.e., BER = 10^{-5}), but the tails will not be long enough to cause a significant increase in round trip delay, so RTD is assumed to remain at 700 millisec. Although this link is composed of more than one transmission medium, its characteristics are combined into those of a single link because the SDLC functions (error correction, etc.) are performed only at the endpoints of the link.

The satellite channel mentioned previously can be

123

9 Typical throughput curve

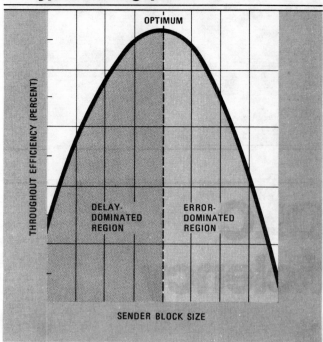

The curves. Although the general shape of the curves will remain unchanged, the curves' position relative to the axes will vary due to the variables affecting throughput.

10 Effect of changing links

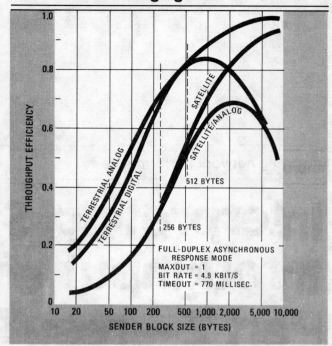

Changing links. Figures 10 and 11 differ only in maxout. Here, at a maxout of 1, all curves are rising at 256 bytes, so the shortest delay terrestrial links are more efficient.

improved by using higher-quality terrestrial digital links for the terrestrial tails so that BER is 10^{-7} and RTD remains 700 millisec. Again, the tails will not be long enough to have significant impact on RTD.

Model results
Results are presented as plots of throughput efficiency versus Sender block size. In each plot, the independent variable, Sender block size, takes values of 16, 32, 64, 128, 256, 512, 1,024, 2,048, 4,096 and 8,192 bytes. The general shape of the curves, illustrated in Figure 9, remain unchanged from plot to plot, but the position of the curves relative to the axes varies markedly. (Figures 1 through 8 appeared in Part 1. Figure 9 was previewed there.) The rising segment, governed primarily by delay characteristics, shifts upward for links with small delay and downward for links of long delay. Similarly, the falling segment is affected most strongly by the error rate so as to shift the curve upward for low error rates and downward for high error rates.

Of interest here are the effects of changing links, of changing link bit rate (BR), of changing data link control (DLC) protocol, and of changing DLC parameters.

Effect of changing links
Studying the effect of changing links is useful since it indicates what will happen to throughput in batch environments when one kind of link is substituted for another. For example, a user may wish to install a satellite link or a terrestrial digital link as a replacement for an existing terrestrial analog facility. The five types of links

which are considered are discussed in the preceding section. Figures 10 and 11 compare these links in full-duplex asynchronous response mode at 4.8 kbit/s. They differ only in maxout: Figure 10 uses a maxout of one, while Figure 11 allows a maxout of seven.

In Figure 10, typical frame lengths for synchronous data terminals (256 or 512 bytes) are marked with vertical lines. All four curves are rising sharply at 256 bytes and, therefore, are influenced primarily by round trip delay at that point. For that reason, the greatest efficiency is afforded by the terrestrial analog link which has the shortest delay and has a 74 percent efficiency. Next in delay, and thus in efficiency, is the terrestrial digital link which has a 72 percent efficiency. Finally, all satellite links coincide at 256 bytes with a 36 percent efficiency.

Predictably, links with smaller delays have better performance in the delay-dominated region, while links with smaller error rates fare better in the error-dominated region. To compensate for long delays, SDLC allows more than one frame to be outstanding at one time, as governed by the maxout parameter. Figure 11 illustrates improvement which may be obtained by using multiple outstanding frames. With maxout = 7, the pure satellite and satellite-with-digital-tails links have advanced to 96 percent efficiency with 256-byte frames. Because of the increased maxout, all curves in Figure 11 peak sooner than their Figure 10 counterparts. For this reason, the 256-byte design point is close to optimum for most links under these conditions. However, Figure 11 also shows that high-error rate

11 Effect of changing links

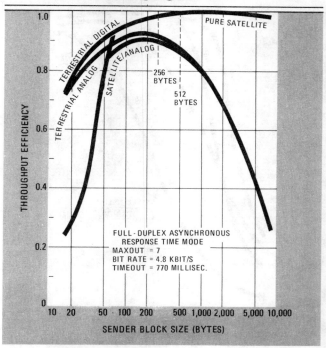

Maxout increase. *Improvement by increasing the maxout to 7 can be seen in all links. Satellite links can be seen to have advanced above 90 percent efficiency in this case.*

12 Effect of changing bit rate

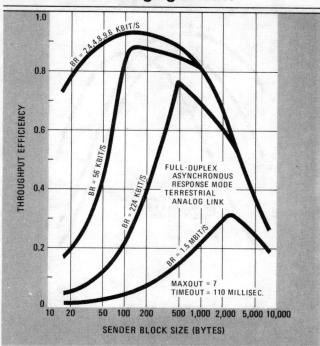

Bit rate effect. *The increase in bit rate can be seen to decrease efficiency and move the curve to the right. Curves coincide in error-dominated portions of the graph.*

links (terrestrial analog and satellite with terrestrial analog tails) begin to fall off sooner in the high-error region than do the same curves with maxout = 1. This is a complex effect which is described in detail later.

Effect of link bit rate
Figure 12 illustrates the effect of changing link bit rate among several values between 2.4 kbit/s and 1.5 Mbit/s on a full-duplex ARM terrestrial analog link. The effect of increasing bit rates is to decrease peak efficiency and move it to the right because less time is being used for actual data transmission, while total time remains almost unchanged. Thus, the curves are similar to curves of increased delay, but they coincide when errors become the driving force on the falling portion of the curve. The 1.5 Mbit/s curve peaks at 30 percent, indicating that maxout = 7 is not sufficient on extremely high-speed terrestrial analog links.

Effect of DLC protocols
Figures 13 and 14 compare the throughput efficiency of the three protocols. In both figures, the bit rate is 4.8 kbit/s, but in Figure 14 a satellite link has been substituted for the terrestrial analog link of Figure 13. The curves coincide for all three protocols when maxout = 1, because in any protocol with maxout = 1 operation is basically half duplex in that the Sender may transmit only one frame, then must wait for a reply. (For this reason, there is no advantage in using full-duplex protocols when maxout is limited to 1.)

In Figure 13, both full-duplex (FDX) protocols are

superior to half duplex (HDX) when maxout = 7, but, for large frames ($\geq$ 500 bytes), the maxout = 7 curves exceed both FDX maxout = 7 and HDX maxout = 7 curves, despite the fact that the FDX and HDX maxout = 7 curves maintain their intuitive relationship. When operating in a terrestrial environment with short delays, the timeout values can be carefully tuned as they have been for the results in Figure 13, where they are set for 10 percent above the terrestrial round trip delay of 100 millisec. Thus, when the maxout is limited to 1, an erroneous frame will be retransmitted 110 millisec. (equal to 33 byte-times at 2.4 kbit/s) after the last SDLC flag has been sent. On the other hand, with HDX maxout = 7, a first frame which is in error will not be retransmitted until all seven frames in the sequence are sent and a round trip delay interval has passed. Clearly, the recovery time for each error is not so great, since each error does not occur on the first frame, but it is always at least as great as the maxout = 1 case and the average is greater. As increasing frame length causes a greater number of frame errors, the increased recovery time overcomes the advantage of having multiple outstanding frames.

Similarly, the recovery time for an error on a FDX ARM link maxout = 7 transmission can exceed the maxout = 1 recovery time, but not to the extent of HDX maxout = 7. Consider again an error on the first frame in a segment. When the Receiver receives the second frame (presumed to be good) the out-of-sequence condition will cause a retransmission request for the first frame. This retransmission request cannot, how-

13 Effect of changing protocol, maxout

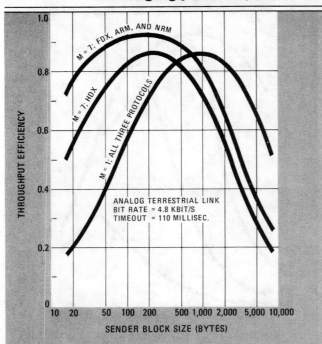

Protocols compared. *FDX ARM and NRM show better efficiency at a maxout of 7, but increasing frame length, which increases errors, overcomes the advantage gained.*

14 Effect of changing protocol, maxout

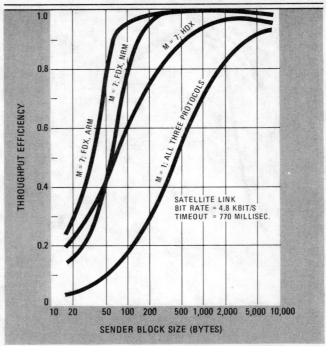

FDX ARM advantage. *With a satellite link substituted for the terrestrial analog link of Figure 13, FDX ARM can be seen to have advantages which didn't show previously.*

15 Effect of changing maxout

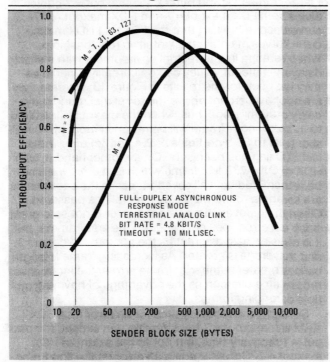

Maxout changes. *The effect of changing maxout from 1 to 3 on an FDX ARM terrestrial analog link can be seen to be significant. A further increase will yield no further gain.*

16 Effect of changing maxout

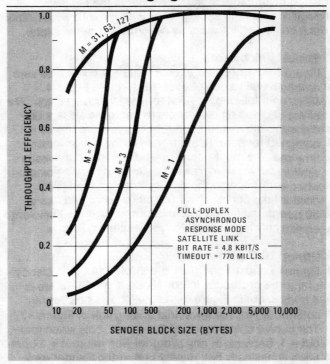

Satellite link. *The maxout changes used in Figure 16 are applied to a satellite link. Performance gains are rapid and, because of greater RTD, maxouts to 31 are useful.*

17 Effect of changing timeout

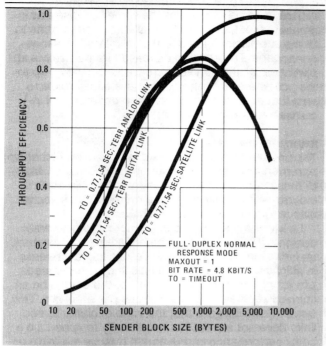

Timeout changes. *The effect of timeout on throughput efficiency is almost negligible in any real situation, but the effect would be somewhat greater at higher data speeds.*

18 Effect of bit error rate

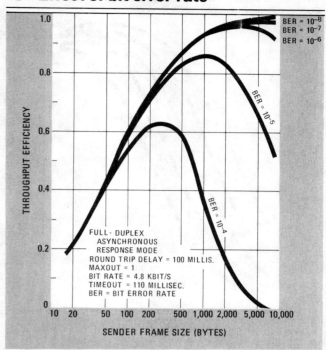

Beyond control. *Once a link has been put in service, the user has no control over bit error rate, which can be seen to have many debilitating effects on throughput efficiency.*

ever, be triggered until the second frame is received, which represents a delay of 600 bytes at the crossover point of the two FDX curves on the graph. In addition, at least 30 more byte-times, representing the propagation delay of 100 millisec., will pass before the retransmission takes place. Thus, the delay for retransmission at the crossover point is 630 bytes. Recall that the delay for the maxout = 1 case was about 33 bytes. Depending on the Sender's retransmission strategy, additional delay may accrue as the Sender waits for a frame being transmitted to be completed.

In Figure 13, the two full-duplex protocols had equal efficiency, but, in a long-delay environment, the advantage of FDX ARM over FDX NRM is evident, as illustrated in Figure 14 where the three protocols are compared at 4.8 kbit/s on a satellite link. (This discussion is limited to maxout = 7 since, as explained earlier, the FDX maxout = 1 cases correspond to HDX.) FDX ARM is the most efficient protocol over all frame sizes, but at short frame lengths (or with long RTD periods) HDX with maxout = 7 is more efficient than FDX NRM. If round trip delay is greater than the time required to transmit M frames, the FDX NRM Sender will have outstanding M frames with a poll bit set at 1 in the first frame, causing the Receiver to acknowledge the receipt of only the first frame. During the next poll cycle, the Sender can send only one frame, the (M + 1)th, with the poll bit causing an acknowledgement of frames through M + 1, such that only M + 1 frames are transmitted in every pair of poll cycles (Fig. 5).

Contrast this with HDX where 2M frames are trans-

mitted in each pair of poll cycles. As frame length increases, however, the advantage gained by overlap of responses with data overcomes this disadvantage and FDX NRM becomes more efficient than HFX—and remains so for all larger frames. If a different strategy is used, it may be possible to eliminate these low-end problems, but a strategy which does not adjust to delay or frame length may have deficiences in other parameter ranges.

Note that when information flows in the secondary-to-primary direction, the primary may respond to each frame. If this is the case, the efficiency is the same as in full-duplex asynchronous response mode.

Effect of changing DLC parameters.
Finally, a general discussion of the effect of changing maxout and timeout values follows. Figure 15 shows the effect of maxout on a FDX ARM terrestrial analog link at 4.8 kbit/s. A change of M from 1 to 3 creates a significant improvement over the operational portion of the curve. For example, at 256 bytes the efficiency improves from 76 percent to 92 percent. On the other hand, due to the well-tuned timeout and relatively high error rate, the error-dominated portion of the curve shows better performance for maxout = 1. Increasing the maxout beyond 3 to 7, 31, 63, or 127 yields no additional improvement on this link because the maxout of three allows enough frames to be available for transmission to eliminate the possibility of inter-sequence delay. Contrast this with Figure 16, which shows the same case for a satellite link. Performance

19 Effect of round trip delay

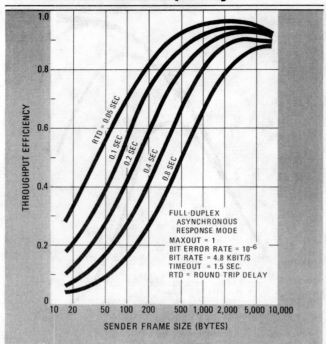

THROUGHPUT EFFICIENCY

RTD = 0.05 SEC
0.1 SEC
0.2 SEC
0.4 SEC
0.8 SEC

FULL-DUPLEX
ASYNCHRONOUS
RESPONSE MODE
MAXOUT = 1
BIT ERROR RATE = 10^{-6}
BIT RATE = 4.8 KBIT/S
TIMEOUT = 1.5 SEC.
RTD = ROUND TRIP DELAY

SENDER FRAME SIZE (BYTES)

Delay effect less. Increases in the round trip delay are not as debilitating as increases in BER. To achieve stability, networks should be designed for the delay region.

gain is rapid as maxout increases from 1 to 3 (60 percent at 256 bytes), and, because of the greater round trip delay, maxout values up to 31 are useful.

Under certain conditions additional maxout is a disadvantage in the error-sensitive region. Earlier, it was explained that half-duplex error recovery time may be less than the recovery time for full duplex. When errors are numerous, this leads to HDX efficiency being greater than FDX.

Large values of maxout may lead to significant efficiency degradations in half-duplex protocols. In half duplex, M (the maxout value) frames are transmitted contiguously and then acknowledged by one response frame. As one would expect, the mean value for non-productive frames (NPF) increases with M; thus one frame error in half duplex requires more frames to be retransmitted as maxout becomes larger. When errors are frequent, the larger number of retransmitted frames means that larger-maxout systems are penalized. This effect is not present in full duplex because, in the overlapped protocol, NPF is not strongly influenced by M, as can be seen from the NPF equations in the panel "Throughput efficiency models," contained in Part 1.

The effect of the timeout on the throughput efficiency is almost negligible in any real situation, as illustrated in Figure 17, where the performance loss due to a double-length timeout is no more than a couple of percentage points. There are other cases (higher speeds, for example) where the effect is greater, but these cases do not represent a desirable operational environment.

An implicit parameter of the models, and of the data

link control, is Sender frame (block) size. Although frame sizes are often constrained by application, an increase in frame size serves the same purpose as increased maxout, i.e. making available enough bits to fill the transmission pipe and thus eliminate inter-sequence gaps. The effect of increased frame size is apparent from all the curves: increased efficiency up to the point where larger frames are so susceptible to errors that efficiency begins to drop because of increased retransmissions.

Interpretation of results

The previous sections discussed in detail how changing parameters modify throughput on various links. Many of these changes have implications either directly or indirectly within other parts of a system. This section discusses some such implications.

Link bit rate is a parameter of interest to network designers. When other parameters are held constant, an increase in bit rate normally results in a decrease in efficiency. However, unless efficiency is reduced proportionally to the speed increase, there will be an increase in actual throughput in bits per second. The trend in tariff filings is that the price of higher speed links does not increase proportionally to speed, so a cost/performance improvement may be available using higher-speed links. The designer must consider, though, whether increased speed will overtax the communications processor or cause undue interference with other operations.

Throughput efficiency is acutely sensitive to maxout in both high-delay and high-error situations, but, on the other hand, the process is insensitive to timeout. Protocol changes are dramatic in long-delay cases, particularly when coupled with increased maxout. Careful selection of maxout and protocol may be the most effective way to obtain high-speed batch throughput over long-delay links. However, the designer must be aware that increasing maxout requires an increase in line buffering.

The parameters studied thus far are those over which the user has some control. Once a link has been put into service, though, the user has no control over the bit error rate (BER) or the round trip delay (RTD) parameters, which are important determinants of throughput efficiency, as seen in Figures 18 and 19. As long as the same link (or a similar one) remains in service, round trip delay will be fairly stable, but the frequency of bit errors may vary widely. Figure 18 shows that large drops in efficiency may occur due to increases in BER when a system is operating in the error-sensitive portion of the curve (or even near the optimum point.) To increase stability, a link should be designed to operate slightly into the delay-sensitive region of the curve. Figure 19 shows that increases in delay are not nearly so debilitating as BER increases. Moreover, the round trip delay values used here are near-worst-case values, so a design point to the left of the optimum will likely result in better-than-predicted performance. In most cases the peaks of the efficiency curves are broad enough so that adjusting parameters for stability reasons will affect efficiency only slightly. ■

Time, not throughput, for net designs part 1: techniques

Kenneth Brayer, The Mitre Corp., Bedford, Mass.

In contrast to a throughput network design scheme, a message delivery analysis permits fast message delivery on very high error rate channels

It has long been believed that there exists some magical optimum block length for data communications networks. This block length, it is said, cannot be traded off against any other design parameter—certainly not against network throughput. This is not true.

As opposed to the narrow inflexible designs which can be achieved with a throughput approach, a wide range of options is available if designers think in terms of speed of message delivery. In fact, it is possible to operate a data communications network successfully with retransmission rates as high as 80 percent. A delivery-time approach to network design reshapes the distribution curve of message delivery times and can form the basis for an entirely new view of network pricing and user charge-back schemes.

If users are willing to wait only a very short additional time for message delivery, or are able to tolerate a few more retransmissions than usual, significant communications saving can be passed on to them. Even a totally performance-minded user can achieve delivery speeds superior to those of a throughput-based system, at no increase in price. These pricing structures will be the subject of part two of this article, which will appear next month. Now, the task is to present the underlying mathematical analysis for those new designs based on the time-delivery concept.

In modern data communications networks, the error control technique of automatic repeat request (ARQ) is used to deliver (hopefully) error-free messages from a message source to a message sink. Typically, the messages are divided into information blocks, often called packets. To these blocks, header identification and error detection parity bits are added. The blocks are then transmitted over a communications channel and are tested for the existence of errors. If errors are detected, retransmission of those blocks in error is requested from the source. This process continues until all blocks are delivered correctly. Until now, the design of such networks has been directed toward describing system structure, selecting codes for achieving low undetected-error rates, and selecting the optimum block length.

Typically, this optimum block length has been selected on the basis of maximizing the efficiency of channel utilization (or throughput of data transmission). This approach has been more than adequate in the past, since the primary users of such systems have been military personnel interested in achieving extremely low undetected-error rates on dedicated circuits.

With the growth of commercial data communications it has become important to minimize operating costs by fully utilizing transmission circuits and equipment;

129

Design equation derived

Equation 1 is derived by letting P_R equal the probability that a block of length L is in error. Assuming that all blocks in error are detected and repeated by the ARQ system, P_R is also the probability of a retransmission.

There is a limit to the number of $(T_2 - T_1)/C$ retransmissions possible before the time to deliver the message is exceeded. The probability of successfully delivering a message composed of T_1 blocks within T_2 tries is the sum of the probabilities of i retransmissions (with i ranging from zero to $(T_2 - T_1)/C$) of incorrect blocks,

$$P_D(t \leq t_0) = \sum_{i=0}^{(T_2-T_1)/C} p(i),$$

where $p(i)$, = probability that i incorrect blocks are transmitted:

$$p(i) = \binom{T_1 + i - 1}{i} P_R^i (i - P_R)^{T_1}$$

Interpreting equation (1), $P_D(t \leq t_0)$ is the sum over all possible numbers of retransmissions ($1 = 0, 1, 2, \ldots, (T_2-T_1)/C$) of the probability of occurrence of blocks with no errors, $(1 - P_R)^{T_1}$, of which there must be a total of T_1, and the probability that i blocks are retransmitted is P_R^i. There are

$$\binom{T_1 + i - 1}{i}$$

ways of selecting the i retransmitted blocks, since the last block must be assumed to be correctly delivered in order to completely and correctly terminate the calculation.

---

simultaneously, it has become necessary to maximize the probability of successfully delivering a message in, at most, a specified time on a continuous basis, within the constraints of available channel capacities.

In contrast to designing networks which optimize throughput by fixing block length, it is possible to select block lengths by maximizing the probability of message delivery within a time constraint. This will achieve a more responsive data communications network than a selection approach which purports only to use the communications links most efficiently. In fact, large inefficiencies in link throughput have no impact on (or relationship to) message delivery performance. This is so because throughput is really only an average parameter, and the optimum value of an average is no optimum.

To design such a network, it is necessary to deal mathematically with the tail end of the probability function. Consider a network with messages divided into a finite number of fixed-length blocks, each containing information bits, overhead (address, etc.) bits, and error-detection parity bits. These blocks are continuously transmitted from message source to message sink without any interblock delays. On reception, the blocks are checked for errors and, for any block found

to be in error, a request for retransmission is issued according to its block number (a portion of the block information content). The retransmitted block is inserted as soon as possible in the data stream going from message source to message sink. However, no block in transmission is terminated in order to allow insertion.

ADCCP format

Since modern networks involve computer-to-computer communications with large amounts of high-speed storage (core or semiconductor) and low-speed storage (disk or drum) available, and since blocks can easily be sorted if received out of order, the "go-back-to-the-rejected-block-and-continue-from-there" type of ARQ system need not be considered. Sorting can be no more complicated than resequencing block storage addresses within a computer.

Also assume that two-way communication is normal and that a format and protocol scheme such as the advanced data communications control procedure (ADCCP) is used. This means that, as part of the overhead field on every block, there is a location for inserting the number of the last block received correctly. ADCCP also allows for the selective rejection of specific blocks. Use of one of these two techniques in conjunction with timeouts will guarantee that no block is lost or long delayed. This subject will be further discussed in part two of the article, where specific design examples for telephone-based computer communications systems will be given.

Throughput Approach

As previously stated the parameter most commonly used to select block length is throughput. There are many forms of the underlying equation for this approach, but they are all some form of the following. The throughput (R) is given by:

$$R = \frac{\text{number of information bits transmitted}}{\text{bits transmitted before accepting the block}}$$

$$= \frac{k}{n + nP(\geq 1, n) + [P(\geq 1, n)]^2 + \ldots}$$

$$= \frac{k[1 - P(\geq 1, n)]}{n}$$

where there are k information bits in a block, n total bits in the block, and $P(\geq 1, n)$ is the probability of at least one error in an n-bit block, commonly called the block error rate.

Throughput is impacted by the portion of the block which conveys no information, $(n - k)/n$, and by the probability that the block will be in error and thus will be retransmitted, $P \geq 1, n$.

Variations of this relationship generally take into account any non-transmission delay time that specific networks may encounter. These variations do not have any appreciable effect on the shape of the throughput curve or on block-length selection. Channel data rate is taken into account by having a different expression for every data rate. Thus, for every data rate, there is a specific optimum block length using this technique.

Hence, there is no design flexibility.

A typical throughput curve is shown in Figure 1. It is an average function. The true error rate is actually varying at any instance. There is some maximum value of throughput less than 1.0 (representing 100 percent throughput). At any instant and for any block length, the throughput will be highest (overhead limited) if there are no transmission errors, and it will be lowest (channel limited) if the transmitted block is in error. There is some block length at which the average throughput is a maximum, although the instantaneous throughput varies. Shorter block lengths are limited in their average throughput by overhead and longer ones are limited by retransmissions. There is no flexibility in this design approach and, in fact, this so-called optimum block length for maximum average throughput does not yield an optimized design. The delivery-time approach, on the other hand, yields a flexible solution which under varying conditions can have different optimum solutions.

Delivery time design

In the delivery-time approach, it is desired to calculate the probability of successfully delivering the message, $P_D(t \leq t_0)$ within a specified time, t_0. The message to be delivered from source to sink on a single data transmission link is divided into blocks. As a minimum, T_1 blocks must be delivered (assuming no retransmissions are necessary), and as a maximum, T_2 blocks can be transmitted in the allotted time. The probability of successfully delivering the message within the given amount of time is given by:

$$P_D(t \leq t_0) = \sum_{i=1}^{(T_2-T_1)/C} \binom{T_1+i-1}{i} P_R^i (1-P_R)^{T_1} \quad (1)$$

where:

$P_D(t \leq t_0)$ is the probability of successfully delivering a message in a time which is within t_0;

T_1 is the minimum number of blocks to be delivered;

$T_2 - T_1$ is the maximum number of retransmissions possible in the given time;

C is one plus the number of time spaces between retransmissions (if separated in time);

P_R is the probability that a block will be in error and therefore require retransmission.

The combinational function,

$$\binom{T_1+i-1}{i},$$

appearing in equation 1 is a statistic which defines the number of ways i items can be selected from $T_1 + i - 1$ items. See the panel, "Design equation derived."
The values of T_2 and T_1 are defined as follows:

$$T_2 = INT(t_0 \cdot Drate \cdot 1/L), \quad (2)$$

where:

Drate is the channel data rate (bit/s);
L is the block length (bits);
t_0 is the maximum allotted delivery time (seconds); and
INT stands for the integer part of T_2 which is caused by the fixed-block-length nature of the ARQ system.

$$T_1 = Ceil(M \cdot 1/(L-OH)), \quad (3)$$

where:

M is the number of message bits to be delivered;
OH is the number of error detection and/or correction parity bits, plus any other non-information overhead;
Ceil represents the upper bound integer operator which yields the maximum possible value of T_1.

Like T_2, T_1 is an integer. This is a result of the fixed-block-length nature of the ARQ technique. The last block in a message, if incomplete, is filled with padding bits. Also, at no additional overhead, a number of identification bits or additional error detection bits (totaling the amount of the padding) can be distributed throughout all T_2 blocks.

To understand the physical natures of INT and Ceil, note that if, in calculating T_1 and T_2, it is found that 7.8 blocks of data exist, then T_1 equal to 8 blocks must be delivered, and if there is time to transmit 11.4 blocks, then only T_2 equal to 11 full blocks can be transmitted.

Important values

The three key parameters in determining $P_D(t \leq t_0)$ are P_R, T_1 and T_2. P_R is, in turn, a function of the communications channel error patterns, and T_1 and T_2 are functions of system design parameters. There is an absolute minimum value of block length (L) given by OH + 1. For any smaller value of L there is no non-overhead information.

The maximum possible block length is determined from the requirement that T_2 be no less than T_1.

The value of $P_D(t \leq t_0)$ for a given number of message bits (M) can be increased by increasing t_0 or Drate

1 Throughput curve

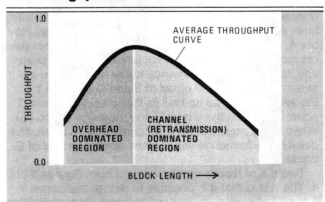

Classify. Regardless of which of the throughput equations is used for a design, the result is always an average function represented by a curve of this general form.

2 Delivery vs time

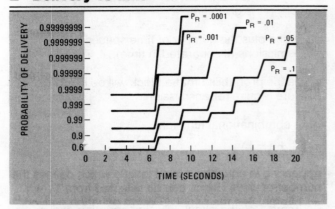

4-kbit message. *Delivery probablity depends on time and error rate. Here a 4-kbit message is studied. The staircase is caused by the fix-length nature of a ARQ system.*

3 Fixed error rate

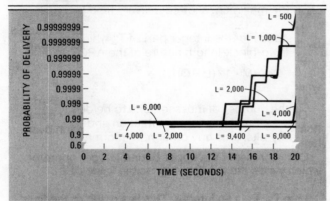

Varying length. *Probability of delivery increases as delivery time grows, but, as can be seen, longer messages will take more time to effect a change in probability.*

4 Retransmission effect

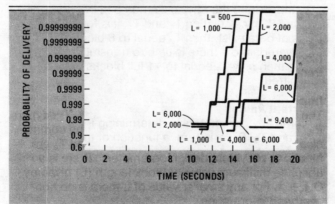

Increased space. *As the time spaces between retransmissions are increased (in this case C = 3) probability of delivery at a given time increases. Data rate is 1.2 kbit/s.*

(both of which increase T_2 while not changing T_1). T_2 can also be increased by decreasing L. Decreasing L also increases T_1, for constant M and OH, but unless L is close to OH in value, the increase in T_2 is greater than that in T_1.

An example of possible delivery probabilities as a function of time and block error probability (P_R) is presented in Figure 2. Extremely high probabilities of delivery can be achieved at error rates on the order of 0.1. The curves are presented at a data rate of 1.2 kbit/s. This value of Drate has been selected because of the availability of real telephone channel error data. This data will be used in part 2 of this article as a vehicle for comparing block length selections based on throughput and the probability-of-successful-delivery criterion.

In Figure 3, the possible trade-offs in block length, probability of successful delivery, and delivery time are detailed. At a block length of 4,000 bits, a message could be delivered in 3.5 seconds with a probability of 0.96. Alternatively, if greater delivery times are acceptable, the probability of success can be greatly increased. At 1,000 bits/block, a probability of 0.9999996 can be achieved at 20 seconds delivery time.

Worst case

In calculating the results of Figure 3 it has been assumed that C (one plus the number of time spaces between retransmissions) is equal to three. This means that every time a retransmission is necessary, a retransmission request is sent back to the source (taking one block transmission time on the link), and since it arrives at the source when another block has already started transmission, the retransmission is held up for one further block time. This represents a worst case situation. It is very possible that two or more messages are to be delivered on the same link during the same time span, as could happen on a message concentration link in a packet-switching network. Rather than considering each message on its own and penalizing it for time when it cannot transmit a retransmission (because another message is sending an original transmission), the multiple messages can be considered as concentrated with no penalty for retransmission waiting time, making C equal to 1. This result is shown on Figure 4, which shows that the delivery time is further decreased with decreasing block length. In actual practice, true system performance will lie somewhere between the results of C equal to 3 and C equal to 1. Performance will be as bad as that calculated with C equal to 3 when there is only one message on the link. When many messages are concentrated on a link, the delivery performance will at times approach that of C equal to 1.

Two major results can be derived from Figures 3 and 4. The first is that it is possible to deliver messages in a specified maximum amount of time with probabilities of success of 0.99999999. That is, only one in 100 million messages would require more than the allotted time. This value falls directly into a grade-of-service quantity that a data communications utility can guarantee its users. The second result is to set aside the concept of throughput from consideration in design of a network. As demonstrated in Table 1, the block lengths which yield the highest throughput are those that require the longest message delivery time and have the lowest probability of success. In Table 1, time is frozen at 18 seconds.

In Table 2, the probability of delivery is fixed at 0.9999, and delivery time for various values of L and C is shown.

The reason that some longer message blocks will be delivered faster than some shorter blocks, as seen in Table 2, is related to the fixed length structure of blocks. Considering the number of overhead bits per block, the values 1,000 and 2,000 bits result in a closer parameter fit to the delivery probability equation than a value of 500 bits does. All of these block lengths are shorter than the throughput optimum value for this channel (1.2 kbit/s) which will be calculated in part 2 and shown to be 9.4 kbits/block.

The alternative approach to block-length selection based on delivery time can be used to find a block length for which, if all other parameters are held constant, a maximum probability of successful delivery will be achieved. This is demonstrated in Figure 5, where, for visual convenience, the probability of failure to deliver a message (which is one minus the probability of success) is presented. BER is the channel bit error rate.

The lowest curve on this figure is for a data rate of 600 bit/s and a BER of 10^{-3} and it shows no optimum. As the error rate decreases to 10^{-4} a clear optimum point is visible, and at an error rate of 10^{-5} the probability of failure to deliver is so small that, for the chosen scale, the whole curve does not fit on the figure. Only the ascending and descending portions of the curve can be shown.

All of these results are at a data rate of 600 bit/s. To demonstrate that this result holds true at higher data rates, the descending portions of the curves at 1.2 kbit/s and 2.4 kbit/s at a BER of 10^{-3} are also presented. The ascending portions of these curves, if drawn, would lie between the ordinate and the ascending portion of the 600 bit/s, BER equal to 10^{-5} curve. All of these curves are for a 12-second delivery time. Figure 6 demonstrates that substantially shorter times at these low probabilities of failure to deliver are possible. Time is related mainly to the channel data rate.

Additionally, it should be clear from Figure 6 that only a slight increase in allowed time will reduce the probability of failure to deliver a message by many orders of magnitude. These results are not limited to the low bit error rate channels. As detailed in Figure 7, such results are easily achievable at retransmission rates of 40 percent.

This is an outstanding result. It has previously been thought, based on throughput analysis, that if the retransmission rate were high, the channel could not be used and should be shut down. In fact, all a high retransmission rate means is that it will take slightly longer for any given message to be delivered. Thus, fast message delivery is achievable at high block error rates

Table 1 Throughput vs block length

BLOCK LENGTH (BITS)	THROUGHPUT	DELIVERY PROBABILITY	
		C = 3	C = 1
500	0.6146	0.9999999+	0.999999999+
1,000	0.8049	0.999999+	0.99999999+
2,000	0.8978	0.999+	0.99999999+
4,000	0.9405	0.96	0.99998
6,000	0.9517	0.97	0.999
9,400	0.9556	0.95	0.95

Table 2 Throughput vs block length

BLOCK LENGTH (BITS)	THROUGHPUT	DELIVERY TIME (SECONDS)	
		C = 3	C = 1
500	0.6146	15+	14+
1,000	0.8049	16+	12
2,000	0.8978	20	13
4,000	0.9405	20	16+
6,000	0.9517	20	19+

and a poor communications channel should not deter a computer communications network.

The design equation relates the performance requirements, $P_D(t \leq t_0)$, and allowable time, t_0, to achieve it, and the system parameters, data rate and block length, to the channel retransmission rate, P_R. An important relationship is the maximum value of P_R versus block length, L, for given design constraints and system parameters. The equation can be solved for this maximum value of P_R as a function of the design parameters. The approach is to subtract the desired value of $P_D(t \leq t_0)$ from both sides of the design equation (equation 1) and apply the Newton-Raphson root-finding technique. In fact, virtually any block length, L, will provide the required $P_D(t \leq 15 \text{ sec. })$ equal to 0.999999. Naturally, there is no solution for $L \leq OH$ and $T_2 < T_1$. As L is varied, the only effect is to change the tolerable maximum block error rate, P_R. If there is such a thing as an optimum block length, it is the value of L for which the largest possible P_R yields the desired $P_D(t \leq t_0)$. As the data rate increases, $T_2 - T_1$ increases to the point where very high values of P_R (e.g. 0.8) can be tolerated, and the performance objectives will still be reached. If no design is possible for a given channel to achieve a given $P_D(t \leq t_0)$, then, by reducing $P_D(t \leq t_0)$ and/or increasing t_0 it may be possible to achieve a design.

Now that the design equation has been presented and used to evaluate the performance of ARQ systems, it is possible to develop a method to use it for other

5 Optimum length

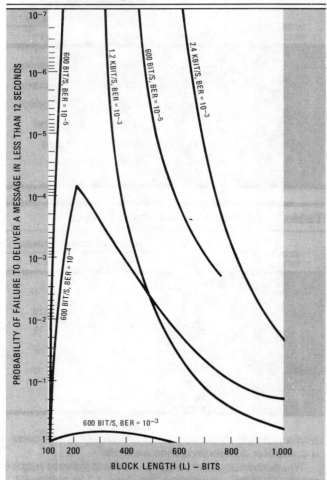

Fixed time. *As demonstrated, there exists an optimum block length for a given delivery time, data transmission rate and bit error rate. Note, OH here is 36 bits/block.*

6 Probability vs time

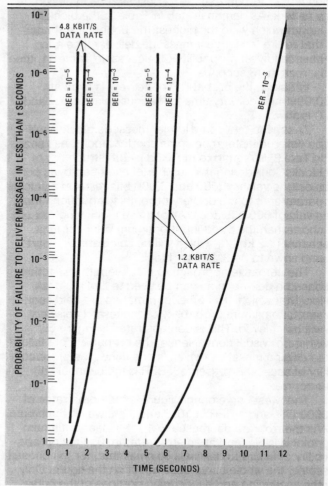

Steep. *The relationship between allowable delivery time and probability of delivery is extremely steep. A small time increase allows greater assurance of message delivery.*

designs. Suppose it is required to design an ARQ network with probability of successful delivery $P_D(t \leq t_0)$ which delivers a message of length M bits within a time t_0 seconds at a data rate of Drate with a residual undetected bit error rate in the delivered message of P_u. The case shall be of one link transmission with no processing delay. However, processing delay can be considered along with l link transmission. Processing delay is incorporated by modifying T_2 or T_1, and l link transmission is incorporated by replacing $P_D(t \leq t_0)$ and t_0 by $[P_D(t \leq t_0)]^{1/l}$ and t_0/l.

An ARQ system design is a three-step procedure:
Step 1. Using the desired value of P_u and a knowledge of the communications channel, determine the necessary number of error detection parity bits (PAR). If any additional identification or overhead bits per block are needed, PAR should be increased by this number after completion of Step 1 to yield OH.
Step 2. Using the values of $P_D(t \leq t_0)$, t_0, M, Drate, and OH, graph the maximum retransmission rate (P_R) that satisfies these parameters versus block length (L). This

step is achieved by solving equation (1) for P_R.
Step 3. On the same set of axes used in Step 2, graph the actual block error rate of the communications channel versus block length.

In order to achieve a successful ARQ system design, it is necessary to find suitable values for the number of parity bits and block length which, along with other parameters, will satisfy the design equation. Step 1 will provide the value of PAR. Since the last block in transmission is a full block (T_1 and T_2 are integer numbers), there may be room in a system design for substantial numbers of filler bits which can be parity bits (i.e., overdesign in Step 1 is not a critical problem). The solution to the design problem is found at the block lengths between the intersections of the graphs of Steps 2 and 3.
Example 1: In this example it is desired to deliver a 5-kbit message at 1.2 kbit/s with a probability of delivery equal to 0.999999 within t_0 seconds on a communications channel exhibiting independent random errors with a bit error probability P(E), and with a residual

134

7 Probability with retransmission

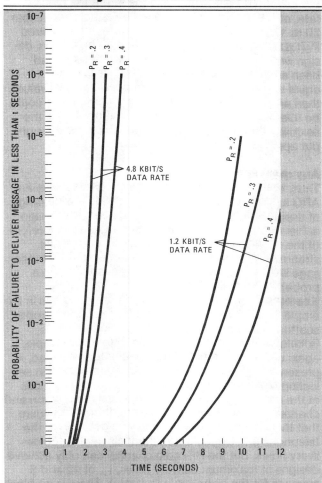

Many errors. *Taking Figure 6 a step farther indicates that even with very poor lines (high error rates) the overall probability of a message delivery is still highly acceptable.*

8 Solution 1

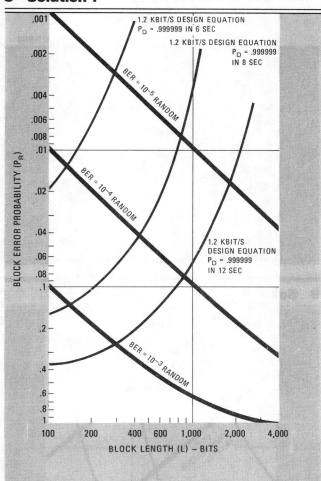

Steps. *By following the three design steps, a solution to the example problem will result in a group of curves similar to these. Remember OH has been chosen at 20 percent.*

undetected bit error rate P_u of 10^{-7}. This is a typical satellite communications channel.

The solution to Example 1 for values of t_0 equal to 6 seconds, 8 seconds, and 12 seconds with values of $P(E)$ equal to 10^{-3}, 10^{-4}, and 10^{-5} appears in Figure 8. The value of OH has been chosen as 20 percent of the block length. Given this value of OH, three curves have been drawn, showing the maximum value of P_R that can be accepted at a given value of L to establish an ARQ system with maximum delivery times t_0 equal to 6, 8, and 12 seconds, while achieving $P_D(t \le t_0)$ equal to 0.999999. Also drawn on this figure are curves of block error rate versus block length for independent random channel error rates of $P(E)$ equal to 10^{-3}, 10^{-4}, and 10^{-5}. An ARQ system design can be achieved at any block length (L) for which the channel block error rate is less than or equal to the maximum block error rate (error detection converts block error rate to retransmission rate) that satisfies the design equation at that block length. For example, at $P(E)$ equal to 10^{-5}, a 12-second delivery time can be

achieved at any block length shorter than 1.8 kbits an 8-second delivery time at any block length less than 812 bits, and a 6-second rate at any block length under 286 bits.

Design Trade-offs

It should be noted that, at the stated block lengths of the above solution, the design is marginal. It is marginal in the sense that, if the channel's parameters are time varying and the block error rate increased at some time in the future, the maximum possible block length would decrease and the system implemented earlier would no longer meet the $P_D(t \le t_0)$ requirement in the given maximum delivery time t_0. If an original design is established at a shorter block length (an overdesign) than the crossover point of the Step 2 and Step 3 curves, the design will better tolerate an increase in channel error rate. Suppose, for example, that a 6-second maximum delivery time with $P_D(t \le t_0)$ equal to 0.999999 is desired, but that, instead of establishing the design for a current channel bit error rate of 10^{-5}

Table 3   Block error rates

CHANNEL	A_1	A_2	CONDITIONS
HF LOWER BOUND (1.2 KBIT/S)	2.3×10^{-3}	.64	$8 \leq L \leq 9,000$
HF UPPER BOUND (1.2 KBIT/S)	1.0×10^{-2}	.52	$8 \leq L \leq 9,000$
TROPOSCATTER (2.4 KBIT/S)	4.8×10^{-4}	.52	$8 \leq L \leq 80$
	2.6×10^{-4}	.68	$80 \leq L \leq 1,500$
	4.2×10^{-5}	.90	$1,500 \leq L \leq 9,000$
TROPOSCATTER (1.2 KBIT/S)	1.4×10^{-4}	.71	$8 \leq L \leq 65$
	8.0×10^{-5}	.78	$65 \leq L \leq 200$
	4.2×10^{-5}	.90	$200 \leq L \leq 9,000$
TELEPHONE (1.2 KBIT/S)	1.23×10^{-5}	.83	$10 \leq L \leq 10,000$

9   Solution 2

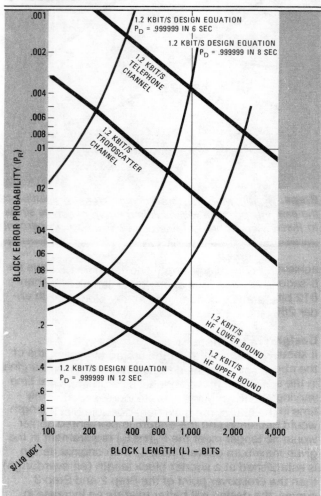

Three media. *For each of the three media described, a unique solution is available. Notice, however, that for the HF radio system no solution is possible within six seconds.*

at L equal to 286 bits, the design were established at L equal to 100 bits. Then, if in the future the block error rate, at L equal to 100 increased by a factor of almost 20 to 1, the system would still operate at the desired $P_D(t \leq t_0)$ equal to 0.999999. In fact, if the original design were at the 12-second delivery point, but had been established at L equal to 100 bits instead of L equal to 1.8 kbits (the maximum possible initial value), then an increase in block error rate of 360 times could be tolerated with no system degradation. This is the flexibility that this approach yields which the throughput approach cannot.

Any message

Thus, the design equation can be used to achieve an ARQ system and simultaneously provide a wide range of design safety margins to the engineer. The design achieved will deliver any M-bit message, and therefore (if the channel is considered to contain an infinite stream of M-bit messages) each and every M-bit message will be delivered, in at most t_0 seconds with a probability of delivery of $P_D(t \leq t_0)$.

Example 2. With the same design parameters as in Example 1, design an ARQ system for telephone, troposcatter, and high frequency (HF) radio channels. Solution to Example 2: The solution to this example, again using 20 percent of each block for overhead, is presented in Figure 9. The solution is embodied in selecting block lengths less than or equal to the values at the relevant intersections of the design equation and channel error rate curves. It is evident from the figure that there is no difficulty in achieving designs for the telephone and troposcatter channels at all three delivery times, but the HF radio channel can only achieve designs at maximum delivery times, t_0, of 12 and 8 seconds for the given value $P_D(t \leq t_0)$. There is no block length for which the HF channel block error rate is less than or equal to the maximum block error rate possible for a t_0 equal to 6-second maximum delivery time; thus an ARQ design cannot be achieved at the given value of $P_D(t \leq t_0)$ equal to 0.999999.

The relationships between block error rate, or retransmission rate, and block length for the above channels is governed by the expression:

$$P_R = A_1 \cdot L^{A_2} \qquad (4)$$

The values A_1 and A_2 which are empirical values related to the length L (as detailed in equation 4) for the applicable ranges of L is given in Table 3.

It must be emphasized that the delivery-time approach does not achieve something for nothing. The throughput approach will deliver a small portion of messages over a finite range of delivery times. The delivery-time approach will increase the numbers of messages which are deliverable in a given time, but there may be some messages which would never be received. This is so because the tail to the right of the density function extends to infinite time. It is this reshaping, along with methods for preventing the tail from going to infinity, that forms the basis for some innovative pricing and user charge-back schemes. This will be the subject of part 2. ■

Time, not throughput, for net designs Part 2: application

Kenneth Brayer, The Mitre Corp., Bedford, Mass.

The message delivery time equation, presented in Part 1, is applied to three telephone channel link designs and compared to a throughput approach

Traditionally data communications network design parameters have been based on optimizing system throughput. This has led to a block length (or packet length) approach that attempts to trade off the amount of time wasted by continuously transmitting a fixed number of overhead bits against the amount of data lost when a block is retransmitted because of errors. However, despite the almost universal acceptance of this method, it is not the most efficient solution to network design.

Rather than the throughput approach, planners should instead think of message-delivery time as the crux of network design. The probability curves resulting from a message-delivery-time design equation, presented in part 1 of this article (DATA COMMUNICATIONS, Oct. 1978, p. 39), are shown in Figure 1, along with the curves based on throughput equations. As detailed in part 1 (and shown in Fig. 1), the message-time approach to network design allows for faster message delivery, higher delivery probabilities, and adaptability to varying channel conditions. Not so obvious, but perhaps even more important, is that a message-time design leads to some fresh strategies for network service charge-back.

Having developed this alternative design equation, it is possible to examine some specific network exam-

ples to test its validity. This is best accomplished by comparing an actual telephone-line data communications network design using both message-time and throughput analysis.

The basic flaw in throughput design is an inappropriate weighting of overhead vs. retransmissions. In throughput design, long block lengths tend to be selected to minimize the percentage of message overhead. But retransmission is truly the predominate problem. For example, if a block has five percent overhead but a single retransmission has the effect of causing three block lengths of time to be lost in delivery, those retransmissions will have a negative impact equal to the overhead of 60 correctly delivered blocks. Thus, the retransmission rate must be less than one block in 60 for the selected block length to be useful. What is the probability of the retransmission rate being this low? This question will be dealt with by means of example.

In the application of the message-time design approach, assume an automatic repeat request (ARQ) scheme is employed. With ARQ there are typically two processors. At a given instant one is the information transmitter and the other is the responder. If two-way simultaneous transmission is possible than an ARQ mode can exist as described or, it is also possible that

1 Probability curves

New curve. *Using a delivery-time message approach to network design, a new probability density function is created. Here, it is compared with a throughput analysis.*

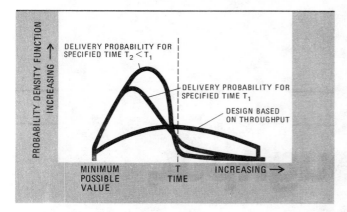

both processors can function both ways simultaneously. In two-way alternate communications one processor transmits messages while the other queues responses. At fixed intervals or when the first processor stops transmitting both processors change functions. In either case, they use the same software. The only difference between the two processor functions is communications expense (a full-duplex channel for two-way simultaneous communications versus a half-duplex channel for two-way alternate communications), and a small amount of switching software in the two-way alternate case. This difference gives rise to the first possible charge-back pricing strategy. That is, if high-speed message delivery is not required, or impossible to achieve, the communications plant cost can be halved by choosing the two-way alternate approach.

The transmitting processor typically divides its messages into blocks and assigns each block a sequence number and an address. It then proceeds to compute error detection parity, append it to the blocks, and transmits the blocks on the channel. If received in error (the parity check fails), blocks are negative acknowledged by the receiver. This negative acknowledgment is placed in a special message field traveling in the reverse direction. It then becomes a positive acknowledgment for all blocks transmitted since the previous negative acknowledgment. As an added precaution, a timeout clock is started when a message is transmitted. If it is not negative acknowledged, or implicitly positive acknowledged by the timeout, the message is transmitted again. This protects against lost messages due to address errors. In conjunction with the delivery probability approach to design, the timeout also allows for an advertised level of service.

Real time execution

In those cases where the negative acknowledgment is received by the transmitter, the block in question is retransmitted. Generally, I/O operations are accomplished via direct memory access (DMA) since time is at a premium. It is possible that under normal

operation both input and output channel may need service almost simultaneously.

To execute the communications procedures in real-time, a reasonably sophisticated set of formats and protocols is required. One set—developed by the American National Standards Institute (ANSI)—is the advanced data communication control procedures (ADCCP). The standard is extensive and designed to cover many general and special cases.

In ADCCP, data link control is defined in terms of various combinations of station configurations. These are:
- Primary link control—called primary station
- Secondary link control—called secondary station
- Balanced link control—called balanced station

The logical functions and protocols of secondary and balanced stations are specified identically with respect to the action taken and the response transmitted upon receipt of a given command. ADCCP specifies only responses. Methods for managing a data link are left to the system designer—although a selection of commands is supplied.

Balanced stations have balanced link control capabilities. The balanced station transmits and receives both command frames (commands) and response frames (responses) to and from another balanced station. It maintains only one information transmission ability to and one information receiving ability from the other balanced station. A station is defined as configurable if it has, as a result of mode-setting action, the capability at different times to be more than one type of logical station (i.e, primary, secondary, or balanced station). In ADCCP there are two logical data link configurations:
- Unbalanced—a primary station and one or more secondary stations.
- Balanced—two balanced stations.

A balanced configuration is made up of two balanced stations connected point-to-point, two-way alternate or two-way simultaneous, switched or non-switched. Both balanced stations have identical command/response and link control capability. The typical data-communications network employs a balanced structure.

Frames blueprint

In ADCCP, all transmissions are in frames, and each frame conforms to the structure shown in Figure 2. Frames containing only data link control sequences form a special case where there is no information (I) field.

All frames start and end with a flag sequence (F) which is used for synchronization. This is a zero-bit followed by six 1-bits followed by a zero-bit (01111110). All stations attached to the data link continuously hunt, on a bit-by-bit basis, for this sequence. A transmitter must send only complete 8-bit flag sequences, however, the sequence 01111110111110 at the receiver is two flag sequences.

In order to achieve transparency, the flag is prohibited from occurring in the address (A), control (C), information (I), and CRC fields. This is accomplished

2 ADCCP frame

Format. *Six frames are defined in the ANSI-developed advanced data communications control procedures (ADCCP). The first and last frames are flag sequences that are used to inform link stations of the start and stop of a transmission. The flags, then, are used to synchronize all data communications. CRC checks for errors.*

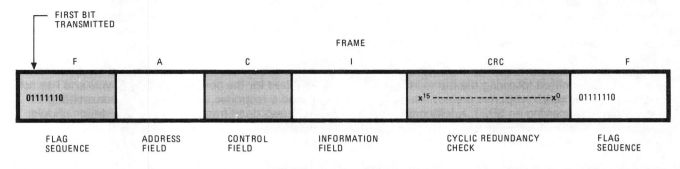

with zero-bit insertion procedure. The transmitter inserts a zero-bit following five contiguous 1-bits anywhere between the beginning flag and the ending flag of the frame. The insertion of the zero-bit thus applies to the contents of the A, C, I and CRC fields.

The receiver continuously monitors the received bit stream, and upon receiving a zero-bit followed by five contiguous 1-bits, the receiver inspects the next bit. If it is a zero, the contiguous five, 1-bits are passed as data and the zero-bit is deleted. If the sixth bit is a 1, the receiver inspects the seventh bit; if it is zero, a flag sequence has been received; if it is a 1, an abort has been received.

Abort is the procedure by which a station in the process of sending a frame, ends the frame in an unusual manner so the receiving station will ignore the frame.

Aborting a frame is performed by transmitting at least seven, but less than 15, contiguous 1-bits (with no inserted zeros). The receipt of seven contiguous 1-bits is interpreted as an abort. Receipt of 15 or more contiguous 1-bits is interpreted as an abort and indicates an idle link state (nothing to transmit). In two-way alternate operation this signifies "your turn" to the other station.

Where station constraints permit, the flag sequence closing a frame may also be the opening flag sequence for the next frame. Any number of complete flags may be used between frames.

The A field contains the link level address of a secondary or balanced station. The field contains a command or response and may contain sequence numbers.

The C field is used by the transmitting balanced station to tell the addressed balanced station what operation it is to perform. It is also used by the balanced station to respond to the remote balanced station. The length of the C field in an unextended control field is one octet. It is two octets long in an extended control field. However the C field is sometimes extended for more complex information.

The I field may be any number and sequence of bits; the data link is completely transparent. Data contained in the information field is unrestricted with respect to code or grouping of bits. An I field length of zero is specifically permitted.

Reduces errors

All frames include a 16-bit cyclic redundancy check (CRC) field for error detection. The contents of the A, C, and I fields (excluding the zeros inserted to maintain transparency) are included in the calculation of the CRC sequence. The CRC is the remainder of a modulo 2 division process utilizing a generator polynomial as a divisor. The generator polynomial is that used in CCITT recommendation V.41 and is: $x^{16} + x^{12} + x^5 + 1$. Those desiring a higher undetected block error probability than the 1.5×10^{-5} this polynomial gives, can transfer two characters from the A field to the CRC field and use the polynomial $x^{32} + x^{26} + x^{23} + x^{22} + x^{16} + x^{12} + x^{11} + x^{10} + x^8 + x^7 + x^5 + x^4 + x^2 + x + 1$ that this author has recommended to U.S. Government standards makers. This polynomial achieves an undetected block error rate of 2.5×10^{-10}, and has been chosen for the Defense Communication Agency Autodin II, the National Airborne Command Post, and the Air Force Sacdin (previously called SATIN IV) nets.

Typically, the C field is implemented in extended form (six characters), and the A field with 18 characters including the addressee, source, block number, priority, and other data link management information. Thus, overhead is 24 characters or 192 bits.

There are two methods for returning negative acknowledgments. They both insert specific bit patterns in the control field. The reject, (REJ) is used by a station to request retransmission of frames starting with the frame numbered N. Frames numbered N-1 (N minus 1) and below are acknowledged. Additional frames pending initial transmission may be transmitted following the retransmitted frame(s). Only one REJ, from a given station to another station, may be established at any given time: another REJ or a selective reject (SREJ) may not be transmitted until the first REJ condition has been cleared by the sender. The REJ is cleared (reset) upon acceptance of a frame with a number equal to the number of the REJ command/response.

The SREJ is used by a station to request retransmission of the single frame numbered N. Frames up to and including N-1 are acknowledged. The SREJ is cleared upon acceptance of a frame with a number equal to the number of the SREJ command/response. After a station transmits an SREJ it may not retransmit SREJ or REJ for an additional sequence error until the first SREJ error condition has been cleared or until a response/command time-out has occurred. To do so would acknowledge that all frames up to an including N-1 were received correctly, where N is the sequence number in the second SREJ or REJ. Frames that may have been transmitted following the frame indicated in the SREJ command/response are not retransmitted as the result of receiving an SREJ. Additional frames, pending initial transmission, may be transmitted following the retransmission of the specific frame requested by the SREJ.

When a frame sequence error is detected, the SREJ is transmitted as soon as possible. Only one "sent SREJ" exception condition from a given station to another given station is established at a time. A "sent SREJ" exception condition is cleared when the requested frame is received. When the station perceives that the requested frame will not be received, because the requested frame or the SREJ was in error or was lost, the SREJ may be repeated.

In the event a receiving station, due to a transmission error, does not receive (or receives and discards) a single frame or the last I frame(s) in a sequence of frames, it will not detect an out-of-sequence exception and therefore will not transmit SREJ/REJ. The station which transmitted the unacknowledged frame(s) shall, following the completion of a system specified timeout period, take appropriate recovery action to determine the sequence number at which retransmission must begin.

With ADCCP it is recommended that a station which has waited for the complete timeout cycle and has not received a response, pause before retransmitting all unacknowledged frames. A balanced station should, in this elapsed timeout case, either retransmit its last single frame or transmit new frames if they are available.

Design equation review
Prior to designing single link computer-to-computer communications for telephone circuits by the throughput and delivery-time methods it is worthwhile to briefly review the design approaches presented in part 1.

The parameter most commonly used to select block length in the past has been throughput. All throughput designs are based on some form of the following:

3 Throughput results

Telephone channel. Curves resulting from a throughput analysis on a telephone link are shown at different data rates. Block overhead is equal to 192 bits per block.

Notice, with the throughput approach to this design, throughput decreases rapidly as block length shrinks. Also, these curves indicate nothing about delivery speed.

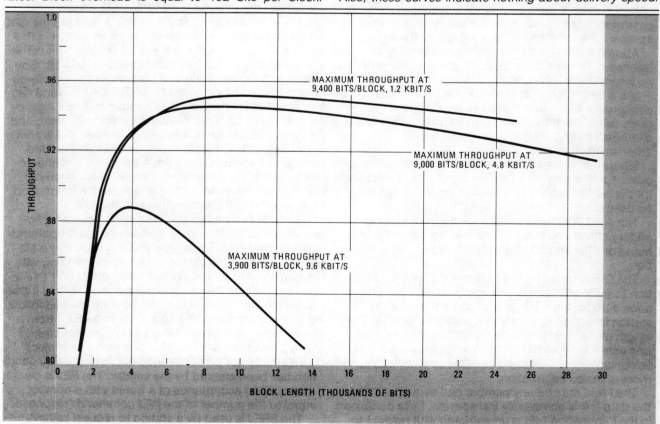

MAXIMUM THROUGHPUT AT
9,400 BITS/BLOCK, 1.2 KBIT/S

MAXIMUM THROUGHPUT AT
9,000 BITS/BLOCK, 4.8 KBIT/S

MAXIMUM THROUGHPUT AT
3,900 BITS/BLOCK, 9.6 KBIT/S

THROUGHPUT

BLOCK LENGTH (THOUSANDS OF BITS)

The throughput (R) is given by

$$R = \frac{\text{number of information bits transmitted}}{\text{bits transmitted before accepting the block}}$$
$$= \frac{k[\,1 - P(\leq 1, n)\,]}{n}$$

Throughput is affected by the fraction of the block that conveys no information, $(n-k)/n$, and the probability that the block will be in error and thus will be retransmitted, $P(\geq 1, n)$. The design objective is to find that n which maximizes R.

An alternative approach is the delivery-time concept. In this approach, it is desired to calculate the probability of successfully delivering the message, $P_D\,(t \leq t_0)$, within a specified time, t_0. The message which is to be delivered from message source to message sink, on a single data transmission link, is divided into blocks. As a minimum, T_1 blocks must be delivered (assuming no retransmissions are necessary), and as a maximum T_2 blocks can be transmitted in the allotted time. The probability of successfully delivering the message within a given amount of time is:

$$P_D(t \leq t_0) = \sum_{i=0}^{(T_2 - T_1)/C} \binom{T_1 + i - 1}{i} P_R^i\,(1 - P_R)^{T_1} \qquad (1)$$

where:

$P_D\,(t \leq t_0)$ is the probability of successfully delivering a message within a time which is t_0,

T_1 is the minimum number of blocks to be delivered,

$T_2 - T_1$ is the maximum number of retransmissions possible in the given time,

P_R is the probability that a block will be in error and require retransmission, and

C is one plus the number of spaces between retransmissions (if separated in time). C will be designated as equal to one in this part of the article.
The impact of other choices for C and the derivation of equation 1 was discussed in part 1.
The values of T_2 and T_1 are defined as follows:

$$T_2 = \text{INT}\,[t_0 \cdot \text{Drate} \cdot 1/L],$$

where:

Drate is the channel data rate (bit/s),

L is the block length (bits),

t_0 is the maximum allotted delivery time (seconds), and INT stands for integer part of.

$$T_1 = \text{Ceil}\,[M \cdot 1/(L-OH),$$

where:

M is the number of message bits to be delivered,

OH is the number of error detection, and/or correction parity bits plus any other non-information overhead, and

Ceil represents the upper bound integer operator which yields the maximum value to T_1.

The design approach is more complicated than that of the throughput approach. It entails a three step process.

Step 1. Using the desired value of undetected error rate and a knowledge of the communications channel, determine the necessary number of error detection parity bits (PAR). If any additional identification or

4 Delivery time results

Speeds. *Designs at 1.2 kbit/s (A), 4.8 kbit/s (B), and 9.6 kbit/s (C) are plotted for a 5,000-bit block with 192 bits of overhead—using the delivery-time approach.*

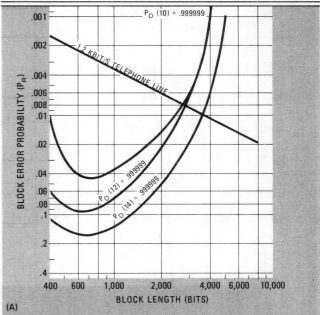

(A)

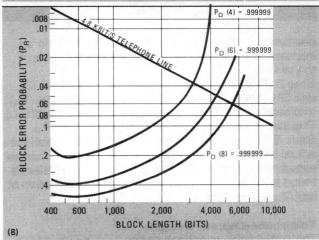

(B)

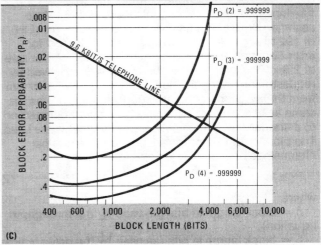

(C)

5 Delivery probability

Degradation. *Delivery probability versus time for a telephone channel with block length selected to maximize the channel's degradation tolerance is detailed. These curves are for a throughput design, but for any combination of abcissa versus ordinate shown, a delivery-time approach can be implemented. Messages are 15,000 bits long.*

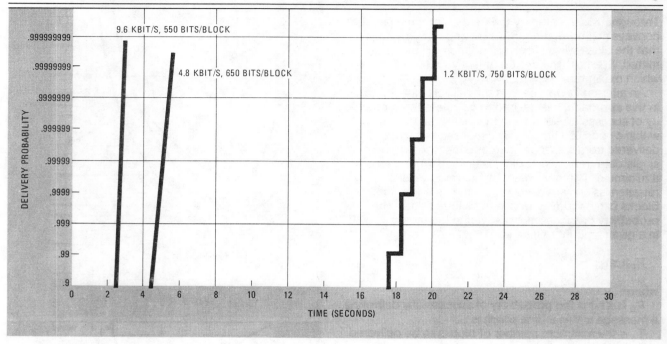

overhead bits per block are needed, PAR should be increased by this number after completion of Step 1 to yield OH.

Step 2. Using the values of $P_D(t \le t_o)$, t_O, M, DRATE, and OH, graph the maximum retransmission rate (P_R) that satisfies these parameters versus block length (L). This step is achieved by solving equation 1 for P_R.

Step. 3. On the same set of axes as Step 2, graph the actual block error rate of the communications channel versus block length. Solution to the design problem is found at the block lengths between the intersection of step 2 and 3 graphs.

Telephone-channel designs

The dialed voice telephone channel will be used for a full-duplex computer communications design. Also assume ADCCP formats and an overhead value (OH) of 192 bits/block. Of these, 32 will be selected for error detection yielding an undetected block error rate of 2.3 x 10⁻. Commercially the channel is achieved by requesting an unconditioned 3.2-KHz, four-wire circuit from the telephone company. Performance will be the same as if two, two-wire circuits of the type connected to a standard telephone subscriber handset were used. The block error rate or retransmission rate on this channel has been measured and found to be:

$$P(\ge 1, n) = P_R = A_1 L^{A_2} \qquad (2)$$

where:

n = block length in bits (as used by the throughput equation),

L = block length in bits (as used by the delivery time

(equation),

n = L, and for $10 \le$ (n, or L) $\le 10,000$
at 1.2 kbit/s $A_1 = 1.23 \times 10^{-5}$, $A_2 = 0.83$,
at 4.8 kbit/s $A_1 = 1.39 \times 10^{-5}$, $A_2 = 0.99$, and
at 9.6 kbit/s $A_1 = 5.58 \times 10^{-5}$, $A_2 = 0.91$

The design for each data rate as achieved by the throughput approach is presented in Figure 3. The block lengths that achieve maximum throughput in a continuous retransmission mode are 9,400 bit/block at 1.2 kbit/s, 9,000 bit/block at 4.8 kbit/s and 3,900 bit/block at 9.6 kbit/s. All three designs yield high throughput but say nothing about how fast a message will be delivered. It should be noted that throughput falls rapidly for shorter block lengths. Thus, short messages will not operate at peak throughput level.

At the chosen block lengths all three channels would exceed the one in 60 of the introductory example by nearly an order of magnitude. Thus, a retransmitted block will cost much more than the per-block overhead in message delivery performance. Since throughput is a statistical average parameter (see part 1) exact calculations of this penalty cannot be made.

Designs for the delivery time approach are presented in Figure 4. The first thing to note is that all designs are for a probability of successful delivery of 0.999999 in a specified amount of time. The primary limit on time is, of course, data rate. At 1.2 kbit/s (Fig. 4A) this probability will be met or exceeded for a 10-second delivery at all block lengths below 2,800 bit/block. Shorter values yield higher values of $P_D(t_o)$ or at the same value of $P_D(t_o)$ they yield margin against future increases in P_R. A block length of approximately 600

6 Probability using throughput

Throughput. *Curves of probability of delivery are plotted using a throughput-selected block length. The throughput approach yields longer delivery times for the same proba-* *bility in a given amount of time as a delivery-time design approach. The staircase shape of these curves stems from the fixed block nature of the ARQ system discussed.*

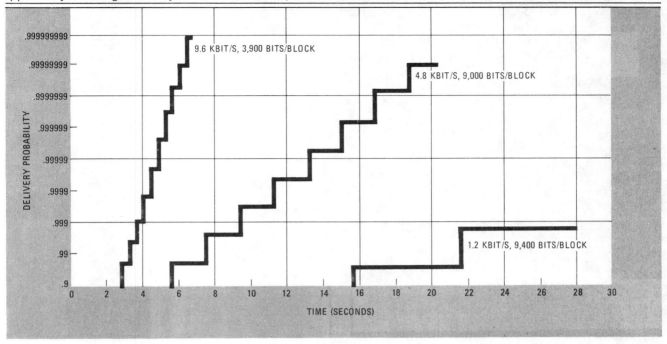

bits yield maximum margin. There are at least two interesting pricing strategies apparent from Figure 4A. Most obvious is that 12 second delivery can be offered at P_D equals 0.999999 while 10 second delivery is actually achieved. Thus, network management can charge more for 10 seconds than for 12 seconds yet implement the same system. The second strategy is to use a lower grade data modem than the one for which the error data was collected. The design will tolerate a higher error rate at shorter block lengths and the utility will save money on modems.

Figures 4B and 4C show performance at 4.8 and 9.6 kbit/s respectively. At 4.8 kbit/s, a 3,500-bit block will achieve a P_D of 0.999999 in 4 seconds. A block length of 4,500 bits will achieve the same at 9.6 kbit/s. A 4.8-kbit/s modem will, however, cost less than half that of a 9.6-kbit/s modem. This means that a user who needs performance no better than 0.999999 in 4 seconds can be interfaced to a backbone system, that is capable of supporting lower times for more demanding users, through the use of a cheaper modem at a lower utility charge. Thus, a system can accommodate different users at different levels of charge and performance by operating a 9.6-kbit/s-backbone system — but interfacing users by matching their individual needs.

An idea of the achievable values of P_D (t_o for the throughput and delivery-time approaches can be seen in Figures 5 and 6. The staircase appearance of the curves is based on the fixed block length nature of the ARQ system. Any value combination, abcissa versus ordinate, shown in Figure 5 can be designed for by the delivery-time approach. Figures 5 and 6 detail the

values achieved using a throughput approach. In this case the designer takes what he gets. The throughput approach always yields higher delivery times for a given P_D (t_o). These two figures have been calculated using a 15,000-bit message length because of the high block length required by throughput design.

Pricing strategies
The key strategy based on the delivery-time approach is shown in Figure 1. At a given desired time the cumulative probability of message delivery is very high with only negligible probability of additional time being required. Thus, a data communications utility could offer a guaranteed delivery time service at a fixed rate — with no charge if the message takes longer to deliver. For example, at 9.6 kbit/s, 2-second delivery of a 5,000-bit message is easily achieved with probabilities greater than 0.999999. Thus, only one in one million messages would take longer than 2 seconds and it would be free.

The cost to the provider would be negligible. A promise of delivery can also be made for failure rates like one in a billion messages at only slightly longer delivery times. The setting of a timeout at just above the promised time (allowing for a final negative acknowledgment) is used to re-establish a message if it is the rare one that is not delivered on time or its address is garbled.

This can be used to increase profit or equitably distribute network costs. Also, this allows users with lesser performance requirements to use slower speed interconnection services to the network backbone. The network of course, provides all these services. Addi-

Pricing strategies

STRATEGY	APPLICABLE PARAMETERS
1. GUARANTEED PERFORMANCE AT NO EXTRA COST	
A. MESSAGE TO BE DELIVERED IN A GIVEN TIME OR NO CHARGE FOR DELIVERY.	PERFORM NORMAL DESIGN AND USE MAXIMUM BLOCK LENGTH AND MINIMUM DATA RATE TO ACHIEVE LEVEL OF PERFORMANCE.
B. TARIFF DISCOUNTS FOR THOSE WILLING TO ACCEPT SLOWER DELIVERY GUARANTEE.	USE LOWER DATA RATE THAN FOR 1A.
C. TARIFF DISCOUNTS FOR THOSE WILLING TO ACCEPT LOWER PROBABILITY OF DELIVERY ON THE FIRST TRY.	USE LONGER BLOCK LENGTH THAN FOR 1A.
D. GUARANTEE PERFORMANCE WILL NOT DEGRADE IN DELIVERY TIME EVEN IF THE DATA CHANNEL DEGRADES.	SELECT BLOCK LENGTH THAT HAS RESIDUAL MARGIN.
2. PRICING ADVANTAGES	
A. SUBSITUTE 2-WAY ALTERNATE FOR 2-WAY SIMULTANEOUS FOR USERS ACCEPTING 1B OR C.	USE 2-WIRE LINES AND MODEMS INSTEAD OF 4-WIRE LINES AND MODEMS.
B. LOWER THE DATA RATE AND SAVE TRANSMISSION EQUIPMENT COSTS ON SERVICE TO USERS ACCEPTING 1B OR 1C.	SELECT REDUCED DATA RATE AND LESS EXPENSIVE MODEMS AND COMMUNICATION LINES.
C. CHARGE FOR DELIVERY SPEED; USE THE SAME DESIGN FOR ALL USERS BUT USE LOWER GRADE TRANSMISSION SERVICES FOR THOSE USERS SELECTING 1B OR C.	USE LESS EXPENSIVE EQUIPMENT AND COMMUNICATIONS LINES FOR SELECTED USERS.

tionally, a user who is willing to forego the delivery time guarantee can be given a lesser guarantee, such as one in one-thousand messages exceeding the specified time. This is achieved by changing that users block length. Users will pay less but are guaranteed less, too.

The design approach also has a built-in ability to adapt to higher data error rates than expected. This can be taken advantage of by using poorer performing modems and reducing the charge to the user or choosing to use these poor modems as a baseline and charging more for a higher grade-of-error tolerance which costs the provider nothing more. A summary of these strategies is presented in Table 1.

By taking advantage of the various market pricing strategies available through the delivery-time approach and not the throughput approach, a computer communication utility can attract users initially and adapt to varying business conditions in the future.

Editors note. Some modifications to part 1 of this article, which appeared last month, are necessary for the full mathematical derivations to be understood. On page 40 in "Design equation derived" the sum of all possible retransmissions should be from $i = 0$, 1, 2, etc. Also, on the same page, in the second line of the throughput equation the third term of the denominator should be: $n[P \geq (1,n)]^2$. On page 41 the lower limit of equation 1 should be zero. In the caption to Figure 4, the quantity C should be equal to 1. ∎

How to determine message response time for satellites

Martin A. Reed and Terence D. Smetanka, International Business Machines Corp.

**Noise and propagation delay
may affect response time,
but an optimum message format
may be found mathematically**

As it becomes more common to use satellite circuits for transmission of data in interactive applications, so it becomes more important for users to understand the factor of propagation delay. There is considerable propagation delay inherent to satellite transmission, and this, along with the high incidence of bit errors on the terrestrial links, can impair efficient operation of an interactive communications hookup.

A mathematical model, presented in this article, helps provide insight on how to minimize link response time. Besides bit-error rate and propagation delay on the satellite link, the model takes into account such parameters as propagation delay on the terrestrial links, the highest number of information frames that can be outstanding and unacknowledged, and the size and number of frames in any one message.

The usual arrangement of a satellite link and its operating environment is for a central computer and a terminal to communicate through a satellite reached by earth stations usually remote from the actual ends of the link. A communications link, called a terrestrial tail, is normally necessary to connect each data processing unit with its respective earth station.

These terrestrial tails are the parts of a satellite transmission circuit most prone to errors. The error rate may range from 1 in 10^3 bits to 1 in 10^5 bits (Ref. 1). The satellite link itself usually has an error rate of 1 in 10^6 bits (Ref. 2), or better. The terrestrial tails are therefore the critical components when considering errors in the overall data link.

There are basically two types of application that will normally make use of a satellite transmission system: batch and interactive. Batch data applications are typically the exchanges of very large blocks of data between separate data processing subsystems. Batch transmissions are usually background operations in which throughput is a key parameter and response time not a critical factor. In contrast, response time is a vital factor in an interactive exchange, since one station must wait for a reply from its correspondent station before the next transmission can proceed. It is essential, therefore, to conduct an analysis of response time when considering the interactive use of a satellite transmission system.

In the satellite transmission system represented in Figure 1, the secondary station—such as a terminal subsystem outside London—generates a message in digitized form. The message is converted to an analog signal by the modem for transmission over the communications links. A terrestrial tail carries it to an earth station in London which transmits it at frequencies in the gigahertz range to a satellite in synchronous orbit

1 Satellite hookup

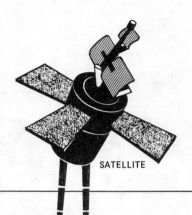

SATELLITE

Tail to tail. A message-and-response sequence on a satellite link must travel four times between satellite and earth, and will develop a propagation delay of nearly half a second. High-speed digital transmission may make this delay a serious problem for the smooth, error-free operation of the link, and steps must be taken to deal with it.

22,300 MILES

CENTRAL PROCESSOR | TERRESTRIAL TAIL | NEW YORK CITY | LONDON | TERRESTRIAL TAIL | INTELLIGENT TERMINAL

PRIMARY STATION | MODEM | EARTH STATION | ANTENNA | ANTENNA | EARTH STATION | MODEM | SECONDARY STATION

35,800 km (22,300 miles) over the Atlantic. The signal is passed on to an earth station in New York City, and then follows a terrestrial tail to the primary station—say a central processor in Albany—where a modem turns the analog signal back into the original digital format.

High-level data link control
The calculation of message response time on satellite circuits is based on transmission under the high-level data link control (HDLC) protocol defined by the International Standards Organization, using a half-duplex, point-to-point circuit. Other high-level, bit-oriented control protocols that might apply are IBM's synchronous data link control (SDLC) (Refs. 3 and 4), and the advanced data communications control procedure (ADCCP) (Ref. 5), the telecommunications standard proposed by the American National Standards Institute; the technique could also be adapted for a full-duplex or multipoint operation.

Any message may consist of one or more frames, and each frame under HDLC is divided into six fields, which perform the various link control functions (Fig. 2): opening flag, address field, control field, information field, frame check sequence field, and closing flag. All are a fixed size, except for the information field, which can range from no bits at all to as many bits as neces-

sary. The flags indicate the beginning and end of the frame. The address field tells which secondary station the frame is going to or coming from. The frame check sequence field is based on a cyclic redundancy check and is needed for detecting the line errors. The information field, if present, contains the user data.

In general, the control field carries the commands and responses required to control the data link. This field also contains two subfields, representing the send and receive sequence counts, N(S) and N(R) respectively. In what is called double-numbering, a station transmitting information frames inserts the number of each one, in sequence, in the N(S) subfield. The receiving station, meanwhile, maintains a corresponding N(R) count, which is incremented upon the receipt of each error-free frame, as long as the received N(S) matches its N(R) count.

The N(R) count thus represents the number of the "next expected" frame to be received. If the received N(S) and the N(R) do not match, the N(R) count does not advance. In such a case, an error will have occurred in the transmission, and the N(R) count will show which frame was the first in error. There is a procedure known as selective reject, whereby only the frame or frames containing errors need be retransmitted, but this requires extensive buffering at both the

2 HDLC frame format

Six fields. *HDLC consists of six fields: The third, the control field, tallies frames transmitted and frames correctly received, and requests retransmission if need be.*

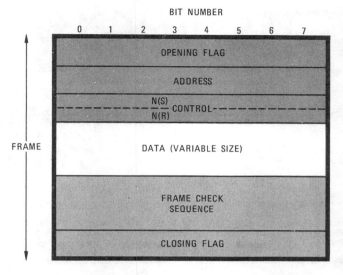

transmitting and the receiving station. This model will instead make use of the GO-BACK-N-ARQ method, an automatic request for repeat of an errored frame and all subsequent frames outstanding and unacknowledged (where N represents the highest number of outstanding frames allowed under a given protocol before acknowledgment is mandatory; under HDLC, N is 127).

Limiting the frames

However, although HDLC allows this relatively large number of outstanding frames under its expanded control operation, if the bit-error rate is high and the data field large it may be undesirable to allow the full 127 frames to be outstanding. In such a case, the number of frames to be retransmitted after an error could be substantial, and thus response time could be significantly degraded. Consequently, a network parameter similar to the MAXOUT option in the IBM network control program (Ref. 6) may be brought in to limit the number of outstanding frames.

When the number of frames in the message is larger than the MAXOUT number, the GO-BACK-N-ARQ procedure allows the retransmission of the frame in error and up to (MAXOUT − 1) subsequent frames, including frames not previously transmitted (Fig. 3). When the number of frames in a message is less than or equal to MAXOUT, the link will operate as though MAXOUT equals the number of message frames.

Thus, the total number of frames transmitted, as well as the number of transmissions required to send a message of B frames, are functions of these four elements: the MAXOUT, the bit-error rate, the number of frames in the message, and the frame size in bits.

Figure 4 details the components of total link response time for each transmission of an exchange of

message and response over the link, where the message is from the secondary to the primary station, as in data entry applications. After the secondary station (in the half-duplex, point-to-point transmission to be used for this model) receives a poll and prepares to send its input message, there is a small delay while the transmission passes physically through the modem; this time is known as the modem transit delay (d_{MT}). There are also propagation delays associated with the terrestrial tails (d_{TP}) and the satellite link (d_{SP}), as the frames are transmitted.

Propagation delays on the two terrestrial tails will likely be not of the same length, because of the different physical lengths of the tails themselves; on the other hand, during any one message-and-response sequence the total of all four delays on the satellite link (up and down for the message, up and down for the response) will be of the same duration. All delays will to some extent contribute to the overhead time.

The actual transmission time of the frames is determined by the data speed of the link — for example, 2,400 b/s, 4,800 b/s, or 9,600 b/s. When the frames are recieved at the primary station, there is once again a modem transit delay. The primary station will then immediately acknowledge the receipt of the error-free frames. When the secondary station receives this ac-

3 Sample transmitting sequence

Requests for repeats. *The receiver requests retransmission of an errored frame and all following frames, but the outstanding frames are held to a manageable limit.*

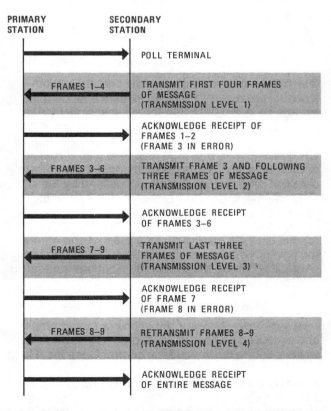

4 Overhead delays on a satellite circuit

Delays, delays. Every element of a communications circuit can contribute to the propagation delay, and delays on the satellite links far overshadow any others.

Because the terrestrial tails will likely be of different lengths, the difference in their propagation delays must be considered when computing total overhead delay.

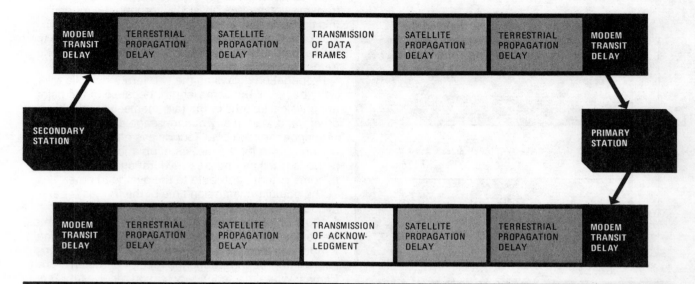

knowledgment, the next sequence of frames in the message can be sent. A link reponse time for a message, based on Figure 4, can now be defined. This response time is the total overhead time due to delays, along with the message transmission time.

Transmission overhead

The total overhead delay incurred in one transmission sequence, as given in Figure 4, is:

$$D = 4d_{MT} + 2d_{TP1} + 2d_{TP2} + 4d_{SP} \quad (1)$$

$$+ \frac{\text{Acknowledgement size in bits}}{\text{Link speed in b/s}} + d_A$$

where d_A represents any additional configuration dependent delays—such as satellite turnaround time, additional system protocol, and encoding/decoding time, all of which are here considered zero.

The number of transmissions required to send a complete message of B frames, with corrected frames, if any, from the secondary to primary station, is called the number of transmission levels (Fig. 3). Link response time (LRT) can then be calculated as:

$$LRT = \frac{(\text{Average number of frames})(\text{Frame size})}{\text{Link speed in b/s}} \quad (2)$$

$$+ (\text{Average number of transmission levels})(D)$$

Equation 2 can also be written as:

$$LRT = \frac{(N_F)(S)}{b/s} + (N_L)(D) \quad (3)$$

where N_F denotes the average number of frames transmitted for a message, including the original message and frames retransmitted because of bit errors in the message; S the frame size in bits; N_L the average number of levels of transmission required for a message; and D the overhead delay for one sequence.

Equation 3 is called the mathematical model for link response time; only D can be readily calculated. N_F and N_L, however, depend on complex functional relationships with such parameters as MAXOUT, bit error rate, number of frames in the message, and frame length in bits.

The factors N_F and N_L can be calculated as shown in the panel "Mathematical model for link response". Although this model may look formidable, it can be executed on a calculator; but it is more efficient, because of the large number of computations involved and the number of iterations required to find optimum values—of MAXOUT, for example—to program the model on a computer. Writing the program will take four to five hours, but each iteration can then be obtained in about one minute of computer run time.

Finding optimum MAXOUT

Two examples have been worked out, and are presented here, to determine the effect of various MAXOUT values and bit-error rates on link response time. The model can also be used to find the effect of various frame sizes and numbers of frames in the message.

Consider the transmission of a message containing 2,048 eight-bit characters from a secondary to a primary station over a 9,600-b/s transmission link. Assume that the circuit has modems with 10 ms transit times. Take the length of each terrestrial tail to be 100 miles, where the propagation delay for this link is 1 ms for each 15 miles (Ref. 7). Acknowledgments are considered to be 56 bits long.

The terms in the expression for overhead delay dur-

Mathematical model for link response

Response time $= \dfrac{(N_F)(S)}{b/s} + (N_L)(D)$

where N_F denotes the average number of frames transmitted, including the original message and any frames retransmitted because of errors; N_L denotes the average number of transmission levels required; and D is the overhead delay incurred during one transmission sequence, calculated from equation (1) in the main text. N_F and N_L are computed from the equations below.

$$N_F = \sum_{j=1}^{L} E_j$$

$$N_L = \sum_{j=1}^{L} V_j$$

where:

$$E_j = M \vee B \qquad\qquad\qquad\quad \text{where } j = 1$$

$$= \sum_{k=1}^{B} (P_{j-1,k} + P'_{j-1,k})\,[M \vee B - (k-1)] \quad \text{where } j > 1$$

$$V_j = 1 \qquad\qquad\qquad\qquad\quad \text{where } j = 1$$

$$= \sum_{k=1}^{B} (P_{j-1,k} + P'_{j-1,k}) \qquad \text{where } j > 1$$

$$P_{jk} = T_{jk}\, p^j q^{k-1}$$

$$T_{jk} = \sum_{n=0}^{(\wedge k + M)-1} (-1)^n\,(C_{j+1-n,n+1})\,(C_{j,k-nM})$$
$$\qquad\qquad\qquad \text{where } k < (M+1) + (j-1)(M-1)$$

$$= 0 \qquad\qquad\qquad\qquad \text{otherwise}$$

$$C_{jk} = \frac{(j+k-2)!}{(k-1)!\,(j-1)!}$$

$$P'_{jk} = \sum_{n=1}^{\wedge(k-M)+M} (C_{j+1-n,n+1})\,(T_{j-n,k-nM}\,pj - n_q k - 1)$$
$$\qquad\qquad\qquad \text{where } M < k < (M+1) + M(j-1)$$
$$= 1 \qquad\qquad \text{where } k = jM + 1$$
$$= 0 \qquad\qquad \text{otherwise}$$

In these equations:

b/s = transmission speed in bits per second;
BER = overall bit-error rate, randomly distributed;
B = message length in frames;
L = total number of transmission levels considered;
M = MAXOUT, in frames;
S = frame size, in bits;
j = particular level of transmission, 1 to L;
k = particular frame, 1 to B;
p = probability of an error in a frame;
q = probability of no error in a frame;
$\wedge\,\alpha$ = least integer greater than or equal to α;
$\alpha \vee \beta$ = the lesser of α and β.

The total number of transmission levels (L) must be set to some practical finite value sufficiently large to guarantee that the average number of frames transmitted on each level—(L + 1), (L + 2), . . .—can be neglected. The specific setting of L depends on the bit error rate (BER), the frame size (S), the message length (B), and the MAXOUT (M), but should be selected so that the average number of frames transmitted on level L is less than 10^{-5}. Since the average number of frames transmitted is a strictly non-increasing function of the particular level of transmission (j), it is possible to ignore all transmissions on levels greater than L.

The expression for frame-error probability (p) can be obtained by noting that if BER is the probability of a bit being in error, then (1-BER) is the probability of a bit not being in error. Thus, $(1 - BER)^S$ is the probability that none of the bits in a frame is in error, and $1 - (1 - BER)^S$ is the probability that at least one bit in a frame is in error. The equations for p and q are then:

$$p = 1 - (1 - BER)^S$$
$$q = 1 - p$$

If the distribution of bit errors is not random, alternate expressions for p and q should be developed from the known distribution.

A 24-page derivation of the mathematical model for the link response time for a message going over a satellite is available from D. Holland, IBM Corp., 65Q202 – 4, P.O. Box 100, Kingston, N.Y. 12401 by requesting IBM Publication TR21.668, April 25, 1977.

ing a message-and-response transmission become:

$d_{MT} = 0.01$ s
$d_{TP} = (100$ miles$)\,(1$ ms $/15$ miles$) = 0.0067$ s
$d_{SP} = (22,300$ miles$)/(186,000$ miles/s$)$
$\qquad = 0.1199$ s
acknowledgment time $= 56/9,600 = 0.00583$ s

Then, from Equation 1 (above), the overhead delay is determined as: D = 0.552 s.

Although HDLC allows up to 127 outstanding frames, it may be advantageous to restrict this limit by means of MAXOUT in order to minimize response time. In Figure 5, the message is blocked into 32 frames, each of which consists of 64 eight-bit characters. The two components of response time are plotted as a function of the MAXOUT setting. The sum of these two

components gives the link response time.

Note that as MAXOUT increases there are more frames retransmitted for each message, as well as a decrease in overhead time, since fewer levels of transmission are required. The optimal value for MAXOUT in this case is less than the number of frames in the message. That is, a MAXOUT of 16 gives the smallest response time, of 4.89 s.

Choice for frames

The user may also have a choice of several different frame sizes. If this is the case, then an even lower response time may be achieved by the proper selection of frame size. Figure 6 gives link response time as a function of MAXOUT for a message blocked into 16

5 Components of link response time

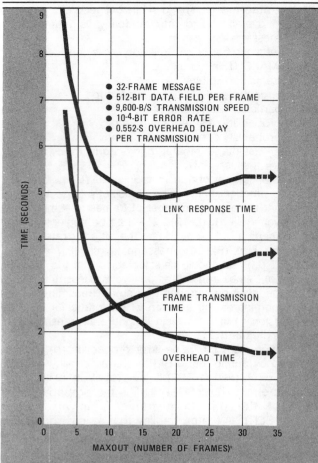

- 32-FRAME MESSAGE
- 512-BIT DATA FIELD PER FRAME
- 9,600-B/S TRANSMISSION SPEED
- 10^{-4}-BIT ERROR RATE
- 0.552-S OVERHEAD DELAY PER TRANSMISSION

LINK RESPONSE TIME

FRAME TRANSMISSION TIME

OVERHEAD TIME

TIME (SECONDS) / MAXOUT (NUMBER OF FRAMES)

Limiting the frames. *Although HDLC allows up to 127 outstanding frames, throughput considerations call for a MAXOUT limit on the satellite link of, say, 32 frames.*

6 Effect of bit errors vs. MAXOUT

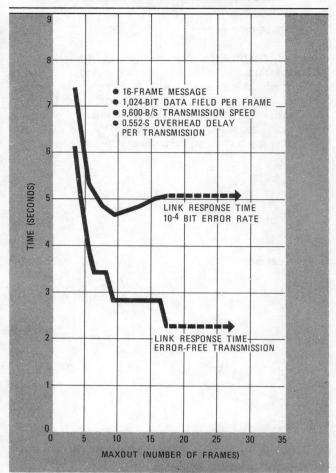

- 16-FRAME MESSAGE
- 1,024-BIT DATA FIELD PER FRAME
- 9,600-B/S TRANSMISSION SPEED
- 0.552-S OVERHEAD DELAY PER TRANSMISSION

LINK RESPONSE TIME 10^{-4} BIT ERROR RATE

LINK RESPONSE TIME ERROR-FREE TRANSMISSION

TIME (SECONDS) / MAXOUT (NUMBER OF FRAMES)

Optimal response. *Response time on an error-free link decreases against MAXOUT. Optimal response occurs where MAXOUT at least equals the number of frames.*

---

frames, each of which consists of 128 eight-bit characters. The optimal response time is shown to be 4.76 s, which is lower than the response time that was previously achieved.

In a second example, the effect of transmission errors on the link response time is demonstrated in Figure 6. In general, the response time of a hypothetical error-free transmission link is a decreasing function of MAXOUT. The optimal value of response time occurs where MAXOUT is at least as large as the number of frames in the message. In this case, the optimal response time is 2.35 s, whereas the optimal response time with one bit in 10^4 in error is 4.76 s at a MAXOUT of eight. Therefore, the effect of transmission errors is to double the best zero-error link response time.

Not only can the proper selection of the frame size and MAXOUT parameters be achieved by using the mathematical model, but cost/performance tradeoffs may also be considered. For example, a higher grade link can reduce the bit-error rate, which will yield a lower link response time (Fig. 6). And a higher speed link will also decrease the link response time, since the

frame transmission time decreases. But a better conditioned or faster link may lead to higher costs. The technique developed here will indicate whether more expensive equipment is justified. ∎

References

1. Martin, J. (1972), Systems analysis for data transmission, Prentice-Hall Inc., Englewood, N.J., p. 202.
2. E. R. Cacciamani and K. S. Kim, Circumventing the problem of propagation on satellite data channels, Data Communications, July/August 1975, pp. 19-24.
3. IBM synchronous data link control—general information, IBM publication GA27-3093-0, 1974.
4. J. R. Kersey, Synchronous data link control, Data Communications, May/June 1974, pp. 49-60.
5. D. E. Carlson, ADCCP—A computer-oriented data link control, Compcon, Sept. 9-11, 1975, 110-113.
6. IBM 3704 and 3705 communications controllers, IBM publications GC-3008-3, 1975, pp. 3-60.
7. Planning installation of a data communications system using IBM line adapters, IBM Publication GA24-3435-5, 1974, pp. 26-27.

Swapping response time for less switch capacity

C. Warren Axelrod, Securities Industry Automation Corp., New York City

If priority operation is invoked, message volume may not outgrow computer limits, but secondary traffic queues will get longer

Before yielding to the pressures of a rising volume of traffic by acquiring more hardware, the network designer might be well advised to ask himself: "Is there a better way?" The way may be better with a message priority mode of operation. In fact, if a realistic evaluation of user response time needs can be made, the findings may well result in fulfilling user requirements at much smaller message-switching capacities.

Messages in a communications system frequently have different priorities. For example, in a stock-market trading environment, it is usually much more important to get an order into the system than to receive an administrative message or an execution report concerning some earlier transaction. Similarly, for a reservations system, the greatest need is to ensure the most rapid transmittal of a reservation request into the computer—the confirmation can often wait a moment or two.

In a study of a major real-time message-switching system, it was found that the capacity requirements could be cut almost in half if users could tolerate comparatively lengthy response times on low-priority messages. From the users' viewpoint, the system under examination accepts input messages (type A) and generates report messages (type B) according to the histogram distribution shown in Figure 1. Note that the system from which this information was collected has

a capacity of at least 3.7 messages per second. At this capacity there is no delay due to queuing, and the response time is equal to the processing time, apart from slight delays that might result from the clustering of messages for random arrivals. No delays will occur for uniform arrival rates.

If the capacity of the system drops below 3.7 messages per second, all messages arriving in a given interval may not be serviced during that interval. In this case, queues will form and the response time will naturally increase as a result.

In Figure 1, the histogram shows arriving message rates (both for type A and type B) for two-minute intervals during a peak 40-minute period. Assuming uniform arrival rates within each two-minute interval, all messages will be serviced under a first-come-first-served discipline immediately upon arrival, for a system with a capacity of 3.7 messages per second or greater. If system capacity is reduced to 3.5 messages per second, a queue will form, as shown by the lowest curve, building to a peak of 130 messages at time interval $t = 10$. However, the queue dissipates by $t = 16$. For a system with a capacity of 3.0 messages per second, the queue reaches a peak of 828 messages at $t = 13$, and then proceeds to fall off.

Reducing capacity still further to 2.5 messages per

1 Message arrivals and queue length—peak period

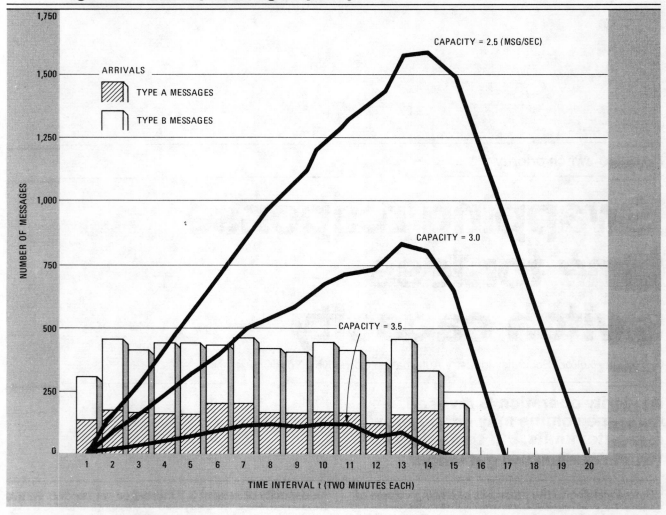

Waiting for the message. *During a peak 40-minute period, type A (input) and type B (report) messages were generated as is shown by the histogram. Assuming all messages are serviced on a first-come-first-served basis, the queue curve applicable to each message is determined by the computer's available switching capacity.*

second causes the backlog to build up rapidly to a peak of 1,585 messages at $t = 14$. Such a situation would require a large memory to store the queued messages. The queue reduces to zero at $t = 20$.

Waiting time vs capacity

Queue lengths translate into waiting time, and in Table 1 the queue lengths and waiting times are shown for various system capacities. Both the maximum and average waiting times are given for the first-come-first-served (FCFS) discipline, in which type A and type B messages are serviced in order of arrival, regardless of message type; and for a discipline in which all type A messages awaiting service are handled prior to any type B messages in the queue.

Under the FCFS discipline, as shown in Table 1, the average waiting time for both message types is lower than for the corresponding average waiting time for type B messages under the priority rule. But, note that

under priority conditions, type A messages do not have to wait, since their arrival rate never exceeds 2.0 messages per second (240 messages in a two-minute interval), the lowest system capacity investigated. However, for a system of capacity 3.0 messages per second, an average wait of 2.5 minutes may be unacceptable for type A messages, but 4.1 minutes may be acceptable for type B messages. The acceptability of a 4.1-minute wait for type B messages, combined with zero wait for type A messages, would indicate that the system capacity is sufficient when the priority rule is in use.

Maximum waiting times are almost the same for both servicing rules since the queue lengths are the same. But, of course, the queue consists of both types of messages under FCFS, and of only type B under priority conditions.

The queue lengths and average waiting times are plotted against system capacity in Figure 2. It is seen that the queues and average waiting times rise at an increasing rate as capacity is reduced. Such a chart is useful in determining desired system capacity. For example, if the priority rule is selected, and a five-minute average wait is acceptable, then a capacity of 2.9 messages per second is appropriate.

Figuring the waiting times

It has been shown that if users' needs are broken down on a priority basis, considerable cost savings may be realized through reduced system size. A method is suggested for selecting the most appropriate servicing rule and system capacity. To enable a message-switch system designer to apply this method, it will be found beneficial to consider how the queues and waiting times are calculated.

A computer program may be used to obtain the results presented here. Alternatively, a set of equations may be derived and the results tabulated. In either case, the logical sequence of steps to be considered is the following:

- The number of arrivals by message type is noted for each time interval.
- If the number of arrivals in the interval is less than the system capacity, the queue, if any, is reduced accordingly. Otherwise, the excess arrivals are added to the queue.
- The queue length is calculated for each interval.
- The average and maximum waiting times are obtained from the queue statistics, which vary with the servicing discipline in effect.

Deriving the equations

To establish the equations let:

t = a two-minute time interval, for example.

A_t = the number of type A messages arriving in time interval t ($t = 1,2,...,n$, where n is the number of intervals under consideration).

B_t = the number of type B messages arriving in time interval t.

I_t = the total number of messages inputted in time interval t.

R_t = the number of messages remaining in the input queue at the end of time interval t.

R_t^B = the number of type B messages remaining in the input queue at the end of interval t.

$R_{d,t}$ = the number of messages remaining in the input queue at the end of interval t with an expected delay of d intervals.

$R_{d,t}^B$ = the number of type B messages remaining in the input queue at the end of interval t with an expected delay of d intervals.

Q_t = the number of messages available for processing in interval t.

P_t = the number of messages processed in interval t.

P_t^A = the number of type A messages processed in interval t.

P_t^B = the number of type B messages processed in t.

C = the processing capacity of the system, assumed constant from intervals t = 1 to t = n.

W_t = the maximum waiting time for messages remaining in the queue at the end of interval t.

W_{AVG} = the average waiting time for all messages arriving in the interval from t = 1 to t = n.

L = the length of the time interval, t (in minutes).

From the above definitions we obtain the following relationships:

$$I_t = A_t + B_t \text{ for } t = 1,2,...,n \tag{1}$$

$$Q_t = \begin{cases} I_t \text{ for } t = 1 \\ I_t + R_{t-1} \text{ for } t = 2,3,...,n \end{cases} \tag{2}$$

where R_{t-1} is the number of messages remaining in the input queue at the end of interval t-1.
For the FCFS case,

$$R_t = Q_t - P_t \text{ for } Q_t \geq P_t, t = 1,2,...,n \tag{3}$$

where $P_t = P_t^A + P_t^B$

For the priority case, since all type A messages are serviced immediately upon arrival and do not appear in the queue,

$$R_t = R_t^B \tag{4}$$

Table 1 Queue lengths and waiting times

SYSTEM CAPACITY (MSG/SEC)	MAXIMUM QUEUE LENGTH (MESSAGES)	FIRST-COME-FIRST-SERVED		PRIORITY FOR TYPE A MESSAGES	
		MAXIMUM WAITING TIME* (MINS)	AVERAGE WAITING TIME* (MINS)	MAXIMUM WAITING TIME** (MINS)	AVERAGE WAITING TIME** (MINS)
2.0	2,423	22	10.5	22	17.2
2.5	1,583	12	5.5	14	9.0
3.0	828	6	2.5	8	4.1
3.5	130	2	0.4	2	0.4
3.8	0	0	0.0	0	0.0

*TYPE A AND B MESSAGES
**TYPE B MESSAGES ONLY

Table 2 Incoming messages and queues

t	A_t	B_t	I_t	Q_t	P_t	R_t
1	140	163	303	303	300	3
2	168	284	452	455	300	155
3	159	259	418	573	300	273
4	154	289	443	716	300	416
5	154	289	443	859	300	559
6	178	251	429	988	300	688
7	188	267	455	1,143	300	843
8	157	265	422	1,265	300	965
9	155	249	404	1,369	300	1,069
10	159	285	444	1,513	300	1,213
11	155	254	409	1,622	300	1,322
12	122	247	369	1,691	300	1,391
13	161	299	460	1,851	300	1,551
14	172	160	332	1,883	300	1,583
15	120	84	204	1,787	300	1,487
16	–	–	–	1,487	300	1,187
17	–	–	–	1,187	300	887
18	–	–	–	887	300	587
19	–	–	–	587	300	287
20	–	–	–	287	287	0
TOTAL	2,342	3,645	5,987	–	5,987	–

Table 3 Delay distribution—FCFS

t	R_t	$R_{1,t}$	$R_{2,t}$	$R_{3,t}$	$R_{4,t}$	$R_{5,t}$	$R_{6,t}$
1	3	3	–	–	–	–	–
2	155	155	–	–	–	–	–
3	273	273	–	–	–	–	–
4	416	300	116	–	–	–	–
5	559	300	259	–	–	–	–
6	688	300	300	88	–	–	–
7	843	300	300	243	–	–	–
8	965	300	300	300	65	–	–
9	1,069	300	300	300	169	–	–
10	1,213	300	300	300	300	13	–
11	1,322	300	300	300	300	122	–
12	1,391	300	300	300	300	191	–
13	1,551	300	300	300	300	300	51
14	1,583	300	300	300	300	300	83
15	1,487	300	300	300	300	287	–
16	1,187	300	300	300	287	–	–
17	887	300	300	287	–	–	–
18	587	300	287	–	–	–	–
19	287	287	–	–	–	–	–
20	0	–	–	–	–	–	–
TOTAL	–	5,218	4,262	3,318	2,321	1,213	134
Δ	–	956	944	997	1,108	1,079	134

Table 4 Delay distribution—priority case

t	P_t^B	R_t^B	$R_{1,t}^B$	$R_{2,t}^B$	$R_{3,t}^B$	$R_{4,t}^B$	$R_{5,t}^B$	$R_{6,t}^B$	$R_{7,t}^B$
1	160	3	3	–	–	–	–	–	–
2	132	155	141	14	–	–	–	–	–
3	141	273	146	127	–	–	–	–	–
4	146	416	146	122	112	36	–	–	–
5	146	559	122	112	143	145	37	–	–
6	122	688	112	143	145	141	145	2	–
7	112	843	143	145	141	145	178	91	89
8	143	965	145	141	145	178	139	128	158
9	145	1,069	141	145	178	139	128	180	143
10	141	1,213	145	178	139	128	180	300	97
11	145	1,322	178	139	128	180	300	300	44
12	178	1,391	139	128	180	300	300	300	43
13	139	1,551	128	180	300	300	300	300	–
14	128	1,583	180	300	300	300	300	203	–
15	180	1,487	300	300	300	300	287	–	–
16	300	1,187	300	300	300	287	–	–	–
17	300	887	300	300	287	–	–	–	–
18	300	587	300	287	–	–	–	–	–
19	300	287	287	–	–	–	–	–	–
20	287	0	–	–	–	–	–	–	–
TOTAL	3,645	–	3,356	3,061	2,798	2,579	2,294	1,804	574
Δ			295	263	219	285	490	1,230	574

$P_t^A \leq C$ for zero waiting time for type A messages. The above equations are used to determine the queue lengths (R_t), as shown in Table 2, for an FCFS case. The A_t and B_t columns of Table 2 are obtained from recorded statistics, in a system described later. (Table 2 also applies in the priority case, except that $R_t = R_t^B$.) In an FCFS example, using Table 2 for t = 4: from equation (1), $I_4 = 154 + 289 = 443$; from equation (2), $Q_4 = 443 + 273 = 716$; from equation (3), $R_4 = 716 - 300 = 416$.

Consider this system which can process 2.5 messages a second, or capacity C = 300 messages for each t = 2 minute interval. In order to obtain waiting times for all arriving messages for t = 1, 2,..., 15, it is necessary to determine the queue characteristics beyond t = 15 until all arrivals have been serviced. This occurs for t = 20 in Table 2 (and Fig. 1). Summing over the 20 intervals, the number of arrivals is equal to the number of messages processed, or

$$\sum_{t=1}^{20} I_t = \sum_{t=1}^{20} P_t$$

and is equal to 5,987.

In Table 3, the FCFS queues (R_t) for each interval t are distributed according to the delay the messages in the queue will experience. For example, at the end of interval t = 4, a total of 416 messages remains to be serviced ($R_4 = 416$). However, since $P_5 = 300$ messages, only 300 of the messages will be serviced with one delay interval in the immediately following interval (t = 5). Under FCFS, the remainder of 116 messages will not be serviced until t = 6. With t = 4, these results are shown in Table 3 as $R_{1,4} = 300$ and $R_{2,4} = 116$. The subscript stands for the delay intervals expected at the end of a time interval. That is, when $R_{d,t}$ is $R_{2,4}$, the messages remaining to be serviced at the end of interval 4 will be delayed until sometime during two intervals later (interval 6). By following this logic for all values of R_t, the $R_{d,t}$ values of Table 3 build up, as shown. By summing each $R_{d,t}$ column of the table, we obtain the total number of messages delayed the column's d intervals or more. Thus, for d = 5,

$$\sum_{t=1}^{20} R_{5,t} = 1,213,$$

which means that 1,213 messages are delayed five intervals or more. Similarly, 134 messages are delayed six intervals or more. However, no messages are delayed more than six intervals. Therefore the 134 messages are delayed just six intervals, so that 1,079 messages (1,213 minus 134) are delayed five intervals. By successively subtracting the total to the right, the number of messages delayed for each time interval is obtained as shown by the bottom "difference" row called delta (Δ) in Table 3. Note that the maximum waiting time is given by the number of intervals represented by the rightmost column (d = 6). Since each interval is two minutes, the maximum waiting time is approximately 12 minutes (see Table 1). If $R_{6,14}$ were 300, the maximum waiting time would be exactly 12 minutes. But $R_{6,14} = 83$ (Table 3). The system can process 300 messages during each two-minute interval. Therefore,

Techniques for analyzing queuing

There are two basic approaches to analyzing queuing systems: deterministic and probabilistic. In the former, the basic data (such as the number of arrivals in a given interval, the service time for each arrival) is assumed to be known, and the results of the analysis are single-valued. For the latter, the characteristics of the system are assumed to belong to probability distributions, such as the bell-shaped normal distribution, and the results are also in probability-distribution form.

Within the probabilistic approach, two techniques are available: analytic and simulation. In the first, applicable to relatively simple systems, equations are developed and solved manually—on a computer, or with a programmable calculator.

In simulation, generally, values of the parameters are selected at random from probability distributions, and the results are determined via a model of the system. In order to obtain realistic results, the simulation model may have to be run hundreds or thousands of times. This often dictates the use of a computer. Simulation has the advantage of enabling the analyst to evaluate more complex systems than analytic methods, and to attain greater accuracy.

Both of the probabilistic methods are useful, if not mandated, at the system planning stage, when the system parameters are not known with precision. When a system already exists, or if accurate system parameters can be obtained from other sources, the deterministic method of this article is preferred, especially for evaluating changes to a running system. Here, the system is modeled to virtually any degree of complexity and level of detail, and the results are calculated for each case, as desired.

the 83rd message is delayed 10 minutes (five intervals) plus (83/300) x 2 minutes of the sixth interval, or 10.6 minutes. Note that the shorter the interval, the more precise the approximation.

Using the differences, D_d, the average waiting time, W_{AVG}, is given by

$$W_{AVG} = L \times \sum_{d=1}^{d\,max}(d \times D_d) \Big/ \sum_{t=1}^{n} I_t \qquad (5)$$

where L is the length of the time interval. Substituting the numbers from Table 3, and with L = 2 minutes, d max = 6 and n = 15 (all messages inputted), we obtain:

$$W_{AVG} = [2 \times [(1 \times 956) + (2 \times 944) +$$

$$(3 \times 997) + (4 \times 1,108) +$$

$$(5 \times 1,079) + (6 \times 134)]] \div 5,987$$

$$= \frac{2 \times 16,466}{5,987} = 5.5 \text{ minutes.}$$

This result is shown in Table 1. For the priority case,

2 Maximum queue length and average waiting time vs. capacity

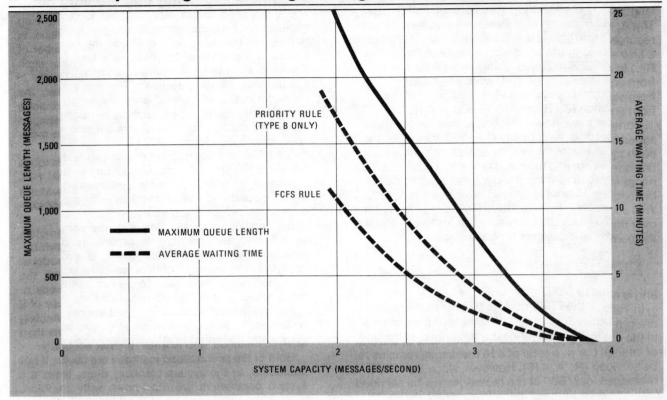

Choosing capacity. *Under priority conditions, if a five-minute wait is acceptable for type B messages, then a system capacity of 2.9 messages per second is sufficient.* *With the first-come-first-served rule prevailing, only a 2.5 message-per-second capacity is needed, but then all messages are subject to the five-minute waiting queue.*

the calculations of maximum and average waiting times are similar to those of the FCFS case. However, the derivation of the queue table in the priority case—Table 4—is more complex. The number of type B messages processed in interval t, P_t^B, is equal to the capacity remaining after the type A messages arriving in interval t have been processed. That is, $P_t^B = P_t - P_t^A$, where $P_t^A = A_t$, priority case (all arriving A messages are processed—see Table 2). For example, for t = 6, $P_6^B = 300 - 178 = 122$. In the priority case, the P_t^B (rather than the P_t used in the FCFS case) is used to determine the elements of Table 4, "Delay distribution—priority case."

Calculating the table
As an example, for t = 3, we have the messages remaining on queue at the end of interval 3, $R_3^B = 273$. But $P_4^B = 146$ messages, so that only 146 messages will be processed in the immediately following interval (t = 4) and the remainder of 127 messages (273 minus 146) will be serviced in t = 5. Thus, $R_{1,3}^B = 146$ (B messages remaining in queue at the end of interval 3 with expected delay of one interval) and $R_{2,3}^B = 127$ (expected delay of two intervals). The other elements of Table 4 are obtained in the same way.

The calculation of the approximate maximum waiting time is the same as for the FCFS case. The formula for

the average waiting time is slightly different from equation (5), since the denominator is

$$\sum_{t=1}^{n} B_t \text{ instead of } \sum_{t=1}^{n} I_t$$

due to applying the average only to type B messages.

The problem of how one can trade off response time against capacity under different service rules is common to many data systems in a variety of industries. Explicit consideration of the service requirements of messages to be handled, and the volume of the messages, should occur at the system design stage in order to determine system capacity needs. The method presented here is ideally suited to evaluating capacity for any no-priority or single-priority system, given knowledge of message arrival rates by type of message. Multiple priority systems can be handled via an extension of the method.

For an established system, where capacity is fixed, the method is valuable in determining the system performance (in terms of response times) for various sequencing rules, such as FCFS and single priority, so that the most effective rule can be instituted.

In all cases, it is merely required to know the arrival distribution by message type and the capacity of the system. The analysis then follows the method described here. ∎

Part 3
Distributed
data processing

Distributed data processing: where we are now

Hal B. Becker, Honeywell Information Systems, Phoenix, Ariz.

Evolution to distributed configuration has occurred for valid reasons, but this evolving—and complex— technique may not be for everyone

Distributed data processing has been around for some time, yet there are many definitions of what that phrase means. As much a concept as a reality, distributed data processing is certain to occupy a strategic place in the application of data communications.

The many variations in defining the concept, however, tend to obscure the real advantages and drawbacks of distributed configurations, which have been evolving for a number of valid reasons. Certainly, one factor has been the explosion of microcomputer and minicomputer technology along with the continuing evolution of the larger mainframe computers. Another factor was the initiation of the network era. Appearing as early as the 1960s as data communications facilities became available, the network was a response to the migration of numerous applications from batch to the on-line environment.

Certainly, it's true that most networks are still configured in the classical "centralized" form. Information and database processing resources, centrally located, are accessed from remote terminals through appropriate data communications or "network processing" facilities. Advances in the various technologies involved made pursuit of the economy-of-scale available through centralization a universal practice.

However, a growing number of users—not neces-sarily gigantic corporations—are discovering complexity-of-scale limitations as they try to achieve economy-of-scale advantages through centralization.

Problems range from the logistics of deploying multiple large-scale systems configured within a single building to unnecessary complexity of data communications processing facilities which feed the information processors and provide them access to surrounding networks.

Current state-of-the-art hardware and software technologies will not support centralization to the degree desired by these users. For them, distributed processing appears to be the answer.

This evolution into the distributed environment can be traced, and consideration of it may provide an insight into some of the motivations involved.

Fairly universal agreement exists within user and manufacturing communities relative to the three basic building blocks or "functions" necessary to configure information networks of all classes. These classes range from the traditional centralized through the newer and evolving distributed configurations. The functions are information processing, database processing, and network processing. Unfortunately, too many industry seers emphasize only the network aspect of distributed processing, but all three elements are equally important to the development of totally distrib-

uted systems. *Information processing,* the manipulation of information to produce the desired result, includes:
- Assembly and/or compilation of various user application programs
- Execution and control of application programs
- Production of output in various user specified media and formats

Database processing is the ability to store potentially large amounts of information in one or more forms available for access by the network and its users. It includes:
- Generation of the database(s) in the appropriate form(s)
- Providing efficient access to the database
- Maintenance of database integrity, including accuracy, restart/recovery, and data protection and security considerations

Network processing is the ability to move information between various locations (nodes) within a network and includes:
- Control of interface between terminal devices and the network
- Control of interface between the various information processors, database processors, and the network
- Control of information movement between terminals and information processors, terminals and other terminals, information processor to information processor, and potentially, between database processors and all of the preceding

Of the three basic functions, the data communications or network processing function is fast becoming a utility—in the sense of a gas or electric company—to the other two. The network's main function is to provide a path and necessary control logic for the interaction between network information processing and database processing resources—and to provide for efficient access of these resources by the various network user classes.

In its utility role, the network processing function is becoming almost entirely application independent. Continuation of this evolution, coupled with maturation of the new "higher level" (above assembly level) languages for network processing, will greatly enhance the function's ability to adapt to the incessantly changing network environment.

Early computer installations with data communications capabilities usually took the form shown in Figure 1. In these installations, all three functions—information, database, and network processing—were contained and executed within the same computer, the information processor.

The growing availability of data communications facilities and increased terminal usage soon produced a conflict. All three functions had to compete for a single set of resources—such as memory and processor time. This conflict quickly reached a level where a single resource, i.e. single central computer, was unable to meet the increasing demands of the three processing functions.

Initially, the conflict was resolved by "separation-of-function" that occurred about 1964. The network processing function was separated from the other two

and placed in a machine designed specifically for data communications tasks (see Fig. 2.). This machine was quickly called the "front-end" or "front-end network processor." By 1974, all of the major computer manufacturers had adopted the front-end philosophy.

The configurations described in Figures 1 and 2 are both of the "totally centralized" network class. Each of the three functions executes at the same, centrally located site within the network topology.

Shortly after the initial separation-of-function occurred, techniques were explored for providing an efficient level of access to the centralized information and database processing resources from remote terminal clusters. This exploration resulted in the configuration shown in Figure 3. A similar, or ideally identical, network processor was configured within the geographically distant cluster of terminals. It provided the cluster with an efficient economical access level to distant processing resources.

Distributed environment beginning
The appearance of distant terminals really marked the beginning of the "distributed environment." As shown in Figure 3, the information and database processing functions remain centralized at site A while network processing is distributed between the front-end at site A and the remote network processor at site B.

Network processing software techniques were developed that recognized this geographic separation and the obvious need for cooperation in providing the function. Figure 3 thus illustrates a partially distributed configuration.

The network processing function was the first to be distributed. Consequently, considerable experience has been gained in this area and the technology is relatively advanced.

Following the first distributed form (Fig. 3) was the initial distribution of the information processing function (Fig. 4). The satellite processor at site C was called a "remote batch" or "remote job entry" processor. It was usually a smaller scale information processor with a line controller that allowed it to interface with a distant "host" processor at site A.

Later versions appeared with multi-line controllers and eventually front-ends, which allowed terminals clustered around site C to access the resources at the same site as well as other distant network-provided resources.

Figure 4 represents another partially distributed configuration. The information processing function is distributed between the larger host at site A and the satellite at site C, the network processing function is distributed between the host at site A, the satellite at site C, and the remote network processor at site B. However, the database processing function remains centralized at site A.

A considerable base of experience exists for the type of partially distributed configuration shown in Figure 4. A great variety of configurations can be implemented using fairly "standard" off-the-shelf products. Usually, the satellite processor will exhibit a functional subset of the host or central site. Also, while a configuration may include a number of satellite sites, it will typically include just a single host site.

The preceding configurations (through Fig. 4) have been available for some time and continue to provide a workable, efficient, cost-justifiable method of providing access to the necessary processing resources for many users. Others, however, who have reached a point where further centralization will not improve efficiency, are closely examining distributed alternatives.

Figure 5 represents just one of a potentially large number of totally distributed configurations. It is totally distributed, since each of the three basic functions—information, network, and database—exists at more than one location. In Figure 5, each function exists at all three locations.

Notice that the configuration in Figure 5 consists of another combination of the same three basic functions—database, information, and network processing—that the earlier configurations utilized.

Numerous possibilities exist relative to the logical design (software) and its integration with the physical configuration shown in Figure 5. A few of them bear on the discussion at hand.

To facilitate the following discussion of totally distributed functions, it will be assumed that the configuration at sites A, B, and C of Figure 5 are identical, the same model and implementation provided by a single manufacturer. In reality, these could be different makes and models. The information processors at sites A, B, and C may be minicomputers, small- or medium-scale units, as well as larger-scale systems. The logical design problems associated with configurations of the smaller scale processors, however, encompass most of the problems encountered with the bigger machines.

A major advantage of the resource-sharing potential

1 Typical centralized processing

Three-function processor. *Information, database, and network functions vie for memory and processing time in the same central computer—the information processor.*

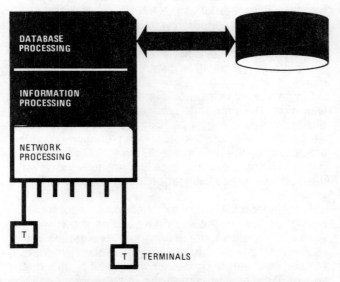

2 Separating front-end processing

Front-end processor. *Despite separation of front-end network processing, the function continues to be executed at the same location and is still centralized.*

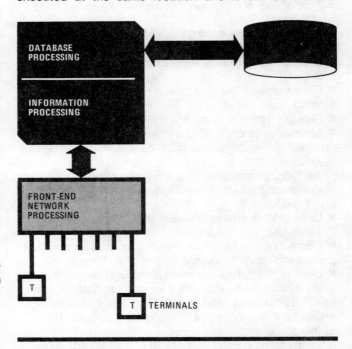

provided by totally distributed configurations is that information and/or database processing loads can be distributed uniformly (in theory) across currently available network resources. Load distribution may occur in a variety of ways.

In perhaps the simplest case, the various application programs are assigned to, and normally executed at the same processing site. Through resource requirements evaluation of the applications and judicious integration of combinations of them within the three sites, a relatively equal load distribution may be achieved. This type of distribution would be fairly stable, interrupted and/or altered only when a failure or other exceptional condition occurs.

Application program distribution of this kind leads directly to the subject of distributing the database(s) associated with and accessed by them. It appears logical to place the database elements, usually accessed by the application process existing at site A, under control of the database management logic resident at site A. Similarly, other database elements would be configured at sites B and C. Known as a partitioned database, this configuration has no single site within a network of this design that maintains a complete copy of the entire database.

Some application program classes executing at their assigned site will require access to information contained in remote partitions of the database. Obviously, the database management logic resident at each of the three sites must distinguish between local and remote database access requests initiated by adjacent information processors. Likewise, each must be capable of responding to requests for database access produced at distant network nodes.

A partitioned database requires that some form of database directory (index of available resources) be available. This directory can range from the database processing functions at the three sites with each maintaining a copy of the directory, to a single copy of the directory maintained at just one of the sites. Evaluation of the trade-offs and selection of a directory implementation can become very complex, particularly when the effect on the information and network processing functions is considered.

Another form of distributed database occurs when each of the three sites maintains a complete copy of the entire database. This is known as a replicated database. The need for a database directory is minimized in this form. However, significant problems arise relative to multiple, conflicting database updates and the need for accurate reconciliation.

Distributed database design considerations and the selection of some form of partitioned and/or replicated database can be more complex than the database directory design previously discussed. This is due, primarily, to the even greater impact of the distributed database on the information and network processing functions. Intersite traffic flow, due to a distributed database and the possible directory function, has a significant impact on network processing throughput with its finite bandwidth limitations. Similarly, throughput and response time characteristics of the application programs executing at the various information processing resources will be affected.

Another distribution variant of application programs involves the use of dynamic allocation algorithms. Application programs are assigned to the information processing sites and resources that, at the time, are most capable of accepting them. In theory, any application program can execute at any site. A given program may execute at site A one time and site B or C another. In this manner, it is hoped that even greater efficiencies via dynamic load leveling will be realized.

Allocation algorithm raises questions
A very obvious requirement of this distributed function type is the dynamic resource scheduling and allocation algorithm. But it raises questions:
- Should the algorithm exist at one site, which would thus control all sites?
- Should the algorithm itself be partitioned, with a piece of it resident at each site?

An intuitive grasp of the desired end result (efficient loading of the network resources) can lead to incredibly complex implementation schemes. Much modeling/simulation research of the various approaches is necessary before workable choices are identified and evaluated.

With application programs traveling around the network, executing programs at first one site and then another, the effect on the associated database activity is potentially significant.

The dynamic scheduling and allocation of the application programs may produce unacceptable traffic

3 Partial distribution

Partial distribution. *Appearance of distant terminals and development of network processing software techniques marked the beginning of distributed data processing.*

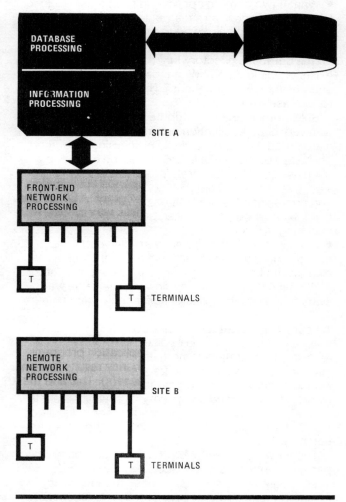

densities at one or more nodes of the network with a relatively static database configuration. This increased density could produce longer response times and/or lower throughput for the executing application program—as well as for other unrelated activities sharing the affected network resources.

Thus, the dynamic scheduling algorithm must evaluate the assignment of a given application program to a given processing resource in terms of its possible undesirable effect on other network activities. It is conceivable that an information processing resource most capable (least busy) of executing an application program could ultimately be the poorest choice due to the effects just described.

An approach that may overcome some resource scheduling/traffic density problems involves the movement of database partitions as well as the application program(s) accessing them. In this way, a high traffic density situation may be avoided and acceptable levels of throughput and response time maintained across the network. Moving database partitions to solve one problem, however, may create others.

■ What if other application programs at local and/or distant processing sites are currently accessing the database partition that is to be moved?

■ What if two or more application programs assigned to different processing sites would like the database partition in question moved to their respective sites?

■ What is the effect of database partition movement on the database directory function? When the directory exists at one location? When the directory exists in its entirety at multiple locations? The questions appear to increase exponentially.

Still another form of distributed function may occur with very large application programs that cannot be accommodated within a single processing resource. These applications would be partitioned and each partition assigned to a separate processing site. The assigned resources would then cooperate in executing and completing the application program. A set of questions, by now vaguely familiar, arises very quickly when exploring this concept.

■ What is the effect on traffic densities, database function, throughput and response time, and other areas as a result of partitioning a large application program?

■ What if it is partitioned statically—the same way every time? Or dynamically—differently every time?

A second separation of function

The preceding discussion of distributed processing reveals that migration of more application programs into the on-line environment frequently results in a similar migration of associated database(s). This and the previously mentioned complexity-of-scale inherent in very large on-line databases (whether centralized or distributed) suggests that a second functional separation may be in order.

The growing dependence on on-line databases capable of supporting heavy access loads produces an increasingly visible conflict. In most offerings today, the information and database processing functions reside in and share a single computer, usually the information processor (see Figs. 2 through 5). The conflict occurs as both functions compete for a single set of resources—such as memory space, processor time, channel time. In a site with heavy information and database processing requirements, successful resolution of the conflict is not always possible—no matter how clever the scheduling and allocation algorithm.

By separating the database function and placing it in an essentially freestanding database processor, certain benefits can be achieved (see Fig. 6). For example, each of the three functions resides and executes in separate processors optimally designed for that function. The information and database processing functions execute more efficiently due to the elimination of complex scheduling algorithm overhead.

Replacing the configuration at each of the three sites in Figure 5 with the configuration shown in Figure 6 and rethinking the discussion in the preceding section (totally distributed functionality) offers intriguing new approaches to some of the problems suggested. It is

conceivable that larger distributed configurations will have one or more nodes consisting of a database processor and a network processor—an information processor is simply not always necessary.

Distributed functionality has been a factor in information network configuration for many years. It will continue to evolve and assume even greater roles in the future. Motivations behind the design of distributed configurations are many—ranging from increased throughput, decreased response times, economic advantages, and the realization that centralization may be difficult, if not impossible, due to complexity-of-scale problems.

The three basic functions, in terms of the distributed environment, include some major objectives in distributing the functions, potential advantages to be realized through distribution, and the major disadvantages that now exist.

The network processing function was the first to be distributed in the early 1960s (see Fig. 3). Prime objectives included moving control of the terminal/network interface out into the network, closer to the terminal clusters. Another objective was reducing data communications costs, primarily in the link (line, trunk) area. Geographic considerations were frequently a factor, and the remote concentrator (Fig. 3) evolved, providing remote terminal clusters with efficient, economical access to distant information and database processing resources.

When the second separation of function occurs (Fig. 6) and increased levels of distributed information and database processing are considered, network processors will be required to provide these distributed resources with access to the surrounding network. Conversely, network processors will provide the various network users with access to the distributed resources.

In some cases, information processing and/or database processing distribution may be considered as a means of alleviating the increasing density of data communications facilities surrounding centralized configurations. Distributed network processing naturally follows.

Distributed network processing advantages

The advantages realized through distribution of the network processing function are many. Among them:

■ Reduced data communications facilities cost

■ Greater user access level to the network and its resources

■ Improved throughput and response time

■ Higher availability and reliability levels through the alternate access and routing logic

The inevitable growth and expansion of the network will be relatively easier to accommodate with increased levels of distributed network processing. Adding or deleting terminals and reconfiguring areas of the network to match changing user requirements will be handled primarily by the network processing function—minimizing the impact on the other two.

While considerable progress has been made with distributed network processing logic, obstacles remain that must be overcome. Newer networks with multiple

4 Distributed information processing

Smaller-scale processors. *Satellite processors initially were called remote batch or remote job entry devices and had a single-line controller interface with the host. Multi-* *line controllers and terminal clusters, allowing local and remote access, were added later. A variety of configurations can be implemented by using standard products.*

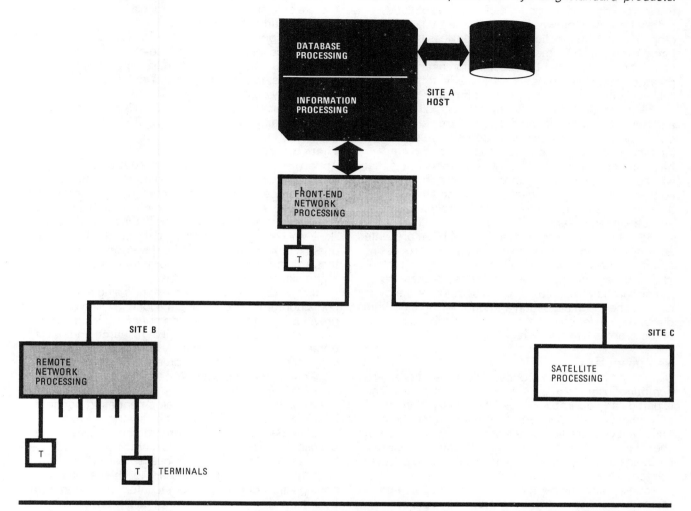

paths between pairs of nodes require more sophisticated routing logic to distribute traffic more uniformly over the paths.

Further, the network must be capable of adapting to load changes imposed by users operating in the various dimensions (timesharing, transaction processing, remote job entry, satellite processing) offered by the network. The network processing logic handling peak early morning periods may not be adequate to handle peaks occurring at other times. This may be due to different combinations of events and require considerably different network processing logic to handle them successfully.

New, higher-level languages for network processing are being developed, but cannot yet be considered mature. These new languages, while not at the compiler level (as are Fortran, Cobol, etc.), are considerably above the assembly level. It is perhaps appropriate to consider them "generator" level languages.

In general, these languages treat network processing

as a set of logic modules that are given a view of the network sector for which they are responsible through a set of attributable tables. Attribute tables define the various interface parameters (physical and logical) presented by the devices (terminals, information processors) that will access the network. Other information relative to addressing, routing, priority, journaling, security, integrity, statistical, and supervisory control logic also is contained in the attribute tables. Attribute tables are then interpretively executed by the logic module set resident in the network processor.

Network changes easily accommodated

A significant, and possibly necessary, advantage of this approach to network processing software is the relative ease with which changes to the network can be accommodated. Terminals, links, and other physical elements can be added, deleted or configured, and the new configuration conveyed to the appropriate network processors quickly. Entry of supervisory mes-

163

sages causing appropriate attribute table changes can be made, in most cases, in an on-line mode, minimizing software rewrite and down-time frequently associated with configuration changes today.

Contemporary network processing usually accepts traffic from devices utilizing different code sets and readily translates between them. But new difficulties crop up when intersection between devices using different protocols becomes necessary. The passage of time seems to promote the proliferation of an even greater number of protocols, particularly at the lower, link level rather than reducing the number.

Link protocols, while useful for masking differences and permitting intersection between terminal devices, do not provide adequate logical control levels for the intersection between coequal information and database processing resources. Higher protocol levels that will facilitate such intersections efficiently are in their relative infancy. A great deal of work and time, unfortunately, is necessary before these protocols will be available to end users.

The network processing function has been presented as a utility to the information and database processing functions. As such, its role in the restart/recovery logic of distributed information and database processing remains largely unexplored. Consideration of the dynamic scheduling allocation and partitioning algorithms discussed earlier provides an insight to the magnitude of the problems requiring resolution.

New user class

Distributed information processing enables a greater number of users to access the function efficiently. This is particularly desirable in view of the availability of new, machine-independent "end-user" languages. These easy-to-use languages are creating a whole new user class which, in turn, acts to compound complexity-of-scale problems already associated with big centralized processors.

Geographic considerations are frequently a major factor in deciding to distribute information processing. Corporations and other organizations with geographically separated elements may find efforts to provide all information processing from a single, centralized site difficult, due to the distances involved.

Corporate merger activity provides another motivation to pursue distributed information processing. Company A, using brand X computers, purchases or acquires control of company B which uses brand Y computers. Both installations are operational, do useful work, and represent substantial system design, development, programming, implementation, and hardware facility investment. Installation interaction is desirable, but replacement of one with a copy of the other so interaction can occur is viewed less than enthusiastically by the principles. Considerable pressure is being applied to computer manufacturers to provide for significantly greater "peaceful coexistence" levels between different machines than are possible today.

Other advantages of distributed information processing may be noted:
- Processing resources are accessible by a greater

number of users more efficiently and economically
- Greater on-line throughput and improved response time
- Improved availability and reliability via the existence of multiple resources
- More efficient utilization of processing resources through uniform load distribution

This last point may provide a stabilization of processing resources, extending the time at which additional facilities must be added to handle increasing loads. In some cases, too, a net reduction in data communications facility costs is anticipated. Reason: a reduction in communications equipment density surrounding large centralized configurations.

There are drawbacks

Appealing as the potential advantages are, there are disadvantages. Frequently, existing autonomous information processing resources located at geographically distant sites and configured with different manufacturers' offerings are to be connected. Since they most likely will be physically and logically different, an adequate set of protocols must be developed to mask these differences and allow interaction—particularly at the higher, user-visible levels.

Further, distributed resource scheduling and allocation algorithms for providing the load leveling discussed previously as an advantage do not exist as standard offerings. It will take considerable research and development before they are readily available. Similar activity must occur in the development of restart/recovery logic and algorithms that will certainly be required in the distributed environment.

A final, very significant development effort concerns information processing operating systems. Present ones are built around the more traditional centralized philosophy. While they can accommodate the host/satellite intersection discussed earlier, the host/host intersection necessary for the various partitionings and/or migration of the information and database processing functions is not easily achieved. It is not a trivial matter to rewrite existing centralized operating systems to produce mature, efficient distributed operating systems.

Distributed database processing is the newest and perhaps least explored of the three processing functions. A variety of objectives, some already discussed, exist for this distribution.

The increasing dependence of information processing on on-line database capability has accelerated its evolution to the point that it will frequently be the most significant of the three. Larger numbers of users (both human and non-human) are demanding increased database access levels. In the process, they're creating a new breed of problems.

Centralized databases frequently cannot provide the desired level of access within response time parameters. This is particularly true as the number of on-line applications with relatively short response time requirements (3-5 seconds) grows. Distributing the database across two or more sites can alleviate this problem.

A second effect is observed when a database is

5 A distributed processing alternative

Uniform processing loads. *Major advantage of resource sharing potential provided by totally distributed configurations is that information and/or database processing* *loads can be distributed evenly across currently available network resources. This type of distribution would be fairly stable—interruptible only under exceptional conditions.*

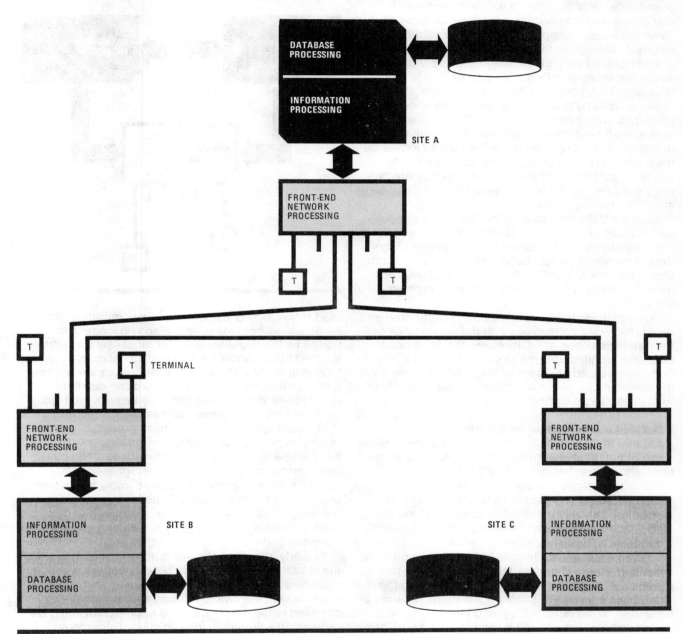

distributed in a manner that maps the geographic distribution of the partition users, distance between users and database is minimized and network processing propogation delays are reduced.

The growth experienced in centralized databases and the size that some have attained produces a complexity-of-scale confrontation similar to that associated with the information processing function. Current technology will not adequately support some of the very large databases being considered. In addition to the improved accessibility provided by a distributed data-

base, it is conceivable that a net reduction in data communications (network processing) costs can be realized. Reason: decreased density of the network processing function that would surround the distributed database sites. The number and bandwidth of links terminating at database sites would be better optimized as would the size and complexity of network processors providing access to the sites.

Being the last of the three to be distributed, the database function exhibits the greatest set of unresolved problems. Database architectures and languages available today, even from a single manufacturer, are frequently physically and logically different. This makes distribution and/or intersection between such facilities difficult to achieve with "standard" implementations. Converting or translating all databases within a proposed network to a single, "standard" architecture that allows such intersection may prove possible in some instances, but appears to be inadequate as a long-term solution to the problem.

An approach with greater long-range potential involves the evolution of a higher-level database mapping language. This, coupled with the new relational databases which lend themselves more readily to such mappings, would permit relatively efficient intersection between different databases or partitions within. Prior to intersection, the elements involved would exchange the mappings associated with the appropriate databases (or partitions). These mappings, when interpretively executed by database management logic, would effect the desired intersection.

All of the difficulties associated today with concurrent multiple access, reconciliation, integrity, and security in centralized databases take on a greater magnitude of complexity when considered relative to distributed database. Considerable research and development is necessary before these and other problems are solved.

Some of these database problems—centralized and distributed—will be resolved with the appearance of the database processor. Others will not. Most current database architectures are structured around the traditional, centralized philosophy. The solution of many of the remaining problems awaits the appearance of mature, distributed database architectures.

Database administrator role grows
Another aspect of distributed databases is the growing role of the database administrator. In many organizations, this person has grown to a level of prominence matching the database itself. His or her importance in a large database-dependent installation is beyond question. The ability of the administrator to function efficiently in all areas and levels of a large distributed database is, however, another question.

Given a suitable architecture for designing and implementing a large distributed database and an appropriate set of efficient languages for accessing it, the database administrator's role begins to track the database itself. While retaining higher control levels over database architectures and languages, the administrator can partition the design and implementation of distributed database sites across the administrators at those sites. In this manner, the various partitions and/or replications can be designed to facilitate the access and usage patterns of the various organizational groups requiring them.

In summary, the distributed environment appears from one point of view to be a revolutionary new concept capable of solving all user problems overnight. But distributed configurations are not for everyone. Many user needs will continue to be satisfied by traditional centralized methods. The attention given distrib-

6 Totally distributed network

More efficiency. Freestanding database processors may be optimally designed for function they are to serve— promoting elimination of complex scheduling algorithms.

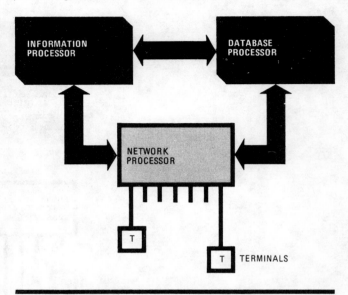

uted technology does not mean that centralized approaches will become obsolete and no longer supported by the manufacturer. But other users will obtain the best price/performance characteristics from partially distributed configurations. Still others will explore totally distributed networks. In any case, distributed environment evolution will produce benefits enjoyed by users across the information network spectrum.

The appearance of the database processor and the second separation-of-function will provide greater levels of efficiency across all three functions. This, coupled with the on-going evolution of higher-level languages will make adaptation considerably easier than present technologies permit. Thus, changes in each of the three functions—information, network and database processing—can be effected with an absolute minimum of disturbance to the other two.

Similarly, the separation-of-function philosophy and the structured approach briefly described will increase considerably the ability to fit the solution (network resources) to the problem (user requirements)—as opposed to the more traditional approach of fitting the problem to a predetermined solution. The process is enhanced by the newfound ability to define a network—any network—as a set of interrelated functions, each of which becomes a smaller, more manageable piece of the whole.

Data processing management roles are beginning to track information network organizations. The emergence and elevation of the database administrator is significant. This manager, in conjunction with coequal information and network processing administrators form a team responsible for providing efficient, economical information network resources accessible by the wide variety of users. ■

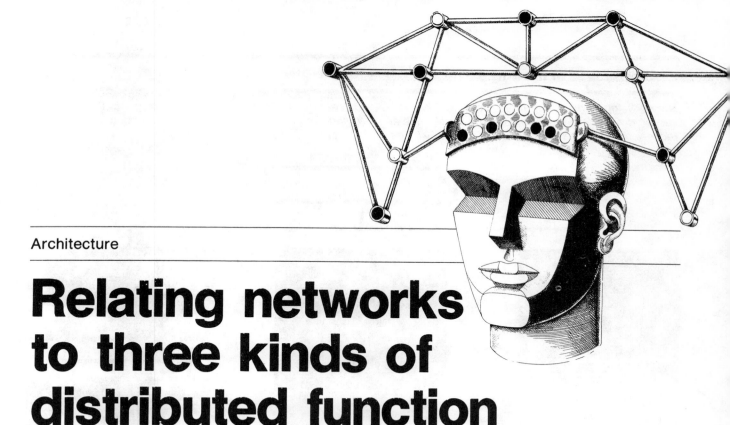

Relating networks to three kinds of distributed function

Dixon R. Doll, DMW Telecommunications Corp., Ann Arbor, Mich.

Each of them — distributed intelligence, data bases or applications processing — needs its own network topology

As minicomputers become cheaper, more efficient and more abundant, users are enthusiastically finding new jobs for them to do. One fast growing area for the minicomputer lies in the various stages of data communications networks, where it is being called on to perform numerous data processing functions.

These processing functions out on the network are commonly lumped together under the generalization of distributed processing. But it is necessary to straighten out the differences between true distributed processing and what has come to be called distributed intelligence.

Distributed processing comes in two different forms: distributed data bases and distributed applications processing. There are several ways in which one or both of these different distributed functions can improve a network's operation. One is better productivity by terminal operators; others are reduced overall network operating costs and faster access to data bases. Users and vendors alike are expecting distributed networks to enjoy exceptional growth in popularity over the coming decade.

Figure 1 (on the next page) compares the three classes of distributed network with the customary approach to data processing using remote terminals — here called centralized processing with central

intelligence. This approach became popular in the late 1960s and early 1970s. The middle 1970s saw the introduction of centralized processing networks with distributed intelligence, which was used mainly for communications control. For the late 1970s and early 1980s, emphasis is expected to shift to true distributed processing networks — which can include distributed database networks and distributed applications-processing networks. It should be noted that any distributed processing configuration can implement in the network the functions of central and distributed intelligence, distributed data bases, and distributed applications processing.

Before discussing distributed intelligence, distributed data bases and distributed applications processing, a few definitions need to be made.

A host computer is a computer — not necessarily a large one — that performs applications processing, accessing of bulk memory (disk packs, for example) and storing data bases.

Centralized processing means that all data processing functions are carried out in a single host computer, large or small, attached to the network. Distributed processing, however, means that two or more host computers, probably with associated bulk storage for necessary data bases, are connected to the net-

1 Alternatives in networks

Network topology. Centralized processing networks can be divided into those with central intelligence and those with distributed intelligence, and each will use a different kind of communications topology. But distributed data base and applications processing networks use either of two kinds of topology.

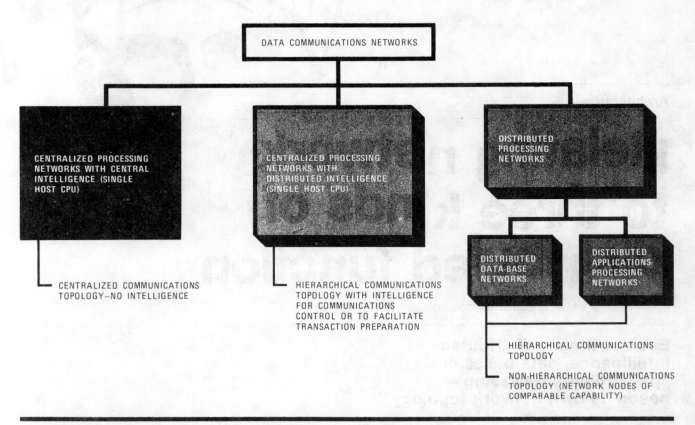

work. The host computers connected to the network can be close together or far apart—in the same building or across an ocean.

Centralized communications topology is the kind of network in which each terminal has direct access to the single host computer, usually on multipoint, multiplexed or dial-up lines, and possibly through a front-end processor (Fig. 2).

Hierarchical communications topology means a network in which terminals connect to multiplexers, multiplexers to concentrators, and concentrators to front-end processors which, in turn, connect to one or more host computers (Fig. 3). In a non-hierarchical communications topology, each of the network's nodes are of roughly the same capability. For example, packet-switching networks, whether private or common carrier, may be used to provide a non-hierarchical structure (Fig. 4)

The term intelligence can he applied both to the data communications network and to certain data processing functions. For example, an intelligent (or programmable) multiplexer can be used in a communications network to provide savings because of line concentration. As a data processing function, however, intelligence applies to such things as ability to

provide prompting statements for a terminal operator or to write a format—for an invoice, for example—on a display terminal screen merely by the operator pressing one function-selection key.

Centralized intelligence

To appreciate the economic and operational benefits of distributed intelligence and distributed processing intelligence and distributed processing, it is appropriate first to consider the older, more common approach—centralized processing with central intelligence. Figure 5 shows the essential time elements to service one transaction for an inquiry/response application taking place on a network without distributed intelligence. Here, the "mask" (or format) is stored in an application program in the single host computer on the network, which has non-programmable, not intelligent, terminals.

The operator wishing to initiate a new transaction begins by depressing a function key, which sends a short message through the communications network to the host computer. The computer activates the appropriate application program, fetches the required mask and transmits the mask to the terminal for display on the screen. Next, the operator enters, edits

2 Centralized communications

Direct access. *Centralized communications networks let each terminal have direct access to the host computer, sometimes through a front-end processor.*

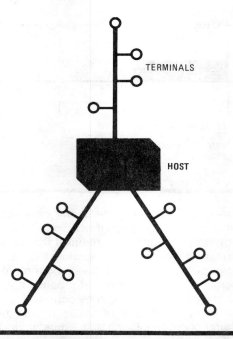

3 Hierarchical communications

Up the ladder. *In a hierarchical communications topology, messages from terminals may flow through several layers of multiplexers and concentrators.*

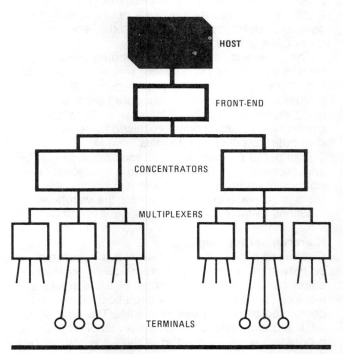

4 Non-hierarchical communications

Same capability. *In a non-hierarchical topology—for example, a packet switching network—each node has about the same processing and data-base capability.*

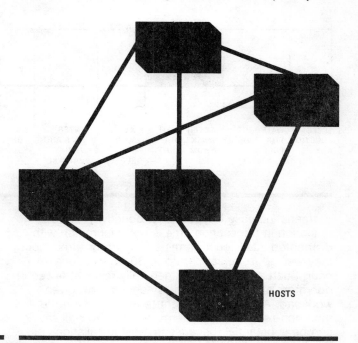

and verifies the variable data at the appropriate places on the mask.

When the operator completes the data entry task, the entire inquiry message is transmitted to the host computer for data-base processing. Finally, the host computer sends back the completed response message for display at the terminal. Then, after a "think" period, the operator can initiate another transaction.

The total elapsed time for the transaction consists of input preparation time, network response time, and operator's thinking time. Several interesting situations are evident in the sequence in Figure 5. For one thing, each transaction requires two input messages from the operator terminal and at least two output messages from the host computer. With distributed intelligence the mask is stored locally, so that the same task can be accomplished with one input message and one (or more) output messages. The lack of intelligence in the terminals, therefore, means excessive communications cost and overhead when the host computer services additional interrupts caused by extra input and output messages to and from the computer. The intelligence in a controller provides all functions for message preparation— which on networks with central intelligence must come from the distant host computer. Storing the mask in the terminal controller greatly reduces the fetch-mask and output-wait times in the input-preparation-time interval, as is shown in Figure 5.

Distributed intelligence, even with centralized application processing and data bases, can result in a

Transaction time. *Without intelligence in the network, an inquiry/response application will require two inputs to the host computer and at least two responses. Intel-* *ligent terminals can eliminate the time wasted in waiting for polling, fetching the mask and waiting for output, thus significantly improving operator productivity.*

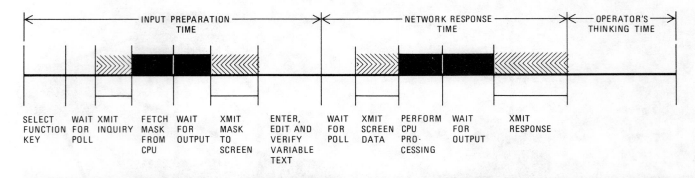

dramatic increase in operator productivity. A 35% reduction in transaction time is not uncommon with distributed intelligence terminals; operator throughput may well go from, say 20 up to 30 transactions an hour. Such an increase will generally result in fewer operators and fewer terminals needed for a given workload. Although intelligent terminals cost more than non-programmable terminals, the over-all saving can be substantial, because in most installations of this kind with central intelligence, personnel costs are the largest single item of expense.

Distributed intelligence may also lead to a smaller host processor, because the host no longer has to supply masks to non-programmable terminals. Furthermore, the host will not be required to handle an excessive amount of unproductive tasks. Looked at another way, the same host computer can be used to supply processing or data-base capability for additional sets of applications.

Distributed processing

A distributed processing network is any end-user network in which application processing and/or data-base accessing (including updates) takes place on two or more host computers in the same network. (Note that certain distributed function terminal systems can be classified as host computers.) A further requirement for a distributed data-base network is that host computers have attached permanent storage disks for on-line data files.

Distributed processing networks can simultaneously support several large computers of the System 370 class, as well as a number of minicomputers. The size of the host computers and their associated bulk memory will depend only on the processing and data-base requirements at each individual location or node in the network.

Users of large communications-based processing networks are beginning to look forward to the day when large centralized computer complexes may not provide enough processing capacity, along with the

necessary quick responsiveness and easy access to vast amounts of data. Even if one large host computer is powerful enough, there remains the possibility that multiple processing nodes, while individually of smaller capacity, might collectively be more economical. Certainly the increased performance and reduced cost of minicomputers—both as communications network components and as application or data-base processing components—has tilted network design in this direction.

There is a strong, unmistakable trend by users seriously to consider networks in which substantial amounts of intelligent processing power and data bases positioned at various stages, or levels, throughout the network. Included in this distributed processing concept is the ultimate possibility of application processing and data-base accessing being done at a number of points throughout a network, with the network, not the operator, locating the required program or data base.

The general motivation for distributed processing then, is to make networks more responsive the user's requirements and possibly to provide significantly greater end-user access to the data bases, as well as to exploit the rapidly falling cost and improved performance of minicomputer-based systems and distributed processing terminals.

Distributed processing, as defined here, cannot be implemented on a network having a traditional centralized intelligent communications topology, since there is no place in the network for the distributed functions to take place.

Hierarchical topology

Distributed processing can, however, be implemented on networks having either hierarchical or non-hierarchical communications topology. Figure 6 shows a hierarchical network of three large host computers connected by high-speed data links. This kind of network is characterized by several levels of nodes. The processing nodes at the top of the hierarchy are generally the large, more expensive host computers with powerful processing capabilities. The lowest levels (the terminals) usually have limited processing ability or none at all. Intermediate nodes, such as the remote job entry (RJE) workstations shown in Figure 6, will enjoy significant processing ability, as well as be able to support local and remote operator terminals.

The distributed processing network is organized and controlled so that simple transactions go to the terminal, or perhaps to the terminal controller. In short, the more work needed for any transaction, the higher up the network will that transaction go. From this come two advantages. One is that communications is limited to what is needed between a terminal and the point in the network at which the processing and data-base accessing takes place. As compared with centralized processing, this, of course, cuts communications line cost, overhead and time. The other advantage is that, again, the host computer is relieved of some communications overhead, as well as

of the processing load now executed at lower levels in the network.

The hierarchical network structure closely parallels the types of reporting relationships found in user organizations. The hierarchical distributed processing network, therefore, appears to be well suited for intra-company operations.

Network vulnerability
One drawback of a hierarchical network, however, is that its operation is vulnerable to line or equipment failures. For example, if an RJE workstation goes out of service, no terminal can communicate with it, although certain tasks executed by the terminal controller with relation to its cluster of terminals can continue. Network availability may be improved only by such costly steps as installing redundant lines, dial back-up facilities, and redundant equipment in certain of the network nodes.

One way to minimize susceptibility to reduced net-

6 Multihost hierarchical network

Power at the top. The processing nodes at the top of the hierarchy are generally large host computers, while the nodes at the bottom generally have only limited *intelligence or none at all. But intermediate nodes, such as a remote job entry workstation, can have significant processing and data-base capabilities.*

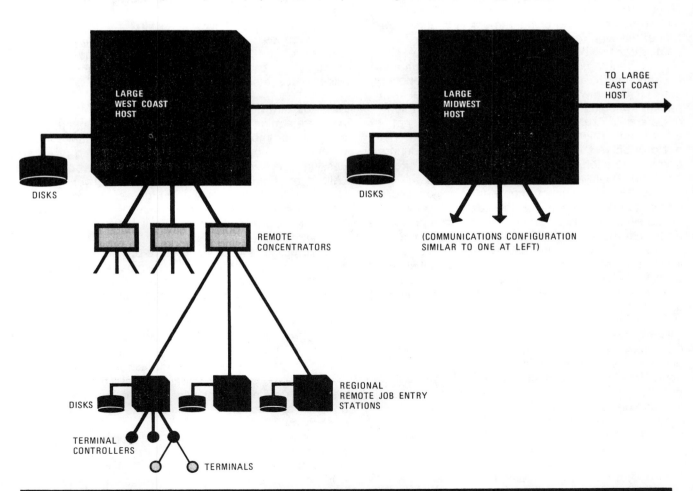

7 Non-hierarchical distributed network

Redundant connections. In a non-hierarchical net-work, each node may be linked to at least two others, something common in packet-switching networks.

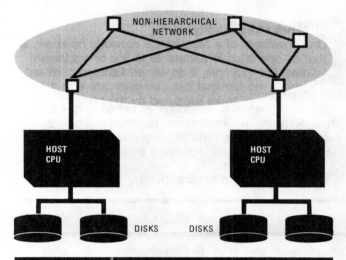

work availability is to use a non-hierarchical or multi-connected communications network, such as those offered by packet-switching carriers. A characterization of this kind of network is shown in Figure 7. Host computers and bulk memory are attached at each node. Often, in non-hierarchical networks, each node is connected to at least two other nodes, a topology that has become quite common and beneficial in packet-switching networks such as the Department of Defense's Arpanet, and the one run by Telenet as a common carrier. The multiple connection of nodes not only offers a variety of message routings during normal operation, but also provides a built-in alternative path should a line or node go out of service.

In such a multiconnected network configured for distributed data bases or distributed applications processing, virtually all of the processing, and storage nodes can be of roughly the same functional capability. Such a configuration, then, would suit the establishment of intercompany networks. Such networks, particularly those for sharing corporate data bases, are expected to form one of the most rapidly growing application areas during the next decade.

Airline reservations
Consider a seat reservations network serving many different airlines. Not only does the computer network handle seat sales and reservations for its own company; any airline reservations computer can trade information with the computer of any associated airline. That is, the reservations computer is able to sell seats from the inventories of other airlines as well as from its own seat inventory. It should be noted that there is no large central computer responsible for the control of the entire data base. In fact, the over-all data base is never processed as an entire unit.

Very few workstations at present support the true promise of distributed processing. What is needed is an intelligent controller, or workstation, that would support a broad variety of peripheral functions, some storage of and access to locally controlled data files, and some applications processing. Moreover, this same controller would perform such data communications functions as concentration, polling, speed and code conversion, and driving secondary lines on its outbound side. The controller would support virtually any type of local or remote terminal. It could provide access to multiple terminals either at headquarters or anywhere in the network.

No longer would users of a variety of terminals attached to the intelligent controller or workstation have to resort to separate multiplexers or concentrators. In fact, the ideal workstation not only could perform local data-base activities when users in the region needed such support, but also could obtain—over the communications network—a subset of some larger file maintained and controlled at one of the host computers. For example, a regional data-base file might obtain from the central host computer personnel information on all electrical engineers employed by the company for scrutiny when a job opened in the region. Any local or remote terminal attached to the workstation would then have access to this data-base subset. Finally, the regional workstation could even serve as a local message switch for administrative messages, with the added capability that messages destined for other regions could first pass through the host computer nominated as network-wide message switch.

Savings and costs
As more equipment reaches the market designed specially for implementing the inseparable requirements of data communications and distributed processing, users will have more choices in network architecture, and in deciding where in the network they want to locate intelligence and processing functions. Undoubtedly savings, better personnel efficiency and improved network performance will result.

Estimates of potential savings made on a few distributed processing networks have provided some insight into changing cost relationships. A comparison between a distributed processing network and one with central intelligence and centralized processing will usually favor distributed processing.

Personnel costs, probably the largest single element of expense, could shrink by 25% to 30%. The cost of intelligent terminals would be more than that of non-programmable units, and there would be an increase in the cost of communications network hardware; but communications line charges could come down by as much as 50%. Finally, the cost of the application processing and data-base storage equipment could also be reduced by as much as 50%. These are general figures; to be exact, each proposed distributed processing or distributed intelligence network must be evaluated in terms of its own tradeoffs and requirements. ∎

Eight factors aid network design and user interface

Charles H. Ruger, Control Data Corp., Houston, Tex.

Matching distributed network users to needed services calls for latest advances in hardware and software

In the following exercise, pick the correct definition. A distributed network is:

    a. a network with host computers and enough terminals to go around.

    b. a network with interconnecting links and intelligent node processors.

    c. a network in which the users are distributed and independent.

    d. none of the above.

    e. all of the above.

If you checked "e," you already have a good idea of what a distributed network is. Indeed, when there are many users sharing several application programs—and the users and the programs are not located in the same place—then the configuration may be considered to be a distributed network. Such a network demands consideration of many aspects by the designer/user. Of these, eight of the most salient are:

- Connection between a host and a network node
- Connection of terminals and remote hosts
- Node modularity and independence
- Node capacity in a shared-load system
- Availability and recoverability of a network node
- Message switching or terminal-to-terminal operation
- Data structure to ensure transmission accuracy
- Trunk protocol for use in inter-nodal transmission

Before discussing each of these aspects in detail, a review of how the distributed network evolved would be beneficial.

The rapid growth of data communications requirements, together with recent significant technological advances, have forced computer manufacturers into major network architectural design efforts. Frequently, these design efforts have been heavily influenced by concepts dictated by limitations imposed by older technology and long-established practice.

Initially, the device generally available for termination of communications circuits was a nonintelligent hard-wired multiplexer. All intelligence required for network control resided, of necessity, in the host processor. The replacement of the hard-wired devices with computers permitted some network control functions to be transferred to a programmable communications controller, generally attached to a host input/output (I/O) channel to serve as a front end. Functions such as data buffering, protocol handling, and error detection and control have been assigned to this communications controller.

These functional reassignments have relieved the host of a significant amount of communications overhead. However, there has been a tendency to retain the elements of network definition and the initiation of

1   A distributed network system

Network independence. *Connecting host computers and terminals to a network is facilitated when the network is regarded an independent entity by the designer.*

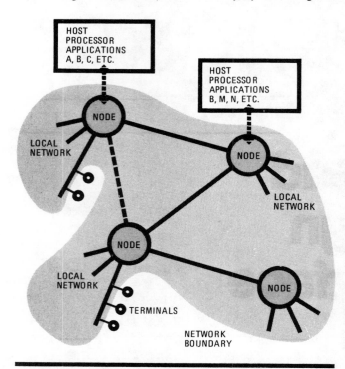

network control functions in a single host. This concept presents a number of problems. Failure of the controlling host can disable the entire network. Implementation of any method of backup is difficult. Terminal-to-terminal communication must usually be accomplished via the host. Control of large networks becomes extremely complex, and may grow to exceed the available resources of the host. Complete definition of each element in the network must reside in the physical unit in which the network control point is located. As a result, small networks will have a disproportionately large control point and cost. Large networks, in which the attached devices such as terminals and host processors often number in the thousands, may outgrow the size and capability of the control point. Both memory and processor time requirements become excessive. It is not unusual for users with even moderate-sized networks to have the communications function use up 40 to 45 percent of the resources of the control point.

Such networks do not lend themselves readily to the environment of constant change which almost invariably exists. The complexity of network definition makes changes difficult to implement with a single control point, and errors in implementation may necessitate halting the entire system.

Network control, monitoring, and supervision functions must be centralized in the control unit. As network size increases, these functions become more complex, with any network reconfiguration error having the potential for a major adverse effect.

With a single control point, network initialization and termination are slow. Both must be accomplished in a hierarchical order, with physical units directly attached to the control point being initialized first, followed by those linked to them. Orderly termination follows the reverse of this procedure.

It is quite common for large users to operate systems obtained from different vendors for different types of applications. For example, one supplier may provide superior offerings in areas of scientific, engineering, and timesharing, while another excels in business data processing. In addition, the acceptance of the merits of distributed processing has resulted in the installation of large numbers of minicomputers scattered throughout the corporate geographic structure, each performing a particular application, but requiring communications linkage with a large computer somewhere in the network. These minicomputers do not lend themselves readily to support of multiple terminal types. Similarly, suppliers of large main frames are often limited in their support of terminal types employing a competing manufacturer's protocol. As a result, freedom of user access to a multiplicity of applications from a single terminal may be impossible, and at best will be subject to severe constraints. Application-to-application communication is similarly restricted. In one known instance, the proliferation of applications processors has been so extensive that six different terminal types are required to access all of the services provided within the system. Suppliers of communications systems generally have not provided the capability required for effective network design in such an environment.

The independent network

These problems are minimized or eliminated when the designer regards the entire network as an independent entity, with both host computers and terminals being attached externally to it. With this concept, host computers may be defined as any intelligent device, large or small, which has as its primary function the execution of user application programs. A communications node may exist at any point at which the installation of a communications processor is justified by network design factors such as circuit economies, numbers and types of circuits and terminal devices, communities of interest, and geographic considerations. The communications processor's connections may be limited to inter-nodal trunks in a large complex network, but the network will also usually support some remote terminals and may have attached host processors (Fig. 1). Application programs—sometimes called services— may reside in the nodal processors as well as in hosts, wherever appropriate. For example, Figure 1 shows that application "B" resides in both host processors.

The user may be an individual at a terminal, or another application program. Users should be able to establish a session—a logical connection to an application—without concern for the application's location or the nature of the host. A terminal may be permanently dedicated to a specific service, or it may be allowed access to a number of services, with the user's point-of-entry node (discussed later) performing the first level of access validation for network security. A response from the service may be required for each user input. Sequence numbers may be generated on input and checked on output to the user. Access requests may be generated by the user's point-of-entry node prior to each input of data, to provide a pacing or throttling mechanism for preventing system overload. A session also may be initiated by an application program in a host. Information as to services available at any time should be retained by each node, based upon information supplied by host computers attached to the network.

1. Connecting a host

Connection between a host and a network node may be accomplished by a unit consisting of one or more microprocessors attached to the host I/O channel. The unit responds to host channel commands, operating in an emulation mode which enables interfacing with a wide range of host processors by consideration of the host software and application program environment. When the host and the communications nodal processor are co-located, the microprocessor unit also may be attached to the node I/O channel to perform a similar function with respect to that processor. When the host and node are geographically separated, communications circuits provide the connection between the microprocessor unit and the nodal processor. With proper hardware and, especially, software design, new types of hosts and terminals may be added without impact upon basic network functions.

Figure 2 shows details of the local channel-to-channel interface. The host channel adapter is a hardware element, designed to specifications of the host supplier for attachment to the appropriate I/O channel. The memory access controller interface unit (MIU) channel adapter is a similar device, designed according to requirements of the communications processor I/O channel. The transform module uses microprocessors to respond to the channel commands of the attached hosts and communications processors, and to permit the flow of data between them through resolution of incompatibilities. Adaptation to a different type of host requires only the appropriate host channel adapter plus reprogramming of the transform module. The microprocessor organization should be adaptable not only to a variety of manufacturers' equipment, but also to the various network access methods—such as IBM's virtual telecommunications access method (VTAM) and Control Data's network access method (NAM)—and their associated software packages. Where system considerations permit, substantial advantages in host overhead reduction and throughput increase may be obtained by use of the microprocessor to make the network appear to the host as one of its standard peripheral devices such as a disk or tape controller unit.

2. Connecting the terminals

Support of the protocols in common use is required for attachment of terminals and remote hosts, and installation of new protocols should be facilitated. Fig-

2 Channel-to-channel interface

Host link-up. *The channel adapters are hardware elements. The transform module's microprocessors are programmable to adapt the network to the type of host.*

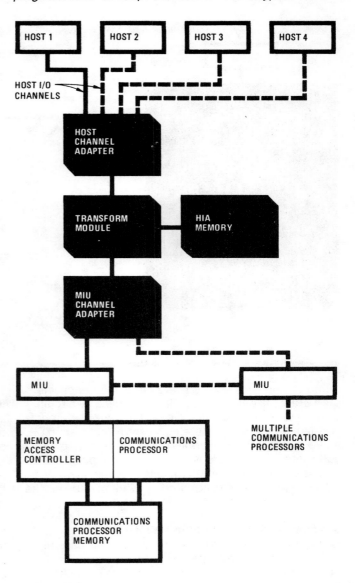

HIA—HOST INTERFACE ADAPTER

MIU—MEMORY ACCESS CONTROLLER INTERFACE UNIT

ure 3 shows the structure of a remote interface applicable to either a terminal or a remote host. A hardware element (modem) provides the physical communications interface to the circuit. A microprocessor incorporated in the line termination subsystem performs data buffering, code conversion where applicable, and character recognition, providing information as required to the interrupt handler software module of the terminal interface package (TIP). This software element, plus the device-dependent logic and protocol handler, are designed to the requirements of the termi-

3 Remote interface structure

Interfacing the terminals. *The hardware element's line termination subsystem uses a microprocessor to buffer data, convert codes, and recognize characters. The soft-ware elements are designed to the requirements of the terminated circuit. New terminal types are installed by adding appropriate new hardware and software modules.*

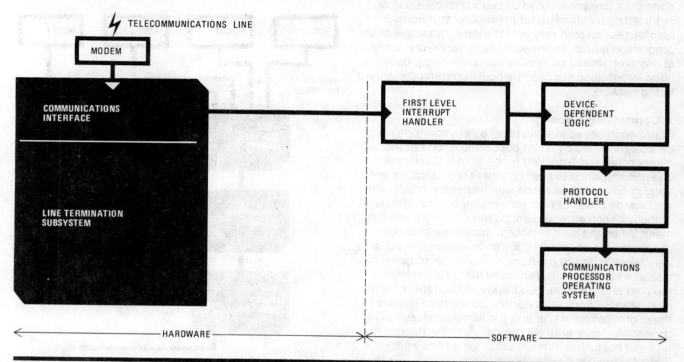

nated circuit. Only one software module for each line protocol is resident in the system, handling all circuits with similar characteristics. Since the entire TIP module is independent of the operating system, installation of a new terminal type by addition of new hardware and software modules creates no disruption of basic system functions. Lines and terminals of types previously implemented on the distributed network may be added and deleted simply by console entries.

3. Node modularity and independence
Modularity of both hardware and software is essential, so that each node may be configured to meet the requirements of its specific area of responsibility. At a minimum, functions may be limited to local network control, protocol handling, error control, data concentration, and perhaps some preliminary editing. Since networks tend to expand, often far beyond expectations, it must be possible to expand each node, or to add new ones, without system disruption.

Many of the currently available communications processors do not provide support for peripheral devices. These devices should not be required for performance of the basic communications functions, but with the concept of total network independence, availability of peripherals as an option provides significant advantages. Since each node is an independent entity, each will originate data which is important to both current maintenance and future planning. The type and location of any malfunction will be detected and re-

ported to the appropriate technical control group. Traffic statistics will be accumulated. This information should be collected and retained at some central point, to provide a source of information as to overall network operational status, and to serve as a basis for subsequent analysis of performance of the various network elements, and for advance planning to avoid the possibility of network overload.

In small networks, this collection may be assigned to an attached host. In large systems, it may be useful to add peripherals to a selected communications node to perform this task. Other optional functions requiring peripherals include traffic journaling, data retrieval, and terminal-to-terminal message switching. Such a node also can provide for mass storage of incoming data in the event of failure of an attached host. Also, storing of output data may be advantageous, permitting the host computer to complete a task without the time constraints which are imposed by characteristics of circuits and terminals.

4. Increasing node capacity
The addition at the communications processor of an inexpensive magnetic tape or disk permits independent initialization of a single node, or concurrent command to initialize all nodes, avoiding the delay occasioned by the progressive initialization which is characteristic of centralized networks. With appropriate peripherals, software maintenance and development may be performed by the nodal processor, retaining the basic

concept of independence from the host.

The capacity of a node in a shared-load system (described later) may be increased further to keep pace with network growth. Additional cabinetry and line termination hardware will add circuit connectability. Expansion of central memory will increase throughput capacity. Further expansion of both circuit termination and throughput capacity may be effected through installation of additional processors in the nodal complex.

The Control Data Cyber 1000 is an example of this type of organization. The basic central memory of 65K words (196K bytes) in each processor may be increased to 256K words to increase throughput by providing additional storage for data in transit. The available pool of central memory may be further augmented by installation of a fixed-head disk file for external storage of non-critical program modules, such as alarms and reports. Basic line termination cabinetry provides for a minimum of 16 low- and medium-speed circuits — up to 9.6 kbit/s. Line termination capacity may be increased to a maximum (per processor) of 128 medium-speed plus 32 high-speed circuits — up to 50 kbit/s. System architecture provides for as many as eight processors in a nodal complex, each with the capacity of the Cyber 1000, as described above.

Expansion is accomplished by field installation. One major node, operating 24 hours a day, 365 days a year, has been expanded from the initial dual processor system to a current total of six, with two more to be added in late 1977. No significant interruptions in the operation of the system have been required during any of these expansion moves.

5. Recovering from node failure
Availability and recoverability of a network node are highly important considerations. In a distributed network, failure of a nodal processor affects only that portion of the network directly attached to that node. While this is acceptable in some instances, for many networks to operate twenty-four hours a day, with an availability in excess of 99%, requires redundant equipment. One method of backup provides a second unit which accepts the same input as the on-line processor, performs the same communications functions, but discards the output. This method provides rapid switchover, but one unit is performing no useful work. A second method permits use of the backup machine for other unrelated tasks. Upon failure of the on-line unit, the task being performed by the backup unit must be aborted, followed by initialization of the communications function. Time is consumed, and operator intervention is required. Malfunction may occur, since the communications software may use resources which were not being exercised by the aborted task.

A third method is offered by a shared-load system, in which each processor services its own specified line group. Processor interconnects provide for intra-node transfers when such routing is required. In the event of processor failure, an adjacent unit is equipped to service the line group of the failed unit as well as its own. Recovery is automatic, without operator intervention. Since it requires only a few seconds, users are normally unaware of the failure. Operator alarms will be generated, so that corrective action may be initiated. The alarm may be displayed at any designated point in the system, so that minor nodes may operate without being attended.

A memory dump or reload and retry are options available to the operator prior to a request for maintenance service, if desired. This backup concept also simplifies planned removal of a processor from on-line status for purposes of preventive maintenance or for software development. Operator action suspends input on circuits attached to the processor to be taken offline, through polling suspension or equivalent action. Output continues to a point at which transfer of responsibility may be made without loss of data, at which time the backup function in the associated processor is activated. The reverse of this process is followed in restoration of the removed unit.

6. Switching a message
Network designers often overlook the common requirement for terminal-to-terminal communications, such as administrative message switching, and that oversight has been known to result in much unnecessary circuit duplication. Network nodes should be optionally capable of performing this function without the involvement of any host processor. This may be accomplished by generating a store-and-forward application program which, instead of being resident in a host, operates in a communications node equipped with mass storage. Users may sign on to the application, as with any other service, and specified terminals may be permanently attached if that is their only function. Messages will be delivered to the addressed terminal whenever it is in a non-busy status. A user who has no permanent location may be assigned a personal identifier which will cause messages to be held in queue for him. He may access the application from any appropriate terminal, obtain a summary display of messages in queue, and request delivery of all or selected items.

7. Molding the data structure
The user's point-of-entry node will check input data for transmission accuracy, if the originating device has provided data for that purpose. In any event, the node will provide the necessary data structure to check transmission accuracy through the network, and will attach an appropriate header.

Information contained in the header may serve a number of useful purposes. The user's point-of-entry node is the only one which needs to be aware of the location and identity of the user and service between which a logical connection exists. However, since the data may pass through other nodes, possibly by circuitous paths, origin and destination indicators are required in the header for routing purposes. These indicators may also be used to advantage by the applications program. If a response is required, the service may simply retain these indicators, reverse and append them to the response, and deliver it to the associated network node without any table look-up for routing

4   Different protocols

Maintaining data flow. Differences between the trunk protocol and the host computer and terminal protocols are resolved by nodes at the points of data entry and exit.

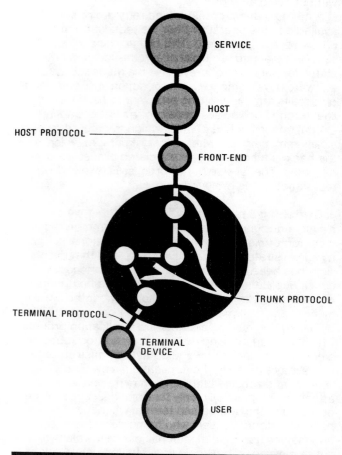

SERVICE

HOST

HOST PROTOCOL

FRONT-END

TRUNK PROTOCOL

TERMINAL PROTOCOL

TERMINAL DEVICE

USER

action on the part of the host computer.

Other information may be included in a data descriptor. An identification of the data code structure is usually required, for use by the exit node in performing code translation. A priority designator may be useful, since the nodes should be capable of multiple priority data handling. Other information may be included in the header as required for implementation of the various session options. Examples include indication as to whether a response or acknowledgement is required, orginating device type identification, message type (such as log-on request, data), and reasons for session termination. Header structure may be completely binary, providing effective use of bit assignment and freedom of adaption to user requirements.

The network should be totally transparent to the user (Figure 1). He should not be required to concern himself with location or characteristics of the host to which he requires logical connection. It should also be transparent to the service to the maximum practical extent. However, physical constraints of terminal devices, such as printer line lengths and card column limitations, together with text formatting considerations

such as columnar arrangement, often require that the application programs be aware of the terminal type in order to produce output in acceptable format. Incorporation of an origin type code in the input header may be used to provide this information.

8. Picking a trunk protocol

The format and protocol used on inter-nodal trunks greatly affect network throughput and response time. Since constraints imposed by existing protocols in the origin and destination devices are resolved at the points of network entry and exit, the designer is free to implement a trunk protocol of maximum efficiency, both to effect circuit economy and to minimize response time.

Figure 4 illustrates the different protocols which may exist between the user's terminal and the host computer. The trunk protocol should provide for simultaneous bi-directional data flow, interspersing of data and supervision blocks, multi-block acknowledgement, and sequence numbers to control acknowledgement. Sequence numbers are also needed to provide for reassembly in the event of out-of-sequence arrival of transmitted blocks at the destination, due to transmission of related blocks via diverse paths.

The protocol should allow the data to transit the network in a user-transparent mode—that is, all bit sequences are accepted and delivered in identical form. Bit-oriented protocols are being developed by standards organizations and by computer manufacturers with consideration for these requirements.

However, in keeping with the concept of total nodal independence, the selected protocol should be one which treats the participants symmetrically, as equals, as opposed to the master/slave relationship incorporated in IBM's synchronous data link control (SDLC). A protocol under development by Control Data—to be compatible with other bit-oriented protocols such as high-level data link control (HDLC) and advanced data communications control procedure (ADCCP)—is the Control Data communications control procedure (CDCCP), which provides this symmetrical relationship for use on trunk circuits, but retains SDLC as a subset for use with devices requiring that protocol. (Reference: *"Control Data's CDCCP—a user's perspective of bit-oriented data link control protocols"* by J.W. Conard, available from the Control Data Corp., Communications Systems Div., 3519 West Warner Ave., Santa Ana, Calif. 92704, attention Mr. S.H. Fischer.)

To sum up, network control may be either centralized or decentralized, but in either case may be performed by network nodes without host intervention. Supervision may be exercised by consoles attached to the nodes, or by any authorized terminal.

The distributed network concept provides complete separation between the application program functions and the network structure, both of which are subject to constant change, but frequently without any specific interrelationships. The user is provided with freedom from constraints in the selection of terminals and hosts, in implementation of new and changed applications, and in virtually unlimited network expansion. ∎

The micro, mini, and mainframe in a DDP network

Terry D. Pardoe, International Management Services Inc., Natick, Mass.

Knowing the capabilities and limitations of the processors available, plus the differences from the DP center approach, should lead to a better DDP design

Network planners and designers have found that distributed data processing (DDP) systems have special equipment needs. To understand these needs, the generic concept of distributed data processing must be examined.

The DDP concept can be defined as "the use of an interconnected family of computers of varying capabilities to supply computational power at all points (geographically or functionally) where it is needed." In contrast to the traditional data processing center approach, the computer is taken to the task rather than taking the task to the computer.

Distributed data processing therefore involves placing computers at end-user locations—such as source-data-entry points, inquiry points, and common-collection points. Since the computational requirements at these points (also called nodes) will vary considerably, full use of the computer spectrum must be made.

The full benefits of a distributed philosophy cannot be realized unless the computational powers placed at each node (or assigned to each function in the case of functional distribution) is carefully examined. This examination should result in a cost-effective match to the requirements, functional expectations, operator-skill levels, data and information needs, and environmental condition of the node.

In many cases, the high-cost mainframe used in most data processing centers is an expensive, overburdened tool that labors to service the computational requirements of both top-level management and bottom-level user. This approach was acceptable when computation costs were high, and data communications costs were relatively low. Today's low-cost micro- and minicomputers, however, make local processing much more practical than moving information unnecessarily to a central point. Distributed data processing is attractive because of the following:

■ It can relieve the burden on existing high-cost, overworked data centers.

■ It provides computational power where it is needed and can be most effectively utilized.

■ It produces a processing structure which is more "in tune" with most organizational structures.

The distributed concept requires, therefore, computational equipment of various levels of processing capability and skill levels. Also needed are flexible and low-cost communications techniques plus the creation of trouble-free complex systems and networks.

The computer spectrum outlined in Figure 1 ranges from simple single-chip microprocessors to the powerful systems found in most large data processing centers. Each of the major categories indicated in the

1 Computer spectrum

Wide range. *The computer spectrum ranges from simple single-chip microprocessors to the powerful mainframe systems found in most large data processing centers.* *Technological advances make it difficult to place absolute definitions on these major classifications. Each could be further expanded to reveal many more computer types.*

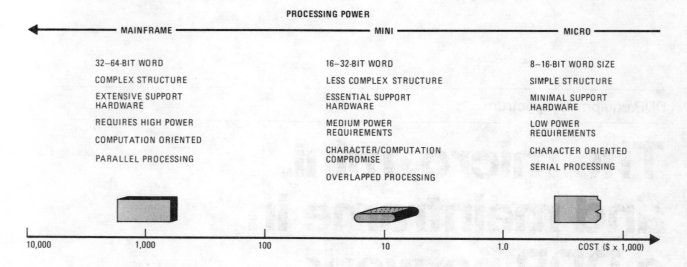

PROCESSING POWER

MAINFRAME ————————————— MINI ————————————— MICRO

32–64-BIT WORD	16–32-BIT WORD	8–16-BIT WORD SIZE
COMPLEX STRUCTURE	LESS COMPLEX STRUCTURE	SIMPLE STRUCTURE
EXTENSIVE SUPPORT HARDWARE	ESSENTIAL SUPPORT HARDWARE	MINIMAL SUPPORT HARDWARE
REQUIRES HIGH POWER	MEDIUM POWER REQUIREMENTS	LOW POWER REQUIREMENTS
COMPUTATION ORIENTED	CHARACTER/COMPUTATION COMPROMISE	CHARACTER ORIENTED
PARALLEL PROCESSING	OVERLAPPED PROCESSING	SERIAL PROCESSING

10,000   1,000   100   10   1.0   COST ($ x 1,000)

spectrum diagram could be further expanded to reveal a range of computer types—each with its own advantages, limitations, and costs.

Equipment overview

Major generic types within the broad micro, mini, and mainframe classifications can—and are—being effectively used in distributed systems. Technological advances make it increasingly difficult to place absolute definitions on these major classifications. However, the following guidelines can assist potential users in understanding the significant roles which the various spectrum members can play in a distributed system.
- Microprocessors and microcomputers. Characterized as low-cost and slow, with limited performance capability and a simple interconnectable structure.
- Minicomputers. Characterized as medium-cost, fast and flexible in performance, and exhibiting high user and environmental tolerance. In operation, they need limited support from computer "professionals."
- Mainframes. Characterized as high-cost, efficient in a batch mode, complex, and requiring sophisticated professional support.

These generalized functional attributes, in turn, lead to the spectrum of potential application areas shown in Figure 2. These areas range from the extensive data processing of "batch" in a general-purpose CPU, to the dedicated control of "real time" in a task-oriented microcomputer. As shown in Figure 2, the minicomputer falls somewhere in between—with some applications that overlap the other two categories.

When applying microcomputers and minicomputers, the systems implementer will be able to utilize a broad array of peripheral devices not normally found in the data center environment. Such devices have "grown

up" with minicomputers, and provide the flexibility, at comparatively low cost, which has ensured the success of thousands of installations. Estimates of the total number of available mini and micro peripherals range from the hundreds to the thousands, but certain generic types become even more important to the distributed system creator.

Figure 3 presents some of these "mini" peripherals and their major advantages (plus) and disadvantages (minus). The range of peripherals available with minicomputers (and even microcomputers) is not limited to these peripherals, but also includes disks, disk packs, reel-to-reel tapes, card readers, paper-tape readers, serial printers, and line printers usually associated with the recognized "standard" data processing environment.

DDP intelligence

Intelligent terminals and terminal controllers are part of the advertised spectrum of equipment which can be used in the construction of a distributed system. Both devices are normally microprocessor-controlled, and as such can be classified (in functional capability) as microcomputers—or even minicomputers.

An essential aspect of the distributed concept is the interconnection of computers. The use of this communications link type implies the use of a range of data communications tools. These tools extend from acoustic couplers (up to 300 bit/s), through standard leased lines (1.2 to 9.6 kbit/s), to wideband groups (19.2 to 230 kbit/s). Special connections and antennas provide microwave and laser transmission up to two Mbit/s.

It is the breadth and depth of the equipment spectrum available which makes possible the matching of user needs and environment at each node. One node type, the microprocessor, represents the lowest cost computational unit available, and therefore can be placed closest to the user. Its extremely low power requirements allows for maximum portability.

Functions which can be assigned to a microprocessor are:
- Control of terminal formatting;
- Performance of simple data editing;
- Control of communications;
- Front-end computing tasks, such as the decoding of machine-readable information;
- Portable low-level processing.

Portable computing represents the ultimate in DDP, since it allows for computation at variable remote points without any specific geographic limitations imposed by a communications network.

Micro's communications role

In a portable device, not only is the microprocessor used to perform DP functions, but it is also used to control data transfers to other systems, perform protocol generation, and control and carry out code construction or conversion. Microprocessors are also used to add error-detection data, and subsequently check errors and request retransmission if needed.

Minicomputers represent the primary component of any distributed data processing system. As such, they serve several functions:
- Data terminal managers
- Local file builders and managers
- Data field, value and format editing, and file look-up
- Message management and communications control
- Output report generation

Minicomputers are affordable local-level computing systems because of their relatively low cost, software support, interactive processing capabilities, and complete range of peripherals. Minicomputers support local needs and can provide the essential distributed functions of moving data upward through a network, extracting information downward from the network, and providing support on behalf of failed systems above.

Minicomputers can be used for both front-end and back-end processing in conjunction with a mainframe computer. In either case, they are being used to relieve the processing burden of the data processing machine by performing repetitive real-time tasks.

Minicomputers also can handle most data communications tasks. Like microprocessors, they can create message formats, control signal generation, and handle error detection and correction tasks. Their high speed and greater processing power suits them for the additional tasks of message routing and switching, handling of a variety of line disciplines and protocols, and concentration of messages for transmission on expensive high-speed lines.

Minis and the system

The data communications use of a minicomputer provides system designers and end users with a number of advantages. For example they:
- Can considerably reduce the communications and applications burden on a host system.

- Can save money by allowing the use of high-speed lines (lower cost per unit of information transferred).
- Allow error control and response to be close to the message source.
- Can provide extensive message validation.
- Supply interrupt structure for message handling.
- Can be provided with software or firmware (read-only memory) modules for specific message handling routines.

To realize these advantages, the distributed concept requires suitable equipment to be placed at identified processing nodes. These nodes normally can be split into four categories: user, local, intermediate, and central (corporate). Figure 4 indicates the probable equipment type to be used at each node level, their cost ranges, and how they interconnect.

The exact definition of node equipment needs will be controlled by its location and data storage requirements. User-level nodes most likely can be serviced with intelligent terminals or microprocessor-based devices, and need a storage capability suitable for transaction logging and small working files. Such requirements can be supplied by cassette tapes (for transaction logging) and diskettes (for working files).

Local level needs — a plant, an office, or a department — can be met by a small minicomputer with local data files stored either on flexible disks or on a relatively small "hard disk". At the local level, additional (historic) data storage may also take the form of punched cards, magnetic tape, or hard copy.

Whether employed at the user or local level, portable computational systems need to have special consideration given to the duration of independent portable

2 Application spectrum

Mixing batch and real-time. The minicomputer's application area falls somewhere between the batch data processor and the real-time dedicated microcomputer.

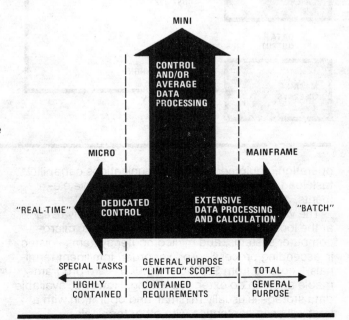

3 Mini peripherals

Pluses and minuses. Peripheral devices not normally found in the data center environment have "grown up" with minicomputers, providing a high degree of flexibility.

Shown here are some major advantages (plus) and disadvantages (minus) of these devices. Also available are the "standard" DP units, such as disks and reel-to-reel tapes.

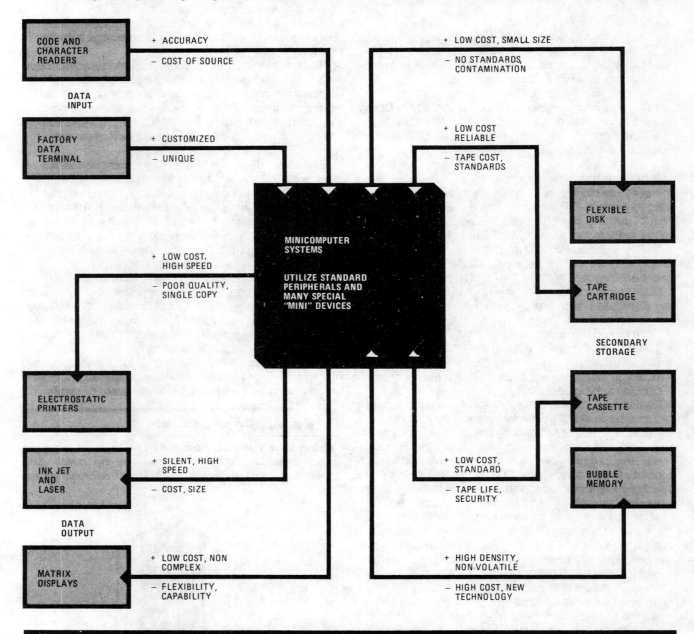

operation, equipment and communications capability, task load-sharing between fixed and portable elements, and backup redundancy.

The various devices which can be effectively used at the local level include intelligent terminals, microcomputer systems, and minicomputer systems—listed in ascending processing-power order. Intelligent terminals—costing from $2,000 to $8,000—are programmable and can do extensive editing. However, available data storage is usually minimal, and operation with a host will be in contention with other terminals.

Adding secondary storage to an intelligent terminal could hike its price to the $20,000 range. But greater local data handling capability is, of course, gained. Potential disadvantages include less central control and a greater impact when inoperable.

Local-level microcomputer systems—costing up to $100,000—provide a high degree of flexibility at a lower cost than minicomputer systems. But—because of their newness—hardware and software support is limited.

At the local level, minicomputer systems—costing

as much as $400,000—provide another order of flexibility, considerable processing power, and a high degree of software support. Of course, users pay for these benefits. And network operation requires rigorous operational discipline to maintain system control over the mini's potential independent functions.

Intermediate-level (Fig. 4) requirements may take the form of communications processing, or communications and data processing. Either one or both functions can be performed by a minicomputer system. If the system is restricted to the communications task, then computer memory storage may be sufficient. But with any level of data manipulation, hard disk storage (for control files, for example) and magnetic tape (for transaction logging and archiving) will be needed.

Corporate level (Fig. 4) needs normally absorb large amounts of processing power. In organizations which have an existing data processing department with mainframe capability, these needs are adequately met. In applications requiring large amounts of corporate processing and the manipulation of huge files, the traditional CPU cannot be replaced. For less complex central requirements, a large-scale minicomputer can be used—particularly if front-end and back-end real-time tasks (on-line processing) have been delegated to additional smaller minicomputers. The resulting configuration will resemble "parallel processing," implemented to maintain minimum response times.

Since the proper availability, usage, and transfer of data are essential ingredients to the successful operation of a distributed system, careful consideration must be given to data storage and movement. Designers should ask:
■ How much should be stored and where?
■ How much can and/or should be allowed to accumulate at any one node?
■ When should it be transferred, and to where?
■ How will it be recovered if damaged, destroyed, or "lost"?

Be prepared for bitters
The distributed concept is not without its problems. The potential system designer, purchaser, or user should be fully aware of them, and take adequate precautions to limit their impact on successful network implementation and operation. In general, most problems fall into one of three categories: technological, functional, or commercial.

The major technological problems are those of compatibility, communications protocol utilization, and speed. Throughout the equipment spectrum, different manufacturers use different interface methodologies, so that random equipment interconnection may not be as easy as it appears on the surface. The biggest single problem exists in the interconnection of minisystems to mainframe computers. This problem is compounded by the absence of a standardized communications protocol between vendors. Designers and users can best protect themselves from these problems by carefully examining available technologies and protocols, and extensively questioning users as well as suppliers to ascertain what combinations work.

4 Node equipment

Levels and costs. Individual end users in a distributed system operate with four node categories of interconnected equipment: theirs, local, intermediate, and central.

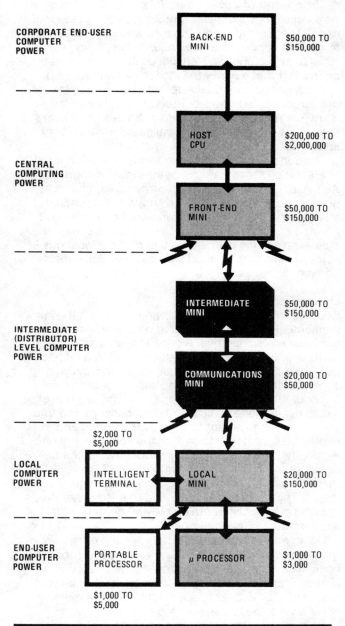

Telecommunications techniques can be expensive. While they are sufficiently fast for most tasks, they appear as a slow element in a distributed system. The efficiency—from a time utilization point of view—of a distributed network may well be limited by the data transmission speed of the communications lines. This type of limitation can be minimized by careful evaluation of data movement requirements and priorities.

Functional problems are associated with either the equipment type used at a particular node, or the total network itself. Use of micro- and mini-based systems at a particular node will limit that node's processing capability. Micro- and minicomputers are, fundamentally, relatively fast (in processing) and flexible (in application), but they are easily overloaded by too much data and slowed by too many tasks.

The specter of inefficient nodal processing can only be exorcised by a concise matching of computational capabilities to node requirements, and rigorous enforcement of non-expansion rules set up during the initial planning phases. Network problems are based on the fact that a heavy reliance must be placed on the proper and continuous operation of a complex set of interconnected devices. Protection against equipment malfunction must, therefore, be designed-in at the earliest possible time and validated at all stages of implementation and consequent operation.

The commercial problems are limited to the natural characteristics of small-computer-systems suppliers. As a rule, they can be characterized as high on technology and low on service and support. This characterization may become an operational problem in distributed environments, where heavy reliance may be placed on service of equipment in multiple locations — some of which are isolated from the traditional major commercial areas.

Unexpected problems
Support, or lack of it, becomes an issue when the implementer is attempting to solve problems which have not been envisioned by the original system components suppliers. The solution does not lie in a plan to purchase all the necessary equipment from a single sophisticated supplier. First, no such supplier exists. Second, any attempt to become this type of supplier would destroy one basic distributed concept: the total spectrum of equipment from all suppliers can and should be considered to service the needs of any node. Again, the containment of this problem area can be accomplished by a careful comparison of the equipment suppliers' capabilities and the nodal requirements. This comparison is needed to ensure that proper backup capabilities are employed, guaranteeing support and trouble-free operation.

But bear in mind that the computer equipment spectrum is continually changing and expanding. Today we have microcomputers; tomorrow it may be picocomputers. Storage technology — currently restricted to magnetic disk and tape, solid state and core memory — may well be totally eclipsed by improvements in bubble memory technology and new amorphous and molecular methodologies.

Consequently, users must be alert to technological advances and be ready to seize innovative opportunity. Users, however, must also beware! The equipment spectrum is broad, and the choices are many. But equipment alone does not a distributed system make. Successful distributed systems consist of equipment plus software, plus management control, plus operational procedures, plus many other important operational tasks. All of these elements must be combined into the most productive and cost-effective package obtainable. ■

Obtaining architectural consistency

Distributed data processing— the key is software

Ernest E. Keet, Turnkey Systems Inc., Norwalk, Conn.

Increased access to a distributed network and programmer-less applications development are two significant benefits forthcoming

It's a product not normally featured (Who wants to look at a photo of a deck of punched cards or at a printout?), but software is the crucial product which will make the distributed data processing network an economic reality. Nearly 70 percent of all medium-scale and larger data processing systems now include networks of terminals. Most of these networks involve interactive applications, usually based on modern visual display technology. While the use of such terminals for interactive program development and time-sharing continues to grow, the real impetus for the growth of distributed data processing (DDP) has been an increasing end-user demand for "instant" data processing at all levels and in all locations of an organization's structure.

Hardware advances are helping the development of DDP. Price/performance improvements in the larger general-purpose computers and additions of peripherals and more powerful software packages to minicomputers are blurring the lines between these two equipment types. As a result, the demand for even more elaborate networks and applications, frequently with interconnected processors and distributed databases, has reached immense proportions.

Despite the great expectations for distributed data processing, recent studies indicate that very few multi-processor networks are now in place. Even fewer have applications installed which involve locally self-sufficient databases which are also available for network-wide access. For example, a recent study of distributed data processing by the International Data Corp. (Waltham, Mass.) found only "a very few pioneering users in specific industries."

A close examination of the few interactive distributed networks now operating would reveal an abundance of special purpose equipment. However, despite the assortment of non-standard architectures represented by today's computer and telecommunications control hardware, such distributed networks can be readily constructed. Hardware is no longer a limiting factor; the available software is, on the other hand, just reaching barely acceptable levels.

Consider the user with a large mainframe who wishes to install a network of terminals, some to be controlled by a locally attached front-end processor and others to be connected to remote (distributed) processors. Both the front-end and the distributed processors are intended to do similar work: control the directly-attached terminals, edit and format the data, and process the transaction using the local (distributed) database. Only those transactions requiring access to the master database or to the full power of the host pro-

185

cessor would demand the host's attention.

To implement this system today, the user must acquire the hardware and software from a variety of sources, and must perform substantial in-house programming. Figure 1 illustrates a network which uses specialized databases at each remote site, and batch transmission for updating the central database management system. Because no interactive processing takes place, architectural inconsistencies are isolated.

Even IBM does not offer a complete solution to interactive DDP. The main processor would require the implementation of programs such as the information management system (IMS) or customer information control system (CICS), in addition to the user's application programs. This step, by itself, is a demanding one requiring skilled systems programmers. A remote site might be able to operate independently, but would have to rely on additional user-developed software to solve the remote-processor-to-host control problem.

In order not to be totally dependent on just one supplier, and to create some price competition, users frequently introduce at least one more vendor—typically a minicomputer supplier—bringing different hardware and different software into the already complex picture. This new vendor may have or may support a database management system, but the chances are great that its architecture will not be consistent with that of the central system, requiring even more expertise and interface programming.

IBM is not alone in its lack of a consistent hardware/software approach. No one vendor—except possibly DPF Inc. (141 Central Park Ave. South, Hartsdale, N.Y.), through its IBM-based Flexicom system—is able to supply hardware and software which are architecturally consistent and allow standard program interfaces in all of the processing nodes in a network: host, front-end, and remote. The missing element in most systems is software which, functioning in each node, can make the other elements appear to be architecturally identical. This is the solution increasingly being proposed by independent software companies.

Costly program development

Another problem has slowed the growth of interactive distributed networks substantially: the high cost of program development, estimated to be up to nine times the expense of programming equivalently complex batch applications. The reasons for the greater expense of interactive (as compared to batch) programs are:

■ Extensive message formatting and editing logic are required which, until the recent advent of parameter-driven systems (discussed later), required extraordinary programming time and effort.

■ Efficient programs are required, which are also more difficult to create. Interactive programs must be modular (that is, functionally segmented) and reentrant (that is, programmed so multiple users can access them concurrently).

■ Interactive testing, debugging, and run-in is considerably more complex.

■ Maintenance is both more frequent and more difficult

1 Distributed data processing today

Specialized databases. Without interactive processing, a currently feasible network isolates architectural inconsistencies, but requires substantial in-house programming.

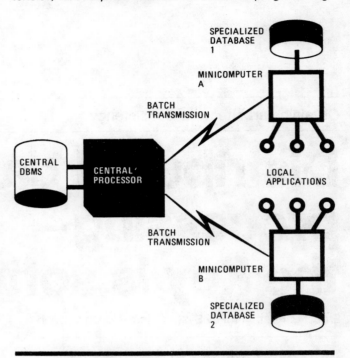

for programming personnel to implement.

Although many batch applications are available on an "off-the-shelf" basis from independent software vendors, very few parameterized interactive applications yet exist. (A parameterized application is one where selectable program options are specified by the user through English-like statements, and thus is more broadly practicable.) The software industry (over a billion dollars in worldwide sales in 1976) has not failed to recognize this need and the resulting market for interactive programming tools. As for distributed data processing, generalized software for such an application is the key to the future of interactive systems.

With minicomputers, however, very few buyers are yet willing to pay more for their software than for their hardware. Nonetheless, full-feature software products are becoming more—not less—expensive. As the software products industry has matured, the quality of its standards, and hence its costs, have increased. Documentation, maintenance, and field-service expenses have forced software prices up rapidly, while hardware costs have continued to drop sharply. This trend will continue until software vendors can plan for markets in thousands of units. Today, only a few such vendors exist, usually with utility programs (such as sorting, program maintenance routines) designed for the large IBM market. At a development cost of over $5 per line of program code, vendors of complex operating systems and application software products—which frequently contain hundreds of thousands of statements—simply could not justify investing in re-

2 Future distributed data processing

370-compatible. *Microprogrammed emulation is enabling minicomputers — as remote network processors — to gain compatibility with IBM System/370 software. These low-* *cost processors, together with a 370-compatible host computer, can constitute the major elements of a distributed data processing network, all operating interactively.*

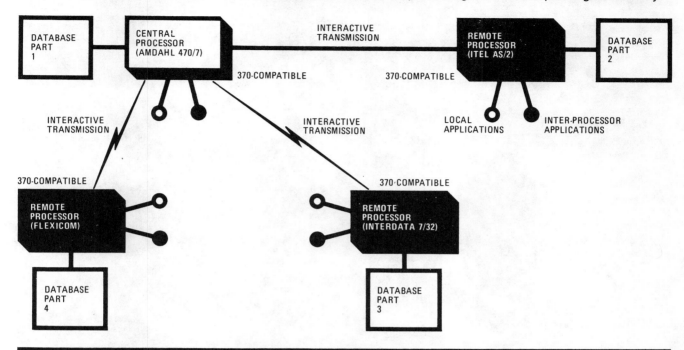

doing their software products for a specialized line of hardware, for sale at reduced prices. As a result, almost all software products sold for the largest machines are simply not available for either the medium-size or small processors.

The future: what to expect

As we have seen, software is the key to the complex application and network development of the future. A more detailed examination of the evolving technology requires some speculation on pending computer and software vendor announcements:

■ Many small to medium-scale computers will acquire full-feature compilers, cross assemblers, and even instructional interchangeability with large systems. The value of the billions of dollars invested in System/360 programming, for example, is clearly attractive to the software-short minicomputer vendor. Expect to see many more entries in the IBM-compatible hardware arena (such as Itel, Amdahl, Control Data), primarily at and below the bottom of IBM's System/370 line.

■ To counter this threat, IBM may well extend its System/370 line (or a compatible new series) downward. To further strengthen its established base, IBM seems to be moving toward integrating previously separable database facilities into the control software.

■ Database manager programs (from independent suppliers) — which operate in a small, directly coupled processor — will offer alternatives to IBM's increasingly "locked-in" approach. Such "back-end" processors will be made available across the entire range of archi-

tecturally compatible equipment.

■ Today's centralized network control will continue to move into front-end and distributed processors, but at an accelerated rate. The interface between database management and data communications control will become more and more standardized as each moves into decentralized processors.

■ Powerful data manipulation and presentation systems (such as information retrieval routines, text managers, pre-programmed data collection systems, and generalized inquiry routines) will become available on a full range of architecturally consistent machines.

■ Application-building software packages, which allow programs to be generated from user-specified parameters, will eliminate much, if not all, of the programming effort involved in interactive data network creation. Inquiry, update, and data capture applications will be specified through an interactive process, involving only systems analysts and users (not programmers).

Hardware: merging designs

In hardware, the merging of minicomputer and large-system designs has already begun. Itel, for example, has announced plans to extend its offering of National Semiconductor's processors to cover the IBM line from System/32 on up. Similar announcements from Amdahl, Control Data, and the emerging Japanese computer industry will not only challenge IBM, but will also severely affect sales of minicomputers and mid-range "midicomputers" (such as Hewlett-Packard's HP 3000). Prospective users are already questioning the

Interactive operation. *Analysts will create complete online applications interrogatively. The steps will include specifying the pertinent database elements, how the data is to be edited and manipulated, and the ultimate presentation media. The computer-driven specification process will be far from "programming" as we know it today.*

logic of buying networks of minicomputers without a consistent architecture for full-scale commercial uses.

Machines at minicomputer prices, but with System/370 software compatibility, will solve the two major small-system problems of architectural inconsistency and limited software. Distributed networks will become easier to implement and will maintain architectural compatibility both with the host processors and with remote units. Operating systems and applications software packages will, for the first time, be interchangeable among central and distributed sites.

Figure 2 illustrates a distributed data processing network made up of IBM 370-compatible, but low-cost processing equipment, all operating on an interactive basis with a compatible host processor. The Interdata 7/32 shown is illustrative of minicomputers which, through microprogrammed emulation, are gaining compatibility with 370 processing gear.

Software: the key
The coming architectural consistency among small and large processors will open up major new markets for software products previously restricted to only the largest machines. This, in turn, will help stabilize the growth of software product prices. Even more important to the designer of complex networks, however, is the value of software interchangeability among interconnected processors of differing sizes. A small division of a large decentralized company, for example, could have precisely the same applications, database structures, and interactive terminal functions—although on a smaller scale—as do its larger affiliates or the company headquarters.

Interconnecting these architecturally consistent nodes into a true distributed data processing network is primarily dependent on software. Software products such as advanced telecommunications monitors (for example, Turnkey Systems' Task/Master) provide the interface between operating systems and user-developed application programs. These software products isolate line control, storage management, and database interface considerations from user programming. In multiprocessor networks, a telecommunications monitor can also provide a common interface for the host and remote processors, while maintaining the functional independence of the remote equipment.

Operating independently of the host increases reliability and reduces loading of transmission facilities. In networks where telecommunications monitors are used, access to another processor is similar to accessing a local file, allowing the construction of complex applications based on distributed databases and processing. The IBM orientation of these products has imposed severe economic restrictions on the size of the smallest processors, as the 370/115 is very expensive by minicomputer or midicomputer standards. These cost considerations will quickly disappear, however, as IBM-compatible small machines are introduced and as the price/performance gains inherent in the System/370 Models 138 and 148 are extended to the lower end of IBM's line of processors.

The distributed network builder who has been focusing on the complexity of developing interactive applications for remote sites would do well to re-examine the trends in large-processor software, as they will soon apply throughout his network. The designer of large networks, for example, no longer considers programming his own data entry systems, database managers, report generators, interactive editing routines, or any of the many data manipulation and presentation systems now commercially available. The ability to purchase these tools "off-the-shelf" has dramatically reduced the cost, time, effort, and risk involved in interactive applications development. Extending these tools to an active network of distributed data processors will have an even more dramatic effect on costs and effort.

Programmer-less development

The high cost of DDP development is directly related to the complexity of the task. Today's software packages offer little help: they are isolated, vendor-specified, and frequently hardware-development solutions to specific problems. Dealing with a single architecture will help control costs for the builder of distributed networks, but other changes will reduce the costs of all on-line development. Most important among these changes will be the continued movement to user-specified applications which eliminate most, if not all, of the programming required to create interactive applications. Such applications are essential to the future of data processing: the 14,000 new programming positions to be filled each year in program development has become a constraining factor on the growth of application programs.

Parameter-driven software packages which allow an analyst or user to specify display formats, report layouts, data editing, data manipulation and formatting, and logic operations, already exist under such headings as "report generators," "query systems," and "data entry packages." The next generation of on-line support software will see these isolated offerings (many of which are for batch-only use today) reborn as integrated systems-building routines. In contrast to the isolated solutions of today, these offerings will be available as building blocks for assembly into a complete application program.

To create a complete on-line application, the analyst

3 Interactive application development

Application creation. Future preparing and debugging of application programs will be done interactively by analysts, permitting rapid reaction to changing requirements.

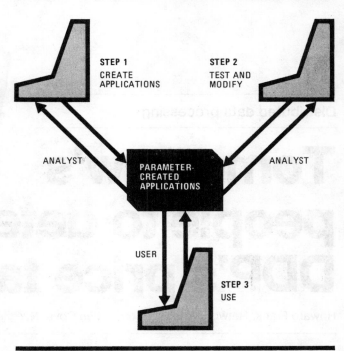

will interactively specify which database elements are involved, how the data is to be edited and manipulated, and the ultimate presentation format and media. This specification process will be computer-driven and interrogative, far from "programming" as we know it today.

The photograph and Figure 3 illustrate the creation of applications by analysts (not programmers) working at interactive terminals. Subsequent testing, use, and modification continue to rely on non-programmer personnel, permitting rapid reactions to changing needs. Such methods will allow even complex on-line applications to be constructed at a terminal in hours, by non-programmer personnel. Although the components of such an application-building program could be assembled today, they exist as high-priced separate offerings from multiple vendors and are available for use on only the most expensive computer equipment.

Until very recently, it was extremely difficult to predict the future of distributed data processing development. It now appears clear that two major trends are evolving: first, the downward propagation and acceptance of IBM System/370-compatible machine features which span the entire range of today's mini-through maxi-processors; and second, the increasing availability of powerful software products which substantially reduce interactive application development complexity. When taken together, these trends foretell an era of rapid application development on truly distributed networks of processors, but with an ever-decreasing demand for specialized hardware and software expertise. ∎

Distributed data processing

Tomorrow's people to determine DDP's price tags

Howard Frank, Network Analysis Corp., Glen Cove, N.Y.

Before deciding to implement DDP today, tomorrow's trade-off between personnel, communications costs needs to be examined

Many factors will affect the decision to implement — or not to implement — distributed data processing (DDP), but the most important of these is not technology or architecture, but the trade-off between personnel cost and communications expenses. The failure of this real issue to surface is understandable, since a truly distributed network is still beyond the capability of current technology. However, once DDP is understood for what it is — and what it is not — the personnel cost versus communications cost trade-off becomes clear.

Users have become dramatically insecure because of the conflicting statements regarding DDP's benefits and drawbacks which have appeared everywhere in the past 12 months. Most are confused at the very least. The confusion is made worse by the fact that before distributed networks actually become practical, new protocols, software techniques, and methods of managing decentralized systems must be developed.

Before describing the cost parameters of tomorrow's DDP network, it is essential first to define what DDP is. The term, distributed, when applied either to a data processing operation or a communications network, is often misleading. Indeed, the degree to which a network can be described as centralized or distributed depends mostly on the state of mind of the observer. For example, a list of the elements of a data processing

operation includes computers, front ends, the physical facility, satellite processors, control units, terminals, and the activities involved in management, maintenance and planning. In one sense, any deviation from an operation with a single centralized computer located in a single facility, which also houses all of the management, maintenance and planning functions, yields a system which is distributed. Obviously, many data processing operations have been distributed in this sense for a long time.

No easy definition
Data communications networks, too — because they are so intimately involved in the data processing function — have similar opportunities for distribution. It's easy to find real world networks which, to some degree, distribute their switching, hardware, storage, topological structure, routing and control, and, in some cases, their management, maintenance and planning functions. Even the classical centralized systems lose that characterization when the location and logical composition of the major network and data processing elements are identified. A network may seem to be centralized, but a close examination of the central switching facility may reveal a number of distributed minicomputers connected in a network of its own. The

point is that with so many elements in a modern tele-processing system, it is not easy to define the term distributed or centralized.

Each network can be characterized only by a multi-directional array of adjectives, and the ultimate characterization of the network, as either centralized or distributed, is largely a matter of the management philosophy or attitude of the network's owner.

The right criteria

The most difficult step in planning a modern teleprocessing system is choosing the appropriate criteria for optimizing the network design. Many planners are seduced by the rapidly decreasing costs of minicomputers, compared to their larger mainframe predecessors. The argument is often advanced that because a large mainframe has a complex operating system, it is inefficient for jobs which do not require such a powerful system. This is true, but its relevance to overall cost minimization is often questionable. By comparing the hardware cost of doing simple calculations on minicomputers and on large central processors, it is easy to see that a small computer wins on a cost-per-computation basis. Similarly, there are few disagreements that large CPUs are more effective than minis for major computations.

Disagreement does begin, however, when one tries to refine notions of computational complexity and efficiency. Indeed, major controversies arise in defining the concept of computational complexity in a precise manner. However, a more fundamental question is whether machine efficiency or cost is even a proper criterion for optimization.

An examination of a few basic considerations which go into the makeup of data processing/communica-tions network costs will show that the answer is no. To calibrate this examination, it will be useful to quote a few estimates advanced by International Data Corp. According to IDC, U.S. EDP (electronic data processing) spending in 1977 will total $35.7 billion (Figure 1). Of this, hardware will make up 40 percent, salaries 30 percent, outside services and software 17 percent, transmission facilities 9 percent, and supplies 4 percent of the overall revenue.

A number of studies conducted over the last few years have pointed out that the cost element distribution for data processing has shifted dramatically since 1970. CPU hardware no longer occupies the dominant position it once held in the total EDP cost picture. A study of the computing bill of the Department of Defense, for instance, shows that hardware costs in 1974 were 20 percent of the total bill, compared to 50 percent in 1968. Moreover, life cycle costs have been found to be dominated by software development and the "people cost" of maintenance, system operation, and management.

Distributed data processing (DDP) is, in part, a reaction toward a need to accommodate ever-increasing amounts of data communications between central processors and remote locations. One major argument for DDP is that it moves processing to the user and thus reduces the volume of data to be sent and the corresponding cost of sending it. Consequently, the decision between centralized and distributed computing depends on the relative costs of computing and communications. Unfortunately, users often consider only the hardware costs when making this trade-off, overlooking the high cost of software, operations maintenance, and management.

In the future, this miscalculation will become critical,

1 EDP's changing cost view

Looking ahead. Electronic data processing planners will have to reorient their thinking to account for major changes in the criteria most crucial to system optimiza-tion. Because hardware costs are falling rapidly, the 1985 EDP budget will be dominated by personnel costs. The contribution of transmission costs will also grow larger.

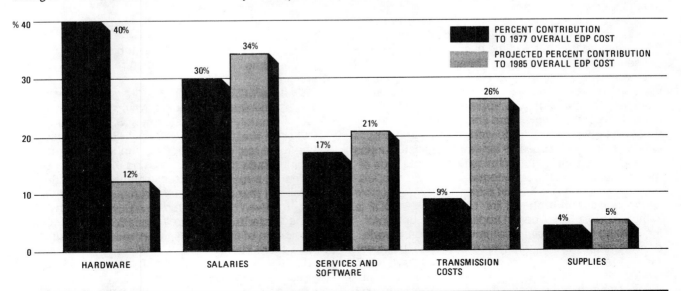

PERCENT CONTRIBUTION TO 1977 OVERALL EDP COST

PROJECTED PERCENT CONTRIBUTION TO 1985 OVERALL EDP COST

	HARDWARE	SALARIES	SERVICES AND SOFTWARE	TRANSMISSION COSTS	SUPPLIES
1977	40%	30%	17%	9%	4%
1985	12%	34%	21%	26%	5%

since the overlooked costs are becoming ever more significant. For example, as Figure 1 illustrates, by 1985, hardware costs are projected to be about 12 percent of the total EDP expenditures within the U.S. and, in fact, salaries will replace hardware as the largest piece of the EDP pie by that time. This will occur because hardware will become cheaper and more effective, thereby reducing its budget contribution.

An Arthur D. Little study projects that microcomputers will increase in capabilities while decreasing in cost by a factor ranging from 15 to 30, minicomputers by a factor ranging from 8 to 15, and large-scale computers by a factor ranging from 3 to 6 by 1985. Figure 2 demonstrates this cost/capabilities ratio as an efficiency factor.

Interestingly, while these efficiency ratios are indeed impressive, their values are less important than their trend. The result of the lower-cost, higher-efficiency trend will be to shrink the hardware portion of the total expense picture, which, in turn, makes personnel cost the most dominant sector of the EDP budget.

Communications lines, leased from common carriers, are also projected to decrease on a cost-per-bit basis, but at a much slower rate. Decreases by a factor of 2 are expected by 1985, but since data transmission requirements are the fastest growing of today's communications needs, the total data communications bill will grow substantially over the next few years. In fact, if personnel costs are ignored, cost projection estimates for data transmission, switching, terminals, modems, CPUs, and storage devices indicate that data communications will occupy about 80 percent of 1985's total EDP budget.

However, personnel costs cannot be ignored. Nowhere will the shift of EDP costs be more dramatic than in the price paid for manpower. Data processing personnel costs have risen inexorably over the last few years, and there is no end in sight. Even with a moderate inflation rate it is likely that personnel costs from both salaries and outside services will exceed 50 percent of the total EDP budget by 1985. This doesn't mean that new or different personnel costs will emerge. However, since there is no real hope of shrinking salaries, as there is with hardware cost, salaries simply become a greater factor in the overall operating expense budget.

When these cost trends for hardware, communications and personnel are combined, a striking result emerges. The trade-off between decentralized and centralized computing will derive primarily from the trade-off between data transmission costs and personnel costs. It would appear, then, that the system which minimizes the total costs of these two factors will minimize the overall EDP budget.

Network contribution

Although most EDP people have a general understanding of the costs associated with running a centralized operation, they are generally unaware of all the elements that go into the total cost of an extensive network-based system. Network elements include communications hardware (processors, modems, multiplexers,

etc.), software, lines, maintenance and operational personnel, start-up and rearrangement expenses, management, and planning.

Currently, the largest portion of these expenses lies in the hardware, software, and line categories. However, as in the overall system, when networks expand, maintenance, operations, and management—all salary intensive activities—will become significantly more complicated. The sources of this complexity are the growing number of uses to which networks are being put in the corporate and government sectors, the more complex environments in which networks are now being built, and the multiplicity of vendors whose products are now found within a single network. Until recently, network management and planning were often neglected areas, and thus their current costs are misleadingly small. Just as the cost composition picture

for data processing will shift over the next few years, the network cost composition picture will change substantially, too.

As with computer equipment, network hardware costs are falling fast. A packet switch which cost $100,000 in 1970 now costs about $25,000 and should cost less than $10,000 by 1980. Conversely, operations and maintenance personnel costs are climbing. Line costs are decreasing at a slow rate, but the demand for lines is increasing at a much faster rate.

It follows then, that in the next few years, network costs, too, will be dominated by line costs, software, and personnel costs. The relationship of this prediction to the one made for overall EDP costs is not merely a simple coincidence.

Efforts to reduce manpower cost are creating an interesting trend in communications, which runs counter to the trend in computation. Network operations

2 Hardware trend (1977 to 1985)

Better and cheaper. *Projected improvements in hardware, along with lower price tags, will result in hardware accounting for just 9 percent of the EDP budget in 1985.*

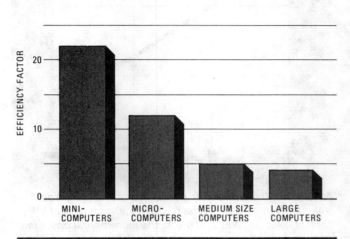

and maintenance activities are becoming more and more centralized, even though the control, routing, and other network elements may be distributed. This trend appears to be accelerating, with new products such as diagnostic devices and automated network control centers now being introduced. Thus, it is not difficult to imagine the anomaly of distributed computation systems being operated over centrally managed, diagnosed and controlled communications networks.

Detailing the cost structure of today's typical network architecture would be useful. The most cost-effective network architecture is generally a multilevel, hierarchical system. Such networks generally comprise what is called a long-haul high-level "backbone" communications system and a family of lower-level, local access networks. In some areas, designers are introducing packet switching into the network's higher levels, but the low-level, local access networks continue to use techniques such as multiplexing, concentration, and polling.

Local access dominates

Additionally, each of the backbone and local access networks can, themselves, be multilevel. That is, in the backbone network, satellites may connect some segments of the system and terrestrial lines may connect others, while in the local access networks, there are hierarchy levels which include in-building distribution networks, terminal controllers, and various degrees of concentration, ranging from polled multidrop lines to multiplexed and concentrated lines.

The planner of DDP networks must have an exacting knowledge of the cost distribution within large scale networks. During the last several years, Network Analysis Corp. has investigated this problem for a variety of existing and planned systems. In virtually all cases, the dominant cost element within the network has been

the local access network. The studies have indicated that local access usually accounts for between 45 and 70 percent of the total communications cost of the system. Backbone switching and backbone communications lines tend to share the remaining cost on about an equal basis.

This conclusion can have a profound effect on the structure of the distributed processing network which aims to minimize total costs, especially since recent tariff trends and new advances in multiplexing and concentration make long-haul communications more attractive, economically, than local access loops. For example, a network structure frequently considered contains a centralized processing center for large jobs, and regionalized processing centers for smaller jobs. Such a structure might be theoretically justified (in a qualitative sense) if, by reducing the communications needed from the user to the central processor, it will significantly reduce the total communications costs. That is, if user-to-central processor communications could be largely replaced by lower-cost, user-to-regional processor communications. However, because of the high cost of the local access portion of the network, the hoped-for line cost saving may never substantially materialize.

Under AT&T's multischedule private line (MPL) tariff, for example, the cost of a 100-mile line is 50 to 60 percent of the cost of a 500-mile line, and up to 43 percent of the cost of a 1,000-mile line. Reducing line lengths by a factor of 5 to 10 only reduces line costs by a factor of about 2 (as shown in Figure 3). In addition, lines from the regional processors to the central processor are then required, and the margin of savings is reduced even further.

Because of the dominance of the local access costs, it is likely that substantial communications savings will be achieved only if the most extreme form of distrib-

uted computing is adopted, with every user having his own processor. Unfortunately, even in this case, if more than occasional communications is required, communications costs are not likely to be reduced as dramatically as might be expected since the economy of scale factor will be working against the user as he reduces traffic. To illustrate, consider that 9.6 kbit/s lines are not four times as expensive as 2.4 kbit/s lines, because the only difference in cost is that of the modems. Thus, traffic reductions alone will not lead directly to major savings. The truth is that each situation will have to be analyzed in very precise terms, balancing the cost of this communication against a personnel budget. Reliance on metaphysical notions, such as the universal "good" inherent in distributed processing, can be a disastrous mistake.

New technology impacts

Over the next five years it is unlikely that the cost of local access from AT&T will be reduced dramatically, because of the absence of any meaningful technological progress in this portion of the common carrier plant and because of the long depreciation periods of current facilities. Innovations in this area from other sources such as Satellite Business Systems (SBS) are yet to be implemented and will not make an impact before 1981 or 1982. Additionally, by that time, the cost of ground stations will play the deciding role in local access satellite economics.

The SBS technology, for example, is based on satellites operating in the 12- to 14-gigahertz frequency range, using a time-division-multiple-access technique. This technology effectively uses satellite capacity and digital transmission. Higher frequencies will allow SBS to locate ground stations in urban areas. Because of these factors, SBS claims that ground stations can be placed on customer facilities and will proliferate widely.

3 Communications cost per mile

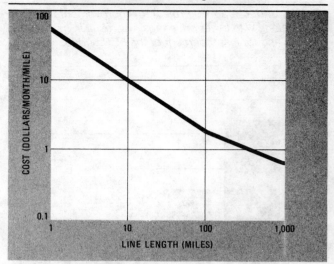

Nonlinear transmission costs. *Private voice-grade lines are clearly not proportional to distance, as a typical MPL tariff shows. Beyond 100 miles, the incremental costs fall.*

Also, users could eliminate many of their "local loop" requirements. What is crucial to this premise, however, is a low-cost ground station, a development which is still forthcoming.

If ground station costs are not significantly reduced, a satellite network structure competitive with a purely terrestrial design cannot have more than a few ground stations, and thus would require a considerable terrestrial local distribution system. This factor is material for two reasons. First, most of the terrestrial facilities in the U.S. are analog. This means that digital satellite systems, when using terrestrial facilities would not, on an end-to-end basis, provide digital service. Second, since technological and tariff trends have been rapidly reducing the cost of long-haul terrestrial facilities at the expense of higher short-haul costs, major savings might not materialize from a hybrid terrestrial/satellite network.

In one sense, the movement toward distributed processing is a result of dissatisfaction with the responsiveness of the traditional centralized data processing operation. In another sense, it derives from the dramatic decrease in cost and increase in capability of processing equipment. However, in the near term, reducing costs by distributed processing will require major reductions in traffic sent and/or substantial labor cost savings.

Since the full ramifications and true labor cost for developing and operating distributed systems are yet to be discovered, the system planner should proceed cautiously before radically altering his organization's data processing environment. At the very minimum, the planner must realize that effective planning of data processing systems is now inextricably tied to data communications and, because of this, a new view of the personnel cost, communications line cost trade-off is mandatory if an optimized system is to result. ∎

Citiproof: new policy validates net's worth

Barry E. Young and Brian Trainor, Citibank, N.A., New York

Distributed information gathering and reporting proves the axiom that time is money for operations as complex as worldwide banking

At Citibank in New York, a distributed data processing network known as Citiproof was developed as a practical response to an overall change in management policy toward customer needs.

In 1976, the bank's data processing operations were reorganized to effect a distributed series of one-to-one relationships with each of the bank's three corporate marketing groups (national banking, world corporation, and international banking). These three groups serve, respectively, U.S. based accounts, multinational corporations (half of which are headquartered in Europ or Japan), and Citibank's 206 overseas branches, subsidiaries, and affiliates.

Management's decision to decentralize back-office operations and give each customer group its own marketing branch was directly responsible for the development of a special data communications network to distribute transaction reporting and other accounting functions among the marketing groups and their particular customers. The network was a direct outgrowth of processing needs. Distributed data processing allows independent data capture and serves the need for consolidated management and accounting information that spans all marketing groups.

The Citiproof distributed data processing network captures data on more than 70,000 customer transac-

tions a day and supports a separate accounting subsystem and a management information system (MIS). Citiproof, itself, is considered a subsystem and it, along with MIS and Accounting, combine to form an all-encompassing integrated accounting and management information system (IAMIS).

Citiproof presently captures transaction data from over 200 video display terminals and keyboard send-and-receive printer terminals located in 170 proofing centers at two New York City locations where clerks make sure that every transaction equals out, or is "proofed," by having the debits equal the credits. Summary records are maintained on more than two million checking transactions by over 100,000 corporate and individual customers.

Transaction processing for bank accounting has customarily been done by traditional keypunch-input, batch-oriented systems using a large-scale computer in a centralized EDP facility. Prior to the Citiproof network, the widely scattered data entry points at Citibank and variety of report formats that were involved in furnishing raw transaction data to such a system led to continual difficulties in credit-debit reconciliation within and between marketing groups. Not only could many errors be expected in data entry, but also, detecting and correcting them after they entered the system was

1 Citiproof subsystem

Distributed data processing. The Citiproof network is a subsystem consisting of a controlling host and six satellite computers that handle all data entry and report functions for three Citibank customer groups and their respective management divisions. Citiproof also ties into Accounting and MIS subsystems to provide overall reports.

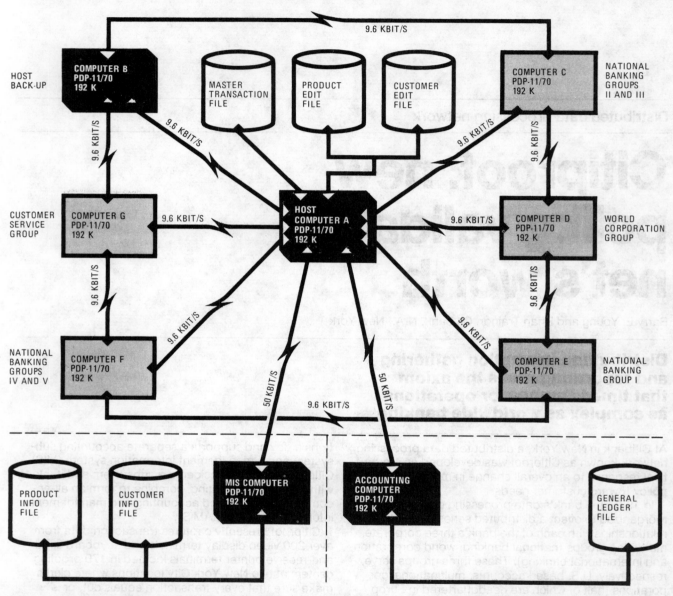

time-consuming and costly. As many as 200,000 transactions might have had to be reviewed before locating an out-of-balance entry.

In the Citiproof network, on the other hand, all of the transaction data that is required in bank accounting is captured only once and in a standard format—and must be verified as a balanced transaction at the point and time of entry. In addition, the many files and databases that are maintained within Citiproof are designed so that there is a clear, easily followed audit trail for every customer transaction. Since the Citiproof network makes the same transaction record available to the Accounting and MIS subsystems in IAMIS, the dis-

tributed data processing network has helped in achieving a consistency among the many accounting and management reports that had been missing with the keypunch-based system of data entry.

The Citiproof network
The Citiproof subsystem of IAMIS is functionally diagramed in Figure 1 together with parts of the MIS and Accounting subsystems. Citiproof is physically configured as a star network and is composed of Computer A acting as the host and six satellite computers joined by leased telephone lines operating at 9.6 kbit/s. An RS-232-C interface is used and all data communica-

tions use the X.25 protocol. Computer A and Computer B, which is used as backup for Computer A and for program development (Fig. 2), are located in the same computer room at the offices of Citicorp accounting information services (CAIS) at 399 Park Ave. Each of the remaining five computers, all located at 111 Wall Street, serves one or more independent banking groups in the Citibank hierarchy.

All seven computers in the Citiproof networking subsystem are Datasystem 570s, made by Digital Equipment Corp. All the Datasystem 570s are identical in hardware and software, consisting of PDP-11/70 computers with 192K words of CPU memory each and operating under the RSTS (resource timesharing system) executive. Applications software was developed by Cibar Inc., Colorado Springs, Colo., in conjunction with CAIS personnel.

Differing OS
The MIS and Accounting computers, also located in the CAIS area at 399 Park Ave. and directly connected to Computer A by coaxial cables are PDP-11/70s with 192K of memory, but differ from the Citiproof network host in that they run under DEC's RSX (real-time executive) real-time operating system. Files and databases for all three IAMIS subsystems are stored on either DEC RP04 or RP06 disk packs.

Communications between computers in IAMIS has recently been placed under the management of the custom-developed Citinet software system. Among other things, the Citinet communications software has increased the computer-to-computer data transfer speed from 9.6 to 50 kbit/s and has permitted direct data transmission via coaxial cables between the Citiproof computers running under the RSTS executive and the MIS and Accounting hosts running under RSX.

The network of small computers provides an overall reliability that cannot be matched by a centralized large-scale facility. If there is an outage in Computer A, manually activated backup switches allow Computer B to take over. An outage in a satellite computer can be covered by a computer serving another banking group since their programming makes them functionally identical. If a line goes out between two computers (or traffic over that line becomes very heavy), Citinet circuit-switching programs seek an alternate route through other lines.

Moreover, the Citiproof distributed data processing network parallels the decentralized marketing and service organizations of the various banking groups. Bank personnel at their terminals in each proofing area, who by definition must be most responsive to the needs of their own customers, send transaction data to their own satellite computer. They are responsible for providing complete information (not just accumulated data), and for validating data at the point of entry.

In a proofing area
The basic record of a customer transaction occurring in any proofing area consists of the following data: A proof/dept. code that identifies the origin of the transaction; a date when the transaction occurred; a cus-

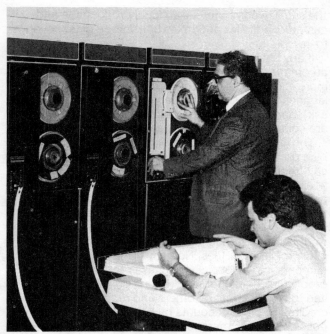

Fig.2—Host backup. Computer B normally operates as a satellite of host computer A and serves Citiproof as a program development tool. It's also the CPU's backup.

tomer account number that identifies the customer initiating or benefiting from the transaction; an account-type code that specifies the type of account (such as demand deposit, borrower, IRS); a transaction code; a compensation method (an indication that the transaction is either fee- or balance-compensated); the volume (this information is optional and records the number of similar transactions that are being entered as a single unit); a local reference number that serves as an audit reference for the transaction; a general ledger account number and debit-credit indicator that shows which general ledger account to debit or credit; a specific amount; and offsetting general ledger account number, debit/credit indicator, and offsetting amounts, all of which provide offsetting data to ensure the accounting integrity of the transaction.

A clerk at a terminal—the Mini Bee 100 is the most common CRT terminal used in Citiproof—actually enters only the customer account number, transaction code, volume, local reference number, and amount. The remaining six types of data in the record are automatically supplied by the satellite computer or are obtained from look-up files for the particular transaction code. The entire transaction record is then temporarily stored in a local transaction file. From start to finish, the clerk spends 10 minutes on all transactions as opposed to three hours in pre-Citiproof days.

As the clerk is entering data (and before the record can be stored on the local transaction file), the Citiproof network software verifies that the customer identification represents a valid Citibank customer account number and that the product or service requested is indeed one provided by that banking group. Verification is accomplished by comparing the customer account number and transaction code with records in the satellite computer's own local product edit and customer edit files and takes an average of 30 seconds to complete.

If any entry is not immediately verifiable, Citiproof automatically prompts the proofing clerk to supply more information. Citiproof recognizes which general ledger account should be debited or credited (or it will ask), and checks that the debit and credit amounts are equal for the particular transaction.

The local reference number entered into Citiproof by a proofing clerk helps to avoid the difficulties that can frequently occur in connection with those transactions that occur between accounts handled in the same proofing area. Before Citiproof, clerks who exchanged many debits and credits within their own proofing area and lost track of the net position within each account were faced with the tedious process of tracking down out-of-balance entries. Now, by using local reference numbers and a special file access program feature, a proofing clerk can request reports on all monies credited to his accounts by others and reports on all monies credited to other accounts by him. For audit trail purposes, the local reference number becomes a part of the transaction record.

There are several types of software-generated reports, based on transaction records and other data maintained in the Citiproof distributed data processing network, that are available on demand at any terminal to authorized persons in a proofing area. The first is an end-of-day report. This is the summary of proof entries for a given day and shows the total debits and credits for each general ledger code. This documentation of the day's accounting entries represents the proofing area's contribution to the bank's general ledger. Next there is a subledger listing, which is a listing of open items on file for a proofing area. The file may be listed for the entire proofing area, for a single customer, or for a range of general ledger account numbers or dates. Finally, there is a transaction listing. This is a listing of all transactions entered within a 24-hour proof period, presented in whatever manner is desired by the user with specific transaction code numbers.

Both CRT and printer terminals—the Anderson Jacobson 630 in Figure 3 is the most common printer terminal used in Citiproof—may be used for entering transaction data and for receiving reports. Proofing personnel may request that particular reports be regularly printed out on a DEC 300 lines-per-minute printer, saving time over the slower, 30 characters-per-second Anderson Jacobson printer terminal.

From Citiproof to Accounting and MIS

As the host for the Citiproof network subsystem (Fig. 1), Computer A is responsible for consolidating transaction records captured by the satellite computers and for updating the files and look-up tables that are maintained locally. At the end of each working day, the local transaction files created at the satellite computers are transmitted at 9.6 kbit/s over leased lines to Computer A to form the merged master transaction file. By 7:30 the next morning (New York time), Computer A will have, in turn, transmitted the master transaction

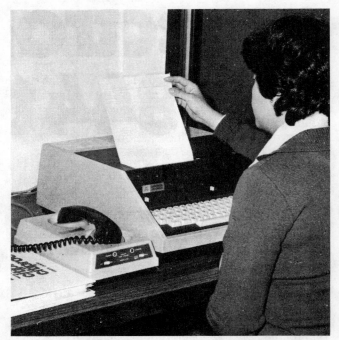

Fig.3—Status reporting. A proofing clerk at a send/receive printer terminal may demand up to four different reports from data maintained in the Citiproof network.

file to the accounting and MIS subsystems, which are the report-generating elements of IAMIS.

In addition to merging the three banking groups' transaction files into the master transaction file and transmitting that to the MIS and Accounting subsystems, the Citiproof network's Computer A retrieves data from the MIS and Accounting subsystems to update the verification files maintained by the satellite computers. Updated information transmitted to satellite computers is stored on disk media until the clerks have time to engage a utility program that reads the files into their computer's memory. The customer edit and product edit files for each proofing area contain the specific products, customers, and general ledger accounts that each area is permitted to post. To make the verification process at the input terminals meaningful, the product edit and customer edit files must be as up-to-date and error-free as possible. Verification data on products and customers originates in the product information and customer information files maintained by the MIS subsystem, and the source general ledger codes are maintained by the Accounting subsystem. Computer A manages the transfer of editing data from the two other subsystems to each of the satellite computers.

The product edit and customer edit files controlled by Computer A (Fig. 1) are automatically updated during the day as changes occur in the MIS subsystem's product and customer information files. Making MIS updated information available to the satellite computers could have been accomplished in either of two ways. First, all the satellites could access the two central edit files controlled by Computer A over the data communications lines. Alternatively, duplicate edit files could be maintained at each of the satellite computers, each satellite, therefore, having complete product and customer edit files for the whole Citiproof network subsystem. The second alternative was selected because, with only one leased line between each satellite and Computer A, there would be no access to these files if the line or Computer A went down. Back-up leased lines could have been provided between Computer A and each of the satellites, but they would be far more costly than the extra disk storage media.

In addition to updating Computer A's edit files, therefore, Citiproof software creates a smaller change-journal file. At the end of the processing day, the change-journal files at Computer A are transferred at 9.6 kbit/s over leased lines to the satellites to produce current edit files for use during the following day. If Computer A goes down, the updating function is taken over by Computer B. This procedure is a significant improvement in speed and accuracy over the former practice of periodically distributing printed lists of new general ledger codes, customers, and products.

Every two weeks, the product edit and customer edit files at each satellite are entirely updated disk-to-disk from Computer A by Citiproof operations personnel. At a line speed of 9.6 kbit/s, this process takes about 30 minutes for each satellite computer. The general ledger codes maintained by the Accounting sub-system's computer are transmitted to the satellites for updating once a week. The send-receive function, made possible by the Citinet data communications network, has simplified and improved interdepartmental transactions, those occurring between proofing areas served by different satellite computers. The need for this capability arises because a transaction entered in one proofing area cannot always be immediately acted on by the proofing area receiving the transmission. This usually occurs when proofing areas are working different hours because of the time-zone separation of the customers.

A banking group can now use the send-receive capability to transmit transactions at 9.6 kbit/s to another group and have it stored there, ready for later attention, without requiring any immediate response by the receiving group. At the beginning of the next working day, a clerk in the receiving group can request a display or printout of the current contents of the send-receive file just as he can request a listing of his proofing area's local transaction file. In addition, authorized persons in the sending group can ask Citiproof for the contents of its section of the receiving group's send-receive file. In the past, even between groups working concurrent hours, the customary approach was to iron out differences revealed in accounting reports the next

4 Accounting subsystem

Account updating. The Accounting subsystem of IAMIS is joined to the Citiproof distributed data processing network subsystem by 50 kbit/s coaxial cables. Its func-tion is to combine all customer transactions into general ledger reports that are reconciled to debit/credit (proof) sheets, and to separate management reports each day.

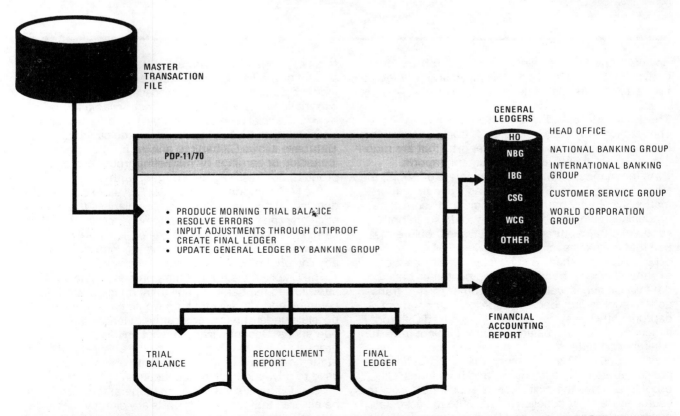

MASTER TRANSACTION FILE

PDP-11/70

- PRODUCE MORNING TRIAL BALANCE
- RESOLVE ERRORS
- INPUT ADJUSTMENTS THROUGH CITIPROOF
- CREATE FINAL LEDGER
- UPDATE GENERAL LEDGER BY BANKING GROUP

GENERAL LEDGERS

HO	HEAD OFFICE
NBG	NATIONAL BANKING GROUP
IBG	INTERNATIONAL BANKING GROUP
CSG	CUSTOMER SERVICE GROUP
WCG	WORLD CORPORATION GROUP
OTHER	

FINANCIAL ACCOUNTING REPORT

TRIAL BALANCE

RECONCILEMENT REPORT

FINAL LEDGER

5 MIS subsystem

Management information. *As with the Accounting subsystem, the MIS subsystem receives specialized reports from Citiproof. The MIS subsystem's function is to provide both bank personnel and customers with up-to-the-minute reports on the status of a customer's balance and shows each banking group's overall contribution.*

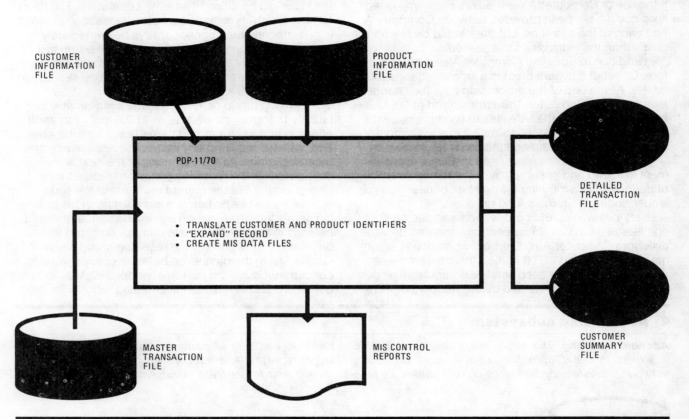

CUSTOMER INFORMATION FILE

PRODUCT INFORMATION FILE

PDP-11/70

- TRANSLATE CUSTOMER AND PRODUCT IDENTIFIERS
- "EXPAND" RECORD
- CREATE MIS DATA FILES

DETAILED TRANSACTION FILE

MASTER TRANSACTION FILE

MIS CONTROL REPORTS

CUSTOMER SUMMARY FILE

day. With the send-receive function, all transactions between groups should be recognized and proofed at both ends before the working day is over.

The Accounting and MIS components of IAMIS
The Accounting subsystem (Fig. 4) combines customer transactions into general ledger reports that are reconciled to proof sheets and management reports.

As the management reporting element of IAMIS, the MIS subsystem (Fig. 5) is viewed as a dynamic information system by both its managers and users. It has gradually grown, and will continue to do so, in both scope of data captured and in the variety of information that it makes available.

Most recently, the MIS subsystem was dramatically expanded when it began receiving customer-balance data via Citinet as well as the customer-related transaction records provided by Citiproof. A second data-capture software system, sometimes called Citiproof II, accepts customer-balance data via Citinet from 19 different computer systems in the areas of loans, demand deposits, TT&L (treasury, tax, & loan), time deposits, letters of credit, leasing, and trust funds. Citiproof II validates the customer balance inputs from the source systems, reconciles balances to the associated general ledger accounts, and feeds management data

to an expanded MIS database. Because the MIS subsystem now relies upon the same sources of data that feed the bank's accounting process, management information is guaranteed to be reconcilable to the bank's financial records. This ability to drive the bank's accounting and MIS processes with the same detailed database allows Citibank to analyze its statements of condition or earnings by marketing group, customer, product, business segment or geography.

The MIS component of the IAMIS system can display detailed customer transactions or balances that comprise any line on Citibank's statements of condition or earnings. Likewise, it can provide on-line CRT displays presenting each organizational unit's contribution to any line on the bank's financial statement.

The Citiproof distributed data processing network has allowed the bank to implement an integrated Accounting and MIS system than would never have been possible under the former struture of large centralized operations. Decentralized transaction capture and processing allows it to guarantee the accuracy of data at the time of entry, and the integrity of the database used to drive the bank's Accounting and MIS processes. Citibank's marketing managers, therefore, can be assured that their MIS reports are directly reconcilable to Citibank's financial statements. ∎

Part 4
Software

An introduction to what makes the hardware run

Gary Audin, Logica Inc., New York City

No matter what his assignment, a professional in networking and data communications needs a basic knowledge of software, this series offers a way to begin that task

Software is a term that is mysterious and remote to many who are involved in data communications, but it cannot be ignored because software is what manipulates, operates, and controls the data communications network.

Hardware is simple and pure and this makes it easy to understand. But, when hardware is manufactured it is something like the philosophers' idea of *tabula rasa*—the blank mind that some say infants have at birth. It has to be taught—or programmed—to do the tasks a network demands. That's where software comes in. The first software a computer has is its instruction set, which is simply a list of jobs and how to do them that the machine understands. This is the computer's "genes," designed into some systems' read-only memory. It's called firmware sometimes. Some software programs, however, have their own built-in instruction sets, so even this basic software doesn't apply. Software, then, is a set of instructions to the computer to tell it how to select job descriptions from its memory to accomplish what the programmer wants it to do.

But how does one write a set of instructions for a computer? That's where all the mystery and remoteness come in. Computer languages can seem forbidding, and the operations of the machine itself can seem intimidating, but that need not be so. Consider software in general:

Do you need a programmer to translate it? No. Do you need specific training? It helps, but it's not essential for data communications professionals. Do you need to learn a new terminology? Definitely. The thing to remember, though, is that all software is aimed at sending signals through the same flip-flops, gates, and circuits and the differences are not in what it says, but how it says it to the computer. The language used may be Fortran, Assembly, Basic, Cobol, or many others, but it's not necessary to learn all these languages, just as it's not necessary to really learn a foreign language to get along nicely in another country on a vacation. A working knowledge of software terminology can be attained fairly easily, and a good understanding of the hardware will serve to help that effort along mightily.

To get started on the path of understanding data communications software, it is necessary first to understand teleprocessing software. Not only does network software implement the movement of data, but it is also responsible for task scheduling, monitoring transactions and messages, and initiating a recovery procedure when the system breaks down. Through all this, it is well to remember, that no matter how esoteric the procedure, the software will still be a list of instructions

1 Communications software

Architecture. *The software system of a data communications network is actually an architecture which contains the functions to schedule, carry out, and cease a task.*

The operating system is the chief task scheduler and the TP monitor works to schedule applications and network control tasks. Terminals connect via access methods.

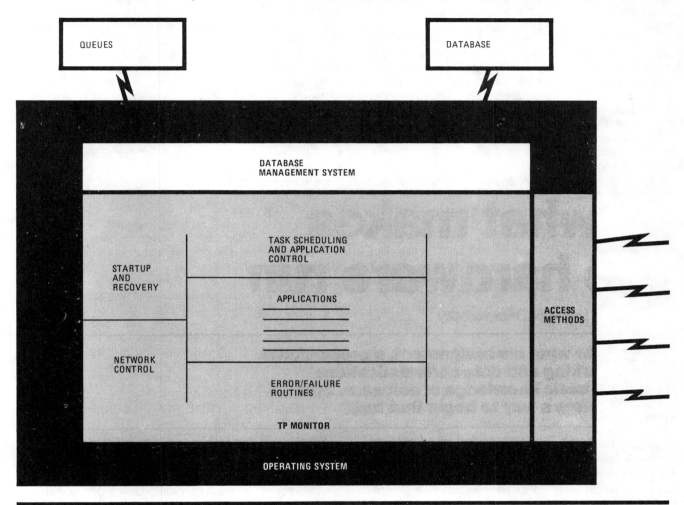

telling the machine how to do a task and when to do it. Some terms need definition before this is continued—using Figure 1 as a guide:

Access method—A collection of programs which directly interface a network.

Operating system—The master schedule for all resources. Provides access to peripheral devices.

Applications programs—Perform the computational analysis necessary to complete a task. Examples include: order entry, file look-up, and data retrieval.

Teleprocessing (TP) monitors—A special set of programs which act as the second in command to the operating system for application and network control.

Database management systems (DBMS)—A set of programs designed to organize information and provide access to it in an organized manner.

Database—The data stored and retrieved by the DBMS.

Queues—The mechanism by which transactions are placed in a waiting line, by priority, for service by an application program, or for delivery to the network.

These definitions are broad, and some variation of these meanings will be offered by others.

One amplification on the above is necessary. The DBMS is not actually part of the teleprocessing software, however it is involved in a majority of the systems encountered.

Now, to focus on the access methods and software systems that are supported by the TP monitor, consider the operating system. As the master scheduler, it could provide supervision of data communications, but it is not the most efficient choice. Therefore, repetitive tasks are usually relegated to the TP monitor. The operating system also supports various peripherals, and it could be used for interfacing the network, but many operating systems primarily support batch-type data communications operations, and as a result, they do not usually include access methods in their design.

The first programs to interface a network must move data (transactions) to and from the computer. To operate, the link protocols asks the CPU something like: Are you ready? The CPU will respond: I am ready, or I receive OK, or not OK, etc. The specific protocol "conversations" are not important. What is important to keep in mind is: each of these exchanges is a group of data bits which defines what is to going to happen next.

The access method software contains programs for sending and receiving each of these conversations. In the access software there are programs for terminal polling. These programs also take care of manipulating and responding to the signals coming from the modem.

The work does not end here. As the access methods go through the protocols, they schedule the use of the system's memory for storing data in transit (this is usually referred to as buffering). Programs also watch for errors and failures which can occur, and inform the teleprocessing monitor of these conditions. Access methods contain files which relate to each terminal and line in the network. The files contain information on the terminal's or line's state, activity, error statistics, and the like.

Access methods are normally provided by the computer vendor. The terminals supported are generally of their own manufacture as well as popular terminals such as IBM's RJE stations, and many CRT and TWX terminals. It is typical that mainframe vendors support a wider variety of protocols than the minicomputer vendors. Minicomputer software itself is more difficult to write and programmers must know a good deal about the hardware involved before attempting to write system software. Minicomputer software is also difficult to test.

TP Monitors

Not every teleprocessing system has a TP monitor. However, the functions that TP monitors perform will be found somewhere in the system software. The need for a control program to keep data flowing in an orderly fashion exists in every data communications environment, regardless of the configuration.

TP monitors can be imbedded in special operating systems, can be part of a DBMS package, or may be a stand-alone package provided by a computer vendor or by many of the growing number of independent software houses.

Whatever the source, the monitor must perform:
- Task scheduling
- Application control
- Resource allocation
- Network control
- Startup and recovery
- Error and failure processing

The level of support to be found for each function varies considerably. The first three are usually well developed while the latter three usually require a user to add more software. Minicomputer vendors, during the past few years, have begun to provide TP monitors, however, because these packages are new, they often require user-designed software to complete a system.

Application control is the prime mover in getting work done. Applications requests must be queued,

then applications must be placed in memory for execution and the results—be it database modification or a system output—must be dealt with to complete the operation. Task scheduling comes into play to keep all work requests in priority order; providing the best overall response time.

Resource allocation programs allocate core memory for loading applications, work queues and provide space for the access methods to empty their buffers (usually to disk storage). The storage of transactions in transit on a disk is also the responsibility of system software.

While a system is operating, the network requires attention. Errors and failures which are detected by the access method must be processed. A number of special programs are called into play to analyze the problems, keep statistics, and provide reports to a remote network supervisor.

Network supervisor

The network supervisor, in turn, may change conditions through console commands. The supervision must be able to start up and shut down in a graceful, orderly manner. All of these functions require significant amounts of software which is generally and incorrectly assumed to be of second-level importance to most system developers.

The ability to recover a system after a failure requires two sets of programs. The first must keep track of what is occurring at every instant, and store all appropriate events in anticipation of a failure. If a failure occurs, the second set of programs is used to re-establish the system, using the stored information.

The second set of programs, once executed and completed (the system is now restarted) is no longer needed. It is stopped and the space it took up to restart the system is once again allocated to the teleprocessing monitor.

A computer network may run out of CPU time as its load increases. A TP system will usually exhaust disk access and core memory space first.

Since queuing to a disk is commonly used, the number of accesses per second available will definitely constrain the number of transactions per second processed by the system.

Also applications programs and the database itself consume access time. This causes a further reduction in the transactions per second processed. A trade-off between these two functions is continually in progress.

The core space used to support an application program is also limited, limiting the number of applications which can operate at one time. The size of an application, and whether it is usable by more than one transaction at one time play an important role in determining system performance.

Next month this series will continue with a further explanation of teleprocessing monitors. The article will explain the need for TP monitors, how they work, and analyze what is currently available to data communications users. A TP monitor manufacturers list will be presented, with a detailed description of each vendor's offering. ∎

Performance: the battle of needs vs desires

Gary Audin, Logica Inc., New York City

When balancing the efficiency of any particular circumstance of programming reality, what is wanted weighs against what is possible

Everyone wants to know a system's capacity in quantifiable terms: what is the capacity in transactions/second, characters/second, processing time, etc? Once an answer is created (not necessarily calculated) another series of questions arises:
- How can the variables be changed to increase throughput?
- How can the variables be changed to reduce response time?
- What is the system's peak by transaction type?
- When does the system start to increase response time?

There are many other variations of these and other questions—all of which may have more than one answer depending upon the variables that are changed.

Before any attempt can be made to answer the questions, a uniform set of definitions must be created which is independent of the communications applications, e.g. message switching, RJE, data collection, inquiry/response. A transaction (message unit or entity) is defined here as a single logical unit of information which is received, processed, and delivered by a computer. A transaction may be a line of text from a teletypewriter, a CRT screen, or a block of characters from another computer. A message to be switched is a single transaction.

The most commonly mentioned parameters for defining capacity, and used to determine performance, are response time (in seconds) and throughput (transactions/second or sometimes characters/second). Response time is the interval between the initiation of transaction transmission (pushing the transmit key) and the delivery of the response (first chracter) to the destination. Throughput is the count of the number of transactions completely serviced in a unit of time. This is a measure of the work performed by a system.

These measurements are affected by the computer hardware, software, and network. Those variables which relate to CPUs, peripherals, and software and their interaction and interference are within the scope of this discussion. The variables which are found in the network will not be discussed in this article.

There are many variables to be considered which affect the capacity of a computer software system. They can be generally listed as follows:
- disk accesses per second available;
- core space available;
- CPU speed;
- CPU instruction set;
- communications equipment (multiplexer or front-end usage and design);
- input/output channel utilization;

- application program design;
- database design; and
- queuing methodology (core or disk).

All of these play varying roles (Fig. 1) in enhancing or reducing the performance of a data communications software system. Some are not even worth considering if their utilization is low (less than 50 percent), but some of these become very important as their utilization exceeds 70 percent.

When a transaction is received by a computer, the variables which hinder throughput may not be found in each stage of a data communications processing system, but they may also be repeated more than once (Fig. 2). Each variable is a tunable element which can be associated with multiple stages. Core space for data communications buffers is a separate problem from core space for application program work areas. Two distinct sets of core space are in use and their size, distribution and activity level (how often they are used and held) vary independently. Each variable will become important as its use goes past 50 percent; therefore, there is not a fixed priority list of variables that should be reviewed. Experience has shown that of all the variables: disk accesses per second; core space available, and CPU utilization are the most commonly consumed resources. They are listed in the order in which most data communications software systems encounter them as problems.

CPU capacity

The ability of a CPU to perform useful work depends greatly upon how much the CPU, with associated software, must do to move a transaction through to the completion of processing. A fine example of this is the amount of work done by a CPU with a hardwired, unbuffered data communications multiplexer. This piece of hardware interfaces modems to a computer channel. The CPU is interrupted for every character sent or received and must fill or empty buffers (which contain the transaction) on a character-by-character basis. This interrupt triggers a program which inspects the character for control and error detection purposes and builds a transaction in a buffer (a section of core memory assigned to a line). The computer time used for a received character may be 50 to 100 microseconds per character, and 35 to 70 microseconds for every character transmitted. Once a completed transaction is received, computer time is consumed while the transaction moves from the buffer to disk and while an acknowledgement is sent back to the terminal.

A buffered multiplexer or front-end does not bother the CPU until a buffer is filled or a complete transaction is received. A comparison of the two data communications interfaces for the receipt of a 200-character transaction looks like this:

Character multiplexer
200 characters per transaction x 75 microseconds per character + 500 microseconds per transaction = 15,500 microseconds per transaction.

Buffered multiplexer or front-end
500 microseconds per transaction.

1 Demand vs capacity

Capacity demands. *In order to achieve a balanced result in software system performance, each area must be given a proportionate share of the total system's capacity.*

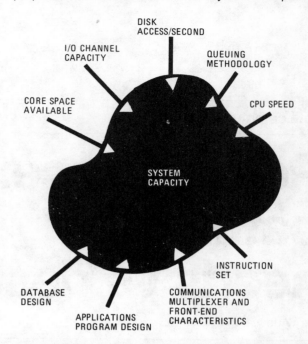

The character multiplexer consumes almost 32 times more CPU time than the buffered multiplexer of front-end. This figure will vary depending upom the CPU speed, instruction set, and the size of the buffer—with the character multiplexer using 20 to 40 times more CPU time. The buffered devices can hold a whole transaction; therefore multiplexers which have buffers that are very small, e.g. two to four characters, are not much better than a single character buffered device. The choice of equipment is obvious, but is not that simple. A whole range of capabilities which vary the CPU time used include:

- character recognition capability;
- error detection;
- block checksum calculation;
- protocol operation; and
- buffer size relative to transaction size.

Effect of software on the CPU

The collection of capacity-data for a network is much easier than for a computer system. There are many interrelationships which make the prediction on computer-system capacity difficult. It is, therefore, only possible to set ranges for the variables rather than determining any absolute limits.

All work performed by a computer is done as a series of instructions organized in groups that handle specific tasks (programs). It would seem that the CPU time consumed can be calculated by multiplying the instruction time by the number of executions and adding them together. This proves difficult to determine since the

2 Performance variables

Change factors. *At each stage of a piece of data's progress through the central processing unit, hardware and software variables determine how quickly and effi-* *ciently the information will be processed. The user must weigh all of the variable factors that exist in the system (hardware and software) to maximize throughput.*

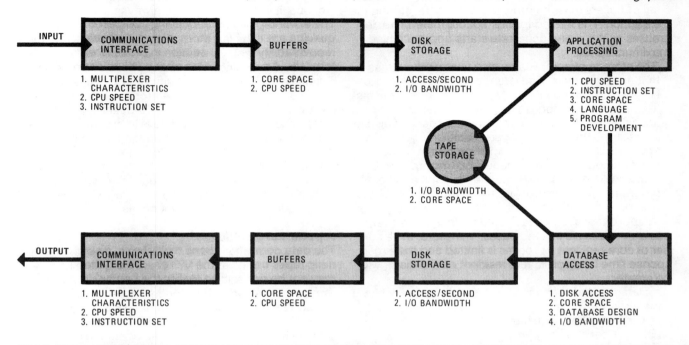

user must know the exact set of instructions used. Usually an estimated "average" instruction time is used, but it is only useful as an approximation.

Therefore, using an "average" instruction time to determine how much CPU time an application program will consume will yield a good estimate. However, if the total estimated CPU time for all programs (operating system, access methods, database management system applications, etc.) reaches more than 80 percent of capacity, then it is reasonably safe to assume the programs are causing system saturation.

The simple calculation of the total execution time will generally produce an estimate of the fastest time possible. There are several reasons why a program will take longer:
■ Every time a program needs to use a busy peripheral, it must wait.
■ An application may be written as several programs which are brought into memory individually. This helps reduce core requirements, but increases the operating system overhead and CPU time.
■ The application may be written in re-entrant code (the program is re-usable by several transactions concurrently) which also increases overhead while reducing transaction response time.
The design of application programs therefore is a trade-off of speed of execution versus response time, overhead, and core utilization. Each system designer will have to negotiate a different set of these variables in response to requirements.

Languages also become an important consideration.

The higher the level, the easier to develop and maintain a program. However, these languages usually produce programs which take longer to execute (more instructions are produced) and consume greater core space. Programs written in languages closer to the computer's fundamental instruction language are generally shorter (less core space used) and faster to execute. These programs, however, require programmer talents which are scarcer, and the programs themselves are more difficult to charge and maintain. Again another trade-off; here it's between system productivity and system development and maintenance.

The allocation of core space
As mentioned, buffers and programs seriously affect how much core is being used. The use of buffers to support the input/output of a transaction to/from data communications interfaces, disks and magnetic tapes will vary with:
■ the number of devices (lines) operating concurrently;
■ the speed of the devices (lines); and
■ block (transaction) length.
The trade-offs for core space in data communications revolve around providing big enough buffers in enough quantity so the CPU does not get interrupted too often. But if the lines are slow, much of the core will be under-utilized (a 100-character buffer takes 10 seconds to fill on a 10-character-per-second line). Also, response time may be increased if it takes a while to determine that a complete transaction has been received—especially when it does not fill a buffer. Enough buffers must

be provided so that once input from a terminal is started, there will be guaranteed space available to receive it. If, however, these data communications buffers must be emptied into disk buffers and the disk is momentarily falling behind in accesses, then an extra set of buffers must be provided to continue storing the transaction. The need for buffer space, therefore, increases as the disk-access rate starts approaching its maximum speed.

The storage of applications also uses work areas that are like buffers. The larger the number of applications which can concurrently exist in memory, the faster the average response time. However, if applications are written as large programs or if the space available is not large, then the response is much longer. If the applications are written as smaller programs, then more can operate simultaneously, but more disk accesses will be consumed in bringing in the additional programs to finish the applications processing. The best of all models would be to have enough space for all applications to reside in core memory. However, this is not possible in most cases. Therefore, the number of core-resident programs is limited and the response time for applications resident on the disk will be greater.

Data communications systems use disks very heavily for storing:

(A) transactions in queue;
(B) applications programs;
(C) databases;
(D) information for recovery/restart; and
(E) copies of the operating system, database management system access methods, etc.

Disks are basic workhorses, but they are limited in the number of accesses per second they can deliver. The use of these accesses cannot exceed a maximum, e.g. 50 per second, therefore:

$$A + B + C + D + E = 50$$

where the sum of all uses is limited to 50. If the database needs more accesses to complete its work, then some other function (usually queuing) must reduce its accesses. This facility is usually consumed first, before CPU utilization or core space.

There are methods which can increase the number of accesses per second available. Fixed head disks, although smaller, produce rates 4 to 16 times faster than moving head disks. The five aforementioned storage functions can be divided between the two types of disks. Transaction queues, copies of application programs, and, possibly, the recovery information are candidates for a fixed head disk. The lower activity functions, which also require considerable storage space (10 to 100 times more than the first three functions) can be economically stored on moving head disks.

If only a moving head disk is available, then the functions and their storage areas should be distributed on the disk by activity. The most active function, queuing, should be placed to minimize head movement with the less active functions stored on either side (with the least active on the outer edges).

This technique reduces the amount of time consumed to move the head to the proper track. It can increase the number of accesses/second available by as much as 100 per cent.

Although a disk is used to hold transactions in queue, it is not necessary to always follow this practice. The advantages of disk-queuing compared to core-queuing are the large storage area available and the recoverability of a transaction in process when a system fails. Anything in core after a failure can be assumed to be lost. In an inquiry situation, this is allowable because a terminal operator can always re-enter without causing a problem. Core-queuing is not acceptable if a database update is in progress or if the transaction has been acknowledged and the operator assumes it is safely stored. Core-queuing simply relieves the disk, but requires considerably more core space. The CPU time consumed is not significantly changed, The response time achieved when using core-queuing, however, is much faster.

A potential bottleneck

The data communications multiplexer, disks, and magnetic tapes units use the I/O channels quite heavily. It may not be possible to realize the bandwidth (bytes or words per second) described in the computer's specifications. Depending upon the system construction, there will be varying degrees of interference between the I/O channels and the operation of the CPU. The cycle-stealing design of most direct memory access (DMA) devices will reduce the effective instruction rate (increase instruction execution time). Disks are usually DMA devices. As the disk access rate increases, with a corresponding increase in total character (byte) transmission, the CPU time available decreases rapidly. It is impossible, in most cases, to have 100 percent CPU time available while the I/O channels are in heavy use.

The data communications interface and magnetic tape drive may be DMA devices, but in a majority of medium and small systems they operate on a character-by-character basis. This consumes considerable CPU time for each character that is moved. If the total line speed and the number of tape reads and writes are low, then there is little to be concerned about. However, several voice-grade lines and dozens of tape accesses/second can significantly reduce the available CPU time.

There are many minicomputers on the market which use a common buss structure to connect the CPU, core memory, and peripherals. It looks good on paper, has a clean design, and works well in low I/O oriented systems. However, the use of core memory by the CPU requires a buss access, so does any access to/from perpherals. Therefore, the more peripheral transfers, the fewer CPU to memory transfer that are available.

Since a peripheral cannot stop in the middle of a transfer, it has a higher priority for a buss access. This leaves the CPU well down in priority. It is possible to create situations where only 50 percent of the CPU time is available because of I/O transfers. Some very high speed disks are so fast that the manufacturers have created bigger minis to support them with special busses which do not interfere with the CPU. However, all the other devices still interfere on the slower buss. CPU time and I/O bandwidth are not mutually exclusive. They cannot be read from a manufacturer's specification and then treated separately. Unfortunately, many manufaturers do not have good models which can determine the system performance when high I/O activity is involved. The user should play it safe and create a design with lots of extra I/O capacity.

Databases influence performance

Database designers can (and often do) construct their structures independent of the data communications environment. This, however, is not effective if the system capacity is to be maximized because databases:

- consume CPU time;
- use many disk accesses;
- require buffers for transfer; and
- consume I/O bandwidth.

Since all these resources are fixed, any consumption reduces their availability to other functions. The structure of a database should be developed to provide easy access to data, the ability to change data, be easily maintainable, and reduce or eliminate multiple copies of data. The goals may, however, conflict with the achievable performance, especially in the consumption of disk accesses. Two different structures may require 2 and 1.5 disk acccesses per request, respectively. These figures do not seem large, but there is a 25 percent difference. Ten requests per second means a difference of five accesses. For a disk capacity of 50 accesses per second, this is a 10 percent difference in consumption fo the whole system. The database designer may have to compromise some of his goals. It does not pay to respond to 10 requests per second if so many disk accesses are consumed that the rest of the system can produce only eight requests per second.

The use of hardware resources in a data communications environment depends heavily on how the software manipulates the available resources. The use of the resources is a multi-dimensional problem where no answer is perfect, but is a compromise. A data communications software system must be tuned in response to the environment. The environment has an annoying way of changing. A successful system is sure to attract more users and uses, more than planned. Going through an exercise to tune the resources is never the end. The tuning exercise may have to be performed every six months and every time a new application is added.

All of this tuning, however, is useless unless adequate statistical information about the actual resource utilization is available. Software and hardware activity monitors and periodic performance evaluation are mandatory. The actual execution time of a program may vary ±25 percent when compared to the calculated time. The published instruction execution times are often conservative, i.e. longer than what can be achieved. The timing and resources reallocation of a software system is never finished. ■

Building block approach shows structure of network programs

Alan P. Rosenberg, Securities Industry Automation Corp., New York

Handling and processing information from points in a network is done in discrete stages, and each step has its own software component

Understanding software, especially the programs for an entire data communications configuration, can be a difficult task the first time out. But, despite the extensive and esoteric customization that is often necessary, any data communications software system contains certain minimum and necessary modules. A discussion of these modules will perhaps aid in the understanding of what has come to be recognized as a vital part of the data communications picture.

The design of complex computer software is still very much an art, although system builders commonly rely on a scientific approach and on a variety of concepts and methods provided by computer science. Often, however, system design depends critically upon past experience and on creative use of resources. The nature of system design as "art-vs-science" probably applies nowhere more strongly than in the area of data communications.

This has historically been the case in the software area for several reasons:

■ users' needs in data communications vary greatly across terminals, disciplines, and applications, and thus require significant customization;

■ in the development of standard software products, data communications stood well behind language processors, general-purpose operating systems, and ap-

plication packages in the priority schemes of hardware manufacturers because of the relative newness of data communications compared with other areas of computer use;

■ user demand for standardized data communications software became significant quite late in the overall expansion of the software marketplace. Hardware vendors were generally slow to realize the marketing value of data communications software as an aid in selling processors, which left early communicators with the task of developing their software on a customized basis.

A major effect of this history is that the fundamental concepts of data communications software are not widely understood. What follows is an introductory description of the basic software components which make up a typical data communications system. While there is much room for variation in the specific set of building blocks, the essential pieces discussed will be found in any data communications processing system.

In order to describe the software components of a typical data communications system, it is necessary to define some basic terms.

A *line* or *circuit* is any physical link connecting communicating devices; neither the physical nature of the medium (copper, microwave, satellite) nor its relative

1 Idealized network structure

Environment. Data communications software operates in a network which is a set of stations controlled by a central computer. Stations may be terminals, terminal controllers, or computers. The links that connect various stations to the central computer may have diverse physical characteristics and may be leased lines or the switched network.

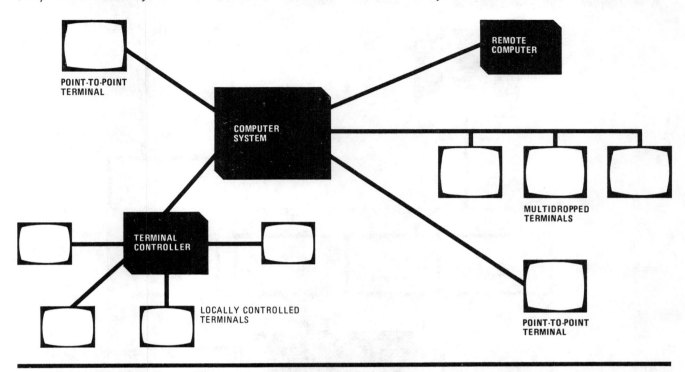

permanence (leased, switched) is important to this discussion. A *station* is any device capable of receiving and/or sending data via a line. A station may be a terminal, a terminal controller, or a computer.

A *network,* for the purposes of this discussion, consists of a set of stations and lines linked to and controlled by a central computer system. While it is understood that certain stations may be computers, and that the central computer functions may be physically dispersed, it is convenient here to view this universe (or network) as a star, in which all stations connect to the (single) central computer. Figure 1 shows a schematic of an idealized network.

A *transaction* is the basic unit of information traversing the network. Examples of transactions include messages in a store-and-forward switching system, inquiries to a remote database, and data in a remote-job-entry or data collection application. A transaction always originates at one station, passes to the central computer, and eventually results in information being transmitted to one or more stations (possibly including the originator). The number of distinct outputs produced as part of processing a transaction is called the explosion factor, and is usually a key input in determining the maximum throughput of the system (the maximum number of transactions which can be serviced in unit time).

Data communications systems are typically characterized by:
- the random arrival through the network of incoming

requests for transaction service;
- the requirement to service multiple users (i.e. stations) simultaneously;
- the requirement to hold and possibly process in-transit transactions within the computer system, often without a pre-definable limitation on the maximum volume of traffic to be accommodated and;
- the requirement to protect in-transit traffic from loss or duplication.

Thus, such systems are usually implemented via real-time, event-driven, multitask software. These terms mean that the system operates in response to external demands for service (events), at a rate consistent with the arrival frequency of such demands (in real time), and in a manner which permits several processing functions (tasks) to run concurrently by capitalizing on the fact that internal processing speeds are orders of magnitude faster that input/output speeds, which are, in turn, orders of magnitude greater than actual line transmission rates.

Figure 2 shows, in block diagram form, the major components in any data communications software system. It should be noted that the operating system component is the heart of the model, providing the connecting links to and among the network, computer peripherals, system-support software, and applications. In many cases, the support software supplied by computer manufacturers is structured so that the lines of demarcation (between operating system and communications services, for example) are blurred.

2 Communications system software structure

Functional divisions. The operating system provides the connecting links among network, computer peripherals, system support software, and applications. Communications services move data across the network. Message management handles transactions within the system. Network management monitors performance.

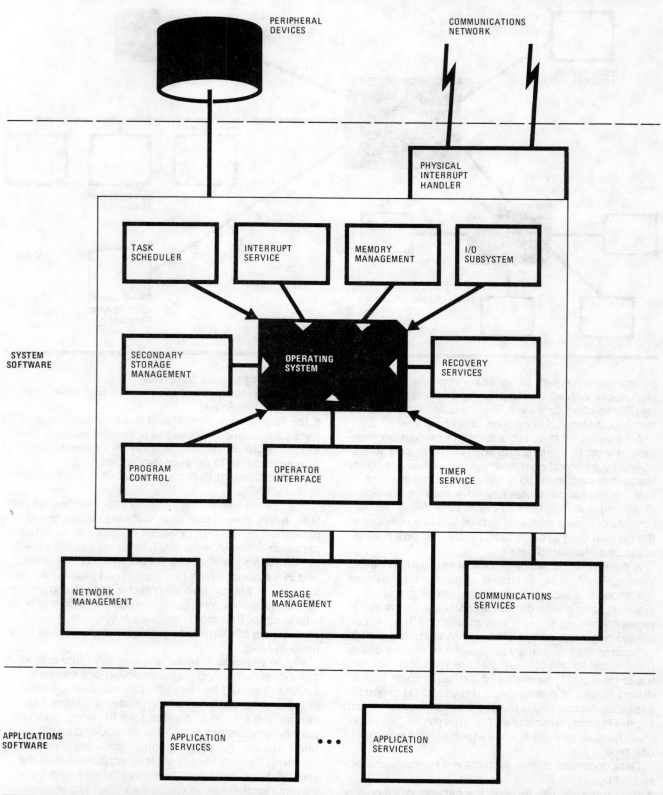

Nonetheless, closer examination will always allow each of the major areas shown in the diagram to be assigned to appropriate portions of the software.

Operating system

The operating system is the manager of such critical system resources as the main memory, the central processor, and the input/output subsystems. An operating system may be either general-purpose, in which case the special requirements of data communications functions are provided by add-on program modules (either purchased or user-developed), or special-purpose, in which event many of these functions will be included.

The major subsystems within the operating system are:

■ Task scheduler—distributes use of the processor among system functions according to demand and priority of operation.

■ Interrupt service—provides the hardware level response to external events, specifically input/output operations. With certain general-purpose operating systems, special physical interrupt handlers may be needed, as illustrated in Figure 2.

■ Memory management—controls the assignment and release of main memory for use as a temporary data residence and work-space. This dynamic use of memory significantly reduces the quantity of storage which might otherwise be required.

■ I/O subsystem—provides for data transfer between software and peripheral devices, usually including communications interface controllers.

■ Secondary storage management—obtains and releases space on disks or other mass storage devices for user information, in-transit message buffering, database structures, transaction logs, and the like.

■ Recovery services—provides for the generation of checkpoints and other records to be employed if system failure occurs. The degree and cost of protection for in-process transactions and data files depends heavily on the particular application.

■ Program control—governs the loading and execution of system and user software modules, including overlay structures used to accommodate programs whose overall size would exceed the amount of memory available.

■ Operator interface—allows external monitoring and control of all system functions.

■ Timer service—allows event initiation based on elapsed time or time of day.

Most operating systems include various additional aids to program development, testing, and maintenance. These include, among others, on-line dumps and traces, and file services.

Communications services

The communications services component of a typical data communications software system is responsible for all activities concerned directly with moving data across the network (i.e. between the central computer and its remote stations). In effect, the communications services subsystem functions as a software front-end between the network with its users and all other software within the system (including the application programs which perform the actual transaction processing operations).

It is usually desirable to design the communications services subsystem with as few dependencies as possible on either the specific applications or the specific types of terminal devices to be used. While this goal can very seldom be completely met, an attempt to reach independence usually simplifies later maintenance and modification of the software. It should be noted, however, that in certain cases considerations such as system-response overhead or development cost may militate against the ideal of maximizing application and terminal independence.

The most important software subsystems within the data communications service area are:

■ Initiation of network service—this includes, on the input side, polling terminals on multipoint lines, answering calls on switched lines, and responding to incoming traffic on contention or freewheeling lines. On the output side, it includes transmission initiation by calling multidrop stations, dialing for switched stations, and sending appropriate bid sequences on contention lines.

■ Message assembly and disassembly—data moving across the network typically appears as a serial stream of characters, and the transmission format is often inconvenient from the perspective of the user application program. Thus, this subsystem provides a logical transaction-oriented interface between the rest of the software and the network, and can remove the need for programs within the system to be concerned with the idiosyncracies of terminal operation or data format. Message assembly occurs upon input from the network and involves composing the data in one logical message or transaction into a standard internal format for subsequent processing. Message disassembly is the same process in reverse. This function also accounts for disparities of terminal type such as code set and text blocking. When data lengths in messages exceed one or two hundred characters, or when transmission speeds are very slow, data will be placed piecemeal in secondary storage to make more efficient use of main memory. In-transit traffic will be moved back and forth between the appropriate processing programs and secondary storage (a technique called staging) when secure message recovery is a requirement, as in a store-and-forward switching application (Fig. 3).

■ Protocol services—this function provides the specific control sequences, data framing, and block construction and interpretation required for communication within the various protocols currently in use. Although modern data communications hardware has assumed many of these tasks (redundancy checksum generation and validation, synchronization-character stripping and insertion, and others), the significant decisions concerning successful receipt and delivery of data traffic must still be made by software. As could be expected, the level of programming to support a complex full-duplex protocol such as IBM's synchronous data link control (SDLC) is usually significantly greater than

3 Staging in-transit traffic

Message management. *The message management subsystem treats transactions as logical units of information. It receives incoming messages from the network via communications software and an initial buffering stage. Messages are queued until they are processed by the applications program and re-delivered to the network.*

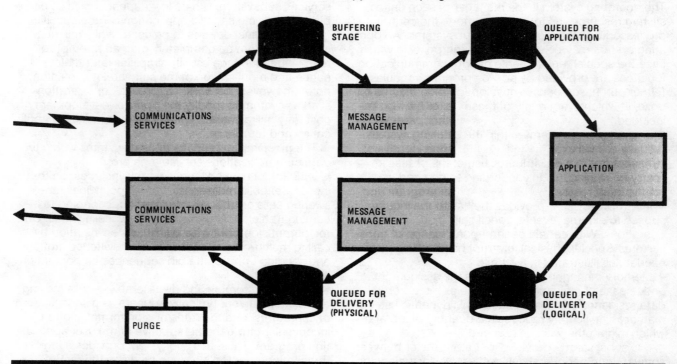

that required to support a teleprinter interface. However, hardware manufacturers seem to be simultaneously increasing the share of protocol handling done by hardware while expanding the functions provided by their standard data communications software facilities.

■ Error detection and retry—the data communications subsystem is typically charged with recognizing network errors, and with initiating appropriate retry measures. Because the expected frequency of errors on a telephone line can be several orders of magnitude greater than that for a computer peripheral (such as a disk drive), network errors are usually treated under a threshold approach. This means that an error or malfunction (such as a parity error or invalid block checksum) is not considered to be a true or "hard" error until a predefined number of retry attempts have likewise failed. The threshold method allows a line or station suffering a transient problem to self-correct without human intervention. Even when a fault condition fails to clear up within the threshold limit, the software may continue its attempts at re-establishing service, although at a lower retry rate to avoid wasting system resources. Of course, any hard failure and its eventual correction will be reported to the operator as part of the network management function.

Message management refers to the portion of the system which handles messages or transactions as logical units of information, generally without regard to actual text content. The message management function receives incoming messages from communications

services and controls their movement through the system (including any processing by applications programs) to the point of presentation to the communications function once again for delivery to the final physical or logical destination (Fig. 3).

Since transaction arrival is a random phenomenon, all data communications software systems are designed so that message service in the network and message processing in the central computer can occur asynchronously.

The software device providing this capability is the *queue*, a first-in, first-out chained list which permits messages to be serviced by the various components of the system at their respective speeds and without the need for complex interlock mechanisms. Hence, the most important message management function is the maintenance of a queuing service for receiving input, processing it, and holding it for output until delivery to the indicated destination is possible. Queue structures often provide two or more priority levels within a queue, so that urgent traffic is not delayed behind normal messages. One of the most significant benefits of a queuing scheme is that application programs can often be designed to operate in a batch-like manner: the program simply obtains the next transaction from an input queue, processes it, directs any output to appropriate delivery queues, and then requests the next input once again. This approach allows applications programs to be developed and tested with a minimum of awareness of the actual on-line nature of the rest of the software. Other message management functions of significance include:

- Routing—selecting the proper destination(s) for arriving transactions. A destination may be a physical station (as in a message-switching application), or an application program within the central computer (as in an order entry or database inquiry application). The routing function also provides for placing outbound messages on queues for subsequent delivery by the communications services component in accordance with the specified destination station(s). It should be noted that transaction routing information may be explicitly carried as part of the message, or may be implied by transaction type, origin, or other parameters. For example, traffic in a message-switching system usually carries explicit destination station identifiers; transactions in a database update application may carry no routing information at all, with implied routing of the input message to an application program and implied routing of the response back to the inquiry originator.

- Validation—the extent to which validation of transaction syntax and content is performed will vary among systems. In general, this function will tend to be included in the message management area when a strong standardization in format is required. A case in point would be large-scale message switching. In other instances, most of the validation required for incoming traffic will be highly application-dependent and thus will most sensibly be incorporated into the individual application functions.

- Purging—since storage for in-transit transactions is usually limited, the removal of transactions from active storage once processing and delivery are complete is a critical function, and it is usually included in the message management area. The purging function commences when a message has been delivered to its eventual destination(s). Any space occupied by the message in the in-transit area (main or secondary storage) is released for subsequent re-use. Depending on the specific application, the purged message may be entered into a historical log for archival storage or redelivery if required later.

Network management

The network management component of a typical data communications software system provides facilities to monitor the performance of lines, stations, and the central computer, and to modify the assignments and functions of the elements of the network. Network management also provides the main operator interface into the system, and is the vehicle for human control over its operation.

Performance monitoring is chiefly concerned with recognition of errors and unusual occurrences. As mentioned previously, errors on communications facilities are much more frequent than on data processing facilities, and hence the threshold approach to error handling is used. The network management subsystem is charged with maintaining accurate error statistics, generating logs of true (i.e. hard) failures, and keeping an updated picture of the state of all central-site and

network equipment. Many network management software systems provide video displays of lines and stations that are not operating correctly, a feature of great benefit to operations personnel when the network is extensive.

Network management software can also detect network-wide problems (such as an unusually large number of messages waiting for delivery in in-transit storage) and can take immediate action or inform the operator with appropriate alarm notifications.

The second major function of network management is control of the network, i.e. providing the operator with the ability to modify the operation or use of any network component. Typical functions provided would include the ability to:

- allow or disallow service to a particular line or station;
- change frequency or order of service;
- establish or remove alternate routing assignments;
- transmit test messages;
- enable or disable selected message or transaction types and;
- display network traffic statistics, error statistics, and equipment status.

It is usually good practice for network management to produce a hard-copy log of all significant events relating to system operation, including operator commands, system failures, network errors, and so on. This kind of documentation can prove extremely useful should problems arise or if detailed studies of the system are required.

Applications

The applications portion of a data communications software system might best be described as the "useful work" part. Everything else is the "overhead" of bringing transaction traffic in and results out. Obviously, the ease of defining and developing applications software depends directly on the facilities provided by the operating system. The applications designer will need to know the manner in which applications receive incoming traffic from the network and pass outbound traffic back, the nature of the database management facilities for user files, and the level of transaction and file recovery supported by the underlying operating system software.

As noted earlier, it is usually advantageous to structure applications modules as serial processing elements which obtain new messages from an input queue and present output to other queues for delivery. If it is necessary to have multiple application paths in parallel, several of these serial modules can be operated simultaneously. The goal is to make the application programs as simple and straightforward as possible, since experience indicates that this is the area of the system most susceptible to change.

The key to intelligent acquisition of data communications software, whether by purchase or development, is complete definition of functional and capacity requirements, and a corresponding understanding of the capabilities of the proposed system. The breakdown into functional areas outlined in the article may be useful in performing the necessary analysis. ∎

The NCP atlas: roadmap to IBM's net control

Albert J. Hedeen, IBM Corp., Research Triangle Park, N.C.

The problem: How do you treat an entire network as a single functioning entity? The solution is control—here's how

Network Control Program (NCP) is a software system used for the physical control of data communications networks under IBM's Systems Network Architecture (Fig. 1). By controlling and monitoring the terminals attached to a communications controller for such functions as polling, addressing, buffering, and code translation, the Network Control Program maintains physical control. In addition, line and terminal problems, both permanent and temporary in nature, are recognized and correction is initiated by the NCP.

The NCP, which resides in an IBM 3704 or 3705 communication controller, can run with either Telecommunications Access Method (TCAM) or Virtual Telecommunications Access Method (VTAM) or with both in a System/370. It supports a wide range of start/stop, binary synchronous (BSC), and synchronous data link control (SDLC) links at line speeds ranging from 45.5 bit/s to 56 kbit/s. In addition, the NCP provides a high-level data communications-oriented macro language to describe the network.

NCP operates with IBM's DOS/VS, OS/VS1, SVS, and MVS operating systems. NCP/VS operates in a single-host environment. ACF/NCP/VS does the same, but can serve multiple local hosts through multiple-channel attachments or multiple remote hosts via data communications links to adjacent 3705s.

The basic concept of NCP is to relieve the host processor's communication access methods of the task of physically controlling a data communications network (Fig. 2). It performs several basic functions including control of attached lines and terminals, error recovery, and the routing of data through the network. Before SNA, a network required each communications access method (BTAM, QTAM, TCAM/EP, and so on) used with a subsystem to contain the program logic for the physical control of the network. Having a single network control program that serves multiple subsystems (such as IMS, CICS, TSO, and JES through VTAM; or CICS and TSO through TCAM) eliminates the redundant logic for network control in each subsystem.

The NCP may be executed in either an IBM 3704 or 3705 communications controller. Major emphasis in this article will be on the IBM 3705.

The NCP resides in the communications controller to control the transfer of data between the terminals and the host processor. Its primary functions are related to the transmitting and receiving of data. The NCP includes routines to initiate error recovery, to record error statistics, and to perform diagnostic tests. These routines enable the program to recover from many transmission errors without user intervention. The NCP performs these error and control-related func-

1 Configuration for network control

Physical control. The Network Control Program is resident in a 3704 or 3705 communications controller and provides a high-level macro language, which is oriented to data communications to describe the network. The NCP can control SNA, BSC, or start/stop terminals simultaneously and routes data to applications programs.

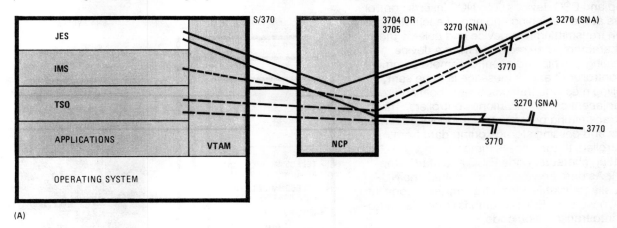

(A)

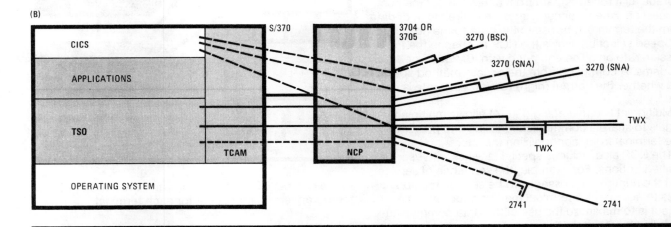

(B)

tions when they are executed by either a local or a remote controller.

Network control program concepts
To control the flow of data through the communications subsystem, the NCP interacts with the communications scanners and the channel adapters. It also communicates with the access method (VTAM or TCAM) in the host processor to control the logical flow of data. Each block of data that passes between the controller and the host processor is preceded by a control-information field that identifies what is in the data unit (user data or a command) and the destination of the data (Fig. 3). Control information from the host is sent by the access method to request the NCP to perform some function, such as activating a line. Conversely, the NCP can send control information to the access method to signal completion of an operation or to report the status of an element of the data communications network. Message data may or may not follow the control information, depending on the operation. The NCP inspects the control-information field

of each block received from the access method to determine its destination, which could be a terminal attached either to the 3705 in which NCP resides or to another 3705 in the data communications network.

The format of the control-information field varies. If the terminal uses start/stop or binary synchronous communications (BSC), the NCP retains the entire control-information field and transmits to the terminal only the message data, framed by start/stop or binary synchronous control characters. If the terminal communicates via synchronous data link control, the NCP retains a portion of the control information and transmits the remainder to the terminal with the message data. Likewise, when SDLC terminals transmit to the communications controller, they prefix the message data with a field of control information.

Standard functions and features
Standard functions of the NCP include those that any transmission control unit performs, such as control-character recognition, communication-line time-out control, error checking, and character assembly and

disassembly. In addition to those functions, the following are standard features of the NCP:

- Polling and addressing multipoint terminals.
- Dialing and answering on the network.
- Inserting and deleting control characters for start/stop and BSC devices. The NCP inserts control characters at the beginning and end of each block of data when transmitting to a device and deletes the control characters when receiving from a device.
- Determining to which adjacent or remote communications controller (if any) a message is to be sent.
- Controlling message traffic between local and remote or adjacent communications controllers. This includes transmitting program load modules to remote controllers and passing storage dump data from remote controllers to the access method.
- Translating character code (BSC and start/stop lines only). As data arrives from a terminal, the NCP automatically translates it from transmission code into EBCDIC. Conversely, EBCDIC data is translated automatically into transmission code.
- Dynamic buffering allocates buffers from controller storage as it receives data from a terminal for the host processor. When it accumulates an entire block of data from the terminal, it transfers the data to the host.
- Speed selection allows the NCP to change the transmission rate on a line equipped with IBM 3872 or 3875 modems. A command from the access method specifies whether the normal (high) rate or a low rate is desired.
- Multipoint line managing (Fig. 4) allows multiple terminals to share a communications line and prevents one terminal from monopolizing the line.

The NCP also includes special facilities with user-defined options. For example, the sequence of service and the number of messages to be sent on multipoint lines to any specific terminal may be specified. The object is to maximize the use of the data communications line by maintaining as many concurrent conversations as possible to satisfy the user-defined sequence for servicing terminal requests. With this feature terminals may be logged into different applications in the host, yet share the same data communications links. It is for start/stop, BSC, and SDLC terminals.

Since NCP enables the attachment of SDLC stations, it must also manage the full-duplex data transmission that can occur on SDLC lines. This function, called duplex-multipoint (Fig. 4) when used on lines with SDLC stations, permits the NCP to receive data from one SDLC station while it is transmitting data to another SDLC station, on the same four-wire link.

The NCP also maintains several types of error and statistic records, and provides panel-display capabilities for diagnostic purposes. Those include:

- Hardware and program-check recording. A record of hardware and program checks is transferred to the host processor for use in determining problems.
- Permanent line-error recording. If normal error-recovery procedures fail, the NCP transfers a communications-error record containing information about the error to the host processor's access method.
- Statistics recording. The program maintains a count

2 Network management host offloading

Consolidation. *A system without the Network Control Program requires each access method to contain logic for physical network control, instead of one program for all.*

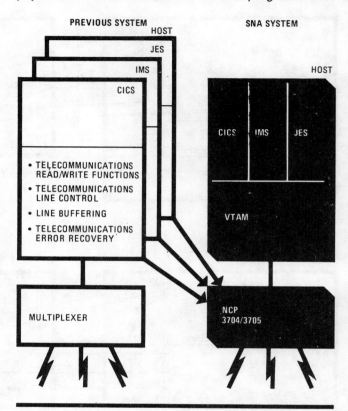

of the number of I/O operations and the number of temporary errors that occur for each terminal.

Functions chosen by need

Many other NCP functions are optional. The user selects the options that meet the needs of the network when the NCP is generated.

For binary synchronous and start-stop communications, the NCP can process blocks of data from either the terminal or the host processor using optional programs called block-handling routines. Selectable as block-handling features of the NCP are date and time insertion, and data correction of text incorrectly entered from a terminal. Additional block-handling routines may be user written and assembled with the controller assembler. Those routines can be included in the program by coding a "generation macro."

Several features that enhance both the error recovery and the diagnostic requirements of a data communications network are available. Among them is critical situation notification (for BSC and start-stop stations only), which can be used to notify terminals when the host processor, channel, or local-to-remote-communications link fails. The user defines a message to be sent to stations in such cases.

Through the 3705 control panel, the operator can request the NCP to perform an address trace that re-

3 Message control

Flow control. Each block of information that is passed between the communications controller and the access method of the host computer is preceded by information that tells what is in the data unit and gives its destination. The access method and the NCP communicate with each other to control lines and report network status.

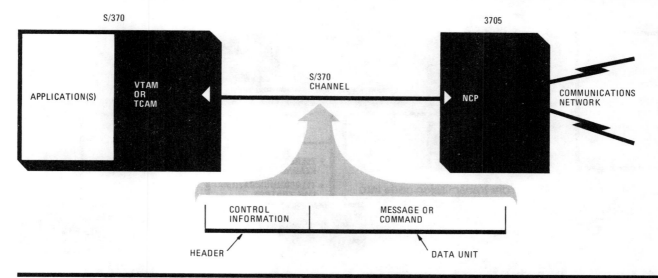

cords the contents of four variables (storage areas and registers) when a specified address in controller storage is accessed. That provides a dynamic-trace facility for diagnostic purposes.

When requested by the host access method, the NCP generates checkpoint records to support the host access method's checkpoint/restart facility. The host access method consolidates and stores the records for use should a restart be required.

On-line terminal testing (OLTT) facilities are available through the 3705 communications controllers. The NCP supports the OLTT functions by recognizing test requests from terminals and executing test routines constructed by an OLTT program in the host processor. For SDLC communications lines, on-line line testing capabilities are available in which the NCP executes test routines constructed by an executive program.

When a transmission error occurs, the NCP attempts to retransmit the data. If initial retransmission is unsuccessful, a pause may be specified and then transmission of the message attempted again. Transit noise or another condition that caused the failure may subside by the time retransmission is again attempted. The number of retries can be user specified for each terminal. That function is included for all terminals unless the user has specified that no retries are to be made.

For certain types of BSC and start-stop terminals, the user may specify an alternate path over the switched communications network that is to be used if the primary point-to-point communication line encounters an error from which it fails to recover. Alternate switched operation is available for local-to-remote or local-to-local connections.

A channel delay feature allows the user to specify an interval, in increments of 100 milliseconds, to be observed before the NCP presents "attention" status to the channel. When a time delay is specified, data arriving from the terminals is stored in the NCP message-buffer pool until the delay interval elapses. Then all the stored data can be transferred across the channel with only one interrupt to the host processor, thus decreasing host processor overhead. The NCP presents "attention" to the channel as soon as it receives enough data to fill all the allotted buffer space in the host-processor access method (VTAM or TCAM) before the specified interval elapses.

If no time delay is specified, each block of data is transferred as soon as it is processed by the NCP, requiring more frequent interrupts to the host processor.

A binary synchronous identification verification feature, available for certain BSC terminals that communicate over the switched network, is useful for limiting access to the network. A list of valid IDs for communications lines on which ID verification is to be used is contained in the NCP. The NCP compares the ID received against those in the list and allows the terminals to connect if a match is found. If no match is found, the NCP can pass the ID information to the VTAM or TCAM or it can break the connection.

For certain low-speed start-stop terminals, multiple terminal access (MTA) allows the controller to communicate with dissimilar types of terminals over the same switched data communications port. When a terminal calls the controller over the MTA line, the MTA option identifies the type of terminal and the transmission code used. The following terminal types are supported by this option:
- IBM 1050 data communications system
- IBM 2740 communications terminal
- IBM 2741 communications terminal
- Terminals using CTP-TWX (models 33 and 35) code at a line speed of 110 bit/s

219

4 Duplex multipoint operation

Line management. *One of the many transmission control functions featured in the Network Control Program is the management of a multipoint line. When data communica-* *tions lines are shared, the NCP prevents the monopolization of the line by any particular terminal. This management system sees to it that all terminals are equal.*

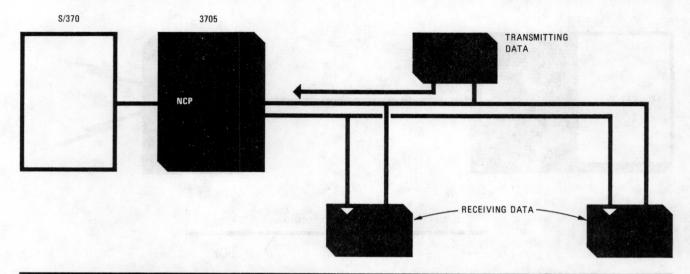

The terminal types, code combinations, and communications lines to be used for MTA are specified as parameters in the NCP program-generation language.

Dynamic control functions from the host access method are also provided to change certain parameters of the NCP. Some of the control functions are standard; others must be specified at NCP generation.

SNA-SDLC terminal and cluster support
For SNA terminals and clusters, the NCP provides a number of program options to manage the devices on SDLC communication lines. Among these program options are the following:
■ Specifying the maximum message size that a device can receive. If a particular message is too long to be accepted by the SDLC station, the NCP will segment it into two or more messages for transmission to the SDLC station.
■ Specifying the number of SDLC frames sent before a data link response is received. Using SNA-SDLC, up to seven message frames may be sent to an SDLC station before a data link response is required indicating the correct reception of the data. The NCP allows this number to be specified for each SDLC device on a communications link thus providing a technique to manage link shareability among the SDLC stations.
■ Pacing the data from host application to terminal user. This function permits the logic supporting the terminal user in an SNA-SDLC terminal or cluster to notify the NCP when it has the ability to accept more data. When NCP receives this response, additional data is sent to the SNA stations for that terminal user.

The NCP also contains SNA logic to manage error recovery and the number of times initial error recovery is attempted, as well as error recovery after a pause between initial and final attempts to transmit a mes-

sage between the host and terminal.

The NCP's primary purpose is to handle data routing and transmission tasks for the network. It is divided into four logical components (Fig. 5):
■ An intermediate network-node component
■ A boundary network-node component
■ A physical services component
■ A BSC/start-stop processor

The intermediate-node component of a local NCP consists of a data-link control, channel adapter I/O supervisor, and a path control to handle the flow of data over the channel interface to the host, the link interface to another intermediate node, or to the boundary node.

In a remote NCP, the intermediate-node component consists of a data-link control to handle data flow over the SDLC link to the local NCP and the link interface to the boundary-network node. All data units transmitted from the host to a terminal enter the NCP through the intermediate-node component.

The intermediate-node component determines whether the received information is destined for a device connected to the local communications controller or for another controller and routes the data unit to the proper component.

A data unit from another controller also enters the intermediate-node component, which routes it to the host interface or another controller.

Data units transmitted from a terminal to the host may enter the NCP at either the SNA-boundary node or the BSC/start-stop processor component. The boundary-node component consists of the logic to attach SNA terminals and cluster controllers. It includes the data-link control (SDLC), path control (routing), and connection-point managers (control blocks) that handle the data flow between this node and an SNA cluster-controller node (for example, 3790) or SNA terminal node (3767). Data units from a cluster controller node or terminal node enter the boundary-node component where they are processed and then transfered to the intermediate node to be sent to the host.

The BSC/start-stop component consists of the start-stop and BSC device support, and the control-command processors used to support these devices.

A data unit from a BSC or start-stop device enters the NCP at the BSC/start-stop support component where it is processed and then transfered to the intermediate node to be sent to the host.

The physical-services component forms an internal path between the various NCP components to handle the NCP control functions.

Network definition
A set of data communications-oriented macros are used to describe the host and network being connected to the 3705 in its native NCP mode:
- The BUILD macro characterizes the 3705 in terms of: channel types, memory size, and network address, and the generation process in terms of type of assembly, program storage area names, etc.
- The SYSCNTRL macro defines what optional features of the NCP are in the generation process (for example, switched network backup).
- The HOST macro specifies buffer size and the number of buffers to be allocated for transferring data to and from the host.
- The CSB macro specifies the types of communications scanners installed and the internal clocking to be used for low-speed lines.
- The GROUP macro defines a set of data communications lines which have similar characteristics such as line-control type and whether they are dial or leased.
- The LINE macro defines a given line by its unique characteristics. Line speed, internal or external modem clocking, half- or full-duplex transmission, and polled or non-polled are some of the items defined.
- The CLUSTER, TERMINAL, and LOGICAL UNIT macros are used to specify physical and logical characteristics of the receiving devices on the data communications lines. The address of the device and any special or optional device features are noted. Maximum data and buffer sizes are specified, as well as other characteristics unique to the terminal being supported.

The NCP-generation process consists of a number of other macros used to define the standard and special requirements of a data communications network. The program is assembled in a sequence similar to the example that appears in the table.

Generating a network control program
NCP generation is a two-stage process consisting of a series of jobs executed under the control of the operating system—either DOS/VS or OS/VS.

Stage one of the generation process is assembly. Either the communications-controller assembler or operating-system assembler prepares a job stream from the program-generation macros that define the program for input to stage two. The stage one output

5 NCP structure

Component parts. The four logical divisions of NCP act to handle different parts of transmission and routing for the network and establish a separation of responsibility.

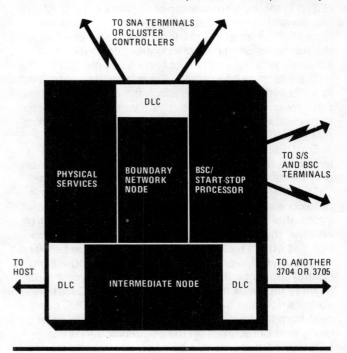

contains data constants, macros that will cause stage two to generate the control tables and conditionally assemble the required program modules, job control statements for stage two, and linkage editor control statements.

In stage two, the communications-controller assembler puts together the control tables as well as those program modules that require conditional assembly. Then the controller assembler link-edits these modules (and other preassembled modules) and puts them into an NCP load-module for later placement into the 3705. A utility program is provided to either load or dump the NCP load module into or from the 3705.

Diagnostic facilities
Several facilities help the user solve problems in the data communications network. Errors in user logic, or malfunctioning lines or hardware frequently can be identified by one of the many traces available.

Each of the traces provides a specific level of information for determining the problem at a particular location or component in the network. Selection of a trace depends on the initial problem characteristics. One type of trace may be able to isolate a problem to a network component. A second trace may then identify the problem within that component.

The data and control information can be traced at various points in the host and the 3705. Figure 6 identifies the traces and the points at which they are made active.

The path information unit (PIU) is a trace of the control fields and optional data between the host and the NCP. It can be in one of two formats, depending on its destination or origin. Format identification zero (FID0) is used to control, transmit to, and receive from BSC and start/stop terminals; format identification one (FID1) is for the transmission of network control information and optional data between the host and the local NCP for an SDLC station. FID1 is also used for the transmission of network control information and optional data between a local and a remote NCP.

The PIU trace can provide the information contained in a PIU in the sequence in which the host access methods presents it to the NCP or vice versa. This can help determine whether or not the proper sequence of commands and responses is being issued.

The line trace helps determine the nature of problems on a communications line; it provides information only for data transmitted over a communications link.

The NCP sends the line-trace data to the host. This data consists of several fields, each containing specific information. One field identifies the type of line control; another, the operation, such as send, receive, or control. Still others relate NCP elapsed time-value between line-trace entries or identify the beginning and ending control sequence for SDLC and BSC line control. Finally, there are fields that differentiate the SDLC station address from the frame being traced, the SDLC control byte from the frame being traced, and the character being sent or received on the communications line.

Address trace can also be of assistance in determining the nature of problems within a communications controller. It is a service aid by which the contents of selected areas of a 3704's or 3705's storage, general registers, and external registers can be recorded at each successive interrupt. The address-trace facility allows the user to select any combination of up to four external registers, general registers, and storage halfwords, the contents of which are to be recorded each time data is loaded from or written into a specified storage address at a specified program level. The recorded data can be displayed on the communications-controller panel or transferred to the host via the dump program. Suspected errors within the NCP can be monitored by recording external registers and changes to storage addresses. This tool is used to identify NCP programming errors or hardware errors that can be identified in external registers.

The channel-adapter trace is a diagnostic and debugging aid that stores those external registers related to the communications controller's channel adapter in a special table. If a channel-adapter hardware error is suspected, this trace can monitor the control-interrupts and data-interrupts at the channel interface. It can also monitor all of the channel's external registers.

The NCP creates miscellaneous data-recorder (MDR) records for the host. The records can be grouped into two types, according to the way they are created and prepared for transfer to the host: MDR records of adapter and program checks and unresolved interrupts; and MDR records of line statistics and permanent line errors.

These records are transferred to the host either when

Program definition

BSC LINK

BUILD—THIS COMMAND DEFINES SUCH PARAMETERS AS CHANNEL TYPE.

SYSCNTRL—A SYSTEM CONTROL PARAMETER WOULD BE, FOR EXAMPLE, SWITCHED NETWORK BACKUP.

HOST—DEFINES SUCH HOST PARAMETERS AS BUFFER SIZE.

CSB—DEFINES PARAMETERS FOR INTERNAL CLOCKS AND SCANNER TYPES.

GROUP—DEFINES SEVERAL LINES BY TYPE (E.G., START-STOP, SDLC, BISYNCHRONOUS).

  LINE—DEFINES INDIVIDUAL LINES BY SUCH CHARACTERISTICS AS SPEED, CODE, ETC.

  SERVICE—DEFINES THE ORDER IN WHICH THE LINES ARE SERVICED (POLLING LIST).

    CLUSTER—DEFINES THE PHYSICAL ADDRESS OF A TERMINAL CLUSTER.

    TERMINAL—DEFINES THE TYPE OF STATION (ADDRESS CHARACTERS, FEATURES, ETC.).

SDLC LINK

GROUP—(SAME AS ABOVE)

  LINE—(SAME AS ABOVE)

  SERVICE—(SAME AS ABOVE)

    PU—DEFINES ADDRESS, DATA SIZE, ETC., OF A PHYSICAL UNIT (SIMILAR TO CLUSTER)

    LU—DEFINES LOCAL ADDRESS, ETC., OF LOGICAL UNIT (SIMILAR TO TERMINAL).

START/STOP LINK

GROUP—(SAME AS ABOVE)

  LINE—(SAME AS ABOVE)

  SERVICE—(SAME AS ABOVE)

    TERMINAL—(SAME AS ABOVE)

    COMP—DEFINES PARTICULAR COMPONENT ON TERMINAL, ITS ADDRESS, AND OPTIONAL FEATURES (E.G., SPECIAL LINE-CONTROL CHARACTERS)

GENEND—PROVIDES DEFINITION NECESSARY TO SUPPORT HIGH-SPEED LINES.

  USING MACROS TO TAILOR THE PROGRAM PROVIDES A FLEXIBLE MEANS FOR ADDING SUPPORT FOR NEW DEVICES OR CHANGING THE REQUIREMENTS OF THE DATA COMMUNICATIONS NETWORK.

permanent errors occur or when the temporary-error counters overflow. They may be analyzed for intermittent and permanent errors of the 3705 hardware and for line errors. If a permanent failure of the NCP prevents the MDR records' being sent to the host, these records are then available in a dump of the NCP.

The dynamic display panel of the 3705 communications controller allows the user to view the interface control word (ICW), or the contents of an external register, and to display or change a half-word of controller storage. The user selects a function by setting the Display/Function Select and Storage Address/Register Data switches on the panel. When the interrupt button is pressed, a panel routine reads the panel switches to determine and then perform the requested functions. This support allows the user to check storage values

Fault diagnosis. *When the network malfunctions, a number of traces can be used to determine the nature and location of the problem. Each of the traces provides a specific level of information for determining the problem at a specific location or component in the network. The type of trace depends on the characteristics of the problem.*

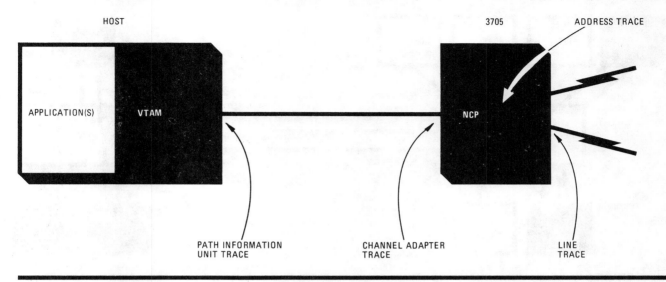

at a point in time and to alter their checked values.

A line-test feature allows the user to address, poll, dial, and transmit to or receive from a terminal. A test is initiated by entering variables through the 3705 panel. A test of lines, modems, and terminals can verify proper operation without a host application program being active.

On-line tests are available from the host processor. They are a user-selected option that provides an on-line maintenance capability. They also provide the customer with a tool to aid in problem recovery. This option supports testing of SDLC, BSC, and start-stop lines of BSC and start-stop devices.

Migration
For current users of the 3705 operating in the emulation program mode, the Partitioned Emulation Program (PEP) function allows a 3705 to contain both the emulation program and the NCP functions. Although the 3705 is logically partitioned to perform the two separate tasks, only a single load module is required. A BSC or start-stop data communications line can be generated as a PEP line to operate in either emulation of native mode with the switching under the control of the systems operator. Therefore, a line used for production purposes under one mode can be used off-hours for testing purposes under the other mode.

Advanced communications function/NCP
The role of a single communications interface for both of IBM's major communications-access-method program products, ACF/VTAM and ACF/TCAM, is provided by ACF/NCP/VS (a program product) that can operate in a multiple-computer-system network environment (Fig. 7). ACF/NCP/VS provides support for channel attachment of up to four hosts in a given net-

work. Major functions selectable with ACF/NCP/VS to enhance primary and backup operations include cross-system message routing for selected devices via a 3705 or a series of local 3705s independent of host control after initial session establishment. This support provides direct communications between locally attached 3705s via an SDLC link and direct routing of message traffic on behalf of adjacent systems without the intervention of its controlling host access method.

The NCP can maintain active user sessions and cross-system routing functions for SDLC devices should its controlling host fail. Also, control of a locally attached ACF/NCP/VS may be assumed by an adjacent host without re-initilization procedures. In fact, these multiple-host environment facilities are directed toward helping minimize disruptions of end users, and to maximize the availability of network and host resources in the event of a host failure or when the host is down for scheduled maintenance.

In addition, full-duplex, wideband support for SDLC lines up to 56 kbits/s is available to enhance the throughput of the 3705's local-to-local or local-to-remote links in a networking environment.

The communications controller
The 3705 communications controller is a modular, programmable unit which can significantly expand the communications capabilities of System/370 mainframes in both single CPU and multiple CPU data communications environments. Because of its programmability, range of features, and storage modularity, the 3705 provides flexible configurations to meet many network requirements.

When operating in its native NCP (ACF/NCP/VS or NCP/VS) mode, the 3705 can be attached to all models of System/370. In emulation program mode (emu-

One interface. Both of IBM's major access methods, VTAM and TCAM, can be interfaced by the Advanced Communications Function version of the Network Control Program. This capability allows many host computer systems, all with a variety of applications programs, to communicate and provide backup for each other.

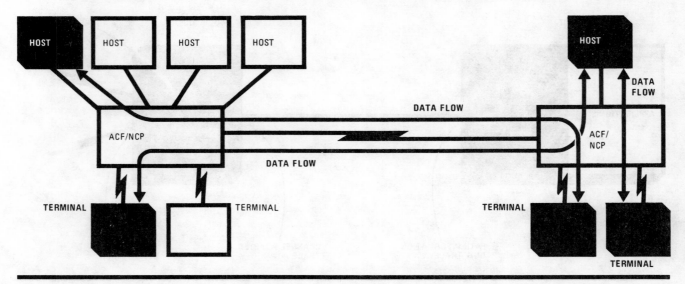

lating the IBM 2701, 2702, or 2703), the 3705 may be used with either System/370 or System/360 hosts.

Both the 3704 and 3705 communications controllers may be configured to operate locally or as remote communications controllers. The 3705 can be configured to operate alternately as a local or remote communications controller. Remote operation is via an SDLC communications link to a local 3704 or 3705 communications controller, which is then channel-attached to the host computer.

The 3705 is available in two models, 3705-I 3705-II, and can consist of up to four modules, depending on the requirements of the data communications network (Fig. 8). The modules house the central control unit, a control panel, a storage area, channel adapters, communications scanners, line interface bases, and line sets. Storage area for the 3705-I ranges from 16K to 240K bytes, in increments of 32K bytes. Its read/write cycle time is 1.2 microseconds. The 3705-II has from 32K to 256K of storage in 32K increments and a read/write storage cycle time of 1.0 microsecond. An enhanced version of the 3705 II can contain storage up to 512 K and has a read/write storage cycle time of 900 nanoseconds. The 3705 supports the attachment of data communications lines from 45.5 bits/s to 56 kbits/s. Up to 352 communications lines may be attached to the 3705 in the NCP mode of operation.

Four types of channel adapters (CA) are available. The Type 1 CA and the Type 4 CA allow local attachment to a System/360 or System/370 byte-multiplexer channel. These adapters contain hardware circuits the program requires to emulate an IBM 2701, 2702, or 2703, as well as allowing operation of the controller in its native mode. When operating in its emulation mode, the controller requires multiple subchannel addresses: one for each communications-line address and one for the native mode's initial program leader (IPL). When the Type 1 CA or Type 4 CA are operating in native mode (NCP), only a single subchannel address is required. The 3704 supports the Type 1 CA, while both Types 1 and 4 may be put in a 3705.

Both the Type 1 and the Type 4 CA transmit data to and from the byte-multiplexer channel in bursts of up to four bytes. When operated in its expanded buffer mode, the Type 4 CA can transmit data in bursts of up to 32 bytes. The Type 4 CA can transfer data in bursts up to 248 bytes when operated in ACF/NCP mode, may be attached to the byte multiplexer, block multiplexer, or selector channel.

The Type 2 and Type 3 CAs, which are available for the 3705 only, operate in the native NCP mode only. They provide for local attachment to a System/370 byte multiplexer, block multiplexer, or selector channel. With the Type 2 or Type 3 CA, the 3705 uses a single subchannel address.

All data transfers between the 3705 storage area and the Type 2 and Type 3 channel adapters are made by cycle-steal operations. That is, when the CA has data to put in storage, it preempts (under hardware control) the necessary machine cycles to transfer the data. Data transfers from storage to the channel adapter also use the cycle-steal technique. A cycle-steal operation is accomplished by hardware circuits and does not affect the logical operation of the program.

A 3705-I communications controller can contain up to two and a 3705-II, four, channel adapters in various combinations of CA types. The base module and the first expansion module can alternately contain a remote program loader (RPL), or both a channel adapter and an RPL.

The central control unit (CCU) contains the circuits and data-flow paths needed to execute the 3705's

NCP dictionary

In this article NCP is used as a generic term that refers to both Advanced Communication Function/NCP/VS and NCP/VS. Similarly, reference to VTAM or TCAM refers to either ACF/VTAM or VTAM and ACF/TCAM or TCAM. Where a particular function is provided by the ACF products only, a distinction has been made.

Access method: A data management technique for transferring data between main storage and an input/output device. Here, data communications access method refers to the data management technique, executed in the host processor, that transfers data between the host processor and the network control program (NCP) in the communications controller.

Channel adapter (CA): A hardware unit in the communications controller that allows attachment of the controller to a System/360 or System/370 channel.

Cluster controller: A device that can control the input/output operations of more than one device.

Communications controller: A type of communication control unit whose operations are controlled by a program stored and executed in the unit. It manages the details of line control and routing of data through a network. It can route data to the host processor or it can route data to or from a cluster controller or terminal.

Communication scanner: A controller hardware unit that provides the interface between line interface bases and the central control unit. The communication scanner monitors communication lines for service requests.

Component: An independently addressable part of a station that performs either an input or an output function, but not both.

Line control character: A special character that controls transmission of data over a start-stop or BSC communication line. For example, line control characters are used to start or end a transmission, to initiate transmission-error checking, and to indicate whether a station has data to send or is ready to receive data.

Logical unit (LU): In SNA, one of three types of network addressable units. It is the port through which an end user gains access to the network in order to communicate with another end user. Through this port a user also gains access to the services provided by the system services control point (SSCP).

Network control program (NCP/VS): A program for the physical control of a data communications network implemented in the 3704 and 3705 communications controllers, and generated by the user from a library of IBM-supplied modules.

Network control program generation language: The set of macro instructions and associated operands by which the user defines for the controller the network configuration and operating parameters of the data communications network.

Path information unit (PIU): The basic unit of transmission in a data communications network. Path information units may request a particular communications operation (request PIU) or indicate the result of an operation (response PIU).

Physical unit (PU): In SNA, one of three types of network addressable units; a PU is associated with each node whose existence has been defined to the system services control point (SSCP). A physical unit controls the resources local to its associated node. The SSCP establishes a session with the physical unit as part of the bring-up process.

Session: (1) The period of time during which a user of a terminal can communicate with an interactive system: usually, the elapsed time from when a terminal user logs on the system until he logs off the system. (2) The period of time during which programs or devices can communicate with each other. (3) In SNA, a logical connection, established between two network addressable units (NAUs), that allows them to communicate. The session is uniquely identified by a pair of network addresses, identifying the origin and destination NAUs of any transmissions exchanged during the session.

SNA terminal: In VTAM: (1) A physical unit, logical unit, or secondary application program. (2) A terminal that is compatible with systems network architecture.

Switched network backup: An optional facility of the network control program that allows the user to specify, for certain device types, a line to be used as a backup line should the primary line become unavailable due to an irrecoverable error.

Synchronous data link control (SDLC): A discipline for managing synchronous, transparent, serial-by-bit information transfer over a communication channel. Transmission exchanges may be duplex or half-duplex over switched or nonswitched data links. The communication channel configuration may be point-to-point, multipoint, or loop. Contrast with binary synchronous transmission and start-stop transmission.

System macro: One of the network control program generation macros that provide information pertaining to the entire controller.

Systems network architecture (SNA): The total description of the logical structure, formats, protocols, and operational sequences for transmitting information units through the communication system. Communication system functions are separated into three discrete areas: the application layer, the function management layer, and the transmission subsystem layer. The structure of SNA allows the ultimate origins and destinations of information—that is, the end users—to be independent of, and unaffected by, the specific communication-system services and facilities used for information exchange.

Telecommunications access method (TCAM): A method used to transfer data between main storage and remote or local terminals. Application programs use either GET and PUT or READ and WRITE macro instructions to request the transfer of data, which is performed by message handlers. The message handlers synchronize the transfer, thus eliminating delays for terminal input/output operations.

Virtual telecommunications access method (VTAM): A set of programs that control communication between terminals and application programs, running under DOS/VS, OS/VSI, and OS/VS2.

instructions and to control the 3705's storage and the attached adapters. It also includes a storage-protection mechanism. The central control unit operates under the control of the 3705 control program, either emulation program or NCP.

The communications scanners provide the connection between the communication-line attachment hardware (line-interface bases and line sets) and the CCU. The primary function of the scanner is to check periodically the hardware associated with each communications line for service requests. Three types of communications scanners (CS) are available: Type 1 CS, Type 2 CS and Type 3 CS. The Type 1 scanner is primarily used with start-stop terminals. When installed in a 3705, the Type 1 scanner supports a maxmimum of 64 half-duplex lines, only one Type 1 can be installed.

The Type 2 scanner in a 3705 supports up to 96 half-duplex lines. This scanner transfers a full byte to or from the CCU. From one to four Type 2 scanners can be installed in a 3705, providing attachment of up to 352 data communications lines.

Finally, the Type 3 scanner supports up to 64 half-duplex lines in a 3705. Depending upon the program buffering options used, the Type 3 scanner transfers up to 254 bytes of data to or from the CCU before interrupting the control program for more data or more buffers. Up to three Type 3 scanners can be installed in a 3705-I, allowing attachment of up to 192 data communications lines (or 256 lines if a Type 2 scanner is included with the three Type 3 scanners). Four Type 3 scanners may be installed in a 3705-II providing for the attachment of up to 240 data communications lines. Type 2 and Type 3 scanners may be mixed in a 3705-II.

Type 1 and Type 2 scanners support both synchronous and asynchronous data communications lines. The Type 3 scanner supports synchronous data commuications lines (SDLC and BSC). All three types support lines of different data rates (line speeds). The line type (SDLC, BSC, or start-stop), character length, bit-clocking mechanism (business machine or modem), installed business-machine-clock speed, and interrupt priority are selected by the program for each interface.

Data communications lines to and from the terminals are attached to the communications controller through a line interface base (LIB). The primary functions of the LIB are to drive and terminate all signals between the communications scanners and the line sets, and to provide bit clocking. The line interface base is transparent to the data transferred and has no effect on the control program except for bit control. The number and type of LIB's vary according to the controller configuration.

As many as 22 LIBs can be installed in a 3705. Several different LIB types are available to meet the needs of a wide variety of line and terminal types. Each LIB type operates identically and is controlled by the communications scanner to which it is attached. However, the design of the various LIB types differs in order to support many line sets and line configurations.

The line set is the hardware connection between the LIB and the data communications line. A given line-set

8 IBM 3705 communications controller

Controller. The 3705 contains modules that house the control unit, control panel, storage, channel adapters, communications scanners, interfaces, and line sets.

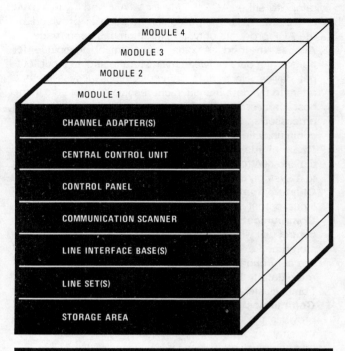

type may support attachment of many different terminals and devices. Therefore, different data sets or modems may be required. A single line set provides the interface for one or two data communications lines, depending on the type of interface.

Data flow
The NCP interacts with the communications scanners and the channel adapters to control the flow of data through the 3705 (Fig. 9).

Data enters a terminal and is received by the line set and line interface base. The communications scanner recognizes when service is required and receives data from the LIB. The program places the data in storage, where it is then available to the channel adapter to be sent to the host-processor channel.

When data is to be transmitted from the host processor to the terminal, the process is reversed. The host channel sends the data to the controller's channel adapter which, under hardware or program control (depending on the type of adapter), places the data in storage. From storage the data is moved to the data communications line via the communications scanner, line interface base, and line set.

NCP-supported devices
The 3705 supports a wide range of terminals and communications systems in the NCP mode including: 1050 data communications system, 2740 model 1 and 2, communication terminals, 2741 communication terminal, 2770 data communication system, 2780 data

9 Data flow

Routing data. The NCP sits between the channel adapter and the communications scanner to assure a proper data flow. The scanner takes in-bound data from the line and passes it to the NCP, which gives it to the channel adapter for routing to the host via the access method. Returning data follows the opposite route on the way out.

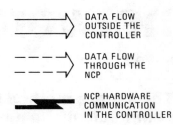

HOST   COMMUNICATIONS CONTROLLER

TELE-PROCESSING ACCESS METHOD — CHANNEL ADAPTER — NCP — SCANNER / LIB — STATION

1 DATA
2
9
10 DATA
4
7
5 DATA
6 DATA

HOST TO STATION

1. HOST SENDS DATA TO THE CONTROLLER
2. CHANNEL ADAPTER NOTIFIES NCP AS DATA ARRIVES
3. NCP PROCESSES DATA, PREPARES IT FOR STATION
4. NCP ACTIVATES COMMUNICATION SCANNER WHEN DATA IS READY TO BE SENT TO STATION
5. DATA IS TRANSMITTED ACROSS COMMUNICATION LINE TO STATION

STATION TO HOST

6. STATION SENDS DATA TO THE CONTROLLER
7. COMMUNICATION SCANNER NOTIFIES NCP AS DATA ARRIVES
8. NCP PROCESS DATA, PREPARES IT FOR HOST
9. NCP ACTIVATES CHANNEL ADAPTER WHEN DATA IS READY TO BE SENT TO HOST
10. CHANNEL TRANSFERS DATA TO HOST

DATA FLOW OUTSIDE THE CONTROLLER

DATA FLOW THROUGH THE NCP

NCP HARDWARE COMMUNICATION IN THE CONTROLLER

---

transmission system, 2972 general banking terminal system, 3270 information display system, 3600 finance communication system, 3614 consumer transaction facility, 3650 retail store system, 3660 supermarket system, 3671 shared terminal control unit, 3735 programmable buffered terminal, 3740 data entry system, 3767 communication terminal, 3770 data communication system, 3780 data communication terminal, 3790 communication system, communication magnetic card selectric typewriter, 5100 portable computer, and 5275 direct numerical control station.

The 3705 communications controller can also connect to the following remote data processing systems operating in a terminal mode: Series/1, System/3, System/7 (operating as a 2740 Model 1 or a System/3), System 32, System 34, 1130 computing system, 8100 data acquisition control system station, and 8100 information systems, System/360 Model 20 with the binary synchronous communications attachment, System/360 Model 25 with the integrated communications adapter, System/370 Model 125 or Model 135 with the integrated communications adapter, and System/360 or System/370 by means of an IBM 2701 data adapter unit, 2703 transmission control, or another 3705 or 3704 communications controller.

The 3705 communications controller can attach terminals with the following controls: AT&T 83B2/83B3, WU 115A, and TWX Model 33/35.

Summary

For its full range of uses, single host-tree networks to complex multiple-host-interconnected networking environments, the NCP provides the functions and operational flexibility necessary to meet increasing data communications demands. At the same time, through programming logic executed within the 3704 or 3705, NCP/VS can relieve host computers of many data communications responsibilites from basic multiplexing to centralized physical network resource management.

NCP provides for a logical separation of functions from the host processor. This leads to better manageability of the system with cleaner interfaces up to the application program level. More host-processor resources become available to application processing and, consequently, more advanced services can be provided to the data communictions subsytems.

ACF/NCP/VS together with the multisystem-networking facilility of the host access method allows for a multisystem-networking environment, where the operation of the network is less dependent on the operation of any particular node in the network, thus minimizing the impact of host failures. ∎

VTAM means software for more logical network management

Sam D. Scott, IBM Corp., Research Triangle Park, N.C.

The access method in a data communications network must know what, where, when, and how in order to move data in and out of a host computer

IBM's Virtual Telecommunications Access Method (VTAM) has been a boon to data communications users because it increases growth potential by providing session services between the host's application programs and the terminals in the network. By doing that, VTAM decreases the adverse effects of changes on applications-program investments. Because IBM's data communications host software products (IMS, CICS, TSO, etc.) have a VTAM interface, a single access method for an entire network provides an economical means of supporting many different on-line requirements. Here is how VTAM works.

VTAM implements Systems Network Architecture (SNA) in IBM 370 or 303X host computers. As an SNA access method, VTAM uses SNA's data formats, data transfers, protocols, and operational sequences to control data communications. The data communications applications programs and VTAM provide the three layers of communications function as defined in an SNA host: applications, function management, and transmission control. Applications are implemented by programs written by the application developers or obtained through IBM. Function management is implemented through VTAM's application program interface. Transmission is implemented by VTAM.

The primary responsibilities of VTAM include start-up, recovery and termination (network control), dynamic connection and disconnection of terminals and applications, and the routing of data between terminals and applications (application services). A terminal can be connected to one application at a time, but has the flexibility to alter this connection should the user choose to communicate with another application in the same host that also uses VTAM. With the Advanced Communications Function (ACF), the responsibility of VTAM is increased to include managing the dynamic connection and disconnection of terminals that have applications running on different hosts. However, the other hosts must also use the ACF versions of the access methods, either ACF/VTAM or ACF/TCAM.

VTAM is designed to take advantage of a host computer that provides virtual-storage (VS) capabilities. VTAM starts itself, based on terminal and application definitions supplied in the form of tables stored on a direct-access storage device (DASD). VTAM can add new definitions while it is running so that additional applications and terminals can become active participants in the network. Thus VTAM adapts itself to supporting both small and large networks. Growth is manageable because additional terminals can be brought into the network as needed. The applications-program interface is supplied in the form of VTAM macros that are compatible across all VS operating systems, such as Disk Operating System (DOS), VS1 and VS2. By using VTAM as a common applications interface, developers of data communications application can concentrate their efforts on delivery of function instead of exhausting their resources on the physical network.

Applications-program interface

The VTAM applications-program interface is in the form of macro instructions that are coded within IBM-supplied programs. IBM programs such as Customer Information Control System (CICS), Information Management System (IMS), Virtual Storage Personal Computing (VSPC), as well as some types of systems control programming (SCP) such as the Time Sharing Option (TSO) and the Job Entry System (JES), have been written to use VTAM. A user-written data processing applications program can be designed and written to use a high-level language, such as COBOL, for its major part. Additional subroutines can be written in assembler language to provide the VTAM interface.

The VTAM data communications macros that provide data transfer between terminals and applications programs are implemented in two forms. The first form consists of macros to support channel-attached IBM 3270 terminals and start-stop and binary synchronous remote terminals controlled by an IBM 3704/3705 communications controller with a Network Control Program/Virtual Storage (NCP/VS). The second form consists of record-mode data communications macros to support channel-attached IBM 3270 and 3790 terminals, remote SNA terminals on switched or leased SDLC lines, and binary synchronous 3270s controlled by NCP/VS. The record mode data communications macros are designed to provide the end-user-to-end-user protocols defined in SNA. These protocols manage data between host applications and intelligent SNA terminals in the network. In addition, the record mode data communications macros in the ACF version of VTAM manage data transferred between two applications programs in either the same host computer or different hosts.

The flexibility of VTAM with terminals is demonstrated by postulating a Multiple Virtual System (MVS) with IMS/VS, TSO, and JES2, using VTAM to support remote IBM 3790, 3270, and 3770 terminals dropped on the same SDLC link. Using the intelligence built into the 3790 cluster controller, one 3790 with multiple display stations can support remote job entry with JES2, on-line applications with IMS/VS and TSO, and off-line user applications executed in the 3790. The 3270 terminals on the same SDLC link can have access to either IMS/VS or TSO along with the 3770 terminals being used for remote job entry. One of the benefits of VTAM is that a given terminal can have access to more than a single host application (like IMS/VS and TSO), thereby reducing data communications line costs and avoiding duplicate terminal costs.

With the advent of ACF, and the ability to network multiple hosts, an application that could not be justified previously because of a limited number of users now becomes possible because more users in the corporate network have access to the program in question.

The interface to VTAM for the remote physical network is provided by NCP/VS in the IBM 3704 or 3705 communications controller, while the start-up of the network is controlled and coordinated by VTAM through NCP/VS. VTAM issues commands to the NCP/VS to start the network in an orderly fashion. The commands issued by VTAM for network start-up can be controlled by user definition and by the VTAM operator facilities. VTAM thus allows the user to activate only that portion of the network requiring access to applications available in the host. Also, terminal-user access of host applications can be controlled based on resource requirements at the host (such as on-line file availability). Similarly, VTAM operator commands allow any part of the remote network to stop receiving services. VTAM, in this case, issues shut-down commands to NCP/VS, which quiesces the portion of the network that no longer requires host services.

VTAM-NCP interface

To control and pass terminal messages between VTAM and NCP/VS, a well-defined interface is used. That interface is currently implemented in two formats, one for NCP/VS-attached SNA terminals, and one for NCP/VS-attached start-stop and binary synchronous terminals. For data transfer between VTAM and NCP/VS, multiple messages for both SNA and non-SNA terminals may be handled in a single input-output operation. VTAM input-output logic for inbound messages for applications programs is driven by an interrupt created by the 370X communications controller.

A user-defined number of VTAM input-output buffers receive one or more messages from the NCP/VS. Thus, during one I/O operation, multiple messages from different terminals may be received by VTAM for distribution to one or more host applications. For outbound messages from applications within the host, VTAM schedules and initiates I/O to transfer one or more messages to the 3704/3705 NCP/VS. Upon completion, the VTAM I/O operation is structured to read any inbound messages the NCP/VS may have received during the VTAM-to-NCP/VS data transfer.

Handling inbound and outbound messages in this fashion provides host efficiencies for attaching terminals by means of older communications controllers that could support only single-terminal message transfers during an I/O operation. The older hardware-oriented methods left all the link protocol responsibilities (polling, addressing, etc.) to the host access method, such as the Basic Telecommunications Access Method (BTAM).

VTAM and the 3704/3705 NCP/VS manage data transfers between themselves by using two different controls. The object is to give better performance and a more uniform response time for inquiry terminals in the network. Either type of control may prompt the 3704/3705 hardware interrupt to inform VTAM that data is formatted in NCP/VS ready for VTAM processing. The first type of control operates through an attention delay that is specified by the user in NCP/VS. The attention delay value, specified in units of tenths of a

1 Dynamic connection

Sessions. *At any one time, a terminal may be attached to only one applications program in the host computer. However, each applications program can be simulta-* *neously attached to several terminal users. These connections, through the use of VTAM, can change dynamically from minute to minute, depending on the user's needs.*

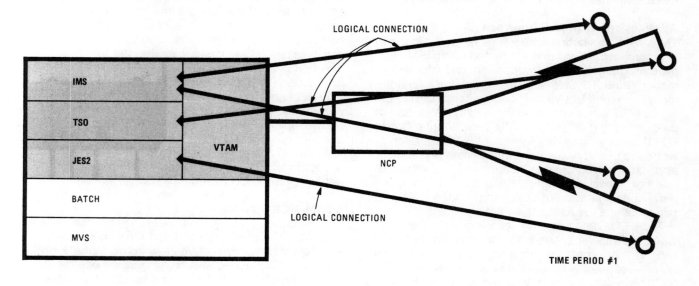

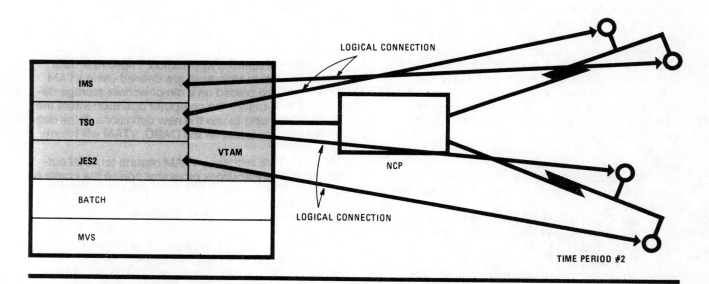

second, controls the maximum time inbound messages can be held in NCP/VS before the communications controller provides a hardware attention interrupt to the host computer. The other type of control is a user-specified maximum number of VTAM message buffers to be used in a single input-transfer operation from NCP/VS to the host. When the NCP has data for VTAM equaling or exceeding the capacity of the buffers before the end of the attention-delay time, the 3704/3705 will provide a hardware interrupt to notify the host of data in the NCP. The ability to buffer and transfer multiple messages in a single input operation from the NCP to VTAM by using the attention delay contributes to upgrading the host's performance.

The ACF has enhanced VTAM by allowing its applications, in the same or different hosts, to communicate with each other. Two widely used applications programs, CICS/VS and JES2, give the user an application-to-application capability when used with ACF/VTAM. JES2 (MVS) is currently available to provide that function for job networking, which is the ability to enter batched data from a remote job-entry terminal. The system then routes the data to the proper host and relays any batched output back to the terminal upon completion of processing.

CICS-to-CICS data communications using ACF/VTAM can be done in the same host or between multiple hosts—the added application-to-application

230

2 ACF session capability

Extension. The Advanced Communication Function allows a network of hosts and terminals with similar access methods to act as one user resource. Host-to-host data communications, along with multi-host access from any terminal in the network, can provide the traffic load to justify previously uneconomic program expansion.

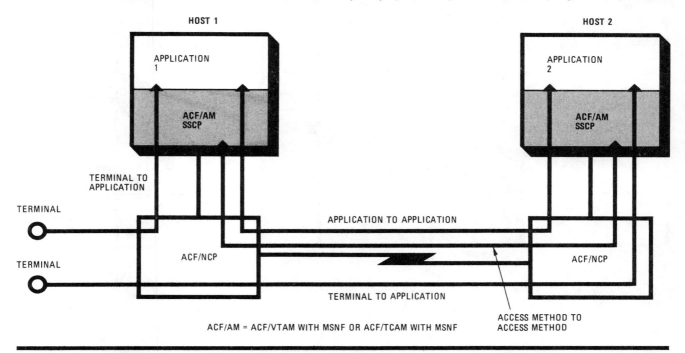

ACF/AM = ACF/VTAM WITH MSNF OR ACF/TCAM WITH MSNF

data communications capability between two IBM hosts is provided by functions added in the Multi-System Networking Feature for ACF/VTAM and in ACF/NCP.

In addition to supporting remote terminals via the 3704/3705 communications controller, VTAM supports the local (channel-attached) IBM 3270 and 3790 terminals, where it performs all the physical I/O operations for data transfer and error recovery.

VTAM services

Network services are performed by specific logic — called the system services control point (SSCP) — within VTAM. The SSCP is responsible for such things as network start-up, recovery, and termination, as well as for dynamically connecting (and disconnecting) each terminal to a given application in the IBM host.

The SSCP becomes active when VTAM is started by the computer operator. Through user definitions, the control point is logically informed of the network resources (which include one or more NCPs with attached links and terminals, channel-attached terminals, and applications eligible to use VTAM). Also through user definitions, all or part of the data communications resources can be put into operation. VTAM reports any failures at network start-up time and continues to bring up as much of the network as possible. After VTAM start-up is complete, the SSCP will service VTAM operator commands. These commands allow a computer operator to define for the SSCP other data communications resources, such as another NCP or a new

data communications application. These new data communications resources are defined using VTAM tables that are placed on a direct-access storage device (DASD) before the computer operator enters the VTAM command to use the new definitions. If the definitions are not found on the DASD, VTAM will inform the operator.

For network recovery, VTAM reports terminal outages to the applications programs and to the computer operating system, then automatically attempts to recover the physical network. VTAM informs the host application program of any permanently lost terminal connections in the network. This keeps the applications program informed of the status of its connections and allows message resynchronization after reconnection has been made.

Another major service is performed by VTAM's SSCP. It monitors connection requests, which can be made by an applications program or by a terminal user. A connection can be made if each data communications resource is available; that is, if the application is running in the host and the terminal is not currently logged onto an application. When an applications program requests a connection to a terminal already logged onto another application, VTAM will inform the application currently connected to the terminal of the pending request. The application, in turn, can honor the request by terminating its connection or it can deny the request.

Thus a single terminal, such as a printer, can be shared by two applications and data can be sent to

231

3 VTAM inbound message flow

Upstream. Messages bound for a host application program are first buffered in the communications controller, then in either a real or virtual buffer under the control of VTAM. VTAM also has the option of placing the message in a secondary storage device before it is finally sent to its destination in the application's work area.

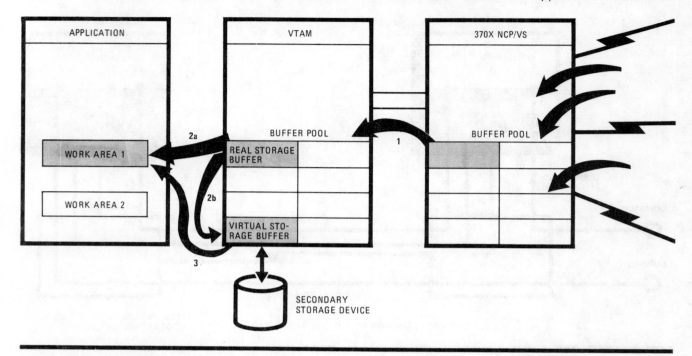

the terminal as it becomes available to the host. Failure to make a connection is reported to the requesting resource, either the applications program or the terminal user. The connection of the terminal user with the application is called a session. Only one session exists for each end user (terminal operator), but concurrent sessions can exist between an application and an SNA terminal with multiple end users (IBM 3790). As in the example described above using MVS with IMS/VS, TSO, and JES2, multiple sessions can exist for terminals residing on the same link. Those connections can change dynamically, based on the terminal user's requirements (Fig. 1).

The ACF has extended the capability of the systems services control point in VTAM. With the Multi-System Networking Feature, the ACF/VTAM SSCP has the ability to communicate with other ACF/VTAMs and ACF/TCAMs that have the Multi-System Networking Feature and that are running in other hosts. This host-to-host communications allows a total network of many hosts and many terminals to be managed in an orderly fashion. (Fig. 2).

Data flow

Before discussing the flow of message data between VTAM and an application, a description of VTAM's message buffers should be reviewed. The message data buffers are created by VTAM at start-up time. The size and number of buffers are specified by the user. However, the program will automatically assign a predetermined amount of buffer space if that information

is not given by the operator at start-up time. Two different message-buffer pools are created: the virtual-storage buffers; and the real-storage message buffers that are used to achieve fast message processing.

For input messages from terminals in the network (Fig. 3), the NCP will physically collect the messages in its storage. Upon 3704/3705 hardware notification, VTAM will read these messages into separate real-storage buffers. Each separate message will start in a new buffer; multiple VTAM buffers will be chained together if the message length requires more than a single buffer. For those applications that have issued a VTAM applications-program message-receive operation (receive or read), VTAM will move the message into the application's message-work area and then designate those buffers available for reuse in its real-storage buffer pool. For those applications that have not issued a VTAM message-receive operation, VTAM will move the message into the virtual-storage buffer pool so that messages become eligible for paging onto a secondary storage device. VTAM keeps track of the messages moved to virtual-storage buffers, so when the application does request message input, VTAM will move the message from the virtual-storage buffer pool to the application work area, where, in this case, the system designates buffers that can be paged as eligible for reuse.

Messages outbound from applications programs to terminals (Fig. 4) are moved from the application's message-work area into VTAM's real-storage buffer pool. VTAM prefixes the message with the proper SNA

4 VTAM outbound message

Downstream. *Data flow management for messages being returned to a terminal in the network begins by moving the data from the applications program's work area to a buffer in VTAM. VTAM sends the message to a buffer in the communications controller, where the message waits until it contains enough bits to form a complete message.*

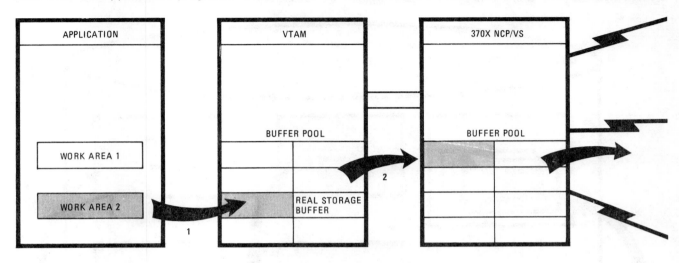

routing control. Multiple messages may be collected from the same or different applications before VTAM schedules the output operation to the NCP. In this way, VTAM can send multiple messages from the host to the NCP in a single transmission. When the NCP indicates that all messages have been received correctly, VTAM designates the real-storage buffers used for output as reusable in the buffer pool.

Since VTAM runs asynchronously with the data communications applications, multiple messages will enter and exit the communications access method, providing more throughput overall. To enhance the flexibility of the buffer management for terminal messages, ACF/VTAM has been designed to allow dynamic buffering. This user-controlled technique, implemented in ACF/VTAM, allows VTAM to add or reduce buffers to accommodate message volume, which results in greater flexibility in determining the number of VTAM buffers required to service message traffic. The technique also permits reduction in the memory requirements for the real-storage message buffers. Although the number of message buffers can grow dynamically, ACF/VTAM can control the number of messages an SNA terminal can send to the host, using a control feature known as inbound pacing.

VTAM generation
Users who need VTAM must have it specified in the operating system (the ACF version of VTAM is an IBM program product and must be ordered separately). As a result of this process, the VTAM code will be placed in a library on a DASD ready to be executed.

The user then creates the proper network definitions that will be used by VTAM at start-up time. There are five different types of definitions that can be classified: (1) NCP terminals, (2) channel-attached terminals, (3) switched SNA terminals, (4) application lists, and (5) VTAM-only parameters (Fig. 5). The NCP/VS definition is the same source definition that is used to create an executable NCP. Channel-attached and switched SNA-terminal definitions, plus application definitions, are tables created by the user. The VTAM-only parameter definition is composed of a few customized parameters for the access method, the most important of which is the buffer allocation. As mentioned in the section on data flow, ACF/VTAM is enhanced to allow dynamic buffer allocation so that the access method can react to different loads. VTAM-supporting documentation provides a formula for calculating the number of buffers required to service the network and its message traffic. In addition to creating the tables for VTAM definitions, the user builds a simple procedure for starting VTAM. All those tables and the start-up procedure for VTAM are stored on a direct-access storage device.

Running with VTAM
VTAM execution begins in the host computer by initiating the start-up procedure. This loads into a partition (region or address space) the VTAM-executable code that begins reading the definitions from the DASD, builds buffers, creates the necessary control blocks, and activates the network. Network activation is implemented in VTAM to provide multiple concurrent network operations that allow VTAM and the NCP to activate the physical network in a quick and orderly fashion. After VTAM is started, host applications may identify themselves to it, and terminal connections can proceed.

VTAM commands exist to display meaningful information about the network. They are used by network operations personnel to determine the status of such data communications resources as terminals, lines,

5 VTAM definitions

Network configuration. *The user prepares his system to properly handle VTAM by defining those elements of the network that will work with the access method. Eligible* VTAM-related configuration elements include NCP terminals, local peripherals, terminals on the network, applications lists, and VTAM-only parameters (buffer allocation).

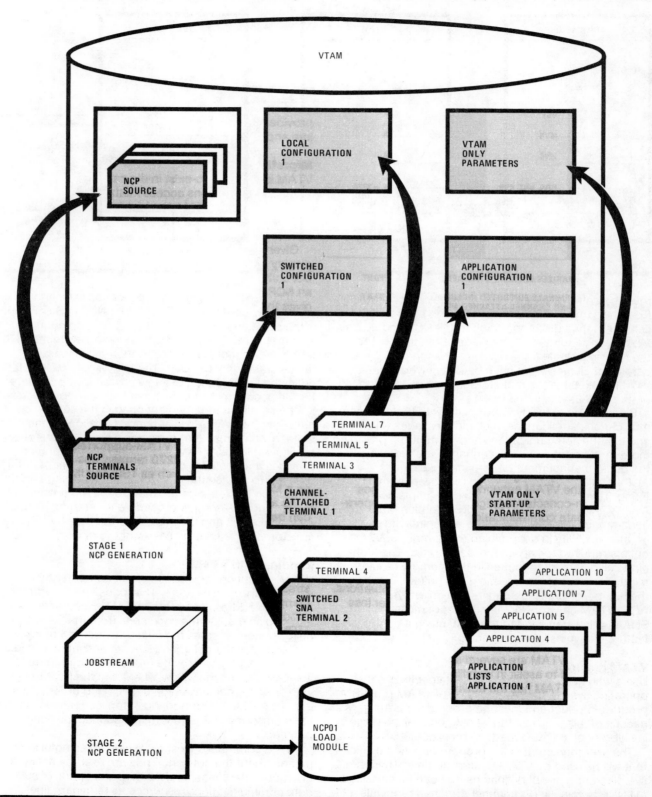

Applications support

APPLICATION	OS	API	TERMINALS
CICS/VS	DOS, VS1, SVS MVS	RECORD	SNA + 3270*
IMS/VS	VSI, SVS, MVS	RECORD	SNA + 3270
TSO	MVS	RECORD	SNA + 3270
POWER/VS	DOS	RECORD	SNA + 3270
JES/RES	VS1	RECORD	SNA
JES2	MVS	RECORD	SNA
JES3 (SCHEDULE RELEASE 9/78)	MVS	RECORD	SNA
IIS	DOS, VS1, SVS MVS	RECORD READ/WRITE	SNA + 3270 2741, TWX
VSCP	DOS, VS1, MVS	RECORD READ/WRITE	SNA + 3270 1050, 2741, TWX

THIS TABLE SUMMARIZES CURRENT VTAM APPLICATIONS SUPPORT

*THE IBM 3270 TERMINALS SUPPORTED INCLUDE THE SNA, BINARY SYNCHRONOUS, AND CHANNEL-ATTACHED MODELS.

NCPs, and applications. The console operator at the host enters the commands, and then documented VTAM messages are displayed (or printed) in response to them. In addition, a VTAM-programmed operator interface exists to allow VTAM commands to be submitted to the access method for processing. A VTAM application using the programmed operator interface can let a terminal in the VTAM network enter VTAM commands to aid in data communications systems management. By doing that, the operator can monitor and act on the VTAM network without interference from system-console messages relating to the operation of the data communications system.

Shutting down the VTAM network is relatively simple. When a console operator calls for an orderly shutdown, VTAM allows all sessions to end normally before terminating execution in its partition. In the case of a quick shutdown, which is designed for emergency situations, halting VTAM execution takes precedence over loss of terminal connections and data.

Service aids
Included with VTAM are several service aids that have been designed to assist in installing and maintaining the network. VTAM has the ability to trace data moving between any terminal or remote application and any application within the host. This data can be captured and written to a host sequential file for printing and diagnosis. Both inbound and outbound data can be captured at the host's interface to the communications controller and at the applications program's interface. Also, the buffer usage in VTAM (operating system type only) can be monitored by using trace facilities, which

help in tuning VTAM buffer usage. The traces can be started and ended by using VTAM operator commands. In addition, the ACF version of VTAM has been enhanced to allow data to be captured in the host for use in tuning the user-defined parameters, such as attention delay, which affect I/O transfer between VTAM and the NCP.

VTAM is designed to take care of malfunctioning network elements. It attempts to detect and handle problems before they become serious. If there is an error, VTAM sends the console operator a message and attempts recovery. If recovery is not possible, VTAM notifies the console operator and automatically provides error records to assist in identifying the problem and its cause.

Migration
VTAM is made to co-exist in the same host with other data communications access methods, such as BTAM and TCAM. Thus VTAM can be brought up or implemented independently in each host, a process that is called migration. Here is one migratory approach.

Given that the data-center host has one IBM 3277 display station attached to a local peripheral IBM control unit, VTAM testing can begin without bringing up an NCP in a 370X communications controller. This gives the system operators experience in: (1) defining VTAM parameters (exclusive of the NCP), (2) providing the VTAM interface in a test application, and (3) operationally starting, managing, and stopping VTAM execution in the virtual operating system. Once that phase of migration has been completed, the installation can use VTAM as the access method to communicate with all channel-attached IBM 3270s. An advantage may immediately be gained by migrating all the channel-attached 3270's to VTAM, because new testing can then begin for a second VTAM-supported application. The channel-attached 3270 terminal has access to multiple applications, such as TSO and IMS running on a MVS-based host.

As a follow-up in this total migration plan, the NCP can be introduced as the next test element. A single data communications link can be used as a test vehicle to obtain experience with VTAM and the NCP. Additional links can then be brought up on the NCP to move the remote network to VTAM/NCP control. To test the stress on VTAM and the applications programs before going into production, a simulator like the program product, called the teleprocessing network simulator (TPNS), can be considered. In addition to providing a production-like environment, TPNS indicates the response time that can be expected under load.

VTAM can also support the central-site management of intelligent terminals. SNA provides architectural compatibility among the access methods that use ACF with the Multi-System Networking Feature. That allows VTAM in one host to communicate via the NCP with TCAM in the same host or with VTAM or TCAM in another one.

SNA adds new capabilities to VTAM, which, by design, can continue to deliver new functions based on rapidly changing technology. ∎

How to access a network via IBM's TCAM

Larry Esau, IBM Corp., Research Triangle Park, N.C.

Software that is designed to grow as user needs change must be flexible enough to accommodate new demands, as well as specialized to fill networking needs

Since 1969, TCAM has proved itself to be a reliable access method to which additional functions and terminal types can be added with relative ease. Its flexibility has made it a strong bridge between the old and the new, protecting the user's investment in application programs and terminals while providing a clear path to the systems network architecture environment.

TCAM—for telecommunications access method—is IBM's primary queued access method that provides high performance, high-level-language-application interface, and comprehensive capabilities for the very large as well as the small teleprocessor user. It supports binary synchronous, start-stop, local attachment, and synchronous data link control terminals, and operates under such IBM programs as operating system/virtual storage 1, single virtual storage, and multiple virtual storage.

Installation of TCAM occurs at system generation time. By specifying that TCAM is required, which is a system generation parameter, TCAM macrocodes and module libraries are created and placed on disks.

The message-control program (MCP), which is executed like any other program in the operating system, is then assembled and control responsibilities are assigned. The MCP can be started and restarted with job-control language statements from the system job queue or by a START command from the system console. Once the MCP has been initiated, TCAM becomes active. The TCAM system programmer can design the MCP in such a way that the network control programs (NCPs), the communications lines, and the terminals will all be brought on line in an active state, or TCAM can require operator control procedures for bringing them up individually. The system programmer can allow the operator to override some start-up parameters by having TCAM request them from the operator. At activation, TCAM builds the required control blocks and opens the required memory areas for handling communications line groups, NCPs, periodic status records, permanent records, and the storage area required if disk queuing is requested.

In many early installations, users were primarily interested in using TCAM's timesharing option (TSO) subsystem. As these customers grew, they began using other facilities available under TCAM; for example, message switching, data collection, and simple inquiry response. Once they started writing TCAM applications, they found the key to TCAM design—the way in which it shields the application programmer from terminal-dependent coding. Also, TCAM allows its application programs to be coded in assembler, Cobol, or PL/1 languages. The application coder retrieves

1 TCAM network components

TCAM components. Along with its own user-defined tables, the message control program includes such TCAM modules as TP interface routines, message handlers, queuing routines, buffering routines, checkpoint routines, operator control, application interface, logging, service aid, and random-access storage in memory devices.

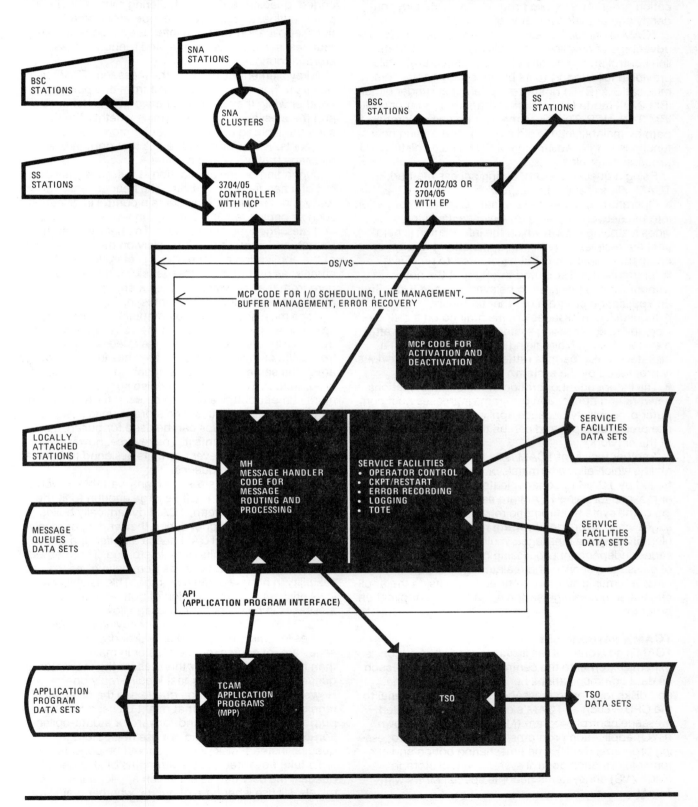

messages and writes messages back to the terminal in the same way a programmer reads and writes to a sequential disk or tape file. That feature allows the separation of the network control performed by TCAM from the message processing performed by the application program. The two programs operate independently and at their own rates of speed.

TCAM is unique because it can allow the user to take advantage of new line protocols (synchronous data link control and systems network architecture) while providing full support to its binary synchronous communications (BSC) or start-stop terminals under either IBM 270X mode (or emulation program mode) or under IBM 3705 NCP. This gives the user an easy migration path by maintaining his old network and adding new functions to take advantage of SNA and its distributed processing terminals.

Being a queued teleprocessing access method, TCAM offers many advantages:

■ Operators at a remote terminal can enter information into the network at their convenience. Queuing provides a staging area in which the information is held until the recipient—either an application program or another terminal—has been prepared to receive it.

■ Information is distributed throughout the network without forcing the input to be synchronized with either an application program or other terminals.

■ If queues of messages are maintained on a disk device, the teleprocessing system can be restarted after a system failure. Maintaining message queues on a disk device also permits retrieval of messages previously processed by the system.

■ The independent operation of the communications network and application programs increases host computer productivity because application programs can use prestored input and can be tested independently of the network.

Another facility of TCAM is its transaction routing ability, which allows terminals or applications controlled by TCAM to communicate with each other. Other reasons for using TCAM are as follows: checkpointing of the system; automatic retransmission of messages when errors occur; warm restart capability; logging of complete messages; multiple routing of messages; independent processing of messages; queuing of messages; service and maintenance capability; extensive terminal support; data-editing outside the applications; and message switching without an application program.

TCAM's environment
TCAM's environment, as illustrated in Figure 1, consists of items external to the central processing unit—such as data communications hardware, telephone lines, and disks for storing messages—and items internal to the CPU—such as TCAM's control program, called message control program (MCP), and roll your own (RYO) application programs, called message processing programs (MPP). The timesharing option and customer information control system/virtual storage (CICS/VS) subsystems become special MPPs with TCAM.

The MCP (Fig. 1) consists of a combination of user code and user-defined tables together with TCAM-provided modules and control blocks. The major programming components of the MCP are the teleprocessing interface routine, message handlers that are user coded, queuing routines, a buffering routine, a checkpoint routine, a restart routine, operator control routines, application-program interface routines, logging routines, service-aids routine, and random-access-storage routines.

A key element of TCAM is the message. TCAM uses buffers to handle messages sent from one point to another while they are in the network. The buffer size and the message length determine whether the message transmitted consists of one or more message segments. A message segment is that portion of a message that will fit into a buffer.

Depending on the application, a message may consist of a header, text, or both. The header, which actually is not required, may contain control information such as origination and destination terminal names, and message type and number. The header's length, format, and content depend solely on the requirement of the application and the user's preference, and are entered as part of the message text, a different procedure from that of systems network architecture headers. The two should not be confused.

Once messages enter the computer system, they are handled by TCAM through the use of buffers and queues. Buffers and main-storage queues are built from units of main storage. All the units in main storage are of the same size, which is specified by the system programmer. The programmer also specifies the maximum number of these units to be used for buffers and for main-storage queues. The storage units assigned to main-storage queues can be used for buffers if the message traffic warrants it. The reverse, however, is not true. TCAM will never use units assigned to buffers as message-storage queues.

Because message sizes are highly variable, it would be inefficient to assign buffers large enough to fit the largest message. Instead, TCAM dynamically builds buffers from the unit pool during the sending or receiving operation. When TCAM needs a buffer or a queue, it is built by linking units of main storage. This method of building buffers and queues from units gives the user flexibility in his use of main storage. This flexibility allows efficient accommodation of both long and short messages in heavy or light message flow.

TCAM also has the capability of having message queues in main storage and on a disk data set. Messages are, of course, queued faster in main storage than they are on disk. For this reason, the main-storage queue is ideally suited for fast inquiry-reply operations. However, the main-storage queue has the disadvantage of tying up storage that might be used for other purposes. Thus a store-and-forward or a data-collection-type operation should not use main-storage queues; instead, disk queuing should be considered.

To take advantage of the strengths of all types of queues, the user can select which applications or terminals will use what type of queue, whether main stor-

2 Routing via DMH and AMH

Message handling. The message from the terminal is examined by the incoming group of the device message handler and is passed through a queue to the outgoing group of the application message handler. The application program processes the message and passes it back through the AMH, queue, and DMH, in reverse order.

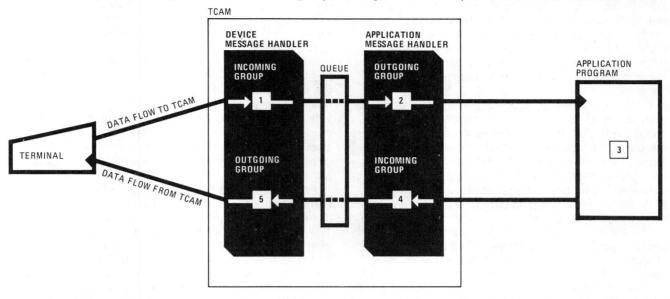

age or disk. In fact, a combination of main-storage queues with disk-queue backup can be used to take advantage of both types of queuing methods.

The facility in TCAM that controls the flow of messages from buffers to queue to destination is a message handler (MH). Message handlers are TCAM's functional management layer. They control the message (data-flow control) from the arrival at the host processor until it reaches its final destination.

MHs are used to isolate the application programmer from device-dependent coding and error-handling code. Separate message handlers can be designed for each group of terminals with similar characteristics.

There are basically two types of message handlers: device (DMH) and application (AMH). The processing of these message handlers are divided into two groups: incoming and outgoing. Figure 2 illustrates how the two types of message handlers work together.

Each of the groups in Figure 2 is further divided into subgroups:
- An inblock subgroup—handles incoming physical transmissions before they are divided into logical messages.
- The inheader and outheader subgroups—handle only the headers of incoming or outgoing messages (first buffer only).
- The inbuffer and outbuffer subgroups—handle all message segments.
- The inmessage and outmessage subgroups—specify actions to be taken after the entire message has been received or sent (for example, checking for specified errors and sending an error message to the source or destination).

A major source of message-handler flexibility is TCAM's option-field capability. These user-defined fields can be set and examined by TCAM to control the path or subgroup to be executed. For example, a user may want to identify, through the use of an option field, whether the terminal is a printer or a screen device.

The user can design and code a message handler to perform different functions on each type of message. The user codes the message handler through the use of TCAM- provided macrocodes. An assembler code can be added to perform functions not provided in a TCAM macrocode, but it cannot be used in the inmessage and outmessage subgroup.

Message handlers can perform the following functions: determine message origin and destination, check and assign sequence numbers, determine message priority, edit message, remove and insert device-dependent code, gather statistics, log message, insert time and date, test for transmission errors, cancel message, generate new messages, and hold message to send later.

Terminal interface

TCAM allows the user to choose whether the terminals are to be controlled through the IBM 270X or emulator program (EP) on the IBM 3705 or through the use of the network control program (NCP). No matter which is selected, TCAM manages the network.

In the EP mode, TCAM supports both start-stop and BSC line protocol. BSC is used for higher-speed data transmission between the central computer and the remote computer or terminal and requires more sophisticated electronics to control the line discipline. The TCAM programmer does not need to be concerned with the differences in transmission techniques except to know the control characters being used to regulate the flow of data on the communications line.

In the MCP, the TCAM programmer develops tables to describe the network to TCAM through the use of TCAM macrocodes. TCAM will control the lines using the information provided to it. TCAM will poll and address the lines automatically to request or send information. TCAM will also support automatic answer, which allows switched terminals to dial the host to retrieve messages in the queue or to send messages to the host.

TCAM supports start-stop, bisynchronous, and synchronous data-link control line protocols in the NCP mode. With NCP, the 3705 communications controllers are programmed control units designed to assume many of the line-control and processing functions for the network (distributed function). The primary function of the NCP is to transmit and receive data as well as to do limited processing on data passing through the communications controller.

The communications controller and the host are physically attached by a System/370 input/output channel, over which TCAM performs all communications with the rest of the network. The basic operating premise is that NCP will be prepared to receive TCAM information as long as NCP has buffers available, regardless of line or terminal availability. However, when NCP has information for TCAM, it presents an attention interrupt over the channel to the host. The host cannot be forced to read from the communications controller, but does acknowledge the attention interruption when ready by issuing a READ command. NCP holds the data ready until TCAM reads it over the channel.

NCP/VS and TCAM communicate over the channel by exchanging information. This information contains control data and, optionally, message data. The control data directs NCP to perform a specific operation. When the operation is completed, NCP responds with corresponding control data, message data, and the completion status of the operation. Thus TCAM directs NCP/VS, which, in turn, controls the network operation and provides TCAM with its resulting data and status information.

In an operating network, NCP receives data from TCAM and remote terminals concurrently. NCP collects the data in communications controller buffers and routes it to its destination when line availability and other conditions permit. Control information and data intended for TCAM are sent to the host processor in a storage-to-storage transfer across the channel. Consequently, TCAM is able to direct the network at channel speeds, while the NCP and the communications controller assume responsibility for line control and data transfer.

Application-program interface
Although free of many real-time network responsibilities, TCAM still must know the structure of all resources that are in the network. This information is provided for both TCAM and the NCP at their respective generations. With TCAM, the network is described through the use of GROUP and TERMINAL macrocodes.

Messages can be generated, or terminal messages processed, through application programs written by the user. TCAM passes messages and inquires to the application programs for processing via a queue and returns messages or responses to their destinations. TCAM also provides a method of tailoring buffers to application programs and handles line control automatically.

In addition, TCAM permits the user to retrieve a message from a message queue's data set on disk after the message has been sent to its destination. It also has facilities to allow the application program to provide network control by examining or modifying the contents of a control block, releasing messages queued for a terminal, and closing down the NCP. All operator control functions are available from application programs.

Application programs run independently of, but in conjunction with, the MCP, usually in another partition or region, but always as a separate task or subtask. If TCAM application programs are not in a separate region or partition, they are attached by the user who writes an operating system macrocode in the MCP.

Messages to be processed are placed in a destination queue by a message handler and routed to the application program. The messages are obtained from the destination queues and transferred to user-specified work areas, where they are processed by application programs. A response message may be returned to the MCP for transmission to a terminal, a list of destinations, or another application program. Application programs are capable of concurrently processing several transactions, using multiple interfaces.

Regardless of the type of processing required, there are several ways to design application support:
- One common method is.to code a separate program for each application, thus each application will have its own interface with the MCP. As shown in Figure 3-A, the message is processed by the appropriate AMH, which, in turn, passes it on to its application program.
- In another situation, it may be more efficient to process the message through a single application program having a single interface to TCAM to perform all of the data processing. As can be seen in Figure 3-B, one AMH is used to pass the message on to the application program, which analyzes the message and routes it to the appropriate processing subroutine.
- Another possibility is shown in Figure 3-C, where an application program is used primarily as a message router to other application programs in the same or other regions. It performs this function by returning the messages to the MCP via a PUT or WRITE macrocode. The AMH in the MCP then routes the message to the next application program. The amount of data transferred from the MCP to an application program by a single GET or READ macrocode of from an application program to the MCP by a single PUT or WRITE is called a work unit. The work unit is processed in an application program's work area. A work unit can be an entire physical message or a record whose length is defined

3 TCAM application design

Application support. *A separate program for each application results in an interface for each program. A single application that performs all processing has one interface* *with the application message handler and three subroutines. Another possibility is to let one program act as the interface as well as the router for all other applications.*

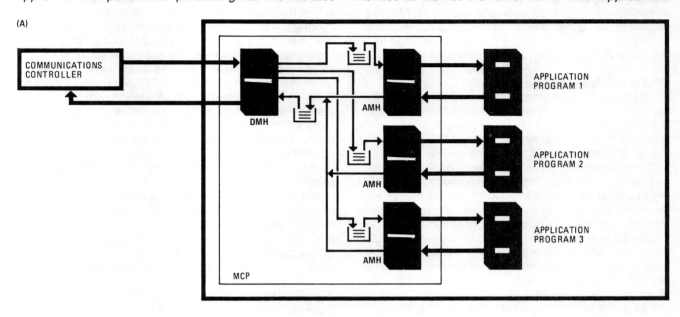

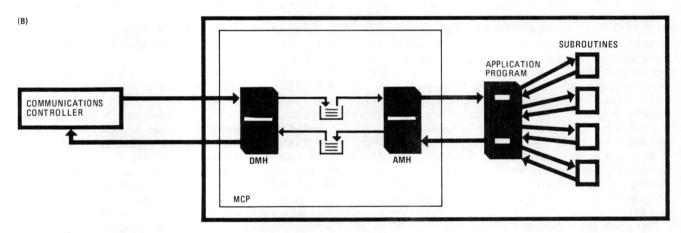

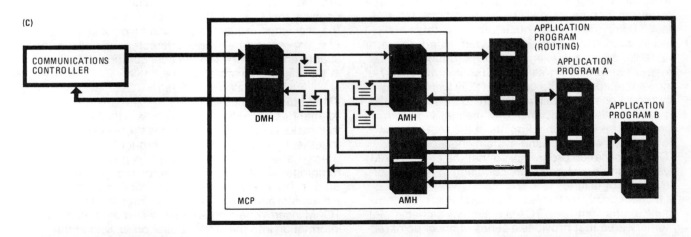

by such delimiter characters as END-OF-BLOCK. A specifically defined amount of data (a work unit) can also be a portion of a message that fits into the work area.

The TCAM checkpoint of the MCP can be coordinated with operating system checkpoints of TCAM application programs by issuing a special TCAM macrocode in the application programs. This allows the MCP and an application program to be restarted at the same point following system failure.

TCAM service facilities

TCAM supports data communications networks with some facilities selected by the user and others provided automatically by TCAM. They include operator control, message logging, checkpoint/restart, I/O error recording, additional debugging aids, and on-line testing.

Operator control allows the user to examine or alter the status of a data communications network in a variety of user-authorized ways. Operator commands can be entered from the system console, remote terminals, and user-authorized application programs.

Various application programs and nonswitched terminals can be designated as operator control terminals. A secondary operator control terminal can send control messages and receive replies; a primary operator control terminal additionally receives I/O error messages. If the primary control terminal becomes inactive, I/O messages are sent to the system console, even when it is defined as a secondary control terminal.

TCAM's message-logging facility enables the user to keep a record in a sequential storage area of either messages or message segments handled by an MCP. Message logging can be useful in accounting, for long-term backup, or for collecting data for exceptional cases. In message switching, the logging of incoming headers may supply all the information needed. In more sophisticated applications, it may be necessary to log complete messages. By determining the flow patterns of message traffic, a programmer can more efficiently allocate the resources of a data communications network. Logging can also aid debugging by allowing the programmer to trace the flow of a message through an MCP.

The checkpoint/restart facility allows the MCP to be restarted after a shutdown or system failure by using information periodically recorded on the status of each station, destination queue, terminal table entry, and invitation list in the system. Upon restart, the terminal table, option table, invitation lists (optional), and internal control blocks associated with stations and lines are restored to the condition they were in before shutdown or system failure. Outgoing message traffic to each destination resumes with the message with the highest priority. Checkpoints of the MCP can be coordinated with operating-system checkpoints of TCAM application programs, so that the entire TCAM system can be restored to its condition at the time of shutdown or failure.

If checkpoint/restart is to be used for a 3705 communications controller, TCAM maintains a checkpoint memory area that provides a series of checkpoint records that correspond to incident records. A record is written each time the status of a link or of a terminal changes in the 3705.

The TCAM MCP or the 3705 communications controller includes a comprehensive set of error-recovery procedures for dealing with the various types of I/O errors that may occur in a data communications environment. If an I/O error is recoverable, the error-recovery procedures usually retransmit the block of data in which the error occurred. If these retransmissions fail to correct the error, it is treated as an irrecoverable error. For irrecoverable errors, TCAM sends a message to the primary-operator control station, writes a permanent error record on disk, and sends a zero-length message with the appropriate message error record to the device message handler so that the appropriate action, as defined by the user, can be taken.

In addition to message logging, TCAM provides error recording and the standard operating system dumps of the MCP partition or region. It also provides some special aids for debugging the telecommunications network and the MCP (Fig. 4).

- TCAM-formatted abnormal end-of-task (Abend) dump, provided automatically when TCAM fails, formats control blocks in the TCAM partition or address space.
- A dispatcher subtask trace used to keep, in main storage, a sequential record of the subtasks activated by the TCAM dispatcher each time a TCAM subtask is dispatched.
- Subchannel trace for an IBM 3705.
- I/O trace for local 3270s or IBM 270X-mode control units.
- A trace of buffer contents and status information.
- NCP service aids—line trace and path information unit trace.
- A dump of the message queue data set, dynamically invoked by a separate TCAM facility, which formats the data set for immediate printing or directs it to tape or disk for later printing.

The teleprocessing on-line test executive (TOTE) is an attached subtask of TCAM that controls the selection, loading, and execution of on-line tests for many devices supported by TCAM. TOTE provides a link between TCAM and device tests written to diagnostic architecture. TOTE schedules and controls the test, conveys messages to the user about the test, prompts the user when requested or when an error in the format of a test-request message is detected, and allows the user to enter changes to the configuration data stored in a configuration storage area.

TCAM message flow

All that has been discussed so far are the components that make up TCAM. Figure 5 ties these components together by tracing a message through TCAM.
Steps 1 and 2: The input message is prepared at a remote terminal and transmitted on a data line.
Step 3: The message enters the host and is stored in a main-storage buffer assigned to that line for input. TCAM inserts chaining addresses and other control information into the stored buffer prefix field of the message. This allows the message to fill multiple buf-

4 Debugging aids

Control traces. Various line and device traces aid the user in determining the nature and extent of networking problems when a TCAM-controlled component fails to function properly. Aside from sleuthing routines, TCAM provides the operator the ability to dump all information for examination when there is an abnormal condition.

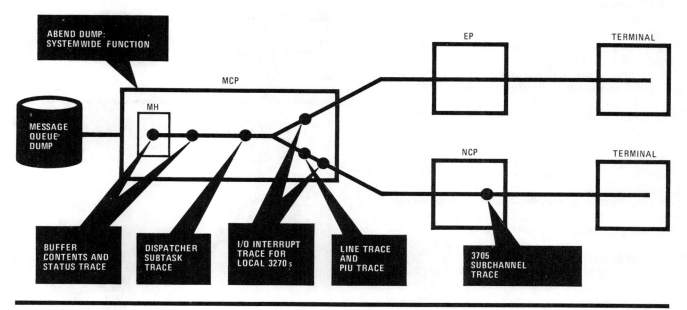

fers that TCAM will chain together to form a message.

Step 4: The incoming message is passed — a buffer at a time — through the message handler's incoming group, which performs the user-selected functions and destination selection.

Step 5: After the message is processed by the message handler, it is forwarded to a destination queue for either an application program or an accepting terminal.

If the message requires no further processing and the destination queue is a terminal, the next operation is Step 13.

The destination queue consists of message segments on direct-access storage devices or in main storage. If the destination queue is located on disk, the buffers are released; if in main storage, the buffers are used to contain the message in the main storage queue.

Steps 6, 7, and 8: The message from a destination queue for an application program is placed in main storage buffers, passed through the outgoing group of an AMH, and kept in a read-ahead queue until the application program requests the buffer or message with a READ or GET macrocode.

Step 9: TCAM passes message data to a user specified work area in the application program. TCAM removes the prefix, which it attached to the buffer, and the application processes the message. The application may return a response message using a PUT or WRITE macrocode to a terminal or another application program for further processing.

Steps 10 and 11: TCAM moves the data from the application program work area into an MCP buffer, in which header or text prefixes are created, and chaining ad-

dresses and other control information are inserted by TCAM. The response message generated by the application can be of any length. After the buffer is filled, it is handled by the incoming group of the AMH assigned by an MCP macrocode.

Step 12: If further processing of the message data by another application is required, the message is queued for that destination and steps 5 – 11 are repeated. If not, TCAM places the processed message on the destinations queue of a terminal.

Step 13: The destination queue for a terminal is like that of an application queue. It is part of the message queue data set and can be either in main storage or on disk. TCAM obtains message segments from the destination queue in first-ended, first-out (FEFO) order within user-defined priority groups

Steps 14 and 15: The message segment is placed in a buffer, and the outgoing group of the DMH for the line or terminal processes the message. The message in this DMH can be translated into the receiving terminal line code, and the required line code inserted along with any other required functions.

Step 16: TCAM transmits the message, minus the buffer prefix it attached, to the destination terminal. As each buffer is transmitted, its units are returned to the buffer unit pool for reuse.

TCAM allows the user to assign priorities to messages and their queues. These priorities will influence the flow of messages within a TCAM system.

Outgoing messages can be queued by destination line or terminal. When queued by line, messages for all stations on the line are placed on one queue. Messages are taken off the queue and sent to the destination on the line in the order received within priority groups. Thus all messages of one priority class on the queue are transmitted before any of the messages on a lower priority queue can be delivered.

When outgoing messages are queued by terminal, one queue is created for each terminal on a line. All messages queued for one terminal are sent before any are queued for other terminals on the line. (This can be modified—using a macrocode in the outgoing device message handler—by limiting the number of messages to be sent to a particular terminal during one contract.) Messages on a queue are sent to a terminal in FEFO order within priority groups.

It should be noted that all switched terminals, buffered terminals, and terminals connected to a 3705 using NCP must be queued by terminal.

Transmission priority is the relative priority between sending and receiving on a line. This is a user option specified by line group. There are three transmission priorities:

- Host receiving has priority over host sending.
- Receiving and sending have equal priority.
- Sending has priority over receiving.

TCAM growth

TCAM's latest versions manage their own SNA formats and protocols and have their own layer structure managers. SNA has three types of network addressable units (NAUs), which are resources in the network addressable by TCAM: the system services control point (SSCP); a physical unit (PU); and a logical unit (LU).

In SNA, a session is a formally bound pairing, or logical connection, established between two NAUs to allow communication between them. A session is identified by a pair of network addresses identifying the origin and the destination NAUs.

Once TCAM is active, the SSCP initiates an SSCP-PU session with each PU in the network (Fig. 6). This session remains established until the PU is deactivated.

After the SSCP-PU session has been established, the SSCP can initiate a SSCP-LU session with the LUs contained within that PU. These sessions also remain established until the LUs are deactivated. Once these two types of sessions are established, an LU can initiate an LU-LU session with another eligible active LU.

Basically, TCAM has three types of primary LUs (Fig. 6). The first type being the TCAM MCP, also called the TCAM LU. If a session is established with this type of LU, the appearance of the SNA terminal will be similar to a BSC or start-stop terminal in that the DMH specified by the GROUP macrocode will be used.

The next type of LU is the device message handler (DMH). Using this type of LU, the user can request a session with any eligible DMH. If a terminal is able to use multiple DMHs, such as one for CICS and another for TSO, the user must use this LU level.

The third type of LU definition is an eligible Tprocess queue. A Tprocess queue is nothing more than a message queue assigned to an application program. Using this type of LU, the DMH should not forward the message. The message will automatically be forwarded to the Tprocess queue that was named in the session request. The device message handler used in this case

5 TCAM message flow

Data flow. *TCAM is composed of components, all of which work together to get the job done. Buffers, queues, message handlers, and interface programs all play a part.*

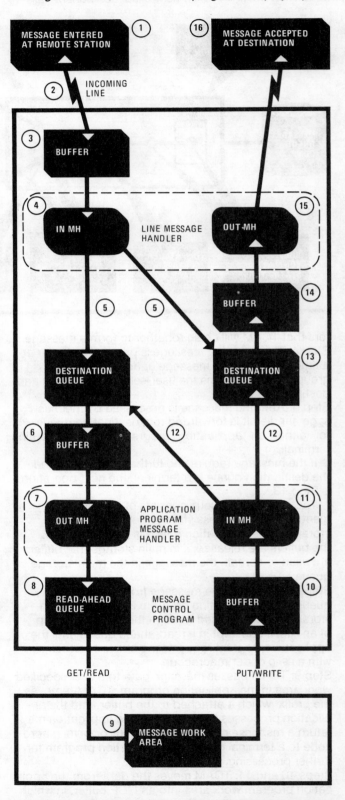

6 TCAM SNA sessions and LU

Sessions. *In the SNA, a session is a formally bound pairing, or logical connection, between any combination of the three different types of network addressable units.*

7 Sessions with transaction routing

Routing. *TCAM can forward messages from a logical unit to an application program independently of sessions, freeing the operator from logging on and off the terminal.*

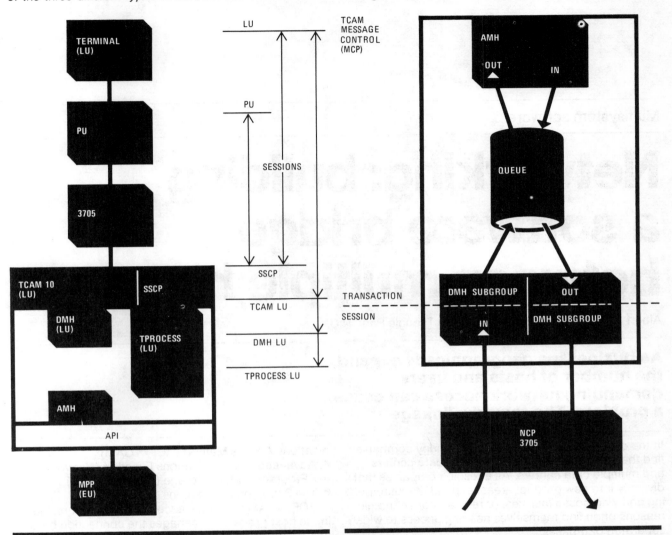

is the DMH specified on the GROUP macrocode.

A secondary LU can establish a session with any of the three types of primary LUs in TCAM (MCP, DMH, or Tprocess). Of course, before an LU-to-LU session can be established, the SSCP-to-PU and the SSCP-to-LU sessions must have already been established.

One of the unique features of TCAM is that even with LU sessions, TCAM still has the full routing capabilities that it had with BSC and start-stop terminals (Fig. 7). If the session is established with either the TCAM LU or a DMH LU, TCAM can forward the message to any application or terminal (SNA, BSC, or start-stop). This routing occurs independently of sessions. In other words, the operator will not have to log on and off the terminal. (TSO users are an exception in that they must log off the TSO MH and log on to a non-TSO MH to gain access to a non-TSO application.)

Termination of a session can occur as follows: the

LU's queue is exhausted and the session had been initiated by TCAM; the DMH executes a "stop session" macrocode, and the terminal operator logs off.

ACF/TCAM

Advanced Communication Function (ACF) for TCAM is available as a program product and runs under the following operating systems: SVS, MVS, and VS1. Previous versions of TCAM permitted only a single-host network configuration, referred to as a single-domain network. ACF/TCAM, with its networking feature, additionally supports a multiple-host-network configuration, called a multiple-domain network.

ACF/TCAM's base product supports only a single-domain network. By ordering the multisystem network facility, which runs with the ACF/TCAM base, ACF/TCAM will support both single- and multiple-domain networks. ∎

Networking: building a software bridge between multiple hosts

Albert J. Hedeen, IBM Corp., Research Triangle Park, N.C.

As businesses geographically expand, the number of hosts and users demanding network access can cause a problem. The remedy: linkage

In the ever-volatile world of business, many companies find the need for multi-host-processor data centers and multiple data centers. As a result, companies that diversify into new product areas, expand manufacturing and warehouse facilities, or relocate for economic reasons often find themselves needing access to widely separated databases.

Moreover, applications resident on one host processor frequently must access data supported by other applications programs in other host processors. Consequently, there is a need for combining multiple hosts into a consolidated network.

Also, security requirements at the data processing facilities within a customer organization leads to the dispersal of host processors to various locations, which further increases the necessity for easy exchange of data between network data processing centers. Because multisystem networking is highly flexible, and provides a multitude of functions, it can be implemented in a wide variety of networking configurations to satisfy a number of requirements. IBM software and hardware products that meet networking requirements are:

■ Advanced Communications Function/Virtual Telecommunications Access Method (ACF/VTAM)
■ Advanced Communications Function/Telecommunications Access Method (ACF/TCAM)
■ Advanced Communications Function/Network Control Program/Virtual Storage (ACF/NCP/VS)
■ The 3705 communications controller.

ACF/VTAM is a single access method that resides in the host processor, manages the connection between end users and applications, and directs the data flow between the two. ACF/VTAM permits applications to share terminals and allows end users at the terminals to access any application in the host processor that is permitted by the user's sign-on and security codes. ACF/VTAM uses the ACF/NCP in the communications 3705 communications controller to manage the physical characteristics of the network. (DATA COMMUNICATIONS, January 1979, p. 77).

ACF/TCAM, like ACF/VTAM, is a single-access method that manages the connection and data flow between the terminal and the application (DATA COMMUNICATIONS, February 1979, p. 89). Unlike ACF/VTAM, ACF/TCAM provides a choice of methods used to manage the connection of the terminal to the application. This choice depends upon the specific version of ACF/TCAM being used, and the application or subsystem being supported.

The types of terminals supported by ACF/TCAM depends upon the type of interface to the programs

1 Sessions

Networking. *The multisystems networking facility (MSNF) is central to ACF/VTAM's and ACF/TCAM's networking abilities. It is the function that permits applications to communicate with other applications, terminals to access applications on their own or other hosts, and for up to four CPUs to share a single 3705 communications controller.*

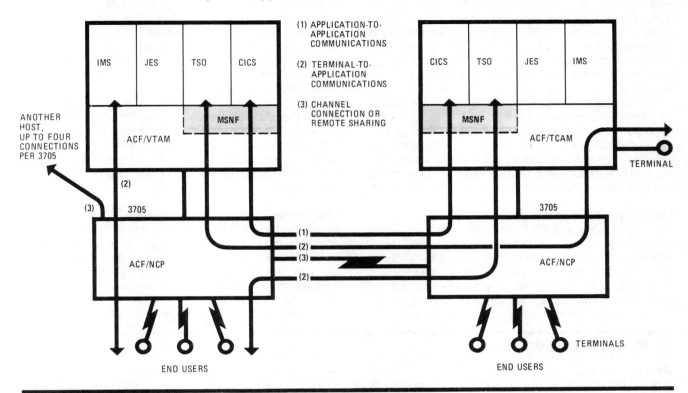

being used. The programs that use the GET/PUT interface (earlier TCAM releases) support the standard start/stop, binary synchronous (BSC) and synchronous data link control (SDLC) devices, while programs that use the systems network architecture (SNA) interface support the IBM 3270 BSC and SDLC devices. The IBM program products that use ACF/VTAM employ the SNA interface to support the IBM 3270 BSC and SDLC devices.

ACF/NCP/VS provides physical control for the attached network. The network control program contains the line control to support attached terminals, error-recovery logic, translation tables for the selected line control, SNA logic to facilitate attachment of SNA devices, and buffering for messages—plus a number of other functions and selectable features required for special types of devices.

The 3705 communications controller contains the necessary hardware and other features to allow it to be attached to the byte, block, or selector channels of a host processor. It also contains the hardware to support the attachment of a variety of line types (leased, switched, or locally attached without a modem) at a variety of line speeds, from 45.5 to 57.6K bit/s (Data Communications, December 1978, p. 51).

The function that permits ACF/VTAM and ACF/TCAM to perform their networking tasks is called the multisystems networking facility (MSNF). In conjunction with ACF/NCP/VS, MSNF (Fig. 1):
■ Permits terminals attached to one host processor to communicate with applications in another CPU, regardless of its physical location.
■ Permits applications in one host processor to communicate with applications in the same or another host processor, regardless of its physical location.
■ Permits one 3705 Model II to be shared (channel connected) by up to four host processors, and be remotely shared (one data communications link away) by up to four host processors.

The MSNF is an optional feature for ACF/VTAM and ACF/TCAM that provides for the interconnection of any combination of System/370 or 303X host processors operating under any mixture of a select group of operating systems, including disk operating systems/virtual storage (DOS/VS), operating system/virtual storage one (OS/VS1), operating system/virtual storage two—single virtual system (OS/VS2 SVS), and operating system/virtual storage two—multiple virtual system (OS/VS2 MVS).

In addition to connecting these diverse operating systems, the MSNF allows the linking of any combination of ACF/VTAM and ACF/TCAM (for example, ACF/VTAM to ACF/VTAM, ACF/TCAM to ACF/TCAM, or ACF/VTAM to ACF/TCAM) on different host processors that may be located in different areas. ACF/VTAM may also be connected through

ACF/NCP/VS to ACF/TCAM with the MSNF on the same host processor.

To establish a network between applications in two different host processors or between a terminal and an application that resides in a remote host processor, two methods of connection are used: multiple channel attachment of host processors from a single 3705 communications controller or a data communications link between 3705s. Up to four host processors can be channel-attached to a single 3705. This provides flexibility for load sharing as well as a back-up facility should some of the network's components fail.

The data communications link between the 3705s at different data centers may be a 56-kbit/s full-duplex synchronous link. The link between two 3705s in a single data center may be a 57.6-kbit/s local attachment (no modems required). SDLC—which permits data to flow in both directions simultaneously—is the line discipline used on this data communications link.

Defining the network
Each application in a host processor that uses either ACF/VTAM or ACF/TCAM must be defined to the access method, as must each terminal, cluster controller, and logical unit. (A logical unit may be a program in an SNA cluster controller, or a display terminal connected to an IBM 3270 communications controller.)

The resource definitions are contained in a logic area—called the systems service control point (SSCP)—of the access method. All resources—whether applications or terminals—defined to this SSCP are considered to be owned by the access method. There is only one SSCP per access method. Each SSCP and the resources defined in it constitute a domain.

When the multisystems networking facility is added to the access method, two additional elements enter the picture: (1) the logic to permit and control cross-domain sessions and (2) a definition of the resources outside the domain that can have access to applications inside the domain.

The logic to control cross-domain sessions is a portion of the SSCP that manages the connection of a resource owned by the SSCP in another domain. The cross-domain resources are applications and terminals owned by another domain (SSCP) that are permitted to establish sessions with applications in the first domain (Fig. 2).

The operator/program connection
Session establishment—the connection between an operator at a terminal and an application program in a host computer—is accomplished using a log-on sequence, which is directed to the host processor that contains the SSCP to which the terminal has been defined. (Fig. 3)

If the log-on is not for an application in the operator's

2 Network definition

Session control. Cross-domain sessions are under the jurisdiction of logic in the systems service control point (SSCP). This logic manages the connection of resources owned by one domain to applications and terminals owned by another domain on another host computer connected to the network, no matter what its location.

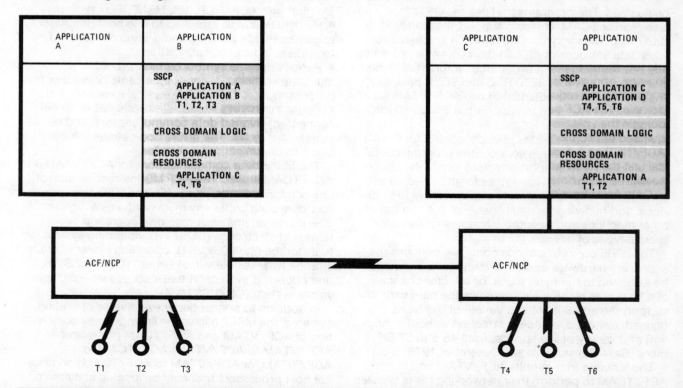

3 Session establishment

Connectivity. *Log-on sequences are commands that establish the connection between a terminal and an application program running in a host. If the log-on is for an application outside the operator's primary domain, the cross-domain logic requests a session on behalf of the operator with the domain that contains the resources.*

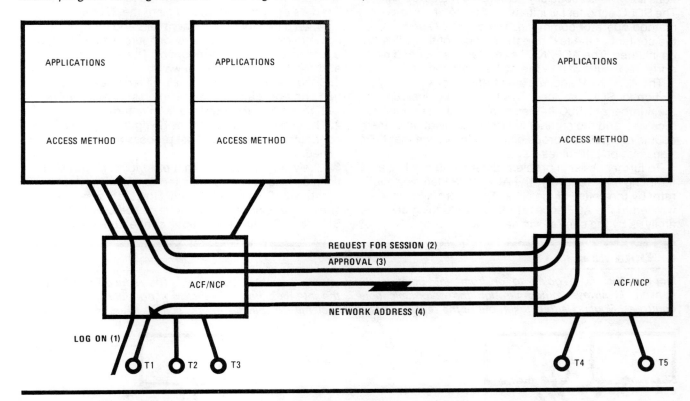

primary domain, the cross-domain logic requests a session on behalf of the terminal operator to the domain that contains the application. This is accomplished by referring to a table that lists the location of the requested application. If it is active and is accepting log-ons, approval is sent by the ACF access method supporting the requested application to the requesting domain. The ACF access method of the requested domain then places the network address of the requested application, via a BIND command, in the ACF/NCP on a control block that represents the logical unit the terminal operator is using. That completes session establishment.

Data flows from the terminal to its target application over the physical path in the 3705s. This path is defined by the user in the ACF network control program and will usually be the most direct route. Figure 4 illustrates examples of data flow that might occur in a multi-data-center environment. Note that the data flows through the 3705 communications controllers from one communications link to the other. The intermediate host processors are not involved in data routing. The path for the response to an inquiry is the same as for the original inquiry.

All references to network resources are symbolic, freeing both the application program and the network operator from concern about the location of a resource within the network. All address translation from the symbolic name to the actual network address is performed by the access method, thus all the symbols used within each domain must be unique. The symbols for resources to be used across domains must also be unique. The same symbol cannot be used by more than one domain.

Network recovery

Even well-designed data communications networks will eventually fail. The failure could be a host processor, a communications controller, a software program, a modem, a data communications link, a terminal, or a cluster controller. The ACF MSNF is designed to aid in network recovery.

Enhanced diagnostic aids—traces and tests—and statistical information are available to diagnose problems and to identify problem areas. Traces examine the data content of a message, the message headers used for routing, and the headers and messages as they are transmitted or received over a data communications link.

To determine if a physical connection exists to the host that owns its terminal, the operator can initiate a connectivity test. This test will validate the path from the terminal to the ACF access method. A connectivity test can be used to assist in determining a problem when a log-on is unsuccessful.

The network operator at the host processor can

initiate an SDLC echo test to an SDLC terminal while messages are being delivered to other terminals on the same link. This test assists the central-site network operator in isolating problems on a data communications link and is especially useful on a multidrop link. The SDLC echo test is initiated by using an access-method operator command. The operator specifies the content of the text and the number of times it is to be initiated. The ACF/NCP executes the test and reports the results of it to the ACF access method.

The ACF/NCP accumulates traffic information by station for SDLC devices. This traffic count includes the number of SDLC frames transmitted, the number received, and the number in error. Examination of these counts can point to drops on a multipoint line that have transmission difficulties.

To further assist in problem-determination while attempting error recovery, the ACF/NCP identifies each retry by the cause of the error. This information is forwarded to the ACF access method for logging and analysis by the central-site network operator.

ACF/NCP/VS release 2, a version of the control program, provides the network operator with the ability to monitor the use of a 3705-II communications controller over a selected period of time. This information is helpful for capacity planning and identifying peak intervals of cycle and buffer use of the 3705-II.

When a network component fails and recovery is not imminent, many users reconfigure the network by bypassing the failed component. The ACF products address this in a number of ways:
1. Should a host processor fail, all terminal-to-application and application-to-application sessions involved with that host processor are terminated.
2. The cross-domain sessions going through the 3705 connected to the failing host processors are maintained.
3. Likewise, the sessions that exist for SNA-SDLC stations on leased lines connected to the failing host processor's 3705 are maintained. However, sessions for start/stop, binary synchronous devices, and SNA/SDLC switched stations connected to that 3705

4 Data flow

Data paths. Data going to or from any point in the network is always routed through the communications controller. Routing is thus taken out of the province of the intermediate host computers. The reduced overhead on the intermediate hosts makes it possible for the central systems to devote more space to data processing.

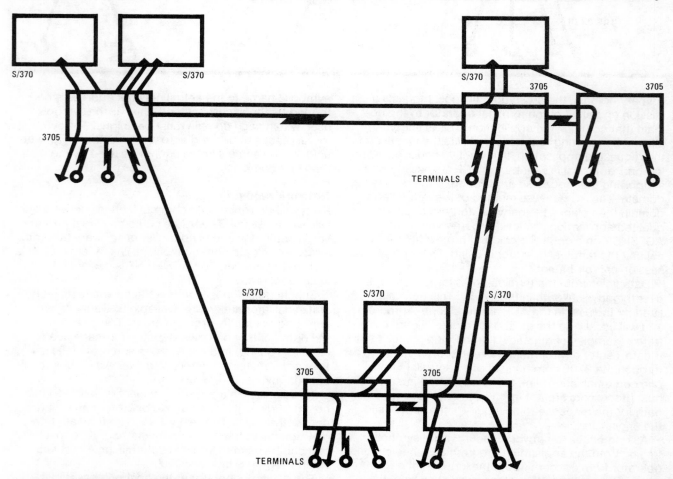

5 Network reconfiguration

Recovery. When any network host processor suffers a failure, network reconfiguration allows another host to acquire a cross-domain communications controller and its attached resources. An activate command from the new host allows it to pick up the failed host's duties without having to reload the 3705 communications controller.

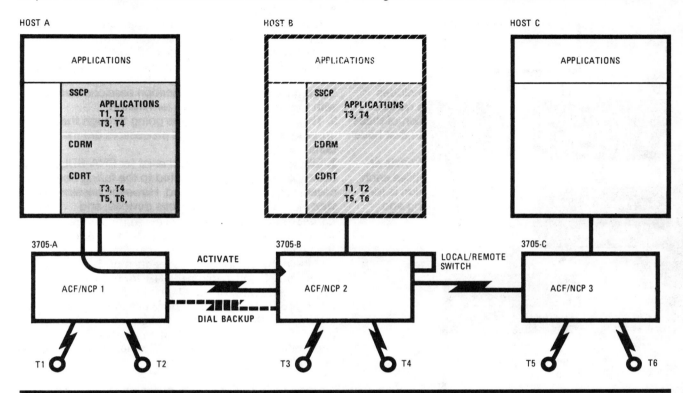

communications controller are terminated.

If Host Processor B (Fig. 5) has failed, network reconfiguration allows another host processor to acquire a cross-domain 3705 and its attached resources. In this example, Host A sends activate commands to 3705-B. The activate commands allow Host A to acquire the resources attached to 3705-B without reloading the 3705. This now provides terminal operators using terminals attached to 3705-B a path to log-on to applications in the network.

If both the host processor and communications controller fail at the same time, but the 3705 can be reactivated, the 3705 and its attached resources can be brought back on line by making the 3705 appear as a remote concentrator. This is accomplished by a feature on the 3705 that allows a switch to be placed in a "remote" position. What had been a local, channel-attached 3705 communications controller can now be down-line loaded with an NCP load module from another data center's host processor.

Should the leased data communications link between data centers fail, a back-up dial link may be used to bypass the failed link. A maximum of three back-up links may be defined. The back-up line is made active through an ACF-access method operator command.

To provide backup for the communications controller, lines and terminals may be defined to two 3705's

connected to a single host processor. Each 3705 is configured to handle all the network resources, but the load is normally split across both of them. If one of the 3705s fails, the lines can be switched over to the second 3705 until the defect is repaired.

Network expansion under control

As the size of a network grows, controlling its resources becomes more complex. What resources should be active? when to deactivate resources? and how backup and recovery should be handled? are but a few of the questions that need to be answered.

As part of the ACF MSNF products, two subsystems are available to provide programmed network control functions: (1) the network operations support program (NOSP) and (2) the network communications control facility (NCCF).

The NOSP functions with only ACF/VTAM R1, an early version of the access method, whereas the NCCF functions with all releases of ACF/VTAM or ACF/TCAM. Each subsystem provides similar functions, and therefore only the NCCF will be discussed here.

The NCCF resides in each host processor and performs the programmed functions of a network operator. The NCCF uses the 3270 family of terminals as network-operator control stations for input messages and responses, and for hard-copy logging of network

6 Migration

Growth. Step-by-step migration improves the network by adding one new component at a time. The user upgrades software by adding new, backward-compatible releases.

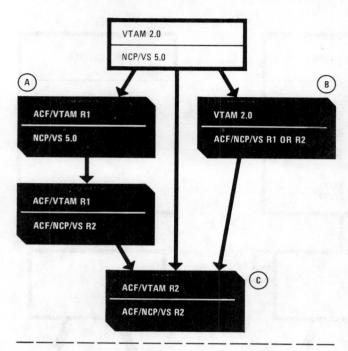

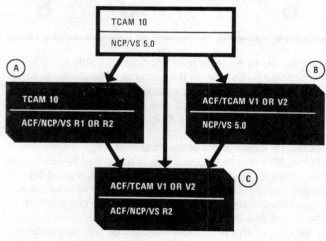

activity. The 3270 network-operator control stations may be attached to the host processor through a local channel or through a data communications link. With this type of flexibility, the stations may be located anywhere to fit a company's requirements. For example, for a three-data-center network, all 3270 network-operator control stations could be located in a central network-control room along with other network monitoring equipment.

The network communications control facility permits the following functions to be performed:
■ Entering of ACF access method commands by the network operator.

■ Operator-to-operator message exchange.
■ Routing of commands from one domain to another and the return of responses. Thus a remote operator in one domain, if authorized, can control resources in another domain.
■ Several network-control operators.
■ User-written exit routines to screen and edit data.
■ Command processors to assist the network operator in controlling the network. For example, diagnostic reduction routines or accounting routines may be written as command processors.
■ Command lists to reduce the amount of information the operator must enter to control the network.
■ Logging of operator interaction with the system.

An IBM-provided command processor that functions with the NCCF is the network problem determination application (NPDA). The NPDA uses the error information collected by NCCF to assist the network operator find problems, and he has access, via 3270 terminal, to accumulated error data and statistics. The NPDA categorizes the error data collected by communications controllers, lines, control units, and terminals in the network.

If the network operator suspects a problem, he logs on the NCCF and invokes the NPDA. From a menu display, the operator selects the mode of display (emulation program, network control program or local mode), and then can show total errors in this mode and, by menu selection, select more detailed error information by category (for example, communications controller, line or control unit).

Communications management configuration
Companies using multi-host processors controlling several data communications networks may be able to consolidate many of the network management and control functions into a single host processor. This type of configuration is called the communications management configuration (CMC).

In this configuration, the network resources—except host applications and local terminals—are owned by the communications management host. That means that the network resources are defined to the SSCP in the CMC host processor. This includes remote communications controllers, data communications lines, and remote cluster controllers and terminals. The communications management host is responsible for network management tasks such as activation, session initiation/termination, configuration changes, and deactivation.

Special network applications, such as message switching, transaction routing, and accounting, can be delegated to the CMC host processor. The ACF access methods may be used in any combination of ACF/VTAM or ACF/TCAM with the multisystem networking facility.

To facilitate TWX and 2741 terminal access to virtual storage personal computing (VSPC) or the timesharing option (TSO) via ACF/VTAM, a program product called network terminal option (NTO) is available for the ACF/NCP/VS. NTO provides an SNA 3767 protocol appearance to the host processor's access method

(ACF/VTAM) for each TWX and 2741 terminal in the network. Data stream mapping is not performed, so the need for changes to existing application programs is minimized. NTO provides access from these terminals to VSPC and TSO. This eliminates the need for a non-SNA access method in the host along with ACF/VTAM to support these applications.

Some types of data must be protected while it is in the network. One way to do that is link-level data encryption; another is session-level data encryption.

Link-level encryption uses an IBM data encryption device between the modem and the data terminal equipment. All characters transmitted over the communications link are encrypted. Encryption on a session level takes place between the host application and the terminal logical unit, and only the data portion of the message is encrypted. The SNA routing header and associated SNA indicators are not encrypted. Encryption between sender and receiver is user defined and may be mandatory or optional.

Migration bit by bit
Migration can be accomplished step by step, improving the network by adding one new component at a time. Networks using the current level of VTAM or TCAM (Fig. 6) can be upgraded to either position A or B. Since ACF/VTAM R1, ACF/TCAM V1, and the current levels of VTAM and TCAM are compatible with ACF/NCP/VS R1 and the current level of NCP/VS, current application programs can be executed with the combinations shown in positions A and B. From either position A or B, it can be one more step to position C, and a complete upgrading of the single-domain system. No recompiling or recording of VTAM or TCAM application programs is required at any step.

Another migration path for both VTAM and TCAM uses the multiple-channel attachment facility of ACF/NCP/VS. Starting with the current level of VTAM and TCAM, upgrading to position A permits the shared use of the ACF/NCP/VS capability. Because the domains of VTAM and TCAM remain completely independent, they can be upgraded separately and at different times to reach position C.

And because the multiple-domain networking capabilities of ACF/VTAM, ACF/TCAM, and ACF/NCP/VS are composites of single-domain networks that have been connected, the same possibilities of coexistence are present. All other data communications access methods and their networks will function independently of the ACF/VTAM and ACF/TCAM domains.

The multiple-domain network is independent of the access methods' operating systems. ACF/VTAM can be executed with either disk operating system/virtual storage (DOS/VS) operating system/virtual storage one (OS/VS1), operating system/virtual storage two-single virtual system (OS/VS2 SVS), or operating system/virtual storage two-multiple virtual system (OS/VS2 MVS). ACF/TCAM can be executed with either OS/VS1, OS/VS2 SVS, or OS/VS2 MVS. Any of these operating systems can be used in the networking environment, and the host computers can be any model that the access methods support.

The key migration for networking is the migration path for single-domain networks. Since cross-domain resource sharing is a new capability, the plan is to minimize the impact of migration on current single-domain network application programs. The execution of new cross-domain application programs cannot proceed until the MSNF of the access method and ACF/NCP/VS have been installed in each host system and each communications controller that will use the networking facilities.

When implementing the migration path for the single-domain networks, the MSNF may be included in the access method during the migration process. While this facility is not required for single-domain networks, it will provide a stable base for current application programs and will be available for later cross-domain networking application programs.

The benefits of interconnection
The MSNF permits applications and selected terminals on one host processor to communicate with applications and programs on another host processor. As a result, data communications networks can grow smoothly from single systems to multiple systems.

Some of the advantages that can be obtained:
- Application sharing across networks gives the terminal operator the ability to access applications on any host processor in a multisystem network.
- Line and terminal sharing permits terminals on the same line to access different applications on different host processors simultaneously.
- The user has a choice of access methods, either ACF/VTAM, which provides a direct-control interface to the network's resources, or ACF/TCAM, for applications that require queuing or a direct-control interface.
- Coexistence with other non-SNA data communications access methods such as the basic telecommunications access method and the sharing of the IBM 3705, using the partitioned emulation program.
- The MSNF gives the user increased systems availability in the event of a host processor failure or deactivation. An adjacent active host processor in the network may take control of the terminals and controllers attached to an inactive host processor's 3705.
- The MSNF has the ability to locate databases and applications in diverse locations for back-up purposes.
- The user gets better balanced host-processor loads through relocation of applications previously residing on one host to several hosts at one or more locations.
- There can be a reduction of development and maintenance costs through the centralization of common editing and validation routines in one host processor with transaction routing.
- The availability of new services by linking systems and applications once not available to the end user.

Multisystem networking is attained by taking advantage of software features in ACT/VTAM, ACF/TCAM, or ACF/NCP/VS, and through hardware features on the 3705 communications controller. Each host in the multiple-system network may employ either ACF/VTAM or ACF/TCAM as the data communications access method. ∎

The TP monitor: know what's important to ask before buying

David Brownlee, Altergo Software Inc., Wellesley, Mass.

Before the decision to go on line is made, system designers must understand the TP monitor function and be sure it supports network objectives

On-line networks, whether local or widely dispersed, cannot function efficiently without a teleprocessing (TP) monitor for controlling the mainframe computer. But before committing yourself to a particular monitor, there are a number of questions that need to be asked and answered.

A TP monitor checklist of 22 questions, along with explanations of their importance (in italic), starts on the facing page. The questions are formulated to evaluate points that pertain to most users' operational environments as well as current and projected network requirements. Providing precise answers to these questions will greatly help to avoid false starts and narrow the field of equipment and software possibilities and, hence, suppliers. In addition to providing a clear picture of user needs, the answers to these questions will help save a lot of time by reducing the number of products that have to be examined—from dozens to no more than three.

It is helpful to assign varying values to each question according to its importance to your installation and objectives. For instance, each question could be assigned a value on a scale from 10 to 50—with the answers being given a score up to the highest value assigned to the question. Each score would depend on a vendor's answer to the question.

Although that is a simple method, it effectively narrows the field of choice. Moreover, if the questions and weighting factors are sent to prospective suppliers, many of them will be able to eliminate themselves before wasting their own, as well as your, time.

In asking these questions, and adding others as individual situations require, it is essential that answers be considered in light of TP monitor objectives—based on user needs—which the on-line-network designer enumerates. The importance of asking the right questions becomes apparent when considering the enormous impact a TP monitor can have on the cost and success or failure of a network.

Essentially, the function of the TP monitor is to keep data flowing in an orderly fashion (DATA COMMUNICATIONS, July 1978, p. 67). To accomplish this, the monitor performs task scheduling, application control, resource allocation, network control, start-up and recovery, and error and failure processing.

TP monitors can be imbedded in special operating systems, be part of a database management system package, or be a stand-alone package provided by a computer vendor or by many of the growing number of independent software houses.

The major objectives of on-line network software:
■ Save money compared with the clerical or

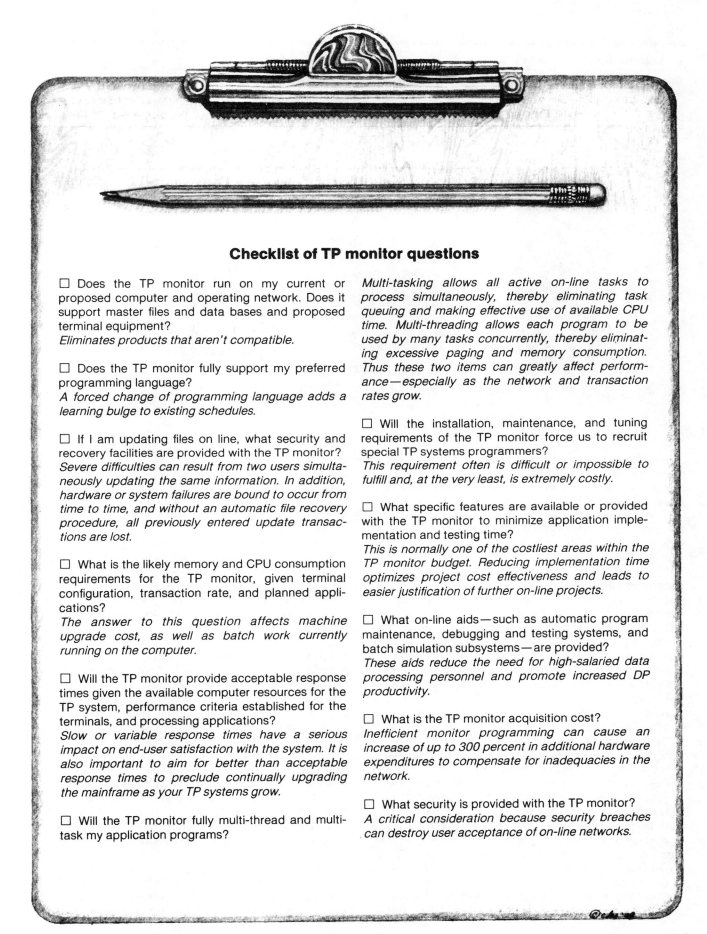

Checklist of TP monitor questions

☐ Does the TP monitor run on my current or proposed computer and operating network. Does it support master files and data bases and proposed terminal equipment?
Eliminates products that aren't compatible.

☐ Does the TP monitor fully support my preferred programming language?
A forced change of programming language adds a learning bulge to existing schedules.

☐ If I am updating files on line, what security and recovery facilities are provided with the TP monitor?
Severe difficulties can result from two users simultaneously updating the same information. In addition, hardware or system failures are bound to occur from time to time, and without an automatic file recovery procedure, all previously entered update transactions are lost.

☐ What is the likely memory and CPU consumption requirements for the TP monitor, given terminal configuration, transaction rate, and planned applications?
The answer to this question affects machine upgrade cost, as well as batch work currently running on the computer.

☐ Will the TP monitor provide acceptable response times given the available computer resources for the TP system, performance criteria established for the terminals, and processing applications?
Slow or variable response times have a serious impact on end-user satisfaction with the system. It is also important to aim for better than acceptable response times to preclude continually upgrading the mainframe as your TP systems grow.

☐ Will the TP monitor fully multi-thread and multi-task my application programs?

Multi-tasking allows all active on-line tasks to process simultaneously, thereby eliminating task queuing and making effective use of available CPU time. Multi-threading allows each program to be used by many tasks concurrently, thereby eliminating excessive paging and memory consumption. Thus these two items can greatly affect performance—especially as the network and transaction rates grow.

☐ Will the installation, maintenance, and tuning requirements of the TP monitor force us to recruit special TP systems programmers?
This requirement often is difficult or impossible to fulfill and, at the very least, is extremely costly.

☐ What specific features are available or provided with the TP monitor to minimize application implementation and testing time?
This is normally one of the costliest areas within the TP monitor budget. Reducing implementation time optimizes project cost effectiveness and leads to easier justification of further on-line projects.

☐ What on-line aids—such as automatic program maintenance, debugging and testing systems, and batch simulation subsystems—are provided?
These aids reduce the need for high-salaried data processing personnel and promote increased DP productivity.

☐ What is the TP monitor acquisition cost?
Inefficient monitor programming can cause an increase of up to 300 percent in additional hardware expenditures to compensate for inadequacies in the network.

☐ What security is provided with the TP monitor?
A critical consideration because security breaches can destroy user acceptance of on-line networks.

1 Large-user network costs

Don't underestimate expenditures. *The graph illustrates real costs—on a percentage basis—incurred by large TP users when they go on line. The actual dollar amount obviously varies considerably from user to user. Experience shows that these costs are invariably higher than the user predicts at the beginning of the project.*

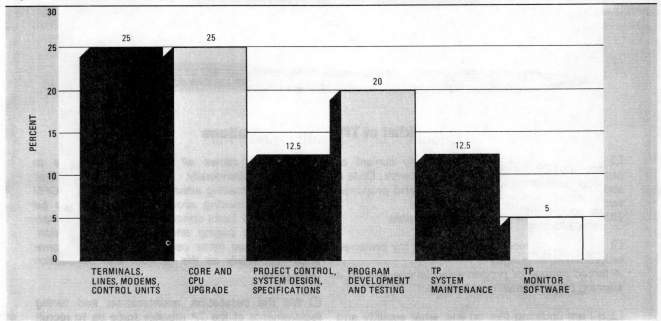

25	25	12.5	20	12.5	5
TERMINALS, LINES, MODEMS, CONTROL UNITS	CORE AND CPU UPGRADE	PROJECT CONTROL, SYSTEM DESIGN, SPECIFICATIONS	PROGRAM DEVELOPMENT AND TESTING	TP SYSTEM MAINTENANCE	TP MONITOR SOFTWARE

batch-oriented system that is about to be replaced.
■ Perform at least some business functions more accurately and faster—thereby enabling management to make better decisions and improve company service and competitive position.
■ Boost productivity of on-line networks.
■ Gain access to information or functions not previously available.

A comprehensive plan

There are likely to be a number of other objectives, depending on individual needs. The ones listed above represent a general overview.

Once a potential user defines network objectives, including the specific applications for which TP plans will be initially justified, there are still many important areas to cover before launching a full-scale project. These include:
■ Determining the type of terminal equipment best suited to network needs.
■ Determining, for remote locations, adequate line speeds and the correct modems, lines, control units, and front-end processing equipment.
■ Determining if the mainframe computer is capable of processing additional on-line applications, and if not, what hardware upgrades will be necessary.
■ Determining if the data processing group is large enough and sufficiently experienced to implement the system design, programming, testing, implementation, maintenance, and user training for the new network.
■ Determining cost.

Choosing mainframe TP monitor software for controlling on-line networks is harder than selecting the necessary terminal and communications equipment—which is readily available in a number of models, capabilities, and prices. (One exception: IBM mainframe computers, for which there is a wide variety of software available from hardware and independent software companies.)

However, the choice of teleprocessing monitor software usually determines the ultimate success or failure of a project. Unfortunately, in the majority of cases, the time devoted to the selection of hardware, equipment, and project design—all of which, of course, are important factors—overshadows the choice of TP software.

Take time to evaluate

Apparently the main reason why thorough software evaluations are often not conducted is that users feel they lack the technical expertise to make the proper analyses; or the time, money, and personnel requirements to make a comprehensive study are greater than users believe practical. Improper TP software can lead to decreased network efficiency. For example, high computer overhead will cause expensive mainframe upgrade, and the selected TP monitor may not be able to perform all project requirements. In addition, terminal response times will suffer, project implementation may be delayed, and the monitor may not be able to support terminal equipment, network architecture, files, or databases.

Indeed, the teleprocessing world is filled with case histories documenting these and other problems. As a result, the final network often includes many compromise solutions that exceed the original budget and

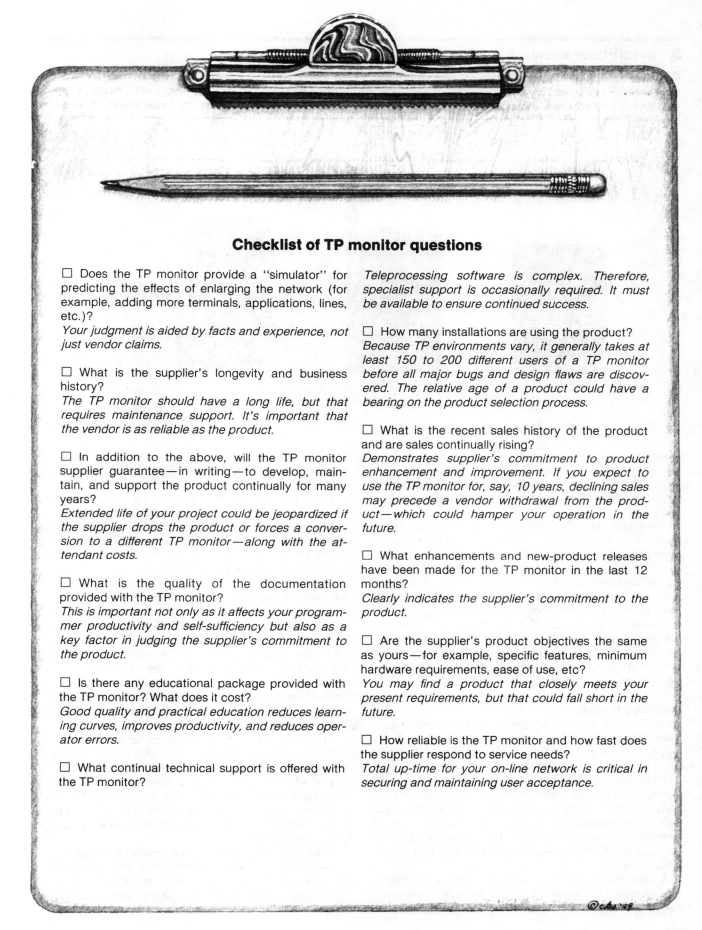

Checklist of TP monitor questions

☐ Does the TP monitor provide a "simulator" for predicting the effects of enlarging the network (for example, adding more terminals, applications, lines, etc.)?
Your judgment is aided by facts and experience, not just vendor claims.

☐ What is the supplier's longevity and business history?
The TP monitor should have a long life, but that requires maintenance support. It's important that the vendor is as reliable as the product.

☐ In addition to the above, will the TP monitor supplier guarantee—in writing—to develop, maintain, and support the product continually for many years?
Extended life of your project could be jeopardized if the supplier drops the product or forces a conversion to a different TP monitor—along with the attendant costs.

☐ What is the quality of the documentation provided with the TP monitor?
This is important not only as it affects your programmer productivity and self-sufficiency but also as a key factor in judging the supplier's commitment to the product.

☐ Is there any educational package provided with the TP monitor? What does it cost?
Good quality and practical education reduces learning curves, improves productivity, and reduces operator errors.

☐ What continual technical support is offered with the TP monitor?

Teleprocessing software is complex. Therefore, specialist support is occasionally required. It must be available to ensure continued success.

☐ How many installations are using the product?
Because TP environments vary, it generally takes at least 150 to 200 different users of a TP monitor before all major bugs and design flaws are discovered. The relative age of a product could have a bearing on the product selection process.

☐ What is the recent sales history of the product and are sales continually rising?
Demonstrates supplier's commitment to product enhancement and improvement. If you expect to use the TP monitor for, say, 10 years, declining sales may precede a vendor withdrawal from the product—which could hamper your operation in the future.

☐ What enhancements and new-product releases have been made for the TP monitor in the last 12 months?
Clearly indicates the supplier's commitment to the product.

☐ Are the supplier's product objectives the same as yours—for example, specific features, minimum hardware requirements, ease of use, etc?
You may find a product that closely meets your present requirements, but that could fall short in the future.

☐ How reliable is the TP monitor and how fast does the supplier respond to service needs?
Total up-time for your on-line network is critical in securing and maintaining user acceptance.

2 Small-user network costs

Expenditures are relative. As with the large user, small-user network costs will vary from company to company. In addition, the small users' six cost areas will differ relative to those of a large user. A small, local network, for instance, does not require long lines, modems, multiple control units, and layers of project-control personnel.

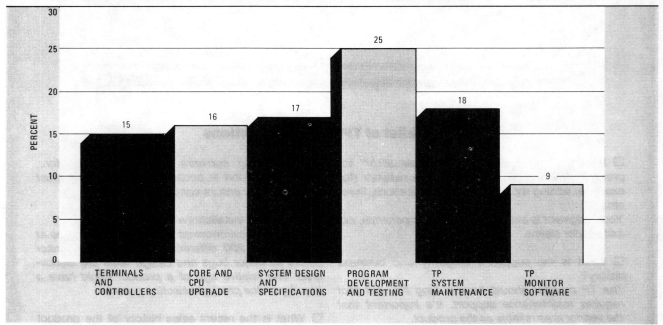

timetable by such a wide margin that justification for the on-line network is lost. Therefore, because of a TP monitor's impact on a project's success, the wherewithal and time must be found to conduct the proper analyses.

Take cost, for instance. Figures 1 and 2 illustrate real costs—on a percentage basis—incurred by very small and relatively large TP users when they go on line. The actual dollar amount obviously varies considerably from user to user, but the graphs serve to illustrate relative costs, which are invariably higher than the user predicts at the beginning of the project.

Choosing the correct TP monitor software, then, is the best way to avoid disaster. Moreover, it avoids a loss of data processing department credibility, a situation that could cause management to view future projects with skepticism.

Finishing the job

After TP monitor selection, the next task is implementation. The steps involved are planning, personnel training, system design and testing, program development and testing, and live production.

To assure success, the TP monitor should be implemented well in advance of TP hardware installation. That will undoubtedly be required to use and test the initial on-line programs. Usually, the teleprocessing monitor has a batch-simulation testing system, so that testing can be done well in advance of terminal installation.

A user must insist that the vendor completely train user personnel in applications and systems programming immediately following TP monitor implementation.

Training flattens the users' learning-time curve and enables the network to achieve maximum productivity quicker.

It is important that data processing department personnel are aware of the major functions and the architecture of the selected TP monitor. This will enable the equipment user to take advantage of software opportunities that could reduce program development time and boost overall network efficiency.

Security breaches

Appropriately designed TP monitors can provide protection against security breaches. Of course, there are likely to be many users and many varied applications running concurrently in the same region or partition of the computer. As a result, the potential for security violations and operational inefficiencies is always present, and thus it is advisable to query the vendor about other standards and procedures that may further ensure security.

Of course, for any network to operate efficiently requires adequate testing, which also applies to the TP monitor. Testing time is somewhat reduced by the availability of sophisticated system testing programs in today's TP monitors. To make certain that the network runs smoothly on the first day of operation, have both your technical staff and technical representatives for the vendor present.

A successful on-line network creates enthusiasm, growth, and cost benefits throughout an organization, but a failure creates despair that can haunt a company—especially its data processing section—for many years. ■

Telecommunications monitors can improve throughput

A Data Communications survey

These software packages are supplied by many vendors. Evaluating and applying them can improve operation of a data communications network

CICS, Intercomm, Task/Master, Environ/1—they are all examples of data communications monitors, but are more commonly—though less precisely—called telecommunications or teleprocessing monitors. These monitors are software packages that supervise the processing of data communications jobs. Why use these monitors? They provide a relatively cheap, but highly efficient way of implementing and processing jobs remotely entered to a processor.

Many people think of data communications in terms of a terminal's transmitting data over a line to a computer. But there is far more to it than that. For example, terminals produce digital data, but most lines can transmit only analog signals. Thus a device—a modem—must be inserted between the terminal and line to convert the digital data. Once data reaches its destination, it must be reconverted to digital data—handled by another modem.

Data reaching the computer must be assembled into a form the computer can work with. Once the data is assembled, the job may then begin to be processed. Likewise, data slated for transmission to a terminal must be coded and assembled into a form suitable for acceptance by the terminal.

If the data communications environment consisted of only one terminal receiving the individual attention of the computer, there would be no real need for telecommunications monitors. Such an environment, however, would waste valuable (and expensive) resources, since the computer would be comparatively idle a good portion of the time.

To maximize the use of resources, users attach many terminals to the computer. A number of computer installations also run local batch processing jobs at the same time remote telecommunications jobs are being processed. Because of line costs and interactive requirements, data communications jobs, however, have the highest processing priority; local batch jobs have the lower priorities.

All jobs run under the supervision of the processor's operating system (OS). This large piece of systems software schedules jobs for processing, initiates the actual processing operation, and services a job's request for data stored on auxiliary devices. In short, it supervises the entire processing operation from the time a job enters the computer until it leaves.

Because of the computer's great speed, the fact that it can perform only one thing at a time is easily forgotten. If it's handling calculations, it cannot be directly handling terminal requests for data. Each request for service must wait its turn. Thus, as the system becomes more heavily loaded, the throughput time for

259

CPU software

System relief. When the operating system devotes time to network terminals, it is likely to become overloaded. A TC monitor will relieve the OS of this network function.

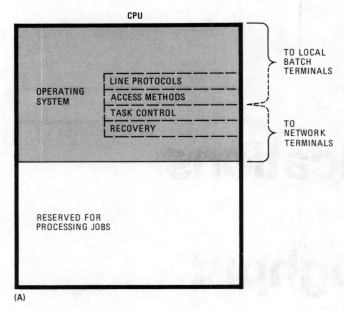

(A)

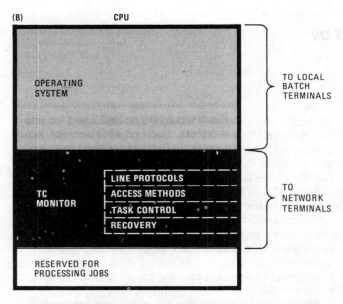

jobs generally increases. In the data communications environment—especially when the computer and terminals interact directly—throughput speeds can be critical. Consequently, the operating system must devote more of its time to servicing these jobs at the expense of lower-priority jobs. Letting the operating system handle all telecommunications functions as the job load builds up, however, is a losing proposition for two reasons: the chances are excellent that the operating system will not be able to provide satisfactory high-priority service after a certain load level is

reached; and as the operating system overloads, it will be unable to provide even marginally satisfactory service to the lower-priority jobs.

Off-loading functions

This processing dilemma could be alleviated if some of the data communications software functions could be "off-loaded" from the operating system, as shown in the figure. Typical functions which can be off-loaded would include:
- Line protocols
- Telecommunications access methods
- Data access methods
- Task scheduling and control
- System recovery

All of these functions can be easily handled through the use of telecommunications (TC) monitors. These monitors generally reside in their own memory region within the computer, or some of their functions are split between that region and the front-end processor. The functions of the front-end processor will be discussed later.

To better understand the extent of TC monitor functions, some review of how data flows should prove beneficial. The flow of information around a network is controlled by a set of rules called line protocols (or line disciplines). These rules ensure that data flows in an orderly manner by determining when terminals may transmit.

If data transmission is taking place over a dedicated line serving only one terminal, no protocol is required. However, since most applications employ multiple terminals, a terminal may not always be ready to receive. Thus protocols are used to control the transmit-receive sequence. In addition to furnishing this service, protocols provide control information (called "framing") to ensure the proper recognition and reception of data. Protocols also determine if transmitted data were received error free. If errors are detected, a retransmission is requested.

Popular protocols.

While there are a number of protocols in use today, the four dominant synchronous ones are:
- Binary synchronous communications (BSC)—a logically half-duplex protocol (i.e., data moves in only one direction at a time, and virtually every transmission requires an explicit response) in wide use for several years. It provides good data error detection and has relatively simple control procedures, but its half-duplex structure makes inefficient use of line facilities. Under certain circumstances, misinterpretation of properly used control sequences is possible. BSC is a character-oriented procedure and is therefore compatible with all existing synchronous transmission control unit (TCU) devices.
- Synchronous data link control (SDLC)—a full-duplex protocol introduced by IBM to supplant BSC and provide more efficient utilization of data links. IBM has adopted SDLC, and a systems/network design structure called systems network architecture (SNA), built around SDLC, as its standard for all future data com-

munications support. SDLC permits two-way simultaneous data transmission, and does not require explicit acknowledgment of each block sent. Error detection is effective, and the control ambiguities of BSC have been eliminated. On the negative side, SDLC is significantly more complex from the control and software viewpoints; it also is bit-oriented, requiring new or radically modified TCU equipment to operate properly.

■ High-level data link control (HDLC) and advanced data communications control procedure (ADCCP) — these are variations of SDLC. HDLC may become a European standard, while ADCCP is a more general ANSI protocol from which SDLC was adapted.

■ Digital data communications message protocol (DDCMP) — a character-oriented full-duplex protocol introduced by Digital Equipment Corp. as its standard for simultaneous two-way data transmission between intelligent devices. An advantage of DDCMP is that it can be implemented using standard character-oriented TCUs.

Asynchronous protocols must also be considered. They are popular in TWX, Telex, and teletype-compatible applications. And a TC monitor can handle modem signal manipulation, and the dialing function.

Adding efficiency
At the computer end of the line, protocols are often implemented in front-end processors. The front-end processor is a peripheral device which allows the computer to communicate more efficiently with the network components. The front-ends range from simple line-handling devices to multiple-line controllers like the IBM 370X series. Minicomputers are also used for this communications function.

While the services provided by the front-end vary, they all furnish two basic capabilities:
■ They provide the interface between the host computer and the terminals.
■ They assemble/disassemble transmitted data, and check for errors. Data is transmitted from a terminal bit by bit over the line, and must be assembled in bytes or words for processing by the computer. Likewise, data from the computer must be disassembled for transmission to a terminal.

The interface services, such as line handling and terminal polling — checking if the terminals are ready to transmit data — relieve the operating system of the chore of performing these tasks. Thus, the operating system can devote more of its time to the constructive processing of jobs.

Additional relief
The use of minicomputers as front-ends also provides another level of processing power to the network. For example, the front-end could be programmed to perform routine processing (such as simple calculations) on incoming data, and then pass the results to the host for more sophisticated processing. It's also possible to use the front-end as a message switcher — again relieving the host from handling this function.

An off-loadable function which works in conjunction with the host operating system is the telecommunications access method. The access method controls the sending and receiving of messages between terminals and the host processor. While the services offered by access methods vary, all provide terminal control and polling. An IBM installation, for example, has the choice of four manufacturer-supplied access methods:
■ BTAM (basic telecommunications access method) provides only basic terminal control and polling services. Additional services must be implemented by the programmer. BTAM runs on all IBM operating systems.
■ QTAM (queued telecommunications access method) is the next step up; it not only controls and polls, but it also queues messages, logs them, allocates resources, and schedules processing. QTAM's services are invoked via macros placed in the application program. (A macro is a single machine instruction equivalent to a specified, often-repeated, sequence of machine instructions.) QTAM is offered with IBM's DOS (disk operating system), DOS/VS (/virtual storage), and OS operating systems. However, it is not offered with OS/VS, SVS (single VS), or MVS (multiple VS). QTAM is popular in teletypewriter applications, rather than "voice-grade" networks. This access method is not usually chosen for new installations, possibly because it does not include BSC.
■ TCAM (telecommunications access method) offers all the features of QTAM, plus network control, checkpoint/restart, and system recovery. Under OS/VS, SVS, and MVS, TCAM replaces QTAM.
■ VTAM (virtual telecommunications access method) incorporates all the facilities of TCAM, and offers the dynamic sharing of network resources [including lines, terminals, and the 3704 and 3705 front-end processors operating in NCP (network control program) mode]. VTAM is available with DOS/VS, OS/VS, SVS, and MVS software packages.

All services offered by these access methods are invoked by the application program. It should be noted that BTAM performs most of the protocol functions (line control disciplines). As one progresses through the other access methods to VTAM, more of the TC monitor functions are performed. But full monitor capability is never achieved.

Selecting a monitor
Protocols and access methods, when managed by the proper TC monitor, optimize a computer's available processing time. While it might seem trite to say that the best monitor is the one which best fits a user's needs, that consideration is often forgotten by technical personnel dazzled by the technical sophistication provided by some systems. It is up to the system manager to provide a more objective view. Before a monitor is selected, the systems design and analysis group should study the overall network requirements to determine the following significant parameters:
■ Throughput — a measure of the amount of work to be performed by the system in unit time. It is often expressed as an average figure for a relatively long time interval (e.g., messages per hour through a message switch).
■ Peak level — expresses the extremes of the work

What's available in telecommunications monitors

MONITOR	VENDOR (PHONE NUMBER)	OPERATING ENVIRONMENT	TASK HANDLING	PROTOCOLS	TERMINAL SUPPORT	TERMINAL ACCESS METHOD	LANGUAGE SUPPORT
SHADOW II	ALTERGO SOFTWARE (617/237-6132)	360/370 DOS, OS, VS	MULTITASK	BSC, START/STOP, SDLC	IBM 2260, 2740, 3270, 3280 3740, 3767, 2780/3780	BTAM & STAM	COBOL, PL/1, ASSEMBLER, RPG II
ENVIRON/1	CINCOM SYSTEMS (513/662-2300)	360/370 DOS, OS, VS	SINGLE OR MULTITASK	BSC, START/STOP	IBM 3270, & OTHER COMPATIBLE TERMINALS	BTAM, TCAM, VTAM	COBOL, FORTRAN, PL/1, ASSEMBLER
GBASWIFT II	GBA INTERNATIONAL (415/924-5792)	360/370 DOS, DOS/VS	SINGLE OR MULTITASK	BSC, START/STOP	IBM 2260, 2740, 3270, 3741, 3767; TTY 33/35	BTAM	COBOL, FORTRAN, PL/1, RPG II, ASSEMBLER
CICS ENTRY	IBM (914/696-1900)	360/370 DOS, DOS/VS	SINGLE TASK	BSC, START/STOP	IBM 1050, 2260, 2740, 2741, 2780, 3270	BTAM	COBOL, PL/1, ASSEMBLER
CICS STANDARD	IBM (914/696-1900)	360/370 DOS, OS, VS	MULTITASK	BSC, START/STOP	IBM 1050, 2260, 2740, 2741, 2780, 3270	BTAM, TCAM	COBOL, PL/1, ASSEMBLER
CICS/VS	IBM (914/696-1900)	360/370 DOS/VS, OS/VS	MULTITASK	BSC, START/STOP, SDLC	IBM 1050, 2740, 2741, 2770, 2780, 3270, 3785, 3600, 3650, 3767, 3790, S/3, S/7, TTY 33/35	BTAM, TCAM, VTAM EXTM	COBOL, PL/1, ASSEMBLER, RPG II
BETACOMM	INFORMATICS (212/481-6800)	360/370 DOS, DOS/VS	SINGLE OR MULTITASK	BSC, START/STOP	IBM 2260, 3270	BTAM, TCAM, VTAM, FTAM	COBOL, ASSEMBLER, RPG II
INTERCOMM	INFORMATICS (212/481-6800)	360/370 OS, OS/VS, MVS	MULTITASK	BSC, START/STOP	IBM 2741, 2780, 3270; PLUS ALL INDUSTRY COMPATIBLE AND OTHERS	BTAM, QTAM, TCAM, VTAM	COBOL, FORTRAN, PL/1, ASSEMBLER
MINICOMM	INFORMATICS (212/481-6800)	360/370 DOS, DOS/VS	SINGLE OR MULTITASK	BSC, START/STOP	IBM 2260, 3270, & OTHER COMPATIBLE TERMINALS	BTAM, FTAM	COBOL, PL/1, ASSEMBLER, RPG II
DATACOM/DC	INSYTE DATACOM (214/526-4280)	360/370 DOS, OS, VS (OR EQUIV)	MULTITASK	BSC, START/STOP	IBM 1050, 1060, 2260, 2740, S/3, S/7; TTY 28/33/35; ALL COMPATIBLE TERMINALS	BTAM	COBOL, FORTRAN, PL/1, RPG II, ASSEMBLER, ALC
TP-2000	MRI SYSTEMS (512/258-5171)	360/370 OS, OS/VS	MULTITASK	BSC, START/STOP	IBM 1050, 2260, 2740, 2741, 3270, 3755; TTY; SANDERS 720; HAZELTIME 2000	BTAM, TCAM	COBOL, PL/1, FORTRAN, ASSEMBLER, FASTER·
COM-PLETE	SOFTWARE AG OF N. AMERICA (703/620-9577)	360/370 OS, OS/VS	MULTITASK	BSC, START/STOP	IBM 2260, 2740, 3277, 3760; ULTRONICS CRT; TTY	BTAM, TCAM, VTAM	COBOL, PL/1, ASSEMBLER, FORTRAN
TASK/MASTER II	TURNKEY SYSTEMS (203/853-2884)	360/370 DOS, OS, VS	MULTITASK	BSC, SDLC, START/STOP	IBM 2260, 2265, 2740, 3270; TTY 33/35; AND OTHERS	BTAM, TCAM, VTAM, GAM	COBOL, FORTRAN, PL/1, ASSEMBLER
WEST I	WESTINGHOUSE (412/256-5583)	360/370 DOS, DOS/VS	SINGLE OR MULTITASK	BSC, START/STOP	IBM 2260, 3270, & OTHER COMPATIBLE TERMINALS; TTY	BTAM	COBOL, PL/1, ASSEMBLER

DATA MANAGEMENT	DATA SECURITY	RECOVERY FACILITIES	PRICE	NUMBER OF USERS
SAM, ISAM, DAM, VSAM; INTERFACE WITH MAJOR DBMS	RECORD LEVEL	CHECKPT/RESTART OR WARM RESTART	$8,000; $240/MON	180
SAM, ISAM, BTAM, VSAM; TOTAL, IMS	FILE PASSWORD	CHECKPT/RESTART, WARM RESTART	FROM $425/MON (DOS) TO $900/MON (OS/VS)	600 TO 700
SAM, ISAM, BDAM, VSAM; TOTAL, IDMS, BOMP, DBOMP, DATACOM/DB, VANDL	RECORD LEVEL	WARM RESTART	$9,000; $400/MON	OVER 100
SAM, ISAM, BDAM, VSAM; VANDL/1	OPERATOR SIGN-ON	NO CHECKPT/RESTART OR WARM RESTART	$235/MON	NOT AVAILABLE
SAM, ISAM, BDAM, VSAM; VANDL/1, IMS-2, DL/I, DBOMP	OPERATOR SIGN-ON	NO CHECKPT/RESTART OR WARM RESTART	$588/MON (DOS); $825/MON (OS)	NOT AVAILABLE
SAM, ISAM, BSAM, VSAM, BDAM; IMS/VS, DL/I, AND OTHERS	OPERATOR SIGN-ON; SEGMENT LEVEL WITH IMS/VS OR DL/I	CHECKPT/RESTART	$475/MON (DOS/VS); $1,000/MON (OS/VS)	NOT AVAILABLE
SAM, ISAM, DPAM, VSAM; TOTAL, VANDL/1 DL/I, DBOMP	RECORD LEVEL	NO CHECKPT/RESTART OR WARM RESTART	$17,500; $489/MON	OVER 100
SAM, ISAM, QISAM, BISAM, VSAM, BDAM; ALL MAJOR DBMS	RECORD LEVEL	CHECKPT/RESTART; WARM RESTART	$38,000 (OS) TO $42,000 (MVS); $1,060/MON (OS) TO $1,173/MON (MVS)	200
SAM, ISAM, BDAM, VSAM	RECORD LEVEL	NO CHECKPT/RESTART OR WARM RESTART	$9,500 TO $11,500; $464 TO $562/MON	150
SAM, ISAM, BDAM, VSAM; DATACOM/DB, TOTAL, IMS	RECORD LEVEL	CHECKPT/RESTART, WARM RESTART	$32,000 OR $940/MON (DOS); $37,000 OR $1,150/MON (OS)	80
SAM, ISAM, BDAM, VTAM; SYSTEM 2000	RECORD LEVEL	NONE	$25,000; $1,000/MON	8
SAM, ISAM, BDAM, VTAM; ADABAS, VSAM	RECORD LEVEL	CHECKPT/RESTART, WARM RESTART	$60,000	40
SAM, ISAM, BDAM; TOTAL, IMS, IDMS, DL/I, DBOMP, CFMS, DATACOM/DB, SYSTEM 2000	RECORD LEVEL	WARM RESTART	$20,000 (DOS, DOS/VS); $44,000 (OS, OS/VS)	ABOUT 300
SAM, ISAM, BDAM, VSAM; TOTAL, DL/I, DBOMP; IDMS DATACOM/DB	TERMINAL/APPLICATION LEVEL	WARM RESTART	$8,500 (LOCAL); $12,500 (REMOTE)	350 TO 400

load distribution, which is a function of the throughput's mean. For example, a message throughput volume of 3,600 units per hour is an average of one message per second. However, the peak loading experienced by this system at certain critical hours of the day may rise to two or three messages per second. In addition to the magnitude of the peak condition, it is important to know the length of the period during which the peak can be expected to persist.

■ Response time—usually defined as the interval between initiation of a transmission by a terminal and receipt of the first character of the response. Requirements for response time are often stated as "mean, 90 percent, 99 percent;" that is, a mean value, a value to be achieved for 90 percent of all operations, and a worst-case value required for at least 99 percent of all transmissions. Response time will be heavily dependent on message volume and size, communications line speed, system capacity, and unit processing load (see the following).

■ Unit processing level—reflects the amount of work required of the system for each message or transaction processed. Contributing factors to this figure are:
a. Communications overhead—physical processing necessary to receive and/or transmit the message.
b. Peripheral I/O overhead—number of disk, tape, or other I/O operations necessary for each message.
c. Central processor overhead—number of actual CPU instructions required for message processing.
d. Queuing overhead—time spent waiting for various services within the system.

These parameters provide a fairly accurate profile of a data communications (DC) system's requirements. They also provide solid evidence for buying or rejecting a certain class of monitors.

Where needed

While access methods provide competent—but rudimentary—services, the more sophisticated DC networks require the additional services of a TC monitor. One drawback of the access methods is that they all require the applications programs be written to take into account the idiosyncracies of the particular access method involved. And all require the applications programmer to have knowledge of the interface problems associated with each.

For example, in constructing the applications program, the programmer often must consider message-formatting requirements, terminal restrictions, polling and addressing, connect/disconnect procedures, error detection, and retransmission. Often, the restrictions of the transmission protocol also become the programmer's headache.

Today's TC monitors make life a lot simpler for the programmer by making the interface considerations the monitor's problem. While the monitor does function under control of the operating system, most of the services provided make the monitor look like a little operating system itself.

An operating system, for example, assigns each job a processing priority; allocates system resources; handles input/output (I/O) requests for data; monitors the processing of each job; and assists the job in restarting when an error occurs. Telecommunications monitors furnish many of these same services—some in conjunction with the OS. The difference is in the level of service provided, and the techniques used to attain them. These considerations make the selection and evaluation of a monitor a bit tricky.

The way in which tasks are handled, for example, can make or break a teleprocessing system as far as throughput is concerned. Some systems will monitor a task to determine how well or poorly it is using system resources. If a job is a "heavy user" of CPU time, it could conceivably prevent other jobs from receiving their fair share of processing time. Monitors quite often will defer processing of a heavily CPU-bound, low-priority job until processing load diminishes.

The accompanying table, "What's available in telecommunications monitors," lists the common characteristics, and approximate prices and number of users, of today's leading monitors. Most of them support the same protocols, and file and telecommunications access methods. By file access method is meant an operating system data access method, such as ISAM (indexed sequential access method), SAM (sequential AM), and DAM (direct AM). These methods organize and control the data used by an application program which receives transactions or messages from the TC monitor.

The monitors all offer the same type of terminal support services. The important differences—in the opinion of many industry experts—lie in:
- Task handling
- Data access/update security
- Recovery facilities

Monitors handle tasks (programs) either one at a time, or many tasks simultaneously. The latter capability is called multitasking, while the former is designated single tasking.

Eliminating idle time

A multitasking system allows more than one job to be processed simultaneously. When one task requires a time-consuming service (such as input/output), or must wait for the occurrence of some other event before proceeding, the computer does not simply remain idle during that period. Rather, it "suspends" the waiting task and "initiates" some other task that is currently able to perform useful work (is "dispatchable"). When the event for which the first task was waiting has occurred, it will become dispatchable and will be initiated in a similar manner. The obvious advantage of multitasking is that the system is always performing useful work even though individual software components may be in temporary waiting conditions.

The two basic prerequisites for multitasking operations are: a breakdown of the system into a set of tasks, each with a relative processing priority; and the ability to recognize the completion of events for which tasks are waiting.

The achievement of the first prerequisite is part of the software design process, and normally includes designating as highest priority a task scheduler routine, whose function is to determine the next task to initiate at any task-change point. The facility required in the second prerequisite is usually provided through an interrupt system, which informs the processor of the completion of I/O, timing, and other events.

Security vital

Data access/security facilities are extremely important, especially where sensitive data is concerned. If, for example, personnel records are being accessed, it would be desirable to restrict the reading of such sensitive data as salary figures.

Access to data is generally accomplished by having the user enter a single password or a series of passwords—depending on the levels of security being employed. Single data password protection to the file level means that anyone knowing the password can read any information contained within that file. More sophisticated systems require passwords to access specific record types within the file, and specific field types within the record.

Password security is often augmented by associating a write-inhibit with certain passwords. Two benefits are gained from this lockout: unauthorized users are prevented from altering the contents of records; and the data remains available for general use.

Some monitors employ a terminal lockout procedure to guard against access by unauthorized terminals. Here, the monitor maintains a table which associates terminals with certain levels of data accessing and manipulation. The problem with this scheme is physically ensuring that only qualified people have access to the terminal.

If the monitor's data security facilities and/or file organization support are too limited, the potential user should ascertain if the monitor will support a more sophisticated database management system (DBMS) such as is now marketed.

Such a DBMS as Cincom's Total, Cullinane's IDMS, IBM's IMS, Infodata's Inquire, Insyte Datacom's Datacom/DB, Software AG's ADABAS—to name a few—combine top-flight security with powerful data handling capabilities.

System failure due to hardware or software problems is inevitable. The trick is to get the system restarted as quickly and easily as possible.

There are two types of restart procedures: cold and warm. Cold restart is the less attractive, for it requires all operations processing at the time of the failure to be cleared and the system restarted. Generally, system log tapes which capture processing data are used during the restarting process. A warm restart, on the other hand, has the capability to resume processing at the point where the failure occurred.

While the accompanying table lists many of the important characteristics of some of the better known and widely used monitors on the market, the chart is only intended to provide a quick reference as to the monitor system's overall capabilities. So, before a TC monitor system is selected or rejected, keep in mind what was stated earlier: the best system is the one which best fits a user's needs. ■

Part 5
Data security

Network security: a top-down view shows problem

Stephen T. Kent, MIT Laboratory for Computer Science and
Bolt Baranek and Newman Inc., Cambridge, Mass.

Providing the security program for data communications networks is not simple, and success is always a relative term; here are the ways and means

Networks span the spectrum from collections of heterogeneous, autonomous host computers to groups of hosts operating under a single authority and cooperating to provide a coherent, supra-computer interface. Correspondingly, the types of measures provided for network security vary over a wide range, depending on the network environment. The selection of an appropriate set of network security measures begins with an evaluation of the threat-environment and an assessment of risks in that environment. Once this procedure has been completed, appropriate security techniques can be selected.

Potential security violations can be categorized on the basis of whether they result in unauthorized release of information, unauthorized modification of information, or unauthorized denial of use of resources. In the context of communications, attacks of the first type correspond to passive wiretapping as in satellite or radio networks, while attacks of the second and third type correspond to active wiretapping.

The development of secure, general-purpose networks has proven to be extremely difficult. However, though a complete methodology for such networks has not been formulated, experience in the development of protection mechanisms for computer systems has resulted in a number of useful principles.

Even when networks consisting solely of secure computer systems become a reality, separate consideration must still be given to security mechanisms in the network itself. There is always the possibility that individual components of the networks could be subverted physically, thus violating some of the basic assumptions on which secure computer systems—and therefore by extension—secure networks are based. Therefore, the following eight design principles should be included in any planning for a secure network:

- Economy of mechanism
- Fail-safe defaults
- Complete mediation
- Open design
- Separation of privilege
- Least privilege
- Least common mechanism
- Psychological acceptability

The first of these principles, economy of mechanism, dictates the use of the simplest possible design that achieves the desired effect. This principle is especially appropriate in the development of protection mechanisms. This is because the design and implementation errors that result in unwanted access paths will not be noticed during normal use. Therefore, techniques such as the line-by-line inspection of software and the physical examination of the hardware that implements protection mechanisms are necessary. A small and simple design is essential if such techniques are to be successfully applied.

The principles of employing fail-safe defaults and complete mediation are complementary. The former requires that access decisions be based on permission rather than exclusion. The latter requires that every access to every object be checked against an access-control database. The former results in a conservative design approach in which arguments must be made as to why objects should be accessible, rather than why they should not. The latter enforces a system-wide view of access control.

The principle of open design states that the configuration of the protection mechanisms should not be secret. Mechanisms should not depend on the ignorance of potential attackers, but rather on the possession of specific, more easily protected keys or passwords. If network security depends only on the secrecy of the keys, then the protection mechanisms can be reviewed by many potential users without the concern that the review itself will compromise the safeguards.

The principle of separation of privilege is based on the concept that a protection mechanism that requires two keys is more robust and flexible than one based on a single key. This principle can be applied to the distribution and use of encryption keys, the interaction among communications security techniques, authentication procedures, and access control mechanisms at the network level.

The principle of least privilege requires that every program and every user of a network should operate by using the least set of privileges necessary to perform a required task. This principle serves to limit the damage that can result from an accident, an error, or the subversion of a network component. The use of this principle to establish "fire walls" is evident in the use of connection-oriented communications security measures and in the use of selective encryption techniques.

The principle of least common mechanism implies that the number of mechanisms available to more than one user and needed by all users should be minimized. Every shared mechanism represents a potential information path between users and must be designed with great care to be sure that it does not unintentionally compromise security. Further, any mechanism serving all users must be constructed so as to satisfy every user, a more difficult job than satisfying one or a few users. This principle motivates the use of connection-oriented communications security measures and influences the positioning of encryption modules in a communications hierarchy.

Finally, the psychological acceptablity principle emphasizes that the human interface must be designed for ease of use. Users should routinely and automatically apply the protection mechanisms available. Also, to the extent that the user's mental image of his protection goals matches the mechanisms he must use, mistakes will be minimized.

The techniques and mechanisms presented here are applicable to a wide variety of environments. To provide a context for discussion, a network model that encompasses packet-switched and packet broadcast network configurations can be assumed. The National Bureau of Standards' data encryption standard (DES) is used as the basic encryption algorithm. Many of the security mechanisms developed are not particularly sensitive to the use of a particular algorithm, and encryption algorithms with similar external characteristics can be interchanged.

Communications security mechanisms generally can be developed independently of communications protocols, although the detailed design of such mechanisms may take into account a particular target protocol. In this article, techniques are discussed at a high enough level that no specific protocol need be assumed. However, the mechanisms can be imagined as being embedded in the information field of an SDLC frame or an X.25 packet, depending on the network architecture employed.

The basic component of the network is the communications subnet, which can be viewed simply as a transmission medium, such as coaxial cable, twisted pair wires with registers, or packet switches connected by leased phone lines.

Network model

The communications subnet serves to connect the hosts on the network (Fig. 1). The model includes four types of hosts: single-terminal hosts, multi-terminal hosts, service hosts, and gateway hosts. A single-terminal host serves to connect an individual user terminal to the network and might be implemented by a microprocessor contained within the terminal. A multi-terminal host (network front-end) serves to connect several terminals to the network. Such a host might be implemented by a microprocessor or by a minicomputer, depending on the number of terminals being served and the level of service provided. The distinction between a single-terminal host and a multi-terminal host is important because the latter is an instance of a multi-plexed communications facility which is concerned with the merging of data streams from the various terminals served.

The service hosts on the net consist of conventional computers providing utility functions, as well as special-purpose hosts providing particular functions. Finally, gateway hosts serve to interconnect two or more networks.

Models of communication security measures

There are two basic approaches to considerations of communications security: link-oriented and end-to-end security measures. The former independently protects messages on each of the communications links, while the latter provides continuous protection for each message from its source to its destination.

There are several places in the network model where communications links can be readily identified. The term link is used in the same context as data link control protocols, e.g., SDLC, HDLC, X.25. Such links,

267

which usually connect the switching nodes in a packet-switched network, may be physically unprotected, and thus may be subject to attack. Link-oriented protection provides security for messages passing over an individual communications link between two nodes. The underlying assumption in providing protection of this sort is that it is much easier to attack the communications link rather than the nodes themselves. Even if this is true, it may not be possible to physically secure packet-switch nodes in the communications subnet as readily as in the terminal and host nodes. Yet, subversion of one of the packet switches results in exposure of all the message traffic passing through that switch, despite the physical security precautions in effect at the source and destination nodes.

Even if all packet switches are located physically near the hosts, and thus are afforded the same level of physical security, subversion of a single packet switch can result in exposure of message traffic between other hosts on the network. In a network where adaptive routing strategies (such as Arpanet) are employed, a subverted packet switch could cause packets to be routed through it almost independently of their source and destination hosts. Thus, link encryption in the communications subnetwork suffers from the problem that subversion of one node could result in exposure of substantial amounts of traffic.

If the only unsecured communications links in a network occur within the communications subnet itself, link-oriented measures have an advantage in that they

1 A network model

Security environment. The protection of data traffic requires attention, no matter what type of communicating device is attached to the network. Single-terminal hosts

connect the user directly to the net. At multi-terminal hosts, service hosts, and gateway hosts, the user's interface is complicated by intervening hardware and software.

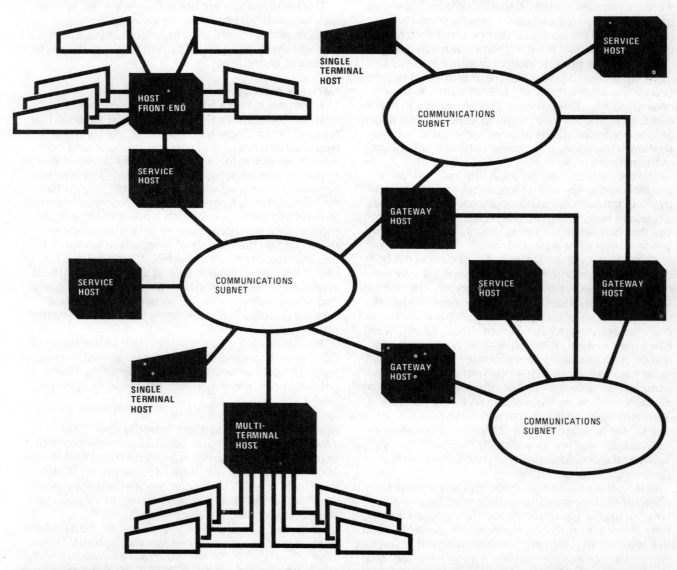

can provide transparent communications security for the hosts attached to the network. If only some of the communications links between terminals and hosts (or between hosts and the communications subnet) need to be protected, security measures for these links can be implemented without affecting the other hosts on the network. The cost of providing link-oriented protection measures on terminal-to-host and host-to-communications-subnetwork links can be borne by the directly affected parties, while the overall cost of link-oriented measures within the communications subnet can be borne by all of its users.

End-to-end measures

Rather than viewing a network as a collection of nodes, joined by communications links, it can be seen simply as the medium for transporting messages. From this perspective, end-to-end security measures protect messages in transit between source and destination in such a way that the subversion of any communications links between the source and destination nodes does not result in the exposure of message traffic. There is some flexibility in defining the points at which end-to-end security measures are implemented: from host to host, from terminal to terminal or service host, or from terminal to process on a service host. By extending the domain of end-to-end security measures, more of the communications path between a user and his computation, or between a pair of users, is protected. However, as the domain of such measures is extended, the range of hardware and software that must interface with these measures may increase.

Connection-oriented security measures constitute a refinement of end-to-end measures and protect each connection individually. Connection-oriented security not only protects that portion of a communications path that lies between the security-defined ends of the connection, but also eliminates undetected cross-talk, whether induced by hardware or software, over that span. In many respects, connection-oriented measures provide the greatest degree of communications security and they are applicable in a wide variety of environments. Moreover, these measures can be employed

by users without affecting other users, and the cost can be borne directly by the benefiting party. Interactive communication provides a particularly rich context in which to examine measures.

In the case of a full-duplex connection between a terminal and a process on a service host, the connection is composed of two independent simplex channels. In many applications, the connection is transitory, e.g., existing for the duration of a single log-in session.

Both the terminal and the host are assumed to reside in secure areas while the remainder of the network may be subject to physical attack (Fig. 2). The terminal may, at different times, be used by various individuals over a range of authorization levels. The host provides services to a diverse user community, not all of whose members employ communications security measures. An intruder, represented by a computer under hostile control, is assumed to be situated in the communications path between the host and the terminal. Thus, all messages transmitted on the connection must pass through the intruder.

Attacks classified

Using the context of the network model and the connection model presented earlier, the types of attacks that can be mounted by an intruder can be classified. It is assumed that the intruder can position himself at some point in the network through which all information of interest to him must pass (Fig. 3). Thus, the intruder is assumed to be in a position to mount both active and passive wiretapping attacks.

In passive wiretapping, the intruder merely observes the packets passing on the connection without interfering with their flow. Intruder observation of the (application level) data in a packet can be termed "release of message contents" and is the most fundamental type of passive wiretapping. The intruder can also observe portions of the packet headers. Even if the data is not intelligible to him, he can learn the location and identities of the communicating processes. Finally, the intruder can examine the lengths of packets and their frequency of transmission to gain knowledge of the nature of the data being exchanged. These latter types

2 A connection model

Communications line exposure. In many cases, it is possible to afford a high level of physical security for the data transmitting and receiving devices. While this is a *desirable goal, it is usually impossible to provide the same physical protection to the transmission media. Wiretapping attacks and countermeasures become complicated.*

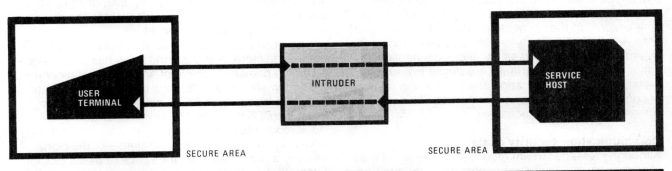

SECURE AREA   SECURE AREA

3 Intruder in internetwork context

Packet network subversion. When packetized data flows through a number of intermediary switching nodes or gateway hosts en route from one secure area to another, there is always the danger of subversion beyond the direct control of the user. It must be assumed that the intruder can cause all data to flow through his own site.

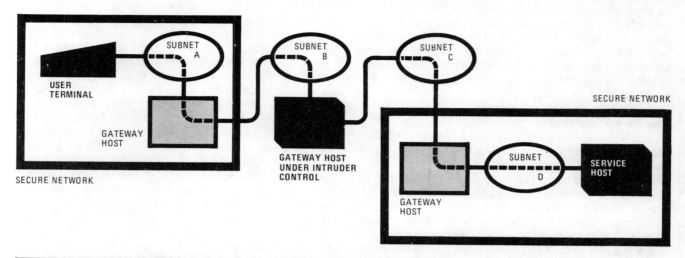

of attacks are usually referred to as "traffic analysis" or "violations of transmission security."

The intruder can also engage in active wiretapping by performing a variety of processing activities on packets flowing past him. These packets can be selectively modified, deleted, delayed, reordered, or duplicated and re-inserted into the connection at a later time, or may pass through unaffected. Bogus packets can be synthesized and inserted into the connection. Acts such as these can be designated "message stream modification" attacks.

Since it has been assumed that the intruder is in a position where all packets of interest flow through his site, he can discard or delay all packets going in either or both directions. Acts of this nature can be classified as "denial of message service" attacks. In the context of packet deletion or delay, the difference between message stream modification and denial of message service attacks is subtle and is a function both of the degree of the attack and the state of the connection. The distinction is made because different types of countermeasures can be employed for each type of attack.

Finally, connections must be initiated in a fashion that supports secure identification of the principles (users, terminals, hosts) at each end and verifies the time integrity of the connection. Attempts by an intruder to violate time-integrity or secure identification constraints can be classified as "spurious connection initiation" attacks. Such attacks are similar in nature to message stream modification attacks, but the context of connection initiation prompts the use of a somewhat different set of countermeasures.

Communication security goals

Although message stream modification, denial of message service, and spurious connection initiation attacks

cannot generally be prevented, they can be reliably detected. Conversely, release of message contents and traffic analysis attacks cannot usually be detected, but they can be effectively thwarted. Mindful of these limitations, five goals are presented for the design of mechanisms that provide communications security:
- Prevention of release of message contents
- Prevention of traffic analysis
- Detection of message stream modification
- Detection of denial of message service
- Detection of spurious connection initiation

Historically, encryption has been employed extensively as a countermeasure against passive wiretapping, thus addressing the first and second goals. Encryption can be used in conjunction with protocols to achieve the third, fourth, and fifth goals. In each case, attainment of the goal is based on the inability of the intruder to subvert the encryption algorithm employed, and the goals can be achieved only problematically.

Data encryption

Encryption serves both as a countermeasure to passive wiretapping attacks and as a foundation on which countermeasures can be constructed against active wiretapping attacks. An understanding of some characteristics of such algorithms is critical to the development of all the countermeasures.

As it appears almost certain that the DES will become a de facto industry standard, it has been selected as the primary example of an encryption algorithm.

Fundamentally, the DES is a block cipher operating on 64-bit blocks, using a 56-bit key. This means of using the DES is referred to as the electronic code book mode (ECB) in an analogy to conventional code books. Each key gives the parameters of the cipher, defining a permutation on the space of 64-bit blocks. Each bit of ciphertext in a block generated by use of

4 Electronic code book mode of DES

Basic scrambling. *Using the National Bureau of Standards' DES as a model, 64-bit blocks of clear data are scrambled through the use of a secret encryption key.* *Enciphered data is exposed on the way to the receiving end where a duplicate key is used to unscramble the message. Success or failure depends on key secrecy.*

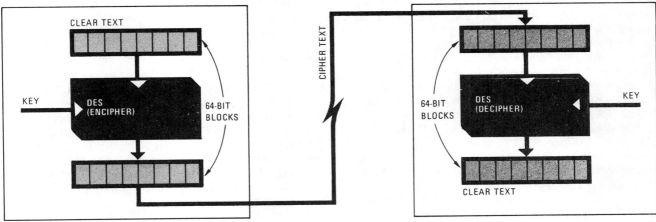

TRANSMITTER

CLEAR TEXT

KEY

DES (ENCIPHER)

64-BIT BLOCKS

CIPHER TEXT

RECEIVER

64-BIT BLOCKS

DES (DECIPHER)

KEY

CLEAR TEXT

the ECB mode is a function of each bit of the key and each bit of the cleartext block from which it was generated. A change of as little as one bit in either the key or the cleartext results in ciphertext in which each bit is changed with approximately equal probability. Conversely, a change in one bit of either of the key or ciphertext will result in changes averaging about 50 percent of the bits of deciphered cleartext.

Although this error of propagation is extensive, it is strictly limited to the block in which the error occurs. Decryption of other blocks is unaffected by such an error. Thus, in the ECB mode, the cryptographic synchrony required for correct deciphering of messages is achieved when both sender and receiver employ the same key and blocks are correctly delimited. Figure 4 illustrates this mode of using the DES.

Enhanced enciphering

An enhanced version of this mode is the chained block cipher (CBC) mode, illustrated in Figure 5. As with the ECB mode, a message is first fragmented into block-sized pieces and padded to occupy an integral number of blocks if necessary. The first block is enciphered as in ECB mode. This ciphertext block is then combined with the second message block and the result is enciphered as in ECB mode. This process is repeated until all of the message is enciphered. Because the ciphertext form of each block after the first is a function of all the preceding blocks in the message, the problem of block-aligned data-pattern exposure is greatly reduced. In this mode, identical cleartext blocks in two messages result in identical ciphertext blocks only if the prefixes of the blocks in their respective messages are identical. Often this apparent deficiency poses no problem since protocol data such as unique sequence numbers will form the beginning of the message and thus will result in a unique prefix for the following text.

The DES also can be used, in several ways, as part of a key-stream generator for a stream cipher. The cipher feedback (CFB) mode of operation transforms the DES into a self-synchronizing stream cipher which can directly operate on a cleartext string from one to 64 bits in length. The cleartext is combined with a matching number of key stream (output) bits generated by the DES block cipher (any remaining DES output bits are discarded). The transmitted ciphertext is fed into 64-bit shift registers that form the input to the basic DES at both ends of the connection, making the key stream a function of all transmitted ciphertext. Figure 6 displays this configuration of the DES for use with eight-bit bytes.

In CFB mode, cryptographic synchrony is achieved only if the sender and receiver use the same key and both shift registers contain the same bit pattern. If an error occurs in the ciphertext stream, a portion of the received cleartext will be garbled, but receipt of 64 bits of error-free ciphertext automatically resynchronizes the cipher. While the number of bits actually garbled by a single-bit error is constant at 65, the number of cleartext bits that might be rendered useless by such an error depends on the length of the cleartext bit strings employed and the granularity of error detection employed in higher level protocols. Initial synchronization of the shift registers requires transmission of 64 bits of "fill."

The data encryption standard (DES) appears to be resistant to conventional cryptanalysis, although it is "breakable" in a theoretical sense and it may be susceptible to "brute force" attacks employing a large, special-purpose, highly-parallel device.

Both the CBC and CFB modes of the DES provide a basis for achieving the first goal, prevention of release of message contents, by being applied to the data to be concealed. Both modes also provide a foundation for the construction of countermeasures to achieve the other goals. Selection of appropriate modes is dependent on both protocol and network environments and influences the type of message-stream modification countermeasures employed.

As noted earlier, protection measures can be link-oriented or connection-oriented (end-to-end) and this distinction is often made in discussing encryption. Both encryption approaches can be used to prevent release of message contents, although link encryption can also provide protection from traffic analysis.

Link encryption can be performed independently on each of the communications links in a network. Stream ciphers are generally employed in link encryption and a continuous stream of bits is maintained between nodes. Because switching (routing) functions are performed only at nodes in a network, both the headers and the data of packets can be enciphered on links. Since many of the links in the network are multiplexed, no segregation of connections on a link is cryptographically enforced. Usually, a different key is employed for each link so that subversion of one link does not result in release of information on other links.

Node security a must

Since information is enciphered only on the links and not within the nodes connected by the links, these nodes must be secure. Although the origin and destination nodes in the network are assumed to be physically secure, the use of link encryption requires the extension of this physical security to all intermediate packet switches and gateways. Not only must these intermediate nodes be physically secure, but the hardware and software that comprise these nodes must be certified to isolate the information on each of the connections passing through the installations. However, even if all the nodes are secure, the use of link encryption as the primary defense against the release of message contents attacks violates the principle of least privilege when there is no need to expose the contents of messages between the origin and destination.

In end-to-end encryption, each message (packet), with the exception of certain header information that must be examined en route, is enciphered at its source and not deciphered until it reaches its destination. A unique key can be used for each connection or a coarser granularity of key distribution can be employed, i.e., a different key can be used between each pair of communicating hosts or a single key can be used over an entire secure subnet. The latter scheme affords end-to-end protection, but does not provide the connection segregation of the former approach. As the range of use of a single key increases, the amount of information exposed in the case of disclosure of that key also increases, but the task of distributing the keys becomes easier.

In accordance with the principle of least privilege, message should be enciphered so that each module that processes a packet has available to it only the information necessary to perform its task. The information in a packet can be hierarchically categorized on the basis of whether the information must be accessible to packet switches and gateways, hosts, or the processes at the end of the connection. Information required at the level of packet switches and gateways cannot be enciphered on an end-to-end basis.

This hierarchic use of encryption can be achieved either by selective encipherment of appropriate information fields or by embedding the information from each level in a protocol layer for the next level and performing encryption on the layered message at each level. In practice, variations on these techniques are employed, using some aspects of selective encipherment and protocol layering.

In dealing with the problem of release of message contents, a technique referred to as "red-black separation" has been developed. Red-black separation attempts to construct a barrier between the secure (red) and unsecure (black) facilities in a communications network. Ideally, red-black separation prevents the transmission of cleartext across the red-black boundary, forcing all the information that crosses the boundary from red to black to pass through an encryption unit. Information flowing in the reverse direction, from black to red, either passes through the decryption unit or through a bypass around it.

Red-black separation has been used extensively in link-oriented encryption devices and can be used in end-to-end encryption as well by placing the communications security device between the host (or terminal) and the communications subnet. Although red-black separation provides a context in which it is easier to certify that only enciphered information (with the exception of limited amounts of addressing and flow control information) crosses the boundary from red to black, this context cannot be used to ensure the isolation of connections back to the origins and destinations in processes. Different levels of encryption can be most easily implemented in a red-black separation context by protocol layering and encrypting the layered message at each level.

Analyzing traffic

Traffic analysis countermeasures center around masking the frequency, length, and origin-destination patterns of message traffic. The precision with which an intruder can carry out traffic analysis directly influences the amount of information that can be gained from the analysis. This precision is a function of several factors including the protocol employed in the network, the transmission medium of the communications subnet, and the operating characteristics of the hosts. For example, origin-destination analysis can take place at several levels in the network environment, enabling an intruder to determine the source of destination of messages at the level of the network, the host, the process, or the specific user(s) involved. The difficulty associated with countering attacks at each level depends heavily on the specific protocol being used and the configuration of the network environment. As is the case with the use of encryption as a countermeasure against release of message contents attacks, traffic analysis countermeasures can be employed on an end-to-end or link-by-link basis. If link encryption is em-

5 Chained block cipher (on 3 blocks)

Strengthening ciphers. A chained block cipher is an enhancement of the basic electronic code book mode of coding. The addition of a prefix to the first block of cleartext ensures that decryption of a full message by an intruder will not only be harder, but also errors introduced by an intruder will warn users of a hostile presence.

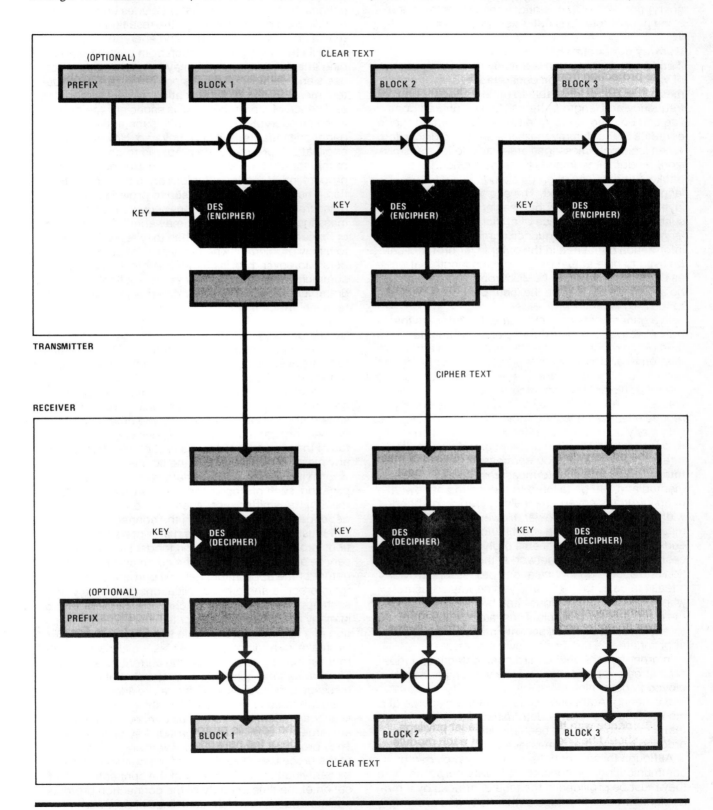

273

ployed, a continuous stream of bits can be maintained between nodes in the communications environment, thus masking the frequency-, and length-patterns of the connection. In situations where communications links are multiplexed among several connections, link encryption also provides origin-destination masking, since packet routing is not visible on the link.

Dummy concealment
If end-to-end encryption is employed, dummy packets of various lengths can be generated whenever actual messages are not available to meet artificially selected frequency and length patterns. An enciphered control flag can be used to indicate to the receiver that the contents of the dummy message are to be discarded. When legitimate messages are available for transmission, random amounts of fill can be included in the packets and an enciphered field can indicate the lengths of the actual text. The encrypted protocol layering approach described earlier is especially well suited to the maintenance of artificial frequency and length patterns. The sequence numbers and length information contained in the outer layer protocol can be used to hide actual frequency and length patterns as dummy packets can be discarded and padding can be stripped away before the inner packet is delivered to the next layer for processing.

In a general network environment, it appears that truly effective end-to-end traffic analysis countermeasures would require both packet embedding and transmission to all possible hosts. Thus, depending on the network configuration and the protocols involved, end-to-end traffic analysis countermeasures can be very wasteful of processing power and can substantially reduce effective network bandwidth.

In many environments, release of information through traffic analysis may be deemed a secondary threat and no specific countermeasures may be instituted. End-to-end countermeasures are easily implemented and can be tailored to reduce the bandwidth of an intruder's covert channels by trading off bandwidth and processing power. However, the cost of masking host level origin/destination patterns using end-to-end techniques seems prohibitive in non-broadcast networks. In such networks, the use of link encryption and secure communications processors provides a feasible basis for traffic analysis countermeasures, while end-to-end techniques can be used to achieve the other protection goals. Thus, a combination of end-to-end and link-oriented security measures may prove appropriate in a number of environments.

In order to achieve the third goal, detection of message stream modification, mechanisms must be employed to determine message authenticity, integrity, and ordering. Authenticity implies that the source of a message can be reliably determined. Integrity implies that a message has not been modified en route, and ordering implies that a message can be located.

Although these functions are usually provided by a communications protocol for reliability purposes, here they must be provided in the face of attacks by a malevolent intruder. Message authenticity and ordering

requirements interact with secure connection initiation and call for the use of distinct encryption keys for each connection. More importantly, the protocol data that provides the basis for authentication and ordering (unique sequence numbers) must be bound to applications data in a fashion that precludes undetected modification of any portion of the resulting message (using error-detection codes and encryption).

While the need for protection from passive wiretapping attacks is apparent, it may be argued that most users and many applications programs can easily detect message stream modification attacks without the assistance of a protocol. This is especially the case when an encryption scheme with substantial error propagation characteristics is employed. However, not all applications programs are prepared to detect attacks of this sort and not all message streams contain the proper kind of redundant information for such detection. Thus, there is good reason to provide detection measures in a communications security protocol. Even messages directed to a user may admit a wide range of "meaningful" contents when they represent answers to a new problem or when they consist of random numbers. Moreover, provision of this protection by the communications protocol frees the application programmer of responsibility for determining how to counter such attacks.

Denial of message service
The fourth protection goal, detection of denial of message service, can be achieved through the use of a request-response protocol.

At each end of the connection, a timer is used to periodically trigger the transmission of a request message that forces a response from the other end of the connection. Each of these messages conveys the status of the transmitter in terms that permit detection of any messages missing from the connection.

Even if no reverse flow of data is required by an application, such protocols require positive acknowledgement of transmitted messages, thus providing a time-dependent integrity check on the connection.

It must be noted that while many interactive applications provide implicit checking for denial of message service attacks because of the command-response nature of the application, general purpose protocols for interactive and other applications cannot rely on such application-dependent characteristics. Moreover, in many instances, the applications program in execution at a service host is unable to predict when a user will make an additional request, especially when that request may be one to abort the current operation. Thus, automatic detection and reporting of denial of message service attacks must be provided.

Countermeasures for accomplishing the fifth and final goal, detection of spurious connection initiation, are largely a function of encryption key distribution. They provide a secure basis for verifying the identities of the processes at each end of the connection and for verifying the time integrity of the connection. Verification of the time integrity of the connection protects against attacks in which recordings of previous legiti-

6 Cipher feedback mode of DES

Stream cipher. The data encryption standard can also be used as part of a key-stream generator. Here, the original data is combined with an equivalent amount of fictional data and normal-sized packets are sent, in which only some bits are part of a real message. Shift registers at both ends contain the same encoding pattern.

TRANSMITTER   RECEIVER

SYNCHRONIZED 64-BIT SHIFT REGISTER INPUTS

KEY — DES (ENCIPHER) — DISCARD — CLEAR TEXT — CIPHER TEXT — DISCARD — DES (ENCIPHER) — KEY — CLEAR TEXT

mate connections allow intruders to mislead or confuse a user, or cause a service host process to perform redundant activities, possibly resulting in errors.

With regard to key distribution, authentication and access control mechanisms are logically and functionally separate, but they are related in that the decisions made by access control mechanisms are based on information supplied by the authentication mechanisms. Both types of mechanisms are, in turn, dependent on communications security measures, since violations of communications security can result in circumvention of the security policies represented by the authentication and access control mechanisms.

Authentication extended
In a security context, the term authentication is often applied to procedures for verifying the claimed identity of an individual, but authentication also can be carried out at the terminal, host, or network level. A number of techniques have been developed for personal authentication, including various password schemes, the use of badges and keys, and physical characteristic measurements such as fingerprints, signatures, and voiceprints.

With the exception of the use of encryption keys for authentication purposes, in a network environment all of these techniques are eventually reduced to the transmission of a stream of bits to the site performing the authentication. Therefore, authentication mechanisms are dependent on communications security measures to prevent the release of authentication information and to maintain the integrity of communications paths after authentication has been performed. The

first of these requirements is met by release of message contents countermeasures while the second, which addresses attacks such as "piggyback" infiltration and "between the lines" entry, is effected by message stream modification countermeasures.

Characterization of authentication techniques according to the lifetime of the information transmitted provides one measure of the damage that may result in the event of exposure of this information. If relatively static authentication information is disclosed, it will enable an intruder to masquerade as an individual for some time. Exposure of more dynamic authentication information may not be usable by an intruder at all. One-time password or encryption key schemes in which the next password or key is transmitted as an epilogue to the authentication procedure are examples of a "chained" form of authentication and do not provide the desired limited-lifetime characteristics. However, these techniques are superior to more static authentication procedures in that they intrinsically prevent spoofing attacks and they alert a user to the disclosure of authentication information by causing the failure of subsequent authentication attempts once the intruder makes use of the exposed authentication information.

Since networks provide convenient access to large numbers of service hosts, users may find it appropriate to have accounts with multiple service hosts. If, for a given user, the same authentication criteria are employed at each host, then subversion of any one of these hosts would permit an intruder to masquerade as the user of all of the other hosts. In the case of dynamic authentication schemes, such as one-time passwords, it could be difficult to maintain synchrony among the corresponding password lists on each of the hosts. As an alternative, the user could employ different authentication information for each host he accesses, but it could prove difficult for a user to maintain all of this information. Moreover, several types authentication techniques do not permit the maintenance of independent authentication information at multiple sites, e.g., fingerprints, voiceprints, and handwriting analysis. If authentication is based on information that is kept secret, as opposed to being physically characteristic of the user, the task of reissuing such information on a periodic basis or in the face of possible disclosure can be complicated when several hosts are involved. If personal authentication is required by the network, independent of authentication requirements of service hosts, then a central authentication service can make life easier even for individuals who access only a single host via the network, since it dispenses with the need for multiple authentications.

Encryption keys constitute an excellent mechanism for personal authentication and the use of a key distribution center can be applied to the problems of managing authentication information as well as encryption keys. A designated, secure, authentication server host can act as a trusted intermediary; carrying out user authentication procedures and forwarding the results to service hosts. It can also generate and distribute keys for establishing connections among terminals and hosts. In this fashion, the problems of proliferation of authentication information and encryption keys can be managed.

Techniques can be employed to minimize the release of authentication information in the advent of subversion of an authentication server. For example, if static passwords are employed, instead of storing the password at the authentication server, the password can be written backwards and this transformation can be stored. This transformation can be applied to a text string submitted as the password during an authentication procedure. If the application of the transformation to the candidate password results in a match with the reversed image of the password under the transformation, the authentication procedure succeeds. In this fashion, subversion of an authentication server would result in release of authentication information only for those users actively engaged in an authentication procedure, since the transformed passwords are useless to an intruder.

Time as a variable
The advent of public-key encryption systems provides a basis for a similar scheme that can be used for time-varying authentication. For example, a user's secret decryption key could be applied to a string consisting of the user's name, the time, and the date. This information could be transmitted along with its enciphered image to the authentication server. The server would apply the public encryption key for that user to the transmitted cleartext, confirming the identity of the user. The authentication server would also check that the time and date included in both the cleartext and ciphertext are approximately current, thus countering

spoofing attacks. This technique does not employ the full "signature" capability of a public-key encryption system, and can be used in environments in which the public-key system is not deemed suitable for communications security purposes.

As an alternative to this approach, an authentication server could store, for each user, the authentication information required by each host accessed by that user. In this context, a user would employ a single means of identifying himself to the authentication server which, in turn, would act as the user's agent in carrying out appropriate authentication procedures. An advantage of this scheme is that it does not require surface hosts to distinguish between connections established using a central authentication server and those in which the user provides the authentication information directly to the host. A user could program different authentication procedures for each host he accesses, and have the authentication server carry out these procedures on his behalf. An authentication server functioning in this fashion appears as a user to each service host and no special provision is needed for users employing this technique as opposed to those who use direct authentication.

Access control
As is the case with personal authentication at the network level, there are various reasons for employing network level access control and several methods for effecting this control. In the simplest case, access control can be used to determine whether or not an individual is allowed to access any of the resources on the network. The granularity of access control exercised at the network level can be refined so that access to individual hosts can be selectively granted or denied to specific users or hosts using a key distribution center to enforce the security policies. Finally, network level access control mechanisms can be extended to include sub-host entities, e.g., processes or files.

Network-level access control mechanisms are appropriate in situations where hosts operate under the auspices of a single authority or where the autonomous authorities controlling individual hosts delegate part of their authority for access control to some trusted intermediary agency.

The concept of jurisdiction arises in discussing centralized key distribution, authentication, and access control. With conventional encryption techniques, interactions between mutually suspicious jurisdictions can be difficult to implement and could require the formation of super-jurisdictions and a jurisdictional hierarchy. The use of public-key distribution or encryption systems provides a means by which these problems can be overcome. The extent to which government regulation affects inter-jurisdictional communications security matters may hinge upon the ability to demonstrate the security of these cryptographic systems.

An expanded version of this article will appear as Chapter 9, "Security in Computer Networks," by Stephen T. Kent, in *Protocols and Techniques for Data Communications Networks*, edited by Frank Kuo, to be published by Prentice Hall in 1979. ∎

Letters to the Editor

Clarification

To the Editor: I have discovered some errors in the published form of my article on network security. The omissions may have resulted from an effort to trim the article to page boundaries, but I hope the material can be presented so that readers will not be misled by the omissions.

In the section on Access Control, a sentence was left out. It should be made clear that network level access control is only providing a database service to the individual hosts since it cannot enforce the security policy within the hosts themselves. Also, the final paragraph of the article should read: "Interjurisdictional interactions are easily implemented so long as the jurisdictions involved are not mutually suspicious. Mutual suspicion complicates matters, requiring a hierarchy of jurisdictions or complex protocol and key distribution arrangements. It seems likely that the hierarchic approach will prove more attractive, but government regulation may influence the choice of configuration or may even prohibit substantial centralization of these functions."

Stephen T. Kent
Bolt, Beranek
and Newman Inc.,
Cambridge, Mass.

Network security in distributed data processing

Hal B. Becker, Honeywell Information Systems, Phoenix, Ariz.

Overview of the various network elements, defined in terms of their security implications, gives users a framework for action

Computer crime, although relatively new in the annals of lawmen, poses a greater problem for operators of the far flung equipment and lines of distributed data processing networks than it did for managers of centralized networks. Security of the systems has become of prime importance as the distribution of the operations has opened up links and increased the difficulty of guarding the many computer and terminal sites.

The untold treasures of data locked in computer memories and the blind (to those who know the key) obedience to orders have proved to be an attractive goal for some unlawful citizens. Consider a typical case: an enterprising young thief managed to gain access to a utility company's computer by buying used telephone equipment, and by retrieving computer listings and operational documents from trash bins. Armed with this simple equipment, he caused several hundred thousand dollars worth of the utility company's equipment to be delivered to him at various addresses. When the delivery arrived, he simply reloaded the equipment onto a legally purchased second-hand company van and drove off. He then sold the equipment—sometimes back to the company from which it was stolen—at an enormous profit.

It was not necessary to gain physical access to either the computer or even to a terminal belonging to the company. The company had sold him the proper access device as scrap and the entry codes and procedures were made available to him through the company's own refuse system.

The ease of access that this young thief enjoyed is not exaggerated and points up the need for security. As data links become more numerous, as in distributed processing networks, and different processing functions are assigned to distant nodes, the security problems intensify. Further examples are cited in the panel: "Security Breaches." However, measures—some easy, some difficult—do exist for providing security to all processors and links in the distributed data processing network.

In centralized configurations and early network implementations, information-, networking-, and database-processing functions were resident in the same computer, usually an information processor. The increasing interference due to competition for a finite set of resources (processor time, memory, etc.), led to an initial separation of function in the middle of the 1960's.

This separation resulted in leaving the information-processing and database-processing functions in the information processor and putting the network processing or data communications function in a separate

1 Separation of functions

Separate processors. *In a distributed data processing network, three basic functions reside in three separate machines. The information processor manipulates data to produce the desired output. The network processor makes sure that the data reaches the proper destination. The database processor stores data for subsequent use.*

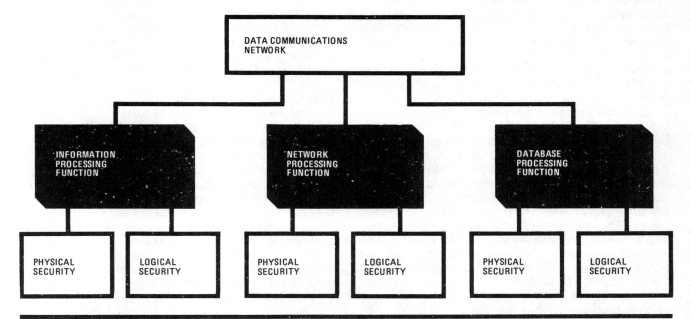

front-end processor. The efficiencies inherent in this approach are attested to by the industry's almost universal adoption of the front-end processor approach to data communications. The separation, also however, changed the security considerations. An additional link was provided which did not previously exist.

The continuing evolution of on-line applications, transaction processing, and other interactive areas has resulted in a greater emphasis and reliance on databases accessible by the data communications network and its users. Predictably, this trend is resulting in increased levels of interference between the information-processing and the database-processing functions which still reside in the information processor.

A second separation of function is about to occur. The database function will be moved from the information processor into a separate database processor. All three of the basic functions—information processing, network processing and database processing—will then reside in separate machines, each optimized for one function. Greatly improved performance will result due to the reduced interference. Security problems, too, can be expected to increase.

The three functions can be defined in terms of their physical and logical function subsets. Physical function subsets consist of the various hardware devices and facilities available to the designers of the network. Logical function subsets consist of software or other stored program logic executed in the various processors. Logical functions control the physical devices of the configuration, and the flow of information within and between the various devices of the network. Figure 1 illustrates the first three levels of a structure that defines data

communications networks in terms of the three basic functions and their physical and logical subsets.

The three basic functions shown in Figure 1 thus become the building blocks for all types of data communications networks, ranging from totally centralized to totally distributed configurations, with many intermediate combinations possible.

In a totally centralized configuration, all three functions—information processing, network processing, and database processing—exist at a single site. This site provides all of the resources required by the terminal users in the surrounding network. In a totally distributed configuration, each of the three functions exists in more than one location.

Intermediate configurations include centralized information processing and database processing with distributed network processing, and centralized database processing with distributed information processing and network processing.

Network relationships

Figure 2 includes the three basic types of nodes which make up all networks.

Source nodes are points at which information enters the network. Source nodes can be such devices as teleprinters and visual display terminals, as well as information processors and network processors.

Destination nodes are points to which information is delivered and leaves the network. Terminals, information processors, and network processors can all act as destination nodes.

Information being routed from its source to its destination can pass through one or more relay nodes. Relay nodes perform two basic functions: to save on line costs and to provide alternate access and/or routing capabilities in networks with high availability requirements. Network processors are active relay nodes. They are program-controlled devices capable of exerting logical control over information passing through them. Passive relay nodes (such as multiplexers and switches) are devices that are not program-controlled and, therefore, can exert little or no logical control over information passing through them.

Figure 3 illustrates a portion of a distributed network. The information processors can come from one or many vendors as long as they work together and can act as both information sources and destinations. Similarly, the terminals clustered around the network processors can be both sources and destinations.

Both the front-end network processors (FNP) and the remote network processors (RNP) can act as information sources, destinations, and relay nodes in the configuration. Since they are program controlled, they are active relay nodes. The frequency-division multiplexer (FDM) is a passive relay node and cannot exert logical control over information flowing through it. The controlling logic for the terminals clustered around the FDM is executed in the remote network processor near the center of the illustration.

As the network becomes more and more distributed security problems change in nature and in difficulty of solution. The remainder of this article discusses distributed-data-processing network security within the framework presented in the first three figures.

Physical and logical security

Network security considerations can be divided into two distinct categories: physical security and logical security. These categories can then be applied to the information processing, network processing, and database processing functions.

Figure 4 indicates the application of physical and logical security to the information and database processing functions. If the entire information processing site is under constant physical surveillance, a first level of security is provided. By limiting physical access through personal recognition and badge or identification card checks, an extra level of security is added. Still greater levels are added by inspecting all personnel for cameras, recording devices, transmitters, receivers, documents carried in and out, and similar measures.

In situations where the processing site is not isolated and where close proximity is easily attained, additional measures may be required. The entire facility, for example, can be placed in a radio-frequency shielded room. This shielding holds in the electrical signals that radiate from operating hardware.

One element of physical security that appears to defy an absolute solution is that of the information that can be carried out of the facility in an employee's head. Stopping someone from memorizing portions of sensitive information can only be achieved by controlling access to the information itself. This leads to a discussion of logical security measures employed within a physically secure processing site.

Logical security measures are those employed to control access to data maintained by the network's information processors. Personnel attempting access can include those authorized for admission to the information processing site and others whose authorization is gained at some remote terminal. Those thus authorized may be further authorized to access either none of the information, or portions of the information, or all of the information. A final class of people includes those who are neither authorized to enter the physically secure facility nor initiate access from a terminal.

Levels of logical security

Several levels of logical security can be used to prevent unauthorized access to information once physical access to the network has been gained. Password sequences of one or more levels can grant or deny further access to the network following the initial connection.

The first level of logical security can simply establish that the user is valid and authorized to connect to the network. A second level can be applied to grant access to such specified dimensions of the network as time-sharing and transaction processing.

Still further levels of clearance can be required for controlling access to the databases maintained by the information processors of the network. Clearance can be assigned on a need-to-know basis.

Additional levels of security within the information processor are attainable through various cryptographic or coding techniques, and secure or privileged software methods.

Figure 4 can also be used to illustrate the application of physical and logical security when dealing with the network processing function. The previous definition of network processing is repeated here to emphasize the separation between the information and network processing functions: network processing is that set of functions necessary for moving the information from the source to the processing site, and on to the intended destination.

The distinction between physical and logical security still exists, but takes a somewhat different form due to the geographic distances between network elements.

In general, maintaining physical surveillance over the entire network is impractical, if not impossible. Exceptions to this include government, military, and other high-security installations.

The next level of organization under the heading of physical security involves the terminals and the communications links. Physical surveillance can usually be maintained over the terminals. This reduces unauthorized access to them and affords some security.

Link surveillance

Physical surveillance of the communications links is the area that presents the greatest difficulty. If the links are contained within the boundaries of the user's property, physical surveillance may be practical. Additional security is provided for such links by burying them in metal conduits in concrete-filled trenches. By doing this, manual access to, and hence tapping, the link is difficult. Additionally, the use of a radio receiver capa-

2 Relationship of network nodes

Nodal composition. *Data entering the network at a source node may originate at any one of three basic devices. When the data is passed to a relay node, it may be manipulated by an active network processor or simply switched by a multiplexer. Destination node devices are the same as source node devices, acting as receptors.*

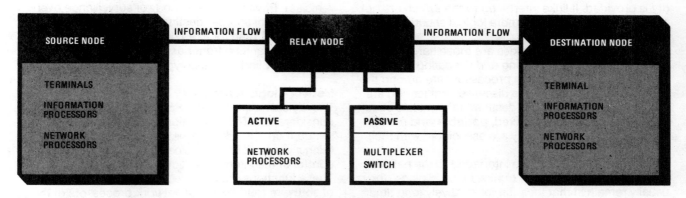

ble of detecting the link's radiated signal becomes difficult, if not impossible.

Commercial network users rely heavily on common carriers for the links that are not contained on their property and, thus, surveillance is usually impossible. For these situations, one or more forms of logical security must be employed.

Security measures applied to the links can vary, depending on a number of factors including: the speed of the link, the coupling and modulation technique used, and whether the link is dedicated or switched.

The logical security techniques for the network processing function are a combination of encryption and access-control procedures at the terminals. Much of the logical security can exist in software modules in network processors. The modules can apply initial tests to requests for access originating from terminals under their control.

While complete clearance for all database activities following access may not be possible at this level, it is possible to screen initial access requests. The security of the software in the network processor itself presents additional problems. Steps must be taken to assure that the software granting or refusing access to terminals cannot be altered.

The security measures provided by the software modules can be static; i.e., they do not change, but remain constant. Other, more complicated, measures involve randomly occurring changes in the procedures that make unauthorized access more difficult.

Network physical security

Figure 5 illustrates the physical functions contained in the network processing hierarchy. These functions form the superset from which the physical configuration for any network is derived. The following paragraphs briefly describe the physical security considerations associated with these functions.

The relay nodes are usually located in places where surveillance and/or controlled access to the site can be maintained. The passive devices (multiplexers) do

not have the secure software problems faced by the active relay nodes (network processors). The growing use of radio links (orbiting satellites and others) presents additional problems, even though physical security can be maintained over the relay node itself. Encryption, scrambling, and other forms of logical security must be applied for these relay nodes.

Coupling devices are those hardware elements used to connect the source/destination devices to the communications lines and trunks of the network. As such, they are usually attached to, or are in close proximity to, the source/destination device itself. The physical security maintained over the source/destination device itself usually can be applied to the coupler.

The distribution function consists of the set of lines and trunks that interconnect the various nodes of the information network. Physical surveillance of the entire configuration is practically impossible for all but the in-plant networks. In-plant is defined as those links that are bounded by public highways and throughfares. This usually places the links on the user's property, where surveillance can be maintained.

Dial or switched links make it impossible to totally prevent unauthorized access attempts. The use of unlisted telephone numbers or private switched facilities provides little security. Eventually, telephone numbers can be determined and methods can be identified that will give access to private switched networks. Various forms of logical security (scrambling, encryption, etc.) are essentially the only security measures available.

Dedicated links provide a slightly higher level of security in that they cannot normally be accessed from a switched link. However, access to utility poles, cables in an underground conduit, and carrier facilities in general is not a difficult task. Higher levels of security for dedicated links must also be obtained through the use of encryption and scrambling techniques.

Reconfiguration switches are frequently used in data communications networks. They can be manual switches requiring an operator to activate them, or they can be under control of an adjacent or distant network processor. Switches are not normally capable of exerting logical control over information flowing through them, and thus do not require any secure software measures. If the switches are configured in locations that are under surveillance, an initial level of security is provided. If links interfaced to the switch are not under surveillance, one or more logical security measures must be employed.

Source/destination devices are those hardware elements capable of initiating and executing access to the network. Information processors are among the source/destination devices discussed earlier and are not covered here. Source/destination terminals occur in three basic categories: fixed, portable, and mobile. Varying degrees of difficulty are associated with their physical security.

Fixed terminals are those interfaced to the network through dedicated lines or trunks. Once in place, they usually remain in that location for relatively long time periods. Surveillance over these fixed terminals is the

Security breaches

These are examples of four basic ways in which the security of data communications networks has been violated in the past.

1. *False disconnect*. A remote terminal user establishes a connection to a central computer port and requests that a particular file be printed out at his location. During the brief period it takes the central processor to retrieve the file, a second terminal is connected to the same port. Then, the port side of the link to the first terminal is disconnected to make room at the port for the link with the other terminal. The first user—unaware of the disconnection—waits for the file to print out while the information is actually being delivered to the second terminal site.

2. *Exploitation*. A remote terminal or computer can use a weakness in the architecture of an operating system to gain unauthorized access to a file's contents. In 1973, a staff group at the Washington, D.C., Naval Research Laboratory used a structural weakness in the operating system of a distant Univac 1107 to gain access to its classified files.

3. *Link failure*. It is possible for critical links in the common carrier network to fail completely. This was the practical result, for example, of the February 1975 fire that destroyed a New York City switching center. Loss of local links to the central office switch frame made network security measures impossible to implement.

4. *Masquerading*. The intruder makes himself and the transactions that he originates appear legitimate to the computer—or the terminals involved. In one instance, an automatic teller machine was ordered from a remote site to discharge several thousand dollars in cash onto the sidewalk, and it did.

Belden Menkus
Consultant and Editor, Computer Security
Bergenfield, N.J.

easiest aspect of physical security to maintain.

Portable terminals are those that access the network through a switched or dial-up interface. Mobile terminals are those that access the network through a radio frequency coupler and link (hard copy teleprinters in vehicles). Physical security and/or surveillance over these types of source/destination devices is obviously more difficult than for fixed devices. Logical security techniques ranging from passwords to cryptography must be applied for these types of terminals.

Network logical security

The logical network functions are the next security consideration. These functions, in various subsets dependent on the individual network, accomplish two things: control of the physical network (Fig. 5); and control of the information flowing through the network. These functions are achieved through the execution of software routines in the network processors of the configuration.

The concept of secure software remains a moving target, and is dependent on a number of considerations. If the network processors are physically secure, one level of security is provided. Access to the operating software modules by way of control panels, supervisory control stations, or remote terminal devices present additional considerations. A network processor capable of software execution with one or more privileged levels provides an additional level of security.

The tables and control fields that are utilized by the protected or privileged software modules must also be

3 Portion of a distributed network

Network interaction. Network processors and multiplexers can come from several different vendors. Their only network requirement is the ability to exchange data.

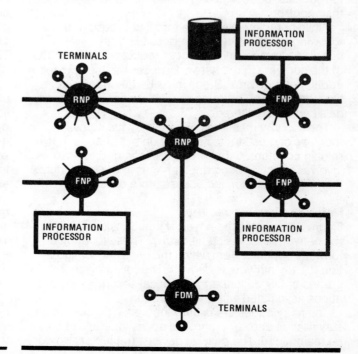

4 Physical and logical security

Security considerations. *Processors must be protected by brains as well as brawn. Allowing the processor to determine if the user is valid is a necessary part of security.*

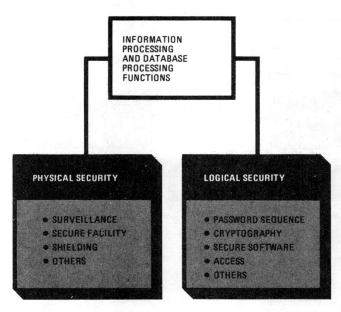

protected. This protection should also include tables in memory and various auxiliary storage media.

The six functions relating to logical security are described briefly in following paragraphs. Those with particular security implications are identified.

The routing function includes those modules required to move incoming information from the source devices through the network to the intended destinations. The lower levels of the routing function include: the addressing codes or techniques employed in the network (implicit, explicit, symbolic, multiple destination, group code, and others), the trunk routing algorithm (implicit, explicit, heuristic, and others), the priority level structure, the security level structure (unclassified, classified, secret, etc.), and similar activities. Secure software procedures should be capable of preventing any unauthorized alteration of the routing tables and/or algorithms that would violate the security level required.

The integrity function consists of three basic components: information integrity, functional integrity, and security itself.

■ Information integrity involves those modules configured to maintain the specified accuracy of the information flow. The techniques employed depend on the physical characteristics of the source/destination devices used. Character parity (odd or even), block check, hash total, cyclic redundancy, and other related techniques are available for use by the information integrity modules.

■ Functional integrity is defined as the ability to detect hardware and software failures occurring in the network. This area should receive appropriately high levels of attention during the design of software for networks

with high security requirements. Any restart/recovery procedures implemented to handle such failures should not be allowed to compromise other security measures.

■ The security within the context of the network structure described above is a relative concept. Security for some classes of networks is limited to establishing the identity of the terminal attempting to access the network. Other networks can require both the identification of the terminal and the human operator, perhaps with a correlation of matching algorithms included. Still others can require the above, and, in addition, extensively structured database access clearance techniques. Several other relative levels exist, up to those military and governmental installations with extremely high security requirements.

The journaling function is the ability to retain, in one or more storage media, copies of information that has passed through the network and was delivered to the intended destinations. The volume of information retained and the time required for retrieval can vary, depending on specific network requirements. Small networks can retain a single, centrally located journal facility, while larger networks can include the journal capability at several locations.

The maintenance of a journal can provide two significant capabilities: the ability to retransmit one or more copies of information previously delivered, and the ability (through analysis of the journal file) to restart and recover from hardware or software failures more efficiently.

This restart/recovery capability is frequently more desirable than having every operator in the network resubmit the entire day's traffic, because it is impossible to determine what was and was not delivered.

The maintenance of such journals presents obvious physical and logical security problems. If the journal media are configured at physically secure locations, logical security measures must be provided to prevent unauthorized access to, and possible alteration of, the journals themselves.

The statistical function involves the collection of a wide variety of statistics concerning the operation of the network itself. These statistics, when compiled into hourly and/or daily reports, are a very valuable technique establishing the performance of a network. In addition to recording the normal traffic flow statistics, it is quite an easy task to record the number of operator errors, unauthorized access attempts, authorized access attempts, authorized accesses at various priority and/or security levels, and other similar security-related statistics.

The hourly and summary statistics and reports can, themselves, require that security measures be applied. It is then necessary to secure the software involved in the statistical modules, and also, to assure that hourly or periodic reports are not routed to unsecure locations or devices.

The utility function is a collection of activities that are not directly related to the main routing, integrity, journaling, and other activities that fall under logical control, but act rather in a supporting role. Code translations, basic format checking (mandatory fields, se-

5 Physical security functions

Weak link. Providing physical security over the entire data communications network presents the most difficult protection problem for the network planner. While relay nodes and source/destination devices can be kept under lock and key, reliance on common carriers for data transfer makes total surveillance of the link impossible.

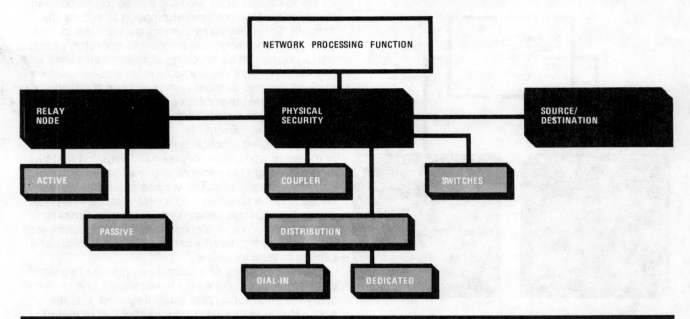

quence numbers, etc.), and destination code validation are examples of utility functions.

Utility functions do not normally fall under the privileged or secure software category. Should any security-sensitive module be required in the utility function, that module—or perhaps all utility modules—can be given appropriate security measures.

The supervisory control function represents perhaps the most security-sensitive aspect of software protection. This is due primarily to the interaction between the network and the personnel designated as supervisory operators.

Small-to-medium scale networks may only require a single supervisory control location, perhaps a single teleprinter. Larger networks can require several supervisory stations, possibly arranged in some hierarchical structure. These structures generally will involve three levels of management.

The first, or master, supervisory level is a single station whose privilege mapping permits it to initiate and execute any supervisory function the network is capable of performing. The intermediate level consists of several supervisory stations—each capable of an individual, possibly unique, subset of the master, supervisory, level functions.

The lowest level is represented by the even smaller subsets that individual terminal privilege mappings permit.

Physical surveillance of all terminals capable of supervisory functions provides an initial level of security. Multiple levels of logical security are needed to assure that only authorized operators are allowed to initiate and execute supervisory functions.

The use of secure software and privileged execution modes within the network processors appears to be mandatory for relatively secure supervisory control.

Proceed with caution

The evolution into the distributed environment creates a question for the user of a centralized network—"Should I convert to a distributed configuration?"

There is no single answer to this question. It can be shown that some users will be best served by a centralized data network. Others, for a variety of reasons, will find centralization difficult, it not impossible, and therefore, must pursue the distributed environment.

Those users following the latter course must do so with an appropriate element of caution. The computer industry, from its inception up until very recently, has pursued a philosophy of centralization. Most, if not all, current hardware and software architectures reflect this trend.

The shift to, or addition of, the distributed philosophy will be a gradual, step-by-step, activity, proceeding only as fast as the exploration of new concepts and technologies will permit. The distributed environment philosophies are not simply a rewrite of the classical centralized concepts.

The security-conscious user is thus provided with an added incentive to explore the security levels provided by the evolving technologies. This article has presented a product-independent frame of reference within which users can: define data networks in terms of basic functions; explore various centralized and/or distributed configurations; and identify the levels of physical and logical security measures required. ∎

Making the digital signature legal — and safeguarded

Stephen M. Lipton and Stephen M. Matyas, IBM Corp.

Basing transmissions on the Data Encryption Standard may be legally valid; more work is needed to reduce the number of signature bits

With the quickened pace of business today, combined with the frequent large distances between the parties concerned, the time required to obtain a signed agreement may undesirably delay a project's inception. Acceptance of an electronic — or digital — signature may remove this legal roadblock. The need, use, and legal significance of one's signature on documents or instruments must be viewed from a perspective embracing several branches of the law, some of which will be discussed later.

All these bodies of law assume, to a degree, a "paper-based" system as the medium for transacting business. However, if such transactions were to be implemented exclusively via an electronic communications system, it would be necessary that the system provide a capability for the transmission of "signed" messages. The term "signed" is used to mean that the recipient could "prove" to an impartial third party (judge or adjudicator) that the content of the message is genuine, and that the message originated with the sender.

Messages are "signed" by appending a special bit-pattern called the "digital signature." The digital signature, in this case, is both message-dependent and originator-dependent.

One possible method for obtaining digital signatures is to make use of a "public-key cryptosystem," a con-

cept invented by Diffie and Hellman (Ref. 1). An approach for implementing public-key cryptosystems has been reported by Rivest, Shamir, and Adleman (Ref. 2), although the cryptographic strength of this scheme has yet to be established.

An altogether different technique, based on conventional cryptographic algorithms such as the Data Encryption Standard (DES—Ref. 3), has been suggested by Leslie Lamport in Reference 1. Since the DES has been adopted as a Federal Standard by the National Bureau of Standards, the underlying principle of DES-based digital signatures has received recognition and acceptance by the relevant scientific community. Therefore, courts would be more likely to accept the validity and uniqueness of such digital signatures.

The authors' analysis shows that protocols for implementing digital signatures will require an initial written agreement (signed in the ordinary sense) between the parties in question. This agreement would contain a complete description of the procedure being agreed to, and, in addition, the bit-patterns which are needed as part of the process of validating signatures. Alternatively, this validation information may be stored in a designated registry.

In summary, the written agreement would provide an independent means for the originator to register his

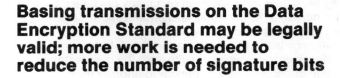

285

non-secret information used in checking signatures, while providing a means for the recipient to be assured of its validity. Hence, with the initial written agreement, it appears that the protocol for digital signatures becomes workable.

Significance of "signature"

The legal significance of one's signature and the use of signed writings bearing such signatures must be viewed from a perspective which encompasses several branches of the law, including, but not limited to: the Statute of Frauds, the Law of Acknowledgements, the Law of Agency, and the Uniform Commercial Code (UCC). In order to appreciate the need for a device or process which may satisfy the requirements of such branches of law in the modern context of electronic or "paperless" signatures, some key areas of the law affecting "signature" must first be considered.

- **Statute of Frauds.** The history of the Statute of Frauds (Ref. 4) commenced in 1677 when "An Act for Prevention of Frauds and Perjuries" was enacted in England. The need for such an act resulted from the peculiar rules of evidence used by English courts during the 17th Century.

For example, two parties—A and B—might enter into an oral agreement for the sale of land. It was pos-

---

See your lawyer first

This is a technical discussion of an approach to solving a legal problem. This article does not constitute advice, and those who intend to implement any of the concepts included herein should first consult their legal counsel.

---

sible for A to sue B and allege that B orally agreed to sell certain land for an X amount (Party A may have never entered into any agreement at all, or the price may have been much greater than X). Under English law, party B could not testify in his own behalf, and lawsuits of this kind were frequently tried with professional witnesses, testimony of friends of the parties, and the like.

Since perjury was commonplace, the defendant in such cases was at a distinct disadvantage. Suppose that party C testified—on behalf of A—that he heard B agree to the sale. How could B bring forth a witness D who could testify that he didn't hear the agreement? The difficulty of B is obvious—that of proving a negative condition.

The difficulty was finally overcome by requiring written evidence that contracts were actually entered into. Specifically, the Statute of Frauds was designed to prevent fraud by excluding from consideration by the courts legal actions on certain contracts, unless there were written evidence of the agreement signed by the party to be charged or his duly authorized agent.

- **Law of Acknowledgements.** There are certain classes of writings which require acknowledgement or proof that the person who signs a document is in fact that person, and that he or she signed the document on the stated date. This acknowledgement or proof is necessary in order that the party who signed the writing may not later claim that his signature is not genuine and thus assert forgery as a defense.

Moreover, there are certain classes of transactions which require that the signature be witnessed by one or more persons. Such classes of transactions may vary according to the local law of the jurisdiction in which the document was executed.

Acknowledgement or proof of signature upon a legal document or instrument may normally be made before a judge, an official examiner of title, an official referee, or a notary public. Essentially, the form of an acknowledgement consists of the following:

On the _____ day of _____, 19____, before me personally appeared [*John Doe*] to me known and known by me to be [*John Doe*] who placed his hand upon said document in my presence and acknowledged same to be his signature.

_____
Notary Public

Such acknowledgements together with the signed document are usually recorded in an official registry, as an office of the county clerk or secretary of state.

- **Law of Agency.** The principles of agency law (Ref. 4) are essential for the conduct of business transactions. A corporation, as a legal entity, can function only through its agents. The law of partnership is, to a large degree, a special application of agency principles to that particular form of business organization. "Agency" may be defined as follows:

Agency is the fiduciary relation [involving a confidence or trust] which results from the manifestation of consent by one person to another that the other shall act on his behalf and subject to his control, and consent by the other so to act. [Restatement of the Law, Agency (2d), p. 7, Sec. 1(1)]

As a general rule, no particular formalities are required to create an agency relationship. The appointment may be either written or oral, and the relationship may be either expressed or implied. There are two situations in which formalities are required: (1) "power of attorney," where a formal acknowledged instrument is used for conferring authority upon the agent; and (2) in a few states where it is required that the act which confers authority to perform a certain act must possess the same formalities as the act to be performed. For example, authority to sign a contract which is required to be in writing must itself be granted by a written instrument.

Generally, the law of agency is applicable in the areas of contracts or commercial paper. A principal—the person from whom an agent's authority derives—is bound by the duly authorized acts of his agent. However, if the agent does not possess the requisite authority (express, implied, or apparent), the principal in most instances will not be bound. An agent who fails to bind his principal to an agreement executed by the agent because of the agent's failure to name the principal, or due to lack of the agent's authority, will usually be

personally liable to third parties. Thus, the correct way for an agent to execute a contract or instrument is to affix the name of his principal followed by his own signature and the capacity in which it is made:

"P" Principal, by "A", as Agent

■ **Uniform Commercial Code.** The Uniform Commercial Code (UCC—Ref. 5) is a comprehensive modernization and compilation of the various statutes relating to commercial transactions. Its primary objective is to provide uniformity of commercial law throughout American jurisdictions (it has been adopted in all states except Louisiana). The present articles relating to commercial paper, banking transactions, and investment securities are "paper-based."

To accommodate electronic funds transfer systems, a special committee was formed to prepare amendments or supplements to these articles. Although the principles governing the transfer of "paper-based" stocks and bonds (see Article 8 of Reference 5, for example) can generally be made applicable to the "paperless" variety, many technical and mechanical changes are needed to apply those principles to certificateless securities.

According to the current (1972) version of the UCC,
"Signed" includes any symbol executed or adopted by a party with present intention to authenticate a writing. [UCC: Sec. 1-201 (39)]
and, in the case of commercial paper,
A signature is made by use of any name, including any trade or assumed name, upon an instrument, or by any word or mark used in lieu of a written signature. [UCC: Sec. 3-401 (2)]

The inclusion of the term "authenticate" within the definition of "signed" is to clearly indicate that, as the term is used in the UCC, a complete handwritten signature is not necessary. This authentication may be printed, typed, stamped, or written; it may be initials or thumbprint. It may be on any part of the document, and in certain cases may be found in a billhead or letterhead. No catalog of possible authentications can be complete, and courts must use common sense and commercial experience in passing upon such matters. The question is always whether the symbol was executed or adopted by the party with the intention at that time to authenticate the writing.

A signature may be made by an agent or other representative, and his authority to make such signature may be established according to the Law of Agency. No particular form of appointment is necessary to establish such authority. However, such a signature may be unauthorized if made by an agent who exceeds his actual or apparent authority. An "unauthorized" signature means one made without actual, implied, or apparent authority, and includes those made by forgers, impostors, and fictitious payees.

The law of commercial paper also recognizes the principle that the drawer—the one who creates a negotiable instrument (a draft, check, note, or certificate of deposit)—has voluntarily entered into relationships beyond his control with subsequent holders of the instrument. The law imposes the responsibility upon the drawer to assure that his own negligence does not contribute to the possibility of material alteration of the instrument later in the chain of transfer.

Contributory negligence

Any person who, by his own negligence, substantially contributes to a material alteration of the instrument, or to the making of an unauthorized signature, is precluded from asserting the defense of alteration or of lack of authority against anyone who has accepted the instrument in accordance with reasonable commercial standards. An example of such negligence is the situation where space is left in the body of the instrument, such as $ 500, allowing the value to be changed to $2,500, or allowing the words " five hundred" to be changed to "twenty-five hundred." It also covers the most obvious case where a drawer makes use of a signature stamp or other automatic signing device and is negligent in controlling access to it.

In banking transactions, verification of signatures is a necessary part of the procedure known as the "process of posting." Completion of this procedure is one of the measuring points in determining where an item is "finally paid" in favor of an innocent holder. Posting involves two basic elements: (1) a decision to pay; and (2) some recording of the payment. In certain instances, the recording may actually precede the decision to pay. That is, provisional debits may be entered, and the decision on the authenticity of the signature may be made at a later time.

As incorporated in the UCC, the concept of finality of payment [Sec. 3-418] states that a drawee (the person on whom a bill of exchange is drawn) cannot recover funds paid to a bona fide holder of a draft or check bearing a forged signature of the drawer (one who draws a bill of exchange, or order for payment), and is known as the rule of *Price v. Neal* [3 Burr. 1354 (1762)]. The rule, as enunciated by Lord Mansfield in 1762, imposed upon the drawee the duty to be satisfied that "the bill drawn upon him was in the drawer's hand" [*Price v. Neal*, 3 Burr. 1354, at 1357] before he accepted or paid it, but that it was not the duty of the good-faith holder to inquire into it.

Many banks today rarely review the signature on a small check for its authenticity. Only in cases of stop payment orders and reports of lost or stolen checks do banks interrupt their otherwise mechanized routines involving such instruments. Generally speaking, losses incurred as a result of forged drawers' signatures are small enough to be absorbed as a cost of operation.

Obtaining digital signatures

In a data communications system, an originator, A, may transmit "signed" messages to a recipient, B, under a defined protocol which requires that certain information be held by both parties. The originator, A, must have information that allows him to generate a digital signature appended to a message to be transmitted to B. The recipient, B, must have information in advance that allows him to validate the digital signature as transmitted by A. Of course, the procedure could be extended to permit two-way communication.

If the originator is concerned that the recipient may later disavow certain messages, he can require that messages be certified. Certification means that if A sends message M to B, then B must send the "signed" message, "B received M from A," back to A. The message M would be repeated in its entirety.

In a public-key cryptosystem (Ref. 1), user A has a non-secret—or public—enciphering transformation (or key), denoted by E_A, and a secret—or private—deciphering transformation, denoted by D_A. When the system possesses a capability for "signed" messages, E_A and D_A are such that,

$$D_A[E_A(M)] = E_A[D_A(M)] = M$$

for any message M. That is, encipherment followed by decipherment is the same as decipherment followed by encipherment. Decipherment/encipherment does not depend on one preceding the other, because the operation is performed on the bits regardless of whether they are plaintext or ciphertext. Both E_A and D_A are efficiently computable (created together) by user A. However, the system is such that the work factor (time,

effort, and resources) to compute D_A from E_A is too great. That is, as a practical matter, given E_A, there is no efficient way of deriving D_A.

Since the process of encipherment or decipherment can be thought of as merely an operation performed upon a string of binary digits, a "signed" message M (treated as a string of bits) can be sent from A to B by deciphering first under D_A (known only to party A) and enciphering next under E_B (non-secret—available to party A, B, and others). The resulting quantity $E_B[D_A(M)]$ is then sent to B, where it is recovered by reversing the process:

$$D_B[E_B(D_A(M))] = D_A(M)$$

$$E_A[D_A(M)] = M$$

That is, party A operates on the message with both A's secret deciphering algorithm (D_A) and B's public enciphering algorithm (E_B). When B receives the result, B operates on it with B's secret deciphering algorithm (D_B), "canceling" E_B. Next, B operates with A's public enciphering algorithm (E_A), "canceling" D_A and recovering the original message, M.

Once the content of M has been verified, the quantity $D_A(M)$ can be used as proof that message M originated with A. Only A could have produced this quantity in the first place, since only A possesses the secret deciphering algorithm, D_A.

A different approach, based upon conventional cryptographic algorithms such as the DES, makes use of a digital signature which is composed of a list of cryptographic keys.

For purposes of notation, let $E_K(X) = Y$ represent the encipherment of 64-bit plaintext X by 56-bit key K. Let $D_K(Y) = X$ represent the decipherment of 64-bit ciphertext Y by 56-bit key K. Unlike the public-key cryptosystem, with the DES, D_K is easily computed from E_K, and vice versa.

The idea is that when the originator wishes to send an n-bit message—whether clear or enciphered—he generates 2n, randomly selected, 56-bit cryptographic keys:

$$k_1, K_1, k_2, K_2, ..., k_n, K_n$$

which are kept secret by the originator. The recipient is given, in advance, two non-secret sets of corresponding 64-bit validation quantities. These quantities must be recorded by the originator in advance both in a prior written agreement with B and others, and in a designated registry. These quantities are:

$$u_1, U_1, u_2, U_2, ..., u_n, U_n$$

and

$$E_{k1}(u_1), E_{K1}(U_1), ..., E_{kn}(u_n), E_{Kn}(U_n)$$

Later, when message M is sent, the digital signature is generated by selecting k_1 or K_1 depending on whether the first bit of M is 0 or 1, respectively; selecting k_2 or K_2 depending on whether the second bit of M is 0 or 1, respectively; and so forth.

The recipient validates this digital signature by assuring that the first 56-bit key in the signature will enci-

1 "Signing" the message

Verifying the signature. *Assuming a 1-bit message, if the bit is 0, S is transmitted as key k_1. The recipient enciphers u_1 with S, and compares the result with $E_{k1}(u_1)$ for verification. If, however, the message bit is 1, S is sent as K_1. In this instance, the recipient enciphers U_1 with S, and then determines if the result is equivalent to $E_{K1}(U_1)$.*

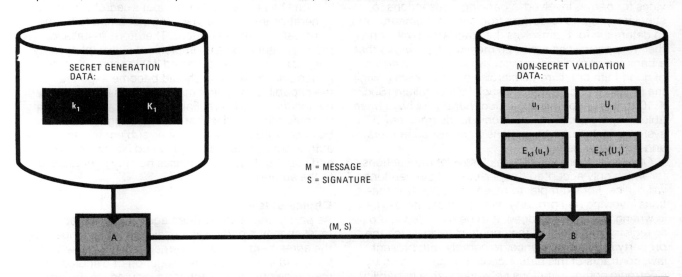

pher validation quantity u_1 into $E_{k1}(u_1)$ if the first bit of M is a 0, or that it will encipher U_1 into $E_{K1}(U_1)$ if the first bit of M is a 1; the second 56-bit key in the signature will encipher validation quantity u_2 into $E_{k2}(u_2)$ if the second bit of M is a 0, or that it will encipher U_2 into $E_{K2}(U_2)$ if the second bit of M is a 1; and so forth.

As shown in Figure 1, for a theoretical 1-bit message, if the bit is 0, the signature S is transmitted as cryptographic key k_1. The recipient enciphers u_1 with S, and compares the result with $E_{k1}(u_1)$. S must be equal to k_1 for the test to succeed. If the test succeeds, both the message and signature are accepted. Otherwise, they are rejected. On the other hand, if the message bit is 1, $S = K_1$, and the recipient enciphers U_1 with S. The result is compared with $E_{K1}(U_1)$ for acceptance of the message and signature.

When the DES algorithm is employed, this approach results in a 56-fold data expansion—56 signature bits for each message bit. (Although the DES requires 64-bit keys to be specified, only 56 of these bits are actually key bits; the other eight bits are used for parity checking, if desired). However, if compression techniques are used, it is possible to reduce the overall number of 56-bit keys that comprise the signature (Ref. 1). Such techniques will not be discussed in this article.

Legalizing digital signatures

In the absence of an omnibus statute governing "paperless" commercial transactions via an electronic communications network, parties are free to enter into their own agreements. However, if disagreements later arise, the party seeking to enforce the contract will prevail only if the agreement complied with certain basic legal requirements. These basic legal requirements may include the statutes of frauds (as imposed by the UCC and/or local law), acknowledgements,

recording, and reasonableness. While modern statutes of frauds require some writing which indicates that a contract for sale has been made between the parties at a defined or stated price, that it reasonably defines the subject matter, and that it is "signed" by either the party against whom enforcement is sought or by his duly authorized agent, we have seen that the requirement of "signed" may be satisfied by something less than a formal handwritten signature. However, a mere pattern of bits, whether in the clear or in encrypted form, would not—as a practical matter—serve as the required symbol in lieu of a handwritten signature, even though executed or adopted by a party with the intention at that time to authenticate a writing. This is because a pattern of bits which is used as a "signature" may be altogether too easily manipulated or forged, and is not part of, or annexed to, a tangible writing. Moreover, unless the pattern of bits were predefined to have a particular meaning to the party receiving it, or unless an agreed-upon code form were adopted by the parties, it would be utterly without meaning.

Therefore, it seems doubtful that, by itself, a special pattern of bits transmitted together with a message and subsequently recorded on some machine-readable media would satisfy the necessary legal requirements of "signature." On the other hand, when an initial written agreement, signed in the ordinary sense, is entered into by the parties in question, it appears that the opposite is true—the legal requirements of "signature" can be satisfied. The initial written agreement, in this case, defines the means and procedures whereby the parties would conduct a series of future transactions, together with an agreed means and procedure for recording the elements of such transactions.

The Universal Commercial Code specifically authorizes parties to vary the provisions of the Code by agreement, except as otherwise stated, and provided that the obligations of good faith, diligence, reasonableness, and care as prescribed by the Code may not be disclaimed [Sec. 1-102-(3)]. The UCC further provides for parties involved in banking transactions to stipulate or agree to deviate from its requirements, and to determine for themselves the standards by which their responsibilities are to be measured, provided that a bank may not disclaim responsibility for its own lack of good faith or failure to exercise ordinary care or limit the measure of damages for such lack or failure [Sec. 4-103]. It is under this exception that banks have been able to operate current electronic funds transfer (EFT) systems, including transactions with their customers and with other banks.

Of course, there are certain classes of transactions for which only accepted "paper-based" conventions will suffice. For example, to be enforceable, transactions involving real property must (in most states) be in writing, be acknowledged, and be recorded in a public registry (the office of the county clerk in which the property is located). Hence, to comply with present law, contracts of this nature could not be handled by electronic communications networks with a capability for digital signatures.

Initial written agreement

With each of the methods for obtaining digital signatures previously described, each party possesses certain secret (or private) information used in generating his own signature, and certain non-secret (or public) information used in checking or validating the signatures of others. Figure 2 depicts the general concept of digital signatures as made feasible through the incorporation of an initial written agreement.

For this protocol to be workable, however, there must be some mechanism for each party to independently authenticate the non-secret signature validation information which he holds. One possible method would be for each party to record his own signature validation information at some agreed-upon registry with recognized and accepted integrity, such as an office of the county clerk or the office of a secretary of state. Another possibility is to include this information within the initial written agreement itself, which was shown to be necessary in order to comply with the underlying legal requirements for conducting "signed" transactions via an electronic network. Recall that in a public-key cryptosystem, the private deciphering algorithm (D_A) cannot be efficiently derived from the public enciphering algorithm (E_A). Likewise, in a DES-based protocol, the private signature keys cannot be efficiently derived from the corresponding public validation quantities.

As to the question of whether or not a person who transmits a message signed with an electronic digital signature is in fact authorized, the procedures necessarily imply that only an authorized agent would have access to the secret information needed to generate the signature. Hence, when the secret information used in generating signatures is stored within a computing system, the burden is upon installation management to assure that this information is kept secret, and that an adequate access control mechanism is in place so that signatures can be created only by authorized users (persons, programs, and the like).

If one has access to a principal's secret signature generation information, he will be deemed to be the principal's authorized agent. Therefore, installation management must also implement sufficient security controls in order to be alerted if this secret signature generation information should become exposed, or if the capability to "sign" messages has been obtained by unauthorized users. Failure of one of the principals to notify other parties that his digital signatures have been compromised and may be subject to use by unauthorized agents may be deemed his own negligence, and might defeat any defenses he may later raise as to the authority of his agents.

Choice of law

As part of their initial written agreement, the parties must specify a particular jurisdiction under whose laws the agreement is to be governed (such as New York law), and the forum for the litigation of disputes which may arise out of transactions executed via the electronic communications system. Where the parties agree to communicate via a common network, and the information needed to validate signatures has been recorded or registered, the jurisdiction wherein such registry is located would be the reasonable and logical choice. Both interstate and international transactions may be accommodated in this manner.

The statute of limitations is a law that defines the period of time within which a lawsuit must be commenced from the time a cause of action accrues. In disputes involving contracts, the period in most states is six years. A cause of action upon a contract may accrue at the time the original written agreement was entered into, or at some time thereafter, when a "signed" message is transmitted. It would appear necessary, therefore, that both parties to a transaction (originator and recipient) retain all data relating to their initial written agreement and to each subsequent "signed" message for at least the period of the applicable statute of limitations.

Regardless of the protocol for implementing electronic digital signatures, the claim is made that if the protocol is implemented as intended, then one can be assured that (1) the sender is not able to later disavow messages as his own, that (2) the recipient is not able to forge messages or signatures, and that (3) both the sender and recipient are certain that the identity of the originator, the timeliness, and the true content of messages can be "proved" before an adjudicator. As a consequence, the following may be said about the judicial acceptance of the electronic digital signature.

The parties may agree or stipulate as part of their initial written agreement that they will be bound by their digital signatures, agree to submit all disputes to an arbiter, and that the concept of digital signatures is cryptographically sound. However, this agreement will not eliminate the possibility of one of the parties later raising the claim that the indicated result lacks validity, that he did not understand the underlying scientific principle (not an unreasonable assertion), or that he was forced to sign the stipulation as a condition of his transacting business with the other party. As a practical matter, therefore, it is prudent to assume that such disputes will inevitably arise.

While various techniques exist for proving the validity of classical signatures (ranging from expert handwriting analysis to the unique properties of handwritten signature acceleration patterns), the resolution of disputes over digital signatures will be based on validation quantities, the cryptographic strength of the algorithms used in the generation of signatures, and the like. Thus, as part of the process of judicial acceptance, the courts must initially pass upon the question of the soundness of the underlying cryptographic technique.

All scientific aids and devices go through experimental and testing phases. During these phases there may be considerable scientific controversy over the validity of the technique, aid, or device. During this period of controversy, there is the danger that a trial of a legal dispute between the parties may result in the trial of the validity of the new scientific technique, rather than a trial of the issues involved in the case. "It is not for the law to experiment but of science to do so." [*State v. Cary,* 99 N.J. Sup. 323, 239 A.2d 680, aff'd, 56 N.J. 16, 264 A.2d 209 (1970)]

When scientific aids to the discovery of truth receive general recognition within the relevant scientific community as to their accuracy, courts will not hesitate to take judicial notice of such fact and admit evidence obtained through their use. "Judicial notice" means that the underlying scientific principle upon which the new device or process is based need not be proved each time the results of the device or process are introduced into evidence.

Judicial notice recognized

As an example of judicial notice, each time a police officer testifies that according to the output display of his radar device the defendant was speeding, he need not present expert witnesses to testify to the scientific foundation of radar — that the radar transmitter and receiver can measure the velocity of a moving target based upon the Doppler effect of reflected waves. Radar has now become generally accepted as a means of measuring vehicle speed. All the officer must prove is that, on the particular occasion in question, his particular radar unit was properly set up, calibrated, and operated. Examples of other scientific principles that have been reduced to practice and are now judicially noticed include the unique properties of fingerprints and ballistics comparisons (Ref. 6).

It would be preferable, therefore, for the digital signature to be based upon the National Bureau of Standards Data Encryption Standard — the DES algorithm. The fact that the National Bureau of Standards has

2 The digital signature concept

Agreeing to the method. *Once an initial written agreement is achieved between parties A and B, the digital signature concept becomes feasible. Adjudication proce-* *dures are specified as part of the agreement, to settle any disputes which may arise out of transactions executed via the connecting electronic communications system.*

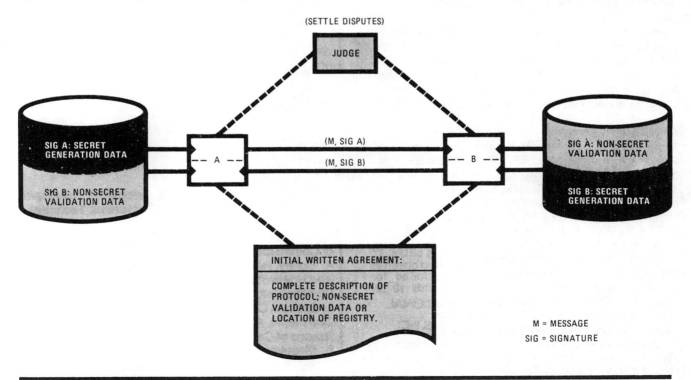

(SETTLE DISPUTES)

JUDGE

SIG A: SECRET GENERATION DATA

SIG B: NON-SECRET VALIDATION DATA

(M, SIG A)

(M, SIG B)

A

B

SIG A: NON-SECRET VALIDATION DATA

SIG B: SECRET GENERATION DATA

INITIAL WRITTEN AGREEMENT:

COMPLETE DESCRIPTION OF PROTOCOL; NON-SECRET VALIDATION DATA OR LOCATION OF REGISTRY.

M = MESSAGE
SIG = SIGNATURE

accepted the DES would, in all likelihood, satisfy the criteria for judicial acceptance of the validity of the underlying scientific principle of digital signatures.

To review the areas covered, parties may enter into contracts or conduct business in any manner they choose. They do so, however, at their peril. Unless certain legal requirements have been complied with, such contracts—while valid—may not be enforceable against a party who attempts to avoid performance.

By entering into a signed written agreement to conduct future transactions according to a predefined procedure involving a digital electronic network, parties to commercial transactions may be assured that (1) the sender is not able to later disavow messages on his own, that (2) the recipient is not able to forge messages or signatures, and that (3) both the sender and recipient are certain that the identity of the originator, the timeliness, and the true content of messages can be "proved" before an adjudicator.

In order that the protocol for digital signatures be workable, each party must be able to independently authenticate the non-secret (public) information which is used to validate the signatures of other parties. This procedure may be accomplished by recording such signature validation information in a designated registry or within the initial written agreement itself. This written agreement may then be recorded in a designated registry. In the event of a dispute, it is assumed that the adjudicator can validate the content of a message and its digital signature using a procedure similar to that used by the recipients.

Each party who enters into an agreement for future "signed" transactions must have sufficient security controls in place to protect his secret signature generation information. If one has access to a principal's secret signature generation information, he will be deemed to be his authorized agent.

Since the DES has been accepted as a Federal Standard by the National Bureau of Standards, the validity of the underlying principle of DES-based signatures has been recognized by the relevant scientific community. For this reason, the courts would be more likely to accept the validity of such digital signatures. ∎

References

1. Diffie, W. and Hellman, M.E., *New Directions in Cryptography,* IEEE Transactions on Information Theory, Nov. 1976
2. Rivest, R.L., Shamir, A., and Adleman, L., *On Digital Signatures and Public-Key Cryptosystems,* Technical Memo 82, MIT Lab. for Computer Science, April 1977.
3. FIPS PUB 46, *Data Encryption Standard,* U.S. Dept. of Commerce/NBS, Jan. 15, 1977.
4. Corley, Robert N. and Robert, William J., *Dillavou and Howard's Principles of Business Law,* 9th ed., Prentice Hall, Inc., 1971.
5. Uniform Commercial Code, *1972 Official Text with Comments,* American Law Institute and National Conference of Commission on Uniform State Laws.
6. Maguire, J. M. and Chadborne, J. H., *Evidence— Cases and Materials,* 6th ed., Foundation Press, Inc., Mineola, N. Y., 1973.

Personal identification devices help to keep networks safe

Paul Meissner, National Bureau of Standards, Gaithersburg, Md.

Hardware that is a substitute for human checkpoints is able to measure personal characteristics and determine identity of users

The numbers of people who have legitimate access to data networks is causing widespread concern over the need to verify their identities, so as to avoid the possibility of others, with no right to be there, making fraudulent or damaging use of the networks.

This problem is becoming especially acute as smaller offices go on line, because the elaborate physical security measures practical for a large central computer site may not be feasible for a local office with a single terminal. And with electronic funds transfer, point-of-sale entry, and credit verification systems entering widespread use, the need for identification devices becomes even more urgent, because the general public has direct access to terminals.

This demand for security has produced a variety of protective devices that check the identity of a person at the terminal before allowing that person to use the network. There are three ways to verify an identity: special information such as a password, the persons' birth place, mother's name, and so forth; a physical item such as a key or an identification card; and personal characteristics such as handwriting, fingerprints, finger lengths, or voice patterns.

The problem with using special information is that anything known to one person may become known to another, while a key or other physical item may be

stolen or duplicated. A personal characteristic, however, can only be presented by its owner. Electronic devices that can identify physical characteristics are being developed, along with associated communications techniques. Only a few such devices have reached the market so far, but their number and use will undoubtedly increase. (A list of some of these products appears in the panel on page 69—Editor.)

A device for the verification of a person's identity compares a measured set of electronic data representing a characteristic of someone claiming to be authorized to use the system, with a set of stored data taken from the authorized person. However, it is sometimes most difficult, when working with body measurements and other human processes, such as speech or writing, to establish accurate reference points and obtain repeatable registration for the measurement and matching of patterns.

Matching fingerprints is a useful technique which can be performed either entirely at the local site, or by reading the prints locally and making the comparison by means of computer at a remote site. No inking of fingers is called for; they are electronically scanned either through a lighted prism or by the reading of a sensitized card on which they have been placed.

In a self-contained system, the image is compared

with one stored on another card or on microfilm, to produce a signal showing the degree of similarity between the two prints. If the similarity is acceptable, the person is cleared. Acceptance or rejection by most identification devices may be signaled by a light or by a readout on a video display terminal. A positive signal may also give access to the network, and can be used besides to release electronically controlled locks.

Remote comparison

A more complex verification method requires transmission of fingerprint signals to a remote computer, either the host itself or a computer at the network control center. This does away with storing the file of prints locally, and so reduces the chance of an intruder gaining access by tampering with the local device. And to keep the data transmission short, only a number of distinctive fingerprint features, called "minutiae", are sent. These features may include ridge endings, branches, or breaks on the fingerprints.

In this method, the user first enters his identity number on a keyboard. This number, along with data representing the minutiae from one fingerprint, is sent to the computer in a combined message a few dozen characters long. The computer calls up its own record of the minutiae and compares the two. If the first test fails, other fingers may be tried, which means that the computer must have several sets of minutiae stored for each authorized user. A legitimate user might be rejected once or twice because of an injury to a finger, or poor positioning of the finger during the test. The computer programs that match the images can take into account a small amount of misalignment, and they are being refined to improve their effectiveness. In one

of these systems, scanning and matching a print takes less than two seconds, and up to 16 terminals may be connected to the verifying computer.

The shapes of hands have been found to present enough variation to provide a basis for checking their owners. The shapes are determined by measuring the lengths of the fingers. In one device, all four fingers of one hand are laid on a surface which has grooves to guide the fingers to the right places. The hand is then illuminated from above and a mechanism under the surface scans it to measure the fingers. Other details can also be checked, such as the translucent portions of the webs between the fingers or the width of the hand. The process takes less than a second.

There is one type of hand-measuring device, however, that does not require communications with another site. The reference profile is stored in scrambled form on a magnetic stripe card carried by the person seeking access, who puts this card in a slot and then places the hand on the scanning surface. The data from the card is unscrambled and compared with the scanner output, and the person seeking access is either accepted or rejected.

Another device transmits the finger measurements to a remote computer where they are compared with appropriate data in a file. In this case the person's identity may be entered by a keyboard, or with a conventional magnetic identification card. The communications requirements of finger measuring devices tend to be modest; the output of one such device is only 13 characters long, and the data representing the measurements is transmitted to the computer at 150 b/s.

Signature verification

Because it may be possible to forge signatures closely enough to pass a machine's inspection, a "dynamic" method of signature verification has been developed which measures such things as the movement of the pen, its force on a pad when a person signs, or both (Fig. 1). These combinations are unique for each person and virtually impossible for a potential forger to detect by inspecting the signature. Sensors, either in the pen or the writing tablet, measure pressures, distances, speed, and even the acceleration and deceleration of the pen.

Writing a signature usually takes four or five seconds. A pen verification device takes this amount of time and a few seconds more to isolate signals representing the signature itself from those that occur, for instance, when the stylus is picked up or put down. Assume that the output signal is sampled 60 times a second and that 10-bit samples are measured in each of three axes. This would produce a data rate of 1,800 b/s, which can easily be transmitted over a voice-grade link.

The signals representing the signature go to a computer, where they are analyzed and a set of characteristics extracted, which are in turn compared with a profile retrieved from storage by the computer. A typical reference file might require only about 300 bits, as against the much larger number derived from the original signature (about 9,000 bits in the example above). The length of the transmissions can be greatly reduced if a microprocessor at the local site is used to compress the data by deriving from it only the most significant characteristics, which are then transmitted.

Image comparisons

There are, of course, devices that simply compare signature images. One such system stores the signature in scrambled form, which can only be deciphered by a special reading device. These systems, however, may be more easily fooled than the dynamic signature readers—those measuring the actual signing process—that have already been described.

One problem with all types of signature verifiers is that many people have more than one way of signing

1 Penmanship. *The Stanford Research Institute signature verifier resolves pressures and displacements into* 20 *characteristics represented by 200 bits of data.*

Personal identification hardware

Fingerscan system scans and matches fingerprints. A central processor can accommodate 16 Fingerscan terminals, expandable to 64. Price range $50,000 to $80,000, plus about $4,500 for each terminal.
Calspan Technology Products, P. O. Box 235, 4455 Genesee St., Buffalo 14221

Identimat hand geometry system can operate as stand-alone device with magnetic-stripe card, or in connection with a user's central computer. Hand geometry reader costs about $5,000; card writer about $5,500.
Identimat Corp., 135 West 50th St., New York City 10020

Signature verification pen, undergoing field trials, measures accelerations and pressures. The device uses a time-shared medium-scale computer, but can be adapted to use a dedicated minicomputer.
IBM Corp., Thomas J. Watson Research Center, P.O. Box 218, Yorktown Heights, N.Y. 10598

Direct fingerprint reader.
Rockwell International Corp., Identification Systems, 3370 Miraloma Ave., Anaheim, Calif. 92803

Signature verification pen and platen (under development). The device uses piezoelectric sensors to measure forces on pen's tip in two axes, as well as pressure perpendicular to the platen.
Sandia Laboratories, Division S133, P.O. Box 5800, Albuquerque, N.M. 87150

Signature verification pen is being designed for production. Pressure is measured in three axes. The device can also be used for data entry of hand-printed characters. Development by Stanford Research Institute, Menlo Park, Calif.
To be manufactured by Xebec Systems Inc., 566 San Xavier Ave., Sunnyvale, Calif. 94086.

Voice authentication system based on high-fidelity speech input and with dedicated minicomputer for processing. A developmental prototype has been used extensively in operational environment. Total voice system for speaker-independent data entry with voice authentication also under development.
Texas Instruments Inc., Central Research Laboratories, Dallas 75222

Signac signature verification system uses an instrumented pen or tablet and measures pressure either along the axis of the pen or perpendicular to the tablet. It uses a dedicated minicomputer, which can also handle other security functions. A microprocessor version is under development.
Marketed by Sentracon Systems, 80 Wilson Way, Westwood, Mass. 02090

2 Preferred performance

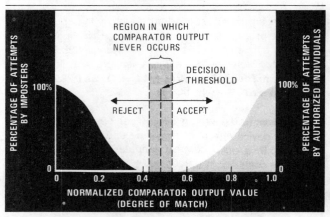

Best results. *A deadband should separate the curve on the left from that on the right, since the device should not accept imposters nor reject authorized people.*

3 Practical results

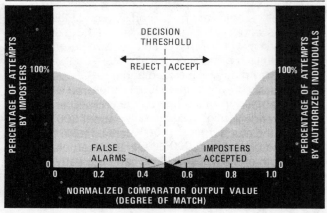

Practical devices. *Some units cannot differentiate exactly between imposters who closely match data in the file, and authentic operators with changeable traits.*

their names. For this purpose, of course, they must sign consistently. An allowance can be made for those whose signatures have excessive variability by broadening the tolerance of the matching process.

An interesting potential application of the signature verification pen is that it can also be used for data entry by means of hand-printed characters. The user first goes through a training routine, in which each character is printed several times to condition the computer to recognize patterns of printing. This process provides the added security of identity verification all the time that data is being entered into the network.

Voice recognition

A computer can analyze digitized voice signals accurately enough to distinguish one voice from another, and to verify a speaker's identity. One such computerized voice verification system is first trained with a vocabulary of selected one-syllable words having prominent vowel sounds, which are the easiest sounds to compare accurately. The person seeking access to the system enters a claimed identity by keyboard to retrieve a reference profile. The system then generates a phrase from the vocabulary, typically four words drawn at random, and presents this phrase to the person over a loudspeaker using prerecorded or synthesized speech. The person repeats the phrase into a high-quality microphone (50 Hz to 15 kHz bandwidth) which transmits the signals to digitizing circuits and then to the computer.

Next, the computer locates specific parts of the speech waveform and matches them against the appropriate reference profiles. If they match within a specified tolerance, the person's identity is considered verified; otherwise, he is rejected, although he may be given a few chances to try again. The reason for using several words from a larger vocabulary is to prevent an imposter from using a recording of an authorized person's voice. Even if the imposter had a recording of the vocabulary as spoken by an authorized user, it

would be quite difficult to pick out the designated words and play them into the microphone in the short time available. As in the case of a signature verification system, the voice can also be used for data entry.

There is considerable controversy as to the possibility of recognizing speakers over ordinary telephone circuits because of noise and loss of fidelity. The quality of these circuits also varies considerably from one connection to another. It is, of course, possible to digitize the voice at the source so that it may be transmitted without distortion, but this would require special equipment for digitizing and buffering the spoken phrases, and would probably increase transmission time considerably, since high-fidelity speech has a higher information content than that transmitted by telephone lines.

Two factors express the effectiveness of an identity verification system: how well it recognizes authorized persons and how efficiently it discriminates against imposters. Both these factors can be tested under laboratory conditions. Failure to recognize authorized persons is expressed as the "Type 1" error rate, or "false alarm rate" (FAR). Failure to bar imposters is the "Type 2" error rate or "imposter pass rate" (IPR). These quantities are calculated as follows: the FAR by dividing the total number of attempts by authorized persons into the number of times authorized persons are rejected; and the IPR by dividing the total number of attempts by imposters into the number of times imposters are accepted.

Necessary tolerances

As mentioned above, it is necessary to provide tolerances in the matching process to accommodate normal variations in the characteristics measured. As these tolerances are made larger, the likelihood of one individual being able to impersonate another becomes greater, which lessens the device's effectiveness.

It is not easy to determine just how much of a mismatch is tolerable. The curve on the left in Figure 2 represents the preferred performance of the device in rejecting imposters, while the curve on the right shows the acceptance of authorized individuals. It would be most desirable if these two curves were widely separated, as indicated in the diagram. This would provide a broad range in which the decision "threshold" could be adjusted. In practice, the curves tend to overlap, as shown in Figure 3, which means that the setting of the decision threshold must be a compromise. The gray area to the left of the decision threshold (labeled "false alarms") indicates degrees of matching which will cause authorized people to be rejected along with imposters. Similarly, the black area to the right of the threshold shows degrees of matching that allow some imposters to get through, along with people properly authorized to operate the system.

If the rejection threshold is set too high, many legitimate users may be turned away, with resulting annoyance and inconvenience, and the need for other means of checking their identities. (Several tries should be permitted before a final rejection is made.) For applications in which the person seeking access is a customer of the system's owner, the rejection rate might be set slightly to the left of the crossover point to avoid the driving away of customers.

Physical security

Aside from the possibility of deceiving the verification system by artificial means, it may be that attempts will be made to bypass the device altogether, which means the verifier should be tamper-proof and its cable protected to prevent anyone tapping in and injecting a false acceptance signal. An encoding device may also be needed to protect signals transmitted to and from remote locations from being recorded and played back into the system as part of an effort to break in.

Costs of verification systems vary considerably, depending in part on whether they require a dedicated processor, or whether the processing and file retrieval can be handled on an existing system. Some verification systems are already being redesigned to make use of microprocessors instead of minicomputers.

The National Bureau of Standards has just published its *Guidelines on Evaluation of Techniques for Automated Personal Identification*, which discusses the factors involved in evaluating devices and the techniques for automatic identity verification. (FIPS Pub. 48, April 1977; obtainable for $3.50 from the National Technical Information Service, U.S. Department of Commerce, Springfield, Va. 22161.) A number of identity verification techniques are now being studied by the NBS, particularly from the standpoint of using them with computer systems and for controlling access to a network from remote terminals.

The NBS is also planning to publish in December a comprehensive guideline on controlling access to computer networks. This will include typical performance data for various identity verification techniques. Another ongoing investigation consists of operational tests of selected devices by the U.S. Air Force Electronic Systems Division, as part of the Base and Installation Security Systems (BISS) program, with the assistance of the Mitre Corp. of Bedford, Mass. ■

Packet networks offer greater security than meets the eye

Grant E. Seal, TransCanada Telephone System, Ottawa, Canada

Despite their "public" nature, packet-switched data communications networks offer users an inherently safe data exchange medium

The introduction of public packet-switching networks is occurring at a time when increasing attention is being focused on database security and user information restrictions. Evidence of the security emphasis is shown by the U.S. Privacy Act of 1974 as well by a general public reluctance to the establishment of computerized financial transaction services.

There are a variety of reasons for this concern. Some are based on the poor performance of traditional data transmission equipment, while others are simply psychological. The very nature of the word "public," for instance, creates an image that a public network is less secure than a "private" network.

It has been suggested that a user of a public packet network might have an opportunity to exploit the network by disrupting service to other users, or to intercept another user's data by manipulating nodal switches. However, this sort of exploitation is not likely to occur on a public packet-switched network.

Because communications processors, which are actually computers, are used to perform a variety of functions within a public packet-switched network (PPSN), the traditional poor security reputation of computer databases adds another concern. Computers have received much negative publicity about being subject to fraud, prone to errors, and have even been tagged as unreliable. A recent study by Institut National de la Recherche Scientifique-Telecommunications (INRS), an affiliate of Canada's Bell-Northern Research, examined the network operating system security features of Bell Canada's X.25 configured public packet network, Datapac. One conclusion reached by INRS was that with a PPSN, unlike a normal computer environment, users only furnish data to the network's nodal processors, and the data is used as an input to programs already running in the node. The user has no control over these programs. Hence, the most powerful tool normally used to penetrate a computer operating system—the writing and execution of user-written programs—is not available to PPSN users. For this reason, nodal processors used in PPSNs are significantly more secure than normal computer systems.

Security is "the freedom from doubt, care and apprehension." In the field of data communications, this meaning is too broad, although ultimately it is what the user is seeking. However, to data network users, security is the prevention of:
- Disruption or denial of use (availability)
- Unauthorized information release (privacy)
- Unauthorized information modification (errors)

One global requirement of public packet-switching networks is to provide a service with high availability;

availability is the likelihood that the network is capable of providing service at any given time. It is dependent not only on the frequency of failures, but also on the length of time it takes to recover from a failure. Poor availability results in unauthorized restriction of user access, and thus, any factor which influences the availability of the service of a public packet-switched network is, in fact, a security concern.

Each network differs slightly in its approach to providing high availability, but a good example can be found in the availability features in the design and operating systems of Canada's Datapac network.

Datapac's switching node multiprocessor architecture allows several processors to share a common workload. Thus, if one processor fails, the node will remain operational. Node software is fault tolerant and is designed to reload and restart automatically in the case of a node failure.

In the case of trunk or node failure, alternative routing paths are selected automatically by the network to bypass the failed component without dropping calls in progress. Each node has multiple interconnections within the network, so there is more than one path between any two nodes.

Most node printed circuit boards can be inserted and removed without interfering with the operation of the node. In particular, line and processor cards can be changed without affecting the overall node operation or the service to customers on other lines.

A network control center (NCC) receives all network alarms, which are automatically generated upon a hardware or software fault. The network also provides node and NCC operators with on-line diagnostics and remote control capabilities. This alarm and control system permits operators to diagnose faults rapidly (remotely, if required), and subsequently control nodal equipment to correct a fault condition. Consequently, the status of the network hardware and software can be constantly monitored by the NCC.

A software control system allows progressive changes in network software and permits recovery of any previous software versions. In Datapac, each node has two magnetic tapes mounted and ready to load; each tape has a complete copy of the node's software.

In addition, a backup copy is available at a data collection center. This ensures that an operationally tested version of node software is always available.

All nodes and the NCC are powered directly from 48-volt telephone central office batteries and, like a telephone network, can function during commercial power failures with no loss of service.

Unauthorized release

User access to PPSNs is controlled by a comprehensive set of communications procedure rules, as in the case of the X.25 protocol. These protocols limit unauthorized access to the network, for example, by allowing calls only to valid network addresses.

Furthermore, dynamic multiplexing of packets from different sources and destinations on each trunk makes it difficult to isolate coherent data pertaining to any one customer or call. Derivation of meaningful information through the tapping of trunks would be nearly impossible. This would be true even when satellite links are used for trunks in PPSNs.

In Datapac, as well as in other PPSNs, protocol violations cause special alarms to be generated and sent to the node and the NCC. An abnormal number of alarms results in subsequent investigation.

In addition, the internal network packet format is different from the customer packet format. The transformation processes are not accessible to subscribers.

Data packets within PPSNs contain an internal destination address in a highly condensed and transformed format, assigned at call setup, which bears no obvious relation to the directory address used by the customers. Thus, it would be difficult for an external observer to identify packets within the PPSN operation as belonging to a particular call or customer.

With most PPSNs, the routing of data is controlled by routing tables in each node. Thus, only the network, and not the subscriber, handles the routing of data. In Datapac, contents of the tables are restricted to specific network personnel and are subject to occasional changes. Destination routing codes are dynamically assigned at call setup and carried with each packet. The codes are protected by safeguards such as cylical redundancy checks (CRCs) and software checksums. Misrouting possibilities are thereby infinitesimal.

Error protection

It is essential that PPSNs maintain the integrity of data which they handle. This means the prevention of unauthorized information modification. That is, PPSNs must provide adequate mechanisms for the detection, correction, and recording of errors. For example, on customer access lines of PPSNs providing X.25 service, error detection is provided by performing a cyclic redundancy check as part of the protocol. This type of error check provides virtually error-free data transmission. (On Datapac's X.25 access service, for instance, the error performance is expected to be equivalent to one undetected error packet in 83 years on a line generating 100,000 packets a month.)

PPSNs also provide additional error-checking features to protect data being transmitted within the network. For example, in Datapac, data transmitted on inter-nodal links (trunks) is protected by a CRC as well as by an end-to-end software checksum. The checksum, a software algorithm, is used to verify data accuracy. This protects the packet against internal nodal errors. The checksum is validated by recalculation at every node as the packet is transmitted through the network. Because the checksum and the CRC apply to both the header and the data of the packet, they prevent both the delivery of incorrect data and delivery to an incorrect location.

End-to-end sequential numbering of the packets within Datapac's network enables detection of out-of-order or missing packets between source and destination nodes; in addition, it makes the injection of false packets into the data stream virtually impossible. Internal network time-outs facilitate recovery from transmission or node failures. These errors are corrected by retransmission on either a link or an end-to-end basis, as appropriate. In order to recover from transmission errors, the source node maintains a copy of each packet it has sent until the destination node acknowledges its receipt. Error performance of trunks is expected to be approximately one undetected packet error in 10^{10} packets transmitted.

Physical security

In addition to the sophisticated network operational features which PPSNs employ to provide data security, many enhance their data security through the use of physically secure locations for key network elements. Nodes, trunk interfaces, the network control centers, and data collection centers are often located in telephone central offices.

Furthermore, all details of network hardware, software, and operation are limited to network personnel on a "need-to-know" basis. With regard to ensuring privacy and secrecy of user data, all network operation personnel are bound not only by explicit PPSN policies, but also by national and regional laws where they exist.

Added security

To this point, the inherent network security features which are, in most cases, transparent to the user have been detailed. However, there are other network and optional features which impact the user and provide additional security. One standard network feature provided by PPSNs supporting the X.25 protocol entails the setting up of switched virtual circuits (SVCs).

Data transfer through PPSNs supporting X.25 is accomplished through the use of virtual circuits. These are not physical connections as in a private-line switched environment. Rather, they are logical associations between two communicating stations using network facilities only during data transmissions. Switched virtual circuits require call set-up and clearing procedures to be carried out.

Whenever an SVC is established, the incoming call packet presents the address of the calling data terminal equipment (DTE) to the called DTE. These addresses are inserted by the network and cannot be tampered with by subscribers. Each DTE on a PPSN has a unique address. The DTE may then selectively accept or reject any call after being provided with the address of the calling DTE, as well as whether or not it was a collect call. Furthermore, SVC calls may be terminated by either end at any time after call setup.

SVC is a standard mode of operation on all X.25-supported networks, but many PPSNs offer options for enhanced security which are usually available at subscription time.

A closed-user group is one such feature. This provides a user with a designated unique set of network access lines and addresses. No network address outside a designated closed-user group can reach any member of the group. The group's identification is maintained within the network and cannot be tampered with by subscribers. This feature enables a user to build his own network on a public network with total isolation from other users.

A collect call blocking feature can prevent all collect calls from reaching a user's DTE. This eliminates the necessity of a user's DTE checking incoming calls for reverse charging and, of course, prevents a user from being charged for any collect calls.

Another feature allows the user to specify logical channels for outgoing calls only. This ensures that a DTE's logical channels are not all assigned to incoming calls, thereby guaranteeing the DTE's access to the public packet-switched network.

A permanent virtual circuit (PVC) feature provides for a permanent, network-recognized association between two DTEs. This service, which is analogous to normal private-line service, requires no call setup or call clearing procedures. The PVC ensures high security because it permits communication capability only between the two designated DTEs at each end of the PVC. No other DTEs can access the PVC.

User responsibility

It must be emphasized that PPSNs do not *replace* user security techniques and procedures, but rather *enhance* existing security. When building a communications system using a PPSN, a user must consider several areas in order to achieve total end-to-end communications security. In addition to selecting the appropriate features, a user must ensure that the physical security of his local facility be adequate, since this is probably the most vulnerable part of the network. Much has been written recently regarding tightening physical security by such means as restricting access to the buildings, locking telephone and computer rooms, installing surveillance equipment, and preventing electromagnetic radiations.

Another measure, which can be implemented to ensure that only authorized DTEs access a user's DTE, is the use of identification schemes such as passwords. (The X.25 call-request packet includes a user data field which can be used for password identification.)

End-to-end encryption and decryption of the data field of packets may be the most effective and low cost method for a user to ensure that his data remains confidential, for this adds another layer of protection to any comprehensive security plan. ∎

Part 6
Testing and
diagnostics

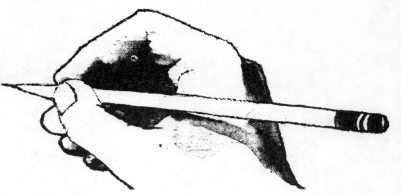

Building a diagnostic center

John E. Nuwer
Atlantic Richfield Co.
Dallas, Texas

Simple as it may seem at first glance, laying out the spatial requirements for a diagnostic test center requires more than a little forethought. Generally, a diagnostic test center (commonly called a tech control center) must, in addition to providing sufficient space for the equipment, allow access to connecting and test points, use only as much cable as necessary, and provide adequate ventilation. Taken one at a time, these considerations may be fairly obvious, but to overlook any one of them is to invite problems later on.

Human factors also deserve attention because the effectiveness of a tech control center is determined to a great extent by the willingness of people to use it. And if its operation involves excessive bending, stretching, or other difficulty in taking readings or making connections, users might try to work around it. The last "Planners Notebook" article (DATA COMMUNICATIONS, Nov./Dec. 1975, pp. 17–23) dealt with selecting and applying the test equipment and patch panels for a tech center. This article covers the layout and installation of this hardware.

The most important consideration in selecting a location is to minimize cable lengths, bearing in mind that to avoid signal degradation, RS-232-C cables should not exceed 50 feet. The optimum location from this point of view is between the modems and the front-end. Moreover, to facilitate access to modems for line and system tests, the modems are often housed right in the tech center.

For distances exceeding 50 feet, cable drivers can extend the usable cabling distances, sometimes by hundreds of feet, depending on the data rate. But be careful. Many equipment manufacturers will not support systems using cable drivers. And when they are used, be sure to test the cables with the tech center's test equipment and also the data processing and communications equipment before the cables are placed in normal operation, to be sure that any signal degradation caused by the drivers and long cables is acceptable.

In designing a tech center for a system not yet installed, the cable routings must be carefully planned and their lengths accurately computed. All obstructions that interfere with direct routing should be carefully taken into account, because 50 feet of cable can easily be consumed, even when the straight-line distance between interconnected units is only a fraction of the 50 feet.

Computer-type cabinets provide the best housing for tech center equipment because rack-mountable units usually conform to their standard widths and can be ordered or fitted with appropriate mounting hardware. Typical cabinets are 6 feet high, 2 feet wide, and 2 to 3 feet in depth, but the deeper cabinets are recommended because space is needed behind the equipment for cables and air flow. Rails are usually provided at the front and rear of the cabinets for mounting the equipment. The standard spacing between rails is 19 inches, the most common width of rack-mounted equipment.

Other desirable features are roller slides and rear doors to facilitate access to equipment, and open cabinet bottoms to permit installation of under-floor cabling. For additional cooling, the top of the cabinet should be open, as well. The cabinets should have hardware for distributing ac power and also loops or ladders for routing cables.

A word about space for cables and connectors—design parameters that are easily underestimated. Providing access to each unit entails the ability to interconnect through a patch panel, also called a patchfield. A full-duplex channel—both channel types can be housed in a single cable—requires four

lines: two RS-232-C-cables for interconnecting the terminal or computer to the modem via the patch panel, and two telephone cables to tie the modem to the line, also through the patch panel. Therefore, as the number of channels increase, the number of cables and connectors needed at the patch panel and the amount of space needed to house them increase fourfold. Still more lines would be required if such items as multiplexers, switching equipment, and spares are also to be tied through the system's tech center.

To assure adequate room behind the cabinet for service workspace, a rule of thumb is that the rear of the cabinet should be at least three feet from the nearest obstruction. Therefore, the total floor-space required for each cabinet is at least six feet of depth and two feet of width.

An alternative to cabinets is inexpensive, open radio relay racks. These are less attractive than computer cabinets, but they are easier to access, and their openness provides better ventilation.

An attractive, albeit more expensive, method of providing access to the patch panel, controls, and indicator lights is to build a wraparound console. But consoles also consume a great deal of floor space. So unless the tech center is used constantly, a wraparound console may not be advisable.

EQUIPMENT MOUNTING HEIGHTS

EQUIPMENT TYPE	EQUIPMENT HEIGHT (RMS)	MOUNTING RANGE (FEET)
CABINET	40	1/2 TO 6
PATCHFIELD (ANALOG AND DIGITAL FOR 12 TO 16 MODEMS)	4	3 TO 5
STATUS MONITORING PANEL (FOR 12 TO 16 MODEMS)	2	5 TO 6
TEST EQUIPMENT	2 TO 4	4 TO 6
MISCELLANEOUS PATCHFIELDS (ANALOG, DIGITAL, SPARE MODEMS ETC.)	2	3 TO 5
ASYNCHRONOUS MODEMS (TYPICALLY EIGHT PER MOUNT)	4	1/2 TO 4
SYNCHRONOUS MODEMS, 2,400 B/S OR LESS (TYPICALLY TWO PER MOUNT)	4	1/2 TO 4
SYNCHRONOUS MODEMS, 4,800 B/S OR MORE	4	1/2 TO 4
DRAWERS (FOR PATCH CABLES, ACCESSORIES)	2 TO 4	3 TO 4
WRITING SURFACES	1 TO 2	3 TO 4

NOTE: DISTANCES ARE FROM THE FLOOR (FEET) OR LOWEST MOUNTING POINT (RMS) TO THE BOTTOM OF THE MOUNTED EQUIPMENT. (1 RMS = 1 3/4 INCHES)

CARRIER LEVEL ALARM INDICATORS PATCH PANEL BIT ERROR RATE TESTER

RS-232-C STATUS INDICATORS

OSCILLOSCOPE

FREQUENCY, LEVEL, NOISE TESTER

PHOTO BELOW

LINE MONITOR

MODEM

BACKUP MODEM SWITCHES

CARRIER LEVEL ALARM DRIVERS

RS-232-C STATUS INDICATORS

RS-232-C PATCH PANEL (NON-STANDARD CONNECTORS)

TELEPHONE LINE PATCH PANEL

BIT ERROR RATE TESTER

REAR OF PATCH PANEL RS-232-C CONNECTORS (NORMALLY CONNECTED)

TELEPHONE LINE CONNECTORS

RS-232-C CABLE

Assembled. The three photographs show a completed tech center with the doors removed. Despite the loose arrangement of units (upper left), the cabling space may be tight (above), especially when the thick RS-232-C cables are connected. The patch panels and status monitors are shown at lower left.

Care must be taken in positioning test equipment, patch panels, and control and indicator panels in the cabinets, so that they are at convenient heights. Test equipment, and control and indicator panels should be as close as possible to eye level, which is four to six feet above the floor. Patch panels can be somewhat lower, from three to five feet. Modems and other equipment not frequently used can occupy the space in the lower three feet.

A list of recommended distances above the floor for various types of equipment is given in the table "Equipment mounting heights." Note that the table specifies equipment heights in RMS units, which stand for Rack Mounting Space (not to be confused with the RMS method of specifying amplitudes of electrical signals). A term frequently used by cabinet suppliers, one RMS unit is equal to a linear distance of 1¾ inches. So 2 RMS equals 3½ inches, and so on.

Patch panels can present some problems in finding enough room to locate all the jacks at convenient heights. Commercial patch panels are designed for 12 to 16 modems and each modem requires two RS-232-C connectors. Experience indicates that the recommended height range provides room for a set of three panels, which can accommodate 36 to 48 modems.

Implementation of the aforementioned features is illustrated in the photographs.

Equipment layout can be simplified by using worksheets, as shown in the diagram for "Arranging the equipment," calibrated both in feet and RMS units. Note that the RMS measurements begin at the lowest possible mounting location, generally six to eight inches above the floor, but the distance in feet is measured directly from the floor. The reason for the discrepancy is that RMS is used to measure *usable* mounting space, whereas the distance in feet—the actual distance from the floor—is used for measuring cable lengths.

The procedure for designing a tech control center is first to estimate the amount of front mounting space needed to house present and future equipment and then to lay out the equipment in the cabinets. The final step is to arrange the cabinets on the floor to minimize digital cable lengths.

The balance of this article illustrates this procedure for a system with 12 low-speed modems, two of medium speed, and two of high speed. Assume that space must also be provided for expansion by 50% to 18 low-speed modems and three each of the medium and high-speed modems.

HOW MANY CABINETS?

ESTIMATING TOTAL MOUNTING SPACE	
EQUIPMENT	**HEIGHT (RMS)**
PATCHFIELD (MOST FOR 12 OR 16 MODEMS; TWO FOR 24 MODEMS)	2 x 4 = 8
STATUS MONITOR (TWO REQUIRED)	2 x 2 = 4
MOUNT FOR ASYNCHRONOUS MODEMS (IF THERE ARE EIGHT PER MOUNT, THREE MOUNTS REQUIRED)	3 x 4 = 12
MOUNT FOR 2,400 B/S MODEMS (IF THERE ARE TWO PER MOUNT, TWO MOUNTS REQUIRED)	2 x 4 = 8
MOUNTS FOR 4,800 B/S MODEMS	3 x 4 = 12
MOUNT FOR TWO PIECES OF TEST EQUIPMENT	2 x 4 = 8
	TOTAL EQUIPMENT HEIGHT = 52 RMS

After choosing the test equipment, obtain the rack-mounting dimensions in RMS units. For the system described above, assume that the test equipment will consist of two patch panels, two status monitor panels, and a bit-error-rate tester. Also assume that the modems will be housed in the tech center, so that their mounting dimensions must also be determined. As indicated in the panel "Estimating total mounting space," the total height of the equipment is 52 RMS units. Computer-type cabinets that are six feet high provide about 40 RMS of mounting space. Taller cabinets are available, but the extra height makes it difficult to reach the equipment on top. As a result, the 52 RMS units of height should be built into a double-width cabinet or two cabinets bolted together. Another advantage of two cabinets is that the equipment can be spread out to assure sufficient cabling space and ventilation. Also, the loose arrangement provides adequate space to build in additional test equipment, should the need ever arise. Note from the photographs on the preceding page that despite the large amount of open space in the front of the tech control center, the rear is crowded with cables.

ARRANGING THE EQUIPMENT

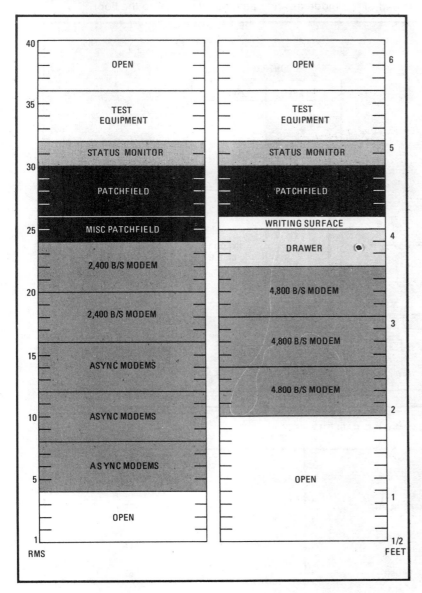

Next the equipment should be laid out in the cabinets, selecting the locations according to the recommended equipment heights. Note from the diagram that a drawer and a writing surface are added. The drawer holds cables, documentation, and other accessories. A "miscellaneous" patch panel also is provided for access to backup modems, special test points, or to expand the patching capability to other units in the system. The need for an extra patch panel often develops as troubleshooting and maintenance techniques evolve.

MINIMIZING CABLE RUNS

Since the patch panel is connected between the modem and the digital equipment, the cable run should be determined by summing the lengths of the cable between the modem and the patch panel and the cable between the patch panel and the digital device. The diagram and table on the next page indicate, for example, that a 24-foot straight-line distance between a modem and computer (indicated as underfloor distance) might require a 60-foot cable.

The problem now is how to reduce the cable length to 50 feet to meet RS-232-C standards. If the digital device and tech center cannot be moved closer to each other, then one way to save a few feet is to use a cabinet without a partition or to drill holes in an existing partition so that the cables connected across the cabinet can be routed directly, instead of around the partition. Another trick is to move the modems and patch panels closer to the floor.

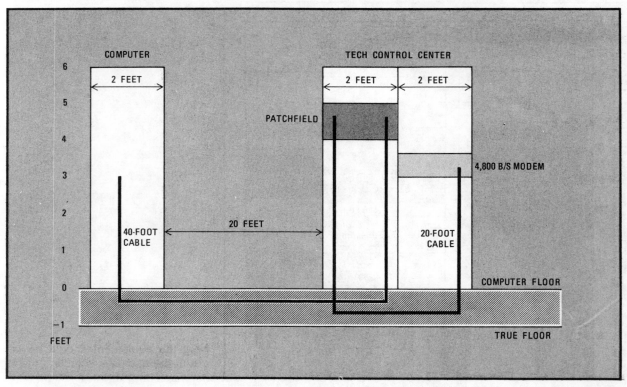

ESTIMATING CABLE LENGTH

CABLE LENGTH FROM MODEM TO PATCHFIELD:

    MODEM TO FLOOR (ASSUMING 1 FOOT OF CABLE IN THE CABINET)   1 + 4 + 1 = 6 FEET

    UNDER BOTH CABINETS   2 + 2   = 4 FEET

    FLOOR TO PATCHFIELD (ASSUMING 1 FOOT OF CABLE IN THE CABINET)   1 + 5 + 1 = 7 FEET

    CABLES USUALLY MADE IN MULTIPLES OF 5 FEET, SO A 20 FOOT CABLE WOULD PROBABLY BE USED   1 + 5 + 1 = 7 FEET

                                               TOTAL LENGTH = 17 FEET

CABLE LENGTH FROM PATCHFIELD TO THE COMPUTER:

    PATCHFIELD TO FLOOR (ASSUMING 1 FOOT OF CABLE IN CABINET)   1 + 5 + 1 = 7 FEET

    UNDER FLOOR (AND BOTH TECH CONTROL AND COMPUTER CABINET)   2 + 20 + 2 = 24 FEET

    FLOOR TO COMPUTER (ASSUMING 1 FOOT OF CABLE IN CABINET)   1 + 3 + 1 = 5 FEET

                                               TOTAL LENGTH = 36 FEET

THEREFORE, A 40 FOOT CABLE WOULD PROBABLY BE USED

What's available in portable data test sets

Portable data test sets shed light on the contents of communications traffic to save time and money

Donald v. Z. Wadsworth
Consultant
Sierra Madre, Calif.

Diagnostics

In many cases, the only economical way to resolve the multivendor finger-pointing problem—whose equipment is at fault?—is with portable data communications test equipment. The test sets discussed here are used at the terminal/modem interface for applications over conventional carrier lines (voice-grade lines at speeds to 9,600 bits per second). This article is intended to guide the data communications user to the best match between his test-set needs and what's available.

The capabilities of 24 data communications test sets, representing 16 manufacturers, are presented under four broad categories in Table 1. Having thus narrowed the selection, the user can make a more detailed comparison with the aid of the second chart (Table 2).

The charts are intended as a first cut in the selection process. Users should base their final decisions on detailed information from the manufacturer and from actual demonstrations. They also should consider qualitative factors such as ease of use, clarity, and completeness of the operation manual, repair-service policy, and reliability.

Despite the current trend toward centralized testing, portable sets still play the major role in data communications troubleshooting. Some fundamental criteria for inclusion in this guide are that the test set must include both a data generator and an analyzer in the same package, be self-contained (function without external equipment such as cathode-ray-tube displays or keyboards, although these could be options), have a carrying handle, and weigh no more than about 35 pounds. Perhaps the most familiar test sets included are Western Electric Co.'s 911 and 914 models. They serve as a good basis of comparison for users since they have influenced the design of some other sets.

Some manufacturers offer models related to the test sets listed. Hewlett-Packard Co.'s 10235A, an addition to its 1645A, provides more complete access and control of the EIA RS-232-C interface and includes analog testing. International Data Sciences offers a family of test sets (1100, 1200, 1300) which culminate in the 1310. Nolton Communications says it is marketing its 1608 test set as two units, the asynchronous 1608A (price range B) and the synchronous 1608B (price range C). Sierra Electronic will be offering a modification to the 920A

BASIC CAPACITIES OF PORTABLE DATA TEST SETS

TEST SET MANUFACTURER AND MODEL	CHARACTER-ORIENTED TESTS	
	ANALYZER	GENERATOR
ATLANTIC RESEARCH MODEL DTS-1 DATA TEK 9600	–	X
ATLANTIC RESEARCH MODEL DTM-1 INTERSHAKE	X	X
ATLANTIC RESEARCH MODEL DTM-2 INTERSHAKE II	X	X
COMPUTING DEVICES MODEL DTS-102 DATA TEST SET	–	–
COMPUTER TRANSMISSION MODEL 350B CHECKTRAN	–	–
DATA-CONTROL SYSTEMS MODEL BA401 BYTE ANALYZER	X	X
DIGITECH DATA INDUSTRIES MODEL 2350 BIT ERROR RATE TESTER	–	–
DIGITECH DATA INDUSTRIES MODEL 2302 BIT ERROR RATE TESTER	–	–
DIGITECH DATA INDUSTRIES MODEL 2652 ANALYZER/FOX GENERATOR	–	X
DIGITECH DATA INDUSTRIES MODEL 2056 DATA TRANSMISSION TEST SET	X	X
DIGITECH DATA INDUSTRIES MODEL 103 PACER	X	X
HEWLETT-PACKARD MODEL 1645A DATA ERROR ANALYZER	–	–
INFOTRON SYSTEMS MODEL TE600 INFOTESTER	X	X
INTERNATIONAL DATA SCIENCES MODEL 1310 TDM-MODEM TEST SET	X	X
MISSION DATA PRODUCTS MODEL 578 DATA ANALYZER	–	–
NOLTON COMMUNICATIONS MODEL 1608 TERMINAL TEST SET	–	–
NU DATA MODEL 922TA MULTIPURPOSE TEST SET	–	X
NU DATA MODEL 922G DATA COMMUNICATIONS TEST SET	X	X
SIEMENS MODEL 920A ERROR TEST SET	–	–
SIERRA ELECTRONIC MODEL 920A ERROR TEST SET	–	–
TELE-DYNAMICS MODEL 7914B MODEM TESTER	–	–
TREND COMMUNICATIONS MODEL 1-8 DATA TRANSMISSION TEST SET	–	–
WESTERN ELECTRIC MODEL 911NA DATA TEST SET	X	X
WESTERN ELECTRIC MODEL 914C DATA TEST SET	–	–

(the 920B) that will include four EIA RS-232-C lead-status indicators.

The criteria eliminate some well-known test sets. Line-monitoring and simulation sets such as Digi-Log Systems' Data Line Monitor 400, General Electric's model TT-1200S Termi Test Program Generator, Spectron's Buffered Data Transmission Simulator, and Universal Data Systems' UDS Data Trap, all require a separate CRT display or a printer for data analysis. Paradyne's 810 Bisync Analyzer and Spectron's Datascope are self-contained but do not provide generation as well as analysis of messages. Cooke Engineering's TC-100 test set qualifies except for portability.

Explanation of features

While most of the features compared in Table 2 are immediately understandable, some need a word or two of explanation. They are discussed in order of appearance in the left-hand column, starting from the top.

Code level. The level of a code is defined in this article as the number of information bits used to encode the characters in an alphabet, generally 5, 6, 7 or 8 bits.

Stop-element length. For asynchronous formats, the stop element consists of a pulse with 1-, 1.42-, 1.5-, or 2-bit intervals, depending on the code and equipment used.

SDLC. Several sets offer automatic SDLC (IBM's synchronous data-link control) capability as an option, and with SDLC, block-check-character treatment is important. While it is not difficult to calculate and manually enter the BCC (block-check character) for BSC (binary synchronous communications) protocols, it is cumbersome to do so for SDLC formats. In such cases, block-check-character entry involves additional manipulations for zero-

| DISTORTION TESTS | | BIT-ORIENTED PSEUDO-RANDOM PATTERN TESTS | LINE PROTOCOL MONITORING/ SIMULATION |
ANALYZER	GENERATOR		
X	X	X	–
–	–	X	X
–	–	X	X
X	–	X	–
–	–	X	X
–	X	–	X
–	–	X	–
X	–	X	–
X	X	–	–
X	X	–	–
–	–	X	X
X	–	X	–
X	–	X	–
X	–	X	–
–	–	–	X
–	–	–	X
X	X	–	–
X	X	X	X
X	–	X	–
–	–	X	–
–	–	X	–
X	–	X	–
X	X	–	–
X	–	X	–

Link test-set makers

Atlantic Research Corp., 5390 Cherokee Ave., Alexandria, Va. 22314.

Computing Devices Co. (a division of Control Data Canada Ltd.), P.O. Box 8508, Ottawa, Ont., Canada K1G 3M9.

Computer Transmission Corp., 2352 Utah Ave., El Segundo, Calif. 90245.

Data-Control Systems Inc., Commerce Drive, Danbury, Conn. 06810.

Digitech Data Industries Inc., 66 Grove St., Ridgefield, Conn. 06877.

Hewlett-Packard Co., 1501 Page Mill Rd., Palo Alto, Calif. 94304.

Infotron Systems Corp., 7300 North Crescent Blvd., Pennsauken, N.J. 08110.

International Data Sciences Inc., 100 Nashua St., Providence, R.I. 02904.

Mission Data Products, P.O. Box 2254, Westminster, Calif. 92683.

Nolton Communications Ltd., Fieldings Road, Cheshunt, Herts., England EN8 9TX.

Nu Data Corp., 32 Fairview Ave., Little Silver, N.J. 07739.

Siemens Corp., 186 Wood Ave., South, Iselin, N.J. 08830.

Sierra Electronic division, Lear Siegler Inc., 10950 Odessa Avenue, Granada Hills, Calif. 91344.

Tele-Dynamics division of AMBAC, 525 Virginia Drive, Fort Washington, Pa. 19034.

Trend Communications Ltd., St. John's Estate, Tylers Green, High Wycombe, Bucks., HP108HW, England (U.S. Agent: W&G Instruments Inc., 119 Naylon Ave., Livingston, N.J. 07039).

insertion and zero-complementing NRZI (nonreturn to zero, inverted). The inverse of these manipulations must be performed on the received message for it to be intelligible. Unlike the BSC protocol with its negative-acknowledgement response, an absent or wrong BCC and zero insertion means a polled station will not reply.

Stored-message generator. Stored messages—generally in a programable read-only memory—are available in such codes as Baudot (International Telegraph Alphabet No. 2), ASCII, and EBCDIC. The stored message may be a standard "fox" (the quick brown fox jumps over a lazy dog's back, 1234567890) or some other combination of characters.

Send RY/U*. Alternating 1s and 0s may be sent instead of information bits in a string of characters by using the character pairs RY for 5-level code and U* for 8-level code.

Character-error count. In comparing test sets it is important to note that, for error-rate determination, parity-error count is generally regarded as being equivalent to character-error count. The latter is obtained by bit comparison of received characters with the generated message. On the average, 80% of the character errors are found by parity checks. Although Table 2 distinguishes between parity-error count and character-error count, the frequently used term "character-error-rate test" (CERT) may be employed to refer to either error-rate determination technique.

Peak- or bias-distortion analysis. Peak distortion refers to peak individual distortion when operating in the synchronous mode (EIA Standard RS-334 explains synchronous distortion) and to peak "gross stop-start distortion," or "telegraph distortion," during operation in the asynchronous mode. This type of distortion is explained in EIA

TABLE 2

COMPARATIVE ANALYSIS OF PORTABLE DATA TEST SETS (PART I)

	ATLANTIC RESEARCH CORP. MODEL DTS-1	ATLANTIC RESEARCH CORP. MODEL DTM-1	PONATIC RESEARCH CORP. MODEL DTM-2	COMPUTING DEVICES CO. MODEL DTS-102	COMPUTER TRANSMISSION CORP. MODEL 350B	DATA CONTROL SYSTEMS, INC. MODEL BA401	DIGITECH DATA INDUSTRIES INC. MODEL 2350	DIGITECH DATA INDUSTRIES INC. MODEL 2302
TRANSMISSION/DATA FORMAT								
TRANSMISSION MODE (SERIAL OR PARALLEL)	SER.	BOTH	BOTH	SER.	SER.	SER.	SER.	SER.
DATA FORMAT (SYNCHRONOUS OR ASYCHRONOUS)	BOTH	BOTH	BOTH	SYN.	BOTH	BOTH	SYN.	SYN.
OPERATING MODE (HALF-OR FULL-DUPLEX)	BOTH	C	BOTH	BOTH	BOTH	BOTH	BOTH	BOTH
CODE LEVEL (NO. CHOICES)	4	4	4	–	4	4	–	–
STOP ELEMENT LENGTH (NO. CHOICES)	3	3	3		4	3		
INTERNAL CLOCK (NO. SPEEDS UP TO 9,600 BITS PER SECOND)	15	15 + F	15 + F	16	ANY	25	11	ANY
INTERNAL CLOCK (MAXIMUM B/S)	9.6 K	9.6 K	64 K	19.2 K	250 K	9.6 K	2.4 K	9.9 K
EXTERNAL CLOCK (MAXIMUM B/S)	YES	20 K	256 K	500 K	2 M	56 K	50 K	300 K
SDLC ZERO INSERTION/DELETION PROCESSOR	–	–	OPT.	–	–	–	–	–
SDLC ZERO-COMPLEMENTING NRZI PROCESSOR	–	–	OPT.	–	–	–	–	–
SIGNAL INTERFACE								
EIA RS-232-C (BIPOLAR, LOW-LEVEL VOLTAGE)	YES	YES	YES	YES	YES	YES	YES	YES
MIL 188C	PART.	PART.	PART.	–	OPT.	–	–	INA
LOOP CURRENT INPUT (20 OR 60 MILLIAMPERES (MA)	BOTH	YES (60)	YES (60)	–	–	–	–	–
LOOP CURRENT OUTPUT KEYER (WET OR DRY)	BOTH	DRY	DRY	–	–	–	–	–
TERMINAL/MODEM HANDSHAKE								
EIA LEAD STATUS (NO. LEADS)	6	23	23	8	10 + D	12	EST.	6
EIA LEAD CONTROL (MANUAL OR AUTOMATIC)	MAN.	BOTH	BOTH	MAN.	MAN.	MAN.	MAN.	MAN.
EIA ACCESS (TEST POINTS OR BREAK SWITCHES)	BOTH	BOTH	BOTH	–	TEST	BREAK	–	TEST
TIME INTERVAL MEASUREMENT (RTS-CTS DELAY)	–	YES	YES	YES	YES	–	–	–
PROGRAMMABLE TIME DELAY	–	YES	YES	–	–	–	–	–
CHARACTER ERROR TESTS								
STORED MESSAGE GENERATOR (NO. CODES)	4	6	8	–	–	PROG.	–	–
STORED MESSAGE LINE LENGTH (NO. CHOICES)	ANY	–	3	–	–	–	–	–
SEND RY/U*	YES	YES	YES	–	YES	YES	–	–
PARITY ERROR INDICATOR	YES	YES	YES	–	–	–	–	–
PARITY ERROR COUNT	EXT.	YES	YES	–	–	YES	–	–
CHARACTER ERROR COUNT	–	–	–	–	–	YES	–	–

Key to symbols and abbreviations

INA: information not available

–: feature not available

ext.: interface provided for connection to external equipment

K: kilobits per second

LRC/CRC: longitudinal and cyclic redundancy checks

M: megabits per second

opt.: options that fit within the carrying case (other options not indicated)

part: compatible with military standard 188C except for output level

prog: programable by the operator

CNS: current level not specified

SDLC: synchronous data-link control

NRZI: nonreturn to zero, inverted

RTS: request to send

CTS: clear to send

BCC: block check character

LRC: longitudinal redundancy check

CRC: cyclic redundancy check

a: based on messages having characters with pseudorandom information bits

b: optional hexadecimal keyboard that fits inside the carrying case

c: full-duplex test capability, except that the monitor buffer logs only half duplex or one side of full duplex

d: additional leads that may be monitored via jump-

	DIGITECH DATA INDUSTRIES INC. MODEL 2056A	DIGITECH DATA INDUSTRIES INC. MODEL 103	HEWLETT PACKARD CO. MODEL 1645A	INFOTRON SYSTEMS CORP. MODEL TE600	INTERNATIONAL DATA SCIENCES MODEL 1310	MISSION DATA PRODUCTS MODEL 578	NOLTON COMMUNICATIONS LTD. MODEL 160B	NU DATA CORP. MODEL 922TA	NU DATA CORP. MODEL 922C	SIEMENS CORP. MODEL 2H2	SIERRA ELECTRONIC DIV., LEAR SIEGLER INC. MODEL 920A	TELEDYNAMICS DIV. OF AMBAC MODEL 7914R	TREND COMMUNICATIONS LTD. MODEL 1-8	WESTERN ELECTRIC CO MODEL 911NA	WESTERN ELECTRIC CO MODEL 914C
	SER.	SER.	SER.	SER.	SER.	SER.	SER.	SER.	SER.	SER.	SER.	SER.	SER.	SER.	BOTH
	BOTH	BOTH	SYN.	BOTH	BOTH	ASYN.	BOTH	BOTH	BOTH	SYN.	SYN.	SYN.	SYN.	ASYN.	SYN.
	BOTH	BOTH	BOTH	BOTH	BOTH	BOTH	BOTH	BOTH	C	INA	BOTH	BOTH	BOTH	BOTH	BOTH
	4	4	–	4	4	3	1	4	4	–	–	–	–	2	–
	2	2	–	3	3	3	2	3	3	–	–	–	–	4	–
	21	ANY	12	15	11	7	10	E	E	11	11	4	10	13	10
	9.6 K	G	9.6 K	9.6 K	9.6 K	1.2 K	19.2 K	9.6 K	9.6 K	9.6 K	9.6 K	1.8 K	9.6 K	1.8 K	2.4 K
	10 K	G	5 M	19 K	200 K	9.6 K	YES	YES	YES	YES	2 M	20 K	100 K	INA	20 K
	–	OPT.	–	–	–	–	OPT.	–	–	–	–	–	–	–	–
	–	OPT.	–	–	–	–	OPT.	–	–	–	–	–	–	–	–
	YES	YES	YES	YES	YES	YES	YES	YES	YES	YES	YES	YES	YES	YES	YES
	YES	YES	OPT.	–	–	–	–	–	PART.	–	–	–	–	–	–
	BOTH	–	–	–	–	–	YES, CNS	BOTH	BOTH	–	–	–	–	BOTH	–
	DRY	–	–	–	–	–	DRY	DRY	DRY	–	–	–	–	DRY	–
	2	23	2	14	8	7	YES	7 + D	11 + D	–	–	5 + D	7	–	8
	MAN.	BOTH	MAN.	MAN.	MAN.	MAN.	YES	MAN.	BOTH	–	MAN.	MAN.	BOTH	–	MAN.
	–	TEST	OPT.	TEST	–	–	TEST	BOTH	BOTH	–	–	–	–	–	BOTH
	–	YES	–	YES	–	–	–	–	–	–	–	–	YES	–	YES
	–	YES	–	–	–	–	–	–	–	–	–	–	–	–	–
	4	PROG.	–	–	A	–	–	4	4	–	–	–	–	2	–
	1	PROG.	–	–	–	–	–	–	3	–	–	–	–	3	–
	YES	YES	–	YES	YES	YES	YES	YES	YES	–	–	–	–	YES	–
	YES	YES	–	–	–	YES	–	YES	YES	–	–	–	–	YES	–
	YES	YES	–	YES	–	–	–	–	YES	–	–	–	–	YES	–
	YES	YES	–	YES	A	–	–	–	–	–	–	–	–	–	–

ers to spare light-emitting diodes

e: crystal-controlled synthesizer allowing selection of any clock period (unit interval) to within 0.0065 millisecond or better

f: internal oscillator for any speed to 1,200 b/s

g: maximum speed of 19 kb/s (standard) or 56 kb/s (optional)

Price ranges: A up to $1,500, B from $1,500 to $2,500, C, from $2,500 to $5,000, D, from $5,000 to $7,500, E, from $7,500 to $10,000

The data presented in the comparative analysis chart are from literature supplied by the manufacturers. For the sake of uniformity, weights were adjusted to include the carrying case.

Standard RS-404 and Bell System Technical Reference PUB 41003. Peak-distortion analysis refers to both synchronous and asynchronous kinds, but not to isochronous distortions. Only three sets in the comparison—the Hewlett-Packard 1645A, the Siemens 2H2, and the Trend 1-8—provide a precise measurement of isochronous distortion as defined in EIA Standard RS-334. Others provide a crude measurement by observation of the deviation of the peak-distortion display from the average value. In any case, the isochronous distortion is never more than twice the value of the synchronous distortion. Bias distortion refers to the elongation of either the mark intervals (marking bias) or the space intervals (spacing bias).

Modulation rate. The distortion display on some data test sets can be used to indicate overspeed, that is, the difference between the modu-

TABLE 2

COMPARATIVE ANALYSIS OF PORTABLE DATA TEST SETS (PART II)

	ATLANTIC RESEARCH CORP. MODEL DTS-1	ATLANTIC RESEARCH CORP. MODEL DTM-1	ATLANTIC RESEARCH CORP. MODEL DTM-2	COMPUTING DEVICES CO. MODEL DTS-102	COMPUTER TRANSMISSION CORP. MODEL 350B	DATA CONTROL SYSTEMS, INC. MODEL BA401	DIGITECH DATA INDUSTRIES INC. MODEL 2350	DIGITECH DATA INDUSTRIES INC. MODEL 2302
DISTORTION TESTS								
BIAS DISTORTION GENERATOR (STEP SIZE)	6%	–	–	–	–	6%	–	–
DISTORTION ANALYSIS (STEP SIZE)	1.5%	–	–	5%	–	–	–	5%
PEAK OR BIAS DISTORTION ANALYSIS	BOTH	–	–	PEAK	–	–	–	PEAK
MODULATION RATE OR OVERSPEED MEASUREMENT	OVER.	BOTH	BOTH	–	–	–	–	–
BIT/BLOCK SYNCHRONOUS ERROR TESTS								
RANDOM WORD GENERATOR (NO. PATTERNS)	2	OPT.	OPT.	4	3	–	3	6
DOT PATTERN/SQUARE WAVE GENERATOR	YES	YES	YES	YES	YES	YES	YES	YES
ERROR COUNT (BIT OR BLOCK)	BLK.	–	BIT	BOTH	BIT	–	BIT	BOTH
BLOCK LENGTH SELECTION (NO. SIZES)	1	–	–	4	–	–	–	6
LINE PROTOCOL MONITOR/SIMULATOR								
MONITOR BUFFER (NO. CHARACTERS)	2	64	1,024	–	–	256	–	–
PROGRAMMABLE MESSAGES/PATTERNS (NO. CHAR.)	4	YES	1,024	–	–	256	–	–
MANUAL PROGRAMMING (KEYBOARD OR BIT SW.)	SW.	SW.	SW.	–	–	SW. B	–	–
NONVOLATILE PROGRAM MEMORY	–	–	YES	–	–	–	–	–
TEST SEQUENCES (PROGRAMMABLE OR STORED)	–	BOTH	BOTH	–	STORED	–	–	–
SELECTABLE CHARACTER TRAP (MAX; NO CHAR.)	1	62	62	–	–	1	–	–
AUTOMATIC ANSWER TO POLL	–	YES	YES	–	YES	–	–	–
BLOCK/FRAME CHECK								
GENERATE/CHECK BCC (NO. LRC/CRC ALGORITHMS)	–	1	4	–	–	–	–	–
BCC ERROR COUNT	–	YES	YES	–	–	–	–	–
BCC ERROR INDICATION	–	YES	YES	–	–	–	–	–
GENERAL								
BUFFER ALPHANUMERIC DISPLAY (NO. CHAR.)	–	EXT.	EXT.	–	–	OPT.	–	–
BUFFER ALPHANUMERIC DISPLAY (NO. CODES)	–	EXT.	EXT.	–	–	OPT.	–	–
BUFFER BIT DISPLAY (BINARY OR HEXADECIMAL)	BIN.	BOTH	BOTH	–	–	BIN.	–	–
PROGRAMMABLE SYNC CHARACTERS (NO. CHAR.)	–	1	2	–	–	1	–	–
ERROR RATE OR COUNT INTERVAL READ-OUT	–	OPT.	OPT.	YES	EXT.	–	EXT.	YES
ANALOG TESTER-VOM, ETC.	YES	–	–	–	–	–	–	–
WEIGHT (LB.)	10	35	35	8	24	18	5	12
PRICE RANGE	B	E	E	A	B	C	A	B

lation rate of the received signal and a standard speed provided by the internal clock. If the internal clock has a fine enough adjustment, it can be used to measure the actual modulation rate of the received signal.

Random-word generator. Up to 6 pseudorandom bit sequences can be stored in the test set—an example is the 511-bit pattern in CCITT Recommendation V.52.

Dot-pattern generator. A dot pattern—that is, a square wave, also known as reversal, or 1:1—is obtained by generating alternate mark and space levels for analysis.

Error count. Error count and error-rate capability are listed separately in the Table 2, although some manufacturers use the two terms interchangeably in their literature. Some of them use the acronym BERT (bit-error-rate test) in this man-

ner. A capability for error-rate or a count-interval readout capability is listed under general features only if the test set provides a direct readout of the error rate or a readout of the total count or time interval associated with an error count.

Nonvolatile-program memory. Sets with this feature have a battery that permits retention of programs fed into memory via the keyboard or bit switches, even though the power is disconnected. The retention varies from two weeks to one year, depending on the test set.

Selectable character trap. In some portable test sets, incoming data can be compared with one or more "trap" characters that the operator has programed into a storage register. When a sequence of incoming characters matches the programed characters, the operator can turn on a trap indicator that will initiate some function, such as trans-

DIGITECH DATA INDUSTRIES INC. MODEL 205GA	DIGITECH DATA INDUSTRIES INC. MODEL 103	HEWLETT PACKARD CO. MODEL 1645A	INFOTRON SYSTEMS CORP. MODEL TE600	INTERNATIONAL DATA SCIENCES MODEL 1310	MISSION DATA PRODUCTS MODEL 578	NOLTON COMMUNICATIONS LTD. MODEL 1608	NU DATA CORP. MODEL 922TA	NU DATA CORP. MODEL 922C	SIEMENS CORP. MODEL 2H2	SIERRA ELECTRONIC DIV. LEAR SIEGLER INC. MODEL 920A	TELE-DYNAMICS DIV. OF AMBAC MODEL 7914R	TREND COMMUNICATIONS LTD. MODEL 1-8	WESTERN ELECTRIC CO. MODEL 911NA	WESTERN ELECTRIC CO. MODEL 914C
6%	–	–	–	–	–	–	3%	3%	–	–	–	–	1%	–
1.5%	–	1%	1%	1%	–	–	3%	3%	1%	–	–	1.5%	1%	5%
BOTH	–	BOTH	BOTH	BIAS	–	–	BOTH	BOTH	BOTH	–	–	BOTH	PEAK	PEAK
OVER.	–	OVER.	OVER.	OVER.	–	–	BOTH	BOTH	OVER.	–	–	OVER.	OVER.	–
–	2	4	3	3	–	–	3	2	1	3	1	3	–	2
YES	YES	YES	YES	YES	YES	–	YES	YES	YES	YES	YES	YES	YES	YES
–	BLK.	BOTH	BIT	BOTH	–	–	–	BOTH	BOTH	BOTH	BOTH	BOTH	–	BOTH
–	1	1	–	6	–	–	–	4	4	5	–	3	–	5
–	1,024	–	1	–	128	64	2	2,048	–	–	–	–	1	–
4	1,024	–	256	–	128	192	3	2,038	–	–	–	–	3	–
SW.	KEY	–	SW.	–	SW.	KEY	SW.	SW. B	–	–	–	–	SW.	–
–	YES	–	–	–	–	–	–	OPT.	–	–	–	–	–	–
–	BOTH	–	–	–	–	–	–	–	–	–	–	STORED	–	–
–	125	–	–	–	1	–	1	1	–	–	–	–	–	–
–	YES	–	–	–	–	–	–	YES	–	–	–	YES	–	–
–	6	–	–	–	INA	–	–	–	–	–	–	–	–	–
–	YES	–	–	–	–	–	–	–	–	–	–	–	–	–
–	YES	–	–	–	INA	–	–	–	–	–	–	–	–	–
–	32	–	–	–	–	–	–	1	–	–	–	–	–	–
–	3	–	–	–	–	–	–	2	–	–	–	–	–	–
–	HEX.	–	BIN.	–	BIN.	BIN.	BIN.	BIN.	–	–	–	–	BIN.	–
–	2	–	–	–	–	1	–	1 OR 2	–	–	–	–	–	–
–	BOTH	–	–	–	–	–	–	–	EXT.	–	–	–	–	EXT.
YES	–	YES	–	YES	–	–	–	–	–	YES	–	YES	–	YES
17	30	22	24	11	8	16	7	14	20	17	7	22	18	35
C	E	B	B	B	A	D	B	C	INA	B	A	B	C	C

mitting an acknowledgment of a poll message to the station where the test set is located. For simplicity, the selected trap character(s) could be the station's address.

Automatic answer to poll. The test set may be used to simulate a polled terminal in a multipoint network. When high-speed synchronous modems are used, it is especially important that the handshaking between the modems and terminal (test set) be automatic. When a test set with this feature receives an inquiry in the BSC poll message, it turns on the request-to-send (RTS) interface lead, waits for clear-to-send (CTS) to be turned on by the modem, and transmits the acknowledgment of the poll. This capability is sometimes referred to as "autoanswer." Almost all sets with this feature also measure RTS-CTS delay listed under the terminal/modem-handshake section.

Programable sync characters. For transmitting text over synchronous data links, one or more synchronization characters are required to bring the receiver and transmitter into the correct character-phase relationship. If the test set has this feature, its receiver circuit is programed with the correct character(s).

After narrowing the field on the basis of this guide, ask the manufacturer about such features as: computer-like software capabilities in the instruction library of the most sophisticated test sets, self-test capabilities (standard with all the sets in the tables), message-release modes, selectable parity bit, procedures for bit and pseudorandom-word synchronization, character-out-of-synchronization indicator and automatic synchronization search, programable-printhead-return delay, and the number of interface cables included. ∎

An orderly routine eases diagnostics on multipoint networks

If point-to-point tests fail to find the problems, check out the polling functions

Ralph W. Lowry
Codex Corp.
Newton, Mass.

Operations

When something goes wrong on the network, the user is no longer merely interested in knowing who or what was at fault. He wants the defect spotted immediately and corrected quickly.

So network diagnostics are more and more being done by the user's staff rather than by vendors' service representatives. Users are getting their own diagnostic devices and hiring trained personnel to operate them, in order to keep their networks going at top levels of throughput. And this is especially important in such real-time functions as banking, credit and reservation systems.

Nowhere is this increasing involvement by users in diagnostics more conspicuous than in high-speed multipoint networks. Point-to-point networks have paved the way in user diagnostics with equipment for analog and digital patching, and line and modem testing. Multipoint networks also need to have these capabilities; but above and beyond this they must have the means to test polling mechanisms remotely, and to correct any defects from the central point.

This article suggests ways to go about testing multipoint networks and restoring them to service after a breakdown.

(The design and use of a point-to-point "tech control" [or diagnostic] center were discussed in two earlier DATA COMMUNICATIONS articles: "Designing a diagnostic center", November/December 1975, pp. 17-23, which covers equipment selection and testing methods; and "Building a diagnostic center", January/February 1976, pp. 33-40, which goes into layout and construction.)

The criteria for point-to-point networks differ from those for multipoint networks in several ways. Many point-to-point applications, for example, are batch-oriented, and although they must satisfy certain time restrictions during a specific operating period, downtime delays can often be tolerated. Multipoint networks, on the other hand, are much more likely to operate in real-time applications, and it is therefore essential that these networks are continuously available.

In a point-to-point network, the failure of an individual component such as a line, modem or terminal merely results in a temporary loss of contact with the one remote point; but in a multipoint network any network defect, such as a break in the

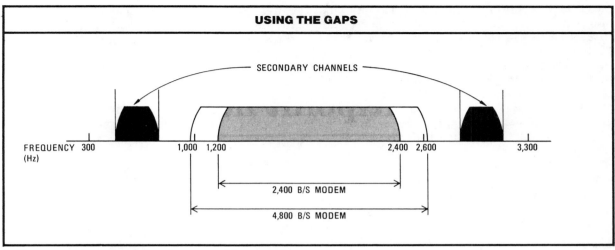

1. The secondary channel makes use of frequencies either above or below those of the main data channel. Control and monitoring signals can be transmitted without interfering with the data stream.

transmission line, will affect all remote points beyond the failure and require a far more complex and time-consuming process to identify the fault and restore service.

What is more, in many cases, point-to-point links operate between large offices with competent personnel to carry out diagnostic procedures on the network and bring in fallback modes to restore operation; in multipoint networks the central point may indeed be staffed by trained technical personnel, but remote points are unlikely to have them.

Because of all this, diagnostic and restoral procedures on multipoint networks must be set up and controlled from the central site. And this underscores the fact that multipoint networks are generally more difficult to troubleshoot than point-to-point, and that repairs must be made more quickly because of real-time use.

Secondary channel

To serve these needs, diagnostic equipment is available from several vendors that allows the user to test and control a multipoint network from the central site. All these diagnostic systems are based on the similar concept of using a secondary channel for monitoring and testing.

In some systems, network control signals can be transmitted at the same time as normal data, using "out-of-band" signaling. Figure 1 shows the frequency spectrum of a standard voice grade telephone line, which covers about 300 Hz to 3,300 Hz. A typical 2,400-bits-a-second modem uses a bandwidth of only about 1,200 Hz, while a 4,800-b/s modem needs one upwards of 1,600 Hz wide. The rest of the line's spectrum is available for a secondary channel, which can be frequency-division multiplexed with the main signal at either the high or the low end. The data signal and secondary chan-

nel can share the same link without interfering with one another.

Figure 2 shows a multipoint diagnostic system with the modem functions broken out in detail. In addition to its basic high-speed transmit (HS-XMT on the diagram) and high-speed receive (HS-RCV) functions the central site has a multipoint diagnostic control module which operates on the secondary channel. Each remote modem has its own address, so that the central site control module can interrogate remote points one by one without interrupting the others.

The multipoint diagnostic control module at the central site can be based on hardwired logic, on a minicomputer or on a programmable microcomputer. The module's main function is to provide the appropriate addresses, command messages and control information to the remote modems by way of the secondary channel. The module is equipped with either selection switches or a keyboard, and has a readout display to show results of tests and control sequences. The control module in each remote modem is either hardwired logic or a microcomputer-based device; it interprets incoming messages from the central site and selects the appropriate response messages.

Three important sets of functions are needed for a multipoint defect-checking system—monitoring, fault diagnosis, and restoral. The monitor mode reports on the status of remote units during normal operation. As soon as a fault has been detected, the system seeks out and diagnoses the malfunctioning element. Finally, a restoral function is needed to make sure that the network operates until the failed element has been repaired or replaced.

Monitoring can be achieved in two ways. One is the continuous mode, where the control module repeatedly polls remote sites with a command to each one to report on its condition. The information sent back to the central site may include the state of such RS-232-C signals as: data set ready (DSR), data terminal ready (DTR), request-to-send (RTS), clear-to-send (CTS), and data carrier detect (DCD). The report might also include the status of the modem's signal quality leads, a confirmation of the continuity of the line, and whether the power in the various pieces of equipment is on or off. When a malfunction is identified, an alarm goes off at the central site or a printer runs off a fault report detailing the cause.

The other monitoring method is selective. A par-

cause it to be cut off immediately, or at least identify the faulty location. Another way to deal with this problem is for the diagnostic system to activate a time-out mechanism (either hardware or software) in the remote site's control unit. This removes a streaming unit from the line after a fixed interval following the last data transmission.

Note that the instantaneous condition respectively of the request-to-send (RTS) and data carrier detect (DCD) signals is not meaningful because these signals are continually changing (between 0 and 1). It is more useful to count up transitions of these signals over a period of time and to report the

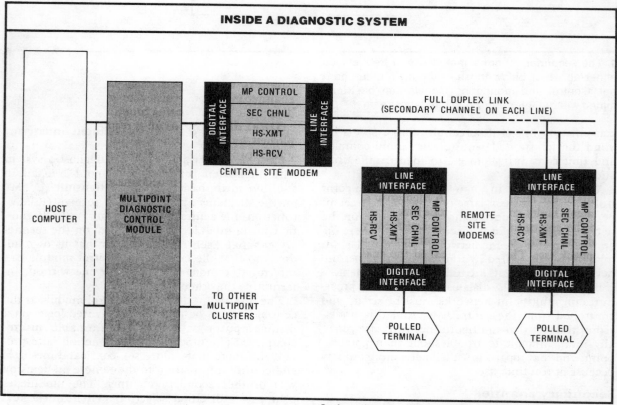

2. A multipoint diagnostic system needs control and monitoring circuits in each modem on the network. The central site initiates tests, monitors results and supervises restoral procedures.

ticular location suspected of malfunctioning is manually addressed and examined over a period of time. Selective tests can be set up after a fault has been identified by the continuous monitor mode, or if problems are spotted by other network diagnostics—usually part of a software polling routine.

An important use of the monitor function is to identify a "streaming" terminal or modem. (Streaming is the term used to describe the condition of a terminal or modem that has locked into a constant carrier signal, preventing normal transmission of data.) Continuous monitoring should automatically identify a streaming terminal and

count in response to a request signal from the monitor. This result should be compared with normal counts so as to see how the network is doing. A poorly operating network will likely produce large number of successive outages during which no data is transmitted. This would show up as a significant drop in the number of signal transitions as against the normal amount, which would warn an operator to test the line.

The monitor, then, is the first line of attack in checking multipoint networks, as it can spot serious malfunctions in modems, terminals and communications links. But although monitoring easily identifies and isolates "hard" system failures, it is not so effective in finding transient problems or in alerting operators to gradual degradation, which may produce loss of efficiency over a long period, but not complete failure.

The first step in diagnosing faults of that kind is to perform the standard tests for point-to-point links, such as modem checks, and analog and digital loopbacks. The next step, if these tests do not uncover any faults, is to conduct a polling test, which checks dynamic multipoint operation.

If there appear to be problems on the link, the operator first checks the equipment at the central site, then addresses the remote location in question and commands a modem check test, switching the remote modem into a self-test mode to learn the status of the signal indicators and the number of errors recorded during the test.

Analog loopback

If the modem check test uncovers no failures, the operator goes to an analog loopback test. This loops the line back on itself at the remote site, returning outbound test data to the central site. The test signal consists of a known data pattern which is synchronized and checked against itself as the data is returned. The central site display then gives a count of the received errors. A high error count indicates a faulty communications link.

If the analog loopback test is satisfactory and reveals no fault, the operator commands a digital loopback test. This is identical to the analog loopback, except that the data is returned from the digital side of the remote modem. This test will show up any fault in the modem.

Successful modem and line tests suggest that the steady-state network characteristics are acceptable. In a multipoint network, however, polling is a dynamic process and requires rapid modem equalization and the initiation of transmission each time a station is polled. A point-to-point system, on the other hand, operates with its modems already equalized and with constant carrier signals.

The next step, therefore, is the polling test, which checks whether the system can change from an idle condition to steady operation without an excessive number of errors. In this mode, the master control transmits a known message to the remote station under test over the high-speed line's main data channel. As the message reaches the remote site, its bit pattern is compared with the known sequence stored there already, and errors can be detected right away. The remote site sends back a count of the errors along with a "canned" response message. Back at the main transmitter, the canned message is also checked for errors against a known sequence. The central site control module then displays any errors on both the outbound and inbound sides, so that the operator can quickly assess the quality of the circuit.

Once a system problem has been identified, the defective unit must be disconnected or bypassed until it can be repaired or replaced. To disconnect a unit, the multipoint control module must be able to set up restoral procedures, again through secondary channel signaling. Among these corrective measures are:

Disconnect and restore. A malfunctioning modem or terminal can be disconnected by a command which disables the remote modem's data channel transmitter. The secondary channel, however, still remains active so that other monitoring, testing and restoral functions can be carried out. A restoral command is used to reconnect the modem or terminal when the time comes.

Low-speed backup. If any portion of the main data channel fails, the secondary channel can be used for transmitting low-speed data. In such a case, the central site control module must be transparent to the low-speed data path. The secondary channel must be returned to normal operation if diagnostic or monitoring functions are required.

Dual dial-restoral. If restoral is to be accomplished by dial-up lines, a full-duplex system requires two lines, as well as a line-sharing device and its associated data access arrangements. The line sharing device broadcasts outbound messages and detects inbound messages on a contention basis. The dial backup can be manual, automatic or a combination of the two methods—manual dialing at the central site and automatic dialing at the remote site.

Spare modem substitution. The central site control unit may automatically switch-in a "hot" (powered) spare at any remote site equipped with this backup equipment. Normally, only a station in an especially remote place, or at a critical dropoff point in the system, would be equipped with a powered spare.

Fallback. It is important in a multipoint network to maintain operation in the face of line quality degradation, as long as the line is still usable. Many modems have low-speed fallback modes for reduced data rates on inbound links, outbound links, or both. Because the number of errors on a bad line can often be cut down by reducing the data rate, a system may still operate under poor line conditions if a low data rate is acceptable.

The control module should be able automatically to switch all modems on a particular multidrop link to any fallback rate, and to restore the system to normal operation when the problem has been cleared up. Fallback may also be necessary in dial backup operation because dialup lines are often prone to errors.

As more and more control circuits are added economically to modem packages, the ability to diagnose problems throughout the system continues to expand. And modems are becoming the focal points for such network diagnostics. ∎

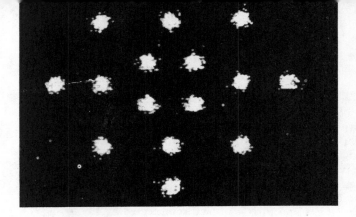

Spotting trouble on high-speed digital data links

Ralph W. Lowry, Codex Corp., Burlington, Mass.

'Eye patterns' are sensitive and versatile tools for speedy, accurate diagnosis of disturbances on communications circuits

The more users know about the current performance of data communications networks serving them, the more quickly causes of trouble can be spotted and identified. The most troublesome and unpredictable parts of a network are the carrier lines, and these are the first places to test when the network goes down. But many users are not experienced in testing telephone lines because of their unfamiliar analog characteristics, so problems in the communications links are often uncovered only after the rest of the system has been checked out.

But there is a simple method for analyzing line characteristics on communications links having modems with quadrature amplitude modulation (QAM) — that is, with twin carrier signals operating at a 90-degree, or quadrature, relationship to each other. These modems are generally used for transmission at 4,800 b/s and up, speeds that have become widely accepted since QAM hardware made its appearance in 1971.

This diagnostic method is an extension of the technique of analyzing "eye patterns" on an oscilloscope, as is commonly done with traditional amplitude modulation modems. (With a QAM modem the oscilloscope pattern bears no resemblance to an eye, although the term has stuck.) An eye pattern is produced on an oscilloscope by plugging it into a special output con-

nector on the modem, or into an accessory unit which converts the modem output into the signals that directly drive the oscilloscope.

Almost every maker of high-speed modems uses QAM today, and to interpret these eye patterns it is necessary to understand the modulation technique. On a 9,600-b/s circuit, four bits (b_1 through b_4 in Figure 1) are modulated at a time. The first pair of bits goes to one modulator (modulator X in the diagram) and the second pair to another (modulator Y). The twin carrier signals fed to these modulators (as already mentioned) are 90 degrees out of phase.

Each modulator changes the amplitude of its carrier signal according to the combination of the pair of bits being transmitted at the moment, and the output of a differential encoder — which contains information on the pair of bits transmitted immediately before. (Each pair of bits can thus assume any one of eight binary combinations, and so can be represented by one of eight amplitude values.) In actual operation a total of seven values are used for each carrier signal. The two resulting carrier signals are united by what is called a summing circuit and the single, complex output signal is put out on the line.

An oscilloscope plot of the X and Y amplitude values shows its QAM eye pattern (Fig. 2). For a 9,600-b/s

1 QAM modulation

Four at a time. Bits b_1, b_2, b_3, and b_4 modulate carrier signals X and Y to one of seven amplitudes. An electronic summing circuit combines the modulator outputs, and the signal is then transmitted on the data link. Such modulation at 9,600 b/s ideally creates 16 different dots arrayed around an oscilloscope's X and Y axes (Fig. 2).

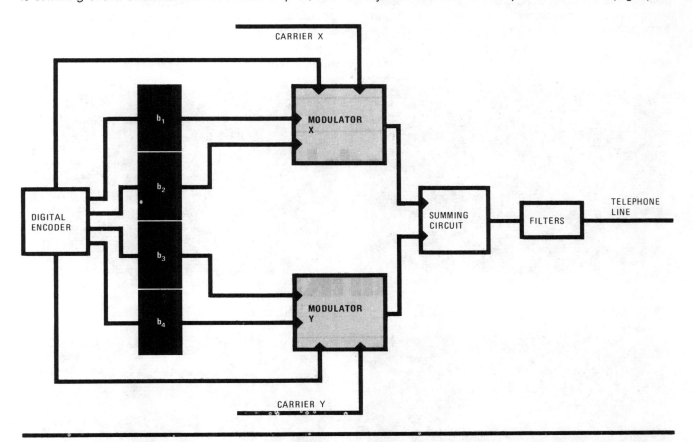

modem the screen shows a 16-point array in which each point corresponds to a four-bit set. For example, as shown in the chart accompanying the patterns, a bit combination "0010" produces a point at 3,3 on the eye-pattern display.

The eye pattern will present a perfect array when the signal is correct in phase, frequency, and amplitude, and has no superimposed noise. But a communications channel is not always so placid, and disturbances will show up as irregularities in the eye pattern.

Line problems

There are two kinds of disturbances that tend to distort received signals. One kind, called steady-state problems, affects the frequency response of the line and produces amplitude and delay distortion. An equalizer circuit in the modem is supposed to adjust for these problems automatically. The other kind of disturbance, spurious or transient line conditions, occurs too fast to be corrected by the equalizer. This group of problems includes such things as random noise, phase jitter, amplitude hits (disturbances), and phase hits.

Random noise, for example, causes the received eye pattern points to be dispersed around their proper positions (Fig. 3a). Similarly, phase jitter causes the

received signal to oscillate back and forth, smearing the dot cluster (Fig. 3b). Gain jitter (Fig. 3c) is characterized by a continuous periodic amplitude error with little or no phase error. Harmonic distortion (Fig. 3d) demonstrates a large amplitude error, again with little or no phase error, and is not so repetitive as gain jitter. An impulse hit (Fig. 3e) can be seen only if an operator is present, because the error gives off a short-term, high-amplitude signal; here the four dots on the eye pattern (from a 4,800-b/s modem) are displaced radially to give the illusion of four more dots. A phase hit of about 20 degrees (Fig. 3f) is characterized by a smear with little amplitude change.

In addition to helping in the diagnosis of line-related, transient effects, a QAM modem can through an oscilloscope provide insight into the transmission line's steady-state characteristics. One such readout displays the modem's tap coefficients (factors introduced by the modem's receiver circuits to compensate for distortion in the signal's quality). In a high-speed, automatically equalized modem, these tap coefficients are analogous to the bass and treble gain control settings of an audio amplifier. That is, a tap coefficient is a positive or negative gain factor developed by the modem's tap circuits, which make adjustments in the received

3 Abnormal line conditions

Patterns tell all. *Transient disturbances on a circuit, such as those represented here, can seldom be corrected by the modem's equalizer. Random noise causes the eye pattern dots to be dispersed around their proper positions; phase jitter causes the dots to oscillate back and forth; gain jitter is characterized by amplitude error; har-monic distortion causes a large amplitude error but no phase error; an impulse hit gives off a short-term, high amplitude so that the four dots (for a 4,800 b/s modem) are displaced radially to give the illusion of four more dots; a phase hit, here of about 20 degrees, is characterized by a smear with practically no change in amplitude.*

(A) NOISE

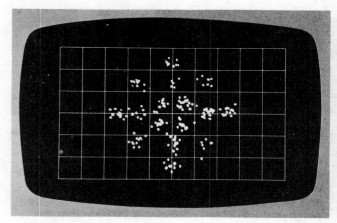

(B) PHASE JITTER

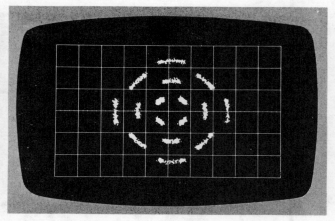

(C) GAIN JITTER

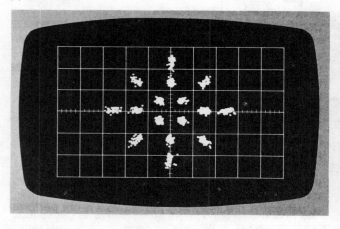

(D) HARMONIC DISTORTION

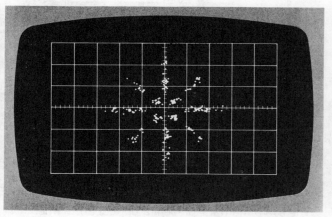

(E) GAIN HIT

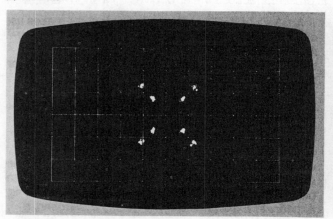

(F) PHASE HIT

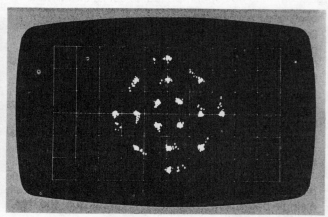

Computerized analysis

The circuit quality monitoring system (CQMS) is Codex Corp.'s microprocessor-based device for the performance of on-line diagnostics. The unit analyzes and displays the received signals and indicates when thresholds are exceeded. It monitors such parameters as phase jitter, amplitude modulation (also called amplitude or gain jitter), noise, band-edge distortion, harmonic distortion, amplitude or gain hits, phase hits, dropouts, and modem retrains. Hits, dropouts, and retrains can be counted either continously or over 15-minute periods, which corresponds to AT&T's standard practice.

The display's outputs are QAM modem eye patterns, tap coefficients, X-Y coordinate error signals, amplitude- and phase-error signals, and a derivative of the eye pattern which displays only the most recent value for each of the allowed dot-cluster positions. Using the replay and expanded time-scale function, each successive eye-pattern value can be observed in slow motion, so that the line's performance can be reviewed.

The CQMS also contains a decibel meter to measure the line-signal level, and a standard bit-error rate test set for use with modems and time-division multiplexers.

The CQMS is at present operated manually, but some automatic features may be added. Functions such as automatic sequencing, error alarm reporting, exception analysis, logging, and statistical monitoring analysis, can be implemented with the appropriate software and peripherals.

---

line signal. Together these circuits form a modem's equalizer. (A typical 9,600-b/s modem has 64 tap circuits.) Because tap coefficients adjust according to the line's characteristics, a display of their values shows the steady-state line conditions. Eye patterns, on the other hand, indicate only transient disturbances. By studying the tap coefficients, the user can determine if the equalizer is operating properly and ascertain whether the line's steady-state parameters are going beyond tolerable limits.

The tap coefficients are depicted by a series of segments in the oscilloscope trace. With an ideal line, only a single coefficient is markedly different from the rest, and is indicated by a single raised segment in the trace. If there is excessive amplitude or phase distortion, sev-

2 Normal eye pattern

Ideal pattern. On a disturbance-free line the 16 dots remain stationary; the eye pattern is fixed on the oscilloscope's screen and symmetrical about the two axes.

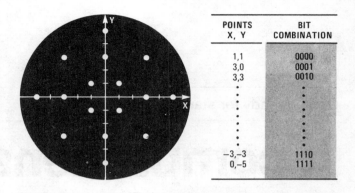

POINTS X, Y	BIT COMBINATION
1,1	0000
3,0	0001
3,3	0010
⋮	⋮
−3,−3	1110
0,−5	1111

eral of the taps will be raised and the largest tap reduced. Careful observation of the tap coefficients provides a qualitative view of the distortion parameters and, with some experience, an operator can decide which patterns of tap coefficients indicate that the quality of the line is not acceptable.

Help from microprocessors

Oscilloscope readouts require interpretation by an operator and can be somewhat confusing, especially when there are several disturbances on the line. For this reason, microcomputers are being used to analyze the high-speed modem signals and indicate directly the nature and relative magnitude of the problems. Microcomputers can be programmed to keep a tally of transient impulse phenomena such as amplitude hits and phase hits, so that an operator need not be present to record these events.

Error signals, eye patterns, and tap coefficient displays can be automatically stored when a burst of errors occurs. The operator can then replay the events to determine precisely why the network is not performing properly, and warn the carrier company of the nature of the line disturbances so that problems can be dealt with quickly.

Analysis of the line with a microcomputer makes use of the fact that line disturbances have their own characteristic "signatures", like those already described for random noise and phase jitter. The microcomputer samples these transient signals and compares their patterns with normal patterns in its memory.

If the errors in the received signal amplitudes correspond to a known disturbance pattern and exceed threshold values, a line disturbance is confirmed and the problem is indicated through an appropriate light output or message printout. An example of a commercial device of this sort is presented in the panel, "Computerized analysis". More about computerized testing appears in *Experiments in line quality monitoring*, a paper by P. Bryant, F. W. Gresin Jr., and R. M. Hayes, in IBM Systems Journal, No. 2, 1976. ∎

A comprehensive approach to network testing

John M. McQuillan and Gilbert Falk,
Bolt Beranek & Newman Inc., Cambridge, Mass.

By checking the data communications network from its components to the finished structure, the designer can test its performance and function

One important task that any organization which operates its own computer/communications network must perform is the development and acceptance testing of the network.

A step-by-step test plan for a data communications network is as essential as a comprehensive design plan. In fact, the test plan can serve as a preview of each of the design decisions to be made in the original specification of the network.

There are five levels of testing. Testing programs are divided into functional tests and performance tests. Functional testing means verifying that the object under test meets such basic requirements as the ability to transmit messages. Performance testing means verifying that the system meets a higher level of requirements such as fast response time, the number of errors transmitted, and reliability.

Level one is associated with individual software routine, or module, testing. At this stage individual modules are tested primarily for operation according to functional specifications. In some cases the performance of groups of modules may be tested as well.

Level two is the testing and measurement of the subsystem. Both functional and performance measurements should be done for individual subsystems. Two kinds of subsystems are distinguished for the purpose of this discussion.

- Data subnetwork subsystems include the data switching node's interface message processors (IMPs) and the front-end processor's terminal interface processors (TIPs) for terminals and/or hosts. Taken together, these facilities are called central offices (COs) for convenience, even if they are not managed in the manner of telephone company central offices.

- While most data communications messages follow a terminal-CO-network-CO-terminal route, some may need an applications and services supernetwork. Both subsystems—the data subnetwork and the applications supernetwork—might include such facilities as message-switching service hosts, network control/monitoring hosts, data sharing/data management hosts, and electronic mail systems. Collections of such computer systems at one location are referred to as service centers (SCs).

Level three corresponds to the testing of entire subnetwork central offices or network service centers. This involves testing to ensure that the individual subsystems within the service centers and the central offices work together. This level of testing also ensures that the data subnetwork COs and the network SCs can communicate with terminal and host subscribers.

Level four corresponds to the testing of combined data subnetworks and application supernetworks. It is not until this level is reached that certain functions of the individual data switches can be exercised. An example of such a function is routing, which requires a test bed of several COs. Likewise, it is not until this level that interactions among SCs can be tested.

Level five is the network testing level. Testing and measurement at this level are focused on the user-to-user functional capabilities, and such performance characteristics as delay, throughput, and reliability.

The following sections describe each of these levels of testing and measurement in more detail. In addition, self-testing capabilities that should be included in the design of the network are described.

Module testing

Sufficient software should exist at the initial testing stages to support individual modules and integrated sets of modules for functional testing, that is, to verify that they meet such qualitative requirements as the ability to send messages. Programs for supporting groups of modules under test create artificial operating environments in order to exercise all the module's functions and are referred to as scaffolding programs (Fig. 1). There are two types of scaffolding programs corresponding to top-down and bottom-up implementation.

Top-down implementation involves writing a program outline first and then filling in the blank spaces as individual software routines become necessary for continued operation. Bottom-up implementation means writing software routines to handle all the jobs a program could ever be expected to do and then fitting them together in the form of a finished program.

1 Scaffolding programs

Program writing. *A scaffolding technique allows the development of a program either from an outline of required parameters or through a building-block approach.*

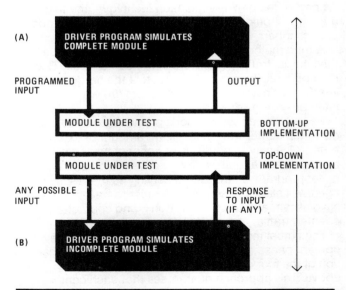

Driver programs (Fig. 1a) associated with a bottom-up implementation generate all the inputs for and accept all the outputs from a module under test. In essence, drivers create the environment of the module under test by simulating all the modules above and below it in the software hierarchy.

A stub program (Fig. 1b), on the other hand, is a dummy program that serves as a place-holder for a blank module during top-down implementation. The minimal requirement for a stub is that it must permit any module under test to continue execution. Therefore, a stub must satisfy any input/output requirements of the module for which it is a substitute. In addition, a stub can be employed as a memory space that records the origin and destination of all messages addressed to it to help build traffic studies, or even to do some initial network exercises prior to final implementation. For example, a stub program could act as an operational module in order to consume execution time and storage space in accordance with estimates for such full-fledged program modules as terminal handlers. In any event, since stubs already satisfy the appropriate interfaces, they should form the basis for subsequent programming, whereas, in many cases, drivers are discarded.

As an example, consider the testing of the source/destination control module in the front end. If this module makes use of the host interface protocol program, which interprets messages to and from hosts, and, in addition, makes use of the operator's console handler, the time-out routine, and various pseudo host programs (which both generate messages and acknowledge their receipt), then the testing of the source/destination control module would involve the use of stubs for each of these as yet uncoded modules. These stubs would then be expanded into the actual operator's console handler module, pseudo host programs, host interface protocol module, and time-out routine. The expansion and subsequent implementation of stubs as actual modules involves the inclusion of capabilities which they received from lower-level programs when they were being used as stubs.

Subsystem testing

Internal software processes should be provided to permit functional and performance testing of COs and SCs. These capabilities will certainly be needed during the initial development period. After the network is completed they will be required for the evaluation of proposed enhancements. In addition, it is likely that they will also be useful in the operational network. The need for such mechanisms is demonstrated by the problem of trying to test the interactions between units of a CO before users are connected.

One solution involves the use of two software processes in the IMP system for the purposes of functional and performance testing. They are message-generator software and message-discard software. The message generator produces bit streams of a specified length and frequency and transmits them. The message-discard software receives messages and ignores them.

Two types of message generators should be used.

2 Subsystem testing

Testing techniques. *The use of traffic generator and bit driver software routines allow the network designer to test the traffic-handling capabilities of both the subsystem front end and the data switching node. The simulated traffic can be used to test either individual units or the entire subsystem before subscribers pay for network services.*

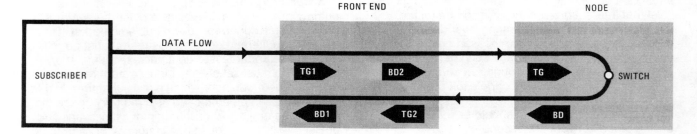

FRONT END   NODE

SUBSCRIBER

DATA FLOW

TG1   BD2   TG   SWITCH

BD1   TG2   BD

TG1 GENERATES TRAFFIC FLOW FROM FRONT END TO NODE
BD2 SIMULATES TRAFFIC FLOW FROM FRONT END TO NODE
TG2 GENERATES TRAFFIC FLOW FROM FRONT END TO SUBSCRIBER
BD1 SIMULATES TRAFFIC FLOW FROM FRONT END TO SUBSCRIBER

These two types are the bit driver (BD) and the traffic generator (TG). A bit driver allows one subsystem to test another subsystem's traffic-handling capacity. These drivers are quite unsophisticated in terms of the traffic they produce, and are associated with the interfaces between modular units. The traffic generators, on the other hand, actually simulate real input which allows functional testing as well as some degree of performance testing.

In contrast to the effect of a bit driver, the module running a traffic generator is being tested as well as being the testing agent. Any particular unit may either be tested or may generate test messages. In the first instance, both the bit drivers and the traffic generators associated with that unit are turned off and the unit is operated from the outside. If one of its traffic generators is on, the unit is the testing agent, even though it may also be one of the units being tested.

As an example of how this internal software is used to test subsystems, consider the case of testing the CO to see whether it is performing its functions properly (Fig. 2). The data switching node can be tested without involving any of the other subsystem units by simply turning on the traffic generator (TG) associated with it. The node is then both the testing agent and the object under test. Now suppose that the traffic-handling capacity of the node must be tested. In this case, the node acts as an operational data switch and the bit driver (BD2) associated with the front end is turned on. The front end is then the testing agent and the node is the object under test.

Finally, consider the case of testing the functions of both the front end and the node. In this case, the traffic generator (TG1) associated with the front end is turned on and the node operates as a data switch. The testing agent is then the front end and the objects under test are both the front end and the node. Although there are many other ways to test a complete service center or central office subsystem, the important point is that there should be a flexible set of software processes for testing each component in terms of its functions and its performance.

Center testing

It is important to have a variety of methods for thoroughly testing the operation of a complete central office or a complete service center. As shown in Figure 3, these include tests for real subscribers' hosts and terminals, simulated subscribers, internally generated traffic, and traffic from other network equipment.

In addition to the network operator, there may be other real subscribers, that is, potential customers of the network, who are willing to use their equipment to partake in some initial system tests. Testing of the centers, however, should not in any way be dependent on the availability of such potential subscribers. Some subscribers can be simulated by an off-line computer. As part of the off-line simulation technique, the test manager should supervise the development of a variety of subscribers who have both hosts and terminals.

A third method of operating a center involves use of the internal traffic generators of the center itself. This method, unfortunately, does not test the hardware interfaces since the traffic generators are part of the internal system software.

None of the above methods provides a way to load down the center with a significant amount of external traffic. One way to do this is to connect two centers back-to-back and allow one to drive the other. The bit driver programs in the center serving as the testing agent will allow the center under test to be loaded with a significant amount of host, trunk, and character-oriented traffic.

The actual testing of a center both during the development phase and after cutover involves a combination of the four center-testing methods described above. This approach guarantees that each center meets many of the required performance specifications

3 Center testing

Test alternatives. To test a network center thoroughly requires several methods. The center's capacity is most severely stressed in pre-operation back-to-back tests.

4 Subnet testing

Center operation. A small test network allows the designer to scrutinize subnetwork components before they are required to handle traffic from real subscribers.

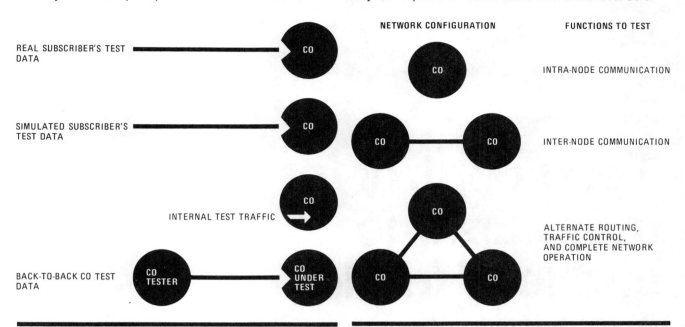

before it is combined with others to form a network.

Programs should be provided both before and after an individual center is put on the network to permit testing of those aspects of the center's behavior that are related to its operation in a distributed network. It is not possible to do this with only a single center. In particular some functions, such as alternate routing, require several centers before they can be exercised at all. This means that a small test network, independent of the operational network, is required. Particular configurations of this test network are used to exercise particular portions of the software.

For example, consider the case of the data subnetwork centers shown in Figure 4. With a single CO, it is possible to test those aspects of behavior associated with communications between the CO, its subscribers, and the network control center. This includes the subscriber access protocol handlers, the input and output handlers, the subsystem-testing software handlers, the terminal command language, and the pseudo-host function in the front end. It takes two COs, however, before those functions associated with communications between two nodes and front ends can be exercised. These functions include the link-control procedure, the store-and-forward function, and the operation of any higher level protocols implemented in the front end. Three COs are required before any aspect of alternate routing can be evaluated. This includes how well the program adapts to communications lines going up and down, or packet-switching node neighbors going down. In addition, a three-node network is required to test adequately the switchover required for hosts connected to more than one CO and aspects of error-

control and flow control where the relay nodes are neither the source nor destination. Adequate testing can be accomplished with a network having no more than three COs.

Network testing

A combination of actual subscribers' equipment, and the ability to simulate subscribers, permits controlled testing and measurement of the subscriber-to-subscriber performance of the network. These tests assure that the level of service to the user of the network is equal to that required by the system specifications. In addition, testing of the interaction between the SCs that form the applications supernetwork, and the COs that make up the data subnetwork, is carried out as part of this phase to make sure that everything works according to plan.

The most visible performance measurements for the user are end-to-end delivery delays for interactive traffic, and throughput capacity for stream traffic. Delay and throughput measurements should be taken by using a variety of specialized software tools. These tools consist primarily of host level traffic generators and analysis programs that run on an off-line computer. Tests should be made that involve modeling a variety of network conditions. Measurement of a subscriber sending to himself should be carried out first. Subsequent tests model one-hop and two-hop paths. Each test should measure delay and throughput under various network loading conditions between zero and maximum load. Loading can be carried out either by additional artificial SC traffic generators or by internal traffic generators in each CO. ■

Tech control for more uptime and less friction

Vic Lester, John Thacker Jr., and Donald Partington, Ashland Oil Inc., Ashland, Ky.

Ashland Oil's network test center gives the firm greater control of network elements and reduces vendor finger-pointing problems

Ashland Oil Inc. places a large amount of trust in good vendor relations and has proved that goodwill pays. Its extensive data communications network is completely tied in to a test center that General Telephone of Kentucky (GTK) bought and leases to the company. Ashland thus avoided the capital outlay needed to buy the test center while it still gets the benefit of the facility at a reasonable monthly cost. The arrangement gives Ashland the ability to spot network problems quickly. For its part, the phone company is assured that its customer is watching the status of a large network and is ready to make tests, call vendors, or inform it of the exact nature of a line problem with the least delay and the highest amount of accuracy. Mutual goodwill has led to mutual interdependence in a test center that benefits both parties.

Ashland Oil's data communications network spans remote departments, divisional offices and subsidiary companies all over the U.S. Its more distant facilities include a Valvoline Oil canning plant in Santa Fe Springs, Calif., offices of Ashland Exploration Inc. in Houston, Tex., and the headquarters of Ashland Oil's construction company—Ashland-Warren Inc.—in Cambridge, Mass. By means of the data communications network, the corporate data center performs many functions for these locations: payroll, general accounting, career profile and personnel records, order entry, cash flow accounting, and other computerized business operations.

As in most private networks, the types of users and the I/O terminals they operate vary widely. The users are divided by function into four major systems. First, there is the information management system (IMS). Here, 120 remote CRT stations are used mainly for transactions on order entry, inventory status reports, accounts payable, and an inventory spare parts system. The second is called Intercom—40 remote and 10 local terminals are used to report cash receipts so as to update the books as soon as receipts clear banks. The third, Atopatcs, is a data collection system in which 20 railroads report the locations of railroad cars over ASR35 teletypewriters. The final system is a configuration of 32 remote job entry (RJE) terminals that submit batch work for processing, including both number-crunching computations and high-volume business tasks such as payroll. Both the IMS and Intercom functions use IBM 3270 CRT display terminals. The RJE stations include a variety of makes—Data 100, Sycor, Univac, IBM,—operating with 2780, 3780, Mod 20, and other protocols.

There are three sets of data communications line configurations in the network: point-to-point (single station), point-to-point (cluster), and multidrop. The point-to-point (single station) configuration in Figure 1A is used for all RJE stations because the very nature of Ashland Oil's RJE operations requires full-time communications between the station and the computers at the corporate data center. The volume of data transfer required to justify an RJE station in the first place is usually so large that a line should be dedicated to that facility alone. Twenty-five of the 32 RJE links are full-duplex, four-wire lines leased from General Telephone of Kentucky (GTK). Dial-up lines are used for the lower-volume traffic on the remaining seven lines.

The point-to-point (cluster) configuration in Figure 1B is used for transaction terminals in the IMS and Intercom systems. IBM 3271 cluster controllers at the ends of these lines handle up to 32 terminals apiece. There are five cluster controllers in Dublin, Ohio, near Columbus (headquarters of Ashland Chemical Co.), one in Chicago, and four in Ashland.

The multidrop configuration (Fig. 2) is used for stand-alone terminals that are likely to be scattered over a limited region, such as at sales offices in the Midwest linked to a bridging junction in Chicago. The typical stand-alone terminal includes a CRT terminal with an associated unbuffered hardcopy printer. An optimum line would have one modem per drop, and up to five drops per line. The multidrop configuration provides more than satisfactory service whenever the data load between the corporate data center and any one terminal is limited. If there is enough work for more than two terminals at a particular location, it is usually just as economical to use a point-to-point (cluster) arrangement.

Finally, there is a microwave link between corporate headquarters at Ashland and the Ashland Chemical

headquarters in Dublin. Six of 24 microwave channels are used for low-cost bulk data communications.

The corporate network includes four low-speed lines (110 bit/s) and five 2-kbit/s dial-up lines for low-volume RJE terminals. The 21 leased lines serving the RJE terminals operate at either 4.8 or 9.6 kbit/s, while the 10 point-to-point (cluster) lines are 7.2 kbit/s. Five microwave channels operate at 7.2 kbit/s and one at 9.6 kbit/s. They are backed up by five 7.2-kbit/s telephone lines.

The major computers in the corporate data center are an IBM 370/158 and a 370/168. There are two IBM 3705 front-end processors (FEPs), which handle the communications tasks associated with the network operation. Either computer can handle (with some impairment of service) all of the data processing tasks received from the network in the event the other temporarily shuts down. In day-to-day operation, the 370/158 handles mainly IMS on-line processing, while the more powerful 370/168 is assigned to the RJE stations, Intercom, and various other terminals such as teletypewriters.

Testing a network

The terminal user is best served by providing him with high accuracy and high availability. To minimize outage time, the network manager must be able to monitor and test communications links, terminals, and modems, wherever they may be located. Once the source of a network problem has been pinpointed, the appropriate vendor—telephone company or modem or terminal manufacturer—must immediately be informed. Accurate diagnosis of the problem ensures that the right vendor is called, and avoids the finger pointing among vendors that is inevitable when no one is certain

1 Point-to-point configurations

Point-to-point. Single-station point-to-point lines operating at either 4.8 or 9.6 kbit/s serve all of Ashland Oil's RJE stations, since the high volume on these links requires full-time communications between terminals and computers. Clustered point-to-point configurations are used to serve interactive management information applications.

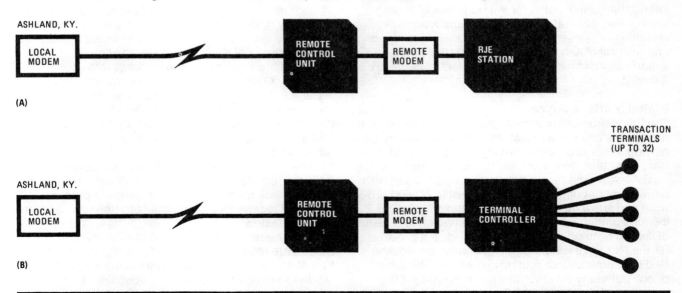

whose equipment is at fault. Network management must recognize that it is serving in an advisory capacity, particularly with regard to the telephone lines. Since the telephone company is responsible for maintaining the condition of the lines, network managers can only indicate where the problem seems to be located so that the telephone company's service organization can proceed with its own diagnostic and testing procedures. Ashland Oil does not believe in using its testing facility as a hammer in dealing with a telephone service organization.

Single site efficient

Integrating the necessary specialized equipment and personnel in a single test center is the most effective method of managing a data communications network that is comprised of a large number of lines. As the Ashland Oil network grew, therefore, a team in the computer science and services department began planning for a test center early in 1974. Although users of the network had been reasonably satisfied with service, it was clear that continued expansion of lines and terminals without a test center would result in less effective service and handling of operating problems.

Eight functions were originally established as necessary capabilities of the test facility that began operation in November 1976. Front-end processor transfer switching involves transferring all digital lines, individually or together, from one FEP to the other. The microwave to leased-line transfer-switching function moves the six microwave channels to leased telephone lines. In addition to the need for transferring lines in the event of an unplanned outage, the microwave channels are shut down twice a year for alignment required by the Federal Communications Commission.

The EIA monitor/test switching function involves accessing lines for passive monitoring and interrupting the data flow in order to test individual communications lines from the EIA side of the modems (bit error rate testing). Communications line monitor/test switching involves accessing lines for passive monitoring, and interrupting signal paths for the purposes of analog testing. Remote station termination and loopback switching isolates modems and terminals for diagnosis and restoral of service. The remote stations may be located any distance from the tech control center in Ashland.

Digital traffic replayed

The EIA instrumentation test function is used to review the conditions on the digital side of the modem by displaying, recording, and replaying data traffic and control characters, and indicates the status of each of the 25 EIA leads. The test center is thereby provided with a means of debugging software and of isolating hardware and firmware problems. Communications-line instrumentation permits orderly observation and testing of lines in both on-line and off-line modes. It provides for the testing of line parameters against previously filed benchmarks as a routine procedure. The telephone company test-facilities function calls for the provision of equipment and space at the test center

for GTK service people to test their own telephone lines assigned to Ashland Oil network. A 200-line patch panel permits GTK to introduce its own test gear whenever the situation calls for it.

The Ashland Oil test center.

The test center was built and installed by T-Bar Inc. of Wilton, Conn. The center is owned by GTK and tariffed to Ashland Oil.

The monitor/test instruments on the analog (communications) and digital (EIA) sides of the local modems at the test center (Fig. 3) are: T-Bar 5911, voiceband circuit monitor (VCM); Halcyon 520-B-07 analog telephone line tester; Spectron model D-601 Datascope digital monitor; ICC 220 bit error rate (BER) tester. These test instruments are connected to the network through T-Bar's analog monitor/test and digital monitor/test switch assemblies. The analog switch assemblies are connected to one control panel and the digital switch assemblies to another. The control panels each include illuminated monitor and test pushbuttons and a three-digit thumbwheel switch. The three-digit switch uses an octal coding method so that it can be manually set to address any one of 512 lines. The total installed line test capacity at Ashland Oil is 88 lines, of which 66 are active now.

In addition to the T-Bar monitor/test switch assemblies, there are T-Bar transfer switches on both the analog and digital sides. On the digital side, the switch is capable of simultaneously transferring all digital lines from modems to a second front-end processor in order to maintain service if one FEP or computer shuts down. It also will transfer lines individually for test and programming purposes and sometimes simply to redistribute the computer load. A separate IBM switch transfers the FEPs from computer to computer.

As part of the network control system, an addressable T-Bar remote control unit has been installed on the analog side of each remote modem (Figs. 1-2). The combination of the T-Bar control panel at the test center and the remote control units on the analog side of each remote modem gives test center personnel the capability of isolating any single line. Dual-tone multifrequency signaling techniques provide addressable remote control of the switching functions.

Each remote control unit will accept three commands in a test sequence. On one command from the T-Bar 4900 control panel, the line is disconnected and terminated with a 600-ohm load. Another command causes the remote control unit to loop the signal back and adds 16 dB amplification. A third command from the 4900 control panel will reconnect the modem to the line. In the disconnect mode, the test center isolates the remote modem and terminal from the line. In the loopback mode, the characteristics of both the send and receive side of the lines together can be monitored or tested.

Since the remote control units are independent of the remote modems, these modems can be any mixture of makes with no effect on test center operations. Modems with built-in loopback capabilities can be tested from the terminals on their digital sides. The

2 Multidrop configuration

Multidrop. *Stand-alone terminals serving such facilities as sales offices are most commonly linked to the rest of the network through modems on a multidrop line. Service from this arrangement is deemed satisfactory whenever the data load is limited. If there is enough work for more than two terminals, a clustered point-to-point line is used.*

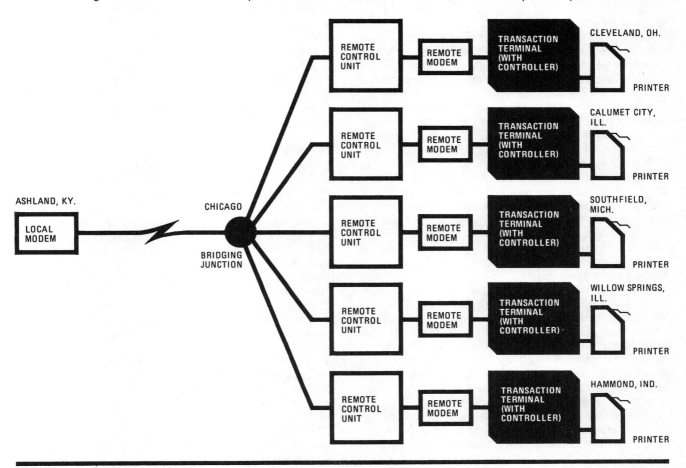

major elements of the test center are all located in a single console (Fig. 4). The analog and digital test instruments are placed at lower left and right, respectively, and the analog and digital monitor/test controls are mounted at the top of the panel.

The video display in the digital monitor presents all transmitted and received data, including control characters, that are flowing between the FEPs and terminals. A line of panel lights indicates the condition of all the EIA leads.

On the analog side of the local modem, transmission can be monitored in any one of three ways. The "eye" pattern on a video display in the analog tester is related to the transmission characteristics of the telephone line. The shape, amplitude and motion of the eye show the characteristics of the telephone line that can be compared to telephone industry specifications. Audio signals monitored over the T-Bar VCM loudspeaker may indicate to the experienced ear the presence of such common problems as noise, crosstalk, and other abnormalities. A dB meter on the VCM loudspeaker measures levels of transmitted and received analog signals. A Halcyon 519-A-02 field test set is also avail-

able for end-to-end line testing by Ashland Oil tech control center personnel. Problems in all line configurations in the Ashland Oil data communications network usually are first observed by a user at a terminal. An RJE terminal operator, for example, will call to say that there are error indications at the terminal or that the terminal just isn't working.

Typical diagnostic procedure
The diagnostic procedure is usually simplest for problems in point-to-point lines. The network manager begins by switching in the digital monitor and observing the send and receive data on the line that apparently has the problem. After confirming that a problem exists on that line (and not in the FEP's transmission), he then checks dB levels and listens to the circuit. If the problem is not apparent in this step, three troubleshooting steps can be taken:

The network manager can place the local modem (in Ashland) into an analog loopback condition and switch the BER tester into the line. If the observed BER is acceptable, the local modem is assumed OK.

With the analog monitor/test switch in the test

331

mode, the T-Bar 4900 control panel can be switched into the line. The appropriate disconnect and loopback addresses are entered to isolate the line from the remote modem. After resetting the analog monitor/test switch to disconnect the 4900 control panel and restore the analog line to its local modem, the BER tester is used to transmit through the local modem onto the send line and back on the receive line. If the observed BER is acceptable, the telephone line is assumed to be operating normally.

After the proper command to bring the remote modem back on the line is entered, the operator of the remote terminal is asked to activate the remote modem digital loopback switch (isolating the remote terminal from the modem). The BER tester is used to transmit through the remote modem and back. If the observed BER is acceptable, the remote modem is assumed OK.

If these three steps thus indicate that the local modem, telephone line, and remote modem are operating properly, the network manager knows that the problem has originated in the remote terminal itself and asks the operator to call the service organization for the manufacturer of the remote terminal.

Analog tests planned

If, however, a possible line problem is indicated by a high reading on the BER tester, the network manager normally calls the telephone company and reports the condition. A procedure soon to be employed will be to test the analog side of the line with the Halcyon line-test unit. Benchmarks that have been previously established on the basis of telephone industry standards will be used as a guide for reporting any difficulties to the telephone company.

The network manager will measure line parameters one by one and compare the readings with the benchmarks. Any parameter indicating cause of trouble will be reported. These parameters include: attenuation in dB; signal-to-noise ratio; phase jitter in degrees peak-to-peak; envelope delay in microseconds; non-linear distortion in dB; C-notched noise in dB; idle circuit noise in dB; and amplitude response. The test center is also able to obtain hit measurements, including gain, phase, impulse, and line dropouts at selected levels, giving simulated error rates. Any parameters that are found to be significantly outside their allowable ranges are also reported to the telephone company for its use in testing. Mutual savings of time and manpower have occasionally been realized by Ashland Oil and the telephone company just by Ashland's being able to furnish a level reading or a selected tone to the telephone company test board.

Amplifier is key

Ashland Oil's successful use of the remote control unit is keyed to an amplifier built within the device. This amplifier overcomes and adjusts the attenuation of the data circuit so that meaningful comparisons to benchmarked parameters can be made. Point-to-point testing is common and has been proved successful. Evaluation of multidrop testing is still under way. Plans include the same basic routine except that, with all points disconnected, loopback tests will be run one at a time, as is done on a point-to-point circuit.

Based on its own experience, Ashland Oil has identified four major benefits deriving from the use of a test center. The first is faster, simpler transfer switching. Because transfer switching involves no more than pressing a button on a control panel, there has been a substantial time saving by network managers. The simplicity of transfer switching means that operators who are not data communications professionals can successfully switch lines from one FEP to the other.

The second advantage derived from operating a test center is reduced testing time. All tests that are valid in a loopback mode can be performed within about

3 Test center layout

Test center. The monitoring and testing equipment located at Ashland Oil's test center includes a T-Bar 5911 VCM, a Halcyon 520-B-07 analog line tester, a Spectron D-601 Datascope digital monitor, an ICC 220 bit error rate tester, and analog and digital monitor/test switch assemblies. A separate switch transfers front-end processors.

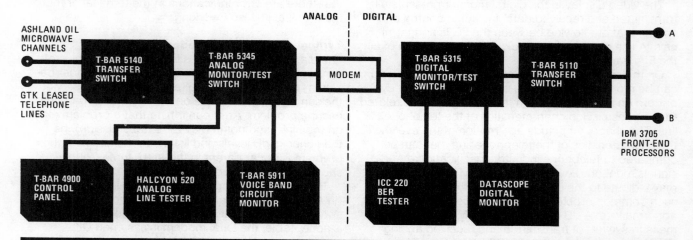

Fig. 4—Control center. *At the Ashland Oil test center, the video display in the digital monitor presents all transmitted and received data. Lights indicate the condition of all leads. On the analog side, transmission is monitored by means of an "eye" pattern display, a voice-band circuit monitor, and a dB level-test meter on the VCM speaker.*

10 minutes. As much as half a day was spent on loopback testing prior to the use of the test center. The only exceptions are end-to-end tests for such parameters as phase shift.

Third, finger-pointing has been eliminated. Since they know the capacity of the test center, vendors willingly accept Ashland Oil's identification of the source of problems. As a result, the rapport between Ashland Oil and its data communications equipment vendors has been appreciably enhanced.

The final point is neatness. Centralization of test instrumentation has reduced the number of cables and minimized confusion. The reduction in the amount of time for transfer switching, problem diagnosis and associated activities was estimated as 174 man-hours each month, plus over $500 a month in telephone company service charges.

However cost-effective in network management, the most important benefit of the test center is superior service to network users throughout Ashland Oil. The improvement is almost impossible to measure, but certainly real in the sense of reduced mean time to repair and faster vendor response at remote terminals.

The test center has been used, to date, primarily for diagnosing and solving problems which have already occurred and which are visible to users of the data communications network. The test equipment and procedures involved in this type of activity can also be used for predicting problems and taking corrective steps before they become visible to users.

Test center personnel are presently benchmarking communications lines before they are put in service. Allowable ranges for specific parameters are being established for all possible combinations of loopback/terminated conditions, depending on the number of points in the circuit. Before long, each circuit will be tested periodically at a quiet time and the measured parameters compared with the benchmark. Any degradation in a data communications telephone line or microwave channel will be noted, and the vendor notified so that the problem can be corrected on scheduled downtime, prior to an actual outage.

Problem prediction is presently being done on difficult lines. Since the test center is monitoring the entire line, it has been able to detect incipient problems before the telephone company becomes involved in end-to-end patching through toll offices. This procedure has been found to be workable only when the telephone company has complete confidence in a test center's diagnostic capability. ∎

A Data Communications Special Report

Network control: managing the data environment

Glenn Hartwig, Data Communications

As it is in nature, the forces required to keep a data network operating are complex links of the same chain

Network control encompasses the basic, interrelated functions needed to keep a data communications network up and running in good shape. Such control is rapidly approaching the point where some users say computers, large or small, must be employed. Until now, slow and steady growth with test equipment, data line monitors, protocol analyzers, and integrated network control systems has been achieved. The next step would also use these approaches, but under computer-based control.

Control by computer, a controversial idea, involves continuous sampling of traffic and the comparison of those samples with predetermined operating parameters. When an out-of-parameter condition occurs, the computer either automatically corrects the condition or notifies the operator to invoke human intervention.

First, consider the basic functions occurring in a network management center. They are patching and switching, monitoring and alarming, diagnostic testing, and repair. Patching and switching bypasses problems occurring on the line, at the modem interface to the line, at the remote terminal, and at the central site front-end processor. The second function is monitoring, the observation of data on the line. Monitoring is used in conjunction with the patching and switching functions. Monitoring the data enables the operator to de-

termine whether he has a problem with the network or if errors are being introduced from outside interference. The third area is diagnostic testing. Once the operator determines that a problem exists on the network, diagnostic equipment is employed to pinpoint the location of the problem. With the problem pinpointed, the operator then makes a personal decision as to what type of corrective action is needed. He may decide that the problem is transient and no action is needed, that the problem requires him to perform repairs, or that something must be replaced and the vendor notified.

All of these have traditionally required active participation on the part of operators at the network control center. However, network control by data communications end users is rapidly approaching the point where the benefits of computer control must be employed. Not only are networks growing in size, but also users are becoming more and more aware of the added expense of operating a network below peak efficiency. What is involved is the need to keep track of large amounts of control information, the ability to act quickly in the event of a severe problem, and the ability to detect the onset of any type of failure before the operator loses the services of his network.

There has been steady growth in the network control equipment field. Vendors worked up from simple jack panels with wires and plugs for manually reconfiguring a network through various levels of sophistication in diagnostic test equipment. Integrated systems for testing lines, the functions of local and remote modems, and some functions of remote terminals are offered by modem makers so their customers can tell at a glance where network problems are coming from.

The next step for network control equipment vendors is to provide these same functions with microprocessor or minicomputer control. Computer-based control, as practiced by such large network operators as Boeing Computer Services Inc. and General Electric Information Services division (GEIS) encompasses completely automatic control systems. The automatic nature of the control provides the user with the flexibility to avoid problems that could in any way affect the reliability or ultimate availability of the network. In both cases the network operating companies were forced to write their own customized software and to effect network control through the use of dedicated minicomputers. In the past, only such large companies as these, along with military and governmental agencies, could afford the expense of automatic network control. Now, both GEIS and Boeing have stated that as much as 90 percent of what they were forced to do on a custom basis could be incorporated into microprocessors and sold to network operators as stock offerings.

Network control equipment manufacturers disagree. What follows is a discussion of the scope and depth of the basic functions of network control, and the opinions of both users and vendors on the degree of automatic control possible in each area. There are no areas of universal agreement. Network control is an open area, resistant to standardization, and as open to the vagaries of supply and demand as any other market area. Often, what is available from one vendor is considered impossible by another. The offerings of all vendors may seem inadequate to some users, but overly sophisticated to others. Some users have little or no interest in the control of their networks, according to some vendors, while the same user requirements are considered by other vendors to be extravagant.

How much network control is available to the user ultimately depends on his own appraisal of the conflicting areas of cost versus the penalty that must be paid for every minute of down time. Included here are such considerations on the user's part as: available capital, the monetary value represented by his data, the willingness to staff his company with specialized network control technicians and managers, and the ability of the user community to offer the vendors a big enough market to encourage their investment of research and development dollars.

In the opinion of Lawrence Kovarovic, vice president of marketing, Digitech Data Industries Inc., the whole future of network control can only be decided by a mandate from the user community. According to him, vendors would naturally be encouraged to enter the automatic network control market if only users would show that there is a real demand and demonstrate that they are willing to pay for high-priced facilities.

The separate areas of patching and switching are

1 Patching and switching

Patching and switching. Automatic or operator-controlled replacement of primary equipment is accomplished through a panel with access to all circuits.

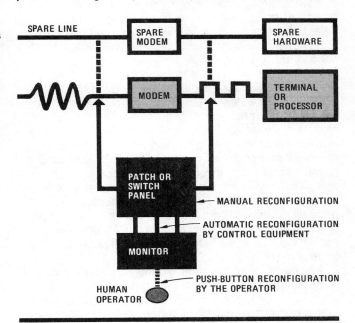

closely identified with each other. According to Robert Brown, manager, preliminary design, Atlantic Research Co., patching and switching are "allied kinds of functions." He said, "Patching provides a manual, physical connection from one circuit to another." This usually means the replacement of discrete components (such as modems) by taking a wire and using it as a means of bypassing the failed component and connecting a good component in its place.

"Switching involves the replacement of a group of components with a backup group of components," Brown said. The difference is in volume, not in function. Additional confusion is added to the picture by the fact that switching is another name for automatic patching, Brown added.

Vaughn Darnel, director of product management, T-bar Inc., said switching is automatic, remote patching that provides a "pre-established alternate condition" for a group of network components. "Most commonly, switching is network reconfiguration done in an emergency mode," he said.

Basically, patching involves the movement of network activity from one component to another on a line-by-line basis, while switching does the same thing for many lines and whole groups of components.

Both patching and switching have been around for a long time. Their development dates back to the earliest attempts by common carriers to keep the lines open. Users employ patching equipment primarily at the central site modem/network-link interface to monitor the quality of the carrier's signal and to compensate for faulty modems. The exception to this occurs when patching takes place at a remote site and the transference of the line from one modem to another is controlled from the central location. This is done by remote control and, according to Brown's definition, falls under the heading of switching.

Switching, when used to designate the transference of a whole group of lines from one component (such as a front-end processor) to another is most often called "fall-back switching." According to both Brown and Darnel, this is the most common type of switching used in network control centers.

Not only are patching and switching "allied functions" that have been around for a long time, but they are also more widely deployed than most other types of network control gear. Edward Siira, national sales manager, Dynatech Data Systems, notes that patching and switching are vital to network reconfiguration in the event of an outage, vendors are thoroughly familiar with the technology involved, and automatic patching and switching equipment has been on the market for some time. Makers of patching and switching equipment all produce automatic as well as manual versions of their gear. Typical among them are Atlantic Research Co., T-bar Inc., Dynatech Data Systems, and International Data Sciences Inc.

Automatic patching can be done locally and remotely, over digital or analog connections, and by either a computer or a human operator (Fig. 1). Further, automatic, computer-controlled, patching and switching can fall into two subcategories. First, there is the situation where network monitoring equipment detects an outage. Computer intelligence is used to recognize the faulty condition and call it to the attention of a human operator. It is then up to the operator to perform the task of reconfiguration. In automatic network control systems, all the operator typically must do is hit a button that engages the proper backup equipment.

In other cases, such as an airline reservations network in which T-bar installed automatic switching devices, any type of human intervention would take too much time. In this case, microprocessor intelligence is employed to check the status of various network components. In the event of a failure, automatic routines that perform the patching or switching operation are immediately engaged. The operator is notified that a patching or switching operation has been performed. He can then perform whatever diagnostic and repair operations are necessary to bring the failed component back to proper operational status. Sensing equipment is used to detect the presence or absence of a signal on a line or from a network component. In the absence of that signal, the automatic patching or switching equipment, through the intelligence of preprogrammed microprocessor control, knows that it is time to act. Because a totally automatic system responds with electronic speeds in the event of an outage, the switching or patching is so fast that there is virtually no downtime. The only problem with this approach is that the equipment is expensive. Even though many of the components incorporated in automatic patching and switching equipment are off-the-shelf items, the ultimate configuration and its cost is up to the user. The higher the level of sophistication, the higher the price.

A big variable in the cost equation of automatic patching and switching for this "dynamic optimization" of network lines and customer equipment, according to Raymond Sepe, vice president of marketing, International Data Sciences Inc., is whether the computer control is provided by the user's mainframe computer or by a microprocessor supplied by the vendor.

Remote control
The price is again increased if the user wants automatic control of patching and switching operation at remote locations. For example, T-bar sells two types of unattended remote control units. One is operated over dial backup lines and utilizes coded signals generated by an ordinary Touch-Tone telephone to effect a variety of patching and switching operations. Equipment for handling up to 16 channels sells for a little over $4,000. A unit that handles only five channels costs about $1,800. A second kind of device that controls patching and switching at remote sites operates over the normal data communications lines. It accomplishes the control of patching and switching operations by sending a predetermined ASCII character—a different character for each control function. This unit in a 16-channel control configuration sells for about $6,700. Again, a smaller unit costs less. Most vendors of patching and switching gear offer equipment similar to the T-bar line of remote control units.

As handy as it may be to have equipment that will patch and switch all by itself, the removal of the human operator can present problems. If, for instance, a transient problem appears and then goes away in a few minutes every day at the same time, automatic equipment may switch to backup equipment needlessly. In some cases there is no substitute for human judgment, no matter how much the user pays, or how much response time is lost.

2 Data trap and display

Signal trap. Most producers of patching and switching equipment offer specialized devices designed to capture and display line events just before a failure occurs.

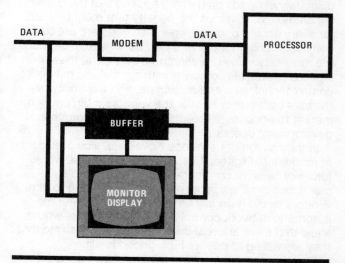

Once the human operator has been firmly established in the user's mind as a necessary component in the network, there are a number of network control devices that will help the operator do his job more efficiently. As stated by Frank Lezotte, technical systems specialist for Intertel Inc., "No network will ever operate itself. This kind of thinking is folly." Since it seems there will always be human involvement to some degree in any network, equipment that monitors the status of the network and tells the operator when something is wrong is invaluable.

Monitoring and alarming

The whole purpose of equipment for monitoring and alarming is to give the operator a head start in deciding what type of remedial action (such as switching and patching) must be taken to keep the network operating at peak efficiency.

As with patching and switching, monitoring and alarming are often referred to together. This is because the human operator can't always sit and watch the status of the data communications network 100 percent of the time. Therefore, monitoring devices often have attention-getting alarms that will alert the operator and help him focus his attention on trouble areas.

The monitoring and alarming functions can either be manual or automatic, again depending on the wishes and needs of the user. The earliest forms of manual monitoring consisted of an operator's trying to collect network information without specialized equipment. At the front-end processor, non-specialized monitoring consists of a teletypewriter that simply prints errors as they occur. There is no indication of the exact nature of the problem, where it is, or how serious it is. At the central processing unit, the total number of transactions-in-error can be stored and dumped at the end of the day. This type of monitoring gives no indication of traffic patterns, and no indication of the exact nature of the problem. As much as any other factor, the lack of a real-time display of errors characterizes the day-end dump type of monitoring as basic in the extreme.

At the modem/line interface, one type of monitoring that has been around since the earliest days of networking involves a continuous audible record. The characteristic sound of data passing through the interface is projected to the operator by means of a loudspeaker mounted on the control console. An experienced operator knows what the data should sound like and can spot any variation in the sound pattern as an indication that something is wrong. This method of fault detection has the advantage of being on-line, but it still does not tell the operator anything specific about the type of problem.

Automatic monitoring

Data network monitoring equipment comes in varied degrees of sophistication and, today, is most commonly located adjacent to the patching and switching modules on the network control equipment rack at the central site. By and large, the same firms that manufacture patching and switching equipment make monitoring

devices. The functions are logically allied because the operator should have an accurate idea of just where the problem is located in order to either patch or switch around it effectively.

However, several manufacturers specialize in producing equipment that monitors data communications network traffic. Among them are such firms as Spectron Corp., Digi-Log Systems Inc., ADC Telecommunications Inc., Digitech Data Industries, Halycon Corp., Hewlett-Packard, and Epicom Inc. In addition, there are modem manufacturers who sell integrated systems that report on the status of networks for which they are the sole supplier of modems. The vendors in this field include, primarily, Racal-Milgo, Codex, General DataComm Industries, and Intertel.

Patching and switching equipment manufacturers offer equipment that will trap and display signals on both the analog and digital sides of the modem (Fig. 2). The same holds true for equipment from specialized manufacturers, with the exception that these vendors generally were the first to offer such extras as buffers that would store the data that immediately preceded the error condition for off-line analysis.

Integrated systems from modem manufacturers often work independently of patching and switching control panels and are concerned only with the condition of modems in point-to-point or multidrop networks. Their function is usually limited to displaying exactly what is wrong with a modem and do not concern themselves with line, terminal, or processor problems.

All of this equipment, however, is more automatic than day-end data dumps or listening for uncharacteristic noise over a loudspeaker. Modems were probably the first pieces of networking equipment to have status monitoring built into them. The standard offering from most modem manufacturers today includes a light-emitting diode (LED) on the front panel indicating the status of every Electronic Industries Association (EIA) connector pin attached to the unit. If something goes wrong with the modem, an operator can tell at a glance which channel is malfunctioning. This contrasts with early modems that either had no status indicator lights or simply had a single light that displayed the existence of a problem, but would not pinpoint it.

The existence of a multitude of lights on each modem is seen as both a help and a hindrance by some network operators. According to David Blevens, manager of data networks for Boeing Computer Services, a diligent operator will go blind staring at banked arrays of modems all day in anticipation of one light going out. More commonly, though, operators will get bored and begin to ignore the modem status lights. This latter condition is in part supported by Gary Angell, product manager, Codex Corp., who says users will ignore even a flickering status light (indicating a marginal operating condition) and wait until either part or all of the network fails before taking any action.

A new series of monitoring products could offer some relief for the myopic network control operator. They generally fall under the title of data traps and operate as follows. The units are attached at the network control console, usually at the patching and

3 Standardizing modem signals

Signal standardization. One unit, functionally stylized here, receives line signals, converts them to modem-acceptable signals, passes them to the receiving unit, and performs these functions in reverse for outbound signals. The advantage that accrues to the operator is that modems from any vendor can interface with the network.

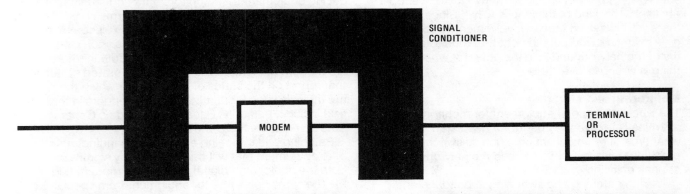

switching interface. They are passive monitors until an anomolous condition is spotted. These data traps are microprocessor controlled and have stored within their software or firmware the operator's preset performance thresholds for a number of network characteristics. The operator is then free to perform other tasks. If and when something occurs that exceeds the operator's specified thresholds, the trap will capture the event and sound an alarm to call attention to the error condition. The System 180 from Racal-Milgo and the DLM II from Digi-Log use microprocessor intelligence to not only trap the erroneous data, but also to automatically run tests to determine the exact nature and location of the fault.

Extended capabilities

Although monitoring and alarming in a network control center generally deal with the functional status of modems and the lines in between, some users have insisted on equipment that will also tell them what's going on with remote terminals and front-end processors. This end-to-end monitoring and alarming capability cannot now be purchased as a standard product from anyone. It must be custom built, either by the user himself or by a vendor on a contract basis. The reason for this, says Codex's Garry Angell, is the lack of an industry standard that would spell out what types of control data should be transmitted on a continuous basis. If such a standard existed, monitoring equipment could then be built with standard components that checked specific parameters on the basis of standardized signals all the way from the most distant terminal, through the remote modem, over the transmission link, through the central site modem, and into the front end of the central processing unit. He believes that advanced monitoring and alarming should be done by the front-end processor because its CPU has the capacity and memory to keep the track of what's going on throughout the entire network.

The most advanced network control systems to date seem to bear out the validity of this approach. In the past, the sheer power needed to accomplish end-to-end monitoring could only be found in host CPUs or dedicated minicomputers with enough processing power to keep track of every signal that passed up and down the network. Airline reservation networks, car rental networks, and network service operating companies such as GEIS and Boeing all depend to one degree or another on the raw computing power available in large scale computers for network monitoring. Dependence on mainframe computers devoted to network monitoring also involves expensive and time-consuming software programming. All of this is generally believed to be beyond the reach of most small- to medium-sized network operators.

The advent of the microprocessor may spell relief for those who need constant monitoring, but can't afford to dedicate an expensive mainframe and customized software to the task. As previously noted, Racal-Milgo equipment will monitor line and modem performance for networks that employ Racal-Milgo modems. Intertel, General DataComm, and Codex have similar offerings for networks using their modems.

Independent monitoring equipment vendors such as Spectron and Digi-Log offer microprocessor-based devices that will perform a thorough job of monitoring a limited number of performance parameters. Theoretically, the extensive use of limited-function microprocessors throughout the network could perform as well as a monolithic, single-site processor. The question still remains, however, as to just how cheaply microprocessors can be built, programmed, and deployed. Ronald Moyer, president of Digi-Log thinks microprocessors will prove much cheaper, even if several are used in the same network. Others in the industry, however, believe that the cost of several microprocessors will be about the same as a central minicomputer.

As with patching and switching, the trend in monitoring and alarming seems to be in the direction of more automation and greater product sophistication. Progress is being impeded, however, by a number of factors. The cost of automatic monitoring and alarming is still high, vendors often view the area merely as an adjunct to other profit centers (the case with modem makers), and there seems to be a need for some form of standardization in the types of signals that will be monitored. Additionally, users are not only leery of the high cost of monitoring equipment (about $6,500 for Digi-Log's DLM II), but also reportedly have little interest in the quality of the network as long as it continues to run after a fashion. Most important, perhaps, is the fact that users have traditionally looked to the vendors to supply the leadership in the monitoring field.

If the present situation of confusion and conflicting areas of interest continues to dominate the attitudes of the vendors, it could be left up to the users to supply the leadership. The idea of users dictating the products that will appear on the market is novel and still in the experimental stage. On one hand, some users feel that no one knows their needs better than the individual network operators. On the other hand, the diversity of network configurations and different data monitoring needs could lead to a situation both unwieldy and impractical. At any rate, the idea seems to be catching on. Atlantic Research recently formed a users' group for companies that installed its Intershake monitoring device. The basic function of the group is to let users communicate and pass new network testing and monitoring software programs back and forth among themselves. Atlantic Research merely acts as a central clearing house for all information, but by doing so, it also gets an idea of what the users want.

Intershake users generally consider both the Intershake device and the users' group to be indispensable. The monitor is used as a debugging device for new equipment and software since it not only lets the user see the data on the line, but also lets him run preprogrammed or canned exercises on new equipment at remote sites.

As for the users' group, Timothy Haake, communications engineer, Monsanto Co., commented, "I don't know of anybody who has not benefited from belonging to the users' group." To his knowledge, only one change has been made to the Intershake device as a result of a user's suggestion. That is secondary, however, to the opportunity to communicate with other users. Interaction with other users saves time for everybody, since everybody contributes programs, thus saving time for other users with similar requirements. According to Haake, "If Atlantic Research, for some reason, disbanded the group, it would be a great loss to the users." He likes the idea of the users' group so much that he further commented that he would be willing to continue the group independent of Atlantic Research and is sure that most of the other members feel the same way.

Diagnostics and repair
Closely following the identification of a problem through the use of monitoring devices comes the final diagnosis of the problem and the restoration of the network. Fault diagnosis is generally accomplished in a manual mode, using much of the same equipment as is used for network monitoring. Monitoring equip-

ment generally has the ability to pinpoint a failure by allowing the operator to check the signals coming from each piece of equipment and to determine whether or not those signals fall within acceptable operating parameters. With the problem pinpointed, patching and switching gear is employed to reroute traffic around the failed component or change the configuration of the network to include backup equipment or communications lines.

In most cases, switching and patching are the only remedial actions that can be taken in network control centers. At one time or another, operations personnel will be called on to switch every line and every piece of equipment from the primary unit to a backup spare while repairs are conducted. Even if equipment is only taken off-line at regular intervals for preventive maintenance checks, patching and switching is the only way to keep the network operational.

Failure prediction
The push on the part of some users in attempting to acquire automatic equipment is not to totally eliminate repairs. The point is to try to predict when a failure is likely to occur and make the repairs before the failure results in a halt in traffic on the network.

The present state of affairs requires that repairs be conducted in a post-failure environment. Predictive analysis equipment would allow repairs to be made in a less hurried, pre-failure environment. Users are asking for network control equipment that will allow them to avoid a failure instead of simply allowing them to recover quickly.

The hope is that, by putting money into the network control center, less money will have to be spent in other areas. For example, Robert McCalley of GEIS and David Blevens of Boeing share the opinion that current fault isolation equipment is of high quality and does a good job of picking out the source of a failure. Neither, however, can tolerate an outage of any duration. Their search, then, is for equipment that can be programmed for predictive analysis. The term predictive analysis covers more than the collection of raw network data. It also includes the summarization of that data and its presentation to an operator in the form of a short trend report or a suggestion that some action be taken to avoid an outage.

As things stand now, the following sequence of restoration events will occur from time to time in most network control centers (see Table). A particular line or piece of network equipment fails, and the operator is notified either by his alarm system or by a customer who calls on the phone to complain of a service outage. The operator can then either immediately switch the customer to all new backup equipment and look for the source of the problem later or use his monitoring and diagnostic equipment to isolate the fault and patch around it—leaving the customer without service for however long it takes to accomplish the repairs.

In an automatic, fault-predictive, environment the scenario is altogether different, as shown in the table under "Prediction." Here, the network monitoring system would tell the operator that a specific link between

Post and pre-failure operator sequences

RESTORATION	PREDICTION
A. FAILURE	A. MONITOR
B. ALARM	B. ALARM
C. SWITCH OR PATCH	C. STATUS DISPLAY
D. DIAGNOSTICS	D. OPERATOR OPTIONS:
E. REPAIR	1) PREVENT FAILURE
	2) ARRANGE BACKUP
	3) TEST BACKUP EQUIPMENT
	4) NOTIFY USERS
	5) SWITCH OR PATCH
	E. DIAGNOSTICS
	F. REPAIR

two cities and affecting X number of terminals is degrading so badly that an outage will occur in an hour. The operator now has time to take several alternative courses of action. The network is still passing data but, by calling the common carrier ahead of time, the operator will be able to determine if the problem can be corrected or if he must activate and test emergency backup lines. Backup modems can be tested ahead of time. In the case of having to replace one high-speed link with a number of slower dial backup lines, the operator can calculate how many lower-speed modems he will need to handle the traffic at both ends. Finally, before the circuit fails he can notify all users that they are being switched to backup facilities and advise them that they may experience a number of different service conditions depending on the speed and quality of the backup lines and modems.

Equipment that warns an operator of an incipient failure would also provide cost savings for the network managers. The network would no longer be required to have as part of its configuration a dedicated standby link. A backup link may only be used on an occasional basis, but it must be paid for on a full-time basis. Lower-speed dial backup facilities may be more expensive than a high-speed dedicated link on a full-time basis, but they are usually less expensive than a dedicated link if used only for short periods while repairs are made on the primary link.

Although this example concentrates on the use of predictive analysis in the detection of an imminent line failure, several other areas of network operation could also benefit. Examples supplied by GEIS include: the ability to detect and display the status of all nodes; the ability to detect and display the status of all links; the ability to introduce new software; the ability to measure overall network performance; and the ability to schedule preventive maintenance.

Network control equipment vendors point out that GEIS is a very large and, in many cases, unique oper-

ation. The claim from the vendors is that GEIS and other large networks of its type will always have to develop customized methods of achieving their goals since the mass market is never going to be that sophisticated. The response of GEIS and Boeing is a firm denial that they are doing anything that is functionally different from any other network operator, no matter what the size. Both McCalley and Blevens claim that 90 percent of the predictive analysis routines that they were forced to write into software on a customized basis could be reproduced in microprocessor firmware—or offered as standard software packages—if there were enough demand to stimulate the interest of computer manufacturers, specialized software producers, or makers of network control equipment. Software development is expensive, and right now no one is willing to risk investment money unless he is guaranteed a profitable market in advance, say those who write their own routines.

Objections

This attitude is affirmed by some network control equipment makers. Says Codex' Gary Angell, "The general attitude is: 'Let someone else do it [offer predictive analysis software.]' The risk is just too high. Who's going to buy it?"

Nor is Angell alone in his assessment. Most network control equipment manufacturers point out that, since each network is configured to the user's individual needs, there is no way the manufacturers could present a standard product line that would give early warning to everyone. The problem, as they see it, is one that includes configuration, protocols, and the make and model of equipment on the line.

The problem with configuration is that most monitoring equipment is designed for point-to-point or multidrop networks. Despite the fact that the software written by Boeing and GEIS can be used in a multiplexed configuration and that the Racal-Milgo System 180 and GDC's Netcon 5 can operate in a multiplexed environment, most diagnostic equipment vendors comment that there is no way analytical tools can follow signals through the time and frequency scrambling process that takes place in a multiplexer. The problem is said to be aggravated when a new piece of data communications gear is added, or when existing remote hardware is moved from one point to another. If any variation in configuration occurs, it is said that the controlling intelligence would have to be changed to take into account the new locations and addresses of every element on the network. Most networks do undergo changes in configuration from time to time. If the arguments of the vendors are valid, the cost would undoubtedly be too high for most users.

The second stumbling block is said to be the wide variety of line disciplines. Network protocols can vary from low-speed asynchronous to very high-speed bit-oriented disciplines. This protocol proliferation is said to make the task of analyzing data for faults dependent once again on complex, customized software. Monitoring equipment would have to be able to switch from one protocol to another and call up the proper analysis routine for the whole network traffic load on a message-by-message basis. The capability has been designed and built by the big network operators, but the cost to the small- and medium-sized network operator would be so high that the market would evaporate.

In the network equipment area, modems seem to cause the most trouble for network control product vendors. They point out that there is no standardization in the modem field. For example, initial handshaking routines vary from manufacturer to manufacturer. If a standard operating procedure existed for all modems, a single piece of diagnostic equipment could perform continuous, on-line monitoring for the whole network. Says Gary Angel, "We need the Electronic Industries Association to step in and produce a standard that would say what remote modems should report to the central site to make monitoring possible in a mixed-product environment." Intertel's Frank Lezotte agrees that there is no standardization in the modem market, but that is the way he prefers it. Says he, "The only way to assure effective fault monitoring is to buy everything from one vendor, no matter what the cost." In a way, that might make more sense than having the EIA step in and proclaim a standard for modem/network interaction. The cost of retrofitting an entire network to conform to a single standard would be prohibitive for all but the most well-financed organizations.

General DataComm Industries does make an item that standardizes the output from any vendor's modem (Fig. 3). The problem here is that the signals can still only be processed by a General DataComm network controller. Nevertheless, the GDC products do allow users with multiple vendor modems to report their status to a single unit at the central site.

The GDC effort is seen as a source of problems by Intertel's Frank Lezotte who dislikes the idea of networks that lack "vendor consistency." He says that several vendors must be called on to maintain such a mixed-modem network.

Integrated systems

Most of Intertel's diagnostic routines are conducted through a test channel within the same line as the data path. According to Lezotte, "If you can run diagnostic routines, the network is fine anyway and there's no sense in taking up space in an on-line channel for diagnostic purposes."

Codex, General DataComm, and Racal-Milgo have an interest in automatic, on-line diagnostics and monitoring and all three sell intelligent network devices similar to the Intertel unit. The basic function of the network control equipment from all four vendors is the same. All units monitor the status of the network and, to varying degrees, diagnose the fault and pinpoint its location. All perform their monitoring and diagnostic functions through a sideband channel in the primary data link.

Codex, however, has a provision for performing certain tests on the main channel since the company believes that reproduction of exact operating conditions is sometimes necessary for effective diagnostics.

Racal-Milgo and General DataComm both have central site network monitor and diagnostics units that employ a microprocessor instead of relying solely on hardwired logic for test purposes. Since the software-based logic used by the microprocessor can be changed, the unit offers a basic flexibility not found in the other units. However, since the user would not normally be capable of changing the software by himself, he must use the device as is. The flexibility provided by intelligence accrues to the vendor, not the user.

The network control packages provided by all four vendors will warn the network operator when lines begin to degrade and all have the ability to report the actual failure of modems and terminals. Predictive analysis for the status of modems and terminals in a standard package does not exist, but certain facts about their status in a "go/no-go" manner can be displayed.

Robert T. Smith, vice president, plans and programs, General DataComm, believes the increasing awareness of the cost of down-time will eventually result in full-scale, real-time diagnostics. Codex' Angell, on the other hand, says that he has seen little demand for equipment to do predictive fault analysis. Even though his company makes hardware that tells the operator about line degradation he states that, "Most users will accept marginal performance right up to the point of failure." The reasoning behind this attitude follows this line, says Angell: The operators feel that anything they do to diagnose their network's problems is a gift to the companies with whom they maintain service contracts. The vendor has contracted to keep the equipment in operating condition. All user-owned network control equipment, to one degree or another, represents a situation in which the customer is put in the position of doing the vendor's job for him.

Several vendors point out that network status information is routinely reported to the host computer of most networks. Since the data already exists in the host, developing predictive analysis is a job for software and no new diagnostic hardware is needed. All that is left to be done, they say, is the development of routines in software that will make predictions on the basis of the data that already exists and display it for the network operator.

This solution sounds simple enough, but problems exist. For one thing, major network users said they were unable to find this kind of software as a standard offering from anyone. This returns the user to the question of whether it is more to his advantage to write the software himself, conduct an extensive search in the hope of discovering the right software, or get by on his present system of post-failure restoration.

A second problem with large, customized software packages that continuously run network status checks is that they require the dedication of a good deal of the front-end processor's time or the full-time use of a dedicated minicomputer. The user must decide if he can afford to use his computing resources in this manner, if he can afford to buy a minicomputer just to watch his network, or if he can afford to wait for microprocessors to proliferate to the point where the network is so full of distributed intelligence that a central intelligence is unnecessary. ∎

Part 7
Communications processors

A Data Communications Special Report

Communications processors — trends and trade-offs

Ray Sarch, Data Communications

Turning out an efficient network requires the proper choice of components. The CP is one device that must be considered in the design

Developing an efficient data network — one that moves data rapidly and is cost effective — is an ever-growing concern of the conscientious user. One way to attain greater network efficiency is through the use of a communications processor.

Recent developments in CP architecture have led to the following:
- Increased use of microprocessors and multimicroprocessors.
- A tendency toward modular use of CP components.
- The placing of more decentralized intelligence (interfacing with network devices as a separate module) away from the CP's central processor, trading off increased central management against reduced central functions.
- Distinct differences in vendor philosophy in regard to how functions are controlled: software, hardware or firmware (microcode), or both.

Before exploring these trends and trade-offs, it would be helpful to define the CP's various forms and purposes. The communications processor is often not a single device, nor are its functions limited to one network location. Basically, a CP is used as (1) a front-end processor, (2) remote concentrator, and (3) message switch. The packetizing processor represents another CP use, but is considered a special form of

the message switch communications processor.

Each of the three basic categories is shown in Figure 1, represented in somewhat simple network arrangements, and explored later in more detail. As a front-end processor (FEP) (Fig. 1A), the CP is located at its host computer. A prime function of the FEP is to relieve the host of network communications overhead.

When physically located at or near the distant terminal devices served, the CP is known as a remote concentrator (Fig. 1B). The connection back to the host may be direct (dashed line, asymmetrical) or through a similar CP acting as an FEP (solid line, symmetrical).

The prime purpose of locating the CP remotely is to reduce the cost of running multiple lines to distant terminals by running fewer to the remote CP. A combination of short runs between the terminals and the remote concentrator plus the CP connections back to the host are usually more cost effective than multiple long runs. In the symmetrical arrangement, when some terminals are located near the host, access to host applications may be made through the FEP rather than through the remote concentrator, as shown in Figure 1B.

Another CP function is store and forward when used as a message switch. Elements of this function exist in the FEP and remote concentrator. But when switching is the primary function, the network may be repre-

343

1 Processor variations

Functional locations. The communications processor's functions are not limited to one network location. As a front-end processor, the CP is located at its host. When located near the distant terminal devices served, the CP is known as a remote concentrator. With its switching function as primary, the processor is called a message switch.

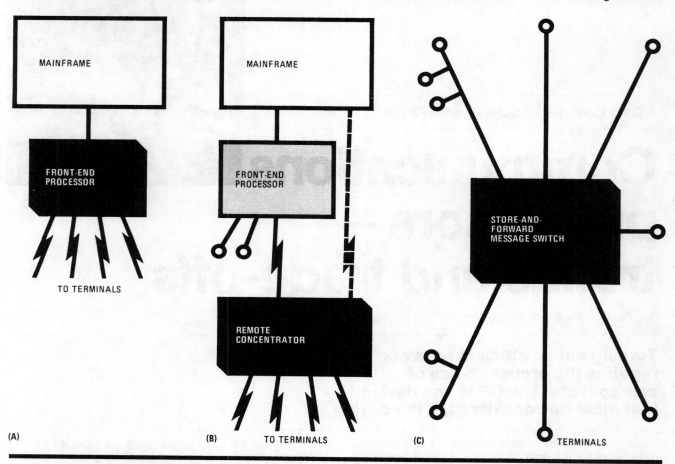

sented more accurately by Figure 1C.

As supplied to the user, a communications processor will resemble a minicomputer or look like an entirely different unit. In the latter case, the equipment is supplied by an independent vendor who designs and builds his own processor. Examples of the independents are Computer Communications, Inc. (CCI) of Torrance, Cal., and Comten, Inc. of St. Paul, Minn. Many minicomputer vendors are also represented by their products in the CP field. Another group of companies increasingly represented is the specialized common carrier, such as Telenet and Tymnet, with their offerings of CPs originally developed for use on their own public packet networks.

Compatible independents

CCI and Comten aim almost exclusively at the IBM user market. Their front-end processors are plug-compatible replacements for IBM's 3704 and 3705 communications controllers, and are upgrades of IBM's hard-wired 270X transmission control units—as are the 370X units. CCI and Comten claim that their units offer greater multi-host support, more ready access to host applications, and support of a greater number of lines and terminals, including non-IBM units.

Where a user has a large system—one with several host computers—employing just one multi-host front-end processor can be very convenient. Hardware costs are lower, and programming is less complex. Comparisons of high-end FEP capacities show IBM's 3705 supporting two hosts simultaneously—or four on a special order. CCI's CC-80 supports seven, and Comten's 3690 can support up to eight.

Even with one host, a front-end processor is effective in relieving a mainframe of dealing with each terminal desiring access to particular application programs. As indicated in Figure 2, the FEP responds to a terminal's application request and gains access to the proper host region. Shown are three typical IBM applications: timesharing option (TSO); information management system (IMS); and customer information control system (CICS). It should be noted that the standard 3705 software does not relieve the host of applications switching. But the independents' FEPs are claimed to control this function, thereby enabling the host to dedicate more of its resources to the applications themselves.

2 Accessing applications

Communicating with the host. *Some front-end processors switch a terminal's application request to the proper host region, thus freeing the mainframe of this function.*

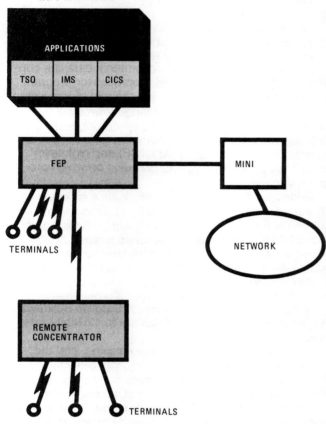

S/370 MAINFRAME

One firm—Comm-Pro Associates of Manhattan Beach, Calif.—claims that it can modify standard 3705 software so that applications handling and other enhancements of the independents are made available on the 3705. This includes increasing multi-host support to four mainframes.

Application programs and multi-host support come together when each host is dedicated to a particular application. Then, a terminal is directed to its application by the FEP switching the request to the proper host. If one host fails, then only that application is lost. Of course, to prevent loss of all applications if an FEP goes down, a back-up FEP should be included.

Networking

When a communications processor is used as a "pure" message switch (Fig. 1C), no connection is needed to a host computer. Only when the network's terminals must also have access to a host's resources—such as particular applications—is switch-to-host connection required.

Although IBM's 3705 should always have access to a host—to the point of not having its own periph-

erals—the independents and the minicomputer vendors provide stand-alone switches. Disk storage and other peripherals are also available.

The CP's network functions—besides being a store-and-forward message switch—include buffering and queuing for load leveling. That is accomplished by what IBM calls pacing, otherwise known as throttling. The technique consists of the processor sensing an impending overflow situation at a receiving device, and either temporarily storing the data that would have caused an overflow, or stopping the sending device until the receiver is ready again.

A CP feature that exercises another form of traffic control is called fast/slow poll. Here, terminals are polled normally—fast—until a terminal does not respond or has no traffic to send. When such non-responses occur, the CP automatically reduces the polling frequency of that terminal. When it again responds with traffic, the terminal is transferred back to a fast-poll mode. The algorithm for establishing polling frequencies and mode criteria are under user control.

It is important to note that the operator of a remote terminal is not aware that he is dealing with an intermediate processor, and not directly with a host computer. In this regard, remote terminal access to host software functions may be compared with Paradyne's Pix offering, which also is claimed to extend host-to-terminal interfaces without affecting host software.

Another network function is logging and journaling. Such information is normally kept on magnetic tape. If this peripheral is not a standard one with the CP, then the data is put on disk and transferred onto tape through another facility—such as at a data processing center.

Collecting and monitoring network statistics is yet another CP function. This data may include line and terminal usage, outages, numbers and types of messages, and repeat-request frequency. By keeping track of connect times, the CP can store—for access by the control console—accounting information such as charge-back data.

Network maintenance is aided measurably by the CP. Both software and hardware "bugs" may be detected, isolated, analyzed, and correction assisted by CP console action. Non-host-dependent diagnostic capabilities are featured in some communications processors, notably those of CCI and Comten.

Network control as exercised by Telenet's TP 4000 processor enables any connected, properly logged-on terminal to run diagnostics on any network-connected TP unit and its lines. In fact, Telenet says that the operational status of connected remote terminals, together with usage statistics, is made available to users.

One notable feature of the communications processor—most apparent with the independent offerings—is the ability to deal with a variety of terminal types, speeds, and codes. Enabling each type to communicate with the others requires CP conversions, which are made possible by a combination of line interface devices and software. Standard speeds and codes are readily handled; non-standard ones may be accepted, but usually require some reprogramming. Similarly, standard protocols—such as asynchronous and binary synchronous (BSC) communications—are accepted by the CP. And those processor vendors who do not yet offer the newer protocols—such as the bit-oriented ones and X.25—are, in general, planning to do so in the near future.

Gateway processor
As public networks proliferate, there will be a growing need for a device on one network to communicate with devices on others. The need is becoming apparent with the various networks in different countries. But political considerations may slow implementation of internation data flow.

However, within the U.S., internetwork transmission may not be as difficult to implement. And with the proper software developed, and the guidance of standards now under consideration, the CP can act as a gateway processor.

There are other situations when the CP, functioning as other than a switch, may operate without a host. For example, if the host computer shown in Figure 2 becomes disabled, the terminals—in the case of many processors—may still communicate with each other. Of course, there will be degraded service. But if the CP is so designed, it may queue application requests until the host is again operational and on line.

To relieve the host of as much of the network operational responsibilities as possible, the efficient CP manages such functions as message routing and network reconfiguration. Routing tables are maintained at the CP. When a table change or update is needed, some CPs require just a console entry for a simple change—such as a terminal identifier to correspond to a new location. But when the update is more complex, the new data is entered as part of an initial program load (IPL) or system generation.

Network reconfiguration data is entered similarly. This routing and configuration information is totally resident in the CP, with the host not involved.

One other network feature a communications processor may have that could be useful is called "pass through." As shown in Figure 2, if access is desired from a terminal to another network (mini-controlled in the figure), the FEP will recognize the request and pass the connection through to the other controlling hardware. This feature effectively widens the numbers of applications and terminals to which a CP-controlled device may have access.

As a network node, the CP combines intelligence with massive switching capabilities. For example, CCI's recently announced CC-85 can handle almost 900 lines. Other vendors claim different numbers—with the processing capabilities also varying. Line speeds range up to 230.4 kbit/s. Facsimile terminals are also being considered as devices for switching by a CP. CCI is working with Rapicom to develop this capability.

Modular structure
Turning from network applications to the communications processor structure proper, the most striking feature is the CP's modularity. As outlined in Figure 3,

Comten's CP, for example, may be divided into five distinct interacting areas. "Minicomputer architecture cannot do the job," says Donald A. Wurden, Comten's director of systems engineering. Comten claims its 3690's throughput is up to about 600,000 characters a second, which is possible, according to Wurden, because of the equipment's distinct communications processor architecture.

The modem interface module (Fig. 3) can be a microcoded or fully programmable device, depending on the modem interface module (MIM) selected. A software-controlled MIM, such as Comten's data link control (DLC) interface, has its microprocessor program loaded at IPL time, together with the rest of the system. The protocols accommodated range from start-stop asynchronous to IBM's BSC and synchronous data link control (SDLC), to the advanced data communications control procedure (ADCCP) and high-level data link control (HDLC)—depending on which program is loaded.

Evidence of the DLC-MIM's intelligence is shown by its expandable capacity to 4,000 instruction words—loaded at IPL time—and 16 kbytes of buffer storage. Up to 32 DLC-MIMs can be attached to each 3690, with each MIM controlling up to 16 lines, at up to 56 kbit/s. When a 230.4-kbit/s rate is required, the MIM handles up to four lines and BSC protocol only—for now. Wurden is also looking at future requirements of coming networks, including that of Satellite Business Systems (SBS). Plans include an 8- to 12-Mbit/s data rate.

With microprocessor prices decreasing, and the growing convenience of using micros as line interfaces, there is a trend to multi-microprocessor configurations. There may be a danger in this trend, however. Arthur Lynch, Data General I/O products manager, says that the overhead in managing all these decentralized processors could take up more CPU resources than can be spared. This argument is countered by Telenet's business planning vice president, Stuart L. Mathison, and other multi-micro-design vendors who are taking a close look at the CPU resources required to manage and control all the jobs that the decentralized micros can handle. So this balancing of multi-micro management against the overhead needed requires some careful design trade-offs.

32- vs. 16-bit word
The word structure a processor uses bears a direct relation to its cost and function. Minicomputer vendors and IBM, among others, have established the 16-bit word as a de facto standard. Lynch acknowledges that a 32-bit structure can support more throughput and more lines, but feels that it can be justified only on large systems, where the 32-bit machine controls an entire network. What is gained with the 32-bit word is more efficient memory addressability.

Comten, for one, is already using the 32-bit structure in its 3690. And CCI's marketing support director, Wilbur W. Marshman, says that his firm is headed in that direction. Despite these developments, Lynch says that he does not expect the 32-bit structure to replace

3 Processor architecture

Modularity. Comten's CP structure is highlighted by its MIM, which, in the data link control version, can "intelligently" accommodate most popular line protocols.

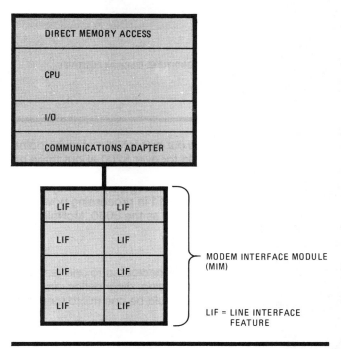

the 16-bit one, because of the cost involved.

As for programming languages, the present standard is Assembly language — not considered a higher-level type. Use of a higher-level language should lead to increased programmer productivity, Wurden says. As a result, Comten is planning to program with PL/1 by early 1980, Wurden adds. CCI's Marshman says that his firm's processors will be programmed with Assembly language at least into next year. But Marshman says that Pascal is being considered.

The I/O structure of communications processors typically uses direct memory access, where processor intervention is not required. This technique enables CCI's memory bus, for example, to attain an internal throughput capacity of about 3.7 Mbyte/s.

Interrupt handling — that is, the method in which a processor recognizes a request for interaction from a terminal — is being approached differently by IBM and by Comten. As Vernon Lizakowski, Comten's director of control software development, explains, the 3705 reacts immediately by either scheduling a task or storing (tabling) the interrupt request at the interface hardware (scanner). This procedure may prevent additional scanning for other interrupts until the processor accepts the first interrupt.

Comten's approach is to table or stack up to 256 interrupts, under I/O control, and not interfere with scanning by the modem interface module (see Fig. 3). The interrupts are examined by the CPU, and the work for each is scheduled at the processor's convenience. The MIM's intelligent functions are thereby not tied up

awaiting response to an interrupt. Other CPs, such as CCI's, operate in much the same way. The essential difference of the two is in the number of interrupts that can be stacked, awaiting CPU action.

Stringing operations

The CP's instruction set — the programmed expressions that specify each of the processor's operations — is different from the mini's. Figure 4 is an example — provided by CCI's Marshman — of one CP instruction. It is really five individual instructions strung together. Comten's programming operates similarly. A non-communications-oriented program could require five separate operations, with the attendant delays between each, resulting in reduced throughput.

The CP operating system (OS) — the software that controls the program scheduling and other management functions — is, of course, communications oriented. This means that all CP operations are in real time, responsive to interactive devices, and not aimed at "number crunching" data processing tasks. The CP resources are designed to respond to network needs.

One mini vendor offering many communications processing features in a remote or distributed environment is Computer Automation (CA) of Irvine, Calif. CA's 16-bit system for access (SyFA) minis establish a virtual network of interactive devices, while maintaining access to host computers (see DATA COMMUNICATIONS, April 1978, p. 21). IBM compatibility is stressed, while support of X.25 packet networks is also claimed.

Continuing the trend of decentralized intelligence, the SyFA network processor has a front-end micro, called a microbooster. Separate FEs are used for X.25 (at up to 56 kbit/s), asynchronous, BSC, SDLC, and line printers. Each has its own 16-kbyte memory. As Carsten Brydum, CA's marketing communications manager, points out — and confirming the CP independents' approach — the SyFA OS manages the micros efficiently because the overhead needed is less demanding of the processor's resources than for the OS to manage each function itself. Each micro is software driven; that is, loading is done from the SyFA mini at start-up with an IPL.

The CA customer is responsible for his own applications programming, similar to the situation with other remote concentration configurations. Future implementations are seen to include integrated voice/data and high-speed satellite applications, Brydum says.

Concentrating on the whole

In contrast with the CA approach is the turnkey system offered by Computer Transmission Corp. (Tran), El Segundo, Calif. Each implementation calls for its own microcoded (fixed) programs combined with Tran's standard line of minis. The communications processors packetize, and X.25 support is available. Jim McNally, Tran's product development director, says that there is an obvious trend to put an increasing number of network functions under microprocessor control. But Tran will stay with the 16-bit word structure, he says.

The increasing use of microprocessors has generally been attributed to reduced costs. The magnitude of

LOGICAL OPERATION (SUCH AS PRODUCT) BETWEEN
REGISTER 3 (R3) AND R4

PUT RESULT IN R5

SHIFT ONE BIT LEFT

TEST FOR UP TO EIGHT CONDITIONS (SUCH AS POSITIVE)

BRANCH ON CONDITION

this reduction is spelled out by McNally when he points out that Intel's 8080 sold for over $200 about three or four years ago. Today, it costs around $4. In addition, a more recent micro such as Zilog's Z8000 may be compared with a DEC PDP-11 in processing power, and is 20 to 30 times as fast as the 8080, McNally adds.

To each its own
He sees each micro chip as dedicated to one task, such as encoding and decoding, diagnostics, and loading control. The ultimate would be one micro for each interface, McNally says.

How cost figures are brought down to the user level is illustrated by a network example. Assuming a 100-terminal configuration, half synchronous and half asynchronous, a three-year CP hardware lease could be budgeted at about $250 per month per line.

Many low-end network applications can be filled by statistical multiplexers, also called intelligent time-division multiplexers (ITDMs). Specifically, referring back to Figure 1, the front-end and remote processors of 1B can be replaced by ITDMs if the required functions can be met. What is gained is lower cost and transparency (DATA COMMUNICATIONS, July 1977, "What intelligent time-division multiplexers offer," p. 29).

A recent arrival in the ITDM field is Micom, with its Micro800. Roger Evans, marketing vice president, says that Micom has gotten out of the CP business because of the customized features demanded by most customers. This requires individualized, labor-intensive programs. And selling unprogrammed hardware "competes with the semiconductor manufacturers," Evans says. He admits that there are firms ready to meet special customer needs, but adds that Micom will stick to its standard product line.

The views of an independent consultant firm, Network Analysis Corp., Great Neck, N.Y., is of particular interest to the potential user. An officer of the company feels that "the CP market has not developed as far as it has to. Statistical muxes have essentially taken away the need for CPs at the lower end. Vendors are making 'dumb' boxes smarter. The problem is to supply more software to maintain the upper end, to make smart boxes smarter." To maximize throughput, he says, the vendor should provide X.25 packet-switch capability as well as migration to a multi-microprocessor mode. ∎

Communications processors keep networks ticking

Gilbert Held, U.S. Civil Service Commission, Macon, Ga.

Communications concentrators and front-end processors have distinct attributes—each is designed to perform specific tasks

Integral to almost every data communications network—and responsible for much of the smooth gear-like meshing of network elements—are two devices which, although consisting of many similar hardware components, must be recognized and utilized as distinct entities. These two devices are the communications concentrator and the front-end processor. Each device is designed to perform specific applications.

Substantial confusion concerning the utilization of these devices can occur due to the multitude of overlapping functions they perform. A front-end processor, in effect, performs concentration functions by concentrating a number of lines into a few data transfer paths between that processor and a host computer. Likewise, a remote network processor can be viewed as performing the functions of a front-end processor when its high-speed data link is used to transmit data directly into another processor.

To alleviate some of the existing confusion about the utilization of these processors, this article will examine the basic components of the devices and the functions they perform, the characteristics that should be investigated for evaluation purposes, and the placement of these devices within a data communications network.

As a general statement, a concentrator is a device

which concentrates M incoming lines to N outgoing lines, where a number of incoming lines is usually greater than—or possibly equal to—the number of outgoing lines. The incoming lines are usually referred to as concentrator-to-terminal links, whereas the outgoing lines are normally called concentrator-to-concentrator or concentrator-to-host links. Although the concentrator-to-host link implies that such lines from the concentrator are connected to the host processor, in actuality they can terminate at a front-end processor which is, in turn, connected to a host processor or main computer.

Depending on the hardware components and operating software one selects, the concentrator can be used to perform concentration, pure contention, store-and-forward concentration, message switching, and remote network processing. Remote network processing is a term some computer manufacturers use to denote concurrent concentration of low-speed terminals with remote batch processing, all on one processor. (For a detailed discussion of the concentrator's message-switching role, refer to "How concentrators can be message switchers as well," DATA COMMUNICATIONS, April 1977, pp. 51-57.)

In a concentration role, concentrators merge the traffic from several low- to medium-speed lines onto one or more high-speed lines, similar to the function performed by a multiplexer. However, concentrators can be programmed to transmit data only from terminals that are active, as opposed to conventional time-division multiplexers in which a fixed fraction of the multiplexed channel is reserved for each terminal, regardless of whether or not the terminal is active.

Concentrators can also be programmed to make the high-speed link more efficient through data compression. A reduction in the average number of bits transmitted per character is made possible by determining the different occurrence rates of characters, and applying an algorithmic code to denote each character. (See the article, "Data compression increases throughput," DATA COMMUNICATIONS, May/June 1976, pp. 65-76.) In addition, if the host computer's native code is different from the terminal's codes, code conversion can be performed by the concentrator, relieving the host processor of this burden.

Interfacing with controllers

The typical hardware components included in a concentrator used in a concentration role are illustrated in Figure 1. The single-line controllers (SLCs) provide the necessary control and sensing signals which interface the concentrator to individual data communications circuits. While single-line controllers can be asynchronous or synchronous, the majority are the synchronous type. The preponderance of synchronous transmission is due to the SLC's normally providing only one—or at most a few—high-speed transmission links from the concentrator to another concentrator or to a host computer (front-end processor).

Since the support of numerous lines would be expensive and would take up a lot of space if implemented with single-line controllers, most communications support for the concentrator-to-terminal links are implemented through the use of multi-line controllers. Multi-line controllers (MLCs) can be categorized by capacity (number and speed of lines supported) as well as by operation: hardware- or software-controlled.

Hardware-controlled multi-line controllers place no additional burden on the concentrator's CPU, the hardware MLC requiring much less operating software than the programmed controller. However, programmed controllers have the lowest per line cost by reducing

1 Concentrator hardware

Components. *Typically, a concentrator used in a concentration role is made up of a central processing unit, a multi-line controller, and numbers of single-line controllers.*

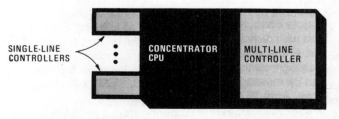

2 Groupings by channel

Foursomes. *In this typical multi-line controller arrangement, each of the four channels in a group must be of the same terminal class, having identical bit rates and codes.*

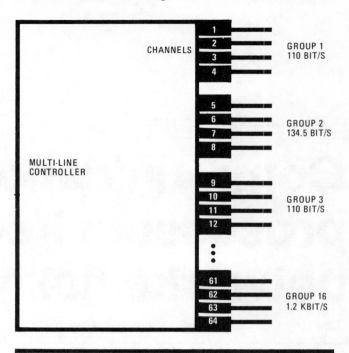

the hardware in the interfaces and the controller to a minimum, although a large burden is placed on the processor. For a programmed controller, all sampling control, bit detection, and buffering is performed by the processor through software control. The amount of processing time required by the operational program is the main factor limiting the number of lines that can be connected to the concentrator via software-controlled MLCs.

To reduce the complexity of circuits in hardware multi-line controllers, as well as to reduce software overhead of programmed controllers, incoming lines are often arranged in groups. These groupings are by bit rate, code level, and the number of stop bits for asynchronous terminal support. Figure 2 illustrates a typical grouping by channel for a multi-line controller. This controller requires a minimum of four channels per group—all four channels of the same terminal class (same bit rate and code). In Figure 2, groups 1 and 3 are of the same class. The MLC may have any mixture of classes, until the number of groups multiplied by four equals the total number of channels supported by the controller (64 in the example).

Although a complete examination of controllers might entail the investigation of up to 50 parameters, Table 1 lists the 13 key types of information that one should ascertain about the different controllers which are supported by a concentrator. Included are those parameters discussed above.

Another area that can have a major bearing on communications costs—and where the cost-cutting implementation is comparatively convenient—are the types of interfaces supported by the controller. If the controller supports directly connected terminals, and the concentrator can be located in the vicinity of a number of the terminals, then connecting those terminals directly to the concentrator will eliminate the cost of installing pairs of line drivers or modems between the concentrator and each applicable terminal. In this case, vicinity means—typically—up to 50 feet for EIA RS-232-C interfacing, or up to about 1,000 feet for a TTY current loop interface configuration.

Pure contention
In essence, a pure-contention concentrator is a port selector. In performing this function, any of M input lines are connected to any of N output lines as one of the N output lines becomes available. The M input lines are commonly called the line side of the concentrator, whereas the N output lines are referred to as the port side—to interface the ports of a front-end processor. The basic hardware components of a contention concentrator are illustrated in Figure 3.

Incoming data on each line of the line side of the device is routed through the concentrator's processor, which searches for a non-busy line on the port side to transmit the data to. The determination of priorities can be programmed so that groups of incoming lines can be made to contend for one or a group of lines on the port side. When all ports are in use, messages can be generated to notify terminals attempting to access the system of the "busy" situation. Through the addition of peripheral storage devices, incoming jobs can be batched to await the disconnection of a user from the system. Then connection to the newly available port side line is made to gain entry to the computational facility, and the stored job is transmitted.

Evaluating the CPU
Although some vendors offer a complete concentration package which includes controllers and CPU, other vendors permit the customer to select the CPU that is to be used for the concentrator. The evaluation and selection of the concentrator's CPU should be accomplished in a manner similar to the evaluation and selection of any stand-alone computer. Both the hardware and software should be evaluated according to user

3   Contention concentrator

Basic hardware. *The input lines from the terminals contend for the output lines to the host ports. Both input and output interface multi-line controllers to the CPU.*

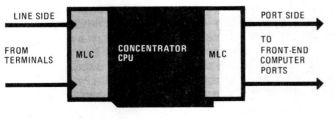

TABLE 1 Controller parameters

Multi-line controller only
Control type—hardware or software
Number of lines supported
Number of lines per class
Maximum throughput

Both single- and multi-line controller
Data codes and speeds supported
Number and grouping of channels
Terminal classes supported
Full-/half-duplex support
Auto-dial/auto-answer interface
Dataset interface
Direct connect interface
Protocols supported
Parity checking

requirements. Thus, if one needs a store-and-forward message-concentration system, emphasis should be placed upon peripheral equipment, data transfer rates, and software appropriate for this particular application. In addition, if the application is critically time dependent, examining hardware reliability by itself may not suffice, and the user will most likely want to consider a redundancy configuration.

As shown in the redundant store-and-forward arrangement of Figure 4, both systems are directly connected to each other by an intercomputer communications unit and share access to incoming and outgoing lines and peripherals via electronic switches. During operation, one system is considered the operational processing or master system, while the other is the slave or standby system, monitoring the master. Upon a hardware failure or power interrupt, the master system signals the slave system to take over processing via the intercomputer communications unit, generates an alarm message, and conducts an orderly shutdown.

Since the slave system has been in parallel processing, it resets all controls and becomes the master system, holding the potential of losing data to a minimum. This procedure can usually be completed within 500 microseconds for processors with a cycle time of 750 nanoseconds or less. In this case, 666 cycles or more (500 microsec ÷ 750 nanosec) are available with that time slot to execute the required instructions to transfer control and effect the orderly shutdown. Actually, just two to four computer cycles are needed for the execution of such instructions.

Switching the message
To effect message switching, incoming data is routed to a central point where messages are concentrated for processing. Then, based upon some processing criteria, messages are routed over one or more lines connected to the system. In message switching, all terminals connected to the system can communicate with every other terminal connected to the system— once the message has been processed and the desti-

4 Redundant message concentration

Store-and-forward. *During operation, one concentrator system is considered the master, and the other is the slave—monitoring the master. The slave system operates in a parallel processing mode. When it senses a failure of the master system, the slave resets all controls through the shared ICCU, and it becomes the new master system.*

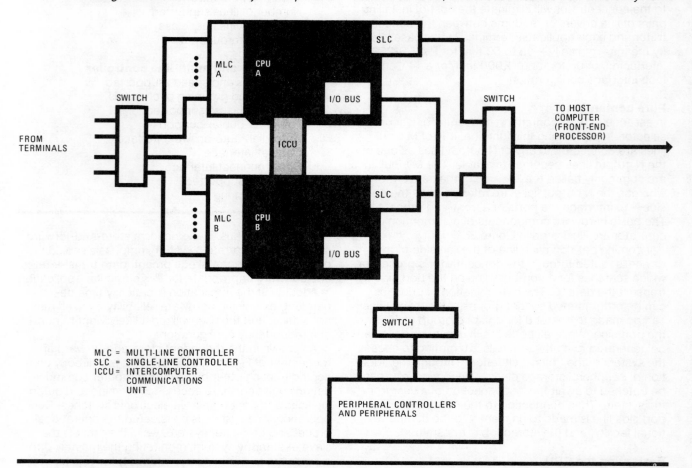

MLC = MULTI-LINE CONTROLLER
SLC = SINGLE-LINE CONTROLLER
ICCU = INTERCOMPUTER
        COMMUNICATIONS
        UNIT

nation data contained in the message is acted upon.

The hardware required for a message-switching system is quite similar to that required by a store-and-forward message-concentration system. The primary differences are the application software, and that incoming messages are not stored, but are processed and then routed over one or more of the incoming lines. And accesses to peripherals such as disks are handled via direct memory access (DMA) channels instead of the lower speed available from data transfers conducted via a processor's I/O bus.

The interface used to transfer data to communications controllers and peripherals is usually determined by the necessary I/O transfer rate. Interfacing may occur at the computer's I/O bus or via such devices as direct memory control (DMC) and direct memory access (DMA). Data transferred on the I/O bus is bit-serial and under control of the program. In the DMC mode, data transfers are effected independent of program control, and data blocks are transferred on a word basis (bit-parallel) to and from any portion of main memory. The DMC mode is used for medium-speed data transfer, and requires a starting and ending

address, as well as the number of characters to be transferred. Although similarly word-oriented and a direct-to-memory medium, the DMA mode requires only the starting and ending address. For high-speed data transfers, the DMA mode is used, but at a cost higher than with DMC. The speed at which DMA permits transfer of data is such that a computer using DMA on a high-speed channel can exchange data with several devices (peripherals) and controllers concurrently on a timeshared basis.

Line and station

In addition to the controller parameters listed in Table 1, the line and station characteristics of the message-switching system—which are a function of both hardware and software—should be determined. Table 2 lists some of the message-switching system characteristics that should be investigated prior to selecting such equipment. These characteristics are discussed next.

The number of stations supported is often far more important than the number of lines supported, since foreign-exchange lines in various cities could each be connected to a channel on the multi-line controller of the message-switching system. This situation would enable a large number of terminals to contend for the foreign exchange line in each city, with each terminal having a unique station code. The station types listed in Table 2 refer to whether full-duplex, half-duplex, or simplex transmission is supported. Message addressing refers to the number of addresses per message, as well as the capability of broadcasting a message to a predetermined group of stations, or to all stations, by using a group code addressing scheme.

Most message-switching software permits several levels of message priority. Examples of priority levels would be Expedite, Normal, and Deferred. A deferred-priority message is transmitted to its destination after normal working hours. A message of expedite priority would preempt any lower priority message being transmitted to an addressee until the expedite message transmission is completed. Depending on the software, some software packages permit any station to assign any message a priority, while other systems can lock out certain stations from assigning one or more specific priorities to a message.

Normally, the maximum length of any message is a function of disk space and system throughput. For all practical purposes, though, users can transmit messages without worrying about their length.

Software for a preferred message-switching system will pre-process the message header as it is entered. Then the user is informed of invalid station codes, invalid group addresses, garbled transmission for both header and text, and any other errors prior to routing of the message. On some systems, a message denoting these errors will also be routed to the message-switching system's operator console, so that the console operator will be able to ascertain user problems as they occur and furnish assistance if required. An example of such assistance is alternate routing, which permits supervisory personnel to route all traffic destined to one station (or group of stations) to some other station. This capability is important if, for some reason, a communications component or terminal becomes inoperative, and there is a station nearby that could handle messages destined for the inoperative terminal.

Line and station "skips" and "holds" supplement alternate routing. The skip command permits the omission of any line or station from the polling pattern. A hold permits traffic to any station or line to be kept from delivery.

Retrieving the message

The journalization characteristic (Table 2) permits every message transmitted from the system to be recorded on journal storage. This storage provides the basis for message retrieval from the journal. However, the type of retrieval permitted varies from system to system. Some systems permit any station to retrieve messages destined only to itself, while other systems permit any station to retrieve any journaled message by sequence number. On some systems the operator can access the journal by either station number, sequence number, or by time of day.

The intercept characteristic permits the central-site operator to have traffic destined for specific lines or stations rerouted to intercept storage. The traffic may then be delivered to the addressed destinations by using a recovery function. The intercept and recovery characteristics are especially important if a large number of lines become inoperative at one time and messages cannot be rerouted to other nearby terminals. Since line losses are of critical importance to a message-switching system, events of this type can normally be expected to cause an alarm message to be generated to a console so the operator can take appropriate action. This action includes notifying the phone company, establishing an alternate route, and notifying

5   Remote network processor

Concurrent processing. *In addition to the standard concentration function, the RNP permits entry of remote batch jobs for transmission to the host computer. Mean-* *while, completed jobs are printed on the line printer, and other jobs are being punched out on the card punch. Some RNPs allow downline program load from the host.*

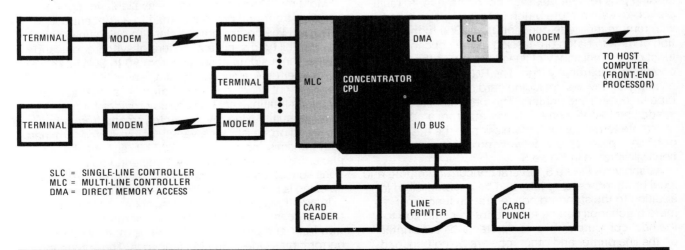

SLC = SINGLE-LINE CONTROLLER
MLC = MULTI-LINE CONTROLLER
DMA = DIRECT MEMORY ACCESS

Host interface. *Although FEPs are similar in design and use components common to those in concentrators, FEPs normally have larger word sizes, faster cycle time, larger* *memory, and permit the interfacing of more communications devices. A local multiplexer is sometimes encountered on FEPs, but is normally not used on concentrators.*

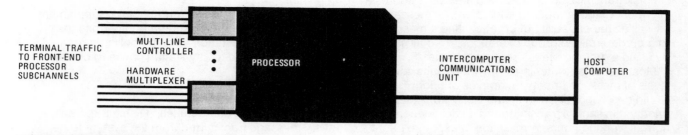

TERMINAL TRAFFIC TO FRONT-END PROCESSOR SUBCHANNELS — MULTI-LINE CONTROLLER — HARDWARE MULTIPLEXER — PROCESSOR — INTERCOMPUTER COMMUNICATIONS UNIT — HOST COMPUTER

Table 2 Switching characteristics

Number of lines supported
Number of stations supported
Line speeds and codes supported
Station types
Message addressing permitted
Levels of message priority
Message length
Input error checking
Alternate routing
Line and station skips and holds
Journalization capability
Retrieval capability
Intercept and recovery provisions
Alarms and reports

the traffic originator of the actions taken—including where transmissions will be received.

Another form of concentrator is a remote network processor (RNP). Besides concentration, it performs the additional function of remote batch processing, thus providing two distinct functions in one package. Remote network processors vary in capabilities—ranging from basic, single-job-stream remote batch processing plus remote message concentration, to multiple-job-stream remote batch processing combined with remote message concentration. Due to the addition of remote batch processing to the concentration function, the efficiency of line utilization to the host computer is extremely high. The RNP may be serving a variety of devices, including card readers, magnetic tape units, and line printers. This peripheral support is in addition to concentrating the data from a number of remote terminals for transmission to the host computer. A typical remote network processor configuration is illustrated in Figure 5.

As shown in Figure 5, several concurrent remote and local batch processing jobs can be accomplished in addition to the standard concentration function. Remote batch jobs can be entered for transmission to the host computer, while completed jobs are printed on the line printer and other jobs are being punched

out on the card punch.

Some remote network processors have a segment of read-only memory which permits downline loading of operational software from the host computer to the RNP. This is a valuable feature since it permits programming changes for new batch and remote terminal equipment to be performed at the central site, and alleviates the necessity of employing programmers at every RNP installation to effect equipment configuration changes.

By offloading work from the host computer, and by blocking the characters transmitted from each terminal into messages, the RNP permits users to better load-balance their computational equipment. In many instances, this load-balancing can alleviate a costly host processor upgrade or the threat of encountering degraded service.

Front-end processing

A front-end processor (FEP) provides a large volume of network communications power in support of a particular computer system. Although FEPs are similar in design and use components common to those in concentrators, normally FEPs have larger word sizes, faster cycle time, larger memory, and permit the interfacing of more communications devices. A typical front-end processor configuration is illustrated in Figure 6.

More multi-line controllers are available for connection to a front-end processor than to a concentrator. The multi-line controllers are close to being universal in their ability to service a mixture of synchronous and asynchronous data at speeds from 50 to 50K bit/s.

Another device encountered on some FEPs, but normally not used on concentrators, is a local communications multiplexer. This device provides for time-division multiplexing, by character, to and from the front-end processor for a variety of low-speed terminals with transmission rates up to 300 bit/s. A local multiplexer can handle terminals with differing communications speeds and code settings. The character demultiplexing is performed in the front-end processor.

In addition to dealing with network and communications processing activities that one normally associates with front-end processors, the FEP is often used to perform message-switching functions. These functions

7 Integrating into a network

Combining devices. *Location 1 uses a standard concentrator for its 32 terminals. Since location 2 has a remote batch processing requirement as well as connecting 12 terminals to the host, an RNP is used. Location 3 has a redundant store-and-forward operation for its terminals. Location 4's front-end uses a contention concentrator.*

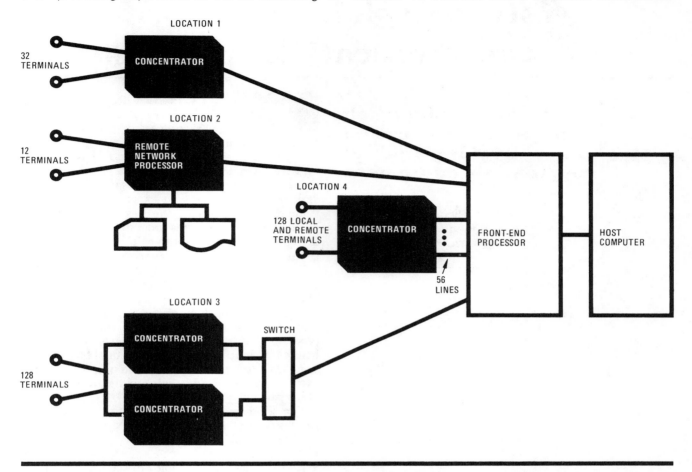

are aided by the FEP's large memory and word size, and by the ready addition of modular software.

Supervising software
The operating system which supervises the overall control and operation of all system functions is the key element of a front-end processor. Although numerous software elements must be evaluated, major consideration should be given to determining supported line protocols as well as supported processor communications. Most vendors divide their supported line protocols into several categories or classes of support. Normally Category 1 refers to vendor-developed and -tested software to support certain line protocols. Category 2 usually references vendor-developed , but non-qualified tested software, which means that the vendor will not guarantee results because the program has not been fully debugged. Category 3 references customer-developed interfaces designed to support certain terminal line protocols.

While the features of front-end processors are similar to those of concentrators, the FEP's reliability and redundancy, as well as its diagnostics, should be more

extensive, since the front-end processor is the heart of a communications network. Figure 7 illustrates a typical data communications network consisting of several different types of concentrators and a front-end processor. This network combines examples of much of what was discussed previously.

At location 1, a standard concentrator is used to concentrate the traffic from 32 terminals onto a high-speed line for transmission to the front-end processor. Since location 2 has a requirement for remote batch processing as well as connecting 12 terminals to the host computer, a remote network processor has been installed to perform these two functions. And since location 3 has a significant number of terminals doing an important application, a redundant store-and-forward message concentrator was installed.

Terminals remaining in the network (location 4) total 128. However, it was felt that at most only 56 would ever become active at any given time. Therefore, to economize on front-end processor ports, a contention concentrator was "front-ended" to the front-end processor, making the 128 channels connected to terminals contend for the 56 front-end processor ports. ■

7 steps to picking the best communications processor

An orderly approach to processor selection avoids pitfalls of inappropriate equipment

Ivan Frisch,
Richard Kaczmarek,
and Benedict Occhiogrosso
Network Analysis Corp.
Glen Cove, N.Y.

Hardware

A great deal hangs on the choice of communications processors. Network performance depends heavily on them, whether they are serving as concentrators, front-end processors, message switches, or packet switches. They also cost up to several hundred thousand dollars each and involve extensive and expensive software development. Still, though the task of choosing one or more communications processors for a network is a complex one and not to be taken lightly, it can go forward in an orderly manner.

The seven-step method presented here guides the user to the most cost-effective of the processors bid by various vendors. As information accumulates, system requirements are steadily refined so that inappropriate or inadequate communication processors are eliminated from consideration well before it is time to ask vendors for final bids. At the same time, the method allows the user to examine existing processors and their architecture in terms of his particular application.

The seven major steps in selecting a communications processor are:

- State the specifications.
- Assign weighting factors.
- Learn what is available in communications processors.
- Compare alternative architectures.
- Model the system and evaluate performance.
- Select a robust design.
- Rank processor designs by performance and cost.

Each of these steps will be discussed in detail. From the outset, though, it is important to realize that the selection procedure is not simply a step-by-step analysis. Rather, it requires iterations, as shown by the feedback loops in Figure 1 (next page) to let knowledge obtained at a later step sharpen the results of preceding steps.

Figure 1 is a flow chart for the seven steps. Note that the user is present in every step. Feedback loop A is necessary since the assignment of weighting factors often focuses on new specification items or variations in existing items that were previously omitted from the specifications statement.

Feedback loop B recognizes that once a qualitative overview has been performed, the relative importance of various functions may change drastically. For example, the selection of a central processing unit (CPU) may become less critical than

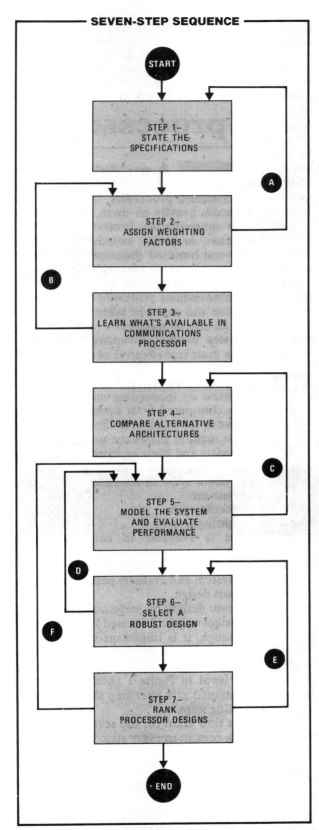

1. This orderly seven-step procedure lets users approach the selection of a communications processor by considering all major factors.

input/output (I/O) capabilities. However, once Step 4 begins, the weighting factors should not be changed since revisions might indicate biases on the part of the user.

Feedback loop C allows for further investigation of the bottlenecks that the systems models will certainly indicate. Feedback loop D is necessary since the actual design procedure will undoubtedly generate further questions that need to be resolved by changing the model. Feedback loops E and F indicate reexamination required for the final decision.

The flow chart provides ample opportunity for feedback and corrections. However, the procedure is fairly straightforward in that all loops, except the last one, go back only one step in the sequence of seven steps. And usually the feedback loops are used just a few times.

Step 1
State the specifications

The set of specifications prepared by the user states what the communications processor is supposed to do, how well it should to it, and, in some cases, even how it should do it. Often, it is unnecessary to state how the processor should accomplish its task, and indeed, the buyer may not want to restrict the bidder's options at this stage. However, if there is a clearcut option, then time and money can be saved by not considering many radical equipment designs and network architectures.

The formulation of specifications is the single most important task in the communications system development. Unfortunately, it is also an extremely difficult one. The specifications must be developed by people who are familiar with both the details of the organization's operational requirements and the state of the art in data communications processors.

On the one hand, the user may initially not know enough about communications processors and networks, in which case the use of outside consultants is warranted. On the other hand, when consultants are used, it is critically important that the user-buyer be aware of all phases of specification development and that he understand the specifications completely. If not, a third party—the consultant—has been introduced between the buyer and his system. For example, it is reasonable to hire an outside consultant to develop processor and network specifications and a project-management plan for a network. But it is important that the plan be implemented by the user so he can retain control.

There are two extremes is specifying requirements for a communications processor. At one extreme are loose qualitative statements such as: "The communications processor must have high throughput capability." At the other extreme, such specific quantitative statements as "The processor must accept 5 megabits/second of traffic at a delay not exceeding 1 millisecond" run the risk of being impossible to satisfy at a reasonable cost. A common but ineffectual solution to this dilemma is to guess at the specification and then pad it "just to play safe." When this happens in estimating, say, the man-years needed for software development, each of several different levels of management may multiply a reasonable estimate by two or three. As a result, the specified programing effort becomes inflated. Estimated programing cost is excessive and, worse still, actual programing becomes a self-fulfilling prophecy, in that many more man-years are expended on it than are actually required.

The communications-processor design later proposed by vendors will not meet all specifications equally well. One processor may have a better response time, another have higher reliability. Therefore, a mechanism must be set up in the specification phase that will let the buyer evaluate quantitatively the systems that are bid later. Hence, the next step in the statement of specifications is to group the individual items in each specification into broad categories that can be evaluated in terms of importance and measured in terms of the offered traffic.

Here, a change in viewpoint is required. In the past, computers have been rated—for example—according to their arithmetic/logic capabilities. That is, processing units were sometimes ranked on the basis of their fixed-point ADD time. This may be appropriate for general-purpose applications. But a computer-based communications processor's overall network function is more important than any one of its capabilities. Thus, arithmetic capabilities not pertinent to the communications processor's overall function are irrelevant. In short, the focus of the specification must be on functional, not structural, requirements.

In the communications framework, typical atributes to be singled out for comparison among different designs from different vendors include reliability and availability, equipment modularity and expandability, security and militarization, and throughput (traffic) and delay. For instance, the request for proposal for the Defense Communications Agency's Autodin II packet-switched network puts great emphasis on the priority structure to be used in the delivery of messages and packets. To prove that their system design meets the specifications on priority handling, it will not be enough for the bidders later on to point to any single feature of their design and equipment. Rather a systematic set of procedures will be required for handling priorities.

Step 2
Assign weighting factors

After grouping the specifications, the user team will assign weighting factors to each item. The

FEATURE	WEIGHTING FACTORS	
	APPLICATION A	APPLICATION B
INSTRUCTION SET CAPABILITY	5	8
NUMBERS OF REGISTERS	10	6
USER MICROPROGRAMING	2	2
DMA CHANNEL	9	4
HARDWARE MULTIPLY/DIVIDE	2	8
STORAGE-TO-STORAGE INSTRUCTION	9	5
NUMBER OF INTERRUPT LEVELS	8	5
INTERRUPT LATENCY	10	5
REAL-TIME CLOCK	8	5

ASSIGNING WEIGHTING FACTORS TO A CPU

weighting factors—ranging, say, from 0 to 10, with 10 being highly important—assess the importance of each item in a specification relative to total system performance. Certain items may be an absolute requirement and will receive the highest weighting factors. Others may be less important and receive a lesser weighting. Besides assigning weights to obvious technical specifications, the buyer must assign weights to such technical risks as a vendor's ability to deliver on time and to maintain hardware and software, as well as his experience in implementing similar systems. The weighting factors reflect the relative importance of desirable functions contained in the statement of the specification.

The table shows how weighting factors may be assigned to the devices comprising the total communications processor. It illustrates how several relevant characteristics for a central processing unit may vary considerably in importance, depending upon its envisioned application. Here, two extreme applications are hypothesized.

Application A requires real-time processing, consists of a one-time software-development effort, and is communications-oriented. A typical example might be a minicomputer-based concentrator. The number of interrupts and the speed with which they are dispatched, and the presence of a real-time clock, are extremely important. For communications, the presence of direct memory access (DMA) and storage-to-storage instructions imply a minimal I/O burden on the processor. Since the programing will be debugged and implemented only one time, a large instruction set can certainly facilitate the development effort but is not critical (hence a weight of 5 for the instruction-set capability). Noteworthy is the relatively low weight given to a hardware-multiply/divide instruction, which will seldom be used in a data-communication-oriented application.

Application B processes batches of data, not in real time, in a scientific-computing environment. Program development is an ongoing function to be performed on line, so that instruction-set capability is deemed relatively important (a weight of 8). Arithmetic capability is required, and hardware multiply/divide is essential. A minimal amount of time-critical I/O is envisioned, so that the presence of DMA and storage-to-storage instructions are not essential.

Finally, user microprograming capability is not regarded as important in either application. Application B's operating system will not permit the programer to access the machine at such a low level, while Application A has no formal requirement for freedom to change the instruction set.

The process of assigning weighting factors is of course very subjective, and should be performed several times during the evaluation of the communications processor—alternating, of course, with

suitable testing of the sensitivity of overall processor performance to each item, as indicated by feedback loop B in Figure 1.

Another example of the weighting of specifications comes from the Advanced Research Projects Agency (ARPA). The people there regarded modularity as of primary importance in specifying their high-speed packet switch. They felt that a modular design would allow them to use a multiprocessor architecture, with a similar processor placed at every node. Furthermore, the design would make adequate provision for growth. But a single-processor architecture with a vendor-supplied operating system would have required a much simpler software effort. It is clear that in ARPA's specifications a greater weighting factor was assigned to modularity than to software simplicity.

Step 3
Learn what's available
in communications processors

Often unfamiliarity with the details of viable alternatives breeds contentment with inferior offerings. The commonest mistake is lack of understanding of the heart of the network's communications processor—the individual minicomputer or microprocessor. Another mistake is to misjudge the potential of multiprocessor architecture as the foundation for a communications processor. Redundancy and clever executive controllers can mask many deficiencies of the individual processor system, but the capabilities of these individual systems often set the ultimate limit to capacity. Thus the user must learn the details of the processors for each system he considers. Ordinarily the vendor is more than willing to provide this information upon request. But the user must still know enough to ask penetrating questions.

After all, vendors typically highlight the virtues of their processor systems. While overt attempts by vendors to mask architectural deficiencies are unusual, these deficiencies will definitely not be made obvious. In addition, many highly touted processor capabilities are not important in a data communications application.

Consequently, a prospective buyer must know what features to look for. Also, he should always be interested in sophisticated features that represent tangible benefits to network performance and flexibility, though he should remember that complexity without purpose often creates unreliability and added expense. Hence, the overview must determine the pros and cons of the particular processor.

Too quick a processor evaluation can result in lost revenues because of inferior performance or wasted expenditures in attaining unnecessary (and often abandoned) goals. Even less important attempts at evaluation can lead to difficulties if standard pitfalls are not avoided. For example, traditional system-evaluation procedures pay an inordinate amount of attention to the central processing unit. But because of advances in integrated-circuit technology, the cost of the CPU is often a small portion of the total system cost, with memory, input/output devices, and line-interface units often costing far more.

Furthermore, in heavily communications-oriented applications the processor is divested of most routine interface responsibilities, with I/O channels and device controllers becoming increasingly important as they take over these tasks.

A classic pitfall is the overeager acceptance of advanced communications techniques. For example, the requirement that the switch be able to support adaptive routing can dramatically improve response times in distributed packet-switched networks. However, adaptive-routing schemes usually entail large processing overhead and may represent an unnecessary and expensive degree of sophistication for light traffic or smaller networks. The fact that adaptive routing has been useful in the past in certain nationwide networks does not mean that it is a valid technique for other networks. Thus, care must be taken to evaluate a processor according to the user's current needs.

Consider a specific example. Based on buffering requirements and memory capacity, a buyer committed to using a particular minicomputer can determine whether he needs one or several machines. Since typical minicomputer memory capacity ranges from 4,000 bytes to 1 megabyte, the requirement looks easy to satisfy. However, the ability to upgrade memory capacity in a cost-effective manner is usually limited by memory-increment size and addressability, which may differ drastically from one vendor's computer to another's. More will be said on this point later.

Step 4
Compare alternative architectures

Having examined the equipment and architectures available from candidate vendors, the buyer must compare the merits of the different communications processors. The result of this process should be a comprehensive tabulation of each system's pros and cons that will help the user assess its ability to meet his requirements.

This step involves the question of taking technical risks. Many risk factors are subjective and are tied to the credibility of the vendor. The history of the vendor is relevant in all of the following areas: commitment to timely delivery, willingness and ability to provide satisfactory maintenance of both hardware and software, and technical support for new applications or system fine tuning.

The novelty of the proposed system is important.

2. Multiple memories can be shared either in a centralized or distributed fashion in a multiprocessor, but the decision affects cost (see Fig. 3).

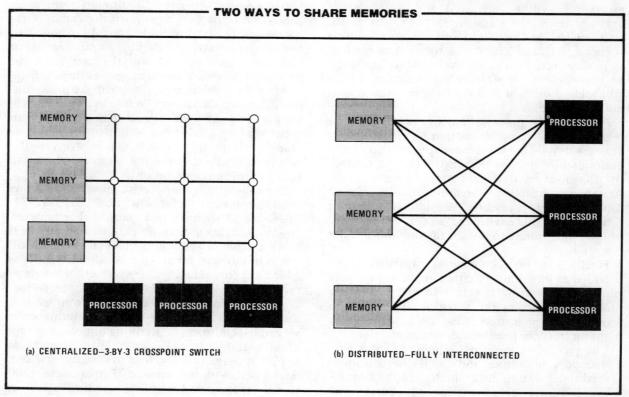

TWO WAYS TO SHARE MEMORIES

(a) CENTRALIZED—3-BY-3 CROSSPOINT SWITCH

(b) DISTRIBUTED—FULLY INTERCONNECTED

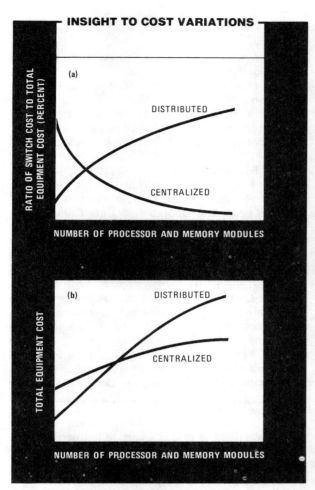

INSIGHT TO COST VARIATIONS

(a)

RATIO OF SWITCH COST TO TOTAL EQUIPMENT COST (PERCENT)

DISTRIBUTED

CENTRALIZED

NUMBER OF PROCESSOR AND MEMORY MODULES

(b)

DISTRIBUTED

CENTRALIZED

TOTAL EQUIPMENT COST

NUMBER OF PROCESSOR AND MEMORY MODULES

3. Just how cost is affected by centralized or distributed design depends on the number of processor and memory modules involved.

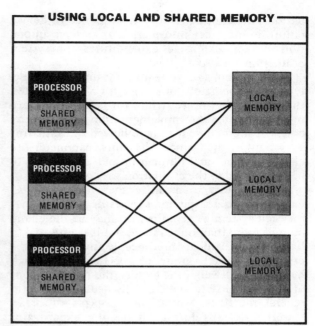

USING LOCAL AND SHARED MEMORY

PROCESSOR / SHARED MEMORY

PROCESSOR / SHARED MEMORY

PROCESSOR / SHARED MEMORY

LOCAL MEMORY

LOCAL MEMORY

LOCAL MEMORY

4. Local (private) memory can be attached to each processor in a multiprocessor, while other memory modules can be shared among the processors.

If the concept is "tried and true," little risk in development is encountered. Use of new technology or radical departures from standard approaches may often provide real breakthroughs in terms of system performance, but they must be thoroughly justified. The vendor's experience in implementing similar systems can dramatically affect the soundness of the design. Where new concepts are used, the vendor should provide test programs to thoroughly verify system performance.

One example of a system approach that involved great risks at its inception but is starting to pay off now is the use of multiprocessors. A multiprocessor consists of several concurrently running CPUs that share access to a common memory and are controlled by a unified and integrated operating system. Its advantages over more conventional approaches are its higher reliability and availability, because it can include one or more "backup" processors, and its greater flexibility and ability to expand because of its modular design.

However, using multiprocessors raises such difficult questions as: How should the work be divided among processors? How should memory be shared by them? How should they be connected together? And do individual processors have adequate interrupt capabilities and address space to operate in a multiprocessor environment?

The Bolt Beranek and Newman Pluribus and the Univac 1100 Series are some examples of multiprocessors. Most minicomputer makers nowadays discuss how their machines can operate in a multiprocessor environment. But several years ago, when ARPA commissioned its Pluribus message processor (IMP) in the form of a multiprocessor, it was taking a gamble that the above questions would be satisfactorily answered for its applications. The fact that companies today benefit from the knowledge gained from the Pluribus shows that the risks were worth taking.

A key question that must be answered at the beginning of the evaluation of alternatives is: How much money should a user spend in verifying that the system will meet the performance objectives? Unfortunately, there is no general formula by which a user can calculate the cost of the verification as a percentage of total system cost. The total amount to be invested in the study is a major management decision, and it depends upon the consequences of system failure, the positive rewards in terms of subscriber satisfaction when the system operates properly, and the user's total projected investment in the system.

For example, if the failure of a device means a communications satellite will be inoperative, then the cost of failure is that of a multimillion-dollar rocket launch. Here an expensive system evaluation is warranted. If the consequence of device failure is incorrect information in a stock quotation system, extensive expenditures for system evaluation are also justified.

But if system failure simply means several teletypewriters being out of service for a few minutes, there may be more time for system experimentation after the implementation stage. In any case, the methodology to be followed in evaluating a system is the same. The only parameters to change are the total number of men and dollars to be committed to the evaluation.

A useful way to organize the alternative-evaluation step is to appoint experts or "champions" for each system. A given person may be the champion of more than one system, but it is essential to have at least two or three people involved in the process. For each group of specifications which have received weighting factors, the pros and cons of each system are argued. This usually occurs in several meetings, which have aspects of brainstorming sessions during which some expert gains insights into his system by comparing it with others. After the sessions, each person can write up a particular aspect of the system—such as reliability and availability—and consider each processor with respect to that characteristic. Alternatively, each person may write up these aspects of each system for which he is expert.

In any case, it is very helpful to tape-record the sessions so they can be replayed while preparing the writeups. This is the first stage in the evaluation procedure at which differences among the proposed systems become apparant. Thus it is one of the most crucial steps. Modularity and expandability are among the issues that arise in meetings of this sort.

Modularity and expandability. Modularity of equipment is often required to allow for expansion to handle future increases in traffic. It implies some form of interconnection among modules. Two extreme possibilities for interconnection are shown in Figure 2. Centralized interconnection uses a K-by-K crosspoint switch. Fully distributed interconnection requires a dedicated link between every processor and memory pair. Assuming an acceptable level of contention for processor and memory resources, both designs may in principle be expanded later to handle increased traffic.

However, there is a hidden cost in upgrading (expanding) the distributed design. As shown in Figure 3a, the cost of the centralized switch becomes a smaller percentage of total equipment cost as the number of processors and memories increases. Furthermore, as shown in Figure 3b, the cost of more cables, special relocation hardware, arbiters, and cable connectors makes the cost of the distributed switch the dominant component of total equipment cost. (An arbiter controls processor access of memory modules in a contention net-

Available models

1. J. Martin, "System Analysis For Data Transmission," Prentice Hall, 1972.
2. J. Martin, "Design of Real-Time Computer Systems," Prentice Hall, 1970.
3. W. Everling, "Exercises in Computer Systems Analysis," Springer-Verlag Lecture Notes in Economics and Mathematical Systems No. 65, 1972.
4. L. Kleinrock, "Queuing Systems," Computer Applications, John Wiley & Sons, 1976.
5. C. Riviere, "Programable Front Ending Beats Computer Upgrading," Data Communications, May/June 1974, pp. 41-48.
6. M. Monroe, "Communications Processor System (CPS): Modeling Approach," Technical Report: RADC-TR-290, Rome Air Development Center, November 1974.
7. W. Chou, P. McGregor, and R. Kaczmarek, "Communications Processor Simulation: A Practical Approach," National Telecommunications Conference, 1975.
8. H. Frank, W. Chou, and R. Van Slyke, "Avoiding Simulation in Simulating Computer Networks," National Computer Conf. 1973.

work.) In addition, the software might be more complex when the resources are fully distributed.

Thus, if system requirements can be assessed at an early enough stage, the centralized approach can offer significant savings by amortization of the switch cost over the network's life. However, because later expansion beyond a certain point is physically impossible with the centralized strategy, the processor and memory must be initially oversized. This situation is evident in the Carnegie-Mellon multiprocessor network which presently uses five of the available 16 memory ports and 1/32 of its total address space. The end result is money spent but not used in the short term.

Microprogramed instruction set. A striking example of the tradeoffs related to microprograming is presented by the Honeywell Series 16 computer and its competitors, the Prime machines. Microprogramed instructions, although aggressively promoted, may have drawbacks. The microprogramed Prime has a somewhat slower average instruction execution time than the hardwired Honeywell. However, one advantage of the microprogramed Prime 300 is that the control store can be tailored by the user to yield an instruction set to meet his own unique requirements. One benefit is greater throughput.

But the successful use of this user-microprograming feature requires a substantial and costly reprograming effort, since not all vendor-supplied software would be compatible with the newly created instruction set. Hence, the user may have a difficult decision to make in evaluating the economic merits of microprograming.

Memory organization. The organization of memory may profoundly influence processor performance. There is a vast array of options that possess significant merits and deficiencies. Multiple memory modules may permit some degree of concurrent access, whether by overlapped read and write cycles in interleaved memories in response to a memory fetch by a single processor, or by the simultaneous access to distinct memory modules by several processors. Usually processor throughput is limited by contention for shared memory modules. Therefore, some form of local dedicated storage can be advantageous. The Bolt Beranek and Newman Pluribus multiprocessor places the most frequently accessed section of the operational software (hot code) in the local (private) memory (Figure 4).

Although cache memories are generally used for high-speed execution of some local code found in a main-memory partition, they can also reduce contention by serving as local storage. The penalty for providing local storage is the replication of frequently used code and the associated redundancy. If the size of the hot code grows too large, the local memory needed to offset contention may also become too large. In these processors, then, the increased performance benefits will be severely offset by memory costs.

Channel efficiency. For real-time data communications, the CPUs of communications processors usually lack the capacity to handle all the input/output (I/O) devices that must access memory. Hence, direct memory access (DMA) is an absolute necessity to off-load the processor. However, using DMA does not altogether solve the problem. A key element in the determination of DMA channel efficiency is where to locate the channel-control word used to monitor and direct the operation of a DMA transfer. The channel control word contains the memory location into which a DMA places data or from which it extracts data. After a DMA transfer, the word is incremented to the next address and tested against an end-of-buffer address. If the word is less than the end-of-buffer address, the next direct memory access transfer occurs. If not, a flag is set and the transfer stops.

When this word resides in main memory, the transfer becomes less efficient, since main memory must be accessed to modify it. When the word is part of the I/O channel, however, the number of main-memory references is reduced, and transfer efficiency increases to a level dominated by channel contention. The most efficient solution is to make the channel control word part of the line controller. As an example, all three communications-control-word options are available on the Prime computer and achieve different channel transfer rates.

Step 5
Model the system and evaluate performance

Selecting a final system from among those submitted by vendors is foolhardy without mathematical modeling and performance evaluation. Until the calculations are done, one cannot be sure of the design. There are always a dozen excuses not to do the calculations: "I have a good feel for the system"; "The calculations are much too theoretical"; "We can always fill in the numbers later". However, the overall study and the qualitative evaluation have served to focus attention on key system features. They must now be rigorously evaluated. Surprises are sometimes in store.

The evaluation may use either analytic or simulation techniques. Analytic methods usually consist of queuing models. Their drawback is that they rely on simplifying assumptions to obtain "closed-form" solutions, so that often these solutions do not accurately reflect the actual operating environment. However, conservative results can be obtained by making appropriate assumptions. Simulation methods can be used to test system performance in exhaustive detail. The methods usually require a great deal of computer execution time and are very costly. Also, they display system behavior only under very specific conditions. The best solution is to use analytic methods with some additional simulation to verify the models.

In addition, money can be saved by doing a careful survey of available programs and system studies before a detailed modeling effort is undertaken. Several general-purpose programs and models can be used to investigate communications processor performance. An excellent survey/summary of most queuing-based analytic models can be found in items 1, 2, 3, and 4 in the list entitled "Where to find available models."

Several in-house software packages have been developed by computer manufacturers and/or system consultants. They often employ a combination of both analytic and simulation techniques to model the system more realistically, yet they avoid the severe computational drawbacks associated with a detailed event-driven simulation. Examples of this type of system include the communications-processor simulation program developed by Network Analysis Corp. (item 7), and the earlier analysis-simulation packages which have found wide application (item 8). Noteworthy systems include a front-end-processor simulation package known as Data Communications Analyzer Model (item 5) and the modeling approach used in the Communications Processor System (item 6).

Consider one simple example of how a detailed calculation can point out a major system bottleneck. A communications processor's operating system requires a control storage area of 100 bytes to

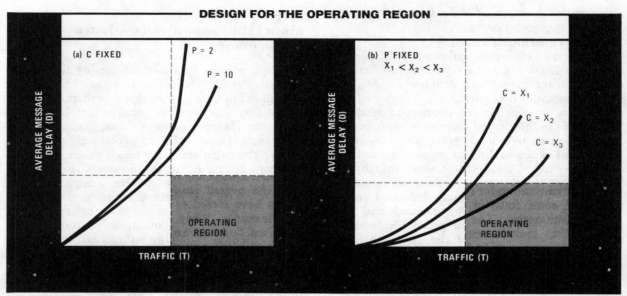

5. Modeling the processors' performance helps to find the number of processors and traffic to reach the robust-design operating region.

control and monitor the status of a message in the system. The control area is used for the entire duration of the message's occupancy of the communications processor system. Also, the communications processor has no secondary storage.

When the processor's operating system can find no available control area, the input message is rejected. The specifications state that no more than one of every 100 messages may be rejected by the processor. The proposed design uses a Honeywell DDP-516 minicomputer with a maximum memory capacity of 64 kilobytes. The operating system and message buffers are known to require 56 kilobytes. Using queuing formulas in a message-switching environment, calculations show that 5 kilobytes are needed—just marginally below the maximum.

Suppose now that management has found their customers unhappy about rejected messages and change the specification so that no more than one of every 1,000 messages can be rejected. Now calculations show that 10 kilobytes are required, for a total of 60 kilobytes—above the maximum. Although the difference of 5 kilobytes seems insignificant, the unfortunate fact is that the maximum memory capacity of the DDP-516 has been exceeded and a second minicomputer is required. If misjudgments of this nature seem unreal, rest assured that they have been made by network designers in the past. In short, the original sizing suffered from lack of robust design, discussed next.

Step 6
Select a robust design

The next step in selecting a communications processor is to use the analytic and simulation models to develop a robust design—one that meets all sys-

tem specifications within a comfortable margin. The goal is to assure oneself that a design is feasible, to obtain an upper bound on cost at a minimum level of processor performance, and to establish a benchmark against which all other designs can be measured. The robust design will also indicate how much of a particular resource, such as memory, is required to meet network specifications comfortably. The way to obtain a robust design is to use consistently conservative assumptions in formulating the model in the previous modeling and evaluation step.

Consider a recent analysis of a multiprocessor-based packet switch configured to handle an input traffic level of T kilobits/second with an average message delay of D seconds. The throughput capacity of the output communication channel was fixed at C kilobits/second. To determine the benefits of multiprocessor operation, the switch performance was evaluated using analytic models. The shaded areas in Figure 5 show the desirable operating region. Clearly, P = 2 processors making up one multiprocessor should not be used since under no combination of D and T does the system perform in the desired operating region. Even a multiprocessor system with 10 processors does not perform properly, in that it is out of the operating region.

Further investigation revealed that the limiting system resource was the communication channel. The C in Figure 5a was too low.

For a system with a few multiprocessors (P in Figure 5b), a relatively modest increase in the output channel capacity to $C = X_3$ improved performance at only a small additional cost.

Eventually, after steps 2 through 6 have been carried out one or more times, as indicated in Figure 1, the system is put out for final bid. Each vendor will respond with his own design. Which one is the best communications-processor configuration?

Step 7
Rank processor designs

The two key selection functions can now be performed: a final quantitative ranking of machines and systems, and an evaluation of their cost. The systems offered are ranked for each specification item that received a weighting factor of 0 to 10 in Step 2. The user team ranks each item in each system from each vendor on a scale, for example, 0 to 1.0. If a particular system scores r_i on item i and has a weighting function of w_i, its overall processor ranking is given by $r_i w_i$. That is, each rank is multiplied by its corresponding weighting factor, as determined in Step 2, and—for each system bid—the products are added.

Just as the assignment of weights is often subjective, so is the assignment of ranks. However, the entire seven-step selection procedure should ease the assignment of ranks and remove much of the uncertainty surrounding them. Nevertheless, even at the very final step, arguments will arise, so the rankings themselves should be studied with regard to their impact on overall processor selection to see if the final score is unduly sensitive to the ranking of one particular item.

During the ranking procedure, the user may find that certain criteria rule out the use of a given equipment or architecture that is favorable in every other respect. For example, in military-based applications, components built to military specifications may be required. Many vendors currently do not market such a "hardened" version of some of their machines, and they are reluctant to reconfigure existing designs to meet military specifications. Furthermore, some vendors have delivered customized versions of their machines but at such severe financial loss to themselves as to preclude similar future ventures. To discover such equipment shortcomings at this stage in the evaluation procedure indicates user and bidder failed to communicate during Step 3.

The final step in system evaluation is the costing of the processor. It is unlikely that processors will be so close in performance that cost will be the primary factor. However, it is likely that some bids will be way out of line. This may indicate that the bidder is upgrading an outdated product and that he is asking the user to underwrite his development costs. In other cases, it may indicate vendor incompetence. Or it may be that the user is being asked to pay for quality.

After this study, the user will be in a position to suggest tradeoffs in performance versus cost and to question bidders intelligently on specific features and the reason for their costs.

A word of caution: Software development, debugging, and maintenance often represent the major percentage of total system development cost. Yet software cost is the most difficult item to estimate. There are many factors to consider. Vendor-supplied compilers and operating systems can ease the implementation of the system. If communications-oriented operating systems are available, these can readily be tailored to the buyer's particular application.

The importance of the availability of existing software cannot be overestimated. Often this consideration could outweigh all others in cost determination. If off-the-shelf software is not available from the vendor or a software house, the development of the programs should be an in-house effort, because trouble is in the air once a third party develops communications code. When third-party software fails to perform, the user can watch an unamusing drama unfold in which the machine vendor and the software-development house point accusing fingers at each other. Suffice it to say that unless the user has detailed knowledge of the programers to be used, experience on developing similar programs, and detailed knowledge of the processors and subroutines, it is extremely difficult to estimate the cost of the software.

The selection methodology described here works for a range of network configurations, from the simplest network to one requiring distributed switching and resource interaction.

By way of an example of what's involved in picking a communications processor, consider a network employing distributed computing resources, distributed multiplexing and concentration, and no resource interaction. A central switch is required to control access between contending terminals, and the switch may be custom hardware or an appropriately tailored minicomputer.

For such a processor, the weighting factors would involve a broad array of functional requirements, as well as a need for expert knowledge of many processor and architectural features. There would have to be extended debates, tradeoffs, and iterated evaluations. The modeling and evaluation of performance mean significant development costs. Further, a robust design involves many complex tradeoffs in order to come up with a wide range of options to meet operating specifications.

However, a much simpler network could mean a simpler processor that would be much easier to pick. For one thing, standard performance models are usually available and, for another, a final decision can be made—with experience—at Step 4, the comparison of alternative architectures.

In conclusion, it must be pointed out that this seven-step methodology is simply an organized approach. It is not a substitute for understanding thoroughly the underlying concepts of network and processor performance. ■

How concentrators can be message switchers as well

Charles J. Riviere and Richard A. Cooper,
CRC Systems Inc., Falls Church, Va.

Besides relieving the host computer of many of its processing tasks, this device shortens delays and may also provide a fallback path

Remote computer-based concentrators that control and organize communications traffic to and from clusters of terminals are growing in popularity. They can be highly economical when it comes to setting up certain kinds of network configuration. What is less apparent is that they can also take on much of the network's message-switching needs and so relieve the host computer of a large part of its network management duties.

Concentrators programmed to do this will naturally not come cheap. But they may well more than make up for the extra outlay by helping to speed up and streamline the operation of the network as a whole, besides allowing a fallback configuration to be worked into the network.

However, a user considering making use of the more complex functions inherent to a concentrator must decide first, whether a concentrator is indeed warranted (whether, in fact, a conventional multiplexer will not do the job), and second, where concentrators are to be placed in the network and how the network is to be configured around them.

In deciding where to put the concentrator, several factors must be brought to bear. It goes without saying that a large regional office with its own computer staff on hand is a more effective place to keep a complicated piece of hardware than a small location that happens to be the central point between a number of branch offices, each with its one terminal. Sound communications management always has a part to play in the placing of network nodes.

Figure 1 illustrates the relationships between the various links in a concentrator network. Each terminal in a cluster reaches the host computer through the concentrator, which is itself remote from the host.

One widely used justification for concentrators is the significant cutback often possible in the total mileage of communications lines making up the network. In Figure 2a, each terminal is connected to the host computer by a single dedicated communications line. However, the judicious use of a concentrator, as in Figure 2b, substantially reduces the total line mileage. But it must be noted that a higher grade of line is needed in parts of Figure 2b—from the concentrator to the host processor and, in certain cases, for lines connecting terminals nearest the concentrator—because more traffic moves over these lines than on the corresponding links in Figure 2a.

Of course, with a multidrop line, more terminals are dependent on a line remaining in service than in the configuration of Figure 2a. But the availability of dial-up as a backup between any terminal and the concentrator eases that situation. If dial lines are used, however, speed of transmission may suffer and contention may become more of a problem, which would result in longer response times. Contention will occur any time the number of terminals dialing in is greater than the number of dial-fallback ports available at the concentrator.

Although the consideration of minimizing total network line mileage is illustrated by the concentrator approach, it is not this consideration that by itself mandates or justifies the use of a concentrator. In such a case, indeed, a hardwired multiplexer would be a more economical solution.

When to use concentrators

It is additional performance and functional requirements that mandate the use of concentrators. Table 1 lists the major features and capabilities often found in these services. It must be noted, however, that they are seldom all found in one unit. A concentrator's mix of capabilities will obviously depend upon the application and the specific requirements of the jobs to be done. The functions represent procedures, time-consuming but necessary, toward the orderly and efficient operation of a network.

The basic data concentrator—having only the starred functions of Table 1—can in a sense be considered as a programmable time-division, statistical and traffic-smoothing multiplexer. (A statistical multiplexer skips idle channels and so allows more efficient use of trunk lines.) By means of its stored logic, a concentrator buffers incoming data and transmits in blocks of characters—multiplexing by block, rather than by character or bit as is the way with conventional multiplexers.

With the large numbers of inexpensive and powerful minicomputers reaching the market, the concentrator has come to be a remotely positioned part of what used to be the host communications and switching functions—that is, capable of all the functions of Table 1. Concentrators bring about two kinds of saving: They reduce line costs and cut down the overhead loads at host processors. They should be used, therefore, when there is a call for a reduction in communications and switching overhead at the host.

One of the most important factors to be considered in designing and setting up concentrator configurations is the level of sophistication at which the concentrator is to function—that is, whether switching, terminal and network management is to be passed to the remote concentrator or retained by the host computer. These decisions must be reached early, because they greatly affect the concentrator's configuration, as well as its size, cost, software sophistication and operational needs.

For instance, consider a case where the concentrator supports a number of terminals grouped in clusters and laid out on multidrop lines. The functional requirements imposed by orderly data transfer between any terminal and the host processor are rela-

Table 1 Network functions

Cluster control
- *Multiplexing
- Terminal "handshake" (control characters) and identification
- Terminal control (such as tab and page feed)
- *Polling and selection of terminals
- *Speed detection/conversion
- Error detection
- Retransmission request (error correction)
- Auto dial/auto answer

***Input Processing**
- Buffer management
- Character assembly/disassembly
- Block assembly/disassembly
- Message assembly/disassembly
- Code conversion
- Data compression
- Line control (such as protocols)

Queuing
- Message queuing
- Overflow management (slow or stop input)

Retrieval
- Message retrieval
- Statistics retrieval (interactive or delayed)

Message Processing
- Message control/accountability (sequence number, origin, format, service message)
- Address validation

Routing
- Table look-up (in data base)
- Local switching
- Message distribution
- Multiple address

Supervisory
- Statistical recording (such as number of messages each hour)
- Journaling
- Soft-fail capability (sending a service message that shutdown is imminent—for example, because of many errors)
- Scheduling (such as retrieval by time or queue priority, or diagnostics dump)
- Line diagnostics/circuit quality monitoring (failure detection)
- Network managing (checking performance)
- Network reconfiguring (after failures or traffic changes—usually operator-aided)
- Intercept (operator-directed)

***Output Processing**
- Multiplexing
- Line control
- Character assembly/disassembly
- Block assembly/disassembly
- Message assembly/disassembly
- Buffer management
- Response to polling and selection by host

Functions of basic (non-switching) concentrator

1 Network terminology

Concentrator basics. *A basic concentrator network is made up of a cluster—consisting of concentrator, terminals and connecting lines—and a trunk channel, which connects the concentrator with the host computer.*

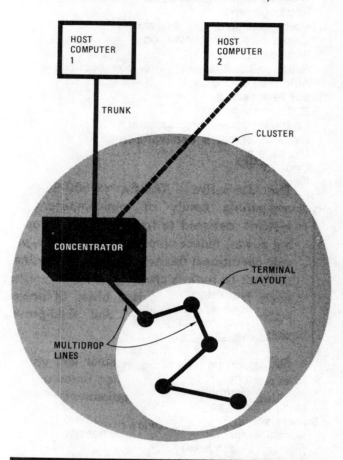

tively uncomplicated. This basic design can usually be set up with a minicomputer-based concentrator and off-the-shelf software. An up-to-date minicomputer will do the job, with appropriate line adapters and enough random access memory for message buffering, and including a real-time operating executive. Any routing of messages between terminals is performed by the host computer, and no switching by the concentrator is required.

Decentralized control

However—and this is where design decisions are important—the problem can grow if the concentrator is to perform local switching, or if a second host is connected (as shown by the broken line in Figure 1). American National Standards Institute (ANSI) specification X3.28 defines this situation as "decentralized control". Here the concentrator no longer acts merely as an intelligent store-and-forward unit but is faced with the much greater responsibility of message switching. In the earlier case the basic concentrator

routed all incoming traffic to the host processor (or to its front end) for any further disposition (multiple distributing, local delivery, journaling and so on). But with the concentrator acting as a message switch, it must itself provide the user community, as well as terminals, network and host processor, with substantial functional and operational support. Table 2 lists the typical additional functions which can be performed by a message switch concentrator, together with a number of examples of these functions.

Table 3 compares the typical delay components found in central (host) message switching with those

---

Table 2 Switching functions

Message processing. The concentrator makes sure that message formats are compatible with network conventions. It handles message accountability and validates each address.

Message accountability. The concentrator keeps track of the sequence numbers and origins of all messages.

Routing. The concentrator translates the destination address, looks up in its address table the whereabouts of the receiving terminal (table lookup), and switches the message to the addressed terminal. This may involve implicit (host-switching) or explicit (concentrator-switching) distribution, multiple addresses, and alternate routing if line or equipment is inoperative.

Message distribution. The concentrator distributes messages to the terminals within its cluster, and between its terminals and the host system or systems, besides handling routing to other concentrators in the network.

Journaling. The concentrator compiles statistical information for all messages it transfers. This may include keeping statistics on lines, and status and activity of terminals, as well as on message history. Retrieval of this information may be initiated by the program or by keyboard entry.

Failure detection. The concentrator may perform failure detection, and reconfiguration and isolation functions around disabled links or other nodes in the network.

Intercept. If a terminal or destination address is found invalid, the concentrator generates an alarm message to the originator.

---

of a local (concentrator) switching configuration. Note that the major delay in the central (host) switch is up to four seconds for processing the message. Total host switching time is from 4.5 seconds to 7.5 seconds, as against the total delay of 1.1 seconds found with the concentrator. When this is multiplied by the number of messages likely to move each day from any one terminal, and by the number of terminals in a cluster, it is obvious how much of its resources a host computer would have to devote to this function. Not only does the concentrator relieve the host computer of this burden, but also—as shown in Table 3—

Table 3   Typical "round trip" delays

FUNCTION	CENTRAL (HOST) SWITCHING	LOCAL (CONCENTRATOR) SWITCHING
CLUSTER PROPAGATION AND TRANSMISSION	1 S	1 S
TRUNK PROPAGATION AND TRANSMISSION	1 S	–
INPUT PROCESSING	6.5 MS	6.5 MS
QUEUING	–	40 MS
MESSAGE HEADER ANALYSIS	–	0.5 MS
MESSAGE RETRIEVAL	–	40 MS
ROUTING	–	3 MS
OUTPUT PROCESSING	12 MS	12 MS
FRONT-END PROCESSING	500 MS	–
MESSAGE PROCESSING	1–4 S	5 MS
RETURN TRUNK PROPAGATION AND TRANSMISSION	1 S	–
TOTAL	**4.519–7.519 S**	**1.107 S**

ASSUME: DATA RATE OF 2,400 B/S;
256 CHARACTERS OF TEXT;
0.5 μS MEMORY ACCESS (CYCLE TIME)

2   Reducing line mileage

Cheaper lines. Line costs are minimized by establishing several multidrop circuits. The multiplexing attribute of the concentrator means that only one port is necessary at the host computer to service each trunk channel.

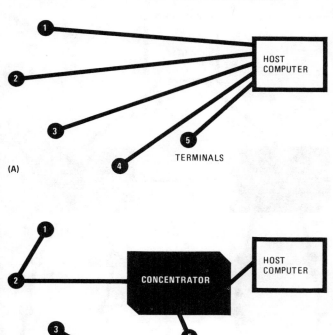

the job moves faster when the concentrator itself does the switching.

An example of a concentrator doing all local switching between terminals is shown in Figure 2b. Traffic between terminals and host computer occurs only to access the host's data base and to deliver and receive daily report information.

Configurations with more than one concentrator-cluster are also possible; Figure 3 shows one with two concentrators, each with one cluster of terminals. Each concentrator handles the switching of messages between terminals within its cluster. But when data is to move from one cluster to another, the message-switching path is through the host. For some messages, switching occurs at the concentrators, for others, at the host computer. If it is found necessary to remove all message switching from the host, a trunk connection must be added between the concentrators governing the various terminals, as indicated by the broken line between the concentrators in Figure 3. With this addition, communications between clusters takes place by way of the switching path between the concentrators.

This concentrator-to-concentrator connection has another advantage. If one host trunk fails, the other trunk, together with the concentrator-to-concentrator trunk, can temporarily handle all traffic between both the concentrators and the host—although performance would suffer somewhat.

Decision considerations

Not only technical and operational factors, but also management convenience, must be taken into consideration before making a decision whether to go to a decentralized control configuration of this kind. The main technical points rest upon whether network traffic volume, distribution patterns, and functional requirements demand the distribution to the remote points of switching, routing, control functions and message accountability (the responsibility for keeping track of sequence numbers and origin of all messages). If these functions are to be dispersed to remote concentrator nodes, the configurations will be far larger and more complex than in those situations where smooth movement of traffic is the concentrator's sole function.

Figure 4 illustrates the differences. In the switching concentrator, more main memory is required to support the added characteristics listed in Table 2, as well as the increased buffer space needed because of longer transit time at the concentrator. Furthermore, extra peripherals will be called for, such as

369

3 Switching concentrator network

Multi-interfacing. *Normally, each concentrator switches messages to and from its own terminals; the host switches between concentrators. With a trunk between concentrators, the host is relieved of all switching.*

4 Concentrator configuration

Added peripherals. *Incorporating the concentrator-switching function demands an increase in the memory size and the adding of peripheral equipment such as disks, magnetic tape and an operator's console.*

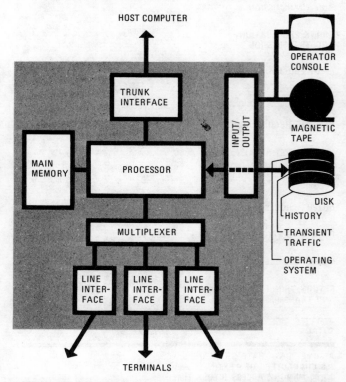

disk mass storage, magnetic tape transport, and an operator's console. In some instances a card reader or other form of binary input may be used for updating and improving the software.

The cost of each configuration reflects differences in complexity and size. Hardware for a non-switching concentrator configuration costs between $12,000 and $25,000, and software between $3,000 and $5,000. For a switching concentrator and its peripherals hardware costs between $40,000 and $100,000, and software between $10,000 and $50,000. If switching between concentrators is required (Fig. 3), core and disk storage needs are about doubled.

Mechanical devices

There will also be significant differences from configuration to configuration in such factors as the reliability and availability of the network. The introduction of mechanical devices, such as disks, may reduce availability of the concentrator node by as much as 5 percentage points (i.e., 98% to 93%). In situations where the network operates 12 hours a day, six days a week, this may mean a difference of more than 15 operational hours every month. Furthermore, the mean-time-to-repair on disk units is considerably higher than on solid state nonmechanical system compo-

nents—which further emphasizes the seriousness of a failure, and introduces, besides, the need for back-up configurations. This in turn will boost costs both of purchase and maintenance, and will mean bigger inventories of spare parts and increased complexity of operations.

However, concentrator switching does appear to be the right solution if the overriding considerations are the relief of the host computer from most communications and switching functions, and reduction in message-switching delays, together with the multiplexing of communications lines.

The ease with which a concentrator network can be upgraded is significant when a user wishes to add telecommunications to a host computer, or when a 10-terminal network is to be enlarged to one with, say, 100 terminals. It will be found that investment in a concentrator network will probably be the most economical solution. By a step-by-step addition of modules and peripherals, a message-switching capability may be added to the concentrator.

A final word of caution: If the plan is for a distributed processing network, its distributed communications aspects must not be brought in as an afterthought. These functions must be considered integral to the whole distributed processing design. ∎

What intelligent time-division multiplexers offer

Ray Sarch, Data Communications

Special features of the smart TDM include concentrator functions, but the conventional mux benefits— especially transparency—stay on

Adding concentrator features to the time-division multiplexer—a long-time network standby—has produced a new network component: the intelligent time-division multiplexer. The ITDM (or smart mux) gets the maximum throughput possible from a high-speed trunk line, while retaining transparency—the most important single attribute of a conventional TDM.

Placing a transparent device in a network means that the device is not sensitive to codes or speeds, and will therefore not require any changes in host computer or communictions software or protocols. On the other hand, adding a concentrator to a network does cause software changes. So the ITDM keeps the transparency of the TDM while incorporating many programmable functions of the concentrator.

Among these functions and other aspects of the ITDM to be discussed are: network configurations, statistical multiplexing, port contention, dynamic bandwidth allocation, data compression, error detection, traffic buffering, automatic detection of rate and code, downline loading, direct memory access, echoplex, and statistic and diagnostic reports.

When a user adds an ITDM to his conventional network, he is adding an intelligent network management function besides those functions enumerated above. The ITDM maintains network control, which is espe-cially important with nodes at locations where personnel may not be trained in network maintenance procedures and supervision techniques.

To better understand how the ITDM fits into the network picture, a review of the TDM and the concentrator would be beneficial. As shown in Figure 1, a typical configuration using a conventional time-division multiplexer (TDM) includes several operator terminals connected to the ports of the remote TDM, and the local TDM connected to the host computer ports. The transmission rate of the high-speed trunk (solid line in Figure 1) connecting the two TDMs equals the maximum aggregate data speed available to all the terminal (or host) lines. For example, if the trunk capacity is 9,600 bit/s, then no more than four 2,400-bit/s terminal lines can be connected.

The primary purpose of multiplexing is to save on line costs. Time-division multiplexing realizes this saving by eliminating the need for extending terminal lines to the host ports. Instead, the high-speed trunk is used by dividing its full bandwidth into a sequence of time segments, with each segment assigned a character (or bit) from each low-speed port. At the receiving end of the trunk, the process is reversed. The bit stream is demultiplexed and the characters (or bits) are assembled into the messages as they appeared at the low-

1 Typical multiplexer configuration

Reducing line costs. *The conventional time-division multiplexer network uses one high-speed trunk line instead of many lines between terminals and host computer.*

With intelligence added to the TDM, it can support more terminal lines than there are host ports, which makes it then possible to introduce another remote multiplexer.

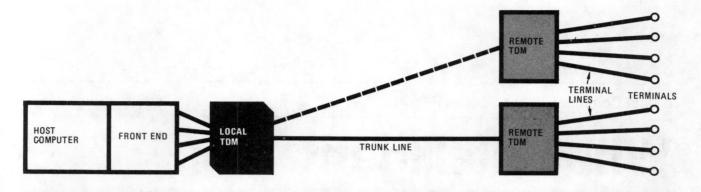

speed ports of the sending (remote or local) TDM.

The conventional TDM is a hard-wired (non-programmable) device which allocates a fixed portion of the high-speed trunk's bandwidth to each of its low-speed channels. Since terminal devices are rarely in operation full time, the fixed allocation scheme uses the high-speed line's capacity inefficently. When a terminal has nothing to send, its allocated time segments—carrying only nulls or fill characters—are still part of the data stream.

A concentrator, on the other hand, uses the high-speed line more efficiently, since it multiplexes by data block, rather than by character or by bit. The block is assembled and stored in a buffer, usually under the control of a minicomputer, with each block consisting of data from a specific terminal. If a terminal is silent, no data blocks are generated, and the only indication of this terminal's existence will be a series of bits in the data stream signifying the unused channel's operational status.

Other programmed features of a concentrator are its network managment functions, which include polling and selecting, speed detection, data compression, buffer management, message assembly/disassembly, and line control (such as protocols). Each application requires its own approach; the concentrator's software is tailored for each case, and the configuration is, by necessity, not transparent.

Configuring the network

A local ITDM communicates with a remote ITDM by using a higher-level full-duplex protocol, such as high-level data link control (HDLC), synchronous data link control (SDLC), or Digital Equipment's digital data communications message protocol (DDCMP)—or variations on one or other of them. The line is typically a 9,600 bit/s or 19.2 kbit/s trunk. The possible interface arrangements include:

■ Two or more hosts to one local ITDM;
■ One or more local ITDMs to two or more remote ITDMs (Figure 1, broken-line trunk and solid-line trunk);

■ Use of the ITDM as a network node, with connections to high-speed remote job entry (RJE) equipment, in addition to conventional user terminals and to other multiplexers.

Among the concentrator functions which the ITDM has adopted is statistical multiplexing. If a conventional remote TDM is connected to a 9,600 bit/s trunk and services user terminals rated at 110 bit/s, the configuration can support 9,600 divided by 110, or nearly 90 terminals. But it can be determined statistically that, at any one time, a certain number of terminals, say 20, are going to be idle. As pointed out earlier, the conventional multiplexer continues to allot high-speed line segments to these idle terminals, sending nulls on the trunk to the local TDM, then on to the host for discard.

Statistical multiplexing eliminates the nulls by allocating trunk line segments only to terminals actually transmitting data. The TDM is driven by time; the statistical multiplexing ITDM is driven by data. Since it was shown in the example that, statistically, 20 terminals are idle at any one time, at least 20 terminals may be added at the remote ITDM without exceeding the capacity of the trunk. The local ITDM will, of course, have to sort out and keep track of host port assignments, since the number of ports at the host remains the same (90 in the example). However, the determining statistics represent only normal conditions. There will obviously be situations when more terminals will seek access than there are host ports available.

Two factors determine if a terminal is to gain access to a host port through a remote ITDM: availability of the host computer port, and availability of bandwidth on the trunk. Port contention will likely take place during times of peak traffic. And transmission delays will result when a terminal operator will hear a busy signal and will have to wait for an available port. Port contention may be considered the penalty paid for the conveniences of statistical multiplexing.

The delays can be minimized, however, by scheduling—where possible—peak periods for different terminals at different times. This may not be as difficult as it sounds, especially if the user's network touches more than one time zone. By considering what delays are acceptable, and establishing a realistic limit on the total number of terminals able to seek access, the user can best reap the economic benefits of statistical multiplexing in spite of port contention.

Another intelligent feature, which also causes contention, is dynamic allocation of the high-speed trunk's bandwidth or number of channels. This feature is realized when a terminal user seeks access at the remote ITDM. With a conventional TDM, each time slot is for a fixed data rate and is not easily changed; the data from each terminal accessing the remote TDM goes into its assigned slot. On the other hand, the ITDM has considerably more flexibility, since there are no assigned time slots and no fixed data rates. Depending at what data rate the terminal operates, as detected by "autobaud" (discussed later), and how much of the trunk's bandwidth is available, the ITDM determines if the traffic can be accepted at that time. So with bandwidth contention, if the terminal seeking access demands more high-speed bandwidth than is then available, it cannot reach a port even if one is available. The remote ITDM will return a busy signal, and the terminal operator will have to try again. The number of available trunk channels is not constant, and depends on trunk capacity (maximum bandwidth)—typically 9,600 bit/s or 19.2 kbit/s—and how much of the bandwidth is not in use at the time.

Compressing data

To make transmission between ITDMs even more efficient, data compression techniques allow information to be sent using fewer bits than when the data is not compressed, or "normal."

The simplest form of data compression calls for the remote ITDM to scan the high-speed data stream, at some time prior to transmission, and pick out repeated characters, such as a string of periods or space characters. The ITDM counts the number of times a character is repeated, then sends the character once, followed by a short combination of bits which represents the number of times the character is to be sent. The receiving ITDM could restore the original data stream, or leave the task to the host computer, whichever is necessary so as to maintain transparency.

A more sophisticated method of data compression is the use of a code that converts frequently used characters to smaller numbers of bits, and allows only rarely used characters to run their normal length or more. A popular method of developing such a code set uses the Huffman coding procedure, detailed in the article, *Data compression increases throughput*, (DATA COMMUNICATIONS, May/June 1976, pp. 65-76). The Huffman code uses an algorithm which lists the characters of a set, such as ASCII or EBCDIC, in the order of their frequency of use. Then assignment is made, for example, of one, two, and three bits to the most often used characters in a particular application. The less often a character is used, the more bits it will have. The least often-used characters can be up to 14 bits long. According to one vendor, however, the average length is about five bits, which improves transmission efficiency by about 55% over the standard eight-bit format. A by-product of variable-length coding is that a certain degree of security is gained in the data stream.

So as to avoid using other than standard software, some vendors do not incorporate transmission encoding and decoding schemes in their equipment. One said he believes in the maxim KISS: "Keep it simple, stupid". The buyer/user is affected only if he decides to have his front-end processor act as the local ITDM. What is gained is the use of only one or two high-speed, rather than of many low-speed ports. But any unusual software requirements, such as those of Huffman coding, become the user's responsibility.

If the buyer/user is considering doing "software demultiplexing" in his front-end processor, thereby eliminating the local ITDM, he should check with his ITDM vendor as to how readily and at what software cost this can be done. Acquiring a local ITDM may turn out to be a better buy.

Error detection

A conventional multiplexer may accept and tag a received character as errored. But no provision is made to correct that error. The ITDM, however, has the ability to correct errors by the automatic repeat request (ARQ) feature, using the cyclic redundancy check (CRC) code to detect errors.

In ARQ, a sending ITDM stores each transmitted data frame while awaiting a positive or negative acknowledgment (ACK or NAK) from its correspondent ITDM. On receipt of an ACK, the sending ITDM discards the stored frame, and continues transmission. If the receiving ITDM recognizes an error in the CRC code of a received frame, it sends back a NAK to the sending unit. The sending ITDM then retransmits the errored frame and all following frames sent while awaiting the ACK/NAK. This process is repeated until the errored frame is accepted as correct, or until a frame transmission counter reaches a preset limit, and causes an alarm to go off.

But ARQ can cause substantial inherent transmission delays. It may be more convenient for a user to tolerate an occasional error—which would be recognized and flagged by the receiving equipment, and could then be corrected by interpretation—rather than accept reduced throughput.

Most ITDM vendors impose ARQ on both synchronous and asynchronous traffic. Even though the synchronous traffic will be monitored again by the host under its CRC-checking protocol, it is simpler not to have to distinguish between the two types of traffic. To apply ARQ only to asynchronous traffic may require additional flag bits to denote the source of the data: from a synchronous or an asynchronous channel or channel group. One vendor, who has not yet completed his ITDM design, suggests use of forward error correction. Although this would require additional coding with each block transmitted (typically at least 165 bits out of a block of 1,000 bits, as compared to 25 bits for a cyclic redundancy check), it would result in errors being corrected at the receiving end—and so avoid retransmission. (For an in-depth discussion of error control techniques, including ARQ, CRC, and forward error correction, refer to *"Error control: keeping data messages clean"*, in Basics of Data Communications, McGraw-Hill Electronics Book Series, pp. 169-173.)

Traffic buffering

As mentioned earlier, unacknowledged transmissions are stored until no longer needed for retransmission. The storage takes place in a buffer which allows dynamic (temporary) retention of a certain amount of transmitted traffic. The prospective user should check the buffer storage capacity of whichever ITDM is being considered for his network. Typically, from 10 to 20 seconds of a user's data may be retained before buffer overflow is threatened. Overflow is likely to occur only during a trunk line outage, or during a noisy trunk line condition causing many repeated transmissions under ARQ, and warning of the overflow's imminence may or may not be provided to the terminals, depending on the sophistication of the circuitry.

One additional buffer consideration which the user should be aware of is the relative "weight" assigned to each terminal port. Even when terminals of identical bit rates are connected to a remote ITDM, it may be possible to program their ports so that one terminal may be treated at a higher priority than the others. Priority is accomplished by emptying the preferred terminal's port buffer at a faster rate than the others. In fact, a series of priorities—or "slot weights", as Codex calls them—may be assigned to establish different buffer-emptying rates for each port. Besides treating certain terminals preferentially, the weighting parameter may also be used to compensate for differing traffic volumes—in addition to what the statistical multiplexing feature accomplishes in this area.

Automatic rate detection

To make most efficient use of its port contention and bandwidth allocation characteristics, the ITDM has a deluxe attribute of the TDM: automatic data rate detection—also known as autobaud or autospeed. Under this feature, a terminal user seeking access to a host computer through a time-division multiplexer must transmit a short group of preliminary characters (usually up to three). The remote TDM analyzes them and determines the terminal's transmission rate. The bandwidth and port contention phases are then exercised, as described previously. Also, when the port on the host (or on its front-end processor, if one is used) is of the autospeed type, the local mux will supply the preliminary characters to the host, which will do its own rate recognition and will accept regular traffic.

Autospeed applies to asynchronous transmission—normally up to 1,200 bit/s. Its widest application is among timeshared service users who dial one particular phone number from terminals of varying asynchronous data rates, and are connected to a modem which accepts that range of rates. Examples of the modems used are the Bell 113B, which handles up to 300 bit/s, and the Bell 202, which handles up to 1,800 bit/s.

Autospeed does not really apply to synchronous transmission, since the applicable modems would require a range of data rates which would make the modem equipment economically impractical at present. And there does not appear to be demand for such an application. However, a minimal form of synchronous autospeed does exist. If a host port can accept, say, either 2,400 bit/s or 4,800 bit/s, then the remote ITDM has that much more latitude in assigning terminals to ports. For example, if all fixed-rate host ports of 2,400 bit/s and 4,800 bit/s are in use, and one multi-rate port for both speeds is still available, then a terminal of either speed can gain access to the host.

Support of any mix of asynchronous and synchronous line speeds is an allied feature of autospeed. The typical asynchronous limit is either 1,200 bit/s or 1,800 bit/s, while the synchronous rates can range from 1,200 bit/s to 9,600 bit/s, or up to 64 kbit/s, in the case of at least one ITDM vendor.

Recognizing the code

A corollary of autospeed is the automatic detection of code or character format. This feature enables the remote ITDM to decipher the preliminary character or characters transmitted to detect the use of either the ASCII or the binary-coded decimal (BCD) code as well as for data rate, as described earlier.

To sum up the gains associated with autospeed, automatic code detection, and line speed mix: The network designer achieves a degree of flexibility which allows him to combine terminals of any speed from different networks (Fig. 1), and to upgrade his terminals—from 10 to 30 characters a second for example—without being concerned with mux changes. With a conventional TDM, mixing speeds is more restrictive, and changing a terminal rate would most likely require a corresponding hardware modification to the multiplexer equipment.

Occasionally, when ITDM program changes are needed, the remote ITDM may be at a location which does not have people who understand software. For this situation, the host-end ITDM may be capable of transmitting any program changes to its remote counterpart—to "downline load" the program. A common loading aid is a keypad, often included as part of the ITDM's front panel controls. Other vendors require a terminal connected to the "loading" ITDM. In either case, the program change is accomplished, usually during off-hours, by "busying-out" user-terminal lines, and sending the new program data from the local ITDM to the remote unit, in the same way that traffic originates from the host.

Vendors disagree on the benefits of downline loading. One company's representative felt that this feature was not important enough to incorporate in his equipment. He felt that, in his experience, a reconfiguration requiring a program change is needed only two or three times a year. Downline loading is sensitive to trunk conditions, he said, which may require many transmissions before the programming process is completed.

The vendor's representative felt that the simplicity of hard-wired program plugs is more appealing to the

2 Echoplex choices

Operator assurance. An "echoplexed" copy of a transmission is returned by the host computer to the sending terminal as verification that the data arrived correctly. An intelligent time-division multiplexer can relieve the host of this processing burden, although the degree of verification is reduced when the host computer is not involved.

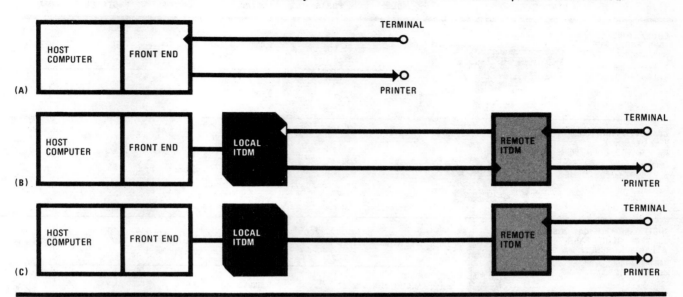

user. These plugs could include jumper wires or small switches, and the combinations of connections or switch settings would determine certain program parameters. Typical "fixed" parameters set by the program plugs are channel address, whether a channel is fixed rate or autospeed, and an autospeed channel's range of data rates.

Views on direct memory access

Another area of vendor disagreement is direct memory access (DMA), a hardware technique used to transfer high-speed data directly between an input/output channel and memory. There appears to be a sharp difference of opinion among ITDM vendors as to the benefits derived from DMA. Western Union Information Systems (WUIS), one of DMA's strongest advocates, claims that this function relieves the microprocessor of having to transfer data to and from memory. Thus, the microprocessor can fulfill its primary supervisory and control functions without the additional burden of data transfer. Other vendors, such as Digital Communications Associates, consider DMA as "based on an obsolete technology," and its use as a "negative feature" and a very limited kind of processing which imposes a more structured program upon the vendor. However, others, such as General DataComm, believe that DMA has a firm position in the future of the software-controlled multiplexer industry.

One reason for the sharply divergent opinions may have been expressed by a WUIS product manager. He said that some vendors choose to use more microprocessing power, rather than direct memory access, because they prefer what they are more familiar with; they are, the Western Union man said, designing "preconceived solutions," while ignoring a somewhat old-

er—but still applicable—data-handling technology.

An operator at a remote terminal usually creates a copy of what is being sent, either on the terminal screen or on an associated printer. This procedure provides no assurance to the operator of the data being received in that form.

Echoplex is a technique which attempts to provide such assurance. With the terminal's line connected directly to a host computer (or front-end processor, as in Figure 2a), the data as received from the terminal is returned to its printer or screen. This method enables the operator to verify that the transmission was received correctly.

Some ITDMs offer the option of relieving the host of the processing time required by the echoplex function. If the local (host-end) ITDM returns the received data (Fig. 2b), then reception is verified for both the terminal and high-speed lines. If the remote ITDM does the echoplexing (Fig. 2c), verification is obtained for just the terminal line.

For low-speed terminals, such as those operating up to 300 bit/s, the delay between transmission and the echoplexed reception may be excessive—causing operator disorientation. In such a situation, full verification may be sacrificed and echoplexing from the remote ITDM is accepted. One vendor refers to this as pseudo-echoplex.

Network reports

With a peripheral printer connected to it, the local ITDM provides statistics and diagnostics. To what extent, however, depends on the particular vendor. As network monitoring information, the statistics may include:

■ High-speed trunk utilization (total traffic trans-

What's available in intelligent multiplexers

VENDOR	MODEL	MAXIMUM NUMBER OF TERMINAL PORTS	MAXIMUM TERMINAL SPEED (BIT/S)	MAXIMUM TRUNK SPEED (KBIT/S)	SYNCHRONOUS TERMINAL PORT PROTOCOL	STATISTICAL MULTIPLEXING (SM)
CODEX CORP. 15 RIVERDAL AVE. NEWTON, MASS. 02195 (617)-969-0600 RALPH W. LOWRY	6030	124	9,600	19.2	BSC	YES
	6040	248	9,600	56	BSC	YES
COMPUTER TRANSMISSION CORP. 2352 UTAH AVE. EL SEGUNDO, CALIF. 90245 (213)-973-2222 J. ROBERT McCONLOGUE	M1318	16	4,800	9.6	ANY	NO
DIGITAL COMMUNICATIONS ASSOC. 135 TECHNOLOGY PARK ATLANTA NORCROSS, GA. 30071 (404)-448-1400 JOHN SNUGGS	SMART/MUX	128	9,600	9.6 (56 PLANNED)	ANY	YES
	MICRO/MUX (REMOTE ONLY)	62	9,600	9.6 (56 PLANNED)	ANY	YES
DIGITAL COMMUNICATIONS CORP. 19 FIRSTFIELD RD. GAITHERSBURG, MD. 20760 (301)-948-0850 DICK HAMPTON	CP-9000	480	64,000	64	BSC (SDLC IN 1978)	YES
GENERAL DATACOMM INDUSTRIES, INC. 131 DANBURY RD. WILTON, CONN. 06897 (203)-762-0711 (UNDER DESIGN) JOHN M. O'NEIL	DATA LINE CONCENTRATOR (BY 1978)	448	56,000	72	ANY	YES
INFOTRON SYSTEMS CORP. 7300 NORTH CRESCENT BLVD. PENNSAUKEN, N.J. 08110 (609)-665-3864 TOM HORNSBY	TL 780 SUPERMUX	128	9,600	9.6	BSC	YES
TIMEPLEX INC. 100 COMMERCE WAY HACKENSACK, N.J. 07601 (201)-646-1155 PATRICK BOURGEOIS	DYNAPLEXER (WITH STANDARD TDM'S)	500	56,000	64	BSC (OTHER PROTOCOLS WITHOUT SM)	YES
	MODIFIED T-96 (LATE 1977)	96	56,000	64	BSC (OTHER PROTOCOLS WITHOUT SM)	YES
WESTERN UNION INFORMATION SYSTEMS 82 McKEE DRIVE MAHWAH, N.J. 07430 (201)-529-6333 RICHARD H. KLING	4100/1	64	1,800 ASYNCH (STANDARD)	9.6	—	NO
	4100/2	64 (128 PLANNED)	9,600	9.6 (DUAL 9.6 LATE 1977)	ANY	YES

ARQ ERROR CONTROL	DATA COMPRESSION		DOWNLINE LOADING	ECHOPLEX	DIRECT MEMORY ACCESS (DMA)
	REPEATED CHARACTERS	HUFFMAN CODE			
YES	NO	YES	YES	YES	NO
YES	NO	YES	YES	YES	NO
NO	NO	NO	NO	NO	NO
YES	YES	NO	YES	YES	NO
YES	YES	NO	YES	YES	NO
YES	YES	YES	YES	YES	ONLY ON PORTS OF 19.2 KBIT/S AND HIGHER
ASYNCH ONLY	PROBABLY	NO	YES	YES	YES
YES	NO	NO	NO	NO	NO
BETWEEN DYNA-PLEXERS ONLY	NO	NO	YES	PLANNED	NO
YES	NO	NO	YES	PLANNED	NO
NO	NO	NO	YES	YES	YES
YES	YES	AVAILABLE EARLY 1978	YES	YES	YES

mitted in, for instance, the previous hour);

■ Trunk error frequency and number of retransmissions;
■ Trunk error types;
■ Buffer activity;
■ Average time length of dial-in connection;
■ Terminal line activity (volume and errors).

When a network problem occurs, the ITDM can also become a diagnostic tool. It assists in localizing and diagnosing the trouble with both its own indicators and the associated printouts. The ITDM can initiate remote and local loopback testing of trunk and terminal lines under off-line or dynamic conditions. At the local site, the entire network may be monitored and abnormal conditions logged, with a note of the time of day.

Diagnostic routines are usually initiated by an operator at the local ITDM. Some vendors offer a "hot" backup unit ready to take over for the primary unit when a failure is detected. The backup unit may be given the task of running noninterfering diagnostics automatically, until it is needed as a replacement.

Some ITDM vendors also provide the modems for the terminal and trunk lines. These modems may occupy circuit board slots in the mux equipment, or could be external to the ITDM, depending on the vendor's design and practice. The buyer/user should include modem costs when comparing ITDM prices.

Who makes intelligent multiplexers

What follows is a list of ITDM vendors, showing to what extent their products include the programmable and disputed features discussed above, and noting any particular claims made by the vendors.

■ **Codex Corp.:** In its microprocessor-controlled 6000 series of intelligent network processors, Codex offers its 6030 and 6040 ITDMs. The 6030, with one to three microprocessors, can handle up to 124 ports at up to 9,600 bit/s, over a trunk of up to 19.2 kbit/s. The 6040, with two to eight microprocessors, handles up to 248 ports at up to 9,600 bit/s, over a trunk of up to 56 kbit/s. With all this microprocessor power, the direct memory access method is, of course, not used. Only half-duplex terminals are supported at present, with synchronous terminal lines limited to BSC protocol. The trunk line protocol is "similar to SDLC", a Codex representative said. Notice of the imminent overflow of a terminal port buffer will not, at present, be passed on to the affected terminal, but this attribute is promised soon as an option. A typical installation of a pair of 6040 ITDMs with a 14-port capacity costs about $35,000.

■ **Computer Transmission Corp. (Tran):** This company's current offerings have a certain amount of intelligence, but do not include statistical multiplexing at present. Tran's microprocessor-controlled M1318 allows for a mix of up to 16 asynchronous and synchronous terminal lines at up to 4,800 bit/s. The high-speed trunk operates at up to 9,600 bit/s. The trunk protocol is Tran's own. Downline loading and echoplexing are not included, nor is data compression or ARQ. Essentially, the only intelligent features are autospeed, programmable network reconfiguration, and diagnostic capabilities. The price is about $5,250 for each M1318. A more competitive stand-alone ITDM—which will include many of the intelligent functions that are not in the M1318—is under development and should be available within a year.

Digital Communications Associates: DCA offers its Smart/Mux series of DEC PDP-8 minicomputer-controlled ITDMs. The company claims that its form of statistical multiplexing is of the most efficient type because it is driven strictly by data traffic. Also, the claim is made that DCA's Smart/Mux has an uncommon networking capability which enables the evolutionary growth of a network while keeping the disturbance to the other elements to a minimum. Up to 128 ports can be supported at up to 9,600 bit/s, with the high-speed trunk aggregate rate at up to 9,600 bit/s; 56 kbit/s is promised. Compatibility "with all industry standard terminals" is claimed, using a protocol converter. The trunk protocol is DDCMP; BSC compatibility to IBM's 2780 and 3780 remote job entry (RJE) data communications terminals is offered. Simple compression schemes are used to compress spaces and redundant characters.

A system consisting of one ITDM at a host site and two remote ITDMs, with the host capacity at 48 ports, comes to about $35,000.

DCA is building a microprocessor version of its Smart/Mux, the Micro/Mux. Size is reduced considerably and initial port capacity is for 62 terminal lines. The equipment is expected to have full hardware redundancy, with the "hot" standby unit running diagnostics until needed. Switchover can be automatic. Initially, the Micro/Mux is intended as the remote device working with a Smart/Mux at the host end. With 30 ports, a Micro/Mux is priced at about $14,500.

■ **Digital Communications Corp. (DCC)**: The multi-microprocessor-controlled CP-9000 can be configured as a concentrator or as an ITDM, according to DCC. As an ITDM, it can be programmed to include all the intelligent functions previously described while maintaining transparency. Up to 480 terminal lines at up to 64 kbit/s are supported, with the high speed trunk operating from 19.2 kbit/s to 64 kbit/s. A "hot" back-up unit may be included, with automatic switchover capability. DMA is available for the highest data rates. Synchronous terminal line protocol is BSC, with SDLC promised for early 1978. Trunk protocol is SDLC. Price information was not made available.

■**General DataComm Industries Inc. (GDC)**: While presently offering conventional TDMs, GDC plans to enter the microprocessor-controlled ITDM market by early 1978 with its data line concentrator (DLC). In spite of the name, the unit is not a concentrator. Its ITDM function descriptions are similar to those of the other vendors. ARQ is planned only for asynchronous traffic, and forward error correction is being considered. The host-end DLC will support up to 64 channels, the remote up to 448 channels, at up to 56 kbit/s. Between DLCs, the rate will be up to 72 kbit/s, "full-duplex type". The direct memory access method will be used. Prices are not yet available.

■ **Infotron Systems**: The Timeline 780 Supermux, or TL780, is microprocessor-controlled. Its more conventional predecessor units, the TL180 and TL240, may be converted to a TL780 ITDM by replacement of certain modules. The Supermux can handle up to 128 terminal ports at an aggregate of 9,600 bit/s. Automatic switchover to a backup unit is offered as an option. Synchronous terminal protocol is limited to BSC. Trunk line rate is also up to 9,600 bit/s, using an "SDLC-like" protocol. Downline loading may be provided in the future if demand becomes apparent. For now, program plugs are used, allowing for uniformity with Infotron's conventional TDMs, which can be expanded and upgraded to a Supermux. No data compression is practiced, "to keep it simple, and to adapt more readily to standard 8-bit software" for front-end demultiplexing, an Infotron representative said. Echoplex is left up to the host computer. A Supermux with 18 terminal ports costs about $7,000.

■ **Timeplex, Inc.**: The company makes a wide range of conventional TDMs, which when used in combination with its network Dynaplexer have intelligence that appears equivalent to that of the ITDMs of other vendors. Timeplex describes its version of statistical multiplexing as data compaction: removing traffic which carries no useful information. There is no data compression. The Dynaplexer can interface up to 12 Timeplex TDMs handling up to a total of 500 terminal ports. Depending on which TDM is used, the terminal line rate can be up to 56 kbit/s. Dynaplexer input and output port rates can be up to 64 kbit/s. Protocol between Dynaplexers is a modified X.25. The price of a Dynaplexer with one link port and one TDM port, plus a TDM handling 96 terminal lines (the T-96) is about $35,000. Timeplex has announced for later this year a modification for the T-96 which will add statistical multiplexing and ARQ as options to this conventional TDM. The cost will be about $5,000 added to the price of the T-96 which, with 96 ports, is $15,000.

■ **Western Union Information Systems (WUIS)**: Featuring direct memory access, the 4100/1 is microprocessor-controlled but does not offer synchronous ports, statistical multiplexing, data compression, or ARQ. The 4100/2, promised later this year, will have all these features. Terminal port capacity is 64 (same as 4100/1), with future expansion to 128 promised. Asynchronous rates of the 4100/2 are up to 1,800 bit/s, synchronous up to 9,600 bit/s, and trunk rate a dual 9,600 bit/s (to two 4100s). High-speed trunk protocol is advanced, such as HDLC or ADCCP. Huffman coding data compression is promised for early 1978, as is a means of local and downline program loading which would not revert to a fixed program upon powering down. This will be achieved by using battery backup power whose capacity is rated at about 96 hours. During regular operation, the battery is kept charged by the equipment's normal power source. The price of the 4100/2 will be $7,500 to $10,000.

The table, "What's available in smart multiplexers", summarizes the preceding information. In addition, the address, telephone number, and a personal contact is provided for each vendor. In some cases, the reader may find that a local technical representative will be more helpful than the home office personnel. ■

How statistical TDMs let network lines support more terminals

Ross Seider, Codex Corp. Newton, Mass.

**A close look at the techniques
shows how STDMs achieve
line economies, and also reveals
pitfalls in queuing delays**

The statistical time-division multiplexers (STDM, and also known as intelligent network processors) became available about two years ago and have proven their worth in reducing line costs. They owe their development to low-cost microprocessors and represent a radical departure from the older frequency-division multiplexers (FDM) and time-division multiplexers (TDM). STDMs offer many efficiencies over the older techniques, but they also exhibit some potential pitfalls, such as excessive queuing delay.

The major difference between FDM/TDM and STDM techniques concerns how the bandwidth of the high-speed transmission line is allocated among lower-speed terminals. In both FDM and TDM, a fixed percentage of the high-speed bandwidth is permanently allocated to each user, usually on the basis of transmission speed. This bandwidth is always committed. Thus, bandwidth (bit rate) is wasted when the terminal is inactive.

STDMs, on the other hand, dynamically allocate bandwidth among active terminals. This means that a user will only be given bandwidth when there is data to send. During idle moments, that bandwidth can be assigned to other subscriber terminals. The microprocessors do this task very rapidly and, theoretically, this allocation process remains invisible to the users.

Most data communications applications have substantial periods of idle time. STDMs use this idle time to handle a larger number of users. For example, a TDM may share a 4.8 kbit/s circuit among four 1.2 kbit/s users. If each user is active less than 25 percent of the time, a STDM could support up to as many as 16 terminals on that same 4.8 kbit/s circuit.

This example is a little too simplistic. Using FDM/TDM techniques, subscriber terminals cannot interfere with each other, because their subchannels are reserved for their use only. Using STDM techniques, channels can interfere with each other in varying degrees. If many channels are simultaneously active, and the sum of this activity approaches or exceeds the high-speed data rate, then transmission delays can grow as that data is queued in the STDM transmitter awaiting transmission on the circuit. The sensitivity of the user application to queuing delays will have a large bearing upon the aggregate supportable input.

Despite the potential delay problem, STDM techniques are more efficient than FDM/TDM techniques in relation to how many users can share a circuit, and are, therefore, very attractive network tools. Other STDM benefits include an error-protected protocol on the high-speed links. Data errors caused by transient telephone-line phenomena will not be seen on STDMs,

1 Frame structure

Overhead. The STDM frame structure can vary depending on activity, but a typical frame might include a variable length data field and overhead. The latter would include, as here, the flag characters, the control characters, the cyclic redundancy checking characters, as well as any addressing octets appearing in the frame's data field.

8 BITS	8	8		8	16
FLAG	CONTROL		VARIABLE LENGTH DATA	CONTROL	CRC

because the device will retransmit the block in error. Diagnostic reports, statistics, reconfigurations, and many more features are available on most STDMs.

Understanding basic STDM operation

The most important function of the statistical multiplexer is to handle data transparently with the least amount of queuing and subsequent delay (Ref. 1). The relative efficiency of a particular STDM technique is best analyzed by examination of the device's frame (or block) structure. A frame structure is needed because the STDM must "block" the data in order to accomplish its error retransmission; and, since a particular user's subchannel is allocated dynamically, data packets from that user must be addressed in some fashion for proper interpretation and routing at the receiver.

The STDM frame structure can vary widely in length depending upon the amount of user activity and the overhead bits that the STDM adds to the frame. A general frame structure might look like Figure 1. In general, under moderate loads, the data field will accommodate all data queued for transmission, up to some maximum, to prevent excessively long frames. In this example, the overhead would include the flag characters, the control characters, the cyclic redundancy check (CRC) octets, and any addressing octets within the variable length data field. An octet is eight bits long, and is often called a byte.

The frame length at any particular level of channel activity (load) is an important performance parameter. Since data arriving at the receiver cannot be released until the CRC characters pass the error-control check, longer frames mean that the data must be held for extended periods of time. The resultant delay can become substantial and seriously degrade throughput.

A first approximation reveals that the end-to-end path delay is equal to the time to transmit one frame: the average data character is buffered in the transmitter awaiting its position in the current frame time for this to occur. After this character arrives at the receiver, it must wait for the last characters of the frame to pass the error-check sequence. This waiting time also averages to one-half frame time. In addition to this, hardware/software delays and character assembly and shifting delays also add tangible delays to the transmission.

A general formula that relates the transmit frame length to the input data load can be derived as follows:

Let F = Frame length (in bits)
OH = Overhead in a frame (in bits)
L = Load of data in the frame (in bit/s)
C = Capacity of link (in bit/s)

To simplify this initial discussion, assume that the load is less than the link capacity ($L < C$). Clearly, L/C is the percent data utilization on the circuit, while $1 - L/C$ is the proportion of wasted bandwidth or overhead. To convert the overhead proportion to bits, multiply by the total frame size F.

$$OH = (1 - L/C)F \tag{1}$$

Solving for F results in:

$$F = (OH)(C)/(C - L) \tag{2}$$

This general formula for frame length (or equivalently, delay) will serve to examine three statistical multiplexing techniques. If F is equated to delay, this can be recognized as a classical queuing theory formula. Equation 2 also has applicability to synchronous protocol performance and has a number of interesting properties that are demonstrated Figure 2.

Figure 2 relates frame length as a function of load for overhead (OH) values of 40, 80, and 120 bits per frame. The family of curves demonstrates that frame structures with greater fixed overhead increase in length more rapidly as the data load increases than do frame structures with less fixed overhead. Similarly, end-to-end path delays grow more rapidly for higher overhead frame structures as the load increases.

The STDM technique that keeps the overhead requirements as small as possible will outperform an STDM with high overhead. This higher performance is seen as less end-to-end path delay, and a higher frames-per-second rate. This reduces buffer sampling intervals and improves automatic request for repetition (ARQ) error recovery. The analysis of STDM techniques is accomplished, therefore, by examination of the overhead (flags, CRCs, addressing octets) introduced by the STDM link protocol.

Figure 3 shows frame length as a function of load, given a fixed overhead of 40 bits per frame. Two link capacities are shown; 9.6 and 7.2 kbit/s. The nonlinear relationship of these two capacities is demonstrated by the divergence of the curves as the load increases. This is a fundamental property of the way capacity affects queuing systems. With light loads, almost no difference in frame length is observable, but the differences increase with high loads.

Since ARQ error-retransmission causes a reduction in effective link capacity, a 9.6 kbit/s data link may be subsequently degraded if the circuit becomes marginal. That is, though the user does not observe data errors, he may notice a reduction in throughput.

Consider now three alternative STDM techniques, simply called Technique A, Technique B, and Technique C. Each has its link protocol described and analyzed, with particular emphasis paid to the overhead per frame that a technique adds.

Structure of Technique A

STDM Technique A uses a full-duplex, bit-synchronous, trunk facility at the standard speeds of 2.4, 4.8, and 9.6 kbit/s. Frames are made up of 8-bit character sequences, and conform to the following structure:

F, A, C, INFO, BCC, Repeats

where

F = Opening flag (8 bits)
A = Link address field (8 bits)
C = Link control field (8 bits)
INFO = Information field (variable length)
BCC = Error-check sequence (16 bits)

The flag field is a unique 8-bit sequence that does not appear normally within any other characters. A technique similar to SDLC's zero-bit insertion is used to maintain this property (Ref. 2). The link address and control fields contain the ACK/NAK codes as well as the transmit and receive frame numbers. The BCC field is 16 bits long and uses a polynominal generator and checker to ensure that the data is received error free.

The variable length information field uses a direct-addressing method to identify up to 63 unique information packets. These data packets can have two formats, depending upon the amount of data to be sent (Fig. 4). Only active channels transmit a packet.

Format A is used whenever there are 3 or fewer characters to transmit. Format B is used when there are between 4 and 63 characters to send. The fixed-frame overhead in this scheme comes from the F, A, C, and BCC fields, and amounts to 40 bits per frame. The addressing characters in Formats A and B represent variable overhead and can be either 8 or 16 bits per transmitting channel, depending upon how busy the sending terminal is. Idle channels would not be addressed within the frame.

As each new terminal turns on, or, as the characters available for transmission exceed Format A's capacity, eight new bits of overhead are added to the frame. Performance for Technique A is shown in Figure 5a.

Once the overhead per frame is determined, the graph of frame length versus load can be constructed using the formula

$$F = (OH)(C)/(C-L)$$

developed earlier. Figure 5b shows a family of curves representing different values of overhead. Here, the heavy line depicts the operating point of the STDM

2 Frame length vs load

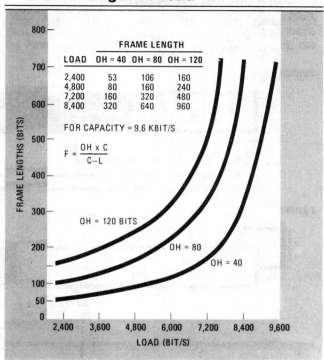

Increase. *An analysis of frame length as a function of data load shows that the combination of heavy data load and great fixed overhead makes length increase rapidly.*

3 Link capacity vs frame length

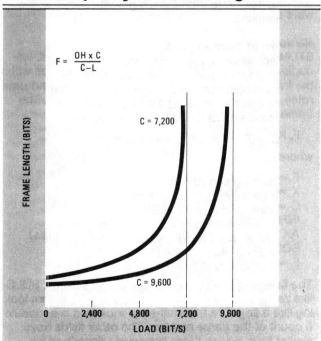

Nonlinear. *Frame length as a function of load analysis reveals a nonlinear relationship between two link capacities. This shows how capacity affects queuing systems.*

4 Data packet structure

Addressing. The variable length information field uses a direct addressing method to identify up to 63 data packets (in binary, ||||| = 63, 64 would require a seventh bit).

Fixed frame overhead equals 40 bits; Formats A and B represent variable overhead. Format A is used for 3 or fewer bits, and Format B is used to transmit 4 to 63 bits.

FORMAT A

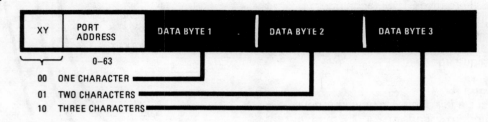

FORMAT B

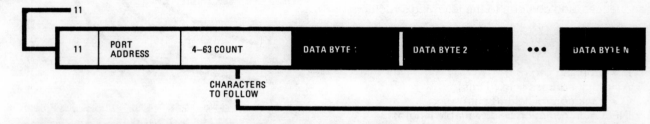

using Technique A. As the load increases, this operating point switches to a higher overhead curve.

If very few channels are simultaneously active, then this technique is probably adequate. But frame length (overhead) increases rapidly as more and more channels become active. This technique is quite straightforward and its simple 8-bit format permits potential software demuxing.

Structure of Technique B

STDM Technique B uses a synchronous bit level, full-duplex protocol made up of variable length fields within the frame. It also operates at standard voiceband data rates, but can also support 19.2 kbit/s service. The frame is made up of the following sequences:

F, X, C, INFO, AK, BCC, F Repeats

where

F = Opening flag (9 bits)
X = Transmit sequence (3 bits)
C = Control/data bit (1 bit)
INFO = Information field (variable length)
AK = ACK/NAK and RCV number field (4 bits)
BCC = Error check code (16 bits)
F = Closing flag (9 bits)

The flag field is a unique 9-bit sequence. Again, SDLC-like zero bit insertion is used to prevent data from looking like a flag. The transmit-sequence field is a modulo 8 count of the frame number. The other fields have similar functions to those previously described for Technique A.

The opening and closing flag and X fields are only sent during error-recovery procedures) thus, they normally do not contribute to overhead. The variable

length information field is segmented into slots, one of which exists for each configured channel module. This slotting technique can be thought of as positional addressing. The data characters' position within the information field defines its address. Slots may contain multiple data characters up to a limit called the slot weight. Slot weight, selectable for each channel, limits the maximum number of characters that may be sent within any one slot. If a slot does not contain the maximum number of characters permitted by the parameter, then a unique XY code terminates this slot and the next slot is started. Figure 6 shows some examples of the XY terminator code in operation.

Of further interest is the fact that the channel's data characters are encoded into variable length prefix codes via a data compression routine. The most frequently sent characters are encoded into short code words (3, 4, or 5 bits long) while less frequent characters are encoded into longer codes (9, 10, 11, or 12 bits long). The result is an average code length of something less than the input character length. The terminator code is a unique sequence, usually 2 bits long (Ref. 3).

The fixed frame overhead for STDM Technique B is 30 bits under normal conditions. Within the information field, the terminator code represents variable overhead and is normally 2 bits per configured channel.

A very desirable feature Technique B is that the overhead goes down as the load increases because the terminator codes are removed as the channel's slot fills with data characters to the slot-weight limit. Overhead as a function of load is presented in Figure 7a, and from this, frame length as a function of load is determined by using Equation 2 and is plotted in Figure 7b. Note that the STDM's operating point switches to

382

5 STDM technique A

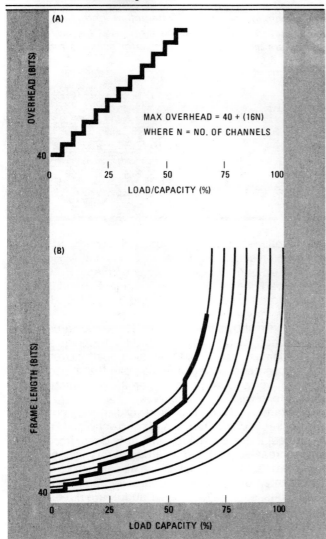

Switching. Each new terminal and overloads add eight bits to frame length. Technique A performance is shown in (a). Frame length vs load (b) illustrates how the operating point switches to a higher curve as frame load increases.

lower curves as the load increases. The data compression feature also has a dramatic effect. When operating properly, this feature acts to expand the data handling capacity of the link. Since a 9.6 kbit/s circuit can only handle 1.2K 8-bit characters each second, the same circuit could support 1.37K characters per second if each character averaged 7 bits in length. Recall an earlier discussion on link capacity. Changing the link capacity (from 1.2K to 1.37K characters per second) has a nonlinear effect on frame length. The capability to send fewer than 8 bits per character on a heavily loaded circuit can make a substantial reduction in end-to-end delay. Also notice that BCD and Baudot codes are transmitted without the need for bit pads because the protocol is bit, not character, oriented. In summary, while the initial overhead per frame may be higher un-

der light loads than STDM Technique A, the overhead of Technique B tends to go down as the load increases. Data compression also aids many applications.

Structure of Technique C

STDM Technique C uses a full-complex, character-oriented, synchronous protocol. Frames conform generally to the same structure as the Technique A STDM, namely:

F, C, INFO, R, BCC, Repeats

where

F = Opening flag character (8 bits)
C = Transmit control bytes (8 bits)
INFO = Information field (variable length)
R = Receive control, ACK/NAK bits (8 bits)
BCC = Error check sequence (16 bits)

These fields have been described before and have equivalent functions within this protocol. Of note is that the fixed overhead per frame amounts to 40 bits.

The variable-length information field uses an addressing method similar to Technique A, but adds an interesting indexing capability that allows STDM Technique C to address additional channels, under certain conditions, without using an additional 8-bit address byte (or octet). There are two types of data messages, identified as shown in Figure 9.

As an example, control byte B could specify to:

- Send a character to the current address
- Increment the address count by two
- Send three characters to this new address
- Increment the address count by one
- Send the last three characters to this address
  As another example, it could specify to:
- Increment the address count by three
- Send six characters to this address

This indexing capability is what differentiates this STDM technique from Technique A. With the one byte of control, STDM Technique C can increment the address count up to four addresses.

The fixed overhead of STDM Technique C is 40 bits per frame and the variable overhead within the INFO field comes from the address byte (Format 1's A bits) and the control byte (Format 2's B bytes). The 8-bit format allows this protocol to be potentially demultiplexed within the host computer.

Note that at least one eighth of the INFO field is variable overhead. The variable overhead in a frame is not only a function of the user data load, but also of which STDM channel addresses are active. If the channel addresses of the active users are greater than four apart in time sequence, the indexing feature is not useful and the required overhead may be greater than the requirements of STDM Technique A. However, under heavier load, the probability of adjacent channel activity (especially if the total number of channels is small) becomes higher and the overhead can be lowered by this feature. The degree to which this becomes more efficient depends greatly on the algorithms used by the microprocessors to construct the frames.

Figure 9a shows frame overhead as a function of

6 Terminator codes

Slot format. *The variable length information field is segmented into slots, one for each channel module. The slots imply positional addressing. If a slot does not contain* the maximum number of characters permitted by the parameter, a unique XY code terminates the slot. If data characters fill the slot, no terminator signal is employed.

CASE 1	NO DATA FROM CHANNEL 10	SLOT 9 | XY | SLOT 11 ↑ TERMINATOR CODE
CASE 2	N CHARACTERS IN CHANNEL 10's BUFFER WHERE N IS LESS THAN THE SLOT WEIGHT	⌐——— SLOT 10 ———⌐ SLOT 9, D1,D2,D3,...DN,XY,SLOT 11 ↑ TERMINATOR CODE
CASE 3	M CHARACTERS IN CHANNEL 10's BUFFER WHERE M IS GREATER THAN OR EQUAL TO THE SLOT WEIGHT	⌐——SLOT 10——⌐ SLOT 9, D1,D2,...D(SW),SLOT 11

7 STDM technique B

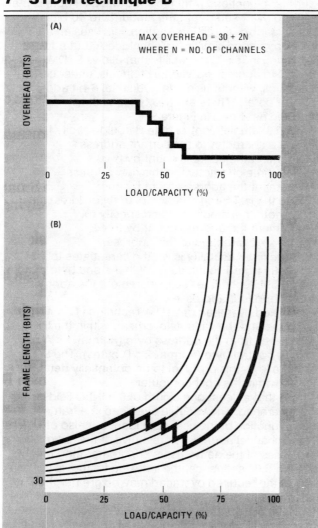

(A)

MAX OVERHEAD = 30 + 2N
WHERE N = NO. OF CHANNELS

OVERHEAD (BITS)

LOAD/CAPACITY (%)

(B)

FRAME LENGTH (BITS)

30

LOAD/CAPACITY (%)

Advantage. *In Technique B, as a channel's slots fill with data to the slot's capacity, terminator codes are removed, and overhead goes down (a). Frame length vs load (b) shows this as operating point switches to lower curves.*

load. Notice that, with light loads, the overhead climbs in a fashion similar to the rise in Technique A. Here, a minimal amount of indexing is taking place. However, as the load continues to grow, adjacent channels become more active statistically and the overhead grows slowly or may even begin to decline.

Figure 9b shows frame length, for various amounts of overhead, as a function of load for Technique C STDM. Initially, the STDM operating point moves to higher overhead curves until the point that the indexing feature begins to take effect, then the operating point moves to lower overhead curves.

In summary, STDM Technique C displays some of the desirable characteristics of the Technique B STDM. In particular, the overhead-per-frame does drop as the load increases, but the magnitude of this savings would be very difficult to predict. Since all characters are represented by 8-bit bytes, character codes of less than 8 bits, such as BCD and Baudot, are not as efficiently handled as in the Technique B STDM.

In any STDM technique, the longer the frame length, the longer the end-to-end path delay. Therefore, keeping the frame length short maintains the response times and throughput which the subscribers want.

In properly designed networks, the average peak load must be well within the link capacity. If not, substantial delay will be encountered. While the peak loads may momentarily exceed the link capacity, this condition should not be maintained for any extended time.

In real world applications, estimating the statistical properties of a pool of user terminals is a very difficult task. The user pool is rarely homogeneous in terms of speed or application, thus making analytical techniques very burdensome. Yet, it is still important to take a first cut at understanding the traffic loads on the terminal in a potential STDM application.

Consider, for example, a pool of M subscriber terminals clustered at a certain location. Assume during the busy hours that all M terminals are actively running an application which involves short, keyboard-entered, messages followed by longer, computer-driven, printouts. The questions to be examined are: What is the average statistical load of the terminals? That is, what is the probability of any terminal's having a character

8 Indexed addressing

Technique C. *In this technique, the variable length information field uses a direct addressing method similar to Technique A's, but also adds (Format 2) an indexing* capability *which enables this technique to address up to four additional channels without using another address byte. Note: one-eighth of INFO field is variable overhead.*

FORMAT 1. ADDRESS-DATA MESSAGE

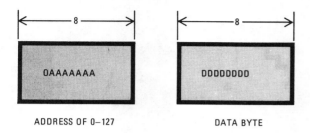

ADDRESS OF 0–127   DATA BYTE

FORMAT 2. MARKER-DATA MESSAGE

1BBBBBBB	DDDDDDDD	DDDDDDDD	./..	DDDDDDDD

CONTROL BYTE   ONE TO SEVEN DATA CHARACTERS

---

to send or receive? Given this probability, how many of these terminals can be expected to be simultaneously active?

The first question can be resolved by actually observing the terminal operator performing the application. The average printout and the time between printouts will give a good estimate of the probability of that terminal's receiving data. Once this probability has been estimated, the second question can be answered using the following formula:

$$P(N) = N^cM \ \ P(ON)^N \ \ (1 - P(ON))^{M-N} \qquad (3)$$

where

N = Number of devices with data to send
M = Total number of devices
N^cM = Number of combinations of devices taken N at a time
P(N) = Probability of N devices being simultaneously active
P(ON) = Probability of N devices' having data to send

The symbol N^cM represents the number of different ways that N devices of M total could be active at a time. This figure can be found in a binomial distribution table, or calculated from the formula:

$$N^cM = M!/(N!(M-N)!) \qquad (4)$$

where the symbol ! means factorial, for example:

$5! = 1 \times 2 \times 3 \times 4 \times 5$ and $3! = 1 \times 2 \times 3$

Consider a network, letting the total number of devices M = 12 and P(ON) = 20 percent the following distribution can be calculated:

P(0) = .068
P(1) = .206
P(2) = .283
P(3) = .236
P(4) = .132
P(5) = .053
P(6) = .015
P(7) = .003
P(8) = .0005
P(9) = .00005
P(10) = .000004
P(11) = .00000019
P(12) = .000000004

From this table, the following conclusions can be drawn: Over 92 percent of the time four or fewer devices will have data to send. This value is found by summing P(0) through P(4).

Likewise, 99.3 percent of the time, six or fewer devices have data to send. If these terminals were 2.4 kbit/s terminals and they were sharing a 9.6 kbit/s circuit, then queuing would occur whenever five or more devices were ON. This condition is found to occur about 8 percent of the time.

During this 8 percent time frame a reduced throughput will be noted on the active terminals. An easy way to view this is to simply divide the circuit speed by the number of active devices:

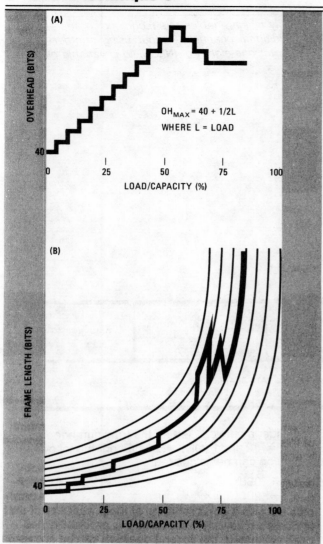

(A)

OVERHEAD (BITS)

$OH_{MAX} = 40 + 1/2L$
WHERE L = LOAD

40

| 0 | 25 | 50 | 75 | 100 |

LOAD/CAPACITY (%)

(B)

FRAME LENGTH (BITS)

40

| 0 | 25 | 50 | 75 | 100 |

LOAD/CAPACITY (%)

Indexing. *Overhead climbs in a fashion similar to Technique A under light Technique C loads with minimal indexing (a). However, as load grows and more channels activate, overhead growth slows; may even decline as in (b).*

5 or more ON	9,600/5 = 1.92 kbit/s or less
6 or more ON	9,600/6 = 1.6 kbit/s or less
7 or more ON	9,600/7 = 1.371 kbit/s or less

In short, if these terminals were 1.2 kbit/s or less, and if the circuit were 9.6 kbit/s, then the link would virtually never run at 100 percent load. ∎

References

Boustead, Carl N., and Mehta, Kirit, *Getting peak performance on a data channel,* DATA COMMUNICATIONS, July/August 1974, p. 39.
Kersey, J. Ray, *Synchronous data link control,* DATA COMMUNICATIONS, May/June 1974, p. 49.
Forney, G. David Jr., and Tao, William Y., *Data compression increases throughput,* DATA COMMUNICATIONS May/June 1976, p. 65.

Part 8
Digitized-voice
and
data-plus-voice

Digitized voice comes of age part 1—trade-offs

Benedict Occhiogrosso, Network Analysis Corp., Great Neck, N.Y.

Digital voice will be mandatory some day, but its benefits can be had now, if the trade-offs and implementations are examined

For well over a decade, telephone common carriers have been converting analog speech into digital formats to maintain compatibility with evolving digital transmission facilities. Such operations—performed by digital channel banks—are generally transparent to users. Nevertheless, in the past, few users required, or even seriously entertained, exclusive reliance on an end-to-end digitized voice transmission system because of the high cost associated with analog-to-digital (A/D) and digital-to-analog (D/A) conversion devices.

However, the cost of both digital transmission service and A/D and D/A conversion hardware is declining. As a result, digitized voice is emerging as a serious alternative to analog service. Moreover, given the continuing proliferation of digital transmission media, and many users' desire to integrate both voice and data in one network, digitized speech has become an increasingly important traffic component in the planning of future systems.

Digital voice communications (DVC) offers users several advantages. Some of these benefits can be realized immediately after a DVC system is installed, while others will only come about within the next few years. Principally, DVC offers:

Compatibility—Because of high conversion costs, compatibility with digital network facilities is not always beneficial in the short term, but eventually, compatibility will be a necessity. This will come about because of the long-range phased elimination of analog-based media by common carriers.

Less degradation—Information transmitted digitally suffers less degradation for a number of reasons. First digital signals are easily regenerated via repeaters. Second, sophisticated error control is more simply applied to digital signals. As a result, analog transmission impairments normally associated with telephone networks—crosstalk, intermodulation interference, echo and filter nonlinearities—can be eliminated. A related attribute of DVC is that any distortion, introduced into speech at the input, can be confined to a source digitizer. Thus, received speech quality can be made essentially distance-independent, a major difference compared to speech quality associated with analog voice transmission.

Secure communications—For many years, the military and several large corporations have desired the ability to transmit conversational speech in a secure (encrypted) fashion. A modicum of protection from eavesdroppers is offered by analog scramblers which alter speech via techniques such as band inversion and permutation, artificial noise insertion, and time inversion. But, these methods often yield high levels of "residual intelligibility" in scrambled speech which may then be discerned by even casual listeners after some brief exposure. Although adequate for many applications, even the most sophisticated analog scramblers do not provide the degree of protection afforded by digital encryption techniques. LSI-based digital encryption devices are also a good deal less expensive than analog scramblers.

It must be noted, however, that while the cost of encryption is generally less than the cost of scrambling, any total cost-comparison between analog and digital secure voice communications systems must also include the associated costs of A/D and D/A hardware.

Reduced bandwidth—By the appropriate choice of a speech digitization technique, voice signals can be compressed in digital form to a point where they require less equivalent channel capacity than the original analog signals. For example, if speech is digitized at 2.4 kbit/s, four simultaneous full-duplex conversations can be multiplexed over a single voice-grade line driven by 9.6-kbit/s modems or 9.6-kbit/s digital trunks. This effectively quadruples communications capacity. Based on current A/D conversion hardware and modem pricing, such "channel-packing" arrangements may not yet be cost-effective, except on relatively long-haul voice-grade channels. However, with the inevitable decline of A/D and D/A hardware conversion costs, these configurations will become increasingly attractive in the future.

Voice/data integration—Once voice has been digitized, it can be freely intermixed with (digital) data traffic. Such flexibility relieves network planners of the burden of separate facilities management for individual dedicated networks. This also enables end-users to take advantage of inherent economies of scale resulting from integration. In addition, integrated systems create an ideal framework for supporting more sophisticated voice-data applications.

Compatibility with computers—Speech in digital form can be readily processed, transformed, and stored by computers. Since current trends indicate that all major communications systems will be computer-based in the future, such compatibility is highly desirable. Obviously, with the appropriate processing capabilities, future communications systems can provide new voice-related services, including automatic speaker authentication, speaker identification, speech recognition, and computer-generated voice answer-back in response to keyed inquiries.

Trade-offs will favor DVC

Many of these advantages are long-term in nature, and, as a result, there are presently issues which could make user adoption of digitized voice communications unattractive. However, since several of these issues are highly technology dependent and cost sensitive, the trade-offs will ultimately favor DVC.

The first trade-off to consider is cost versus voice digitization rate (VDR). Currently it is not very expensive to digitize speech at bit rates above 16 kbit/s. The techniques are well understood and the complexity of the conversion hardware is minimal. For useful DVC,

however, high VDR has limited practical appeal due to the high transmission cost associated with even a single conversation. From the standpoint of bandwidth efficiency, the lowest possible VDR is always desirable. However, the cost of low VDR conversion devices is still quite high. Therefore, trade-offs between conversion device costs and transmission bandwidth must be made in order to arrive at the most cost-effective strategy.

To analyze this trade-off, an optimum voice digitization rate must be determined. Combining transmission costs and hardware conversion costs, as shown in Figure 1, a total-cost curve can be computed. From this graphic view, the "optimum" VDR is found at the point of least cost. Figure 1 is only a representative analysis of a DVC cost picture, and any actual costs trade-off must take into account such real factors as specific tariff charges, conversion device costs, and network topology.

Voice "quality" must also be considered. Voice quality is both difficult to define and difficult to quantify. Yet no single characteristic of DVC is more crucial to the user. Perceptual voice quality encompasses several different characteristics. The barest requirement is intelligibility or, stated simply, the listener's ability to understand what the speaker is saying. Several devices which operate at low VDR can distort specific phrases and impair intelligibility. Other digitization techniques provide adequate intelligibility, but sound synthetic or machine-like. In many instances, therefore, voice naturalness is also required.

At higher VDRs, additional speaker-related attributes are easily preserved, such as a listener's ability to recognize the speaker, and even discern his emotional state. In order to reduce VDR, some speech characteristics are compromised. This degradation depends, however, not only on the VDR, but also on the digitization technique used. Systems exist which sacrifice several aspects of voice quality, and yet are still per-

1 Trade-off speed and cost

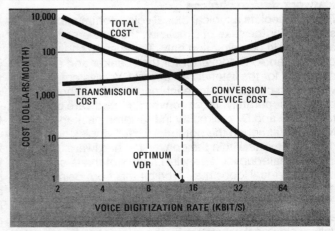

Optimum. *Above the optimum VDR, transmission costs dominate, while below, conversion device costs take over. Note that these curves are only representative samples.*

2 Format conversion

Considerations. *Several design considerations underlie the use of A/D and D/A converters in a digital voice communications system. The most crucial of these are the conversion devices' location relative to the handset, using local loops and switched networks, employing multiplexed or per channel usage, and the type of digitization used.*

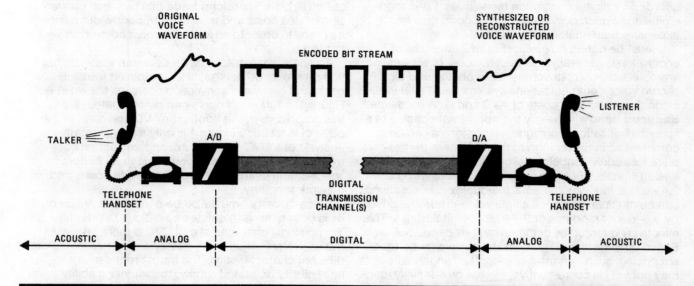

ceptually tolerable. Although these may be adequate for some users, most demand a technique that at least maintains the same quality guaranteed by the telephone network.

Finally, there is the cost of an interim reliance on modems. In the event a user desires to reap the benefits of DVC, but still derives transmission bandwidth from analog facilities, modems are required. In many cases, the combined modem and speech digitization hardware cost may outweigh the advantages of "going digital," and it is more economical to remain analog. This, however, is only a short-term condition that will change as more digital communications facilities become available from common carriers.

Network design choices

Figure 2 depicts a typical digital voice communications system. For the sake of simplicity, the conversation is examined in one direction only. The system shown provides an A/D converter for the speaker and a D/A converter for the listener. An actual DVC system provides both converters for each participant. Although pictured separately, most conversion hardware contains A/D and D/A circuitry in the same package. Note that although the potential for full-duplex communications exists within the conversion hardware, the inherent half-duplex (two-wire) nature of the telephone network's local loops may prohibit this from being realized in many installations.

At the input, acoustic pressure created by the speaker's voice is converted into a time-varying, continuous-valued electrical waveform by the microphone contained in the telephone handset. This analog speech is then transformed by an A/D conversion device into a digital bit stream. The encoded information is then

transmitted to the listener over telephone lines.

At the receiving handset, the digital voice is reconverted by the corresponding D/A device into an analog waveform. This is then used to drive the speaker in the listener's handset, thereby generating an acoustic output. Note that the intervening digital transmission channels connecting the talker-listener pair may be switched or point-to-point, and inherently digital or analog (with modems).

Several design concerns related to the use of A/D and D/A hardware in this DVC system must be addressed. These include:

- Location of speech digitizing devices
- Shared or dedicated use of DVC hardware
- Digitization technique and bit rate

The conversion hardware in Figure 2 can be positioned in several places: as an integral part of the telephone handset, as a stand-alone local adjunct to the telephone, or as part of local or remote switching/transmission facilities. The projected DVC environment, digitizer cost, switching technology involved, and underlying applications are all factors in determining where the conversion should be performed and if the hardware should be shared.

Locating hardware

When digitizers are relatively expensive, it is not cost-effective to dedicate one for each incoming local loop at a backbone switch, or as an integral part of the telephone handset. In such instances, resource sharing among many users is necessary. For example, most common carriers use time-division multiplexing to distribute digitization hardware among several active conversations via channel banks. Additionally, digital local loops may be unavailable to a user. This requires the

3 Options

Options. Three categories exist for the placement and usage of digitization hardware: Strategy A, multiplexed usage as part of the transmission facility; strategy B, digitizing at a PBX; and strategy C, digitization performed within a telephone handset. The choice depends on individual local tariffs and the type of service the user needs.

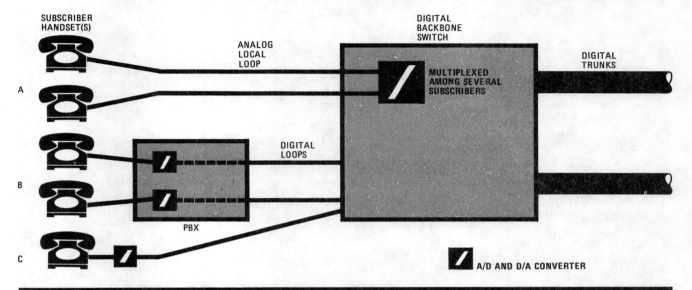

voice signal to remain analog for a portion of the route in order to retain compatibility with local transmission facilities. Such a class of subscribers is exemplified by strategy A in Figure 3.

There are instances in which digitization is a prerequisite for communications. For example, security considerations may dictate the use of end-to-end digital encryption, or compatibility with digital transmission media may be necessary.

If digitization of individual handsets is not cost-effective, alternatives do exist. A PBX could uniquely associate digitizers with incoming or outgoing calls as a natural part of access control. This prevents the establishment of conversations for which conversion equipment is temporarily unavailable. Strategy B in Figure 3 represents this class of users.

Finally, digitization performed at the handset level is desirable if the cost of the conversion device is sufficiently low (strategy C in Fig. 3). The benefits of mass production, realized by the inclusion of digitizers within handsets could bring about cost reductions in the digitizer itself. Moreover, once speech has been converted into digital form at an end-user level, alternative local access topologies (apart from the ubiquitous star configuration used in the analog local loop) move within the realm of possibility.

The final design consideration concerns the techniques used to convert speech from analog-to-digital and vice-versa.

Converting speech to digital

All human languages consist of certain basic sounds called phonemes. English, for example, has approximately 40 phonemes. In normal conversational speech, at most, 10 phonemes per second are uttered; there-

fore, if six bits are used to encode each phoneme, a bandwidth of 60 bit/s is required to transmit human speech. Table 1 lists several major voice digitization techniques, and illustrates the typical range of associated voice digitization rates at which "acceptable" quality speech may be obtained.

Caution must be exercised in order to reconcile the apparently large differences between the VDR which is theoretically required and that which is realized in practice, since a great deal more information than only speech is normally conveyed. For example phrasing, stress, articulation, and emotional content are all important parameters of conversational speech. Indeed, purely computer-driven synthesis techniques yield a singularly monotone output, yet have achieved rates as low as 75 bit/s. But, these devices are not applicable for conversion of user-generated speech in real time applications.

Quantizers, vocoders

Even among the digitization techniques employed in conversational speech, there still exists a wide disparity in VDR (two orders of magnitude in Table 1). A rule-of-thumb is that as VDR decreases, device costs increase and perceptual "quality" deteriorates.

Speech digitization techniques can be subdivided into two general categories: the less expensive, high VDR waveform-reconstruction strategies and the more expensive, rather sophisticated, low VDR analysis-synthesis strategies.

Waveform-based techniques, as their name implies, generate output speech which *looks* like the original analog input speech waveform. Analysis-synthesis methods generate output speech which *sounds* like the original input speech. However, the output speech

Table 1 DVC techniques

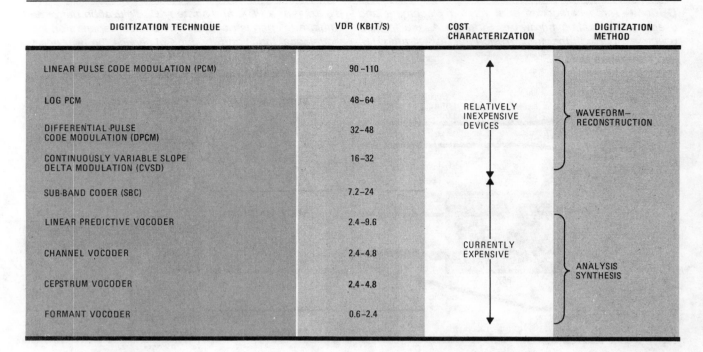

DIGITIZATION TECHNIQUE	VDR (KBIT/S)	COST CHARACTERIZATION	DIGITIZATION METHOD
LINEAR PULSE CODE MODULATION (PCM)	90–110		
LOG PCM	48–64	RELATIVELY INEXPENSIVE DEVICES	WAVEFORM–RECONSTRUCTION
DIFFERENTIAL PULSE CODE MODULATION (DPCM)	32–48		
CONTINUOUSLY VARIABLE SLOPE DELTA MODULATION (CVSD)	16–32		
SUB-BAND CODER (SBC)	7.2–24		
LINEAR PREDICTIVE VOCODER	2.4–9.6		
CHANNEL VOCODER	2.4–4.8	CURRENTLY EXPENSIVE	ANALYSIS SYNTHESIS
CEPSTRUM VOCODER	2.4–4.8		
FORMANT VOCODER	0.6–2.4		

waveform may bear little resemblance to the input speech waveform.

Moreover, analysis-synthesis devices can be speech-actuated so that no information is transmitted during extended silence periods, thereby reducing the average voice digitization rate. Waveform-based techniques usually generate a continuous output bit stream. Devices employing the waveform-based method are generally referred to as quantizers, while devices employing the analysis-synthesis techniques are referred to as vocoders (voice coders).

A detailed analysis of the major digitizing techniques will be presented in part two of this discussion, appearing next month. For the present, however, it must be pointed out that the indicated VDR associated with each technique in Table 1 represents the typical bit rate required for acceptable voice quality. Each technique's VDR may be increased or decreased, but either change will have an effect on quality. For instance, in many of the strategies, detailed in Table 1, the voice quality associated with different techniques is not comparable.

Table 1 contains both commonly used digitizing techniques, as well as many techniques still considered experimental.

The most widely used method of digitizing voice is pulse-code modulation (PCM). It is employed by carriers worldwide, and, in fact, implementations of PCM have been standardized by CCITT for voice digitization. With PCM, analog inputs are low-pass filtered and sampled at a fixed rate. The sampled waveform is quantized to a discrete level and then encoded. The VDR in PCM depends on the sampling rate.

A technique known as companding is often used to reduce the analog signals' dynamic range. Compand-

ing takes advantage of the human ear's operation, which is logarithmic—with higher sensitivity at lower amplitudes. Two standard companding techniques—μ-255 and A-law—are used most often. Both techniques employ fixed digitization rates.

Differential pulse-code modulation (DPCM) differs from PCM in that it uses the difference between sample amplitudes and not the actual value as in PCM. Delta modulation (DM) is a special case of DPCM, which approximates a speech waveform with a staircase function. By employing automatic gain techniques, the staircase can be made to adaptively track the analog waveform. A special form of adaptive DM is called continuously variable slope delta modulation (CVSD). CVSD varies the staircase step size as a function of its average signal power. Recently LSI-based CVSD devices have become cost competitive with PCM at equivalent performance levels.

Another voice digitization technique, sub-band coding, is still largely experimental. Sub-band coding techniques divide speech into continuous sub-bands, and each sub-band is quantized independently. Experiments indicate that sub-band coding provides greater control of quantization errors and can improve signal quality.

What's available
The preceding are all waveform reconstruction techniques. The other digitizing scheme, analysis-synthesis, uses vocoders, which exploit certain intrinsic properties of human voice. By digitizing only these parameters, a significant reduction in VDR can be achieved. As Table 1 points out, a number of different vocoder types are employed in reconstructing waveforms. Their differences will be examined next month. The choice of a

Table 2 The DVC marketplace

MANUFACTURER	DEVICE	CONVERSION TECHNIQUE	VDR (KBIT/S)	APPROXIMATE PURCHASE PRICE	COMMENTS
FULLY CONTAINED UNITS					
E–SYSTEMS P.O. BOX 6118 DALLAS, TEXAS 75222	VADAC 5	CHANNEL VOCODER	2.4 OR 4.8	$14,000 (UNIT COST)	ALL-DIGITAL. COMPLETELY SELF-CONTAINED UNIT; 54 BIT FRAME FORMAT; 22.5 MILLISECOND ANALYSIS INTERVAL. OFFERS EIA RS232, CCITT V.24 COMPATIBLE INTERFACE. ADDITIONAL OPTIONS INCLUDE PBX INTERFACE AND PUSH-TO-TALK FOR HDX OPERATION.
TIME AND SPACE PROCESSING, INC. 10430 N. TANTAU AVE. CUPERTINO, CALIF. 95014	TSP-100	LPC	2.4	$13,000 (UNIT COST)	COMPLETELY SELF-CONTAINED UNIT; MICROPROCESSOR BASED; 54 BIT FRAME FORMAT; 22.5 MILLISECOND ANALYSIS INTERVAL. OUTPUT STREAM COMPATIBLE WITH RS-232, CCITT V.24 OR MIL-188C. OPTIONS INCLUDE PUSH-TO-TALK, ECHO SUPRESSOR DISABLE. OFFERS SELF TEST CAPABILITY.
INTERNATIONAL COMMUNICATION SCIENCES 9000 MASON AVE. CHATSWORTH, CALIF. 91311	ICS TELEMUX	LPC	2.4 OR 4.8	$16,000 W/INTERFACE MULTI-PLEXED (UNIT COST/ CHANNEL)	COMPLETELY SELF-CONTAINED. REQUIRES SITE-DEPENDENT INTERFACE ATTACHMENT. OFFERS OPTION OF MULTIPLEXING FROM 1 TO 4 FDX CONVERSATIONS OVER A VOICE GRADE LINE. SEPARATE MULTIPLEXER ENABLES INCORPORA-TION OF DATA AT 300 BPS WITH DIGITIZED VOICE. RS-232 AND CCITT V.24 INTERFACE COMPATIBILITY.
CHIPS FOR INCLUSION IN FULLY CONTAINED UNITS					
PRECISION MONOLITHICS, INC. 1500 SPACE PARK DR. SANTA CLARA, CALIF. 95050	DAC-76	PCM	64	$19 IN QUANTITY	EMPLOYS μ255 COMPANDING LAW; REQUIRES ADDITIONAL FILTER CIRCUITRY FOR IMPLEMENTATION. A-LAW COMPANDING TO BE SHORTLY INTRODUCED.
SIGNETICS 811 E. ARQUES SUNNYVALE, CALIF. 94086	ST-100	PCM	64	$ 7 IN QUANTITY	EMPLOYS μ255 COMPANDING LAW; REQUIRES ADDITIONAL FILTER CIRCUITRY FOR IMPLEMENTATION. A-LAW COMPANDING TO BE SHORTLY INTRODUCED.
HARRIS BOX 883 MELBOURNE, FLA. 32901	HC-55532 HC-55516	CVSD CVSD	32 16	$27 IN QUANTITY $27 IN QUANTITY	BOTH CHIPS REQUIRE EXTRA BANDPASS FILTERS FOR IMPLEMENTATION AND INCLUDE CIRCUITRY FOR AUTOMATIC NOISE SQUELCH; SYLLABIC FILTERS AND SIGNAL ESTIMATE FILTERS ARE INCLUDED ON THE CHIP.
MOTOROLA BOX 20912 PHOENIX, ARIZONA 85036	XC3417 XC3418	CVSD CVSD	8–32 16–64	$ 7 IN QUANTITY $10 IN QUANTITY	EMPLOYS I^2L TECHNOLOGY; 3417 USES 3 BIT STEP-SIZE ADAPTATION ALGORITHM FOR GENERAL APPLICATIONS, 3418 USES 4 BIT ALGORITHM FOR HI-PERFORMANCE USE. CAN BE CLOCKED AT VARIABLE RATES ALLOWING A RANGE OF VDR. EXTERNAL FILTERS STILL REQUIRED.

speech digitization technique is a non-trivial affair; there exists a variety of competing strategies, each differing in device cost, complexity, VDR, quality of synthesized speech, and performance in the presence of errors. Given the current scarcity of self-contained, off-the-shelf devices, however, this issue is largely of academic concern for users.

Moreover, in addition to the high cost of low VDR devices, the absence of well-defined, widely recognized standards may prove to be an obstacle for end-user adoption of DVC, particularly in the low VDR arena. Table 2 lists several presently available voice digitization devices.

Quantizers for OEMs

The marketplace is divided between relatively inexpensive, high VDR quantizers implemented as LSI chips, and expensive low VDR vocoders, which are completely self-contained stand-alone units that can be directly interconnected with existing telephone handsets. Note that the prices indicated are for a single device, and that two such units are required in order to sustain a conversation. The LSI chip offerings are generally available at quantity discounts in lots of at least 100; the vocoder prices are current unit cost, although quantity discounts are available from the indicated vendors.

Obviously, quantizers are directed at original equipment manufacturers (OEMs) interested in A/D and D/A conversion hardware for inclusion in products targeted for users. Additional quantizers not included in Table 2 include: A two-chip PCM coder-decoder from National Semiconductor; a single-chip PCM device from Motorola and a CVSD offering from Signetics. In addition, many instrumentation vendors manufacture LSI-based A/D and D/A devices. Most chip-based quantizers require additional interface circuitry on the chip, for attachment to a microphone or a handset, and filtering. The future development outlook portends the integration of filter circuitry on the chip within two to three years. If this prediction holds, chip devices may ultimately be used by telephone equipment designers in place of conventional channel banks.

Little vocoder activity

The low VDR vocoder marketplace currently has only a handful of competitors, catering primarily to the military and select commercial users. All units listed are stand-alone, and require no interface circuitry apart from external modems for transmission over voice-grade analog lines. Multiplex arrangements can be implemented with time-division multiplexers, available in some cases from the vocoder manufacturer. All systems also permit the attachment of external encryption devices for secure voice communications. Several discussions indicate that the existing high cost associated with off-the-shelf vocoders can be significantly reduced by LSI-based implementations. At present, however, the market for low-bit-rate DVC is untapped, and there is inadequate motivation for most manufacturers to commit themselves to monolithic implementations. Configuration details for deployment of these vocoders vary, depending on the specific system. The interested reader is referred to the appropriate vendor literature for further information.

In the future, a number of additional applications tangentially related to end-user communications, but presently regarded as "blue-sky," could be supported on a large scale in a digital voice environment. Packetized voice is one example.

Once speech has been encoded in digital form, it can be handled in a fashion similar to data traffic. Speech packets could be formed and transmitted in a store-and-forward manner through a packet network. Although new protocols would be required for accommodating speech packets (due to their different error and delay performance requirements compared to data), there exists a potential for saving of transmission bandwidth by a combination of packet switching and speech-actuated vocoding. By not transmitting information, or utilizing communications facilities during periods of silence, approximately a 50 percent reduction in bandwidth requirements can be realized.

The future reliance on DVC will also spur the growth of man-machine communications applications on a network-wide basis. Speech is man's most natural form of communications, and thus, ample motivation exists for "communicating" with computers in this manner. The widespread existence of digitized voice using quantizers and vocoders will facilitate such applications and, with additional research, will transfer them from the laboratory environment to on-line services.

Synthesized answerback

Computer-generated answerback already exists in the analog world, and is used extensively in banking and order-entry applications. A synthesized voice could be used in response to user-entered queries via standard keyboards or dual-tone multifrequency keyboards (such as AT&T's Touch-Tone pad).

Both speaker identification ("Who is this individual?") and speaker authentication ("Is this person who he says he is?") could be supported under DVC. As we shall see next month in part two, vocoders intrinsically generate certain unique parameters of voice, such as pitch. These parameters can then be used to verify or determine the caller's identity. The potential for erroneous identification is much higher when analog signals are used for this, due to noise. In DVC using vocoders, however, the vocoder supplies the raw speech parameters required for identification.

Finally, the support of speech recognition and speech understanding systems, under which users can verbally input commands and/or data to a computer (although still a major research topic at many universities and laboratories around the world), would be facilitated in a digitized environment.

As noted, part two of this article, which will appear next month, will discuss various voice digitizing techniques in detail and will relate these techniques to the important parameters in digital voice communications, including voice digitization rate, voice quality, and mode of operation. In addittition, part two will contain an extensive list of reference material which is recommended for further study. ∎

Digitized voice comes of age part 2—techniques

Benedict Occhiogrosso, Network Analysis Corp., Great Neck, N.Y.

"Going digital" with voice traffic involves a number of crucial decisions, but none more important than choosing a digitization technique

Several design questions must be answered before a digital voice communications (DVC) network is implemented. These center on where to locate digitization hardware, how to employ the hardware most efficiently, and finally, which digitization technique to use.

Part one of this article, published last month, outlined the global trade-offs associated with DVC, surveyed the status of the marketplace, and detailed various DVC techniques. The examination continues this month with a more detailed look at the most widely used speech digitizing techniques.

Speech can be digitized according to two general strategies: waveform reconstruction or analysis-synthesis. Waveform reconstruction-based methods generate an output speech envelope which *looks* like the original input voice signal. Analysis-synthesis digitization, used in vocoders (voice coders) produces output speech which *sounds* like the original input voice signal, but the speech envelope may look quite different from the original input signal.

Today's technology enables devices employing waveform reconstruction, called quantizers, to be developed as large-scale-integrated (LSI) circuits which are much less costly than vocoders. However, quantizers are not stand-alone units. They are only part of a voice digitization circuit, which must also include additional filtering, power supplies, and telephone interface circuits.

Waveform reconstruction can be used to digitize both voiced and non-voiced analog signals. Analysis-synthesis, on the other hand, is principally used to digitize certain parameters of speech.

The earliest developed, and still the most widely used digitization method is pulse-code modulation (PCM). Its operation, illustrated in Figure 1, was first developed by Alec Reeves, in 1937. At the transmitter, input analog voice is low-pass filtered, to an upper frequency limit between 3.2 and 4.0 KHz, and sampled at the Nyquist rate, which is twice the highest frequency component of the sample. Hence, if the analog signal is filtered between 3.2 and 4.0 KHz, its Nyquist rate will fall between 6.4 and 8.0 KHz.

The amplitude for each sample of the analog waveform is then mapped into one of a set of discrete fixed-amplitude levels. This process is called quantization. Each quantized level is next encoded into a binary format suitable for transmission. The quantized waveform represents an approximation of the original waveform, altered only by the quantization noise (solid color area in Fig. 1).

At the receiver, the digital bit stream is reconverted to a discrete-level approximation of the original input

1 PCM digitization

Basic PCM. *Pulse-coded modulation produces a waveform which, when reconstructed, differs from the original input signal by the addition of a quantization noise signal.*

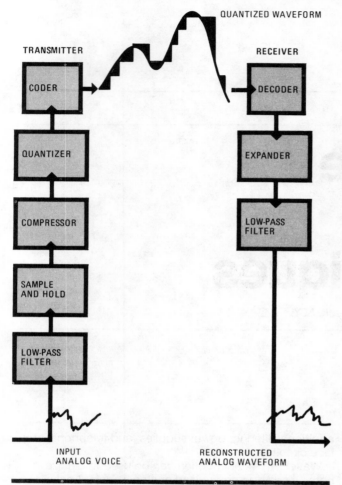

and low-pass filtered. To guarantee acceptable quality speech with linear PCM, a voice digitization rate (VDR) between 90 and 110 kbit/s is required. To reduce VDR, advantage can be taken of the fact that the amplitude response of the human ear is logarithmic—with greater incremental sensitivity at low sound intensity levels. In addition, small input levels occur more frequently than large levels in conversational speech.

Log PCM

Both of these characteristics can be exploited by using a compander (compressor-expander), a device which boosts small-signal amplitudes, but attenuates larger levels. This, in effect, alters the input signal's dynamic range, while increasing its amplitude resolution in a region where the ear's sensitivity is greatest. Companding can be regarded as a means of spacing the quantization levels in a non-uniform fashion in accordance with anticipated input signal levels. Companded PCM, also referred to as log PCM, yields acceptable voice quality at VDR of 48 to 64 kbit/s. The VDR in both

PCM and log PCM depends on the sampling frequency and the number of quantization levels.

Due to maturity of the PCM technology, a number of standards exist. For example, the Bell System D2 channel bank used in the North American telephone network samples analog inputs at an 8-KHz rate, quantized to 256 (2^8) levels. This yields a VDR of 64 kbit/s. D2 employs the μ-255 companding law which has an input (x)-output (y) characteristic given by:

$$y = \frac{\ln(1 + \mu x)}{\ln(1 + \mu)}, \text{ where } \mu = 255 \tag{1}$$

The actual implementation uses a 15-segment piecewise linear approximation of equation (1). Different PCM companding algorithms, such as the A-law compander, are used in other countries (notably Japan). Conversion circuitry has been developed which permits the transmission of information between systems using different companding schemes. Both μ-255 and A-law companding fix the position of quantization levels, and are often referred to as instantaneous companding. Variations in the instantaneous companding law used in PCM, such as adaptation of quantization levels in real-time as a function of the input waveform, have also been proposed, but have not found widespread use due to their high cost and the complexity of their coding and decoding circuitry.

Differential PCM

An extension of the PCM scheme is differential pulse-code modulation (DPCM). DPCM takes advantage of the fact that consecutive samples of input speech, generated at the Nyquist frequency, are highly correlated. DPCM transmits not the amplitude of the current sample, as in PCM, but the difference between the amplitudes of the current and previous samples. This results in a lower voice digitization rate for an equivalent voice quality.

Figure 2 details a basic DPCM codec (coder-decoder). At each sampling time, the difference between the current input and a predicted value of the current input (based on fedback previous samples) is quantized, encoded, and transmitted. In the simplest variation, the predicted value of the current input is a weighted version of the previous sample's first-order predictor.

More sophisticated strategies compute the predicted value based on a linear combination of k previous samples, using the relationship:

$$\hat{y}_i = \sum_{n=1}^{k} a_n y_{i-n} \tag{2}$$

where the coefficient a_n remains fixed during the conversion.

Referring to Figure 2: At each sampling instant, the difference, d, between the current sample y_i and a predicted estimate $\hat{y}_i$ is quantized, encoded, and transmitted. The predictor forms a weighted sum of previous sample estimates, offset by the quantized difference signal, $\hat{d}$. The quantizer step size may be adapted by adding a quantizer memory and utilizing an adaptation algorithm (AL). The most complex DPCM variations permit the adaptation of quantization levels (as a function of input signal power); hence some adaptation memory may be introduced in order to dynamically modify the quantizer's step size. This technique is referred to as adaptive differential pulse-code modulation (ADPCM). Perceptual listening tests have demonstrated equivalent voice quality between ADPCM digitized speech at 24 kbit/s and PCM digitized speech at 42 kbit/s. (Ref. 1).

Delta modulation

A special case of DPCM, in which the difference signal (residual) is quantized into only one of two levels and encoded using a single bit, is referred to as delta modulation (DM). DM compensates for the simplicity of the quantization strategy by sampling the input speech waveform at a much higher rate than the Nyquist frequency. This increases the correlation between successive speech waveform samples. A first-order predictor ($\hat{y}_i = a\,y_{i-1}$) is almost universally used for DM. The implementation of a delta modulation codec is particularly straightforward and inexpensive, and, as a result, it has attracted considerable attention for use in speech digitization.

As illustrated in Figure 3A, delta modulation approximates input speech waveforms by a staircase function of fixed step size. The transmission of a binary one increments the receiver's output by the step size; the transmission of a binary zero decrements the receiver's output by the step size. Two types of quantization distortion can result: slope overload noise, in which the input signal changes too rapidly for the quantizer to "keep up," and granular or idle noise, in which the input signal is not changing appreciably, causing the quantized waveform to "hunt" around for the true value. Because of these distortions, DM does not track an input waveform as well as PCM.

Although slope overload noise is the primary source of tracking error in DM systems, it has been empirically demonstrated that, for some VDRs, the granular distortion is the principle form of degradation of the speech's perceptual quality (Ref. 1). The establishment of an optimum fixed step size as a trade-off between slope overload and granular distortion has been attempted. This is, however, not of practical significance, given the low cost and simplicity of adaptive techniques.

Adaptive DM methods

By appropriately modifying a quantizer's step size magnitude, a more accurate representation of the input waveform can be obtained, as in Figure 3B. Automatic step-size adaptation, employed in adaptive DM (ADM), is equivalent to companding in PCM. The principal

2 Differential PCM operation

DPCM codec. *At each sampling instant, the difference (d) between the current sample, y_i and a predicted estimate, $\hat{y}_i$ is quantized, encoded, and transmitted. The predictor forms a weighted sum of sample estimates and offsets the quantized difference, $\hat{d}$. The step size can be adapted with memory and an adaptive algorithm.*

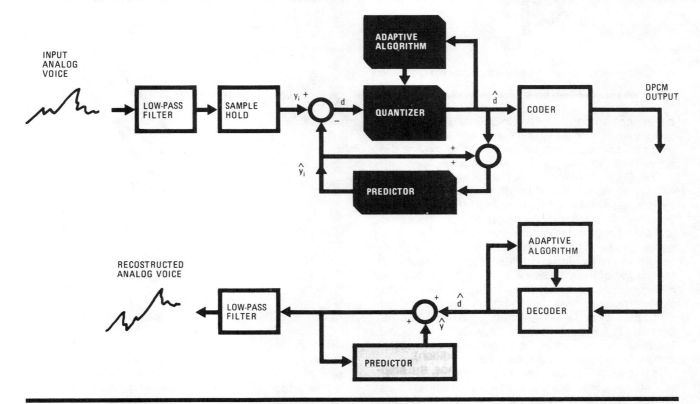

3 Delta modulations

Staircase. Delta modulation can employ fixed step sizes (A), or variable step sizes (B) which adaptively track the input speech, using automatic gain control techniques.

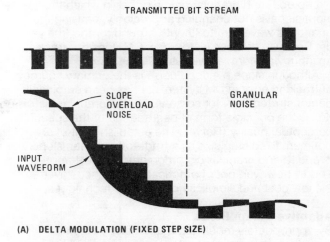

(A) DELTA MODULATION (FIXED STEP SIZE)

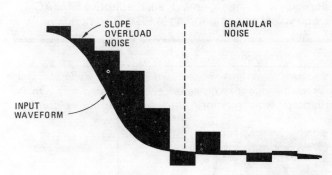

(B) ADAPTIVE DELTA MODULATION (VARIABLE STEP SIZE)

differences among ADM techniques are sampling frequency, minimum and maximum step sizes, and the step-size adaptation algorithm (when to change the quantizer's step size, and by how much).

One extremely popular technique is continuously variable slope delta modulation (CVSD), which alters the step size based on a measure of the average signal power. In CVSD, the reconstructed waveform's slope is always proportional to the signal's rms (root-mean-square) value. If several (typically three or four) consecutive binary ones are in the output bit stream, the magnitude of the step size is increased by a predetermined multiplying factor (MF). If three or four consecutive zeros are present in the bit stream, the step size is reduced by an MF. Such changes in the step size continue to a maximum or minimum MF, based on consecutive occurrences of the zeroes or ones (these occurrences are called a coincidence condition).

In the repeated absence of coincidence, the step-size MF reverts to a predefined nominal value. Since speech can exhibit abrupt increases in intensity level,

but generally decays at a slower rate, many ADM circuits provide larger MFs for step-size increase than for a step-size decrease. Both MFs may be chosen independently, based on the desired performance. Although a variety of ADM implementations exists, no universally accepted standard algorithm has been recognized (unlike PCM). However, as a consequence of the continued activity in ADM, several standards can be expected to emerge.

SNR comparisons

Objective measures of performance, such as signal-to-noise ratio (SNR), are frequently used as a means of comparing the waveform-reconstruction digitization techniques. SNR measurements, however, are not always representative of the actual differences in perceptual quality. For example, as shown in Figure 4 (from Ref. 1), ADPCM has an 8- to 12-dB SNR advantage over log PCM, independent of VDR. Log PCM is superior to ADM at high VDR, but inferior at lower VDR.

One noteworthy advantage of DPCM and ADM over PCM is their superior quality in the presence of channel noise. Because DPCM and CVSD use feedback mechanisms in quantizer level adaptation, a single-bit error may propagate in time and generate several erroneous codec outputs over successive sampling intervals. Under PCM, however, a single-bit error is confined to the current sample, with no subsequent error propagation.

Nevertheless, the perceptual quality associated with PCM is inferior to that encountered with DPCM and CVSD. In PCM, an incorrect bit in a sample can generate an error spike—which can give the listener a painful

4 SNR comparisons

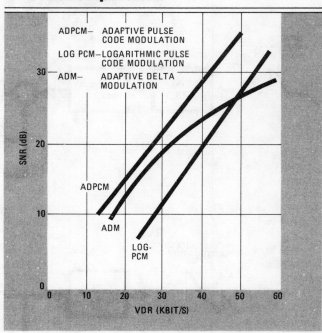

Ranking. ADPCM has the best signal-to-noise ratio performance, but at low VDR the gap narrows, and its higher codec costs may outweigh its SNR advantage.

398

sensation resulting from the high-volume transient—while CVSD errors produce only a minor transient noise. This is because PCM transmits a speech sample's actual amplitude level, whereas CVSD encodes a measure of the difference between the current and the previous samples. The greater magnitude of a PCM error spike renders the reconstructed speech errors more annoying to the listener.

Many other voice digitization techniques have been developed recently, but their use is still largely experimental. One of the most promising of these is the sub-band codec developed at Bell Laboratories. (Ref. 2). Under conventional waveform reconstruction techniques, input speech is band-limited (filtered), sampled and quantized. However, the quantizing distortion which is introduced (see Fig. 1) is not equally detectable at all frequencies in the speech spectrum (300 Hz to 3.2 KHz) since the contribution to overall speech intelligibility is non-uniform across the voice spectrum. In particular, lower-frequency bands (300 to 600 Hz) contribute more to overall intelligibility than higher bands (2.3 to 3.2 KHz).

By fragmenting the speech spectrum into sub-bands and preferentially coding (assigning a larger number of bits per sample) to the lower-frequency bands, the distribution of quantization noise can be controlled, and an improvement in overall signal quality is realized. Experiments indicate that sub-band coded speech at a VDR of 9.6 kbit/s is comparable to ADM speech at a VDR of 19 kbit/s. Because of this, sub-band coding may ultimately fill a gap between inexpensive, high-VDR waveform reconstructions such as PCM and CVSD, and the sophisticated, but currently expensive low-VDR devices (vocoders).

Analysis-synthesis techniques

By analyzing human voice characteristics at the talker's handset, vocoders can achieve much lower VDRs than quantizers. These characteristics, standard in all human speech, are encoded and transmitted to the listener's vocoder, where they are then used to synthesize a replica of the original speech. No attempt is made to preserve the exact shape of the original speech waveform. In fact, extreme waveform accuracy is not essential for the listener to perceive good quality synthesized speech. Vocoders, therefore, exploit many of speech's inherent redundancies to attain low VDR, but at much greater device cost.

The essential speech features used in vocoder analysis-synthesis are illustrated in Figure 5. An electrical analog model for speech generation (Fig. 5A), and the short-term amplitude spectrum of a typical voiced sound are detailed (Fig. 5B). Sounds can be subdivided into two classes: voiced (such as ''ee,'' in eel) and unvoiced (such as ''ss,'' in hiss).

During the production of voiced sounds, the vocal cords are tensed and vibrate at a fixed frequency referred to as the pitch. During unvoiced sounds, the vocal cords are relaxed and do not vibrate. All air generated in the chest cavity, whether it is modulated by the vocal cords (voiced sounds) or not (unvoiced sounds), passes through the vocal tract and ultimately

5 Analog voice model

Speech production. *A model for speech generation illustrates the major parameters of human speech, such as pitch, gain, and voiced or unvoiced discrimination.*

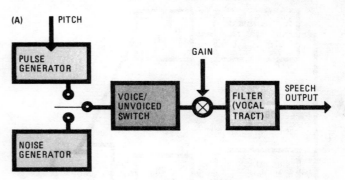

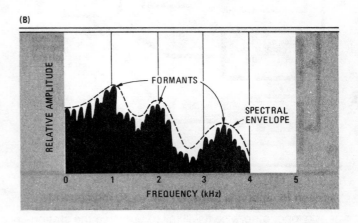

exits via the mouth, where it is perceived as speech.

The vocal tract is a non-uniform tube which acts as a time-varying filter to determine the sound. The short-term amplitude spectrum of Figure 5B illustrates that a voiced sound is a composite of an excitation function (determined by the pitch frequency of vocal cord vibration) and an envelope function (determined by the vocal tract shape.) The peak frequencies of the spectral envelope are referred to as formants, and correspond to the vocal tract's resonant modes of vibration; the position of the formants changes in accordance with the muscular changes in the shape of the talker's vocal tract.

Although the model in Figure 5A cannot simulate all speech sounds, it is adequate for most applications. Consequently, if the source vocoder can analyze basic speech parameters: voiced or unvoiced sound, pitch, gain (a measure of sound intensity), and spectral envelope (filter coefficients) determined by the vocal tract shape, the destination vocoder can synthesize a replica of the input speech. These parameters are extremely important for speech perception, since the human ear essentially performs a spectral analysis of speech and is extremely sensitive to pitch, but relatively insensitive to phase.

Vocoders periodically analyze a portion of input

6 The channel vocoder

Analyzer, synthesizer. *In the analyzer (A), a composite signal is formed by digitizing speech parameters and transmitting them to the synthesizer (B), where the signal* *is decomposed into its constituent parts. The speech parameters are then combined and used to produce a synthesized replica of the original input waveform.*

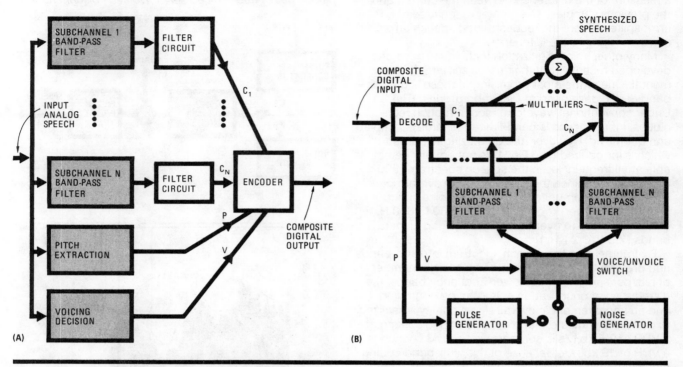

speech for intervals between five to 30 milliseconds (time windows). The time window's duration must not be too long; otherwise it will fail to preserve the stationary nature of the speech waveform, thereby complicating the analysis. However, there is no motivation for using an excessively small time window since speech parameters change slowly with time, and are limited by the rate of motion of the muscles and speech organs. The digital representation of speech within a time window is referred to as a frame.

The major differences among vocoders is the manner in which the basic speech parameters are extracted. Many vocoders also can be augmented by speech-activity detectors, so that no information is digitized during silent periods such as conversation lulls.

The first vocoder
The channel vocoder was the first analysis-synthesis device, developed by Homer Dudley about 1929. It was originally conceived as a means for the efficient transmission of voice signals, but not necessarily in digital format. In the mid-1950s, attention focused on channel vocoder usage in speech digitization. To this day, the channel vocoder's underlying operational principles—shown in Figure 6—remain unchanged.

A bank of band-pass filters is used to partition the speech spectrum into contiguous frequency subchannels. Each subchannel's signal component is then rectified, integrated, and low-pass filtered (as shown by the filter circuit in Fig. 6A) in order to obtain an esti-

mate of the spectral envelope (C_i) within that subchannel. Separate circuitry is employed to determine the pitch frequency (P), the voiced/unvoiced status (V), and, the gain. Each parameter is then digitally encoded (often using PCM, or perhaps DPCM, for selected features which exhibit a high degree of interframe correlation), and a composite digital signal is formed and transmitted to the receiving vocoder.

The synthesizer portion of the receiving vocoder decodes the composite bit stream, breaking it into its constituent signals, which are then used to create a replica of the original voice. Either a pulsed-periodic input at the pitch frequency (for voiced sounds), or random noise (for unvoiced sounds) is used to excite a filter bank whose output is then weighted by the spectral envelope signals (C_i) (Fig. 6B). The channel vocoder typically reduces the VDR to the range of 2.4 to 9.6 kbit/s. For example, using a 54-bit/s frame format with a time window of 22.5 milliseconds, a 16-channel vocoder requires a VDR of 2.4 kbit/s.

Although the voice quality is determined by the number of subchannels and their associated bandwidths (which are typically chosen to be unequal), the major performance factors are the pitch estimation and voiced/unvoiced decisions. Errors in extracting either of these parameters can render the synthesized speech particularly annoying and occasionally unintelligible. The computation of both parameters is a nontrivial processing operation, although all-digital implementations have somewhat simplified their determination.

Many variants of the original channel vocoder have been proposed, but have found limited application due to the high device cost which existed at the time of their introduction (Ref. 3), and their replacement by alternative digital hardware implementations.

Cepstrum, formant and voice-activated
Other strategies which have withstood the test of time include the cepstrum and formant vocoders. Both rely on separate logic for pitch estimation and voiced/unvoiced discrimination, but employ markedly different techniques for estimating the shape of the spectral envelope. The cepstrum vocoder uses a process known as homomorphic filtering (Ref. 4) in order to separate the excitation (pitch) and envelope (vocal tract) information. VDRs in the range of 2.4 to 9.6 kbit/s have been found to yield adequate speech quality.

The formant vocoder can operate at very low VDR (0.6 to 2.4 kbit/s), since it only transmits the location/amplitudes of the spectral envelope's peaks, but not its detailed shape (Fig. 5A). The formant vocoder has not found widespread use outside the laboratory because of the extreme difficulty of real-time formant tracking. In many instances, formant tracking is even more problematical than pitch estimation, and extreme accuracy can be obtained only at great expense.

Voice-excited vocoders employ a technique similar to channel vocoders for spectral envelope estimation, but overcome the problem of pitch estimation and voicing decisions by more elaborate processing (Ref. 5). Operating between VDR of 7.2 and 9.6 kbit/s, voice-excited vocoders have exhibited better quality than either the channel or cepstrum vocoders at the same VDR.

Linear predictive vocoder
Several of the implementation problems which plague channel, cepstrum, and formant vocoders stem from the fact that their operations are mostly performed in the frequency (spectral) domain. Consequently, there often exists a need for extremely tight filter specifications, or spectral analysis with fast Fourier transforms (FFTs). Both of these requirements are expensive. Linear predictive coding (LPC) offers the capability for obtaining the majority of the speech parameters directly from the time waveform. LPC techniques were applied to speech analysis-synthesis first in 1971 (Ref. 6). The LPC method is an alternative strategy for obtaining the speech's short-term amplitude spectrum (Fig. 5B). The analyzer portion of the linear predictive vocoder attempts to estimate the input speech as the weighted sum of k previous samples, as stated by equation (2).

As in DPCM, this is referred to as the kth order predictor. However, unlike simple DPCM (in which the a_n remains fixed), the predictor coefficients, are periodically updated to minimize the average energy in the error signal representing the difference between the current speech sample's amplitude and its estimate. Stated mathematically, this is: min $[E (\hat{y} - y)^2]$. The predictor coefficients which minimize the error signal are found by solving a set of simultaneous linear equations (Ref. 7), which are readily implemented in an all-digital fashion. This computation is performed for successive time windows.

The underlying physical significance of the LPC speech analysis method is illustrated in Figure 7. The human vocal tract is essentially a non-uniform tube, but as Figure 7 points out, it can be approximated by a piecewise cylindrical model. Each of the consecutive cylindrical segments is of equal length. The number of segments is determined by the predictor order, k. The value of the predictor coefficients, a_i, in Equation (2) provides a measure of each segment's cross-sectional area and volume.

Linear prediction thus provides a method for estimating the shape of the vocal tract at periodic intervals (Ref. 6). The predictor coefficients are updated as a function of the sound uttered, in accordance with changes to the vocal tract shape. The order of the predictor (number of cylindrical segments) determines the accuracy with which the vocal tract can be modeled. This represents an important design consideration in LPC, and it is the subject of continuing research. The predictor order must be chosen as a function of the waveform-sampling rate and the envisioned VDR. The waveform sampling rate is typically higher than the frame-generation rate at which updated values of the predictor coefficients is transmitted.

The predictor coefficients are then used in the synthesizer portion of the receiving vocoder as inputs to a digital filter which represents an approximation to the spectral envelope. Together with pitch, voiced/unvoiced/discrimination and gain parameters, output speech can be synthesized at the destination vocoder. Hence, the LPC predictor coefficients, a_i, are functionally analogous to the subchannel signal components C_i of the conventional channel vocoder.

A representative frame format for a tenth-order LPC vocoder is shown in Figure 8. Note that more detailed coding is performed for the lower-order coefficients, which, in general, determine the spectral envelope's gross shape, than for the higher-order coefficients, which provide more detailed information. Refinements to the basic LPC technique include the use of modified sets of coefficients, and variable frame rate transmission, (in which speech is periodically analyzed, but only those parameters which have significantly changed since the last frame are transmitted).

A related voice digitization technique which predates the LPC vocoder, known as adaptive predictive coding (APC), transmits both the periodically updated prediction coefficients and the error signal (difference signal of the actual input speech and its estimate); the error signal is used in place of the separate pitch, gain, and voicing parameters individually computed by the LPC vocoder. APC is a more sophisticated variant of ADPCM in which the predictor coefficients no longer remain fixed. However, digitization of the error signal, normally results in an excessively high VDR (8 to 20 kbit/s). In this range, other techniques (such as CVSD) may be more economically attractive.

Voice-quality comparisons between different vocoder types rely exclusively on perceptual listening

7   Vocal tract

Voice model. *The human voice tract, essentially a non-uniform tube, is modeled under LPC as a series of equal-length cylindrical segments. The number of cylinders* *depends on the predictor order, and the value of each predictor. The coefficients are a measure of each cylinder's cross sectional area along with its cylindrical volume.*

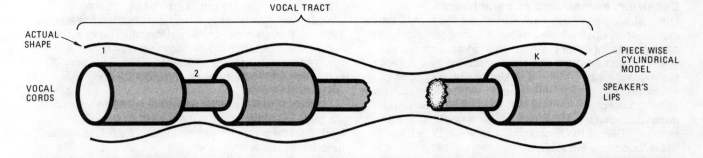

tests, as there is no quantitative measure of voice quality for vocoders similar to SNR used for quantizers. Although, at present, no unanimous opinion exists on the relative performance between various vocoder types, many listeners indicate a preference for LPC-vocoder speech over channel vocoders at the same VDR. LPC, however, does not perform as well as the channel or cepstrum vocoders in high-bit error rate (BER) environments (1 to 10 percent BER), but this error-rate region is of little practical use, except in some military applications. (Ref. 8).

An additional problem present in LPC is the unpleasant distortion which results in the synthesized speech in the presence of background acoustic noise at the talker's vocoder. But, additional cancellation techniques have been proposed which attempt to eliminate these effects. Finally, even with high-speed LSI implementations, sophisticated voice digitization techniques, such as LPC, may require an inordinate amount of processing time, thus prohibiting their use in real-time. In such instances, trade-offs between the superior voice quality possible with a large number of predictor coefficients and the excessive computation required for their update may have to be exercised. In order to

achieve low VDRs, vocoders remove many inherent speech redundancies. But, unfortunately, this renders vocoded speech more susceptible to channel errors than quantized speech. Hence, some form of error control may become necessary. Many data communications error control techniques which automatically retransmit incorrect blocks, are not applicable for digitized voice, because they impose excessive delay. Forward-error correction (FEC) is therefore required. But the long checksum characteristic of most FEC schemes is equally undesirable if applied to the entire vocoder-output frame because of the resulting transmission overhead. Therefore, FEC has been used sparingly on relatively few crucial parameters, such as pitch, voiced unvoiced determination, and the low-order filter coefficients with good results.

Voice quality encountered under error-free conditions (found in a laboratory) may not be indicative of what exists in an actual transmission environment. Even such apparently biased comparisons as those made between CVSD quantized speech at VDR of 16 kbit/s and LPC vocoded speech at VDR of 2.4 kbit/s must be weighed against the communications channel characteristics. In the absence of errors, CVDS would

8   LPC output format

Window. *Using a time window of 22.5 milliseconds, a VDR of 2.4 kbit/s is realized in an LPC scheme. More accurate coding is performed for the lower order coefficients (a_1 to* *a_4) which determine the general shape of the envelope, than for the higher order coefficients, which are used to provide the detailed refinements in the output speech.*

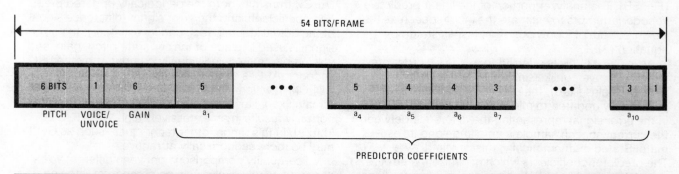

generally be preferred. However, if both CVSD and 2.4-kbit/s LPC are transmitted, using the appropriate modulation techniques on channels possessing identical analog bandwidth and signal-to-noise ratio, the larger transmission bit-error rate which would result for CVSD (because of its higher VDR,) could render it perceptually inferior to LPC (which has both a lower VDR and a lower BER). ■

References

The following list of references is by no means exhaustive, but should point interested readers to more technical aspects of speech digitization. The first eight are referenced in this analysis, while the remaining 11 are presented for further reading.

1. Jayant, N., "Digital Coding of Speech Waveforms: PCM, DPCM and DM Quantizers," *Proceedings of the IEEE,* May 1974, pp. 611-632.

2. Crochiere, R., and Flanagan, J., "Sub-Band Encoding of Speech," *ICC '77* pp. 293-296.

3. Flanagan, J.L., *Speech Analysis Synthesis and Perception,* Springer-Verlag, 1972.

4. Rabiner, L., and Gold , B., *Theory and Application of Digital Signal Processing,* Prentice-Hall, 1975.

5. Schroeder, M., "Vocoders: Analysis and Synthesis of Speech," *Proceedings of the IEEE,* May 1966, pp. 720-734.

6. Atal, B., and Hanauer, S., "Speech Analysis and Synthesis by Linear Prediction of the Speech Wave," *Journal of the Acoustical Society of America,* Vol. 50, No. 2, pp. 637-655, 1971.

7. Makhoul, J., "Linear Prediction: A Tutorial Review," *Proceedings of the IEEE,* April 1975, pp. 561-580.

8. Coulter, D., "Low Bit Rate Speech Transmission," *Proceedings of Princeton Conference on Digital Communications,* March 1977.

9. Jayant, N. (ed.), *Waveform Quantization and Coding,* IEEE Press, 1976.

10. Bayless, J., et al., "Voice Signals: Bit-by-Bit" *IEEE Spectrum,* October 1973, pp. 28-34.

11. Goodman, D., "Trends in Digital Coding of Speech Signals," *Proceedings of Electro '77,* pp. 15/3.1.1-5.

12. Falk, H., "Chipping in to Digital Telephones," *IEEE Spectrum,* February 1977, pp. 42-46.

13. Rosenthal, L., et al, "Automatic Voice Response: Interfacing Man with Machine," *IEEE Spectrum,* July 1974, pp. 61-68.

14. Aaron, M., "Digital Channel Banks: Genealogy and Anatomy," *Zurich Seminar on Digital Communication,* 1976, pp. 36-46.

15. GTE, "PCM: Concepts, Developments and Potential," *Telecommunications,* September 1975, pp. 36-46.

16. Messerschmitt, D., "Speech Encoding for Digital Transmission," *Eascon '76* pp. 88-A to 88-G.

17. Harris Corp., "CVSD—Analog to Digital Transmission with a Change," *Electronic Products Magazine,* pp. 51-52, May 1977.

18. Sambur, M., "Recent Advances in LPC Speech Vocoding," *ICC '77,* pp. 297-300.

19. "Digitized Voice Moves Closer," DATA COMMUNICATIONS March/April 1976, pp. 9-10.

Plan today for tomorrow's data/voice nets

Howard Frank, Network Analysis Corp., Great Neck, N.Y.

Communications managers, by planning now, can have a powerful influence on how data/voice integration is put to the most efficient use in their companies

Today, integrated data and voice communications is one of the hottest prospects around. In just a few years—perhaps as few as 5 to 10—user attention focused on the marriage of data and voice will increase dramatically. The catalysts will be the increasing availability of digital transmission facilities and of all-digital hardware, both for central offices and for private branch exchanges (PBXs).

The benefits of data/voice integration—economy of scale in equipment purchasing, efficient facilities utilization, and common network planning and management—will result from the implementation of new network technologies, lower-cost hardware, and switching disciplines.

Until recently, it was commonly believed that circuit switching was best suited to voice traffic as well as longer data messages, while packet switching was better for short interactive messages. Recently, however, packet switching has emerged as a preferred approach for many data communications.

Surprisingly, detailed studies of voice traffic and switching technology with a large database (represented by the future requirements of the U.S. Department of Defense) are indicating that packet switching may also be the best technology for voice. If borne out, these results have enormous implications for net-work users in the next decade. Even if this should be the case, having 10 years to plan, today's planner must focus on existing hardware, facilities, and techniques in order to move incrementally to more cost-effective network configurations. It is essential that communications managers understand the elements of networks, sources of cost, the opportunities for cost savings and performance improvement and the options available over the next few years to achieve a more effective organizational approach to integrated networking.

Perhaps the most crucial of these concerns is the day-to-day operational costs of a network. Notwithstanding the multiplicity of new carrier and transmission offerings which have become available in the last few years, the most significant factor in pricing of transmission services has been the AT&T tariff structure, because, in the main, other transmission suppliers have set their tariffs to compete with AT&T. An important factor in this area has been the introduction of the AT&T multi-schedule private line tariff known as MPL. This tariff has the effect of decreasing significantly the cost of long-haul lines (1,000 miles or more) at the expense of significant increases in the cost of short-distance links. This means that exceptional care must now be taken to configure new networks and reoptimize existing ones. It must be remembered that the

1 Line implementations

Saving. Concentrating more traffic from additional terminals requires higher-speed lines and additional multiplexing hardware, but saves overall communications costs.

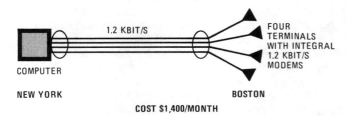

COST $1,400/MONTH

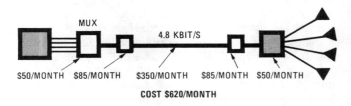

COST $620/MONTH

---

cost of local access usually accounts for much of the total communications costs and often dominates total line costs. Trends in both AT&T's and their competitors' tariffs are reinforcing this domination, and the ability to multiplex and concentrate traffic into high-speed lines at the long-haul network level is making this domination absolute.

Total network costs can be divided into components of hardware, software, lines, maintenance, start-up and rearrangement, management, and planning.

Costs for most communications hardware is subject to the same rapid drops as for computer hardware, and for essentially the same reason—the introduction of microprocessors and large-scale integration. The trend can be expected to continue in the future. While it is relatively easy to understand the cost component of network hardware, predicting the cost of the network itself is not as straightforward. This difficulty stems from the variety of ways in which networks can be configured and the many opportunities for intelligent cost reduction by proper selection of alternatives.

Multiplexing saves

Suppose, for example, we wish simply to connect four terminals with integrated 1.2-kbit/s modems located in Boston with a computer located in New York, as shown in Figure 1. Under the MPL tariff, the cost of four leased lines would be $1,400 per month. An alternative would be to multiplex these terminals onto a single 4.8-kbit/s line. Including the costs of the multiplexer, the higher-speed modem and the line, this new configuration would cost $620 per month. Forty-four percent of this amount is hardware, while 56 percent is the line cost. Thus, assuming that there is no change in the line cost, and assuming fully amortized hardware, the cost of the multiplexed configuration could drop by a maximum of 44 percent.

A more complex example of the same issue is illustrated by the terminal selection problem for a large timesharing network. In a specific problem investigated by Network Analysis Corp., a network utilizing multiplexers and low-speed, unbuffered terminals was found to cost $50,000 per month. Moreover, network costs were predicted to increase to $76,000 per month when future traffic and terminal increments were taken into account. An alternative to the existing configuration was to utilize higher-speed, buffered terminals on a multidrop line configuration. With this revision, the network cost was $25,000 per month for the existing traffic and was projected to increase to $38,000 per month with future traffic growth. The significant reduction in line cost resulting from the multidrop rather than the multiplexer configuration was partially offset by the increased cost of the terminals. However, the savings over a three-to-five-year period generated a capital pool in excess of $1.5 million for the purchase of terminals.

This example has three main points: first, the precise definition of the network problem and its boundaries is crucial to the planning process. Second, it is extremely difficult to project a network's cost without detailed analysis of the specific situation. And third, intelligent network analysis can have a major impact on ultimate data system cost. Moreover, because of the growing utilization of digital voice, the techniques developed for data network planning and optimization are now becoming applicable to voice transmission.

PBX the key

Turning to hardware components for voice networks, the PBX is emerging as a significant network element whose role will be vital to the operation of future integrated networks. In recent years a number of new computer-controlled PBXs have been developed by the Bell System and their competitors. Not the least of their advantages is that they replace large and inflexible electro-mechanical devices with small, quiet devices with few or no moving parts. The new PBXs also offer convenience, flexibility, efficiency, control, and accounting advantages over their electro-mechanical predecessors.

Two features offered by computerized PBXs are of particular interest to larger organizations and will play a significant role in the evolution of integrated voice/data networks. The first of these is the ability to act as a trunk switch for tandem tie-line networks. The other is the ability to perform digital switching functions for a terminal-oriented data network.

As a voice switch, the computerized PBX uses either pulse-amplitude modulation (PAM) or pulse-coded modulation (PCM). For example, the AT&T switches of the Dimension series are PAM type while the Northern Telcom SL-1 switch is PCM. The line interfaces of these devices convert analog voice from the telephone sets into PAM or PCM signals respectively. Then, after the signal makes its way through the switch, the analog signal must be reconstituted. With the PCM-type switches, however, it is possible to interface directly (without conversion) to digital transmission lines. Thus,

PCM switches can be used to switch data in conventional digital form.

For example, a modification of the SL-1, called the SL-10, was used as a packet switch for the Canadian Datapac data communications network. In the very near future, the modern computerized PBX will allow major organizations to use the same network and switches for both data and voice.

Vocoder cost falling

In conjunction with the digital PBX, another device, the vocoder (voice coder) provides the link which will allow voice to be treated as data and consequently be amenable to data network optimization techniques.

A vocoder converts analog waveforms created by speech into digital bit streams. The techniques used to digitize speech vary in cost and complexity from simple analog-to-digital (A/D) converters to sophisticated devices employing predictive coding techniques.

The current standard for digital speech transmission through common carrier facilities is at 64 kbit/s, using very low-cost devices called codecs (coder/decoders). However, vocoders are now available which can code voice data at rates as low as 2.4 kbit/s with reasonable quality. While these vocoders are still relatively expensive ($10,000 and up), projections indicate that within five years their cost could be reduced to several thousand dollars and longer term forecasts suggest that, with a mass market, their cost could decline to several hundred dollars.

To see how vocoders might be used within a private communications system, consider the voice multiplexing situation represented by Figure 2. In this example, several voice-grade leased lines connect digital PBXs. Embedded in each PBX is a bank of vocoders. When a user requests a line, depending on the code he selects, he may be routed through the vocoders instead of being directly connected to the line. Since current modem technology allows voice-grade analog lines to be operated at 9.6 kbit/s, several voice streams could be multiplexed onto such a line.

These lines could be either digital or analog. For example, with 2.4 kbit/s vocoding, four voice conversations could be multiplexed onto a single voice-grade line. Thus, if an organization had four leased lines between two points, three lines could be eliminated.

Let's look at the economics of such a situation under the current AT&T MPL tariff for analog circuits. Under this tariff, New York-to-California lines cost approximately $1,400 per month; Washington, D.C.-to-Chicago lines cost about $550 per month; New York-to-Boston lines are approximately $350 per month. To operate a multiplexed data link, modems and multiplexers would be required in addition to the vocoders. The modems and multiplexers could be standard off-the-shelf products without any special features. The cost for a standard four-line configuration at both ends would be roughly $600 per month. Assuming that the capital costs of the vocoders were amortized at a rate of 3 percent per month, eight $10,000 vocoders would lead to a monthly vocoder operating cost of $2,400 or a total operating cost of $3,000. If these devices were used to eliminate three of the four New York-to-California lines of our example, a reduction in line costs of $4,200 would occur. This would be partially offset by the increase in costs arising from the vocoders, modems, and multiplexers ($3,000), but a net savings of $1,200 per month would result.

Price breaks

To further elaborate, Table 1 shows the savings resulting from using vocoders at various prices for several typical line locations. As is evident, the price breakpoints where vocoders become cost effective are $15,000 each for New York-to-California lines, about $5,000 for Washington-to-Chicago lines and about $2,000 for New York-to-Boston lines. Thus, even for the low-cost New York-to-Boston lines, this arrangement of vocoders would become economically attractive within about five years. (Note: the parentheses indicate a loss small enough to be considered a breakeven in the analysis.)

To achieve these savings, the vocoders must be employed at the PBX or other switch level, and shared by all the telephones served by that switch. If vocoders were placed directly within the telephone, a much larger number would be needed, and their cost would have to be much lower to provide equivalent savings. However, such an arrangement could be justified if there were a need to secure voice communications through

---

2 Voice multiplexing

Key. *Although the digital PBX is the key element in a private integrated network, vocoders are also required to convert the analog voice traffic of the network into a* *digital format. The maximum number of vocoders needed for any single line is equal to the line's data rate in bit/s divided by the vocoders' voice digitization rate in bit/s.*

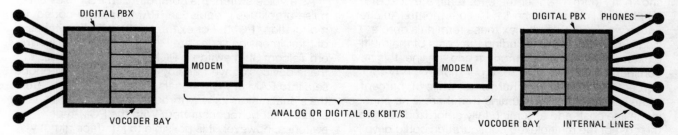

Table 1 Savings via multiplexing

PURCHASE PRICE OF VOCODER	N.Y.–CALIFORNIA	WASHINGTON, D.C.–CHICAGO	N.Y.–BOSTON
$15,000	$ 0	$ *	$ *
10,000	1,200	*	*
5,000	2,400	(150)	*
2,000	3,120	570	(30)
1,000	3,360	810	210
500	3,480	930	330

*VOCODER IMPLEMENTATION MORE
EXPENSIVE THAN FOUR LEASED LINES.

encryption. In this case, encryption devices would be placed at the telephone between the vocoder and the PBX and a secure end-to-end path between telephones would result.

Management integration

Communications systems integrating can be divided into management and technological integration. Management integration can be as straightforward as using the same staff to plan or operate separate voice and data networks. Since people cost is becoming a larger percentage of the total life cycle cost of communications systems, this approach can lead to significant savings over the long run.

Another type of management integration involves the use of economical offerings from the common carriers to lower the cost of leased or dial-up lines. For example, the AT&T Telpak tariff allows a user to arrange the billing for his leased lines (without physically reconfiguring his network) to take advantage of substantial bulk discounts. As a consequence, a large user can often radically reduce the cost of lines leased for data if he leases a large number of lines carrying voice between the same points. Similarly, a user who must communicate with a large number of locations from a single central point can often lower his cost by using WATS (wide area telecommunications service). If the WATS lines are suitably chosen, data traffic can often be served at only a small incremental cost.

Technical integration

Since voice communications hardware is rapidly moving from electro-mechanical analog to solid-state digital technology, opportunities for integrating voice and data communications in a technical sense are growing. There are a number of ways to technically integrate these requirements onto common facilities. The simplest of these may be referred to as time window sharing of lines. This approach essentially involves using a voice facility for data during periods of the day or evening when there is no voice traffic requirement. Imple-

mentation of such a technique requires scheduling of data traffic such as batch or facsimile, and is generally available to users who employ dedicated leased voice facilities. However, for all but the lowest-speed, half-duplex data traffic, electronic four-wire PBXs or switches capable of handling full-duplex transmissions with tolerable error rates are generally also needed to take advantage of such an approach.

Efficient networking

Another benefit of integrating voice and data requirements is the more efficient use of facilities. This benefit is derived from the mathematical properties of the traffic processes governing performance of communications lines.

Voice network performance is usually expressed by the relationship between two quantities: Erlangs and blocking probability. An Erlang (E) is a measure of traffic offered to the system and is expressed as the number of calls arriving each second multiplied by the average number of seconds per call. Thus, one Erlang of traffic represents the requirements for a single voice-grade channel. The blocking probability (P) represents the probability that a call cannot be completed because of the unavailability of facilities. Circuits for typical voice systems are engineered at P between 0.01 and 0.03. Thus, for such systems, one to three calls per hundred will be blocked because all facilities are in use.

It is possible to relate traffic load and blocking probability P for a simple system consisting of several parallel circuits by the formula:

$$P = E^N/N! \bigg/ \sum_{k=0}^{N} E^k/k!$$

where N = number of parallel circuits, and ! = factorial i.e. (4! = 4 x 3 x 2 x 1 = 24).

For instance, if calls (which can be either voice conversations or data transactions) arrive at the rate of one every 10 minutes and each call is one minute long, E is equal to 1/600 times 60 or 0.1. Table 2 relates the percentage of calls blocked for E of 0.1, 0.2, 0.3, and 0.4 for a path served by one, two, or three lines.

This very simple table illustrates two important points. First, suppose we have 0.1 E of voice traffic and 0.1 E of data traffic, each being separately served by single lines. A typical voice or data call will then be blocked 9.1 percent of the time. By combining the voice and data requirements and pooling both lines through a common access point (e.g. a PBX), we will have 0.2 E of traffic being served by two lines and the resulting call blocking rate will be reduced to 1.6 percent. Thus, the shared access arrangement using the same total number of lines results in a blocking rate only one sixth as large as the separate access rate.

Now consider a case with 0.2 E voice traffic and 0.2 E of data traffic. Suppose we seek a blocking rate no greater than 2 percent. This means that to serve these requirements separately we will need four lines, two for voice and two for data. However, the combined load of 0.4 E can be served on a shared basis by three lines, with a blocking of 0.7 percent. Thus, the shared configuration allows us to reduce cost by eliminating a line while improving performance.

In general, combining separate voice and data facilities will always result in improved performance. Often, performance levels will be improved to such a point that lines can be removed without violating the original system performance constraints.

More sophisticated techniques for integrating voice and data utilize more dynamic sharing of switching and transmission facilities. For example, it is well known that more than one half of the time occupied by a typical voice conversation is composed of periods of silence. During the past two decades, numerous techniques have been developed to take advantage of this fact by using both analog and digital techniques to compress the conversations of a number of speakers onto a smaller number of channels. The earliest strategy was the Bell System TASI (time assignment speech interpolation) in which channel capacity is allocated to a conversation only when appropriate hardware detects that a party is actively speaking. Once the channel is seized, the speaker is given access to the channel as long as this stream of speech continues. During periods of silence, the channel is relinquished and becomes available to other speakers.

Digital variations of the original TASI concept, such as digital speech interpolation and speech predictive encoding, have also been implemented. These systems "freeze out" speakers when the number of active speakers temporarily exceeds the available channel capacity. This results in clipping and segmentation of certain conversations with an associated loss in intelligibility for the callers.

Mixing speech and data

Refinements of the TASI concept based on digital encoding techniques which reduce the bandwidth per active speaker to accommodate additional speakers also have been implemented. Two such techniques are adaptive pulse-code modulation and variable-rate adaptive multiplexing, both developed by the U.S. Army. In these systems, when the number of active speakers exceeds the channel capacity during overflow periods, performance degradation is shared among all speakers by reducing the sampling rate per conversation. Thus, no single call is degraded much.

Table 2   Blocked calls

ERLANGS (E)	NUMBER OF LINES		
	1	2	3
0.1	9.1%	0.5%	0.02%
0.2	16.7%	1.6%	0.1%
0.3	23.1%	3.3%	0.3%
0.4	28.6%	5.7%	0.7%

The interpolation of data into speech silence periods is an ideal approach to utilize idle channel capacity without degrading either the speech or data. This is especially true for data that can be delayed by a few tenths of a second, since it can then be readily fitted into the silence periods as they occur without violating the time constraints on data delivery. An important development which contributes to this technique is packet switching. Packet switching of voice is a natural way to take advantage of the burstiness of speech in a network environment and prevent network resources from being inefficiently dedicated to speakers during silence periods. Under this scheme, both voice and data are accommodated by the store-and-forward packet-switched concept, but different packet sizes and different transport protocols are used for data and speech. Research on packet switching of voice is in its infancy, but analyses of this approach by Network Analysis Corp. have already shown that substantial savings over traditional approaches are possible.

The future

For large organizations, there are significant advantages in integrating voice, message, data, and facsimile requirements:

■ Voice circuits not utilized after business hours will be available for data, message, and facsimile (electronic mail) traffic on off hours.

■ If separate groups of circuits for voice, message, and data are combined, the number of facilities can be reduced for the same grade of service.

■ The individual requirements of voice, message, and data at a site may not justify the economics of a leased circuit, but the combined requirements might.

■ An integrated network will facilitate the use of new digital communications channels and service offerings when these become available.

Because of the radical reduction in cost of digital logic, it is now relatively inexpensive to perform analog-to-digital conversion of voice and facsimile data and to perform sophisticated digital switching. Combined with the fact that digital transmission has more tolerance to noise than analog transmission, and that switching, compression, encryption and other added value services can be more easily implemented digitally, these advances result in a steady trend toward integrating all modes of communication onto digital channels. Sophisticated digital switches are being developed which will be able to switch voice, data, message, and facsimile in any combination. While the specific characteristics of these new networks are now unknown, a pattern has emerged which allows us to predict the architecture of the future integrated network (Fig. 3).

The network will have a backbone that is primarily digital, connecting a set of either public (owned by a carrier) or private (owned by the user) switching nodes. Initially, these switching nodes will be based on circuit-switching technology. They will then most likely be replaced by hybrid switches combining the best elements of the circuit-switching technology with packet switching. Ultimately, they may become pure packet

3 Future net

Benefits. Economies of scale in purchasing, integration of local and long-haul access, and common planning are only three of the many benefits promised by integration.

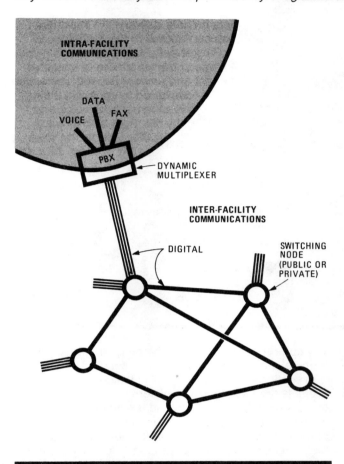

switches serving both voice and data. The switching nodes will be linked via common carrier digital lines, either terrestrial or satellite.

Connected to the switching nodes will be local access trunk lines emanating from PBXs. For a long time, many trunks will remain analog if routed on terrestrial facilities.

Future technological efforts will center on the local access area, with the PBX as the center of interest. The future PBX will be the interface between growing intra-facility networks and the outside world. In addition to its most advanced current features and elements, it will contain banks of low data rate voice digitizers and dynamic multiplexers to interpolate various classes of traffic during idle transmission periods, and it will also be able to interface directly to remote PBXs, packet switches, and a variety of other network controllers.

The future integrated network is technically feasible now. Many of its necessary components exist. Within the next five to seven years, the costs of these components will become low enough to allow large organizations to begin cost effective implementation.

The planning process for the telecommunications

function has been observed to range from merely fixing things when users complain to implementing truly sophisticated procedures which are derived from modern business planning methods as practiced by some of the world's larger corporations. Because of the complexities, both organizational and technical, in planning for an integrated network, it is clear that a sophisticated approach is a necessity.

A framework of an effective telecommunications planning process consists of three elements: the communications plan, a system development methodology, and the telecommunications budget process. The communications plan is a long-range strategic plan. The planning should be comprehensive and include data, voice, message, and facsimile services. Managerial as well as technical issues must be considered. Once the basic strategy is at least tentatively identified in the communications plan, one can turn to the tactical issues of procurement and implementation which are dealt with using a suitable system development methodology. Finally, the cost estimates derived from the system development methodology together with ongoing operational cost projections can be used to develop the telecommunications budgets required.

Define strategy

The communications plan is a document defining the strategy for telecommunications support in an organization. It is a contract between the providers of telecommunications services, the users, and management. As such, it is a dynamic process rather than a static document and is a means of continuing, systematic, communications between management, users, and providers. It specifies measurable objectives to calibrate progress.

A possible outline of a communications plan is depicted in Table 3. The system concepts and objectives section of the plan specify the conceptual basis for the communications system development. Examples of issues to be resolved in this section are: should voice, data, message, and facsimile requirements be handled on separate networks or on integrated networks? Should the network(s) be distributed or centralized? Should data networks be packet switched, circuit switched, or both? How does the data processing function relate to data communications? Should computer processing be partitioned by function or by geographical distribution of users?

Communications network management concepts should also be set out here. They can sometimes be profound. If a technically integrated network is the overall objective, management functions must be integrated also. Issues such as budgeting and pricing for integrated network services must be resolved. For example, should users be charged for the communications facilities they use? Phasing, cutover, and other time related strategic issues should also be treated here. This section essentially is a summary of the results of the communications plan.

In the next section, the services offered by the communications system should be expressed in a narrative way. The description should be purely functional and

Table 3 A communications plan

SECTION	ELEMENTS	EXAMPLES OF ISSUES
1	SYSTEM CONCEPTS AND OBJECTIVES	SEPARATE OR COMBINED FACILITIES, DISTRIBUTED OR CENTRALIZED
2	SERVICES OFFERED	CURRENT SERVICES AND EXPECTATIONS OF NEW OFFERINGS
3	ASSUMPTIONS ABOUT THE PLANNING ENVIRONMENT	EXTERNAL: REGULATORY, POLITICAL INTERNAL: STRUCTURE, TYPE OF BUSINESS
4	TECHNOLOGY FORECAST	TRENDS AND THEIR EFFECTS ON FUTURE
5	USER REQUIREMENTS (QUANTIFIED)	DATA RATES, ERROR RATES, TRAFFIC DENSITY, FUTURE AND CURRENT
6	CURRENT SYSTEM	SYSTEM TYPE AND PERFORMANCE
7	ACHIEVEMENT OF PLAN OBJECTIVES	RECENT ACCOMPLISHMENTS
8	FUTURE OBJECTIVES	PLANNED CHANGES
9	STATUS OF PROGRAMS	OVERALL PROGRESS

written from the users' point of view. That is, it should identify what requirements are satisfied by the communications system, not how they are satisfied. The requirements should be clearly related to the business objectives of the users. In creating this description, users should be surveyed as to significant future plans which will require communications support.

The third section attempts to summarize the assumptions which must be made about the environment in which planning is taking place. These assumptions are divided into two categories. The first are external conditions and include assumptions about the economic, political, regulatory, legal, and technological future. The second class of assumptions concern the internal environment, namely the future structure and nature of the business.

In section 4, future technology and its impact on the communications planning process is evaluated. In a field as technically volatile as telecommunications, the importance of this stage is obvious. While predicting the future in detail is difficult, the basic trends are clear. Technology now in development is the technology that will be available in the 1980-to-1985 time frame.

The user requirements are given in a quantitative form in section 5. They are also identified in terms of communications characteristics, such as number of messages, bits per second, peak-to-average traffic ratios, and the like. Requirements should be specified for the current system and estimated in the same quantitative terms for specific future time periods. This data is then used in design studies to evaluate alternative communications system architectures. In the sixth section, the current system is defined in more detail.

The current performance is treated quantitatively in terms of standards that have been set.

In sections 7, 8, and 9, specific tasks, programs, or projects are defined, using system development plans to implement the concepts and the architecture defined in section 1. Section 7 summarizes those parts of the communications plan which have been completed recently. Section 8 covers those tactical steps which are to begin in the near future. Finally, section 9 summarizes the status of programs in progress.

Implementation of the elements of the communications plan is accomplished through system development plans. Many system development methodologies are available. All share these essential characteristics:
- The system development is broken into discrete steps.
- Each step is given precisely definable objectives.
- At the end of each step, a specific management decision is made to continue, re-do or abort.

It is useful to indicate potential programs which must be addressed along the route to the integrated network of the future. These include:

Telecommunications management—This function has changed dramatically in the last decade. Ten years ago, telephone network management involved selecting the proper colors and numbers of buttons on telephones. It is now becoming imperative for organizations to revise these structures to deal more adequately with the challenges to come. Issues such as the proper organizational and physical location for this function as well as appropriate levels of support, required skill sets and interface to the telecommunications users must be considered and resolved before substantive

4.—Graphics. *For a voice/data network, a system-wide PBX evaluation is critical. In the photo, a Network Analysis Corp. researcher is evaluating alternate PBX configura-* *tions on a graphic terminal display. The program is a computer-aided design tool which includes system-wide parameters of an existing data communications network.*

progress can be expected by corporate management.

Telecommunications database—The establishment of a corporate telecommunications database requires a current inventory of telecommunications facilities including PBXs, numbers of telephone sets, leased lines, WATS lines, data terminals, and other communications equipment. Communications requirements, including performance standards, and traffic requirements are part of the database. This should be quantitative information which can be used as input to procedures for projecting future traffic, and as input for communications design tools.

Shared domestic voice network study—Many large organizations, often with sales in the billions of dollars, do not operate rationalized shared voice facilities. For these organizations, an early step would be to discover if there are substantial cost reductions or other benefits to be gained through an intra-organization private voice network using either dedicated or switched lines. If so, individual system development plans would then be created to structure and implement the network.

Data network integration—Data communications networks within large organizations have evolved on an application basis so that a single organization may operate many such networks. The initial step toward ultimate telecommunications integration is the step-by-step integration of these data networks. In some instances, a single corporate data network will emerge. In other cases, especially for those involving inflexible existing hardware and architectures, several networks may operate in parallel until they are replaced by more flexible arrangements at the end of their life cycles.

Organization-wide PBX evaluation—Because of the lack of centralized telecommunications expertise, local telecommunication managers are often dependent on their telephone company representatives for planning support. In the area of PBX selection, this can have significant disadvantages. First, unless the telephone company's representative is particularly diligent, he may not help the local manager evaluate newer telephone company options which could substantially decrease telecommunications costs. He will certainly not help the local manager evaluate the cost and functional advantages which can be obtained by using interconnect PBXs.

The objective of this study would be to identify the cost-savings and benefits which can be achieved by alternate PBX configurations and by defining a system-wide PBX strategy. This activity should be coordinated with the shared domestic voice network study, since the PBXs would be an important component in any such network (Fig. 4).

First-level data integration—The objective here is short-term savings by sharing lines for data and voice. Using lines for voice during the day and for data at night is one example.

Charge-back feasibility study—It is possible to change user habits by selective pricing. Evening discounts, for example, will encourage use of lightly loaded facilities.

Taken together, these suggestions can, in themselves, yield significant payoffs along the route to an integrated network. Moreover, planning for the integrated network of the future can directly impact the concept of the office of the future, and can lead to big savings in corporate communications. ∎

Computerized PBXs combine voice and data networks

Nicholas S. Fiekowsky, Economics & Technology Inc.

Private branch exchanges that are programmable by hardware will come into their own as long-range digital transmission improves

One of the biggest advantages to a computerized private branch exchange, or CBX, lies in its ability to move both voice and data signals over the same high-grade all-digital circuits at high speeds. But there is more to the CBX (an outline of which appears in Figure 1) than just a computer replacing the standard relay logic of an ordinary PBX.

The electronic switching system of the CBX has evolved from the mechanical devices previously used, and most contemporary units employ some form of time-division multiplexing. These two improvements mean that the CBX can be much more than a high-powered switchboard; it can in fact serve as the keystone of an integrated voice and data network and handle data communications equipment and digital transmission lines.

For many users, integration of voice and data communictions networks can lead to increased economy and efficiency. Often the same individual staff member handles both networks, and both have many problems in common. Since the CBX and its technology are still developing, knowledgeable data communications managers may be able to influence the design and features of new units. The CBX can generate data on usage, traffic, and other parameters that reflect the way a company is conducting its communications, and this data should be of the greatest interest to cost-conscious corporate managers.

Computer control and time-division multiplexing present a number of features and capabilities available to a CBX's user. They include easier data transmission at higher speeds — for example, in timesharing and electronic mail applications — easier access to digital transmission media, and minicomputer or microprocessor-controlled features. An understanding of a CBX's operation provides a foundation for dealing with its present capabilities, as well as with its potential for greater usefulness in the future.

The control computer is the heart of a CBX. The computer drives the time-division multiplexing network, acting on data from its random access memory as well as on information provided by interface equipment such as an adapter to the trunk telephone lines.

As with most data communications applications, the inadequacy of any one component can limit the performance of the whole unit. For example, the CPU spends a certain amount of time processing each request for a connection, either from a directly connected station or from a remote unit communicating over a tie line. The CPU must also support foreground and background activities involving network maintenance and information output. As the number of calls placed

1 Computer-controlled PBX structure

The CBX itself. *A central processor is the heart of a computerized switchboard. The processor's intelligence keeps control over the flow of data and voice connections.*

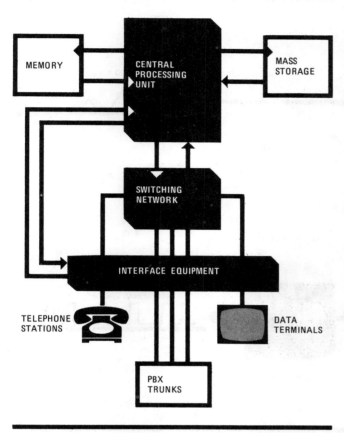

on the network rises the CPU may be overloaded—which will result in long waits by dial-up terminals for their connections.

To get around these inadequacies, the designer of a network can either increase the CPU's speed and capacity, or assign more functions to the interface equipment. In small systems the processor may handle all the tasks—controlling lights and signaling, and even interpreting the Touch-Tone signals coming from the stations. Most CBXs, however, use discrete tone decoders and other circuitry for these tasks, with the CPU issuing occasional control words or reading information from the data bus. The interface equipment will generally detect ringing on incoming trunk calls, put a ring signal on called station lines, and report on station status to the processor; the processor still exercises direct control over the switching network.

The time-division multiplexing feature of the CBX is vital to its operation from a data communications point of view. This process sometimes acts to limit the speed at which information can be sent through the network. On the other hand, some technologies are directly compatible with direct transmission of digital signals, and suggest a broad range of applications in the future. Such technologies range from the traditional space

division (a switching matrix providing physical connections and using conventional reed relays or solid state devices) to the different forms of time-division with pulse amplitude modulation, pulse code modulation, and delta modulation.

Time-division multiplexing involves the sampling of the voice signals, and their transmission over a common path divided into time slots. Connections are established by assigning the parties to complementary slots. Station A might transmit on slot 4 and receive on slot 12, while station B operates inversely. When the conversation is completed the computer automatically reassigns the time slots to other stations or trunks. The network operates in a four-wire, full-duplex mode, the transmit and receive paths being electrically separate, as they are on most private lines. This means that the CBX can act as a high-quality tandem switch; it makes connections between four-wire private lines in a four-wire mode and so avoids the kind of degradation in transmission quality often to be found in the two-wire switching used in most PBXs.

Different techniques

Modulation techniques vary. Some equipment uses pulse amplitude modulation (PAM) (Fig. 2a). This method involves sampling voice signals at a high rate and injecting them onto a wide bandwidth link at the appropriate time. PAM limits the number of voice signals which may be carried by a single link, and does not have any advantages for data transmission.

Pulse code modulation (PCM) (Fig. 2b) resembles a modem working in reverse—taking an audio signal and translating (quantizing) it into a data stream by way of an analog/digital converter. The voice signal is first sampled, as in PAM, but the amplitude is then measured and represented as an eight-bit binary number. This number is injected onto the line at the proper time for transmission. PCM allows the digital link to carry more slots, and has greater immunity from noise, than does PAM; more important, PCM can be adapted to carry data directly by using digital termination devices (usually printed circuit boards in the CBX) instead of the usual modems.

The third TDM technology, delta modulation, is similar to PCM, except that here the CBX, instead of coding the signal's amplitude, notes the difference in amplitude from the last sample and transmits that value. Although this method is electronically easier to implement, it involves some reduction in the quality of voice reproduction over the circuit.

Rockwell International's Collins Radio Group has produced a CBX that can handle both time-division and frequency-division multiplexed signals. The system is based on an in-house coaxial cable, with certain channels dedicated to television transmission (for example, for a closed circuit security operation) and others to voice and data. Within the voice channels, the signals are encoded by a time-division technique. Connections are set up when the CBX's communications controller assigns circuitry in the Collins custom-made telephone sets to the picking up and transmission of data within certain time slots. The system can also

2 Modulation techniques

Signal sampling. Pulse amplitude modulation (PAM) multiplexes analog signals but gives no advantage to data transmission. Pulse code modulation (PCM) trans- lates analog signals into digital data in the form of an eight-bit number. When injected onto the line, this data can be delivered direct to processors on the network.

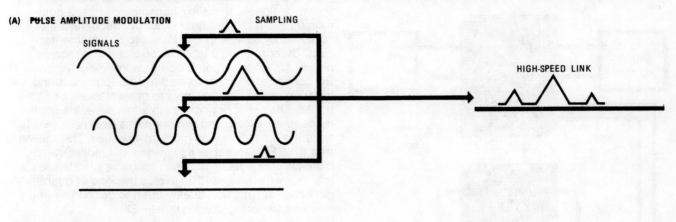

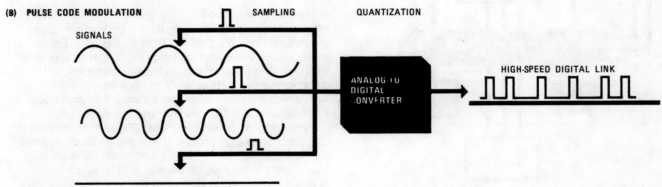

transmit data through a frequency-division multiplexer, since some of the available television frequencies could be assigned to high-speed data use, or subdivided to provide several low-speed channels. A single coaxial cable can carry the entire communications spectrum for an installation, and the communications controller can manipulate entire television frequencies as well as voice channels within the cable.

Digital transmission capability
Both PCM and delta modulation have an advantage shared by no other internal switching and transmission technique—the analog signals are converted to digital data streams and internally handled as such (Fig. 3). This means that a data stream can be introduced to the CBX from a terminal or computer, at a much higher speed than is at present usual under these circumstances, and the machine will have no trouble accepting and switching it. The eight-bit data words are no different from the encoded voice signals normally handled—which does away with the need for modems.

This digital ability means that telephone lines within an office building can easily handle as much as 64 kb/s, as against the present limit of 9,600 b/s for data transmitted over an outside telephone line. When a CBX encodes a voice signal for its internal switching network it must sample the voltage level on the telephone line 8,000 times a second. The voltage level of each sample must then be measured and transmitted as an eight-bit number to allow accurate reproduction. The CBX is therefore carrying 64,000 bits each second for each analog telephone line it is connecting. If the telephone lines were replaced by high-speed digital links, the sampling and coding stages could be eliminated and the network would simply accept data at 64 kb/s from the terminal or computer at the other end of the wire, and carry this data through its network in the way it would an encoded telephone conversation. One CBX, therefore, can serve an organization's entire telephone and data transmission needs.

Uses of data transmission
The natural suitability of some CBXs for many data communications needs opens a large number of possibilities, including more flexible timesharing configurations, electronic mail, high-speed facsimile transmission, and easier sharing of communications facilities between voice and data users. Although most of these techniques are not in use today, they will probably be introduced in the near future through such transmission

3 Digital transmission through a CBX

Handling high speeds. *The CBX acts as a funnel through which both digital and analog transmissions are placed on a high-speed link. In the case of digital entry termi-* *nals, only the speed of the signal is increased. When an analog message is to be transmitted, it is given digital form before being put out on the 64 kb/s link.*

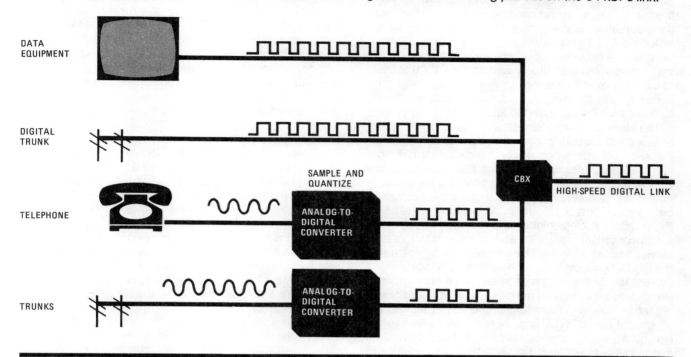

services as the high-speed data offering planned by Satellite Business Systems. A well planned telephone and data network will be able to accommodate these developments. This planning calls for close coordination between those responsible for data communications and for voice facilities both at the network design stage, and at the time for specifying equipment expected to fill present and future needs.

Electronic mail (Fig. 4) is a label that can be applied to a wide range of practices, such as facsimile transmission, communicating word processors, and sophisticated packet-switching networks. These different practices call for different types of equipment and transmission lines. After facsimile, the most successful form of electronic text transmission probably lies in the word processing technique. Different offices within an organization can transfer documents by entering them in a local word processing terminal connected through the telephone system to a remote terminal, and transmitting the message as a data stream.

At present, word processor-based transmission is mostly done through modems over voice-grade lines, usually after normal business hours when rates are lower or dedicated lines are open. More sophisticated schemes have a store-and-forward message switch with a buffer, which calls each word processor in turn and receives all its messages, then calls each terminal back and reads out documents addressed to it. This procedure is only practical, however, if each word processor in the network is fitted with its own modem.

A CBX using digital transmission can make the process more efficient. Each word processor can be given a direct digital connection at the CBX. This immediately speeds up the process, because transmission can now take place at 64 kb/s instead of 9,600 b/s. The CBX's intelligence can be used to help control the local terminals and to select the appropriate transmission line to distant points on the network. If conventional lines are used to reach distant locations, only one modem is needed—at the CBX—instead of one for each trunk connection. If the organization uses digital connections for data, the CBX can access these at night for the electronic mail, when there is less demand for them.

Timesharing applications

As with electronic mail, the CBX's main virtue in a timesharing application is that it eliminates the need for most modems, replacing them with more straightforward data converters, that will act as interfaces between the CBX and the data terminals. There is little advantage to this technique for fixed in-house connections, but in cases where terminals contend on a dial-up basis for ports either on a single computer or on several different computers, the CBX acts as a hardwired front-end processor for simple line control and replaces a set of modems, and perhaps line controllers as well. A CBX also directly interfaces with the digital network, allowing terminals easy access to a digital link that ties the CBX to a distant computer. This provides the timesharing user more cost-effective access to the distant machine than would separate voice-grade lines for each terminal.

Before it went out of business, Datran introduced end-to-end digital transmission, on either a full-time or part-time basis, for commercial customers. Satellite Business Systems will offer exclusively digital service. It is inevitable, as computer-to-computer communications continues to grow, that other common carriers, including AT&T (which already features Digital Data Service) will provide more digital—as opposed to analog—transmission services. Just as the CBX transmits at 64 kb/s over its internal network for each signal it handles, long distance transmission in a digital form also requires 64-kb/s capability.

The high-density transmission media already current or being introduced (microwave, coaxial cable, satellite, and fiber optics) generally use digital formats for more flexibility, easier design, and better performance. Finally, higher speed data lines can easily be derived from a digital medium, and the cost for this service will be low since straight digital transmission is cheaper than digital/analog/digital conversion.

Network planners will be able to cope with this new service in several ways. The simplest will be to treat the digital line merely as a cheaper way to perform current tasks, and stay with multiplexed networks similar to present ones, but making use of the advanced digital multiplexing techniques (such as PCM, and delta, described earlier). Those networks would have concentrators with simple digital-to-digital connectors instead of conventional modems.

Voice or data

A high bandwith digital line can be run directly into a CBX using digital signal encoding, and the CBX can then supervise a computer's use of the channel for voice and data, conversing with a similar machine at the distant end for more efficient control. If there is no demand for data transmission at a given time, the channel capacity can be subdivided into 64-kb/s segments and used for voice connections. As data demand increases, the CBX releases larger portions of the line's capacity for data use, probably in 64-kb/s increments. As voice traffic is relegated to fewer virtual links in the channel, the delay in getting an open line will rise and calls must be completed over other, analog, lines. The CBX can even be programmed to shift a conversation from one path to another without interrupting the call, in order to make way for the transmission of a digital message.

The data devices could be terminated as digital stations on the CBX, using it for local connections as well as for those to distant points. Alternately, all data terminals and computers could connect to a multiplexer which would share control of the digital trunks with the CBX and its voice traffic.

As the practice increases of transmitting short data bursts to diverse locations, users will make more use of packet-switching services, either over private networks or those provided by common carriers. In a sense this is a switchboard data service, and the CBX can be equipped to support the service, using its digital transmission and computer control. The Canadian Datapac network is run with Northern Telecom SL-10s, a modified version of their SL-1, which is a commercially available CBX that makes use of pulse code modulation switching.

As digital transmission becomes more common, a wider range of products designed expressly for data communications within that format will certainly become available—for example, terminals operating under a digital protocol. Data communications managers should realize that the telephone equipment manufacturers are already producing suitable equipment, and that integration with regular analog voice communications offers considerable economies.

Encoding, compression

The newest crop of high-speed facsimile devices use digital encoding and data compression to achieve a transmission time of less than 30 s for an 8½-inch by 11-inch sheet. Since the digital signal must go through a modem, and is limited to 9,600 b/s, a CBX offering digital transmission at 64 kb/s makes a somewhat less expensive and much faster device possible. Long distance transmission at these speeds would obviously require a suitable all-digital data link to the distant machine. If such links are available for computer use, the CBX offers a straightforward means for one facsimile machine to reach another.

The programmability of the CBX is likely to make a wide range of features available. At this point most of the development effort has been concentrated on voice applications, but a few features have been introduced which are useful for data transmission, including data privacy, data restriction, and queuing. These capabilities make it easier to integrate data applications into the CBX. The same programmability that enables the device to support these features also helps protect users from obsolescence, since program modifications and updates can easily be put into effect by means of changes in the software.

Another feature of a CBX is that it can communicate with a user while a call is in progress by injecting tones onto the line to show that another caller is waiting, or that a high-priority user is about to exercise an override privilege and break into the conversation. These same tones would cause severe errors if they were introduced onto a line carrying data or facsimile signals.

The data restriction feature permanently marks a line and prevents the CBX from injecting any signals into an established connection. Data privacy gives the same insulation but allows the user, by special access codes, to control the protection. The full features of a line can thus be exercised if it is used for voice, and it can be restricted while a facsimile machine or data terminal is in use.

Tie lines and special trunks, such as WATS lines, are expensive, and the traffic on most networks can justify only a small number of these lines. Normal fluctuations in traffic can lead to long stretches of time when the network is idle, while overloads may develop during busy periods. While users may be inconvenienced during times of overload, when access to the network is

4 Electronic mail

Electronic mail. *After facsimile, word processing is the most used form of text transmission. Most present word processing systems rely on relatively slow analog trans-* *mission (A), but a CBX with its buffered message switch (B) allows the use of high-speed digital transmission from one end of the link to all other points on the network.*

(A) WORD PROCESSOR TO WORD PROCESSOR

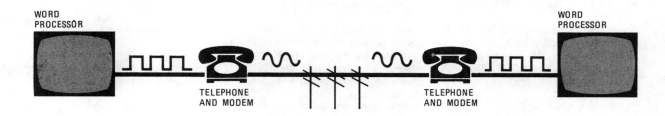

(B) COLLECTION AND REDISTRIBUTION WITH A CBX AND MESSAGE SWITCH

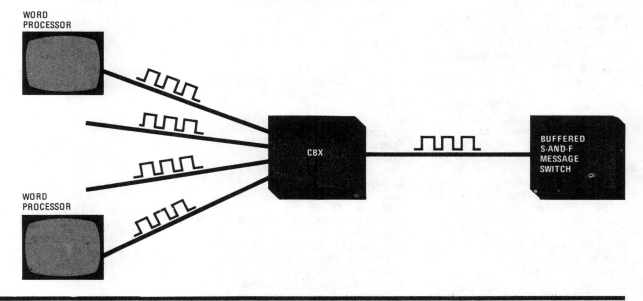

difficult, the idle periods show that additional lines would not be justified. Queuing provides a partial solution to this problem.

Special code

If someone placing a call gets a busy signal when trying to use one of the trunk groups, a special code can be entered in the CBX to tell it that the caller is willing to join the queue waiting for a free line. Once a line in the group is released, the CBX rings the caller (which may be a dial-up terminal), and when the instrument there is picked up, the connection to the line is established. If the caller enters the full number of the call's destination, the machine will automatically dial this number over the line. This procedure eliminates idle intervals on a trunk group during periods of heavy demand, and reduces the number of attempted calls made during these times. Instead of sitting idle for indefinite amounts of time between calls, a line is in use continuously, since a new call can start almost as soon as the pre-

vious one is ended. Users are taken care of first-come, first-served, and can attend to other business while waiting for a line. This feature is helpful on the special lines used for credit verification, for example, and allows satisfactory service to be achieved with a smaller number of lines.

The CBX, with its programmability and digital transmission techniques, has developed a new series of possibilities for designers both of voice and data communications networks. Although useful features are already available for data communications, more of the potential will be realized as digital transmission media, and devices such as digital facsimile machines, become more widely available.

The hardest job at present is to forecast future needs and applications, and to assure that new CBX installations will support them. The most successful users will be those who remember that their CBX is built around a computer and take full advantage of its flexibility and power along with a digital switching system. ■

INDEX